MW01715079

Osborn/Osborn

Public Speaking

Seventh Edition

Trusted

Innovative

Student-Focused

With expanded coverage of persuasion, new end-of-chapter exercises, fully integrated technology, and new up-front material designed to get students ready to present right away, the Seventh Edition of *Public Speaking* is more interactive and student-focused than ever. Centered around three core objectives-preparing students for civic life, respecting the diversity of the audience, and sensitizing students to the ethical impact of their words-the text continues to offer both practical advice for public speaking and an understanding of why such advice works.

The Seventh Edition introduces two new models of oral communication—**the Mechanical Model** and **the Identification Model**—designed to help students better understand the elements that influence oral communication. The Mechanical Model addresses the physical and technical constraints that shape communication, while the Identification Model points out the ethical consequences of oral communication. These concepts are brought to life through examples from real, student, and professional speeches; new Discussion and Application exercises at the end of each chapter; and a variety of boxed features throughout the text. While the trusted content and distinctive features of the text have been maintained, *Public Speaking,* Seventh Edition continues to evolve and adapt to changing times and the needs of its student audience.

"We've never been content with 'cut and paste' revisions. Every photo, every graphic, every chapter and every sentence must rejustify itself. The basic test is: How could this better advance the learning process?"

SUZANNE OSBORN

"We're really excited about our new chapters on persuasion. The emphasis on ethical argument is right for our time. The Toulmin model should help students master the reasoning process and put it to work in their speeches."

MICHAEL OSBORN

Trusted Content...Adapting to Changing Times

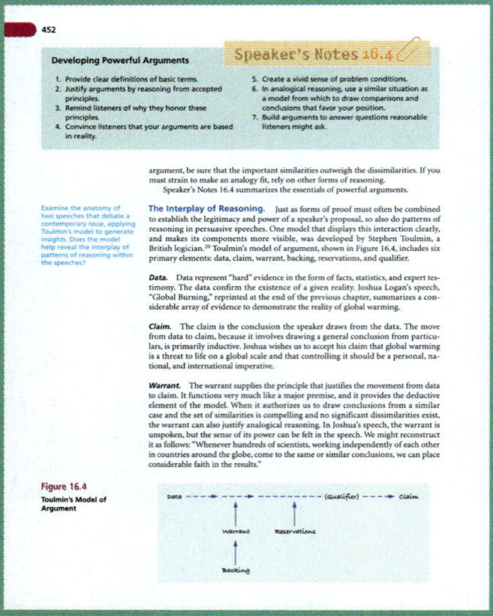

Enhanced Coverage of Persuasion Chapters 15 and 16 have been restructured to provide a clearer, more ethically defensible discussion of persuasion. In addition to expanded coverage on ethics and forms of proof, the concept of argumentative persuasion has been developed to emphasize the ethical importance of reasoning in areas such as the formation of public policy. Also, a new section on Listening to Persuasive Speeches addresses both how to be a thoughtful, active listener, and how—as a speaker—to anticipate and respond to questions from listeners. Chapter 16 also introduces the Toulmin model of proofs to help students grasp how to make reasoning work productively in persuasive efforts.

New! Discussion and Application Exercises at the end of each chapter allow students to practice skills in small group settings or on their own. These varied activities can be used in-class to promote discussion or assigned as homework.

New! Chapter on Communication Anxiety (Chapter 2) addresses this important subject when your students need it most-as they are preparing to give their first presentation. This chapter flows well into Chapter 3, Your First Speech.

New! Stairway to Speech Success Model in Chapter 3, Your First Speech, lays out the speech development process from start to finish to help students get started on preparing their first presentation. Osborn, Public Speaking, 7/e, is one of the only books to have a full chapter dedicated to the first speech—often one of the most challenging assignments for both the student and instructor. This chapter helps to facilitate this first assignment.

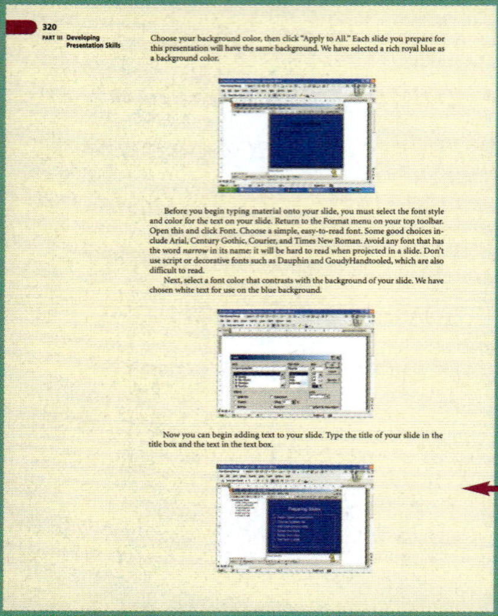

New! PowerPoint Tutorial at the end of Chapter 11 offers instructions (including screenshots) on how to operate PowerPoint and how to use PowerPoint as an element of a presentation.

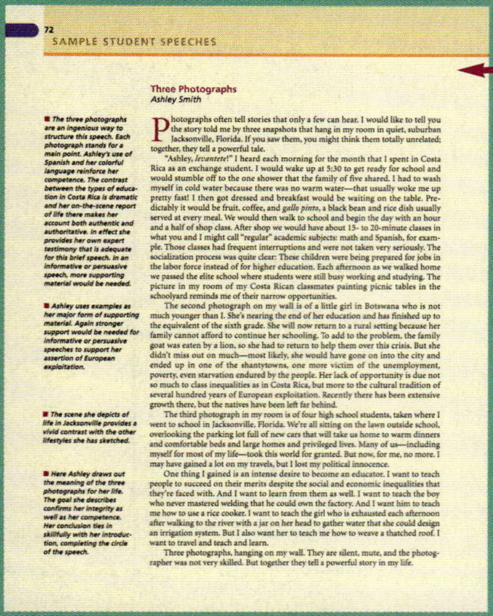

Annotated Sample Student Speeches illustrate how the theories and principles discussed apply in real life. The Seventh Edition uses more real-life examples of student speeches than any other text on the market.

Updated Ethics Alert! boxes highlight ethical concerns or issues as they arise in the context of content—to continually remind students of the importance of ethics in public address, rather than confining the subject to a chapter on its own.

Updated Speaker's Notes provide students with useful suggestions for improving their presentations, and reinforce key principles and concepts.

Integrated Technology...a Turnkey Solution for Your Public Speaking Classroom

New to the Seventh Edition of *Public Speaking*, technology icons throughout the margins of the textbook point students and instructors to interactive exercises and resources available on the updated VideoLab CD-ROM and revamped Online SpeechStudio in Eduspace®.

VideoLab CD-ROM

The VideoLab CD-ROM is an interactive study tool for students that can be used independently or in class. It provides digital video of student speeches that can be viewed in conjunction with corresponding outlines, manuscripts, notecards, and instructor critiques. A series of drills to help students analyze content and delivery follows each speech. The VideoLab CD-ROM comes packaged with the textbook at no extra cost.

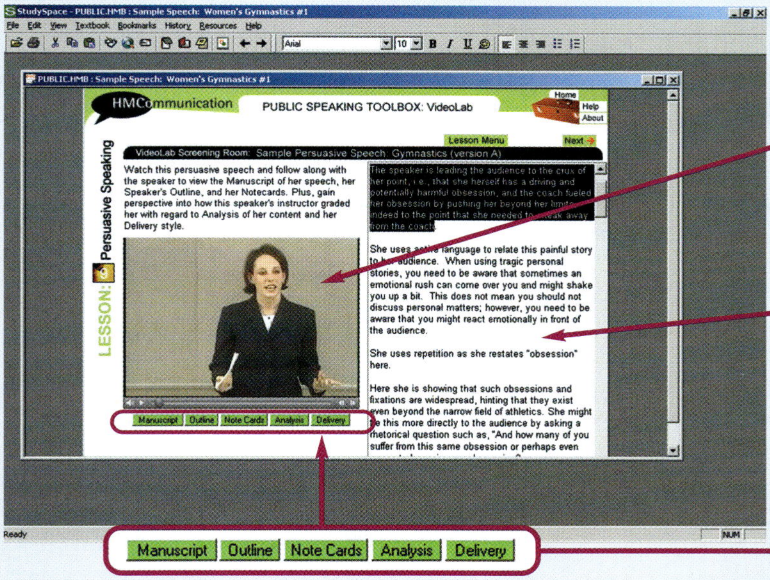

The updated VideoLab provides new digital video of twelve, real-life student speeches organized into ten lessons.

Instructor analysis helps students learn how to give constructive feedback.

Students can view the speech manuscript, outline, note cards, and instructor analysis along with the video.

Each lesson contains a series of questions on concepts such as listening, delivery, organization, and audience analysis that provides an interactive way for students to test and improve their knowledge and skills.

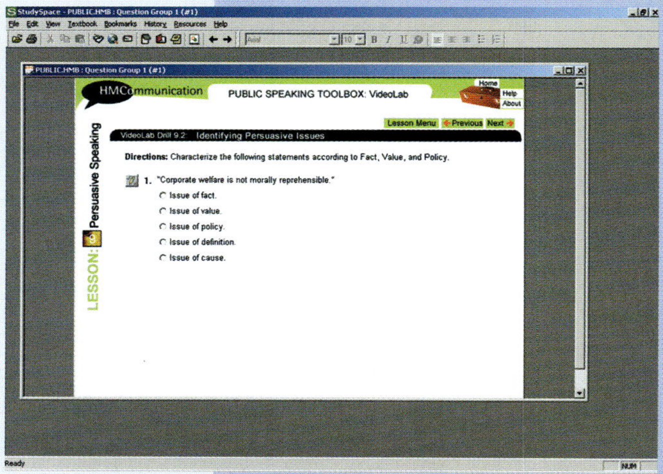

Online SpeechStudio in Eduspace

Ready to use, and easy to integrate into any public speaking course, the Online SpeechStudio in Eduspace powered by Blackboard™ extends the mastery of public speaking skills beyond the classroom. This interactive speech preparation toolkit and course management system helps students learn to model and compose organized, thoughtful speeches and build an online portfolio of their work. With resources tailored to all of the major types of speech design, the Online SpeechStudio gives students hands-on practice with every stage of the speech development process—from selecting a topic and audience analysis, to outlining and critiquing.

The Online SpeechStudio gets students thinking about what they want to say and how they want to say it with a host of self-assessments, worksheets, and tools—including a new PowerPoint tutorial and a new speech outliner tool.

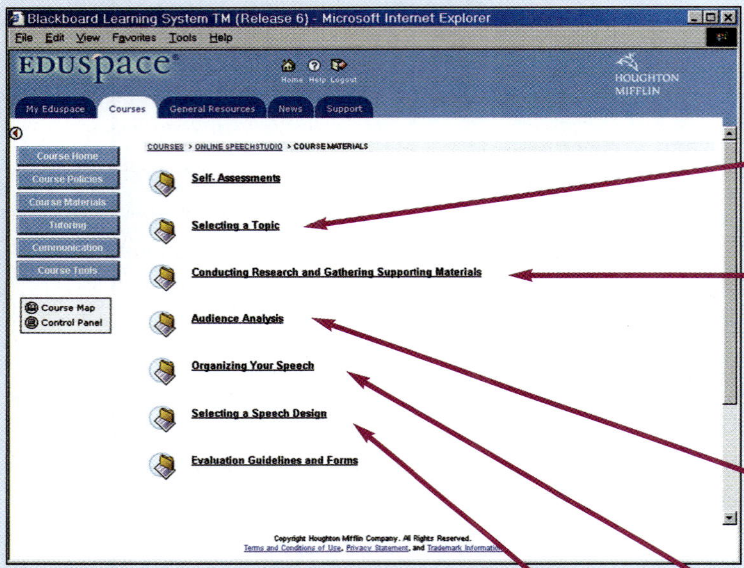

Selecting a Topic helps students think critically about personal knowledge and experience, audience interest, and focus as they work toward choosing the right topic.

Conducting Research assists students in conducting strategic and thorough research to back up arguments and support points.

Audience Analysis helps students assess an audience in terms of attitude, environment, logistics, and occasion.

Organizing Your Speech helps students write with focus.

Selecting a Speech Design features nine common design types students can use to determine which speech design to choose and when.

A Complete Package for Instructors and Students

Instructor Supplements

Annotated Instructor's Edition (0-618-53196-3) includes general and ESL teaching tips for every chapter.

Instructor's Resource Manual, available online, is completely updated and revised. Part I of the manual includes:

- Overview of the purpose and philosophy of the course
- Information on preparing a syllabus
- Sample syllabi
- A variety of speech assignments
- Information on evaluating and grading speeches
- Troubleshooting guide with teaching strategies for new instructors
- Bibliography of resource readings

Part II offers a chapter-by-chapter guide to teaching Public Speaking, including:

- Learning objectives
- Suggestions for teaching
- Lecture/discussion outlines
- Classroom activities
- Transparency/handout masters
- Bibliography of readings for enrichment

Instructor Textbook Website with Online Test Bank also includes an online IRM, PowerPoint slides, exercises, and other ancillary material.

HM ClassPrep CD-ROM (0-618-53201-3) includes digital versions of the IRM, Test Bank, and PowerPoint slides.

Student Speeches Video (0-618-53199-8) and **Video Guide** (available online). The Student Speeches Video offers a selection of new, real-life student speeches, while the accompanying online Video Guide contains the text of each speech, an evaluation of the presentation, discussion items, and commentary.

Great Speeches Video (0-618-31275-7) features contemporary speeches by Jimmy Carter, George Bush, Lyndon Johnson, Geneva Overholser, and Cesar Chavez.

"Using Visual Aids" Video (0-618-22367-3) shows students how best to use visual aids (i.e., video clips, charts, special guests) in a presentation.

Student Resources

Student Textbook Website includes chapter-specific test questions, student speeches with relevant exercises, vocabulary flashcards, and updated links to relevant websites.

VideoLab CD-ROM, packaged with the student text, offers student speeches, analysis, exercises, and tips to help students develop and deliver their own speeches.

Online Speech Studio in Eduspace is a speech preparation toolkit that gives students hands-on practice with every stage of the speech development process, including selecting a topic, conducting research, audience analysis, organizing a speech, and critiquing. Recently enhanced, the Online Speech Studio now also offers:

- **PowerPoint Tutorial,** which provides students a step-by-step guide on how to use PowerPoint efficiently when giving a speech.
- **Speech Outliner,** which offers students a self-directed, step-by-step electronic process for outlining speeches.

Multicultural Activities Workbook, (0-395-83994-7) a student workbook with hands-on activities including checklists, surveys, and writing assignments, geared towards a multicultural classroom.

Motley, *Overcoming Your Fear of Public Speaking,* (0-395-88459-4) written by a well-respected researcher and communication anxiety specialist, this brief handbook focuses on approaching a speech as a communication task rather than as a performance. This guide offers assistance to every student who suffers from speech anxiety.

Speech Prep Workbook, (0-618-53197-1) developed and updated by Suzanne Osborn, contains materials for activities mentioned in the text and skeleton outline formats for the major speech designs.

Classical Origins of Public Speaking, (0-395-65347-9) written by Michael Osborn, offers a concise overview of classical Greek theory on the nature and importance of public speaking.

About the Authors

Michael Osborn, Ph.D. is retired from the University of Memphis, but continues to teach by appointment every other semester at schools such as the University of New Mexico and Vanderbilt University. A past president of the National Communication Association, Mike earned his Ph.D. in rhetoric from the University of Florida and is recognized as a leading scholar in the field of public language and rhetoric.

Suzanne Osborn, Ph.D. has held faculty positions at the University of Memphis, Indiana University, and Christian Brothers College where she taught courses in public speaking and organizational communication. Suzanne has a degree in psychology from the University of Memphis and is the author of a hybrid communication text and a public speaking workbook, both published by Houghton Mifflin.

Public Speaking

PUBLIC SPEAKING

SEVENTH EDITION

MICHAEL OSBORN
University of Memphis

SUZANNE OSBORN
University of Memphis

HOUGHTON MIFFLIN COMPANY
Boston New York

Publisher, Humanities: Patricia A. Coryell
Senior Sponsoring Editor: Mary Finch
Development Editor: Julia Casson
Senior Project Editor: Fred Burns
Editorial Assistant: Brett Pasinella
Manufacturing Coordinator: Chuck Dutton
Senior Art and Design Coordinator: Jill Haber
Senior Composition Buyer: Sarah Ambrose
Marketing Manager: Elinor Gregory
Marketing Assistant: Evelyn Yang

Photo credits may be found on page 556.

Custom Publishing Editor: Peter Nowka
Custom Publishing Production Manager: Tina Kozik
Project Coordinator: Kim Gavrilles

Cover Design: Emily Quillen

Printed in the United States of America.

ISBN: 0-618-66892-6
N-05265

2 3 4 5 6 7 8 9 – WP – 07 06 05

Houghton Mifflin
Custom Publishing

222 Berkeley Street • Boston, MA 02116

Address all correspondence and order information to the above address.

Houghton Mifflin's VideoLab

Lesson 1: Public Speaking 101
Speech of Self-Introduction

Lesson 2: Audience Analysis and Adaptation
Persuasive Speech: Child Protection

Lesson 3: The Importance of Listening
Persuasive Speech: Chicago Mass Transit

Lesson 4: Gathering Materials to Support Your Ideas
Informative Speech: Depression

Lesson 5: Organizing and Outlining Your Speech
Informative Speech: Overcoming the Fear of Public Speaking
Persuasive Speech: Olestra

Lesson 6: Delivering Your Speech
Persuasive Speech: Native American Symbols

Lesson 7: Language Use
Persuasive Speech: Corporate Welfare

Lesson 8: Informative Speaking
Informative Speech: Milk Additives

Lesson 9: Persuasive Speaking
Persuasive Speech: Woman's Gymnastics (version 1)
Persuasive Speech: Woman's Gymnastics (version 2)

Lesson 10: Ceremonial Speaking
Ceremonial Speech: Seizing Opportunities

Minimum System Requirements

General
RAM: 128 MB minimum, 256 MB recommended
Resolution: 800x600 minimum, 1024x768 recommended
Hard Drive space: 20 MB minimum

Windows
Windows XP, 2000, 98/ME
Internet Explorer 6.x, 5.5, 5.0.
Netscape 7.x, 6.1, 6.2.

Macintosh
OSX 10.3, 10.2, 10.1 (Native OSX support)
OS 9.2
Internet Explorer 5.x
Netscape 7.x, 6.2
Safari 1.x

Getting Started

Windows

Insert the CD-Rom into your CD-Rom drive. The program will autorun. From the Welcome screen, click Enter. From the Table of Contents page, select a lesson to begin. If the program does not autorun, access your CD-Rom drive by clicking My Computer, or through Windows Explorer. Open the contents of your CD-Rom drive. Then click on Start to launch the program.

Macintosh

Insert the CD-Rom into your CD-Rom drive. The VideoLab icon will appear on your screen. Click on the VideoLab icon. Then click on Start to launch the program. From the Welcome screen, click Enter. From the Table of Contents page, select a lesson to begin.

Technical Support

Call Houghton Mifflin Software Support at 800-732-3223 between 9am and 5pm (EST) Monday through Friday.
Email support@hmco.com. We respond to email within 24 hours.

Please have the following information available when you call Technical Support: Computer Operating System and Version, and Browser Type and Version.

Dedication

We dedicate this edition of *Public Speaking* to Optimist International, which sponsors the annual Communication Contest for the Deaf and Hard of Hearing. This event, supported each year by nearly 300 Optimist Clubs, has helped convince countless young people that they have worth, and that an impairment does not mean that they can't communicate with others. In particular, we want to express admiration for our friend, Otis Gray, Memphis Optimist, who has been the inspiring angel behind the event. His vision and determination originated the contest in Memphis, and made its development into an international event not only possible, but inevitable.

Contents

Preface

The study of rhetoric, as applied in public speaking, is returning to its traditional place at the center of the liberal arts. The great events and controversies of our time have reaffirmed this classical centrality and have elevated the importance of our discipline on the nation's education agenda. Issues such as determining the validity of evidence, assessing the adequacy of proof, and deciding when conclusions are justified in the light of proof and evidence are re-emerging not just as personal and pedagogical concerns but as a crisis at the heart of social and political life. We believe strongly that education should equip students to deal with these critical issues of deliberation and communication. The seventh edition of *Public Speaking* has been revised and renewed in the spirit of this conviction.

Long-time users of our book will recognize that we have made significant changes while preserving the virtues that have characterized past editions. We hope you will share our enthusiasm over both the changes and continuities in the Seventh Edition.

The Spirit of Our Book

From its first edition, *Public Speaking* has stressed three objectives: preparing students for civic life, respecting the diversity of the contemporary audience, and sensitizing students to the ethical impact of their words on others.

Ancient educators recognized this study as the core of a liberal education. What other discipline, they argued, requires students to think clearly, be attuned to the needs of listeners, organize their thoughts, select and combine words artfully and judiciously, and express themselves with power and conviction, all while under the direct scrutiny of an audience? The challenge to teach such a complex range of abilities has always been difficult, but today it is especially so, as people struggle to define what it means to be human in the context of social situations. Civic engagement is the site of this ongoing struggle; the task of communication educators is to empower students in social, economic, and political situations that require public speaking skills. Not only personal success but also the fate of communities may depend upon the outcomes.

Another core objective of our book is to illuminate the role of public speaking in a diverse society. Adjusting to a diverse audience is a challenge ancient writers could not have anticipated. The increasing cultural diversity of our society adds to the importance of public speaking as a force that can counter division. Thus, cultural diversity is a theme that remains constant in our book.

We continue to believe that a major goal of public speaking is to make students sensitive to its potential impact on the lives of others. Because of the pervasive importance of values and ethics, we discuss ethical considerations throughout the book. For example, we direct the attention of students to ethical concerns as we consider listening, audience analysis and adaptation, cultural variations, topic selection, research, ways of structuring speeches, presentation aids, use of language, and the consequences of informing and persuading others. In particular, the persuasion chapters have been revised to develop a new ethical concept: *argumentative persuasion*, emphasizing the centrality of reasoned proofs, is advanced as an antidote to that *manipulative persuasion* evident in much contemporary communication. The development of argumentative persuasion extends a moral axiom that has characterized our book since its inception: the speaker's obligation to offer listeners *responsible knowledge*.

For all these reasons we continue to believe that a college course in public speaking should offer both practical advice and an understanding of why such advice works. We emphasize both the *how* and the *why* of public speaking—*how* so that beginners can achieve success as quickly as possible, and *why* so that they can manage their new skills wisely. Consistent with this philosophy, we base our practical advice on underlying principles of human communication. As we advise readers on structuring speeches, we show how various speech designs connect with basic psychological concepts of "good form," explaining why some speeches succeed and others fail. We ground our advice on informative speaking in the principles of learning theory, and our suggestions on persuasive speaking on research from social psychology, philosophy, and the communication discipline. Our approach is eclectic: we draw from the past and present and from the social sciences and humanities to help students understand and manage their public speaking experiences.

The Roman educator Quintilian held forth the ideal of "the good person speaking well" as a goal of education. We join him in stressing the value of speech training in the development of the whole person. We also suggest that education in public speaking is excellent training for leadership. In addition, understanding the principles of public communication can make students more resistant to unethical speakers and more critical of the mass-mediated communication to which they are exposed. The class should help students become both better consumers as well as producers of public communication.

We have continued throughout the book to follow the metaphorical themes of the student as climber, builder, and weaver to represent the important dimensions of personal growth and development that the public speaking class makes possible. The student learns to climb barriers of personal and cultural interference that block authentic communication. The student also learns how to build ideas, mastering how and when to use different designs and forms of supporting materials. Finally, the student learns how to weave words into a clear, colorful fabric of communication and how to fashion a tapestry of argument out of evidence and proof. Mastering these central metaphors is the key not only to effective communication, but also to successful living.

Innovations in the New Edition

The seventh edition of *Public Speaking* is marked by seven significant changes: (1) the development of dual models of oral communication, (2) a separate new chapter on communication anxiety, (3) a separate new chapter on topic selection and evaluation, (4) a separate new chapter on research for public speaking, (5) an expanded development of narrative as a form of supporting material and as a design for structuring speeches, (6) substantial revision of the persuasion chapters, and (7) a number of important new themes and concepts woven into the fabric of the book.

Dual Models of Communication

We have long had the uneasy feeling that reducing oral communication to a single model that emphasizes the technical features of speaking is a mistake. Such a model can result in over-simplifying, if not misrepresenting, the subject. To counter this problem, we have developed dual, complementary models that provide together a more complete portrayal of the rich and complex process of communication that occurs in successful speaking.

The first of these models, the mechanical model, developed out of the study of electronic communication in the Bell Telephone Laboratory around the middle of the twentieth century. The mechanical model helps students understand the physical and technical constraints that shape communication. Such concepts as "interference" and "feedback" are gifts of this model.

The second model, the identification model, is based on the work of communication theorist Kenneth Burke. This model is helpful in pointing out the major ethical consequences of oral communication, especially the effects of transactional and transformational communication.

Together, these two models function more adequately to describe the "yin and the yang" of public speaking, the essential technical and ethical/spiritual features of the subject. They reflect a consciousness that communication is both a craft and an art. They justify two levels of awareness as the book develops: a recognition that speakers must master techniques, but also an admonition that their words shape—for better or worse—the human condition.

Separate New Chapter on Communication Anxiety

All of us are aware of the corrosive effect of fear on oral presentations. To help students handle this fear, we have changed what was an appendix in the sixth edition and moved it near the beginning of the book (Chapter 2). Our intent is to encourage students to confront and control the symptoms of anxiety early in the course so that the problem becomes manageable and not an impediment to their development as speakers.

We describe communication anxiety as a normal response to an abnormal situation. Our goal is to help students channel their anxious energy into constructive energy so that it plays a productive role in their communication experiences.

Separate New Chapter on Finding Your Topic

Getting off on the right foot by finding and focusing a speech topic that is appropriate to the speaker, the audience, and the assignment is vital to success in the course. For this reason, we have developed what was once part of a chapter into a separate chapter (Chapter 6). We offer a creative synthesis that integrates a number of techniques that are too often used in separate, willy-nilly approaches to the subject.

We divide topic selection into three phases: discovery, exploration, and refinement. During the discovery phase, the student applies the techniques of brainstorming, interest charts, and media prompts to uncover promising topic areas. To explore and narrow these areas into topic possibilities, we teach students how to apply the non-directive technique of mind-mapping and the directive technique of topic analysis.

During the refinement phase, we show students how to frame the general purpose, specific purpose, and the thesis statement of the topic they have selected. The process of refinement is like looking at a topic through lenses of a microscope so that it emerges in clearer and sharper form.

Separate New Chapter on Researching Your Topic

Central to our book is the idea that the ethical speaker must demonstrate *responsible knowledge* of the major facts and issues surrounding a subject. The business of developing such knowledge through research is now covered in a separate chapter (Chapter 7). We show students how to develop and follow a strategic research plan. The chapter is followed by a comprehensive list of Internet resources, categorized by general topic areas. Of special interest is the new chapter's discussion of accessing and using the invisible (deep) web. Also valuable is its section on evaluating Internet research, which presents criteria for evaluating advocacy, information, and personal websites.

New Emphasis on Narrative

The ability to tell a story, whether it be one's personal story or some beloved cultural legend, can be vital to a speaker's success. In Chapter 8 we have expanded our discussion of narrative as a form of supporting material, incorporating the important work of Professor Walter Fisher of the University of Southern California. In Chapter 17 we have provided a discussion of narrative design, which differs from the linear, logical patterns typically used in public speeches. Speakers who use narrative design follow a dramatic pattern of development, in which they develop a prologue that foreshadows the story, a plot, and an epilogue.

Substantial Revision of the Persuasion Chapters

The uncertainties of our time demand a renewed insistence on the centrality of reasoned discourse in the work of persuasion. We offer a substantial revision of our persuasion chapters (Chapters 15 and 16) in response to this need. Changes in our model of the forms of proof especially reflect this new awareness. Personal, emotional, and cultural forms of proof remain important, but within a framework that assures the primacy of responsible reasoning. Additionally, we have developed the concept of argumentative persuasion to emphasize the ethical importance of reasoning in the formation of public policy.

Along with this change of emphasis, we give renewed attention to the thoughtful listener. Such a listener will ask certain questions of the persuader. Showing the speaker how to anticipate these questions and plan in response to them underlies the structure of our revised Chapter 16. In this chapter we introduce the Toulmin model of proofs to help students grasp how to make reasoning work productively in persuasive efforts. To make the discussion more precise, we have divided persuasive speaking into three types: fact, value, and policy. The result of these changes, we believe, is a clearer, better structured, and more ethically defensible discussion of persuasion.

New Themes and Elements

Longtime users will also recognize other changes in our book:

- Expanded, step-by-step tutorial at the end of Chapter 11 on how to prepare simple slides for presentations using PowerPoint. The chapter also includes cautions on how *not* to misuse this popular new technology.
- Renewed emphasis on the practical "how to" dimension of the text. Part of this new emphasis is the addition of "Discussion and Application" items at the end of each chapter.
- Expanded use of the Speaker's Notes, Ethics Alert!, and InterConnections features of the text. These popular innovations from previous editions are introduced as highlighted, boxed inserts in each chapter. They help focus the reader's learning experience, raise ethical considerations at vital moments, and offer opportunities for learning enrichment.
- Introduction of "Stairway to Speech Success" model in Chapter 3 to help students integrate and assimilate the advice on developing their first speeches.

- Expanded use of the "Ladder of Listening" model in Chapter 4 to reinforce the importance of critical and constructive listening within the communication experience.
- Development of the concept of *integrated communication* in Chapter 13 to emphasize how the convergence of presentation and content factors in a speech can create a compelling communication experience for all participants.
- A treasure trove of new examples from student and professional speeches, along with favorites from previous editions.

Distinctive Features of Our Book

A textbook is a rhetorical product: it must constantly adapt to the changing times and needs of its student audience. Nevertheless, some features have remained constant and distinctive across the many editions of our book.

- *Responsible knowledge as a standard for public speaking.* In order to develop a standard for the quality and depth of information that should be reflected in all speeches, we offer the concept of *responsible knowledge.* This concept is developed in detail in Chapter 7, in which we discuss the foundation of research that should support speeches.
- *Special preparation for the first speech.* As teachers we all realize the importance of the first speaking experience to a student's ultimate success in the course. Yet much useful advice must be delayed until later chapters as the subject of public speaking develops systematically over a semester. Having experienced this frustration ourselves while teaching the course, we decided from the outset to include an overview of practical advice early in the book that previews later chapters and prepares students more effectively for their first speeches. This overview is provided in Chapter 3.
- *Communication ethics.* We have always discussed ethical issues as they arise in the context of topics, rather than confining the subject to a chapter on its own. *Ethics Alert!* helps us to highlight these concerns as they develop chapter-by-chapter within the situations to which they apply.
- *Internet research.* Recognizing that today's student often turns to the Internet for information and opinions, we offer a variety of resources to enrich the research experience, provide standards for evaluating what students find there, and develop a plan to help them use such materials judiciously. Chapter 7 offers an extensive directory of websites, selected specifically for their relevance to student speakers. *InterConnections.LearnMore,* offered in most chapters, highlight online educational opportunities throughout the book.
- *Enriched treatment of listening.* Our discussion of listening is distinctive in three important ways. First, we introduce the concept of listener apprehension, which is presently receiving considerable attention in listening research. This new concept identifies an important challenge that both speakers and listeners must overcome. Second, we offer a model of the *ladder of listening* to help students understand the various kinds of listening and the relationships among them. Third, we enlarge the focus on listening in order to emphasize its constructive as well as critical dimensions.
- *The importance of narrative in public speaking.* We discuss narrative as an important form of supporting material and as a previously neglected design option. We also identify appeals to traditions, heroic symbols, and legends—all built upon

narrative—as an important emerging form of proof (*mythos*) in persuasive speaking.

- *Improving language skills.* We offer a cohesive approach to teaching language skills that emphasizes understanding the power of language, applying standards so that this power is not diminished, and learning special techniques that can magnify this power at important moments in speeches. Among the standards is learning how to avoid grammatical errors that make listeners cringe.
- *Enhanced understanding of ceremonial speaking.* The study of ceremonial speaking too often has been treated as a collection of "occasional speech" assignments, combined with little rationale into a chapter that sometimes seemed tagged on at the end of a book. We provide coherence and dignity for this subject by pointing out the importance of ceremonial speaking in society, and by indicating how two powerful concepts, one offered by Aristotle and the other by Kenneth Burke, can be combined to generate successful ceremonial speeches, especially speeches of tribute and inspiration.

Plan of the Book

Public Speaking is designed to help beginning students build knowledge and skills step by step. Positive initial speaking experiences are especially important. For this reason, Chapter 2 helps apprehensive students control communication anxiety as they stand to speak for the first time. Chapter 3 offers an overview of advice to help students design and present successful first speeches.

In the chapters that follow, students learn how to listen critically and constructively, analyze their audiences, select, refine, and research speech topics, develop supporting materials, arrange these materials in appropriate structures, outline their thinking, and create effective presentation aids. They also learn how to manage words and present their messages. Students become acquainted with the nature of information and how to present it, the process of persuasion and how to engage it, and the importance of ceremonial speaking in its various forms. Appendix A, "Communicating in Small Groups," describes how to use public communication skills to participate effectively in small group interactions.

Teachers may adapt the sequence of chapters to any course plan, because each chapter covers a topic thoroughly and completely.

Detailed Plan of the Book

Part I, "The Foundations of Public Speaking," provides basic information that students need for their first speaking and listening experiences. Chapter 1 defines public speaking as communication, highlights the personal, social, and cultural benefits of being able to speak effectively in public, and emphasizes the ethical responsibilities of speakers. Chapter 2 helps students come to terms with communication anxiety, so that they can control this problem early in the course. Chapter 3 offers practical advice for organizing, practicing, and presenting first speeches. Chapter 4 identifies common listening problems and ways to overcome them, helps students sharpen critical thinking skills, and presents criteria for the constructive evaluation of speeches.

Part II, "Preparation for Public Speaking," introduces the basic skills needed to develop effective speeches. Chapter 5 emphasizes the importance of the audience, indicating how to adapt a message and how to adjust to factors in the speaking situation. Chapter 6 provides a systematic way to discover, evaluate, and refine speech topics. Chapter 7 shows how to research these topics, emphasizing the importance of acquiring *responsible knowledge*. Chapter 8 identifies the major types of supporting materials gathered from such research, including facts and statistics, examples, testimony, and narratives. The chapter shows how to bring supporting materials to life through comparison, contrast, and analogy. Chapter 9 shows how to develop simple, balanced, and orderly speech designs, how to select and shape main points, how to use transitions, and how to prepare effective introductions and conclusions. Chapter 10 explains how to develop working outlines, refine them into formal outlines, and derive key-word outlines for use during presentation. An extended example in Chapters 8, 9, and 10 illustrates how a speech on an environmental topic might develop from its initial conception to its final presentation.

Part III, "Developing Presentation Skills," brings the speaker to the point of presentation. Chapter 11 explains the preparation of presentation aids, including PowerPoint presentations. Chapter 12 provides an understanding of the role of language in communication and offers practical suggestions for using words effectively. Chapter 13 offers exercises for the improvement of voice and body language and helps students develop an extemporaneous style that is adaptable to most speaking situations.

Part IV, "Functions of Public Speaking," discusses informative, persuasive, and ceremonial speaking. Chapter 14 covers speeches designed to share information and increase understanding. The chapter discusses the different types of informative speeches and presents the major designs that can be used. Chapter 15 describes the persuasive process, focusing on how to meet the many challenges of persuasion. In Chapter 16 we develop the concept of argumentative persuasion, helping students develop strong, reasoned cases to support their positions. The chapter also identifies the major forms of fallacies so that student speakers can avoid them and detect them in the messages of others. Chapter 17 explains how to prepare effective ceremonial presentations, including speeches of tribute and inspiration, speeches introducing others, eulogies, after-dinner speeches, and speeches presenting and accepting awards. The chapter explains the narrative design, often used in ceremonial speeches.

Appendix A, "Communicating in Small Groups," introduces students to the problem-solving process and to the responsibilities of both group leaders and group participants. This appendix also provides guidelines for managing informal and formal meetings, and explains the basic concepts of parliamentary procedure. Appendix B provides a number of student and professional speeches for additional analysis.

Learning Tools

To help students master the material, we offer a number of special learning tools.

- We open each chapter with a table of contents and learning objectives that prepare students for efficient and productive reading.
- The epigrams and vignettes that start each chapter help point up the topic's significance and motivate readers.
- We use contemporary artwork and photographs to illustrate ideas, engage student interest, and add to the visual appeal of the book.
- Examples illustrate and apply the content in a clear, lively, and often entertaining way.
- Speaker's Notes, Ethics Alert!, and InterConnections.LearnMore features help students learn the essentials, apply what they are learning to ethical issues, and pursue additional information using the Internet.

- Annotations in the chapter margins cue students to learning enrichment opportunities offered in the VideoLab CD-ROM and Online SpeechStudio supplements provided with the book.
- We end each chapter with In Summary, Terms to Know, and Discussion and Application features that further reinforce learning.
- Sample classroom speeches found at the ends of many chapters illustrate important concepts. The annotated speech texts show how the concepts apply in actual speaking. Appendix B contains additional speeches for analysis that cover an interesting array of topics, contexts, and speakers.
- A glossary at the end of the book defines Terms to Know in a comprehensive, accessible format.

Supplementary Materials

The following materials are available to adopters of *Public Speaking:*

For Instructors

- An ***Instructor's Annotated Edition*** includes general and ESL teaching tips for every chapter.
- The ***Instructor's Resource Manual*** that has been completely updated and revised by Michael Vickery of Alma College. Part I of the manual includes sections on the purpose and philosophy of the course, preparing a syllabus, various sample syllabi, an assortment of speech assignment options, a discussion of evaluating and grading speeches, a troubleshooting guide with teaching strategies for new instructors, and an extensive bibliography of resource readings. Part II offers a chapter-by-chapter guide to teaching *Public Speaking,* including learning objectives, suggestions for teaching, lecture/discussion outlines, classroom activities, transparency/handout masters, and a bibliography of readings for enrichment. This comprehensive manual can be used as a text for training teaching assistants.
- A ***Test Bank*** prepared by Jim Parker of Vanderbilt University is provided separately from the IRM to provide test security.
- A ***PowerPoint Program,*** useful as a lecture supplement, created by Todd Frosbish, assistant professor at Fayetteville State University, is available on the Houghton Mifflin website.
- The ***HMClass Prep™ Instructor's CD-ROM*** contains digital versions of the IRM, a computer-generated test bank, and the seventh edition PowerPoint Slides.
- ***Student Speeches Video*** offers a selection of student speeches accompanied by a guide that contains the text of each speech, an evaluation of the presentation, discussion items, and commentary.
- ***Contemporary Great Speeches Video*** is the latest compilation in the series from the Educational Video Group.
- The ***Instructor companion website*** contains updated links, exercises, and other ancillary material for both instructor and student use.

For Students

- The ***Speech Preparation Workbook*** developed by Suzanne Osborn that contains materials for activities mentioned in the text and skeleton outline formats for the major speech designs.
- The ***Classical Origins of Public Speaking*** supplement written by Michael Osborn that offers a concise overview of classical Greek theory on the nature and importance of public speaking.
- The ***PowerPoint Tutorial*** prepared by Martin McDermott of Brookdale College, is available online and will give students a step-by-step guide on how to use PowerPoint efficiently when giving a speech.
- The ***VideoLab CD-ROM*** offers student speeches, analysis, exercises, and tips to help students develop and deliver their own speeches.
- The ***Online SpeechStudio*** in Eduspace is a speech preparation toolkit that gives students hands-on practice with every stage of the speech development process, including selecting a topic, conducting research, audience analysis, organizing a speech, and critiquing.
- The online ***Speech Outliner*** offers students a self-directed, step-by-step electronic process for outlining speeches.
- The ***Student Companion Website*** includes chapter-specific test questions, vocabulary flashcards, updated links to relevant websites and additional communication career resources.

Acknowledgments

Many people have helped improve *Public Speaking* over its two decades of existence. For this edition, we especially thank Kristen Desmond LeFevre, special projects editor, for her many astute suggestions. Julia Casson, development editor for communication at Houghton Mifflin, devoted herself to completing our project as it entered its final phases. Elinor Gregory, marketing manager, has helped *Public Speaking* find its audience. Mary Finch, sponsoring editor for communication, has offered encouragement and support at critical moments.

We are grateful to our colleagues listed below whose critical readings have sparked the many improvements in the Seventh Edition.

Linda Atwell, George Mason University
Mark Banks, Slippery Rock University of Pennsylvania
Marcia Berry, Azusa Pacific University
Andrew Billings, Clemson University
Vincent L. Bloom, California State University, Fresno
John Campbell, University of Memphis
Terry M. Cunconan, Central Missouri State University
Michael Eaves, Valdosta State
David Foster, University of Findlay
Deborah Hefferin, Broward Community College
Richard Ice, St. John's University/College of St. Benedict
Timothy James, Community College of Southern Nevada

Corwin P. King, Central Washington University
Jan A Kruse, Western Michigan University
Katherine L. Nelson, Barry University
Jean E. Perry, Glendale Community College
Paul Siegel, University of Hartford
Sharon S. Smith, Middle Tennessee State University
Dick Stine, Johnson Community College
Mary E. Triece, University of Akron
Nancy J. Wendt, Oregon State University
David Williams, Texas Tech University

List of Speeches

Self-Introductory

Topic Briefing

Informative

Persuasive

Ceremonial

The Foundations of Public Speaking

PART I

1 Public Speaking and You

This chapter will help you

- realize how a public speaking course can help you
- understand public speaking as communication
- recognize your ethical responsibilities as a speaker

OUTLINE

The ability to make a good speech is a great gift to the people from their Maker, Owner of all things.

OGLALA SIOUX

Mary was worried about taking public speaking. She had put off the course as long as she could, but finally she had to take it in order to graduate. At the first class meeting, she saw about twenty-five other stone-faced students who looked as uncomfortable as she felt. Because dropping the course was not an option, she steeled herself to stick it out.

Mary's first oral assignment was a speech of self-introduction. As she prepared her speech, it dawned on her why she found her major, marine biology, so fascinating. When she spoke, her enthusiasm for her topic helped relieve her nervousness. Although her speech was not perfect, she did some things very well. Listeners could now see her as an individual. She had built up credibility for her later informative and persuasive speeches on the fate of the oceans.

As she listened to others speak, Mary's fears began to recede. Many of the speeches were interesting, and she joined in the discussion of what worked well and how the speeches might be improved. The stony faces of her classmates began to chip away to reveal the human beings they had masked.

Mary began to care about her classmates and to take pleasure in their successes. As she researched her speeches, she kept their interests in mind. She sought out facts, opinions, examples, and stories that they would find useful and compelling. Toward the end of the term it dawned on her: she had become a speaker! She believed she could meet the challenges of speaking and listening whenever they should arise in her later life beyond the classroom.

Our "Mary" represents the many successful students we have known in our years of teaching public speaking. You also may wonder why you are taking this course, even whether you can make it through the semester, let alone be successful. To make yourself into a "Mary," you must commit yourself to the work required to be successful. You must decide that you want to learn more about public speaking, that you will select meaningful topics, that you will treat listeners ethically, and that you will listen constructively to others. In this chapter, we will say more about why your public speaking course deserves your commitment, introduce this art you will be learning more about, and explain why it requires your utmost ethical sensitivity.

Public Speaking? Why Me?

Some students bring a negative attitude to the public speaking class. "Why do I have to take this course? I'm not going to be a public speaker. Besides, I'm terrified. I don't have anything to say, and if I did, I wouldn't know how to say it." Disguised in these questions and complaints are genuine fears and some ignorance. The good news is that the worst complainers often have the most to gain from a public speaking class.

Learning to present yourself and your ideas effectively in public settings can help you handle some important moments in your life: times when you need to speak to protect your family's interests, or when your values are threatened by the action or inaction of others, or when you need approval to undertake some important project. In such situations, family, spiritual, and material values may all depend on your ability to speak effectively.

Moreover, the principles you learn in this class can make you a more astute consumer of public messages. They will help you sort through the barrage of information and misinformation that bombards us on a daily basis. Developing public speaking and critical listening skills can produce profound personal, social, and cultural benefits.

Personal Benefits

When you stand up before others to speak, *you* are the focus of attention. At first this may seem strange, and you may feel awkward—even a little uncomfortable. You may experience one or several of the following doubts and problems:

- You might feel nervous. *But what if your public speaking course could help you learn to control your fear, to convert your nervous energy into an exciting presentation of yourself and your ideas?*
- You may wonder how and whether you can hold attention. *But what if your public speaking course could help you learn how to use striking facts and figures, offer colorful examples, and tell fascinating stories?*
- There may be moments when you mumble and stare at the wall. *But what if your public speaking course could help you learn to smile and make eye contact with listeners, and speak forcefully about important matters? What if you become a compelling, eloquent speaker?*

You have much to gain personally from this course, if you are willing to invest yourself in it. The skills you develop should help you develop confidence, project your best self to others, and earn for your ideas the attention they deserve. In short, they should help you become a more effective person. Consider the following:

- **You will learn more about yourself.** To select a promising topic, you must explore your own interests and values. To prepare a substantive message, you must expand your knowledge. Preparing an effective speech sparks creative self-expression as you combine ideas and information in new ways.
- **You will learn about others.** To tailor your message to your audience, you must become sensitive to their needs and interests. In your public speaking classroom, you will encounter many diverse voices. Public speaking experiences invite us to listen to each other, to savor what makes each of us unique and valuable, and to develop an appreciation for the different ways people live. Your experiences in this class should bring you closer to meeting one of the major goals of higher education: "to expand the mind and heart beyond fear of the unknown, opening

them to the whole range of human experience."[1]

- **You will learn to be a more effective listener.** Listening is a part of communication that is often neglected, even though we listen far more than we speak. You will learn the twin arts of critical and constructive listening, so that you can recognize the flaws and deficiencies of messages as well as appreciate their virtues and worth.

The skills you learn in your public speaking class can help you in many ways. Learning to present yourself well can be an asset in job interviews.

- **The personal growth you experience in a public speaking class can help you in other classes, in campus activities, and in later life.** On a practical level, the ability to communicate ideas effectively is vital to getting a good job and advancing professionally. Each year, the National Association of Colleges and Employers (NACE) surveys hundreds of corporate recruiting specialists. On the basis of a survey of 294 employers in various fields, NACE isolated eleven fundamental skills that recruiters seek in job candidates. *The most important of these skills—at the top of the list—was oral communication.* NACE concluded: "Learn to speak clearly, confidently, and concisely."[2] In a similar study, 250 companies surveyed by the Center for Public Resources rated speaking and listening as among the most critical areas in need of improvement for people entering the work force. Martin Ives, vice chair of the Governmental Accounting Standards Board, commented, "The difference between an average career and a 'special' career is the ability to communicate orally and in writing."[3] Finally, an American Council on Education report, *Employment Prospects for College Graduates,* advises readers that "good oral and written skills can be your most prized asset" in getting and holding a desirable position."[4]

- **The abilities you develop in this class also can help you be a more effective citizen.** If you think you may never have to speak outside the classroom, picture the following scenarios:

The local school board has announced that it plans to remove *A Catcher in the Rye, Huckleberry Finn, Of Mice and Men,* and *To Kill a Mockingbird* from the high school library. It will hold a public hearing on this issue at its next regular meeting. You disagree with the school board's decision and decide you must attend this meeting to speak out for your principles and for the rights of your children.

You have just rented an off-campus apartment. It isn't until after you move in that you discover that the faucets leak, the wiring is dangerous, and you're about to be run out of the place by roaches. The landlord refuses to do anything about the problems, and the city's rental properties department gives you the runaround. To protect yourself and other students caught up in similar situations, you decide to attend the next City Council meeting and to speak up during the time reserved for public participation.

Speaker's Notes 1.1

Public Speaking Can Help You

1. increase your confidence in your ability to speak in public.
2. learn more about yourself and others.
3. learn how to develop effective content for your speeches.
4. exercise your ability to use words precisely and colorfully.
5. become a more compelling speaker.
6. learn more about informing, persuading, and inspiring others.
7. develop the art of constructive listening.
8. become a more critical consumer of messages.
9. become more sensitive to the ethical dimensions of communication.
10. prepare for those times when your ability to communicate will determine success or failure.
11. expand your career options and enhance your attractiveness as a candidate for rewarding positions.
12. develop your understanding of important public issues.
13. become a more effective citizen.

Anna Aley, a student at Kansas State University, was living in similar substandard off-campus housing. She brought that problem to the attention of her classmates in a persuasive speech (see Appendix B). Her listeners then asked her to represent them by presenting the speech at a campus public forum. During that presentation, Anna made such an impression that the local newspaper printed the text of her speech and launched an investigation of off-campus housing problems. The paper followed up with a strong editorial, and the mayor established an enforceable rental inspection program in Manhattan, Kansas. When we called him, the mayor told us: "Anna's speech certainly made a difference in our community." Although this story is unusual, speeches—even speeches given in classes by students—are a vital part of citizenship.

- **A final personal bonus of your public speaking class is that it makes you an active participant in the learning process.** You don't just sit in a class, absorbing lectures. You put communication to work. The speeches you give illustrate the strategies, the possibilities, and the problems of human communication. As you join in the discussions that follow these speeches, you learn to identify elements that can promote or block communication. In short, you become a vital member of a learning community. It is no accident that the words *communication* and *community* have such a close relationship.

Public speaking is vital to the maintenance of a free society. The right to assemble and speak on public issues is guaranteed by the Bill of Rights.

Social Benefits

In a recent class we taught, student speakers criticized the support of Latin American dictatorships, attacked and defended the policy of preemptive warfare, criticized the fast food industry, condemned intolerance of gays and lesbians, urged support for Special Olympics, and argued for and against state lotteries. Viewpoints from all sides were heard, and sometimes the discussion was heated. Nevertheless, everyone remained civil, even when there was strong disagreement.

Clearly, the kind of open discussion encouraged in speech classrooms constantly stirs society's pot. Public speaking tests and critiques public policies, urges support for good causes, proposes new programs and attitudes, and urges the reform of flawed institutions. In these ways, public speaking classes often become dynamic laboratories for the democratic process.[5]

The political system of the United States is built on faith in communication. If we citizens are the last repositories of political power, then our understanding must be nourished constantly by a full and free flow of information and discussion. When we speak in public meetings and vote in elections, our power must be exercised wisely and justly, or our system will become merely a legalized form of mob behavior, what Alexis de Tocqueville once described as "the tyranny of the majority."[6] At the very least, we must be able to listen critically to those who represent us, advise them of our positions, and evaluate their performance at election time. We should be able to take part in public discussions in which we learn from others, develop convictions on important issues, and speak our minds effectively. This class prepares you for such responsible citizenship.

Being able to speak without fear and to hear all sides of an issue are rights basic to our social system. Our nation's founders realized the crucial importance of freedom of speech when they wrote the First Amendment to the Constitution:

> **Congress shall make no law respecting an establishment of religion, or prohibiting the free exercise thereof; or abridging the freedom of speech, or of the press; or the right of people peaceably to assemble, and to petition the government for a redress of grievances.**

Why is freedom of speech so important? The answer is simple. When public decisions are open to public discussion, power is distributed among the people. Those in power don't like to give it up, so they often resent those who exercise their freedom by speaking out. Freedom of speech is our most controversial, as well as our most fundamental, freedom.

The importance of public speaking in democratic societies has a long and rich history. The study of public speaking as we know it today had its origins in the ancient Greek academies, where the curriculum included mathematics, music, gymnastics, and **rhetoric**, or public speaking. During the Golden Age of Greek civilization, about 2,400 years ago, Aristotle and other leading intellectuals taught rhetoric to the citizens of Athens. Public speaking was especially important in that society because there were no newspapers, and books were not readily accessible. It is hard for us to imagine a time before the invention of the printing press (or the Internet, for that matter), but clearly oral communication made society possible. Nor were there professional lawyers or judges. Juries composed of hundreds of citizens decided legal cases, and the contending parties had to speak for themselves. Rhetorical skills also were needed because all citizens were expected to participate in the assembly that established the laws of the land. Finally, rhetorical skills were an important component of the great public rituals, when heroes were remembered and their exploits were celebrated in speeches such as Pericles' *Funeral Oration.*

Aristotle organized and systematized the study of rhetoric.[7] He described three major forms of public address:

- **forensic:** speeches that argue guilt and innocence in legal settings

InterConnections.LearnMore 1.1

Freedom of Speech

Thomas Jefferson Center for the Protection of Free Expression
http://www.tjcenter.org/about.html
A unique nonpartisan organization devoted to the defense of free expression in all its forms.

Philosophers and Freedom of Speech
http://www.sjsu.edu/faculty/Brent/190/speechlinks.html
San Jose State University web site offering a variety of links to freedom of speech sites, many containing texts of historical documents.

American Library Association Office for Intellectual Freedom
http://www.ala.org/Content/NavigationMenu/Our_Association/Offices/Intellectual_Freedom3/Default622.htm
A quick guide to intellectual freedom resources on the Internet, with links for easy access.

The Freedom Forum
http://www.freedomforum.org
A nonpartisan international foundation dedicated to free press, free speech, and free spirit for all people.

First Amendment Cyber-Tribune
http://w3.trib.com/FACT/index.html
An excellent resource for anyone wanting to learn more about the First Amendment. Contains links to recent news stories and other web sites of interest.

Raphael's painting shows "The School of Athens" where rhetorical skills were part of the basic curriculum.

- **deliberative:** speeches that debate public policy in legislative settings
- **epideictic:** speeches that celebrate special occasions

He also identified three forms of influence that determine whether listeners will accept what speakers say:

- **logos:** proofs that are based on reasoned demonstrations
- **pathos:** appeals to audience feelings
- **ethos:** perceived personal qualities of the speaker

Aristotle stressed the importance of logic in the public arena and of using examples and narratives to illustrate points. He further suggested that speeches should have effective structure:

- an **introduction** that gains attention, creates favorable impressions of the speaker, and makes clear the purpose of the speech
- a **body** that develops, demonstrates, and proves the speaker's message
- a **conclusion** that reminds listeners of the speaker's main points, amplifies the importance of the choices they must make, and leads them to the point of decision

Aristotle's *Rhetoric* laid the groundwork for later Roman rhetoricians. Cicero, who was a celebrated speaker as well as renowned writer, described rhetoric as "an art made up of five great arts." In his greatest work, *De Oratore,* he identified the following "great arts":

- **invention:** the discovery and selection of ideas, themes, and lines of argument for a speech
- **arrangement:** the placement of these ideas in appropriate order
- **style:** the expression of these ideas in effective language
- **memory:** the storage of these ideas in the mind for recall during speaking
- **delivery:** the presentation of the ideas to an audience

Quintilian, perhaps the greatest of the Roman communication educators, later elaborated on the five great arts in his *Institutio Oratoria.* He also stressed the importance of ethics, defining an ideal orator as a good person speaking well. Like Quintilian, *we stress the ethical importance of public communication.* We begin our treatment of communication ethics in this chapter and continue this emphasis throughout the text.

Although more than two millennia have passed since these classical theorists wrote and the media of public communication have changed dramatically, much of what they said still holds true today. Many of the topics addressed in this text update and expand on their work. Their ideas provide the foundation for understanding the social benefits of public speaking as an expression of political freedom and as an instrument of civic power and improvement.

Cultural Benefits

Several generations ago, when you listened to the radio or read magazines, you would find one striking assumption: America was the best of all possible worlds. This attitude typified our **ethnocentrism**, the tendency of any nation, race, or religion to believe that its way of seeing and doing things is right and proper and that other perspectives and behaviors are incorrect. Ethnocentrism can touch everything from the clothes we wear and the food we eat to the values we affirm. It can shape our most basic ways of thinking about our world.

In the first half of the twentieth century, the idea of America as a "melting pot" suggested that as various groups of immigrants came to this country, they would be melted down in some vast cultural cauldron into a superior alloy called "the American character." This metaphor reinforced ethnocentrism and expressed cultural arrogance. It created a **stereotype**, a generalized

InterConnections.LearnMore 1.2

Classical Origins of Public Speaking

Forest of Rhetoric [Silva Rhetoricae]
http://humanities.byu.edu/rhetoric/silva.htm
A guide to the terms of classical and Renaissance rhetoric, with sample rhetorical analyses or extended examples for each major entry. Developed by Professor Gideon O. Burton of the Department of English, Brigham Young University.

History of Rhetoric
http://www.uta.edu/english/V/histrhet.html
A site developed by Professor Victor Vitanza of the University of Texas at Arlington, with links to many documents and other materials relevant to the history of rhetoric.

Aristotle's *Rhetoric*
http://classics.mit.edu/Aristotle/rhetoric.html
The W. Rhys Roberts translation of the full text of this document, made available through the Massachusetts Institute of Technology.

Plato's *Phaedrus*
http://ccat.sas.upenn.edu/jod/texts/phaedrus.html
The B. Jowett translation, made available through the University of Pennsylvania.

Rhetoric and Composition
http://eserver.org/rhetoric/
Offers a variety of resources relevant to classical rhetoric, including texts of Plato's Gorgias *and* Phaedrus, *Aristotle's* Rhetoric, *and selections from Cicero.*

Speaker's Notes 1.2

Ten Timeless Lessons from the Ancient World

1. If you want to convince listeners that you have a good message for them, you must first convince them that you are a good person.
2. If you want strong commitment from an audience, you must engage strong feelings.
3. If you want commitment to last, you must be able to show that your arguments are based on sound, logical interpretations of reality.
4. When speaking on matters of guilt or innocence, you must emphasize the morality of past actions.
5. When speaking on matters of future policy, you must stress the practical advantages of proposed plans of action.
6. When celebrating great achievements, you must emphasize the values that make them great.
7. Your speech should be based on a thorough investigation of a topic, so that you have the widest possible range of choices as you select ideas and materials for emphasis.
8. You should follow an order of ideas that leads listeners to greater illumination and stronger conviction as you speak.
9. The right words will make your points come to life in images that your audience will easily remember.
10. The more you can speak in a direct, conversational way from a pattern of ideas imprinted in your mind, rather than by reading a prepared text or reciting a memorized script, the better the quality of communication you will achieve.

picture of a race, gender, or nationality that supposedly represents the essential character of the group.

The stereotype accompanying the "melting pot" seemed harmless enough on the surface: it offered an image of the ideal American citizen. However, that citizen usually had a white male face. Asians, Native Americans, and African Americans did not mix readily into a common pot. Moreover, often these people—and others—did not wish to lose their ethnic identities. Within the melting pot, women simply disappeared. It was hard to champion the economic and political rights of women when the ideal citizen was always pictured as a man. Elizabeth Lozano summarizes the shortcomings of the melting pot stereotype and proposes an alternative view of American character:

> **The "melting pot" is not an adequate metaphor for a country which is comprised of a multiplicity of cultural backgrounds. . . . [W]e might better think of the United States in terms of a "cultural stew" in which all ingredients conserve their unique flavor, while also transforming and being transformed by the adjacent textures and scents.[8]**

A public speaking class is an ideal place to savor this rich broth of cultures. As we hear others speak, we often discover the many flavors of the American experience. If you examine your own identity, you may discover that you yourself are "multicultural." One of your authors describes herself as "part Swedish, part Welsh, part German, and all hillbilly." The other is Scottish, Irish, and English with a dollop of Creek Indian.

As we strive to understand our own and others' unfolding identities, we must continue to guard against the subtle intrusion of stereotypes into our thinking. If we look inside ourselves honestly, we may discover many stereotypes already at work, whether they are of Latinos or athletes or "rednecks." They may seem like useful habits of thinking because they simplify human interactions and are endorsed by our social group. Unfortunately, stereotypes can be quite damaging. They can be negative and scornful, and they may keep us from seeing the true value of a person who just happens to be a Latino, or an athlete, or a Southerner. They can block our ability to communicate with others. Perhaps the best protection against stereotyping is to remember that in the final analysis, we are talking to individuals.

One of our favorite metaphors for the complex culture of the United States was introduced in the conclusion of Abraham Lincoln's first inaugural address, as Lincoln sought to hold the nation together on the eve of the Civil War:

> **The mystic chords of memory, stretching from every battlefield, and patriot grave, to every living heart and hearthstone, all over this broad land, will yet swell the chorus of the Union, when again touched, as surely they will be, by the better angels of our nature.[9]**

Lincoln's image of America as a harmonious chorus implied that the individual voices of Americans will not only survive but will create a more beautiful music than that of any one voice alone. Lincoln's vision holds forth a continuing dream of a society in which individualism and the common good can not only survive but can also enhance each other.

In your class and within these pages, you will hear many voices: Native Americans and new Americans, women and men, conservatives and liberals, Americans of all different colors and lifestyles. Sometimes these voices may seem bitter, alienated, or dispossessed, but all of them are a part of the vital chorus of our nation. The public speaking class gives you an opportunity to hear these voices and to add yours to them.

Public Speaking as Communication

Seeing yourself as public speaker may at first seem difficult, especially if you think of public speaking as a mysterious skill possessed only by a privileged few. But you have actually been preparing for public speaking for a long time. As an infant, you developed the most essential tool of the speaker—language. When your grandfather showed you how to catch a fish or your mother cautioned you to stay away from fire, you were introduced to two of the great functions of human communication, *informing* and *persuading*. Later, as you developed friendships, you began practicing interaction skills that are vital to communication: how to listen as well as speak.

Public speaking expands the conversational skills we have been using all our lives. However, some distinctive features make public speaking a unique form of communication.

Public Speaking as Expanded Conversation

Public speaking retains three important characteristics of good conversation. First, it preserves the natural directness and spontaneity of informal talk. Second, it is colorful. And third, it is tuned to the reactions of listeners.

Public Speaking Preserves Conversational Directness and Spontaneity. Even though a speech has been carefully researched, thoughtfully prepared, and well rehearsed, it should sound conversational and spontaneous as it comes to life before an audience. Those words bear repeating: *A speech comes to life before an audience.* Consider the following opening to a self-introductory speech:

> **It may seem hot here today, but it's not near as hot as Plainview, Texas, where I was born and raised. I almost said "roasted." John has just told us about the joys of urban living. Now you're going to hear about what you might call a "country-fried" lifestyle.**

Compare that opening with:

> **My name is Sam Johnson, and I come from Plainview, Texas.**

The first version seems fresh and spontaneous. The "us" and "you," along with the casual humorous remarks, suggest that the speaker is reaching out to his audience. The second, unless presented with a great deal of oomph, will sound quite ordinary. The first opening invites listening; the second invites yawning.

Public Speaking Is Colorful and Compelling. We often enjoy talking with some people because their speech is colorful. Consider the following development of the "heat" theme from the preceding example:

> **That place was so hot it would make an armadillo sweat! It was so hot that rattlesnakes would rattle just to fan themselves!**

Compare those words with the following:

> **The average summer day in Plainview was often over a hundred degrees.**

The literal meaning of both statements is not that different, but the first contains the kind of colorful conversational qualities that listeners usually enjoy.

Public Speaking Is Tuned to Listeners. Like a good conversation, a good public speech is tuned to listeners. As you talk with people in social situations, you monitor their reactions. If they look confused, you try to explain yourself more clearly. You may give an example or tell a story. If they frown, you may rephrase an idea or present evidence that supports your views. If they smile or nod, you may feel you have the green light to develop your thoughts.

If good conversations are interactive and audience centered, effective speeches are even more so. From the very beginning, a speech must be planned with the audience in mind. Then, as the speech is presented, speakers must be constantly aware of the reactions of listeners and make on-the-spot adjustments. Your entire speech should be designed to answer the questions that audiences will instinctively ask:

- Why should I be interested in this?
- What do you mean?
- How do I know this is true?
- What can I do about it?

You must give listeners a reason to be interested in the introduction of your speech, or you will lose them before you ever get started. Your speech must be clearly organized and your language simple and direct so that listeners can understand what you mean. You must provide facts and figures, examples, and expert testimony to demonstrate the truth of your statements. If your speech is persuasive, you must give listeners clear indications of what they should believe or do.

It seems clear that public speaking—far from being a mysterious skill—is a natural expansion and application of abilities we develop from our earliest years. On the other hand, some features make public speaking distinctive (see Figure 1.1).

Distinctive Features of Public Speaking

What makes public speaking distinctive as a form of communication is the relationships among a set of nine elements: speaker, message, medium, listener, response, interference, setting, purpose, and consequences. These elements interact with one another in ways that can affect those who participate and the world around them. They constitute a dynamic, interactive communication process.

Figure 1.1
Chatting or Speaking?

Conversations	*Public Speaking*
1. Audience-centered	1. More listener-centered
2. Loosely organized	2. Better organized
3. Off the top of your head	3. Grounded in responsible knowledge
4. Often no clear purpose	4. Has a clear purpose
5. Informal language	5. More formal language
6. Speaker/listener change roles	6. Speaker/listener roles clearly defined
7. Informal environment/small groups	7. More formal environment/larger groups

This charismatic speaker seems dynamic and likable.

Speaker. In public speaking, speaker and listener roles are clearly defined. Public speaking spotlights the role of the **speaker**. As Aristotle pointed out, our impressions of speakers affect how we respond to what they say. We are more inclined to react favorably when we think speakers know what they're talking about and when we trust them. These qualities of competence and integrity form the basis of **credibility**. Aristotle also noted that audiences respond more favorably when speakers seem to be people of goodwill—when we find them to be likeable and attractive. Modern researchers have uncovered still another important speaker characteristic, forcefulness (or dynamism).[10] Some speakers strike us as vital, action-oriented people. When important interests are at stake and action seems called for, we may turn to such people to lead the way. These qualities of likeableness and forcefulness combine to form the basis of **charisma**.[11] Taken together, credibility and charisma make up Aristotle's idea of ethos.[12]

Watch the **VideoLab Lesson 1 Screening Room: Sample Speech of Introduction** and answer the questions in Drill 1.1. Think about the nine distinctive elements of public speaking while watching the video. VideoLab

Message. Successful public speaking offers a **message** that is designed to serve the speaker's purpose and to meet audience needs. It should be based on responsible research and careful thought, and it should be internally consistent and complete. Its aim is to coax an audience into giving sympathetic attention to the speaker's ideas. It has been carefully worded and rehearsed so that it achieves maximum impact. The

Speaker's Notes 1.3

Public Speaking: A Dynamic Process Involving Interactions Among Nine Key Elements

1. **Speaker:** The person who initiates the communication process
2. **Message:** That fabric of words, presentation aids, gestures, and vocal cues that conveys the speaker's ideas and feelings
3. **Medium:** The channel (air, electronic media) through which the message travels
4. **Listeners:** Those receivers who interpret the message and can make it effective
5. **Response:** What happens during and after the speech as a result of hearing it
6. **Interference:** Factors that disrupt the communication process
7. **Setting:** The physical and psychological contexts in which the message is presented
8. **Purpose:** What the speaker wishes to accomplish
9. **Consequences:** The actual impact of the speech: both its immediate effect and its long-range influence on speaker and listener behavior and identity

message is the product of the speaker's **encoding** processes—the effort to convey through words, tones, and gestures how the speaker thinks and feels about the subject. Audience members respond by **decoding** the message, deciding what the speaker intended and determining the value of the message for their lives.

Shaping a message is a basic public speaking skill; therefore, it is a central focus of this book. Becoming a master of the message is a goal you can achieve through practice and constructive advice from your teacher and classmates.

Medium. The **medium** conducts the speaker's message. When public speaking takes place in a direct, face-to-face encounter, the medium is the air through which the sound travels. When a speech is presented outside or in a large auditorium, a microphone and amplifiers may become part of the medium. We tend to take the medium for granted until we discover something wrong with it, such as poor acoustics.

Public speeches can also be transmitted through the electronic media of radio, television, video- or audiotapes, and CDs. Such media can have major effects on the entire communication process. For example, radio emphasizes the attractiveness, clarity, and expressiveness of a speaker's voice. Television brings a speaker into a close relationship with viewers, so personality and physical appearance take on added importance. The medium can even shape the message. When speakers want coverage on the evening television news shows, they must compress important ideas into twenty-second sound bites, and the language must be immediately clear and colorful. We say more about media presentations in Chapter 13.

Listener. A constructive **listener** is supportive, yet listens carefully and critically. As we shall see in Chapter 4, such listeners seek the value in all messages. Because the fate of a message depends on how listeners respond to it, the audience must be at the center of your thinking as you plan, prepare, and present your speeches. What needs or problems concern them? What subjects interest them? What biases could distort their reception of messages? These questions are crucial to the selection of your topic and to the way you frame your message. Moreover, you should be sensitive to the fact that your words could affect the lives of listeners and even their perceptions of themselves.

Constructive listeners encourage speakers, listen to speeches with open minds, and emphasize the positive values of messages.

Remember that listeners do not come to a speech with a blank slate. Their minds are filled with past experiences, information or misinformation about a topic or speaker, attitudes and values, aspirations and fears. All of these factors influence how listeners will respond to your speech. We cover audience analysis and adaptation in Chapter 5.

Response. The **response** to a speech is what happens as a result of the speech. One of the things that makes public speaking dynamic is its interactive quality. While you are speaking, listeners are responding. As they respond, so should you. This makes every speech an interaction in which listeners and speakers constantly adjust to each other. These on-the-spot adjustments lend an unpredictable quality to public speaking that can make it an interesting and exciting form of communication. Note the adjustment that one of our speakers made to feedback during a speech on the dangers of global warming:

> **Some of you are frowning, and I can hardly blame you. This is really hard to believe. But here is how *Time* magazine interprets these recent scientific discoveries: "Except for nuclear war or a collision with an asteroid, no force has more potential to damage our planet's web of life than global warming." Yeah, I know. Tough words. But is it an exaggeration? More and more scientists don't think so. We can't afford to ignore the threat, hoping it will be untrue or that it might just go away.**

The fact that you can't always predict the adjustments you must make during a speech simply means that you must prepare all the more carefully. This student was ready for the "frowning" response he got to his speech and was able to adjust to it.

The technical term for the response listeners make during a speech is **feedback**. Feedback is important because it can improve the quality of communication. It can alert speakers to problems, signaling that some listeners didn't understand a point, or that others were drifting away, or that still others want more evidence before they are willing to grant a point. Therefore, good speakers will constantly monitor feedback so that they can adapt to the audience. Specific ways to adapt to feedback when making a presentation are covered in Chapter 13.

Interference. **Interference** (or noise) can enter at any point in the process to disrupt the effectiveness of communication. Interference can range from physical noise that impedes the hearing of a speech, such as a plane flying over the building, to psychological "noise" within speakers and listeners that prevents them from connecting. Three forms of interference are especially troubling: communication anxiety, listener distraction, and cultural barriers.

The first is *communication anxiety.* Fear is an understandable reaction to public speaking experiences. The situation may seem strange, and speakers may feel exposed and vulnerable. Listeners may seem distant, unfriendly, or threatening. Novice speakers learn to control their fears and to convert them into positive energy that adds sparkle and power to their speeches. But at the outset, these feelings can interfere with effective communication. We address the problem of communication anxiety in Chapter 2.

A second form of interference is *listener distraction,* which imposes a barrier between an audience and a message. Listeners may decide that a topic doesn't concern them and lapse into daydreams. They may be distracted by worries over an upcoming test or dreams about the weekend ahead. Limitations in the physical setting, such as poor acoustics or a noisy environment, can add to the distraction. The result is psychological drift away from the speech. The message never reaches the listener, and there is no true response to the speech.

A third important form of interference is *cultural barriers.* People from different backgrounds may view each other suspiciously. Speakers may misjudge how certain listeners will respond and as a result make poor adaptations that the listeners resent. Listeners may fear hidden agendas and close their minds to the speaker's words. Stereotypes involving race, gender, lifestyle, religion, nationality, and so forth can clutter our heads with prejudice that blocks the fair reception and interpretation of messages. The result is psychological distance and misunderstanding—the opposite of what speakers hope to achieve.

Fortunately, what you learn in this class can help you overcome the problems of interference. *The art of public speaking is to overcome interference so that genuine communication can occur.*

Setting. A speech occurs within a physical and psychological **setting** that can determine how well it succeeds. The physical setting in which a speech is presented can include such factors as the time of day the speech is given, the amount of time allotted for the presentation, the place of the presentation, and the size and arrangement of the audience. For example, when speaking outside, a speaker may need a more forceful presentation than when speaking in a small room. A larger audience may require a more formal manner of presentation than a smaller audience. The very quality of the physical setting can affect the speech. For example, one of the most profound discussions of the ethics of communication, Plato's *Phaedrus,* takes place in a woodland setting that frames and colors its message appropriately.[13] In this lovely pastoral scene, Socrates envisions an ideal communication that promotes spiritual growth for both listeners and speakers.

One classroom setting in which we taught recently required us to open windows and doors because the air conditioning was inadequate. As a result, speakers often had to contend with unpredictable distractions from outside. In addition, the room had an oblong shape, shallow in depth but wide, so that listeners were spread out in front of the speaker. This required speakers to shift attention from side to side to maintain eye contact. Most of our students learned to adapt to this setting.

The psychological setting for a speech includes such factors as the occasion for the speech and the context of recent events. The occasion for a speech sets the stage for what listeners expect. If they anticipate an informative presentation on investing in the stock market but instead hear a sales pitch for mutual funds, they may feel exploited. Recent events can change the climate of communication overnight. If you have planned a speech attacking oppressive campus security and a major crime occurs on campus shortly before your presentation, you may need to adapt your message to fit the changed situation. We cover adaptations to setting in Chapter 5.

Purpose. People seldom speak in public unless they have a **purpose** or motive. A purpose can be complex, private, and psychological: speakers may speak because they like the sound of their own voices or because they like attention. Or they may speak out of a need to define themselves and to establish their presence—to have some impact on the course of events. What makes public speaking a useful art is that most people speak because they have ideas to share. They know something that may be valuable to others. It does not diminish the importance of their contribution if public speaking also satisfies inner needs.

Although purposes vary according to the speech and speaker, it is possible to identify three general purposes: the *informative purpose,* the *persuasive purpose,* and the *ceremonial purpose.* In Part Four of this book we examine these purposes in depth and detail.

Consequences. Successful speeches obviously have impact. As a result of such speeches, listeners learn, often decide to change their minds or to take action, or join in celebrating someone's accomplishment. Moreover, if we could see the communication process at work in a speech, we might note a constant play of interactions among the elements we have identified. We might also see the spiritual impact of communication on the identities of speakers and listeners, as participants change or become defined in certain ways . These effects would all represent the **consequences** of public speaking, especially the ethical impact of transactional communication and transformational communication.

Transactional communication suggests that successful communication goes beyond personal achievement and the sharing of vital information, ideas, and advice. It also implies the shaping and sharing of selves. In the introduction to *Bridges Not Walls,* the interpersonal communication scholar John Stewart notes: "Every time persons communicate, they are continually offering definitions of themselves and responding to definitions of the other(s)." Therefore, Stewart suggests, communication is an ongoing transaction "in which who we are . . . emerges out of the event itself."[14] We agree: *Public speaking is often a self-creative event in which we discover ourselves as we communicate with others.*

This may seem like a mystical idea, but we can see it at work when many speeches work together over time to create the identities of speakers and audiences. Consider what happened during the civil rights movement from 1956 to 1968, when it was led by Martin Luther King Jr. During those years, King repeatedly identified himself with Moses. He spoke as though he had been destined by God to lead his followers out of semislavery. His followers, many of whom had suffered from degrading identities assigned to them for generations, were redefined by his rhetoric as the "Children of Israel."[15] Through the many battlefields of the civil rights movement, where they would be beaten, jailed, and some of them killed, these people were moving toward a Promised Land. King was still offering visions of that land on the night before he was assassinated.

This example illustrates not only transactional but also **transformational communication**.[16] The figure of King grew and expanded into epic proportions as his leadership emerged. His followers were transformed into heroic figures as they marched through one ordeal after another. These transformations indicate how people can grow and enlarge when they interact in ethical communication. In contrast, deceitful and dishonest communication may stunt the process of spiritual growth.

This is what Plato told us long ago in the *Phaedrus*. Plato realized that ethical communication that respects the humanity of listeners and nourishes it with responsible knowledge encourages the spiritual growth of both speaker and listeners. As you develop in your public speaking class, you may notice the growth in yourself. You may also see your classmates change in response to good speeches throughout the term.

Finally, as rhetorical scholar Lloyd Bitzer has noted, successful communication builds **public knowledge**, what we as a community decide is worth knowing.[17] Public speaking expands and builds this knowledge base. It develops the scope and accuracy of our public awareness. In these fundamental ways, then, for the speaker, listener, and public knowledge, public speaking can be both transactional and transformative. These consequences make participating in public speaking and public listening both ethical and significant. They suggest why you are in this class and how you might benefit from it.

Models of Communication

Thus far in our discussion, we have been following the features of two quite different models of the communication process. These models are complementary, in that their strengths and weaknesses compensate for each other.

The first is the **mechanical model**. Widely used in communication textbooks, this model developed out of the study of electronic communication in the Bell Telephone Laboratory around the middle of the twentieth century.[18] Our version of this model, adapted for the public speaking class, appears in Figure 1.2. In this model, we see that the speaker has initiated a message within a certain communication setting. The message flows through the medium of air until it is received by an audience member. Along the way, the message passes through various forms of interference that can distort its intended meaning. As identified earlier, such noise can include communication anxiety, listener distraction, and cultural barriers. All of these can cause the listener to "receive" a message that is different from what the speaker intended. The listener in turn reacts to the message he or she has received, sending response cues back to the speaker in the form of feedback. These cues must

Figure 1.2

Mechanical Model

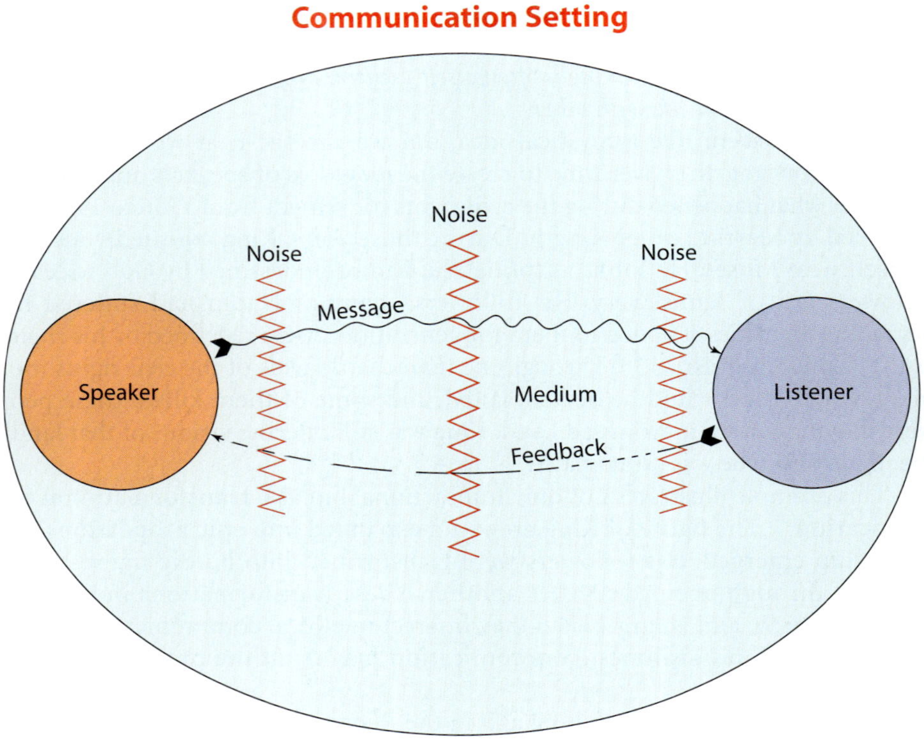

travel through the same forms of noise back to the speaker, sometimes causing the speaker to misread the listener's reaction.

The mechanical model thus dramatically illustrates how a simple act of communication can result in confusion and misunderstanding. The model is useful for describing the physical features of communication, such as speaker, receiver, medium, message, setting, interference, and response. It is less effective for exploring intangible and ethical features, such as the psychological setting, purpose, and consequences. It offers a partial (although helpful) diagram of what is an enormously complicated process.

The second model is what we call the **identification model**. Based on the work of theorist Kenneth Burke, this model is especially useful in representing the major ethical consequences of public speaking.[19] In the *precommunication* stage shown in Figure 1.3, we see a speaker and a group of listeners before a meaningful communication interaction has occurred. The figures are smaller, separate from each other, and indistinct, suggesting that identities are relatively unformed. In the *postcommunication* stage, we see speaker and listeners after the transactional and transformational processes of an ethical communication act. As a result of that act, the scattered listeners have been joined into an audience, and audience and speaker have been brought together so that they now share an identity, an area of *common ground* (they have become, Burke would say, "consubstantial"). They have also been enlarged by the act of communication, made more knowledgeable and powerful. Finally, their identity outlines are now well defined, suggesting that communication has helped reinforce who they are and how they should act.

The story of the civil rights movement under King's leadership would be an excellent illustration of the process indicated by this model. So also would Lincoln's "Gettysburg Address," in which the people of the United States were redefined and transformed as "The People," and Franklin Delano Roosevelt's "First Inaugural" address, which established and defined FDR's forceful leadership during the depression and redefined the role of citizens as soldiers in a battle against adverse economic forces.

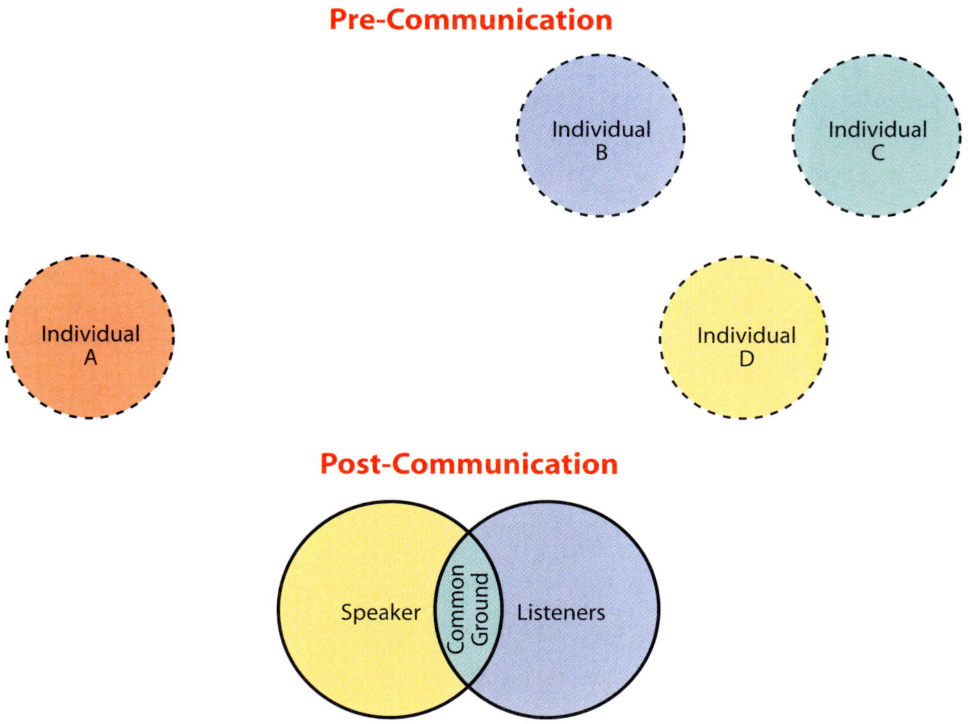

Figure 1.3
Identification Model

The identification model also suggests how unethical acts of communication might be represented. In one form of undesirable communication, such as the rhetoric of racism, the act of communication drives groups of people further apart rather than bringing them together, and, while defining them (undesirably), reduces their moral stature. In another form of evil communication, as in Hitler's rhetoric of national socialism, speaker and listeners do come together in a shared identity, but that identity, judged on moral grounds, is vicious and depraved, because it depends upon the degradation, if not the destruction, of others.

Taken together, the mechanical and identification models provide a more complete portrayal of the rich and complex process of communication that can occur in successful public speaking.

Ethical Public Speaking

In this time of spin doctors, misleading advertising, and cynical disinformation campaigns, communication ethics has become a vital concern. **Ethics** is the moral dimension of human conduct—the way we treat others and want to be treated by them in return.

Because it is so important, ethics is covered in many places in this book. You will find these places highlighted with an "Ethics Alert!" throughout the text. In addition, the code of ethics of the National Communication Association, the "Credo for Ethical Communication," is reprinted in this chapter's "Application" section on page 26. In this final section we shall discuss the two major considerations that underlie ethical communication: *respect for the integrity of ideas* and *concern for listeners.*

Respect for the Integrity of Ideas

Respect for the integrity of ideas involves speaking from responsible knowledge, using communication techniques carefully, and avoiding plagiarism.

For additional information on ethical speaking, go to **Drill 1.3: The Ethics of Public Speaking.** VideoLab

Speak From Responsible Knowledge. Over 2,400 years ago, Plato complained that political speakers were ignorant of their subjects but that they shamelessly paraded their ignorance before the public anyway. He accused speakers of pandering to public tastes and making listeners feel satisfied with themselves when instead they should feel the need for improvement. The skepticism and cynicism many Americans feel concerning public affairs and politicians suggest that things haven't improved much since Plato's time.

No one expects you to be an expert as you speak in class. You should, however, make an effort to acquire **responsible knowledge** of your subject. As we note in greater detail in Chapter 7, responsible knowledge of a topic includes

- knowing the main points of concern.
- understanding what experts believe about them.
- being aware of the most recent events or discoveries concerning them.
- realizing how these points affect the lives of listeners.

Responsible knowledge requires that you know more about a topic than your audience so that your speech has something useful to give them.

Consider how one of our students, Stephen Huff, a student at the University of Memphis, acquired responsible knowledge for an informative speech. Stephen knew little about earthquakes before his speech, but he knew that Memphis was on the New Madrid fault, and that this could mean trouble. He also knew that a major earthquake research center was located on campus. Stephen arranged for an interview with the center's director. During the interview, he asked a series of well-planned questions: *Where was the New Madrid fault, and what was the history of its activity? What was the probability of a major quake in the near future in the area? How prepared was Memphis for a major quake? What kind of damage could result? How could his listeners prepare for it? What readings would the director recommend?* All these questions were designed to gain knowledge that would interest and benefit his listeners. Armed with knowledge from the interview, Stephen went to the library and found the readings suggested by the director. He was well on his way to giving a good speech. Acquiring responsible knowledge requires time and effort, but it is well worth the work.

Use Communication Techniques Carefully. The line between ethical and unethical uses of speech techniques can be easy to cross unless you are careful. For example, you may wish to quote authorities in support of your position. When used ethically, this technique helps establish the credibility of ideas by demonstrating that they are not simply your opinions but are verified by experts. You must be careful, however, to avoid abusing this technique by **quoting out of context**. This unethical use of a quotation distorts its meaning. In effect, it lies to the audience. Harper Barnes, movie critic for the *St. Louis Post-Dispatch*, describes a typical case of quoting out of context:

> **Jan Boyar of the *Orlando Sentinel* recently reported a fairly egregious example. . . . An ad for the Richard Gere–Sharon Stone stinker "Intersection" attributed this line to Boyar: "Sizzling! Hot stars, steamy sex." He replied, "What I actually wrote was that the premise of 'Intersection' is 'considerably**

less sizzling' than those of other movies ... and those sex scenes, which I called only 'ostensibly steamy,' are, I noted, 'presented in a deliberately unsexual way.' As for the ad's suggestion that I had characterized Richard Gere, Sharon Stone, and Lolita Davidovich as 'hot stars,' that much is correct. But I would now add that they're not quite so hot after appearing in 'Intersection.'"[20]

In more serious situations, quoting out of context can produce disastrous effects. A high point of Dr. Martin Luther King Jr.'s famous "I Have a Dream" speech came when he said that he wanted his children to be judged "not by the color of their skin but by the content of their character." Tom Teepen of the *Minneapolis Star Tribune* argues that when you hear that quote "being piously invoked these days, you can be sure black folks are about to get nailed again":

Gov. Pete Wilson flew the quote like air cover over his political turnaround when he supported the referendum that killed affirmative action in California. A man whose lawsuit has all but cleared the University of Texas law school of black students crowed, "It's kind of finishing Dr. King's dream. . . ." Colorado Attorney General Gale Norton cited King, too, in her effort to end scholarships to the state's colleges and universities targeted for black students. Mississippi Gov. Kirk Fordice used the quote to explain why he was appointing only white men to the board that runs the university system. Robert Brustein, theater critic and artistic director of the American Repertory Theater, cited King in condemning the formation of black theatrical companies. And on and on goes this political grave robbery.[21]

Teepen's point is that King's words were quoted not only out of the context of his speech but also out of the context of his life. Such citations subverted all that King had fought and died for as a civil rights activist. Be sure to quote people carefully and to reflect the true spirit of their meaning.

As we discuss the use of supporting materials in Chapter 8 and developing evidence and proofs in Chapter 16, we will be especially attentive to the potential for ethical abuse.

Avoid Plagiarism. **Plagiarism** is *presenting the ideas or words of others as though they were your own, without acknowledging where the ideas or words came from.* Most colleges consider plagiarism a major infraction of the student code and impose penalties ranging from grade reduction to suspension. Learn the particular policies at your school. These can usually be found in the student handbook or on your college web site. Your communication department or instructor may have additional definitions and rules governing this problem.

Plagiarism comes in various degrees and forms. We shall discuss blatant forms, more subtle forms, and how to avoid the traps of plagiarism into which one can stumble.

Blatant Plagiarism. Plagiarism is *blatant* when a speaker intentionally steals an entire work from another source. Examples of blatant plagiarism might include using a speech or outline offered by a friend or found in fraternity or sorority files on the Internet, or in another public speaking text. One truly reckless student once memorized the text of a student speech from an earlier edition of this book and presented it in class as his own effort. Unfortunately for him, the instructor had taught from that earlier edition and recognized the material.

The shortcut that blatant plagiarism provides simply does not justify the risk. Many departments maintain files of speech outlines, instructors discuss speeches with each other, and there are even software programs that uncover Internet plagiarism.

A related form of such plagiarism involves pirating and parroting a magazine article. You walk on the ethical side of the line when you *discuss* an article you have read, pointing out why you agree or disagree with it. You step across the line when you *present* the article or a substantial part of it as though it were your own creation.

Related to this practice is what we call "cut and paste" plagiarism, which involves lifting passages verbatim from more than one source, then splicing them together into a "speech." It is unethical to simply rearrange the order of ideas or change a few words, and then claim the material as your own.

Beyond the ethical considerations involved in plagiarism, there are also some very practical ones. Speeches that are blatantly plagiarized are usually not very effective because they don't have your stamp of commitment in them or your own personal touch. If the thoughts are not really yours, it will be hard for you to present them effectively. They just won't seem authentic. They may also be dated in terms of their information and examples, or they may be irrelevant to your particular audience. Speeches plagiarized from magazine articles or essays will usually lack the conversational style that marks genuine oral language. In "cut and paste" plagiarism, the ideas usually won't flow smoothly, a red flag for any suspicious listener. Finally, when you plagiarize a speech, you are cheating yourself. It's like "sending a friend to practice tennis for you—you'll never score an ace yourself!"[22]

More Subtle Plagiarism. You must also guard against more subtle forms of plagiarism, many involving the abuse or neglect of citations or oral credits. You must always credit your sources when you are using a direct quotation from either a published or an unpublished work. You should also provide citations if you are paraphrasing someone's ideas or opinions. Be careful about relying too much on any single source of information. Gather facts and ideas from a variety of sources, develop your own thinking about what they mean to you and your listeners, and present them in your own words.

You should credit any especially colorful or striking language that you pick up from someone else and use in your speech. For example, had we started this paragraph on citations by asserting, "A citation is not a traffic ticket," but neglected to say that we found this quotation in a document published by the Georgetown University Honor Council, we would have been guilty of plagiarism.[23]

When you quote someone or borrow ideas and information, let your listeners know. Rather than simply saying:

> **The dean of the College of Communication at Boston University resigned after he presented a commencement address that was plagiarized.**

say instead:

> **According to the *Boston Globe* of July 2, 1991, the dean of the College of Communication at Boston University presented a plagiarized speech at the university's commencement ceremonies that year. Then on July 15, the *Washington Times* confirmed that the president of the University had accepted the dean's resignation, saying, "It's the duty of all responsible scholars and writers to credit their sources."**

It doesn't make sense not to credit your sources. Citing them strengthens your speech. It shows that you have prepared carefully. It also associates your thinking with that of respected experts, publications, or opinion leaders.

Avoiding the Traps of Plagiarism You may stumble into plagiarism because of the traps of time and careless research practices. Be sure to allow enough time to prepare thoroughly for your presentation. Not only will this allow you to acquire responsible knowledge, but it may also reduce the temptation to take the easy way out by copying from someone else's work.

Ethics Alert! 1.1

Avoiding Plagiarism

1. Don't present or summarize someone else's speech, article, or essay as though it were your own speech.
2. Draw information and ideas from a variety of sources; then interpret them to create your own point of view.
3. Don't parrot other people's language and ideas as though they were your own.
4. Always provide oral citations for direct quotations, paraphrased material, or especially striking language, letting listeners know who said the words, where, and when.
5. Credit those who originate ideas: "John Sheets, director of secondary curriculum and instruction at Duke University, suggests there are three criteria we should apply in evaluating our high schools."
6. Identify your sources of information: "According to The 1998 *Information Please Almanac,* tin cans were first used in 1811 as a means of preserving food"; or "The latest issue of *Time* magazine notes that ..."
7. Introduce your sources as lead-ins to direct quotations: "Studs Terkel has said that a book about work 'is, by its very nature, about violence—to the spirit as well as the body.'"
8. Allow yourself enough time to research and prepare your presentation.
9. Take careful notes as you do your research, so that you don't later confuse your own thoughts and words with those of others.

As you do your research, take careful notes. Be sure to put any quotations or striking words you might want to use in quotation marks so you will know whose they are when you are ready to compose your speech. Even our greatest scholars are not above stumbling into this trap. Doris Kearns Goodwin, a Pulitzer Prize–winning historian, had to make a humiliating confession in a recent issue of *Time* magazine. Writing of her blunder, she said, "Citation mistakes can happen. I failed to provide quotation marks for phrases that I had taken verbatim, having assumed these, drawn from my notes, were my words, not hers [referring to another author's book]." The lesson should be clear: As you make notes on your research, keep your own ideas separate from the quotations or paraphrasing you draw from others.

Concern for Listeners

Recognizing the power of communication leads ethical speakers to a genuine concern for how words affect the lives of their listeners. We end this chapter by introducing two related ideas: how the "other" orientation of public speaking requires us to be more ethically sensitive, and how applying universal values may help us overcome the challenge of audience diversity.

Developing an "Other" Orientation. In our opening vignette, Mary began her public speaking class with a great deal of concern about her own fate. During the class, however, as she came to know and like her classmates, she prepared her speeches more with them in mind. In so doing, Mary developed an "other" orientation and grew away from **egocentrism**, the tendency to believe that our thoughts, dreams, interests, and desires are or should be shared by others. In their book *Communication Ethics,* Jaksa and Pritchard give this example: "After offering a lengthy explanation of the importance of egocentricity in Kohlberg's theory of moral development, [one of the authors of this text] ... was greeted with this response from a student. 'I think I understand what egocentric thinking is. Here's an example. You're interested in Kohlberg. So you assume we are, too.'"[25] The discipline of the public speaking class encourages an "other" orientation and the expansion of the self that this implies.

Applying Universal Values. If the members of your class represent many cultures, each offering a different outlook, how can you frame a speech that will communicate and appeal across these many different audiences-within-an-audience?

One answer to this dilemma has been offered by Rushworth M. Kidder, former senior columnist for the *Christian Science Monitor* and president of the Institute for Global Ethics. In his book *Shared Values for a Troubled World,* Kidder describes what he calls a **global code of ethical conduct**, centering on the deeply and widely shared values of *love, truthfulness, fairness, freedom, unity, tolerance, responsibility,* and *respect for life.*[26] If Kidder is correct, appeals to these fundamental values should resonate in any culture and should be well received by the diverse members of your public speaking class. We shall say more about how to effectively engage such values in Chapter 5.

In Summary

How a Course in Public Speaking Can Help You. This class deserves your commitment because of the significant benefits it offers. Personally, you should benefit from the opportunity to grow as a sensitive, skilled communicator and from the practical advantages such growth makes possible. You should also become a more effective member of society. Self-government cannot work without responsible and effective public communication, and public speaking is the basic form of such communication. The public speaking class can expose you to different cultures as you hear others express their lifestyles, values, and concerns. Such exposure can counter ethnocentrism, the tendency to feel that our way of living is the right way.

Public Speaking as Communication. Public speaking builds on the basic communication skills we originally develop as we acquire language and learn how to converse with others. As expanded conversation, public speaking preserves the natural directness and spontaneity, and the colorful and compelling qualities, of good conversation. Like conversation, public speaking is tuned to the reactions of listeners.

What makes public speaking distinctive are the relationships among nine elements. Audiences respond to the first element, *speakers,* in terms of their *credibility* and *charisma,* which together constitute their *ethos.* The second element, *message,* is the speech itself, which represents the speaker's *encoding* process. The third, *medium,* transmits the message to *listeners.* Listeners themselves form the fourth element. They do their work by *decoding* the message, and their *response,* in the form of *feedback,* provides the fifth. *Interference,* the sixth element, recognizes the possibility of distortion and misunderstanding at any point in the communication process. Major forms of it are speaker apprehension, audience distraction, and cultural barriers. The physical and psychological *setting* in which the speech is presented represents the seventh element. The eighth, *purpose,* recognizes that people speak out of some intention or need. The book identifies three major categories of general purpose: speeches to inform, speeches to persuade, and ceremonial speeches. The ninth element, *consequences,* measures the immediate effect of speeches and their ethical impact in terms of their transactional and transformational effects. As they interact with each other, these nine elements constitute public speaking as a dynamic process.

Ethical Public Speaking. Ethical considerations in public speaking are inescapable. Ethical public speaking respects the integrity of ideas and focuses on the impact of communication on listeners. Respect for the integrity of ideas means meeting the demands of *responsible knowledge,* carefully using communication techniques, and avoiding such practices as *quoting out of context* and *plagiarism.* Responsible knowledge requires having up-to-date information on the major points of a topic, knowing what the most respected experts have to say about them, and understanding how these points affect your immediate audience. Quoting out of context deceives listeners concerning the intention of a quotation. Plagiarism is intellectual theft. Being convicted or even suspected of such a crime can do grave damage to the speaker's ethos.

Concern for listeners comes as you develop an "other" orientation in your public speaking class to balance the *egocentrism,* or excessive preoccupation with the self, that you may bring to such a class. You can adapt to the many cultures that may be represented in your class if you base your appeals in the deep and widely shared values of a *global code of ethical conduct.*

Terms to Know

rhetoric
forensic
deliberative
epideictic
logos
pathos
ethos
introduction
body
conclusion
invention
arrangement
style
memory
delivery
ethnocentrism
stereotype
speaker
credibility
charisma
message
encoding
decoding
medium
listener
response
feedback
interference
setting
purpose
consequences
transactional communication
transformational communication
public knowledge
mechanical model
identification model
ethics
responsible knowledge
quoting out of context
plagiarism
egocentrism
global code of ethical conduct

Discussion

1. Look for symptoms of ethnocentrism and egocentrism among newsmakers of the day. What impact do these attitudes have on events and on the ethos of those who speak in connection with them? Share your ideas in class.
2. Identify some stereotypes at work in your own thinking and your conversations with friends. Why do these stereotypes exist? What is the result of their existence?
3. Discuss how the ethics of communication might be applied to advertising. Bring to class examples of advertisements that you think are ethical and unethical and explain why.
4. What personal and social benefits are lost in societies that do not encourage the free and open exchange of ideas?
5. Do you agree that it is better to think of American culture as a "stew" or "chorus" rather than as a "melting pot"? Can you think of other desirable metaphors for American identity?

Application

1. Visualize yourself as the speaker you hope to become by the end of this class. What specific skills will you have to acquire to make this ideal a reality? For example:
   A. Will you have to build confidence by developing knowledge on specific subjects that interest you?
   B. Will you need to learn more about your audience, so that you can speak directly to their interests?
   C. Will you need to learn more about the techniques of speaking, such as how to develop your ideas, prove your points, tell stories that

people will enjoy, or use language that people will remember?

D. Will you need to learn more about presentation techniques such as PowerPoint?

E. Do you need to work on your voice and body language to make them better able to convey your thoughts?

Plan a work schedule for a model week—from the time you wake up until "lights out"—that will enable you to meet your responsibilities. Leave plenty of time to work toward your goals in the public speaking class.

2. The National Communication Association has adopted the following code of ethics concerning free expression:

Credo for Ethical Communication

Questions of right and wrong arise whenever people communicate. Ethical communication is fundamental to responsible thinking, decision making, and the development of relationships and communities within and across contexts, cultures, channels, and media. Moreover, ethical communication enhances human worth and dignity by fostering truthfulness, fairness, responsibility, personal integrity, and respect for self and others. We believe that unethical communication threatens the quality of all communication and consequently the well-being of individuals and the society in which we live. Therefore we, the members of the National Communication Association, endorse and are committed to practicing the following principles of ethical communication.

- **We advocate truthfulness, accuracy, honesty, and reason as essential to the integrity of communication.**
- **We endorse freedom of expression, diversity of perspective, and tolerance of dissent to achieve the informed and responsible decision making fundamental to a civil society.**
- **We strive to understand and respect other communicators before evaluating and responding to their messages.**
- **We promote access to communication resources and opportunities as necessary to fulfill human potential and contribute to the well-being of families, communities, and society.**
- **We promote communication climates of caring and mutual understanding that respect the unique needs and characteristics of individual communicators.**
- **We condemn communication that degrades individuals and humanity through distortion, intimidation, coercion, and violence and through the expression of intolerance and hatred.**
- **We are committed to the courageous expression of personal convictions in pursuit of fairness and justice.**
- **We advocate sharing information, opinions, and feelings when facing significant choices while also respecting privacy and confidentiality.**
- **We accept responsibility for the short- and long-term consequences for our own communication and expect the same of others.[27]**

Working in small groups, discuss how you would adapt this general credo into a specific code of ethics for use in your public speaking class. For example, your group might develop a series of action statements ("We endorse . . . , we condemn . . . ," etc.) that touch upon such issues as establishing your class as a haven for dissent, endorsing respect for diversity of views and lifestyles, seeking the truth through research before forming opinions for your speeches, and insisting upon honesty in attributing ideas to their sources. Each group should present the code it proposes to the class, and the class should determine a code of ethics to be followed during the term.

3. Begin keeping a speech evaluation notebook in which you record comments on effective and ineffective, and ethical and unethical speeches you hear both in and out of class. As you observe speeches, ask yourself the following twelve questions:

(1) How did the speaker rate in terms of ethos?

(2) Was the speech well adapted to its listeners' needs and interests?

(3) Did the speech take into account the cultural complexity of its audience?

(4) Did the speech make an effective connection with universal values?

(5) Was the message clear and well structured?

(6) Did the medium pose any problems?

(7) Was the language and presentation of the speech effective?

(8) How did listeners respond, both during and after the speech?

(9) Did the setting have any impact on the message?

(10) Did the speech overcome interference to achieve its goal?

(11) Did the speaker respect the integrity of ideas by developing an original speech that demonstrated responsible knowledge and a careful use of communication techniques?

(12) Did the speech have any transactional or transformational significance for its listeners?

Notes

1. Arati R. Korwar, *War of Words: Speech Codes at Public Colleges and Universities* (Nashville, Tenn.: The Freedom Forum First Amendment Center at Vanderbilt University, 1996).

2. "Be the Person Employers Want to Hire," *Job Web and Job Choices Online*. http//www.jobweb.org/jconline/Tips/tips4.shtml (5 July 1998).

3. Sandy Hock, "Communication Skills Top List of Student Advice," *Accounting Today* 8, no. 5 (1994): 27.

4. From Kathleen Peterson, ed., *Statements Supporting Speech Communication* (Annandale, Va.: Speech Communication Association, 1986).

5. Jill J. McMillan and Katy J. Harriger, "College Students and Deliberation: A Benchmark Study," *Communication Education* 51 (2002): 237–253.

6. See his discussion in Part I, Chapter 15, of *Democracy in America,* first published in 1835.

7. Aristotle, *On Rhetoric,* trans. George A. Kennedy (New York: Oxford University Press, 1991).

8. Elizabeth Lozano, "The Cultural Experience of Space and Body: A Reading of Latin American and Anglo American Comportment in Public," in *Our Voices: Essays in Culture, Ethnicity, and Communication,* ed. Alberto Gonzalez, Marsha Houston, and Victoria Chen (Los Angeles: Roxbury Publishing, 1994), p. 141.

9. T. Harry Williams, ed., *Abraham Lincoln: Selected Speeches, Messages, and Letters* (New York: Holt, Rinehart and Winston, 1964), p. 148.

10. See the discussion summarizing ethos-related research in James C. McCroskey, *An Introduction to Rhetorical Communication* (Englewood Cliffs, N.J.: Prentice Hall, 1993), pp. 78–98, and a critique of such research in Gary Cronkhite and Jo Liska, "A Critique of Factor Analytic Approaches to the Study of Credibility," *Communication Monographs* 43 (1976): 91–107.

11. *Fortune* magazine offers an interesting discussion of the importance of charisma in American business in Patricia Sellers, Shaifali Puri, and David Kaufman, "What Exactly Is Charisma?" *Fortune,* 15 Jan. 1996. http://www.pathfinder.com/fortune/magazine/1996/960115/charisma.html (15 May 1998).

12. Book 2.1 of the *Rhetoric,* trans. Lane Cooper (New York: Appleton-Century-Crofts, 1960), p. 92.

13. *The Dialogues of Plato,* trans. Benjamin Jowett, in Great Books of the Western World, vol. 7 (Chicago: Encyclopaedia Britannica, Inc., 1952), p. 116. See also the analysis by Richard M. Weaver, "The *Phaedrus* and the Nature of Rhetoric," in *Language Is Sermonic,* ed. Richard L. Johannesen, Rennard Strickland, and Ralph T. Eubanks (Baton Rouge: Louisiana State University Press, 1970), pp. 57–83.

14. John Stewart, ed., *Bridges Not Walls: A Book About Interpersonal Communication,* 5th ed. (New York: McGraw-Hill, 1990), p. 22.

15. Malinda Snow argues that the flight of the children of Israel from Egypt has been a suggestive comparative theme for African Americans since the days of slavery. See her "Martin Luther King's 'Letter from Birmingham Jail' as Pauline Epistle," *Quarterly Journal of Speech* 71 (1985): 318–334.

16. This concept may be closely related to an idea developed by famed historian James MacGregor Burns. Burns describes "transformation leaders" as those who "elevate, motivate, define values, offer vision, and creatively produce reform and at times revolutionary developments in the face of unusual opportunities and challenges" (as summarized in David M. Abshire, "A Call for Transformational Leadership," *Vital Speeches of the Day,* 1 May 2001, p. 432). Among the American presidents, Abraham Lincoln and Franklin Delano Roosevelt clearly exemplify transformational leaders. Presumably, transformational leadership is enabled by transformational communication, such as one sees in Lincoln's Gettysburg Address and in Roosevelt's First Inaugural.

17. Lloyd F. Bitzer, "Rhetoric and Public Knowledge," in *Rhetoric, Philosophy, and Literature: An Exploration,* ed. Don M. Burks (West Lafayette, Ind.: Purdue University Press, 1978), pp. 67–93.

18. Claude E. Shannon and Warren Weaver, *The Mathematical Theory of Communication* (Urbana: University of Illinois Press, 1963). Shannon's first classic essay on the subject appeared originally in 1948 in the *Bell System Technical Journal,* and a companion essay appeared in 1949 in *Scientific American.*

19. See especially Burke's discussion of identification and consubstantiality in "The Range of Rhetoric," in *A Rhetoric of Motives* (Berkeley and Los Angeles: University of California Press, 1969), pp. 3–43.

20. Harper Barnes, "'Distorted!' 'Pretentious!' 'Arrogant!'" *St. Louis Post-Dispatch,* 28 July 1994, p. 1G. Reprinted with permission of the *St. Louis Post-Dispatch,* copyright © 1994.

21. Tom Teepen, "Twisting King's Words to Give His Antagonists Comfort," *Minneapolis Star Tribune,* 14 July 1997, p. 9A.

22. "Avoiding Plagiarism: Mastering the Art of Scholarship," Student Judicial Affairs, University of California, Davis, October 1999. http://sja.ucdavis.edu/sja/plagiarism.html. (15 Jan. 2001).

23. Georgetown University Honor Council, "What Is Plagiarism?" (1999). http://www.georgetown.edu/honor/plagiarism.html. (17 Jan. 2001).

24. Doris Kearns Goodwin, "How I Caused That Story," *Time,* 4 Feb. 2002, p. 69.

25. James A. Jaksa and Michael S. Pritchard, *Communication Ethics: Methods of Analysis,* 2nd ed. (Belmont, Calif.: Wadsworth, 1994), p. 94.

26. Rushworth M. Kidder, *Shared Values for a Troubled World: Conversations with Men and Women of Conscience* (San Francisco: Jossey-Bass, 1994).

27. Credo of Ethical Communications; National Communication Association. Used by permission of the National Communication Association.

Managing Your Fear of Speaking

2

OUTLINE

This chapter will help you

- realize you are not alone in your fear of public speaking
- understand the nature of communication anxiety
- learn ways to control communication anxiety

Bravery is being the only one who knows you're afraid.

DAVID HACKWORTH

Professor, could I talk with you for a few minutes? I'm supposed to graduate this semester, and I've put off taking this course until now. Well, actually I started it twice before and dropped it after the first couple of classes. I've got to make it through this time or I won't graduate. But, the idea of speaking to a group makes me so nervous I don't think I can handle it. Everyone else seems more confident than me. Can you help me?

Would it help to know you're not alone? For years survey after survey has placed public speaking at or near the top of the list of people's fears.[1] Jerry Seinfeld once observed that since most people prefer death to public speaking, almost anyone would rather be in the coffin than delivering the eulogy at a funeral. For many of us, however, this is no laughing matter.

The National Communication Association recently commissioned the Roper Starch polling organization to conduct a nationwide survey to determine how comfortable and effective people feel communicating in different situations.[2] Figure 2.1 shows that most of us are more comfortable in one-on-one interactions or talking on the phone than we are at speaking up in meetings or giving a speech. Indeed, many people are *not comfortable* speaking up at a meeting, and even more are not comfortable giving a presentation or speech.

Almost all college students are uncomfortable when they have to address a class. International students and students from marginalized cultural groups often have a great deal of apprehension. Once, when we were teaching a public speaking course in summer school, a student confessed that she was enrolled at another college but was taking the course with us so that if she didn't do well it wouldn't spoil her GPA and keep her out of medical school. Her fears were unfounded. The text of her excellent first speech, "My Three Cultures," has been a staple in all previous editions of our text and is included in Appendix B.

USA Today once opened an article on "stage fright" with the following lines: "Laurence Olivier had it. Carly Simon has it. So does Barbra Streisand. Some Olympic athletes, executives of Fortune 500 companies, tenured professors and high-powered sales people have it."[3] Prominent sports figures also have such fears. "Pro-golfer Annika Sorenstam was so afraid of public speaking that she said there were times when she would intentionally finish second to avoid giving a victory speech!"[4] An article for computer specialists suggested that "most technical professionals would rather plunge hot needles into their eyes than be forced to stand up and address a room full of people."[5] Your speech instructor may even have some communication anxiety, but you probably won't be able to detect it. Even your authors have experienced this problem. Here is the story of our own communication anxiety:

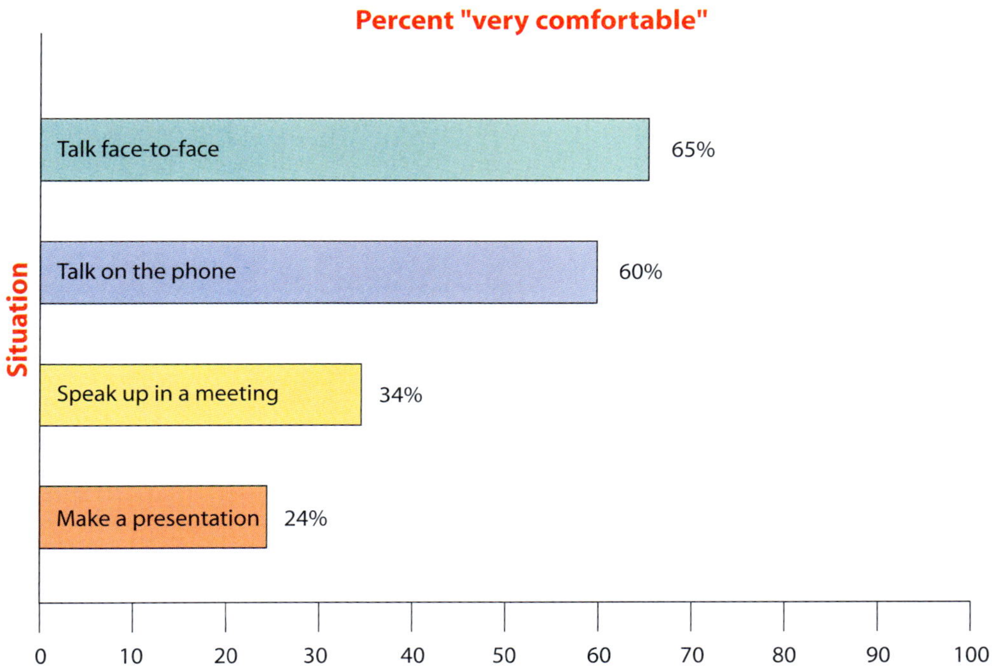

Figure 2.1
Communication Comfort

A Confession

As college professors and authors, we have had a lot of experience speaking both in and out of the classroom. Being the authors of a public speaking text puts even more pressure on you. When you earn your bread and butter by telling others how to do something, they expect you to be able to do it yourself—and do it much better than most other people. Even with all our experience, every time we face a new group—a class of undergraduates, a group of graduate assistants hoping to learn how to teach this course better, our publisher's sales representatives, fellow citizens at community meetings, or our professional colleagues at conventions—we feel the burden of this pressure and get a healthy dose of stomach butterflies.

Pro Golfer Annika Sorenstam once avoided press conferences because she suffered from communication anxiety.

Surprised? Still think that everyone else is more confident than you are? The late Edward R. Murrow, a famous radio and television commentator, once said: "The best speakers know enough to be scared. . . . The only difference between the pros and the novices is that the pros have trained the butterflies to fly in formation."

Steve Raymund, chairman and CEO of Tech Data Corporation (the world's second largest wholesaler of PC products), lists "more confidence to speak in public" as the one thing he would most like to change about himself. His approach to the problem is simple and effective: "If you must conquer it, you must know it. To know it, you have to study it. Then, study it some more."[6] We will follow Raymund's recommendation in this chapter by investigating the nature of this fear and by telling you what you can do about it. Our goal is to help you train your butterflies to fly in formation.

Understanding Communication Anxiety

You may have noticed that earlier in this chapter we put the words *stage fright* in quotation marks to indicate our reservations about this typical way of describing public speaking fears. *Stage* suggests theater, and *theater* suggests performance. However, a public speech is not a performance, but an interactive communication event.[7] The simple use of the words *stage fright* sets a speaker up for an array of dramatistic disasters. If you think of your speeches as performances, you will cast yourself in the role of an actor. Just as actors don't necessarily believe what they are saying, performers may not think of their speeches as authentic commitments to communicate. Their messages may be something they say simply for effect. If you cast yourself into the role of a performer, you are also likely to think of the audience as critics and then try to please them rather than communicate with them. To discourage this distorted way of thinking about public communication, we avoid the term *stage fright.*

Go to the **SpeechStudio** and take the Self-Assessment Test: **A Personal Report of Communication Apprehension (PRCA).** How does communication anxiety affect you in different situations?

Go to http://college.hmco.com/eduspace/

One way to discuss such fear is to describe it as "public speaking anxiety." Our preference, however, is to use the term **communication anxiety** to refer to those unpleasant sensations a speaker may experience before or during a presentation. Our rationale is that the fears associated with public speaking go beyond the event itself. They are deeply rooted in the chances people take during authentic communication. To communicate in public, people must open their hearts and minds to the scrutiny of others. This experience can result in personal growth and self-enhancement. But opening up to others also involves risk; thus the anxiety of speakers is understandable. We begin by examining some of the symptoms of communication anxiety, some of the reasons why you might feel anxious when you stand up to speak, and some of the specific things people are concerned about.

Symptoms of Communication Anxiety

It's the night before you are scheduled to make your first oral presentation in class. You turn off the lights and go to bed, but you just can't get comfortable. You toss and turn, get up and plump up your pillow. You try to distract yourself by reciting the alphabet backward. It doesn't work, so you lie there in the dark worrying. The more you think about your speech, the more anxious, tense, and irritable you become. You notice the sound of music from next door, so you get up, tromp down the hall, burst into the room, and yell, "Will you turn that down! I've got to give a speech tomorrow, so I have to have a good night's sleep!"

Finally, morning comes. You're sitting in class waiting for your turn. You can't listen to the other speeches because you feel miserable. You hear your name called. Your stomach drops. Your hands begin to sweat. Your heart races. Your ears feel hot. Your mouth feels dry. You plod to the podium and look up at the audience. Your knees start to shake. You grab hold of the lectern for support.

InterConnections.LearnMore 2.1

Communication Anxiety

Speech Anxiety
http://chattanoogastate.edu/cde/anxiety
An online resource for working through communication anxiety prepared as a class project under the direction of Debra Jones, Chattanooga State Community College.

Stage Fright
http://www.selfgrowth.com/articles/zimmer5.html
A self-help article, "Transforming Stage Fright into Magnetic Presence," prepared by Sandra Zimmer, consultant and director of the Self-Expression Center, University of Houston.

Overcoming Speaking Anxiety
http://www.selfgrowth.com/articles/laskowski.html
Useful advice from a professional speaker on coping with communication anxiety.

Any of these symptoms sound familiar? What you are experiencing physically is a natural "adrenaline rush." It's the same type of physical reaction you might experience if you suddenly encountered a bear in the wilderness, or a mugger on a dark city street. These are the symptoms you usually associate with fear. They make up the "fight or flight" readiness that can help you through a difficult situation. But when it's your turn to speak, neither fight nor flight is an appropriate response. You've got to give that speech.

Most likely you won't have *all* of these symptoms of communication anxiety, but you may well have some of them. If you didn't, you wouldn't be normal. *Moreover, a little bit of communication anxiety is a good thing.* It can "psych" you up for your presentation. However, too much nervousness can be paralyzing and is a cause for real concern.

The symptoms of anticipation and excitement we experience when we challenge ourselves are much like the symptoms of communication anxiety.

You may be surprised to learn that a little bit of communication anxiety is a good thing. How can this be? The absence of any nervousness may suggest that you don't care about your audience or your message. We recently taught a student who announced to the class that she never had any "stage fright" because she had been very successful in high school speaking contests and was used to "performing" before a group. She couldn't understand why she was required to take this course. She was indifferent to learning what the course had to offer and indifferent in her preparation. She never really listened when others were speaking, because she didn't think she could learn anything worth knowing from her classmates. She also didn't listen to her instructors, because she felt she already knew all she needed to know about public performances. After all, she had experience and had been successful–she had the trophies to prove it. Perhaps because of this attitude, her classroom speeches sounded as though they had been dredged up from her high school forensics files (perhaps they were). They weren't tailored to her audience or the assignment. Her delivery was smooth. Her presentations were performances in the truest sense of the word. But she came across as pretentious. She never connected in any meaningful way with her audience. *She never communicated with them.* That we were never able to teach her the true meaning of communication–with all its risks and rewards–is one of the failures of our career as educators.

So where do you stand in terms of your personal communication anxiety? One way to estimate how much communication anxiety you have is to complete the questionnaire in Figure 2.2.

You may be surprised to find that you didn't score as

high on this scale as you thought you might. If your score is higher than 120, you should arrange a meeting with your instructor to discuss the problem.

Why Public Speaking Can Be Frightening

Right about now you may be thinking, "Well, perhaps I'm not alone, but I'm still pretty uptight about giving a speech. I'm afraid I'll do or say something stupid. Or, I'll forget something important. Or, my classmates will make fun of me." These are very common concerns, so let's investigate why speaking before a group can be frightening. As we cover these concerns, we'll do some reality testing.

The most debilitating anxiety about public speaking typically takes place before you ever reach the podium. Your worries may begin when you register for the course, when a speech is assigned, or while you are preparing your presentation. In outside-the-classroom situations you may begin to get nervous when you know you will be "called upon to say a few words," or when you have a report to make to a work group, or when you feel impelled to speak up before others on a cause you really care about. The nervousness that comes before you make a presentation we call **anticipatory anxiety**.[8]

Because you usually know well in advance that you will be giving a speech, there is a lot of time to build up fears. Understanding the causes of this anxiety can help you cope with it. Later in this chapter, we will give you some concrete suggestions for channeling your nervous energy into a constructive direction. Some of the sources of anxiety are external to the person, more involved in the situation. Other sources lie within the person.

External Factors

Let's begin with two of the more rational reasons why people are not comfortable speaking before a group: the unfamiliarity of the situation, and the importance of the occasion.

Unfamiliarity. Addressing a large number of people face to face is not an everyday occurrence for most of us, and we tend to be somewhat ill at ease in unfamiliar situations. Chances are you want to do well, but you don't know whether you can be successful. Whenever we embark on a new adventure, there is always some element of uncertainty that can cause anxiety. Fortunately for most people, familiarity with the situation tends to reduce anxiety. Practice your speech before a group of friends. Enlist your roommates, sorority sisters or fraternity brothers, or your family to be an audience. Practicing gives you increased familiarity with the speaking situation. Although it may not "make it go away" as you might wish, it can help reduce anxiety to a manageable level.

Importance. Anxiety can also be increased by realizing that you usually will have to speak in public only on *important* occasions, when a lot depends on how well you express yourself. When things are important to us, we tend to worry about them before they ever happen. This anticipatory anxiety is often worse than the anxiety you may experience during the presentation of your speech. It can cause sleeplessness and irritability. Prepare your speech well in advance of your scheduled presentation. If you put off preparing your speech until the night before it is due, you will simply magnify your normal anxiety level as well as compromise the quality of the speech. Try to find something relaxing to do the night before you are scheduled to speak. Watch a silly television show or go to the movies, take a long walk with a friend, or listen to someone else's problems and think about how you might help him or her.

Speaker's Notes 2.1

Common Causes of Communication Anxiety

1. Unfamiliarity with the situation can cause anxiety.
2. The importance of the occasion can make you uptight.
3. Anxiety sensitivity, the fear of fear itself, can magnify apprehension.
4. Perfectionism, the dread of making a mistake, can make you uncomfortable while speaking.
5. Audience misperceptions such as picturing your listeners as predators or faultfinders, can make you nervous.
6. The expectation of dire consequences or humiliation can make you dread the speaking experience.

Internal Factors

How nervous you actually feel about giving a speech also may be related to your personality. This nervousness is not always rational, but it can become a problem if you let it. You may believe you don't have a great deal of control over these factors, that it is simply the way you are; but understanding them may help you cope with them.

Anxiety Sensitivity. You may be the type of person who interprets even the weakest of the symptoms we discussed earlier as signs of fear. If you are like this, you can blow your nervousness all out of proportion. Psychologists call this tendency **anxiety sensitivity**.[9] It is a fear of fear. You think you're afraid so you become more afraid. Knowing that fear feeds on itself, *you must try not to get too anxious about normal anxiety*.

It is important to remember that the physical symptoms you may experience before or during speaking are also associated with other types of reactions that we do not usually call fear. For example, do you remember ever being so excited on Christmas Eve that you couldn't sleep? How did you feel when you heard the first strains of the processional for your high school graduation? What kind of feelings have you had before a big date with a special person? Did you call these feelings "fear" or "excitement"?

Perfectionism. Another personality factor that contributes to communication apprehension is **perfectionism**. As a beginning speaker you may believe that your speech has to be perfect for it to be effective. No presentation is ever perfect. Even former president Ronald Reagan, who was known as "the great communicator," bumbled some lines and repeated himself in his presentations. It's all right if you make a few mistakes, and besides, your listeners probably won't even notice them unless you call attention to them.

Audience Misconceptions. If you expect yourself to be perfect, you may also think that the audience expects you to be perfect. You may picture your listeners as predators lying in wait, ready to pounce on any little mistake you might make, eager to make fun of you like

InterConnections.LearnMore 2.2

Stress Management

Stress Management
http://www.unl.edu/stress/mgmt/
Developed by Wesley E. Sime, Department of Health and Human Performance, University of Nebraska-Lincoln. Provides information necessary for understanding stress and guidelines for coping with stress, including training in relaxation techniques.

Beating the College Blues . . . Stress Reduction Tips and Strategies for College Students
http://www.isma-usa.org/isma/article0701.htm
Prepared by Betty C. Carlson, Chaminade University. Offers useful suggestions for coping with college life on the International Stress Management Association web site.

Top Ten Strategies for Wildly Effective Stress Management
http://caps.unc.edu/MStress.html
Counseling and Psychological Services web site at the University of North Carolina. Provides excellent suggestions for coping with the stress and strain of college life.

Stress, Inc.
http://stress.jrn.columbia.edu.
Lighthearted web site helps place stress in perspective.

Figure 2.2

A Gauge of Communication Anxiety

For an electronic version of this test, go to the **SpeechStudio** and take the Self-Assessment Test: Personal Report of Public Speaking Anxiety.

Go to http://college.hmco.com/eduspace/

Directions: Assume that you have to give a speech within the next few weeks. For each of the statements below, indicate the degree to which the statement applies to you within the context of giving a future speech. Mark whether you strongly agree (SA), agree (A), are undecided (U), disagree (D), or strongly disagree (SD) with each statement. Circle your SA, A, U, D, or SD choices. Do not write in the blanks next to the questions.
Work quickly: just record your first impression.

___	1. While preparing for the speech, I would feel uncomfortably tense and nervous.	SA5	A4	U3	D2	SD1
___	2. I feel uncomfortably tense at the very thought of giving a speech in the near future.	SA5	A4	U3	D2	SD1
___	3. My thoughts would become confused and jumbled when I was giving a speech.	SA5	A4	U3	D2	SD1
___	4. Right after giving the speech I would feel that I'd had a pleasant experience	SA1	A2	U3	D4	SD5
___	5. I would get anxious when thinking about the speech coming up.	SA5	A4	U3	D2	SD1
___	6. I would have no fear of giving the speech.	SA1	A2	U3	D4	SD5
___	7. Although I would be nervous just before starting the speech, after starting it I would soon settle down and feel calm and comfortable.	SA1	A2	U3	D4	SD5
___	8. I would look forward to giving the speech.	SA1	A2	U3	D4	SD5
___	9. As soon as I knew that I would have to give the speech, I would feel myself getting tense.	SA5	A4	U3	D2	SD1
___	10. My hands would tremble when I was giving the speech.	SA5	A4	U3	D2	SD1
___	11. I would feel relaxed while giving the speech.	SA1	A2	U3	D4	SD5
___	12. I would enjoy preparing for the speech.	SA1	A2	U3	D4	SD5
___	13. I would be in constant fear of forgetting what I had prepared to say.	SA5	A4	U3	D2	SD1
___	14. I would get uncomfortably anxious if someone asked me something that I did not know about my topic.	SA5	A4	U3	D2	SD1
___	15. I would face the prospect of giving the speech with confidence.	SA1	A2	U3	D4	SD5
___	16. I would feel that I was in complete possession of myself during the speech.	SA1	A2	U3	D4	SD5
___	17. My mind would be clear when giving the speech.	SA1	A2	U3	D4	SD5
___	18. I would not dread giving the speech.	SA1	A2	U3	D4	SD5
___	19. I would perspire too much just before starting the speech.	SA5	A4	U3	D2	SD1

Figure 2.2
(Continued)

___	20. I would be bothered by a very fast heart rate just as I started the speech.	SA5 A4 U3 D2 SD1
___	21. I would experience considerable anxiety at the speech site (room, auditorium, etc.) just before my speech was to start.	SA5 A4 U3 D2 SD1
___	22. Certain parts of my body would feel very tense and rigid during the speech.	SA5 A4 U3 D2 SD1
___	23. Realizing that only a little time remained in the speech would make me very tense and anxious.	SA5 A4 U3 D2 SD1
___	24. While giving the speech I would know that I could control my feelings of tension and stress.	SA1 A2 U3 D4 SD5
___	25. I would breathe too fast just before starting the speech.	SA5 A4 U3 D2 SD1
___	26. I would feel comfortable and relaxed in the hour or so just before giving the speech.	SA1 A2 U3 D4 SD5
___	27. I would do poorly on the speech because I would be anxious.	SA5 A4 U3 D2 SD1
___	28. I would feel uncomfortably anxious when first scheduling the date of the speaking assignment.	SA5 A4 U3 D2 SD1
___	29. If I were to make a mistake while giving the speech, I would find it hard to concentrate on the parts that followed.	SA5 A4 U3 D2 SD1
___	30. During the speech I would experience a feeling of helplessness building up inside me.	SA5 A4 U3 D2 SD1
___	31. I would have trouble falling asleep the night before the speech.	SA5 A4 U3 D2 SD1
___	32. My heart would beat too fast while I was presenting the speech.	SA5 A4 U3 D2 SD1
___	33. I would feel uncomfortably anxious while waiting to give my speech.	SA5 A4 U3 D2 SD1
___	34. While giving the speech I would get so nervous that I would forget facts I really knew.	SA5 A4 U3 D2 SD1

To determine your score:

1. Fill in the blank next to each item with the NUMBER accompanying the response you circled. BE CAREFUL to enter the CORRECT NUMBER. NOTICE that the numbers printed with the responses are not consistent for every question.
2. Add up the numbers you recorded for the 34 questions. The sum is your public speaking apprehension score.

Interpretation:		
	34-84	low
	85-92	moderately low
	93-110	moderate
	111-119	moderately high
	120 +	high

Source: Adapted from "Personal Report of Public Speaking Anxiety" by James C. McCroskey. Appeared in "Measures of Communication Bound Anxiety," Speech Monographs 37, (1970), p. 276. Used by permission of National Communication Association.

InterConnections.LearnMore 2.3

Help for Perfectionists

Perfectionism
http://www.potsdam.edu/COUN/brochures/perfectionism.html
Online brochure prepared by the SUNY Potsdam Counseling Center. Discusses the self-defeating nature of excessively high and unrealistic goals.

Perfectionism: The Double Edged Sword
http://isis2.admin.usf.edu/counsel/self-help/perfect.htm
Developed by the Counseling Center for Human Development at the University of South Florida. Defines perfectionism as a compulsive striving toward unrealistic goals motivated by a fear of failure.

Perfectionism
http://www.nexus.edu.au/teachstud/gat/peters.htm
Popular article by Carol C. Peters. Discusses the relationship between giftedness and perfectionism, the quest for self-actualization, and the productive management of perfectionism.

kids in grade school. In reality, most audiences, especially college classroom audiences, want speakers to succeed. If you look out in the audience and see someone frowning, that person is probably worried about his or her own upcoming speech or some personal problem, rather than preparing to pounce on you. No one expects you to be perfect except yourself.

You also may worry that everyone in the audience will know how uptight you are. Actually, most listeners won't know this unless you tell them. They are not clairvoyant! One time we were taping student speeches for a teaching video. One person began her speech with an excellent interest-arousing introduction. About two minutes into the speech she stopped, looked at us, and said, "I can't do this! I'm too nervous." We have used the tape of this speech in many classes. We show the speech up until right before the student stops. Then we ask the class to estimate how anxious they think this speaker is. Typically they say, "She's not at all nervous," or, "She's very poised." Then we start the tape back up and show the segment where she quits. The class is typically quite surprised, but the lesson is clear.

Dire Consequences. You may believe that as soon as you stand up to speak something dreadful is going to happen to you–you'll throw up or pass out. This seldom happens, even with the most anxious students. In our many years of teaching we've never seen a student throw up or pass out in a public speaking class.

Specific Fears That Bother Speakers

Two recent surveys of both the general population and college students identified some *specific* fears that people have regarding public speaking.[10] The fears cited by

You may feel that the audience is just waiting for you to make a mistake, but in truth, most audiences want you to succeed.

the general public are listed in Figure 2.3. The students surveyed also mentioned negative consequences (e.g., bad grades) as a major concern. Let's look at these fears and see how troublesome they can be.

Negative Consequences. Anticipating negative results was an important consideration with students who were surveyed, but not with the general population group. For students, the negative consequences were typically related to the grade they might receive on the speaking assignment. Although this may seem like a rational cause for concern, it really diverts your focus from what should be your main concern.

If you prepare your speeches solely for the purpose of making a good grade, you are not going to be a very successful speaker. *Your main purpose for speaking must be to communicate something to your audience*–to provide them with new, interesting, or useful information or to convince them to change their ways of thinking or behaving. Beyond this, although students sometimes insist that they are most anxious about the grade they will get, they are typically just as anxious when making ungraded presentations.

Trembling or Shaking. Approximately 80 percent of the general population polled indicated that they were afraid they would tremble or shake while making a presentation. This was the most common specific fear mentioned in the surveys, and it may well be the most common physical reaction. Indeed, as you make your first presentations, your hands may tremble a bit or your leg muscles may begin to twitch. Is this really all that bad? Chances are you will be more aware of the trembling than anyone in your audience. And, if listeners do notice it, what will they think? That you're a failure? That you're incompetent? Or, that you–*like them*–are somewhat uncomfortable in front of a group?

Actually, some slight trembling may have a positive effect on how the audience reacts to you. Psychologists call this the "pratfall" effect. When people in a position of power or authority (as you are when you give a speech) make a minor mistake, they appear more human and make it more likely that people will respond positively to them. Trembling probably won't affect how competent people think you are, but it may make you seem more likeable.

Is there anything you can do to control your trembling? Probably not as much as you would like. The best thing you can do is focus on your message and not on your mannerisms. It might also help to plan some purposeful physical activity, like gesturing with your hands or walking around from behind the lectern, to give your energy a positive channel for expression. Another good idea is to incorporate a presentation aid into your speech. As you point out the features of a model or refer to

Figure 2.3

Specific Public Speaking Fears

Type of Fear	Percent Reporting
Trembling or shaking	*80%*
Mind going blank	*74%*
Doing or saying something embarrassing	*64%*
Unable to continue talking	*63%*
Not making sense	*59%*
Sounding foolish	*59%*

the figures on a chart, you give your body a positive way to work off some tension.

Mind Going Blank. The second most common specific fear people reported was that they were afraid their minds would go blank, that they would not remember how they had planned to say something or what they intended to say next. Back in middle school or high school, probably all of us had the experience of memorizing a passage to recite in class–the Gettysburg Address, a scene from Shakespeare, or a poem–and drew a blank about halfway through our performance. It can be traumatic standing in front of a class full of adolescents who just can't wait to make fun of you. Your college classroom audience will be far more forgiving, but having your mind go blank is one of the major pitfalls of memorized presentations. It is one of the reasons that we do not recommend memorizing your speeches (as discussed in Chapter 13).

An effective speech is presented extemporaneously–prepared and practiced, but not written out and memorized. If you practice your speech using a key-word outline and keep the outline handy as you present your speech, drawing a blank should not be a major problem for you. If after all this, you do experience one of those rare dreaded moments when you simply can't think of what to say next, go back over what you have just said in different words. Audiences expect summaries in speeches, and going back over your material to that point should help get you back on track.

Even if you don't say exactly what you had planned to say exactly as you had planned to say it, the audience won't know this unless you tell them. Furthermore, what you say on the spur of the moment may actually be *better* than the exact wording you had planned.

Embarrassing Yourself. Whenever you appear before a group to make a presentation, you are putting yourself in the spotlight. The spotlight is bright, and it shows all the things you might like to hide. As a speaker, you are conspicuous. All eyes are on you. One of our public speaking students several years ago brought home the meaning of this to us. She was a cheerleader at Indiana University. One day she came into our office to ask for advice on controlling her communication anxiety. "You're nervous about speaking to twenty students!" we exclaimed. "Why, every weekend you're out there in front of sixty thousand people at the stadium!" "That's different," she replied. "Out there I'm not really in the spotlight. Those sixty thousand fans are focused on the game. In this class the twenty students are focused on me."

What can you possibly do during a speech that would be really all that embarrassing? Tremble in front of people–we've already discussed that. Forget how you planned to say something–no big deal. Mispronounce big words or technical terms–look them up ahead of time. Flub a word–everyone does this from time to time. Save being embarrassed for the truly ludicrous things that might happen in your life, and keep in mind that you will survive even those.

The first class one of your authors ever taught in college was a large lecture class held in an auditorium, complete with a lectern on a stage. During the first exam a student asked her to cut off the air conditioners that were making a racket.–Klumpt! Bang! Rattle! Whoosh! You know how they sound. She shut off the air conditioner on one side of the stage and was walking across to the other side, not looking where she was going, and tripped over the base of the free-standing chalkboard, falling flat on her face in front of 250 students. Now, that's embarrassing, especially for a first-time graduate student teaching assistant. She was praying there'd be a trap door she could fall through, but of course there wasn't. To her amazement, however, no one was laughing. The expressions on the faces she could see were ones of concern. She picked herself up, brushed the dirt off her clothes, and muttered something like, "Grace is my middle name!" The students' looks changed from

concern to relief when they realized she wasn't hurt. To her everlasting surprise, the sun rose as usual the next morning. And regardless of how embarrassed she had felt, she had to show up for the next class and lecture on the topic of the day.

Chances are nothing like this will happen to you in your public speaking class, but if it does, you will survive it, and you may be even stronger because of it. No one is going to make fun of you, regardless of what happens.

Unable to Continue Talking. Although almost two-thirds of the people in the general population survey mentioned this as a specific concern, it very rarely happens even to the most anxious of students. This concern is closely related to having your mind go blank, a rare occurrence that can be handled by referring to a keyword outline or by summarizing previously covered material.

On very, very rare occasions a student may experience a panic attack. You're going along presenting your speech, everything is going well, when you suddenly feel overwhelmed with fear for no apparent reason. Not only are you afraid, but you also realize that the fear is irrational, and you think perhaps you're "losing it." You really want to drop your notes and bolt for the door. Don't do it! Decide to weather the storm. Mark Twain once said, "Courage is resistance to fear, mastery of fear, not absence of fear." A panic attack is usually short. It may last only a few seconds (although it may feel as though it's going on forever). Keep talking. Look for the friendliest face in the audience and direct your words to that person. Accept your fear for what it is, a temporary aberration. Chances are it will not happen again, but if you are concerned about this, schedule an appointment with your instructor to discuss it.

Not Making Sense and Sounding Foolish. Most speakers who don't make sense and therefore sound foolish do so because they have not adequately prepared for their presentations. The remainder of this book is devoted to helping you prepare and present speeches that do make sense and sound intelligent. You will learn how to analyze your listeners and how to adapt your messages to their needs and interests. You will learn how to gain responsible knowledge through research and how to use this material to support your ideas. You will learn how to structure and organize your messages clearly and how to use oral language effectively. All of this information will help ensure that you make sense and don't sound foolish.

On the other hand, if you take your assignments lightly, don't adequately prepare, and don't practice for your presentations, you've earned the right to be anxious and to suffer the consequences.

Presentation Anxiety

Presentation anxiety, the discomfort one can feel while actually presenting a speech, is the counterpart of anticipatory anxiety, which builds up before a speech. Although different, these two forms of discomfort can be related. How much anxiety you experience when actually presenting your speech may be a function of how much anticipatory anxiety you build up. If you can keep your anticipatory anxiety under control, you've won most of the battle. Expect to be most nervous when you first begin your speech.[11] Then, as you get used to the situation and as the faces before you become more familiar, you should gain confidence. Research shows that as you get into the delivery of your speech, your nervousness will diminish. Prepare your introduction carefully, and practice it until it flows easily. Keep your focus on the essence of your message–what you want to communicate to your audience.

Controlling Communication Anxiety

You've probably heard a lot of advice about how to control your nerves. For example, picture the audience sitting there naked. (Try this and you might be quite distracted.) Another pearl of wisdom is to take a really deep breath each time you feel yourself getting anxious. (Do this and you'll start hyperventilating.) Or–and this is probably the worst advice we've heard–cut back on your preparation because "in general, the more you prepare, the worse you will do."[12] The people who offer such wisdom may mean well, but quick-fix techniques don't work.

You also may have been told that taking a public speaking class will cure you of your communication apprehension. One of the biggest myths about a public speaking class is that it can or should rid you of your natural fears. *There is no cure for communication anxiety, but there are things that can help you keep it under control.*

Research shows that the techniques we will discuss in this chapter do help and that they work best when used in combination.[13] So try one thing and then another until you find what works best for you. The techniques that we will consider are selective relaxation, attitude adjustment, visualization, and skills training.

Selective Relaxation

A good starting point in learning how to handle your anxiety is to master the art of **selective relaxation**. Begin practicing this technique now before your first speech. Practice doing it several times a day until the technique becomes second nature. Follow the sequence outlined below:

1. Find a quiet place where you can be by yourself. Sit in a comfortable chair or lie down, close your eyes, and breathe deeply in through your nose and out through your mouth. You should feel yourself beginning to relax.
2. Once you feel yourself relaxing, begin slowly repeating a special word, such as *one*, each time you exhale. Let your mind drift freely. You should soon feel quite relaxed.
3. While you are relaxed and breathing deeply, practice selectively tensing and relaxing different muscle groups. Begin by tensing your feet and legs: curl up your toes, tense your arch, tighten your calves, lock your knees, contract your thigh muscles. Hold this tension for several seconds and concentrate on how it feels. Not very comfortable, is it? And even with the tension concentrated in the lower part of your body, it's not all that easy to continue deep breathing.
4. The next step is to concentrate on breathing deeply again, repeating your special word as you exhale and consciously letting the muscles relax.
5. Move the tensing and relaxing up your body: practice it on your abdominal muscles, your hand and arm muscles, your neck and head muscles. After you have done this a number of times, simply repeating your special word should trigger a relaxation response.

One good thing about this exercise is that once you have mastered the technique, you can practice it unobtrusively in many situations. While you are sitting in class waiting to speak, tense your feet and leg muscles; then relax them. If you find yourself getting nervous while you are speaking, repeat your special word to yourself. The word alone may be enough to help you relax and return your concentration to your message. If this doesn't work as well as you would like, try tensing and relaxing a hand as you speak. (Just be sure it's down at your side where it can't be seen.)

Attitude Adjustments

Throughout this chapter, we have stressed the importance of thinking of public speaking as an interactive communication act and not as a performance. Bringing this off may require some attitude adjustments.

Communication Orientation.

When you adopt a **communication orientation** to public speaking, you concentrate on your message and your audience, not on yourself. Select a topic that is so exciting and interesting that your worries about yourself will fade into the background. Choose a topic that brings important new information or a new perspective to the audience, and then concentrate on communicating it effectively to them.

One of the most communication-apprehensive students we ever taught actually left the room in the middle of her first speech to get a drink of water and try to compose herself. While she was in the hall, we discussed with the class how we as an audience might help her. When she came to our office after the speech, we tried to work with her on focusing on her message and her audience. Her second effort was a little better. She stopped during her presentation to try to "pull herself together," but she managed to finish without leaving the room. Her third speech (persuasive) was a totally different story.

The student worked during the day as a dispatcher for a major interstate trucking firm. She presented a speech urging her classmates to lobby their congressional representatives to vote in favor of a truck safety bill that was pending in Congress. This topic was very important to her. Her speech was filled with interesting examples of near catastrophes that this legislation would make less likely. She knew her topic. She knew it was important. She got so caught up with her message that she forgot to be anxious. The audience was spellbound. When she finished, there was a moment of silence while it all sank in, then spontaneous applause–applause for a speech well given and applause for a speaker who had conquered her personal demons.

Cognitive Restructuring.

Another attitude adjustment involves changing the messages you send to yourself about your public speaking experiences. The psychologists call this **cognitive restructuring**. All of us send messages to ourselves about our behavior. If these messages are positive, they can act as self-fulfilling prophecies that help us function better. Positive messages can also boost your self-confidence. When you have faith in yourself, you are better able to withstand nonconstructive criticism from others. Early in her career Rosie O'Donnell appeared in a talent show. The producer told the other contestants, "She'll never be famous. She's too tough. She's too New York. And, she's too heavy." Rosie's reaction? "He's gonna feel like a jerk when I'm famous!" [14]

On the other hand, if the messages we send ourselves are negative, they may become suicidal predictions that invite failure. To practice cognitive restructuring, you need to identify the irrational negative messages that you are sending yourself about public speaking and replace them with positive, constructive messages. For example, instead of telling yourself, "I'm going to sound stupid," say, "I've worked hard on this speech and I know what I'm talking about." Replace, "Everyone in this class is more confident than I am," with, "I am as confident as anyone in this class." For "I really don't want to give this speech," try, "I've got a chance to offer my ideas to others."

Right before you stand to speak, summarize these positive messages into a final encouraging pep talk to yourself: "I've worked hard for this moment. I've got a good message, and I'm well prepared to present it. Now it's time to put it across, and I can do it."

Speaker's Notes 2.2

Techniques for Handling Communication Anxiety

1. **Selective relaxation** helps reduce anticipatory anxiety, shaking hands, and wobbly knees.
2. **Attitude adjustments** help you focus on your message and change negative self-messages.
3. **Visualization** techniques prepare you for your presentation by implanting a positive image of success in your mind.
4. **Skills training** makes you more competent and therefore more confident as a speaker.

Visualization

The championship game of the 1999 Women's World Cup Soccer game was tied at the end of play. This meant that China and the United States each had five penalty kicks to determine the winner. Before one of China's kicks, the camera zoomed in on Briana Scurry, the American goalkeeper. She had a look of intense concentration on her face. The announcer commented, "She's visualizing blocking this next kick."

Professional athletes have long used this technique to improve their performances. You can also control communication anxiety with **visualization**, in which you systematically imagine yourself succeeding as a speaker, and then practice your presentation with that image in mind.[15] To make visualization work best, you need to develop a script in which you picture a day of success from the moment you get up through the moment when you enjoy the congratulations of your classmates and instructor for your excellent speech. A sample script is provided at the end of this chapter. Amend it to fit your own needs and personality. To use this technique most effectively, you start off with relaxation exercises and then run your script for success through your mind. Do this several times throughout your preparation, and then again immediately before you present your speech.

Star athletes often use visualization as a means of preparing for success.

Skills Training

Think back to a moment in your childhood when you acquired a new skill. It might have been learning to swim or using a computer. The more you learned and the more you practiced, the more confident you became. The more confident you became, the less afraid you were. Before too long you were jumping into the deep end of the pool without hesitation, or solving a complex computer problem without asking anyone for help. The same type of relationship exists between knowledge, practice, confidence, and public speaking. When you feel you know how to prepare a speech and when you have adequately practiced your presentation, you will feel more confident and will have less communication anxiety.

Although learning the fundamentals of public speaking is important, it is also important to have substantial knowledge of your topic if you want to speak confidently about it. Select a topic you already know something about, and then build a body of responsible knowledge to supplement that basic information. Go to the library, access the Internet, and interview a local expert. Then you will be prepared to speak with authority and confidence. (Read more about researching in Chapter 7.)

Keep in mind that practicing is an important part of your preparation. Highly anxious students often spend a lot of time researching and organizing their speeches, but then they don't spend enough time actually practicing their presentations.[16] So practice, and then practice some more. The more you master the presentation of your message, the more confident you will be.

A final word of advice: When you rise to speak, ACT CONFIDENT even if you don't feel that way. Walk briskly to the front of the room, look at your audience, and establish eye contact. If appropriate to your topic and purpose, smile. Whatever happens during your speech, remember your listeners cannot see or hear inside you. They only know what you choose to show and tell them. Show them a controlled speaker presenting a well-researched and well-rehearsed speech. Never start your speech by telling the audience how frightened you are. When you come to the end of your message, maintain eye contact for a short time, and then walk confidently back to your seat. Even though you may feel relieved that your speech is over, don't say "Whew!" or "I made it!" And never show disappointment with your presentation. You probably did better than you thought.

Do these techniques really work, and is such advice helpful? Research related to communication anxiety has established the following conclusions: *(1) Such techniques do work, and (2) they work best in combination.*[17] Controlling anxiety takes time. As you become more experienced at giving speeches and at using the suggestions in Speaker's Notes 2.3, you will find your fears lessening, and you will be able to convert more of your communication anxiety into positive, constructive energy.[18]

VideoLab

Keep **Lesson 1's VideoLab Coach: Tips to Remember** in mind when preparing for your speeches.

Speaker's Notes 2.3

Ten Helpful Hints

1. Prepare a well-researched and carefully organized message.
2. Practice your presentation until it flows smoothly.
3. Focus on communicating with your audience.
4. Practice selective relaxation.
5. Replace negative, self-defeating statements with positive ones.
6. Visualize yourself being successful.
7. Select a topic that excites you.
8. Master your topic so that you can speak with authority.
9. Act confident, even if you don't feel that way initially.
10. Take advantage of other opportunities (classes, social groups, etc.) to practice speaking in public.

In Summary

Communication anxiety is a widespread problem that bothers many public speaking students. It can be especially debilitating to students who think that everyone in the class is more confident than they are. We use the term *communication anxiety* rather than *stage fright* because public speaking is interactive communication and not a performance.

Understanding Communication Anxiety. Communication anxiety typically results from an adrenaline rush that may be accompanied by butterflies in your stomach, sweating, heart palpitations, a dry mouth, and shaking extremities. The symptoms are always more obvious to the person suffering from them than to any observers. There is an upside to communication anxiety: it can energize your performance. A lack of any anxiety usually results in an uninspired presentation.

Public speaking can be frightening because it is not an everyday occurrence and because you usually speak in public only on important occasions. If you suffer from *anxiety sensitivity*, your fear of fear itself may make the situation worse. If you are a *perfectionist*, you may put undue pressure on yourself. You may also see the audience as predators lying in wait to make fun of you, when in reality most college student audiences want speakers to be successful. If you are like most students, you are probably sure that everyone can tell how nervous you are, but this is not usually the case. You may think that as soon as you rise to speak something dreadful will happen to you, but this rarely happens.

Some of the major fears that make up communication anxiety include our anticipation of trembling or shaking while speaking, having our mind go blank, embarrassing ourselves, being unable to continue talking, not making sense, and sounding foolish. Many of these fears are irrational.

Ways to Control Communication Anxiety. There is no quick fix for communication anxiety, but there are several things you can do to reduce your discomfort. You can practice *selective relaxation* to reduce bodily tension. You should adopt a *communication orientation* rather than a performance orientation, keeping your focus on your message and its value for your listeners. Practice *cognitive restructuring* so that you replace negative messages to yourself with positive ones. Develop and enact *visualization* scripts that picture you succeeding as a speaker. Learn and practice speaking skills so that you develop greater confidence. These techniques usually help, and they work best in combination.

Terms to Know

communication anxiety
anticipatory anxiety
anxiety sensitivity
perfectionism
presentation anxiety
selective relaxation
communication orientation
cognitive restructuring
visualization

Discussion

1. Interview teachers of the classes you are taking this semester to determine whether they ever had or have problems with communication anxiety and what they did or do to overcome these problems.

2. Write down three negative messages you often send yourself, such as "I'm going to forget what I want to say." Restate these messages in more positive ways, using the principles of cognitive restructuring. For example, the message just quoted could be restated as, "My key-word outline will ensure that I keep my place." Share these with a small group of your classmates. Were there any similarities among the negative messages? Could your classmates offer or could you offer them any suggestions for improving these restatements?

3. Make a list of all the questionable things you may have tried to control your communication anxiety, such as avoiding eye contact or reading your speech (or even delaying taking the class!). In what ways were these efforts self-defeating? Which of the positive techniques we have discussed (selective relaxation, communication orientation, cognitive restructuring, visualization) do you think might work best for you? Why? Share these insights with your classmates.

Application

1. List the three major reasons that you are afraid of making a speech. Try to be precise as you complete the expressions "I'm afraid that . . ." or "I'm afraid because . . ." Go over your list and classify each of these fears as rational or irrational. Now develop a plan to counter them. Try to use selective relaxation, cognitive restructuring, visualization, and speech practice techniques. Which of these proves most and least useful in controlling your fears?
2. Write out your own script for success for the presentation of your first speech in this class. Provide your instructor with a copy, and then use it as you prepare for your presentation.

Notes

1. The Gallup Organization, "Snakes Top List of Americans' Fears" (19 Mar. 2001). http://www.gallup.com/poll/releases/pr010319.asp (20 Sept. 2003).
2. National Communication Association, "How Americans Communicate" (undated posting). http://www.natcom.org/research/Roper/how_americans_communicate.htm(25 June 1999).
3. Nanci Hellmich, "Lifting the Curtain on Stage Fright: Anxiety at Performing Is Normal, But Panic Can Become Paralyzing," *USA Today*, 13 Aug. 1996, p. 6D.
4. Ed Sherman, "It's Not the Novelty, It's the Challenge," *Chicago Tribune*, 22 May 2003, p. 1. Online at http://www.chicagotribune.com.
5. Rochelle Garner, "Bore No More," *Computerworld*, 5 Apr. 1999, p. 54.
6. Pedro Pereira, "Top 25 Executives: Steve Raymund," *Computer Reseller News*, 17 Nov. 1997, p. 129.
7. Michael T. Motley, *Overcoming Your Fear of Public Speaking: A Proven Method* (Boston: Houghton Mifflin, 1997).
8. Ralph R. Behnke and Chris R. Sawyer, "Milestones of Anticipatory Public Speaking Anxiety," *Communication Education* 48 (April 1999): 165–172.
9. Jennifer D. Mladenka, Chris R. Sawyer, and Ralph R. Behnke, "Anxiety Sensitivity and Speech Trait Anxiety as Predictors of State Anxiety During Public Speaking," *Communication Quarterly* 46, no. 4 (Fall 1998): 417–429.
10. M. B. Stein, J. R. Walker, and D. R. Forde, "Public Speaking Fears in a Community Sample: Prevalence, Impact on Functioning, and Diagnostic Classification," *Archives of General Psychiatry* (February 1996): 169–174. *Thrive Online Health Library*. http://www.thriveonline.com (July 1999). Amy M. Bippus and John A. Daly, "What Do People Think Causes Stage Fright? Naïve Attributions About the Reasons for Public Speaking Anxiety," *Communication Education* 48 (1999): 63–72.
11. R. R. Behnke and C. R. Sawyer, "Milestones of Anticipatory Public Speaking Anxiety," *Communication Education* 48 (April 1999): 165–172.
12. Harvard University, *Public Speaking Home Page*. http://gseweb.harvard.edu/~westma/pubspeak.htm/ (28 July 1999).
13. Randolph W. Whitworth and Claudia Cochran, "Evaluation of Integrated Versus Unitary Treatments for Reducing Public Speaking Anxiety," *Communication Education* 45 (1996): 228–235.
14. Melina Gerosa, "Rosie Revealed," *Ladies Home Journal*, February. 1999, p. 118.
15. Joe Ayres and Brian L. Hewett, "The Relationship Between Visual Imagery and Public Speaking Apprehension," *Communication Reports* 10 (1997): 87–94.
16. Joe Ayres, "Speech Preparation Processes and Speech Apprehension," *Communication Education* 45 (1996): 228–235.
17. Whitworth and Cochran, pp. 306–314.
18. Mike Allen, John E. Hunter, and William A. Donohue, "Meta-Analysis of Self-Report Data on the Effectiveness of Public Speaking Anxiety Treatment Techniques," *Communication Education* 38 (1989): 54–76.

SAMPLE VISUALIZATION SCRIPT*

You see yourself getting up in the morning, full of energy, full of confidence, looking forward to the day's challenges. You are putting on the right clothes for your speech. Dressing well makes you look good and feel good about yourself, so you have on just what you want to wear. As you are going to your speech classroom, you feel very confident, so confident that others comment positively on your appearance and demeanor. You feel thoroughly prepared for your speech. You have really researched the topic you will be speaking about today.

Now you see yourself in the room where you will present your speech, talking comfortably with others in the room. The people to whom you will be presenting your speech are quite friendly and warm in their greetings and conversations prior to your presentation. You feel absolutely sure of your ability to present your speech in a forceful, convincing, positive manner.

Now you see yourself approaching the area from which you will present your speech. You are feeling very good about this presentation. You see yourself presenting your talk. You are quite brilliant and sound like a polished professional speaker. You see your listeners nodding their heads in agreement. They are smiling at you, providing feedback that says you are "on target."

Your introduction to the speech goes the way you planned. In fact, it works better than you had expected. The transition from the introductory material to the body of the speech is smooth. As you come to the body of your speech, the first major point emerges as you expected. Your evidence supporting the point is relevant and evokes understanding from the audience. All your main points flow in this fashion. As you wrap up your main points, your concluding remarks seem to be a natural outgrowth of everything you have done.

All your concluding remarks are well received. When you finish speaking, you feel your speech could not have gone better. Your introduction worked well, your main points were clear, your evidence was strong, and your conclusion ended the speech with style and flair. In addition, your vocal variety added interest. Your pauses punctuated important ideas, and your gestures were purposeful. You see yourself answering audience questions with confidence. You see yourself receiving the congratulations of your classmates. You see yourself relaxed and pleased with your speech. You are filled with a sense of well-being. You congratulate yourself on a job well done!

* Adapted from Joe Ayres and Theodore S. Hopf, "Visualization: Is It More Than Extra Attention?" *Communication Education* 38 (1989): 2–3.

Your First Speech

3

OUTLINE

This chapter will help you

- prepare and present your first speech
- manage the first impressions you make on others
- develop a speech in which you introduce yourself or someone else

> *Without speech there would be no community. . . . Language, taken as a whole, becomes the gateway to a new world.*
>
> ERNST CASSIRER

Jimmy Green worried about his first speech. What he had read about managing his communication apprehension gave him some comfort: at least he knew he was not alone in his performance anxiety. But he had read only two chapters in the text, and he didn't feel he knew enough to get up and speak without making a fool of himself. To top that off, his instructor had assigned a speech of self-introduction. Jimmy felt that nothing exciting had ever happened to him. What could he talk about? After working through the self-awareness inventory discussed later in this chapter, Jimmy decided to talk about growing up in rural Decatur County. He opened his speech by referring to the song "A Country Boy Can Survive." Then he captivated his urban audience with graphic descriptions of jug fishing for catfish and nightlong barbecues where "more than the pig got sauced."

Many of us just can't see ourselves as "public speakers," especially when faced with our first speech. We doubt that we have anything interesting to say, and even if we did, we're not sure we could say it effectively. We are then pleasantly surprised when we not only survive our first speech, but actually do some things very well.

The first speeches in a class can help build a communication climate that nurtures effective speaking and listening. No matter what the exact nature of your assignment, your first speech serves three useful purposes.

- First, it gets you speaking early in the course so that you don't have time to build up an unhealthy level of communication apprehension.
- Second, it allows you to try out some of the basic skills needed to develop a speech and present it effectively. Much of what is in this chapter will be covered in more depth and in greater detail later in the text. Here, we simply want to provide you with enough advice to increase your chances of success the first time you address the class.
- Third, your first speech gives you an opportunity to present yourself as a credible source of ideas. As we noted in Chapter 1, people are more likely to respond favorably to those whom they respect and like. In this chapter we show you how to get off on the right foot by managing the all-important first impressions you make as a speaker. We conclude this chapter with some special advice on developing a speech in which you introduce yourself or a classmate.

Before the opening round of speeches, you and your classmates are usually strangers. These first speeches are often called "icebreakers," because they give members of the class a chance to know each other better. You will probably discover that your classmates are both diverse and interesting human beings behind the masks. What you learn about them will help you prepare later speeches and give you insights into their knowledge, interests, attitudes, and motivations. Because it is easier to communicate with people you know, after a while you should feel more comfortable about speaking before the class.

Planning Your First Speech

So now you have your first speech assignment. Whatever it may require, the planning, thought, creativity, and excitement of presentation are all up to you. But at the moment, standing before the class and saying something sensible may seem like a remote possibility. The challenge may seem large, and the more you think about it, the larger it becomes. Take comfort, however. A distant goal can be reached and brought down to size if you take the right number of steps, one by one, to reach it. Eventually you will be standing at the lectern before your classmates, well prepared to present an interesting speech. This stairway to speech success appears in Figure 3.1. Follow it as you prepare each of your speeches.

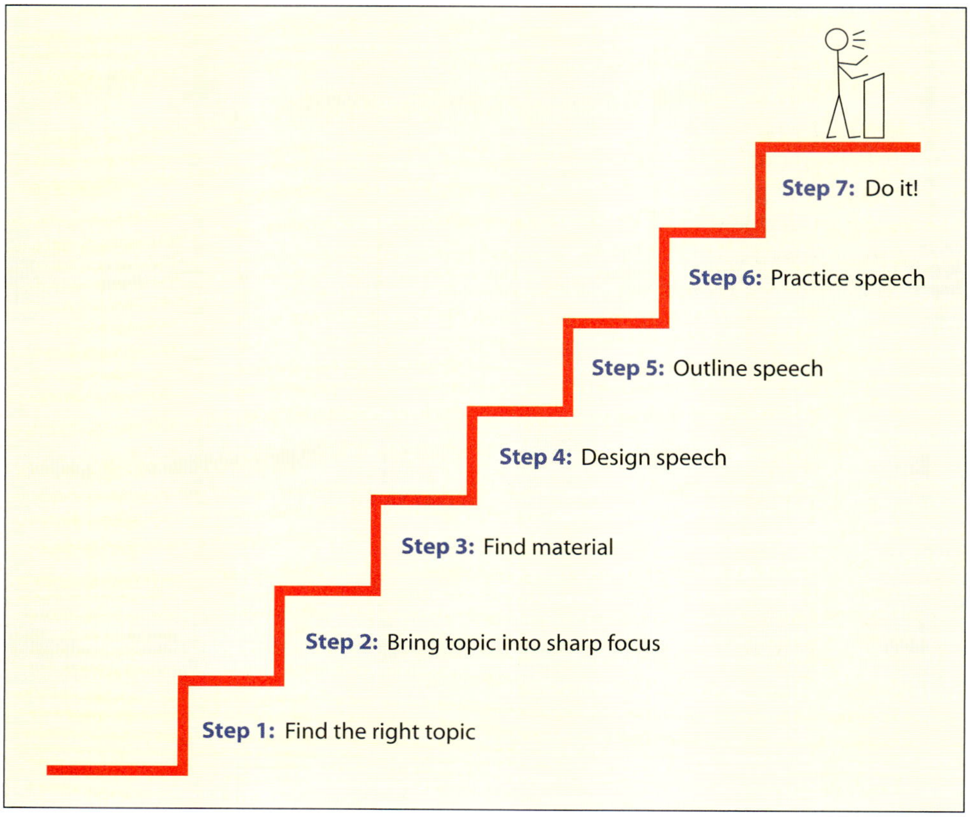

Figure 3.1
Stairway to Speech Success

As you prepare for your first speech, go to **VideoLab Lesson 1's Next Step: Preparing Yourself to Speak.**

One thing is immediately clear. To climb this stairway requires some time. You can't delay speech preparation until the night before you have to present your first speech. Take the first step well in advance of the day you are to speak. Schedule your preparation so that you have enough time to climb steadily toward your speech, without skipping or hurrying any of the steps. It is better to devote an hour each day to speech preparation over five days than to cram five hours of desperate preparation into the night before you speak. A speech needs time to jell, and you need time to reflect on it. Your wise investment of time now will pay big dividends later.[1]

Step 1: Find the Right Topic

The nature of the first speech assignment will often narrow your search for an appropriate topic. For example, if your teacher asks you to introduce yourself or a classmate, the topic area is predetermined: your personal experience or that of the other person. Or, the assignment may have some other slant that limits the universe of topic possibilities.

Nevertheless, within that narrowed scope of selection, you will still have to make important choices. The exact topic you select should be appropriate to you and your listeners. Ask yourself:

- What am I most interested in?
- What would I hope to accomplish by speaking on this subject?
- Do I know enough or could I learn enough to give a responsible speech on this topic?
- Can I make the topic interesting to my audience?
- Can I share information or experiences about the topic that might enrich my audience's lives?
- Will I be able to present this speech in the time allowed?
- Might this speech help me give later, related speeches?

Jimmy Green's first speech, "My Life as a River Rat," drew directly on his background growing up along the Tennessee River. He knew that listeners love stories, and he had some good ones to tell. If he could share his culture with them and give them a few enjoyable moments, he thought he could satisfy the assignment of introducing himself as a unique individual. Because he had timed himself as he rehearsed his speech, he could relax during the actual presentation, knowing that he would be within acceptable time limits. By the end of the speech, he had not only met the assignment: he had also created a favorable impression of himself and built credibility for his later speeches on environmental policy.

Step 2: Bring the Topic into Sharp Focus

A topic search may produce a promising subject for your speech, but often these subjects are far too vast and general to cover in a short classroom speech. Beth Tidmore, a student in our class at the University of Memphis, decided she wanted to give her self-introductory speech on the university's rifle team. As a member of this team, Beth became an All-American during her freshman year, and at the time of this writing she is a prospect for the United States Olympic team. Beth knows so much about her sport that she could have talked about it for hours, but she had only a maximum of five minutes.

Clearly, Beth needed to narrow and focus her topic; she needed to develop a slant that her listeners might find interesting. She might have explained how rifle matches are scored, or how an expert shooter executes a successful shot. Beth decided that these were technical approaches that might not be so interesting to a general audience that lacked any orientation to the sport. Instead, she opted to tell her listeners how and why she became a shooter. She opened by talking about the commitment her mother made when she bought Beth the expensive rifle she would need to develop her skill. She went on to describe the price she had paid in time, hard work, and dedication to reach the top of her sport, as well as the personal satisfaction she got from her success. She concluded by saying that she felt her mother's faith had been vindicated. Her speech fascinated her audience and won their admiration. All of us cheered her as she went on that spring to win the gold medal in the Junior Olympics competition held at Colorado Springs.

Beth's speech illustrates two important principles of focusing a topic:

- *You must have a clear idea of what you want to accomplish given the time available.* Beth wanted to tell us how and why rifle competition had become a central passion in her life.
- *You should be able to state the message of your speech in a single simple sentence.* Beth's message was that faith and commitment can be justified by hard, determined, and dedicated work.

When you have properly focused your topic, you will be ready to take the next step toward speech success.

Step 3: Find Material to Develop Your Speech

Once you have a topic a vision of what you want to accomplish, and a clear idea of your message, you can start putting together material to support your ideas and make them come to life. The four basic forms of supporting materials are narratives, examples, testimony, and facts and statistics.

Your personal experiences can provide examples and narratives for your speech.

Narratives. **Narratives** make characters come to life in stories that add interest and authenticity to a speech. For your first speeches—especially for introductory and self-introductory speeches—stories are especially vital. They help develop a feeling of closeness between the audience and the speaker. Through the stories they tell, speakers can create desirable impressions of themselves or the classmates they introduce. They can seem more human, more approachable. Good stories invite listeners to become close observers of an event or part of the action: therefore, a good story is a shared adventure.

Beth Tidmore's narratives helped listeners relate to her topic.

Beth Tidmore opened her speech, "Lady with a Gun," with a story of her mother's commitment to her:

I'm sure everybody has had an April Fool's joke played on them. My father's favorite one was to wake me up on April first and tell me, "School's been canceled for the day; you don't have to go," and then get all excited and say "April Fool!" . . .

Well, on April first 2000, my mother said three words that I was sure weren't an April Fool joke. She said, "We'll take it." The "it" she was referring to was a brand-new Anschutz 2002 Air Rifle. Now, this is $2,000 worth of equipment for a sport that I'd been in for maybe three months—not long. That was a big deal! It meant that I would be going from a junior-level to an Olympic-grade rifle.

Somebody outside of the sport might think "Eh, minor upgrade. A gun is a gun, right?" No. Imagine a fifteen-year-old who has been driving a used Toyota and who suddenly gets a brand new Mercedes for her sixteenth birthday. That's how I felt.

And as she was writing the check, I completely panicked. I thought, "What if I'm not good enough to justify this rifle? What if I decide to quit and we have to sell it, or we can't sell it? What if I let my parents down and I waste their money?" So later in the car, I said, "Momma, what if I'm not good enough?" She said, "Don't worry about it—it's my money."

Beth's story illustrates excellent narrative technique. Her use of **dialogue**, the actual words exchanged between characters, brings listeners close to the event. They become eavesdroppers to the conversation. Notice that she uses *internal dialogue*, her conversation with herself, as well as *external dialogue*, as she talks with her mother. Notice also the superb use of **analogy**, as she invites listeners to compare her feelings with those of someone who has just received a Mercedes. The analogy highlights the significance of the gift to her. Finally, notice how well Beth builds suspense: had she been able to justify the purchase of such an expensive gift? She aroused our curiosity for the rest of the speech.

Stories should be short and to the point, moving naturally from the beginning to the end. Just as in Beth's speech, the language of stories should be colorful, concrete, and active; the presentation should be lively and interesting.

After describing her success in national and international competitions, Beth concluded with another story that both balanced and completed her opening narrative:

So not long ago, I asked my mother, "How did you know?" She said, "Ah, I just knew." I said, "No, Mom—*really*. How did you know that you weren't

going to waste your money?" She got very serious and she took me by the shoulders and she squared me up. She looked me right in the eye and she said, "When you picked up that gun, you just looked like you belonged together. I knew there was a sparkle in your eye, and I knew that you were meant to do great things with that rifle."

So, thanks, Mom.

Examples. **Examples** illustrate points, clarify uncertainty, and make events seem authentic. When listeners ask, "Can you give me an example?" they are requesting clarification and reassurance. An example says, in effect, "This really happened." It takes a point out of the abstract and places it firmly in the concrete. To illustrate her abstract claim that it is good business to serve the needs of disabled people, Karen Lovelace described a group called Opening Doors, which encourages companies to improve travel for the disabled. "One hotel chain that has used this program is Embassy Suites. Their staff is taught by Opening Doors to problem-solve based on guests' needs. And you'd better believe that the word gets around to disabled travelers!" This example made her claim seem well grounded.

To illustrate her point that she was a lover of reading, Erin Evans introduced a number of brief examples: "In high school the classics came into my life. I loved *The Great Gatsby, Medea*, and then my senior year I met a real challenge—Dostoyevsky. It took me more than two months to get through *Crime and Punishment*, but it was time well spent!"

Whether you are piling up a number of brief examples or developing one example in great detail, remember their function: *they help listeners grasp your point*. As with stories, you should use colorful, concrete, and active language in your examples.

Testimony. **Testimony** offered by experts or other respected people can strengthen the authority of your speech. Along with facts and statistics, testimony becomes more significant as you present more substantive informative and persuasive speeches later in your class. When you quote the words of others, you call them up as though they were *witnesses* to support a point you have just made or wish to make. As she developed her speech supporting better service for the disabled, Karen Lovelace quoted Sandy Blondino, director of sales at Embassy Suites Hotels, who confirmed that the hospitality industry is now more receptive to disabled travelers. She concluded with Ms. Blondino's exact words: "But that's just hospitality, right?" She followed up this *expert testimony* with *prestige testimony* by quoting former President Clinton: "When I injured my knee and used a wheelchair for a short time, I understood even more deeply that the ADA isn't just a good law, it's the right thing to do." When you quote expert testimony, be sure to mention the expert's credentials including when and where she or he made the statement you are quoting.

If you were to cite Nancy Reagan's support for stem cell research in your speech, you would be using prestige testimony.

Facts and Statistics. **Facts and statistics** help turn assertions into well-documented arguments. For example, to support her idea that American business has a legal as well as a moral obligation to reach out to disabled persons, Karen Lovelace offered factual information from the Americans with Disabilities Act:

The ADA said that "privately owned businesses that serve the public such as restaurants, hotels, retail

> **stores, taxi cabs, theaters, concert halls, and sports facilities are prohibited from discriminating against individuals with disabilities." The ADA went on to say that "companies have an ongoing responsibility to remove barriers to access for peoples with disabilities."**

Additional information showing the percentage of American businesses that remain out of compliance with the act and demonstrating how that percentage has changed very little over the past decade added statistical support to Karen's call for reform.

Similarly, to support her point that Native Americans are victims of social injustice, Ashley Roberson used an array of statistical evidence:

> **Did you know that Indians have one of the lowest life expectancies of any population living in this hemisphere, second only to those living in Haiti? And did you know that the suicide rate among American Indians is seventy percent higher than that of the general U.S. population? Or, did you know that in 1999, Indians suffered 124 violent crimes for every 100,000 people—two and a half times the national average?**

The effective use of facts and statistics helps convince listeners that you know what you are talking about and that you didn't invent something. To find such supporting materials, you will have to invest an afternoon in the library or make careful use of Internet search engines.

As you do this investigation, be sure to record the *who, where*, and *when* of the key nuggets of information you discover. In your speech, use this additional information to *document* your claims. For example, Ashley's facts and statistics would have been more effective had she introduced them with the following statement: "According to a Princeton research survey reported in the *Washington Post* of March 15, 2004, Native Americans are our most abused Americans."

Taken as a whole, stories, examples, testimony, and facts and statistics provide the substance that makes us take a speech seriously.

Step 4: Design Your Speech

Your speech should have a **design** or plan that arranges your material in an effective order. Your ideas should fit together in a way that is easy for your listeners to follow and understand. Your design should also help you achieve your purpose. Three kinds of designs often used in first speeches are categorical, cause-effect, and narrative.

Categorical Design. The **categorical design** is a logical pattern that develops a subject according to the natural or customary divisions—or categories—within it. Martha Larson introduced herself by explaining how she was shaped by the neigh-

Speaker's Notes 3.1

How to Develop Your First Speech

1. Tell stories that carry your message.
2. Give examples that clarify your points.
3. Cite experts or highly respected people who support your point of view.
4. Present facts and statistics that make your ideas credible.

borhood where she grew up. She began with the *setting*, a description of a street scene in which she captured sights, sounds, and smells: "I can always tell a Swedish neighborhood by the smell of *lutefisk* on Friday afternoons." Next she described the *people*, focusing on a certain neighbor who influenced her. This man, the local grocer, "loved America with a passion, helped those in need, and always voted stubbornly for the Socialist Party." Finally, she talked about the *street games* she played as a child and what these taught her about people and herself. These "setting-people-games" categories structured her speech in an orderly manner.

Martha's speech also suggests how the introduction, body, and conclusion of a speech should be closely related. Her introduction, in which she aroused interest and set the mood for what would follow, was the opening street scene. In the body of her speech, in which she demonstrated her points and answered the questions raised in her opening, Martha described the people of her neighborhood, using the grocer as an example. She also described the childhood games that reinforced the lessons of sharing. Her conclusion clarified the point of her speech:

> **I hope you have enjoyed this "tour" of my neighborhood, this "tour" of my past. If you drove down this street tomorrow, you might think it was just another crowded, gray, urban neighborhood. But for me it is filled with memories of colorful people who cared for each other and who dreamed great dreams of a better tomorrow. That street runs right down the center of my life.**

Cause-Effect Design. Should you decide to tell about a condition that had a great impact on you, a **cause-effect design** might be most appropriate. Since this design follows the natural pattern of cause and effect, it also is a logical design. It helps you explain a situation, and it can be quite useful as you introduce yourself or others. Maria One Feather, a Native American student speaker, used such a design in her speech "Growing Up Red—and Feeling Blue—in White America." She treated the condition of her background as the cause and its impact on her life as the effect.

Narrative Design. The **narrative design** structures your speech by developing a story from beginning to end. In contrast to a logical design, such as cause-effect, a narrative design is, by its nature, dramatic. It focuses not so much on a sequence of points as on a sequence of events or scenes in which characters interact. Introduction, body, and conclusion all become part of the narrative structure. Consider Beth Tidmore's dramatic story of her rise as a competitive shooter. The speech develops not so much by making points as by describing selected scenes in a kind of mini-drama: beginning with the story of her mother's commitment to her, then her personal, relentless pursuit of excellence, which was followed by a sketch of her success in rifle competitions, and, finally, her tribute to her mother's faith. The message emerges with the developing story, as Beth celebrates the virtues of commitment, dedication, discipline, achievement, and family love.

The various designs available to develop your speeches are discussed in more detail in Chapters 9, 14, 16, and 17.

Speaker's Notes 3.2

Ways to Structure Your First Speech

1. Use a categorical design that divides a subject into areas of interest.
2. Use a cause-effect design that pictures a subject either as the cause of an effect or as the effect of a cause.
3. Use a narrative design that moves from scene to scene in telling a story.
4. Be sure that you have an effective introduction, body, and conclusion.

More on Introductions, Bodies, and Conclusions. In addition to arousing interest and preparing listeners for the rest of the speech, your introduction should also build a good relationship between you and your audience. That, of course, fits in with the general idea of making a good impression in the first speech. The best introductions are framed *after* the body of the speech has been planned—after all, it is difficult to draw a map if you don't yet know where you are going.

The body of the speech is where you satisfy the curiosity aroused in your introduction. The body includes what are called the main points, the most important ideas in your message. In a cause-effect design, the body will consist of two main points: the explanation of a cause of some condition, and the elaboration of its effect. In a categorical design, the body will develop two or three major divisions of the subject: you won't have time to do more than that, and your listeners would probably get lost if you tried. In our earlier example of a Swedish neighborhood, the division into setting, people, and games establishes the main points of the speech. In a narrative design, the body develops the major scenes necessary to establish the story.

The conclusion often summarizes your main points and ends with reflections on the meaning of the speech. Good conclusions are easily remembered—even eloquent. Sometimes they quote well-known people who state the point very well. They may tie back to the introduction, completing a symbolic circle in a way that the audience finds satisfying. You will find more on developing introductions, bodies, and conclusions in Chapter 9.

Transitions. As you design your speech, you should also be planning transitions. **Transitions** help you move from one point to another. Transitions are bridging devices such as "having shown you the cause, I will now show you the effect," or "let's now consider another part of this problem," or "after I warned him, let me tell you what happened." Transitions also remind listeners of the point you have just made, and preview what is going to happen next in the speech. Oral connectives like "first," "second," and "finally" can also work as transitions. Marie D'Aniello's first speech, "Family Gifts," which appears at the end of this chapter, illustrates the skillful and subtle use of transitions.

Step 5: Outline Your Speech

Preparing an outline allows you to put your design down on paper so that you can see more clearly whether it will work. The outline should contain your introduction, the message you want to get across, your main ideas and their subpoints, and your conclusion.

Full outlines help you during speech preparation, but you should not use them during presentation. At that time, the outline should be imprinted not on paper but—for the most part—in your mind. We will say more about outlining in Chapter 10.

In the following outline for a self-introductory speech, several critical parts—the introduction, message, and conclusion—are written out word for word. They set forth the meaning of your presentation and make your entrance into and exit from the speech smooth and graceful. Thus, it is important to plan them carefully, even though you may make changes while speaking to adjust to the immediate situation. To encourage spontaneity, the body of the speech is not written out.

"Free at Last"
by Rod Nishikawa

Introduction

Attention-Arousing and Orienting Material: Three years ago I presented the valedictory speech at my high school graduation. As I concluded, I borrowed a line from Dr. Martin Luther King's "I Have a Dream" speech:

"Free at last, free at last, thank God almighty we're free at last!" The words had a joyful, humorous place in that speech, but for me personally, they were a lie.

Message: I was not yet free, and would not be free until I had conquered an ancient enemy, both outside me and within me—that enemy was racial prejudice.

Body

I. When I was eight years old I was exposed to anti-Japanese prejudice.
   A. I was a "Jap" who didn't belong in America.
   B. The bully's words burned into my soul.
      1. I was ashamed of my heritage.
      2. I hated having to live in this country.

[Transition: So I obviously needed some help.]

II. My parents helped me put this in perspective.
   A. They survived terrible prejudice in their youth during World War II.
   B. They taught me to accept the reality of prejudice.
   C. They taught me the meaning of *gaman:* how to bear the burden within and not show anger.

[Transition: Now, how has *gaman* helped me?]

III. Practicing *gaman* has helped me develop inner strength.
   A. I rarely experience fear or anger.
   B. I have learned to accept myself.
   C. I have learned to be proud of my heritage.

Conclusion

Summary Statement: Practicing *gaman,* a gift from my Japanese roots, has helped me conquer prejudice.

Concluding Remarks: Although my Japanese ancestors might not have spoken as boldly as I have today, I am basically an American, which makes me a little outspoken. Therefore, I can talk to you about racial prejudice and of what it has meant to my life. And because I can talk about it, and share it with you, I am finally, truly, "free at last."

Rod's three main points are each supported with facts, examples, or narratives. The outline uses Roman numerals to indicate main points, capital letters to indicate subpoints, and Arabic numbers to indicate sub-subpoints. These numerals and letters are indented appropriately to show their relative importance in the structure of the speech.

Step 6: Practice Your Presentation

You are almost there. After you have developed and outlined your first speech, you are ready to practice your presentation. *An effective presentation spotlights the ideas, not the speaker, and is offered as though you were talking with the audience, not reading to them or reciting from memory.*

Spotlight the Ideas. The presentation of a speech is the climax of planning and preparation–the time you have earned to stand in the spotlight. Though presentation is important, it should never overshadow the substance of the speech. Have you ever had this kind of exchange?

"She's a wonderful speaker—what a beautiful voice, what eloquent diction, what a smooth delivery!"

"What did she say?"

"I don't remember, but she sure sounded good!"

As you practice speaking from your outline and when you present your speech, concentrate on the ideas you have to offer. *You should have a vivid realization of these ideas during the moments of actual presentation.*[2] Your thoughts should come alive as you speak.

Speak Naturally. An effective presentation, we noted in Chapter 1, preserves many of the best qualities of conversation. It sounds natural and spontaneous yet has a depth, coherence, and quality not normally found in social conversation. The best way to approach this ideal of improved conversation is to present your speech extemporaneously. An **extemporaneous presentation** is carefully prepared and practiced but not written out or memorized. If you write out your speech, you will be tempted either to memorize it or read it to your audience. Reading or memorizing almost always results in a stilted presentation. DO NOT READ YOUR SPEECH! Always keep in mind that *audience contact is more important than exact wording.* The only parts of a speech that might be memorized are the introduction, message, conclusion, and a few other critical phrases or sentences, such as the wording of main points or the punch lines of humorous stories.

Prepare a Key-Word Outline. If you feel the need for a reminder during presentation, use a **key-word outline**, a shorter version of your full-sentence outline that you should also use as you practice. Relying on the key-word outline will help you sound more conversational and spontaneous. *Never use your full outline as you present your speech.* You will lapse into reading if you do.

As its name suggests, the key-word outline contains only words that will prompt your memory. It can also contain presentation cues, such as *pause here* or *talk slowly.* Although the full outline may require a page or more to complete, the key-word outline should fit on a single sheet of paper or one or two index cards. To prepare it, go through your full-sentence outline and highlight the key words in each section. Transfer these to a sheet of paper or index cards to use as prompts as you speak. The following key-word outline is based on the outline presented earlier.

Note that Rod's key-word outline reminds him not only of the flow of ideas, but also of his presentation plan. It is the "game plan" of his speech.

"Free at Last"

Introduction

"Free at last"—high school valedictory speech

Not free—enemy outside and within was racial prejudice

Body

I. Encounter with bully
- A. "Jap," didn't belong [Mime bully]
- B. Words burned in soul
  - l. Ashamed of heritage
  - 2. Hated living in America [Pause, smile]

II. Parents help
- A. Survived much worse
- B. Taught me to accept reality
- C. Taught me *GAMAN* [Pause and write word on board]

III. *Gaman*—inner strength
- A. No fear or anger [Stress]
- B. Accepted self
- C. Proud of heritage [Pause]

Conclusion

Gaman from my Japanese roots helps conquer prejudice

Also an American. Can talk about it: therefore, "free at last"

Rehearse Your Speech. Speech classrooms often have a speaker's lectern mounted on a table at the front of the room. Lecterns can seem very formal and can create a barrier between you and listeners. Also, short people can almost disappear behind a lectern. If their gestures are hidden from view, their messages may lose much of the power of body language. For these reasons, you may wish to speak either to the side or in front of the lectern.

If you plan to use the lectern, place your key-word outline high on its slanted surface so that you can see your notes easily without having to lower your head. This will help you maintain eye contact with your listeners. Print your key-word outline in large letters. If you decide to hold your outline and note cards, don't try to hide them or look embarrassed if you need to refer to them. Most listeners probably won't even notice when you use them. Remember, your audience is far more interested in what you are saying than in any awkwardness you may feel.

Imagine your audience in front of you as you practice. Start with your full outline; then move to your key-word outline as the ideas become imprinted in your mind. Maintain eye contact with your imaginary listeners, just as you will during the actual presentation. Look around the room so that everyone feels included in your message. Be enthusiastic! Let your voice suggest confidence. Avoid speaking in a monotone, which never changes pace or pitch; instead, strive for variety and color in your vocal presentation. Pause to let important ideas sink in. Let your face, body, and voice respond to your ideas as you utter them.

Test your speech preparation on the **Online Speech Studio's Checklist for Speech Preparation** under **Organizing Your Speech.** **Go to http://college.hmco.com/eduspace/**

Step 7: Step Up and Do It!

It's your moment to speak. You've earned it. Now enjoy it with your listeners.

Managing the Impressions You Make

As you step to the lectern to speak, your listeners will begin to form impressions of you that will influence how they respond to your message. The ancient writers on rhetoric believed that these personal impressions could even determine the fate of a speech. Aristotle called these impressions **ethos**. A person with high ethos will be listened to with respect; therefore, ethos also is a key ingredient in leadership. If you are to be successful in later speeches and in later life, you must begin to build high ethos. You can do this by helping listeners form favorable impressions of your competence, integrity, goodwill, and dynamism. In this section we explore each of these components, including ways you can encourage these impressions.

Competence

Competent speakers seem informed, intelligent, and well prepared. You can build a perception of **competence** by selecting topics that you already know something about and by doing the research necessary to qualify yourself as a responsible speaker. You can further enhance your competence by quoting experts and citing authoritative sources who support your position. For example, if you are speaking on the link

Figure 3.2

The Components of Ethos

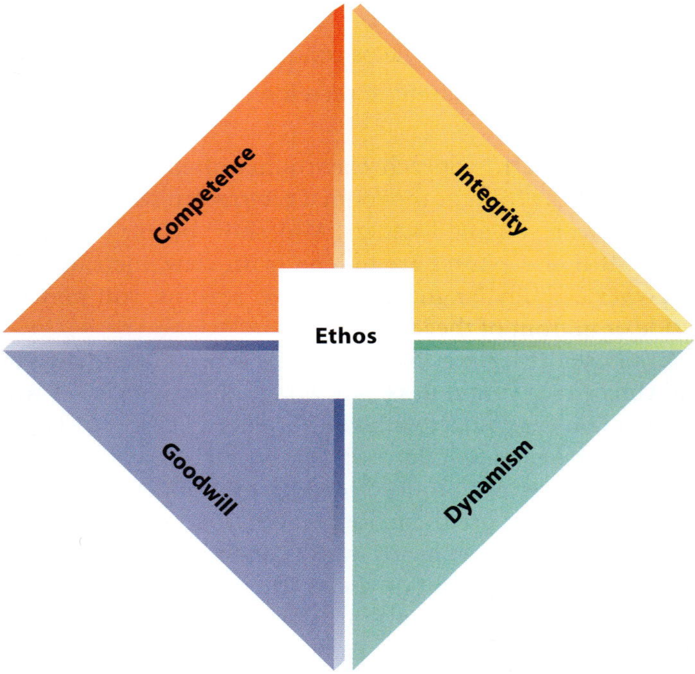

between nutrition and heart disease, you might quote a prominent medical specialist or a publication of the American Heart Association: "Dr. Milas Peterson heads the Heart Institute at Harvard University. During his visit to our campus last week, I spoke with him about this point. He told me . . ." Note the competence-related elements:

- The speaker cites the qualifications of the expert, noting his connection to a prestigious institution.
- The quotation contains recent information.
- The connection between the expert and the speaker is direct and personal, suggesting a favorable association.
- The speaker shows that he or she has prepared carefully for the speech by interviewing a visiting expert.

When you cite authoritative sources in this way, you are "borrowing" their ethos to enhance your own. Remember though that borrowed ethos enhances but does not replace your own. Personal experience related as stories or examples can also help a speech seem authentic, bring it to life, and make you appear more competent. "Been there, done that" can be a very effective technique. Your competence will be further enhanced if your speech is well organized, if you use language ably and correctly, and if you make a polished presentation.

Integrity

A speaker with **integrity** seems ethical, honest, and dependable. Listeners are more receptive when speakers are straightforward and concerned about the consequences of their words. You can enhance your integrity by presenting all sides of an issue and then explaining why you have chosen your position. You should also demonstrate that you are willing to follow your own advice. In a speech that calls for commitment or action, for example, it should be clear to your listeners that you are not asking more of them than you would of yourself. The more you ask of the audience, the more important your integrity becomes.

How can you develop impressions of integrity? One of our students, Mona Goldberg, met this challenge in a number of ways. Mona was preparing a speech on welfare reform. The more she learned about the subject, the more convinced she became that budget cuts for welfare programs were unwise. In her speech, Mona showed that she took her assignment seriously by citing many authorities and statistics. She reviewed arguments both for and against cutting the budget and then showed her audience why she was against reducing aid to such programs. Finally, Mona revealed that her own family had had to live on unemployment benefits at one time. "I know the hurt, the loss of pride, the sense of growing frustration. I didn't have to see them on the evening news." Her openness showed that she was willing to trust her listeners to react fairly to this sensitive information. The audience responded in kind by trusting her and what she had to say. She had built an impression of herself as a person of integrity.

Goodwill

People of **goodwill** seem to have our interests at heart. They are not self-centered; rather, they think and act in terms of what is good for the group or community to which they belong. We like such people and enjoy their company, perhaps because we feel that they like and enjoy us.

Audiences are more willing to accept ideas and suggestions from speakers who radiate goodwill.[3] A smile and direct eye contact can signal listeners that you want to communicate. Sharing your feelings as well as your thoughts conveys the same message. Speakers with goodwill also enjoy laughter at appropriate moments, especially laughter directed at themselves. Being able to talk openly and engagingly about your mistakes can make you seem more human and appealing as well as more confident.

The more speakers seem to be people of good will, the more audiences want to identify with them.[4] **Identification** is the feeling of sharing or closeness that can develop between speakers and listeners. It typically occurs when you believe someone is like you—that you have the same outlook on life or that you share similar backgrounds or values. Identification is more difficult to establish when the speaker and listener have different cultural backgrounds. In such situations, speakers can invite identification by telling stories or by using examples that help listeners focus on the experiences or beliefs that they share. Even though she was speaking before a class that included students from all sections of the United States, Marie D'Aniello encouraged identification in her self-introductory speech by developing a theme everyone could share family pride. At one moment in her speech, Marie pointed out how she had drawn inspiration from her brother's athletic accomplishments:

The character and personality of a speaker can influence how well a message is received. Likeableness is an important component of speaker ethos.

The Ethics of Ethos

Ethics Alert! 3.1

1. Do the research necessary to become a responsible speaker.
2. Be sensitive to the impact of your words on others.
3. Present all sides of an issue fairly before explaining your position.
4. Be honest about where you stand on your topic.
5. Acknowledge any possible differences between your own beliefs, values, and attitudes and those that some of your listeners may entertain.
6. Show how these differences might be bridged.
7. Demonstrate that you are willing to follow your own advice.
8. Trust your listeners if you would have them trust you.

When I think of glory, I have to think of my brother Chris. I'll never forget his championship basketball game. It's the typical buzzer beater story: five seconds to go, down by one, Chris gets the ball and he drives down the court, he shoots, he scores! . . . I'll never forget the headline, "D'Aniello saves the game!" D'Aniello, hey wait, that's me. I'm a D'Aniello. I could do this too. Maybe I can't play basketball like Chris, but I can do other things.

After this speech, which appears at the end of this chapter, it was hard not to like Marie. This aura of goodwill, combined with other favorable impressions of her competence, integrity, and confidence, created respect for her point of view.

Goodwill can also be enhanced by appropriate touches of light humor. For example, Marcos White, a point guard for the University of New Mexico basketball team, endeared himself to listeners during his first speech. Marcos introduced himself as the son of an African American father and a Mexican mother: "I guess," he said, "that makes me a blaxican."

You should dress nicely when you present your speech as a sign of respect for your listeners and your assignment.

Audiences often identify with speakers who talk or dress the way they do. They prefer speakers who use gestures, language, and facial expressions that are natural and unaffected. However, you should speak a little more formally than you do in everyday conversation out of respect for the communication situation and the audience. Similarly, you should dress nicely for your speech, but not extravagantly. You want to honor and respect your listeners, but not to create distance between yourself and them by language or dress that seems either too formal or too casual.

Dynamism

James Norton, who introduced his classmate, Rosamond Wolford, as an accomplished violinist, later confessed that he was nervous before he gave his speech. He was not sure how it would be received, and he worried that he might make a mistake. But when James walked in front of the room to speak, he seemed confident, decisive, and enthusiastic. In short, he conveyed the qualities of **dynamism**. Whatever he might have secretly felt, his audience responded only to what they saw and gave him high marks for his commanding presence.

At first you may not feel confident about public speaking, but you should act as though you are. If you appear self-assured, listeners will respond as though you are, and you may find yourself becoming what you seem to be. In other words, you can trick yourself into developing a very desirable trait! When you appear to be in control, you also put listeners at ease. This feeling comes back to you as positive feedback and further reinforces your confidence.

One of our students, John Scipio, was at first intimidated by the public speaking situation, but John was blessed with two natural virtues: he was a large, imposing person and he had a powerful voice. And then he found a subject he truly believed in. When John presented his classroom tribute to the final speech of Dr. Martin Luther King Jr., he radiated dynamism, in addition to competence, goodwill, and integrity:

> **When I asked him during a telephone interview why he thought Dr. King was such an effective leader, Ralph Abernathy said, "He possessed a power never before seen in a man of color." What was this power that he spoke of? It was the power to persuade audiences and change opinions with his words. It was the power of speech.**
>
> **In his speech, Dr. King had to give his people hope and motivate them to go on. He spoke to all of us, but especially to those of us in the black community, when he said, "Only when it is dark enough can you see the stars." And when he talked of standing up to the fire hoses in Birmingham, he said, "There's a certain kind of fire that no water can put out."**
>
> **And on the last night of his life, with less than twenty-four hours to live, he was still thinking—not of himself, but of our nation: "Let us move on," he said, "in these powerful days, these days of challenge, to make America what it ought to be."**

To appear dynamic, you must also be decisive. In persuasive speeches, you should cover the important options available to your audience, but by the end of the speech there should be no doubt where you stand and why. Your commitment to your position must be strong.

Finally, you gain dynamism from the enthusiasm you bring to your speech. Your face, voice, and gestures should indicate that you care about your subject and about the audience. Your enthusiasm endorses your message. We discuss more specific ways of projecting confidence, decisiveness, and enthusiasm in Chapter 13.

Introducing Yourself or a Classmate: An Application

Instructors of public speaking assign a variety of first speech presentations. Among the most frequently used are those that ask you to introduce yourself or a

InterConnections.LearnMore 3.1

Ethos

Ethos (Ethical Proofs)
http://www.lcc.gatech.edu/gallery/rhetoric/terms/ethos.html
Highly readable discussion of ethos as one of the three major sources of persuasion, prepared by Yasmin Hussain of the Georgia Institute of Technology.

Credibility: Perceptions of Competence, Character, and Good Will
http://www.abacon.com/pubspeak/analyze/notecred.html#top
Excellent discussion of the three major classical components of ethos.

Online Lesson: Ethos (Credibility)
http://jan.ucc.nau.edu/;sc315-c/class/sales/ethos/lesson3-1-2.html
Interactive lecture on ethos in sales persuasion prepared by Kurt Billmeyer of Northern Arizona University.

Establishing Ethos Online
http://lor.trincoll.edu/;writcent/warriner.html
An interesting article, "Email Debate and the Importance of Ethos," on developing ethos in online interactions, prepared by Professor Allison Warriner, Department of English, California State University, Hayward, as part of the Electronic Democracy Project.

classmate. The speech of introduction can help warm the atmosphere in the classroom, create a sense of community, and provide an opportunity for the speaker to develop initial ethos. The speech also has practical applications beyond the classroom. In later life, you may be called on to introduce yourself or an organization to which you belong. Typically this will be part of a longer speech. When she spoke to the Republican National Convention in 2000, Condoleezza Rice introduced herself as a future leader in the Bush administration as she praised the party's candidates. When the commandant of the Coast Guard spoke before the National Press Club, he introduced that branch of the military in order "to raise the visibility of . . . current and future Coast Guard service to America."[5]

A classroom speech of introduction is usually quite short. Since there is no way to tell an entire life story in a short speech, you have to be selective. What you should avoid is simply giving the audience a few superficial facts, such as where you went to high school or what your major is. Such information reveals very little about a person and is usually not very interesting.

One way to introduce yourself or others is to answer this question: *What is the one thing that best describes me or the person I am introducing as a unique person?* You should then develop a speech around the answer that will build positive ethos for later speeches.

To help stimulate your creativity, what the ancient writers on public speaking called your "inventional processes," conduct a **self-awareness inventory** in which you consider the following possibilities:

VideoLab

View a sample speech at **VideoLab Lesson 1's Screening Room: The Speech of Self-Introduction.** After watching the speech, complete accompanying **Drill 1.1.**

1. *Is your cultural background the most important thing about you?* How has it shaped you? How might you explain this influence to others? In her self-introductory speech, reprinted in Appendix B, Sandra Baltz described herself as a unique product of three cultures. She felt that this rich cultural background had widened her horizons. Note how she focused on food to represent the convergence of these different ways of life:

   In all, I must say that being exposed to three very different cultures—Latin, Arabic, American—has been rewarding for me and has made a difference even in the music I enjoy and the food I eat. It is not unusual in my house to sit down to a meal made up of stuffed grape leaves and refried beans and all topped off with apple pie for dessert.

2. *Is the most important thing about you the environment in which you grew up?* How were you shaped by it? What stories or examples demonstrate this influence? How do you feel about its effect on your life? Are you pleased by it, or do you feel that it limited you? If the latter, what new horizons would you like to explore? In his self-introductory speech, "My Life as a River Rat," Jimmy Green concluded by saying:

   To share my world, come up to the Tennessee River some fall afternoon. We'll take a boat ride north to New Johnsonville, where Civil War gunboats still lie

on the bottom of the river, and you will see how the sun makes the water sparkle. You will see the green hills sloping down to the river, and the rocky walls, and I will tell you some Indian legends about them. We'll "bump the bottom" fishing for catfish, just drifting with the current. And if we're lucky, we might see a doe and her fawn along the shoreline, or perhaps some great blue herons or an eagle high overhead.

Jimmy's descriptions of nature conveyed his feelings about his home without his having to tell us about them.

3. *Was there some particular person—a friend, relative, or childhood hero—who had a major impact on your life?* Why do you think this person had such influence? Often you will find that some particular person was a great inspiration to you. Here is a chance to share that inspiration, honor that person, and in the process, tell us much about you. In her speech to the Republican Convention, Condoleezza Rice spoke of her grandfather's influence on her:

Granddaddy Rice . . . was the son of a farmer in rural Alabama, but he recognized the importance of education. Around 1918, he decided he was going to get book-learning. And so he asked, in the language of the day, where a colored man could go to college. He was told about little Stillman College, a school about 50 miles away. So granddaddy saved up his cotton for tuition and he went off to Tuscaloosa.

After the first year, he ran out of cotton and he needed a way to pay for college. Praise be, as He often does, God gave him an answer. My grandfather asked how those other boys were staying in school, and he was told that they had what was called a scholarship. And, they said, if you wanted to be a Presbyterian minister, then you can have one, too. Granddaddy Rice said, "That's just what I had in mind." And my family has been Presbyterian and college-educated ever since.[6]

4. *Have you been marked by some unusual experience?* What was it? Why was it important? How did it affect you? What does this tell us about you as a person? Ashley Smith decided to speak on what she had learned from her experiences as an exchange student in Costa Rica and Botswana. After she told stories to illustrate how peoples' lives were controlled and limited in those countries, Ashley confided—in a speech that is reprinted at the end of this chapter—that her travel experiences had made her want to return as an educator:

I want to teach people to succeed on their merits despite the social and economic inequalities that they're faced with. And I want to learn from them as well. I want to teach the boy who never mastered welding that he could own the factory. And I want him to teach me how to use a rice cooker. I want to teach the girl who is exhausted each afternoon after walking to the river with a jar on her head to gather water that she could design an irrigation system. But I also want her to teach me how to weave a thatched roof. I want to travel and teach and learn.

5. *Are you best characterized by an activity that brings meaning to your life?* Remember, what is important is not the activity itself but how and why it affects you. The person being introduced must remain the focus of the speech. When you finish, the audience should have an interesting picture of you. As she reflected on her identity, Julie Cunningham decided that the most meaningful thing in her life was her participation in a weekly off-campus ritual:

Every Sunday morning before sunrise I arrive out at Shelby Forest State Park with a few friends of mine. My responsibilities are to gather wood and sweep the area for our sweat lodge. The sweat lodge is a Native American ceremony of spirituality and purification, and the lodge itself represents the womb of mother earth. You crawl in for the sweat ceremony, and when you crawl out you are reborn to this world.

Go to the **SpeechStudio** to fill out the **Self-Awareness Worksheet** under **Selecting a Topic.**

Go to http://college.hmco.com/eduspace/

6. *Is the work you do a major factor in making you who you are?* If you select this approach, focus on how your job has shaped you rather than simply describing what you do. What have you learned from your work that has changed you or made you feel differently about others? In introducing Mike Peterson, Carol Solomon told how his work as a bartender had influenced him. She explained that his job involved more than just mixing drinks—that it had made him an observer of people.

   He sees them when they are happy, when they are celebrating a promotion or a grandson or an anniversary. He sees sad lonely people, trying to make a connection, and he sees the other people, the predators, who try to take advantage of them. He hears a lot of good stories, and thinks maybe he'll be a writer so he can tell some of them. If we're lucky, Mike might even tell us about the land shark who got hooked by the hooker.

   After her speech the audience saw both Mike and his work in a new light. Carol's introduction also communicated a favorable impression of her as well.

7. *Are you best characterized by your goals or purpose in life?* Listeners are usually fascinated by those whose lives are dedicated to some purpose. If you choose to describe some personal goal, be sure to emphasize why you have it and how it affects you. Tom McDonald had returned to school after dropping out for eleven years. In his self-introductory speech he described his goal:

   Finishing college means a lot to me now. The first time I enrolled, right out of high school, I "blew it." All I cared about was sports, girls, and partying. Even though I have a responsible job that pays well, I feel bad about not having a degree. My wife's diploma hangs on our den wall. All I have hanging there is a stuffed duck!

   As he spoke, many of the younger students began to identify with Tom; they saw a similarity between what caused him to drop out of school and their own feelings at times. Although he wasn't "preachy," Tom's description of the rigors of working forty hours a week and carrying nine hours a semester in night school carried its own clear message.

8. *Are you best described by some value that you hold dear?* How did it come to have such meaning for you? Why is it important to you? Values are abstract, so you must rely on concrete applications to make them meaningful to others. As she described her commitment to the value of justice, Valessa Johnson also established her goal, to become an attorney, and paid tribute to her personal role model:

   If you go down to 201 Poplar at nine o'clock in the morning on any weekday, you will find yourself faced with hundreds of individuals and their quest for justice. Many of these will be convicted, and rightly so. Unfortunately, while

Speaker's Notes 3.3

Self-Awareness Inventory

1. Was your *cultural background* important in shaping you?
2. Was your *environment* a major influence?
3. Did some *person* have an impact on you?
4. Were you shaped by an unusual *experience*?
5. Is there an *activity* that motivates you?
6. Has your *work* had a major impact on who you are?
7. Does some special *goal* or *purpose* guide the way you live?
8. Does a *value* have great meaning for you?

they're incarcerated, the illiterate and unlearned will remain so, as will the unskilled and the uncrafted. Who's going to stand for these so that they have an alternative to standing in the revolving doors of the criminal justice complex? Or better yet, how about the ones that are truly innocent? Oh yes, that's right, not everyone in the court system, not everyone institutionalized, is guilty. Who is going to stand for these? I will.

You know, we were once blessed with a true advocate for justice, attorney Barbara Jordan. She fought a long, hard battle to ensure that we all abided by the constitutional creed "All men are created equal" and "justice for all." Someone has to continue to beat the path of justice for all men. That includes black men, white men, yellow men, brown men, and women. Someone has got to continue to fight the good fight. And I submit to you that I am that someone.

When Valessa concluded, no one questioned the sincerity of her commitment to justice and to her chosen career.

As you explore your own background or that of a classmate, we suggest that you ask all the probe questions within the self-awareness inventory. Don't be satisfied with the first idea that comes to you. You should find this thorough examination of yourself and others to be quite rewarding. Just remember: You are not on a tabloid talk show. You don't want to embarrass listeners with personal disclosures they would just as soon not hear. If you are uncertain about whether to include personal material, you should discuss it with your instructor. The general rule to follow is, *When in doubt, leave it out!*

To critique a self-introductory speech, go to the **SpeechStudio** and fill out the **Evaluation Form for a Self-Introductory Speech.**
Go to http://college.hmco.com/eduspace/

In Summary

Many of us underrate our public speaking potential. As you prepare your first speech, you can develop basic skills in selecting and polishing speech topics, structuring and outlining your speech, and practicing for presentation. You can communicate favorable impressions of yourself, useful for later speeches. You can contribute to the transformation of the class into a learning community favorable for the cultivation of communication skills.

Preparing Your First Speech. Effective preparation requires that you take a number of steps toward speech success. First, select a topic that is appropriate to you, your listeners, the assignment, and the time limits assigned for your speech. Second, narrow and focus your topic until you have a clear idea of your message and of what you want to accomplish. Third, seek *narratives, examples, testimony,* and *facts and statistics* that will make your points interesting and credible. Fourth, design your speech so that your ideas fit together in a cohesive pattern. Often used patterns for the first speech are the *categorical design*, the *cause-effect design*, and the *narrative design*. Develop an introduction, body, and conclusion so that your speech forms a satisfying whole. Provide *transitions* between the various parts of your speech. Fifth, outline your speech so that you can check on the soundness of your design. The outline should reveal the overall structure of your ideas and should include transitions to help you move from one point to another. Sixth, practice your presentation. Develop an *extemporaneous presentation* that avoids the faults of reading and memorization. Keep the spotlight on your ideas, and strive for a conversational presentation. As you practice the speech, use a *key-word outline* to jog your memory.

Managing the Impressions You Make. Listeners acquire positive impressions of you based on your ability to convey competence, integrity, goodwill, and dynamism. These qualities make up the ancient concept of *ethos*. You can build your perceived *competence* by citing examples from your own experience, by quoting authorities, and by organizing and presenting your message effectively. You can earn an image of *integrity* by being accurate and complete in your presentation of information. You can promote *good will* by being a warm and likeable person who invites *identification* with listeners. *Dynamism* arises from listeners' perceptions of you as a confident, enthusiastic, and decisive speaker.

Introducing Yourself or a Classmate. A speech of introduction helps establish you or the person you introduce as a unique person. Prompted by your *self-awareness inventory*, it may focus on cultural background, environmental influences, a person who inspired you, an experience that affected you, an activity that reveals your character, the work you do, your purpose in life, or some value you cherish.

Terms to Know

narrative
dialogue
analogy
examples
testimony
facts and statistics
design
categorical design
cause-effect design
narrative design
transitions
extemporaneous presentation
key-word outline
ethos
competence
integrity
goodwill
identification
dynamism
self-awareness inventory

Discussion

1. Although we have defined ethos in terms of public speakers, other communicators also seek to create favorable impressions of competence, integrity, good will, and dynamism. Advertisers always try to create favorable ethos for their products. Bring to class print advertisements to demonstrate each of the four dimensions of ethos we have discussed. Explain how each ad uses ethos.
2. Select a prominent public speaker and analyze his or her ethos. On which dimensions is this speaker especially strong or weak? How does this affect the person's leadership ability? Present your analysis for class discussion.
3. Political ads often do the work of introducing candidates to the public and disparaging their opponents. Study the television or print ads in connection with a recent political campaign. Bring to class answers to the following questions:
   a. What kinds of positive and negative identities do the ads establish?
   b. Which of the forms of supporting material (narratives, examples, testimony, facts and statistics) do they emphasize?
   c. Which of these ads are most and least effective in creating the desired ethos? Why?
   d. Which of the self-awareness inventory questions discussed in this chapter might explain how the candidates are introduced?

Application

1. As the introductory speeches are presented in your class, build a collection of "word portraits" of your classmates as they reveal themselves in their speeches. At the end of the assignment, analyze each of these "autobios" to see what you have learned about the class as a whole. What kinds of topics might your classmates prefer? Do you detect any strong political or social attitudes to which you might have to adjust? Submit a report of your analysis to your instructor, and keep a copy for your own use in preparing later speeches.
2. Prepare an outline of your first speech. On an attached page identify the kind of design you are using (categorical, cause-effect, narrative, etc.), and discuss why this design is most appropriate to structure your speech. Turn this outline and rationale in to your instructor.
3. Summarize your own adventure of preparing for your first speech. Which of the steps identified in this chapter were most difficult for you? Why? What have you learned about speech preparation that might be useful for your next speech? Submit your report and analysis to your instructor.

Notes

1. John A. Daly, Anita L. Vangelisti, and David J. Weber, "Speech Anxiety Affects How People Prepare Speeches: A Protocol Analysis of the Preparation Processes of Speakers," *Communication Monographs* 62 (1995): 383–397.
2. Donald C. Bryant and Karl R. Wallace, *Fundamentals of Public Speaking*, 4th ed. (New York: Appleton-Century-Crofts, 1969), p. 233.
3. James C. McCroskey and Mason J. Teven, "Goodwill: A Reexamination of the Construct and Its Measurement," *Communication Monographs* 66 (1999): 90–103.
4. Kenneth Burke, *A Rhetoric of Motives* (Berkeley and Los Angeles: University of California Press, 1969), pp. 20–23.
5. James M. Loy, "Proud of What We Do for America," speech to the National Press Club, Washington, D.C., 24 Feb. 2000, *Vital Speeches of the Day,* 15 June 2000, pp. 517–520.
6. Condoleezza Rice, "American Dream for All of Us," address to the Republican National Convention, Philadelphia, 1 Aug. 2000, *Vital Speeches of the Day,* 15 Aug. 2000, pp. 653–655.

Three Photographs
Ashley Smith

■ *The three photographs are an ingenious way to structure this speech. Each photograph stands for a main point. Ashley's use of Spanish and her colorful language reinforce her competence. The contrast between the types of education in Costa Rica is dramatic and her on-the-scene report of life there makes her account both authentic and authoritative. In effect she provides her own expert testimony that is adequate for this brief speech. In an informative or persuasive speech, more supporting material would be needed.*

■ *Ashley uses examples as her major form of supporting material. Again stronger support would be needed for informative or persuasive speeches to support her assertion of European exploitation.*

■ *The scene she depicts of life in Jacksonville provides a vivid contrast with the other lifestyles she has sketched.*

■ *Here Ashley draws out the meaning of the three photographs for her life. The goal she describes confirms her integrity as well as her competence. Her conclusion ties in skillfully with her introduction, completing the circle of the speech.*

Photographs often tell stories that only a few can hear. I would like to tell you the story told me by three snapshots that hang in my room in quiet, suburban Jacksonville, Florida. If you saw them, you might think them totally unrelated; together, they tell a powerful tale.

"Ashley, *levantete*!" I heard each morning for the month that I spent in Costa Rica as an exchange student. I would wake up at 5:30 to get ready for school and would stumble off to the one shower that the family of five shared. I had to wash myself in cold water because there was no warm water—that usually woke me up pretty fast! I then got dressed and breakfast would be waiting on the table. Predictably it would be fruit, coffee, and *gallo pinto*, a black bean and rice dish usually served at every meal. We would then walk to school and begin the day with an hour and a half of shop class. After shop we would have about 15- to 20-minute classes in what you and I might call "regular" academic subjects: math and Spanish, for example. Those classes had frequent interruptions and were not taken very seriously. The socialization process was quite clear: These children were being prepared for jobs in the labor force instead of for higher education. Each afternoon as we walked home we passed the elite school where students were still busy working and studying. The picture in my room of my Costa Rican classmates painting picnic tables in the schoolyard reminds me of their narrow opportunities.

The second photograph on my wall is of a little girl in Botswana who is not much younger than I. She's nearing the end of her education and has finished up to the equivalent of the sixth grade. She will now return to a rural setting because her family cannot afford to continue her schooling. To add to the problem, the family goat was eaten by a lion, so she had to return to help them over this crisis. But she didn't miss out on much—most likely, she would have gone on into the city and ended up in one of the shantytowns, one more victim of the unemployment, poverty, even starvation endured by the people. Her lack of opportunity is due not so much to class inequalities as in Costa Rica, but more to the cultural tradition of several hundred years of European exploitation. Recently there has been extensive growth there, but the natives have been left far behind.

The third photograph in my room is of four high school students, taken where I went to school in Jacksonville, Florida. We're all sitting on the lawn outside school, overlooking the parking lot full of new cars that will take us home to warm dinners and comfortable beds and large homes and privileged lives. Many of us—including myself for most of my life—took this world for granted. But now, for me, no more. I may have gained a lot on my travels, but I lost my political innocence.

One thing I gained is an intense desire to become an educator. I want to teach people to succeed on their merits despite the social and economic inequalities that they're faced with. And I want to learn from them as well. I want to teach the boy who never mastered welding that he could own the factory. And I want him to teach me how to use a rice cooker. I want to teach the girl who is exhausted each afternoon after walking to the river with a jar on her head to gather water that she could design an irrigation system. But I also want her to teach me how to weave a thatched roof. I want to travel and teach and learn.

Three photographs, hanging on my wall. They are silent, mute, and the photographer was not very skilled. But together they tell a powerful story in my life.

Family Gifts
Marie D'Aniello

Lorraine, John, John Victor, Christopher, Michael, and Anthony. That's my family. My mom, my dad, and my four brothers—that's my life. Together these people have shaped me as an individual. Growing up in a small town with a large family teaches you a lot, especially if you grow up like I did, with a lot of love, a little money, and a whole lot of gifts. Not tangible gifts like clothes and jewelry (although those are nice, too), but gifts like strength, and glory, and pride, pride not only in myself, but also in them and in my family name. I am Marie D'Aniello . . . a D'Aniello. I belong to them like they belong to me. I'm a little bit like my Mom and a little bit like my Dad. I can work like my brother John and play like Chris. I can dream like Michael and love like Anthony. I'm Marie, exactly like no one but a little bit like everyone.

■ *This speech records one student's appreciation of her family's meaning to her life. Even from the printed transcript, one can sense Marie's command of oral rhythm. Her sentences flow in a pleasing way that reinforces the meaning of her words. The speech is woven around three themes, each connected with a member of her family. This strategy seems casual because like most good art, it conceals itself. As a result, we don't think of Marie's technique, we think of her message.*

Every now and then I hear people say things like, "You know, my family just doesn't understand me." Well, yeah, I feel that way too at times. My family's not perfect. We have our hard times and disagreements. But I always walk away from these spats with a little more knowledge about myself. Maybe I learn that I'm stronger than I thought. That strength comes from my Mom.

It takes a strong woman to work a full-time job, hold together a family, and raise five children. But my mom does it all. I can remember when I was little waking up at night and listening to the sound of the vacuum cleaner. My Mom would stay up all night, cleaning the house and making sure everything was ready for the next day. She never complained about the hard work. She just did it because she loved us.

I never realized the influence my mother had on me until I went away. Now that I'm here, a thousand miles away from her, I sometimes see her smiling and working the night away. And when I get a grade and I don't think it reflects my effort, I can hear my Mom saying, "You're worth more than this, Marie. You'll get it next time." My Mom's strength has given me my own strength and my own perseverance. I know these qualities are the keys to glory.

When I think of glory, I have to think of my brother Chris. I'll never forget his championship basketball game. It's the typical buzzer beater story: five seconds to go, down by one, Chris gets the ball and he drives down the court, he shoots, he scores! We all rush the floor, everyone. But Chris doesn't care about anyone else. All he looks for is us, his family. He wanted to share his glory with us. I'll never forget the headline, "D'Aniello saves the game!" D'Aniello, hey, wait, that's me. I'm a D'Aniello. I could do this too. Maybe I can't play basketball like Chris, but I can do other things.

■ *Marie uses a story to describe her brother's glorious moment. Note how she re-creates the excitement of the situation and how she focuses on his gift of inspiration to her.*

So I started trying harder in school, "applying myself," as they say. And I had my own taste of glory. I became a valedictorian, won a scholarship, and now I'm here at Vanderbilt. Unbelievable. After I watched Chris drive toward the hoop to score the winning basket, I wanted to "drive" toward my future. And you know what? I just might make it!

And even if I don't make it, at least I'll try and I'll have my pride. At least, that's what my Dad always says. He knows about pride. He knows what it's like to be scorned because you don't make as much money as other people or because you don't have an impressive job. My Dad is a small-town mechanic. He couldn't go to school, so he taught himself everything he knows. And he knows a whole lot, not just about cars, but about honor. I hear my Dad all the time, saying, "Marie, whatever you do, just try to put your whole heart into it. Make it count. Take pride in it." Not a day goes by that I don't hear those words. Because of him, I take pride in my work and I take pride in myself.

■ *Marie's praise of her father's pride and sense of honor was presented to an audience of students from mainly affluent families. The story reminded listeners that the most valuable gifts may not be material, and that you can't always measure the worth of a person by wealth or formal education.*

I practiced my speech in front of one of my friends, and she said, "Marie, are you sure you're really talking about yourself?" Yeah, I am. When I talk about my family,

■ ***In her conclusion Marie counters an impression that her identity relies too much on her family. She affirms that because of their influence she can be the individual that she is.***

I'm talking about the main sources of myself. They've given me a world, but it's not like I'm trapped in it. I can go anywhere and do anything because of the gifts they've given me. Strength, glory, pride—thank you, John, Chris, Michael, Anthony, Mom, and Dad. You've made me an individual, Marie D'Aniello, a little bit different from each one of you, and a little bit like all of you.

Becoming a Better Listener

4

OUTLINE

This chapter will help you

- appreciate the benefits of effective listening
- understand the process of listening
- overcome barriers to listening
- improve critical listening skills
- evaluate messages constructively
- become a more ethical listener

Easy listening exists only on the radio.

DAVID BARKAN

You walk to the front of the room, ready to make your first presentation. You pause to make eye contact with your audience. This is what you see:

In a far corner of the room, a student is frantically trying to finish her accounting homework. A ledger is open on her desk, a textbook is open on her lap. Her eyes move from the book to the ledger. She never stops writing, and she never looks up.

In the other far corner, a student is sleeping off the effects of last night's party. His eyes are closed. Occasionally his chin drops to his chest, and he jerks himself up and tries to look alert, but within twenty seconds he has dropped off again.

Finally, you spot an attentive face—someone who actually looks as though he's ready to listen. His desk is empty except for a notebook. He is sitting alert, a pencil in his hand. His eyes are on you. He looks interested in what you have to say.

A good listener can be hard to find! Legend has it that President Franklin Delano Roosevelt was bemused by the poor listening behavior of people who visited the White House. To test his notion that people didn't really listen, he once greeted guests in a receiving line by murmuring, "I murdered my grandmother this morning." Typical responses ran along the lines of "Thank you," "How good of you." or other platitudes of polite approval. Finally he met someone who had actually listened and who responded, "I'm sure she had it coming to her."[1]

Poor listening can exact a large price, both globally and personally. Nations may make up their minds about the intentions of other nations, and then refuse to listen to information that does not support their conclusions. People in groups may make poor decisions, swayed by the power of a group member's dominant personality. Juries may not render fair verdicts because they have not learned how to apply critical listening and thinking skills. If you are not listening effectively in a classroom, you will find it hard to do well in the course.

Fortunately, effective listening can be learned.[2] In this chapter we consider why you should want to become a better listener, and we describe the process of listening. We discuss the main causes of poor listening and suggest ways to overcome them. Next, we look at the development of critical and constructive listening and tie these skills into the evaluation of speeches. Finally, we consider your responsibilities as an ethical listener.

The Benefits of Effective Listening

Why should you want to become a better listener? Both in corporate America and in the classroom, listening—whether effective or ineffective—makes a difference.

Listening in the Workplace

Consider the following scenario:

> **John, a truck driver who was carrying a load of lettuce, called his dispatcher early in the morning. "Where do you want me to take the load?"**
>
> **"Jackson," she answered, and gave him the street address.**
>
> **Later that afternoon, John called her back. "Well, I'm in Jackson, and I can't find the address," he reported.**
>
> **"I've got it here, just as clear as can be. It says, get off I-40 at exit 82 and. . ."**
>
> **"Wait a minute," John interrupts. "I came down on I-55."**
>
> **"I-55? In Jackson, Tennessee?"**
>
> **"Hold it. You didn't tell me that. I'm in Jackson, Mississippi."**
>
> **"Well why didn't you ask me?" she countered. And while they argued over who was more to blame, the poor speaker or the poor listener, a huge load of lettuce began to wilt under the Mississippi sun.**

Variations of this story are played out in different forms every day, at all levels of American society. Who can say how much time and money are lost each day because of poor listening? This is why companies assign so much importance to listening in their hiring (and firing) decisions. The truth is, effective listening can mean the difference between success and failure–both for individuals and for companies. A survey of over four hundred top-level personnel directors suggests that the two most important factors in helping graduates find jobs are speaking and listening abilities.[3] Another survey of major American corporations reports that ineffective listening leads to ineffective performance.[4] If you listen effectively on the job, you will improve your chances for advancement.

Companies that encourage people at every level to develop effective listening skills enjoy many rewards. Employees are more innovative when they feel that management will listen to their ideas. Morale improves, and the work environment becomes more pleasant and productive.

Do you know the differences between a good and poor listener? Go to **VideoLab Lesson 3's Next Step: Good Listeners vs. Poor Listeners.** VideoLab

Listening in the Classroom

Now consider another scenario:

> **It is a warm spring day. Marie's body is sitting in her management class, but her mind is wandering somewhere else, fluttering between her memories of the past weekend and her anticipation of the summer ahead. In the background her instructor's voice drones on, but the words don't register, not until the professor says: "Now, I know that Marie has worked in this kind of environment, and she can tell us what it's like. Marie, will you describe it for us?"**

Have you ever lived through this kind of nightmare? If so, we won't have a hard time convincing you that effective listening is also important in the classroom and in the here-and-now of your life. Effective listeners read assignments ahead of time to familiarize themselves with new words and to lay a foundation for understanding. Stu-

dents who listen effectively earn better grades because they learn to concentrate and identify what is important in a message.[5]

Effective listening is particularly important in the public speaking class. By listening carefully to the speeches presented in your class, you can learn about the topic of the speech and also which speaking techniques work best and under what circumstances. Good listeners can provide the kind of feedback that helps speakers adjust their messages. A good audience can also help ease a speaker's anxiety by creating a supportive environment. As a listener, you can show support by being pleasant and responsive rather than dour and inattentive.[6] Give speakers your undivided attention, and nod occasionally in response to what they say. Show respect for them as people, even if you disagree with their ideas.

The ability to listen effectively is valued in the workplace.

Effective listeners also can give speakers a psychological boost. How many times have you had people really listen to you? How frequently have your ideas been taken seriously? If your answer is "seldom," you may be in for a pleasant surprise. You will discover that there are few things quite as rewarding as having people really listen to you and respect what you say.

The ability to listen effectively can help you in your other classes.

The Neglect of Listening

Given the obvious importance of listening in our personal lives and in the economic life of the nation, why is it so neglected by educators? Although we spend most of our communication time listening, we receive less formal training in listening than we do in speaking, writing, or reading.[7] Perhaps educators assume that we naturally know how to listen well, despite a good deal of evidence to the contrary. Listening may be undervalued because we associate it with following, not with leading. Or, in a society that values action, we may see speaking as active and listening as passive behavior.

Other cultures place a higher premium on listening. Some Native American

Listening is a highly valued skill in many Native American cultures.

tribes, for example, have a far better appreciation of its importance. The council system of the Ojai Foundation has three main rules for conducting business: "Speak honestly, be brief, and listen from the heart."[8] For the Blackfeet tribe, listening is a way of opening themselves to the sacredness of their surroundings.[9] The Lakota also recognize the value of listening:

> **Conversation was never begun at once, nor in a hurried manner. No one was quick with a question, no matter how important, and no one was pressed for an answer. A pause giving time for thought was the truly courteous way of beginning and conducting a conversation. Silence was meaningful with the Lakota, and his granting a space of silence to the speech-maker and his own moment of silence before talking was done in the practice of true politeness and regard for the rule that, "thought comes before speech."[10]**

We will take to heart these lessons from the Ojai Council and the Blackfeet and Lakota people, and regard effective listening as absolutely essential to successful communication.

The Process of Listening

Listening is a process that extends from the most primitive kind of auditory awareness to the most sophisticated forms of reception. You can think of the various phases of this process as though they formed the rungs of a ladder. When people are strangers or when they are suspicious of each other, they sometimes build invisible walls for protection. If communication is to occur, speakers and listeners must somehow climb these walls. The Ladder of Listening shown in Figure 4.1 illustrates the sequence of steps one must master to accomplish this climb.

Discriminative Listening

Listening is much more than a mere awareness of sounds in our environment. But before there can be listening, there must be hearing. **Hearing** is an automatic, involuntary process in which sound waves stimulate nerve impulses to the brain. Therefore, hearing is the basis of **discriminative listening**, the first rung on the ladder, in which we respond to the sounds of our aural world.

InterConnections.LearnMore 4.1

Listening

International Listening Association
http://www.listen.org
The official web site of the International Listening Association, dedicated to improving listening skills, with links to exercises and resources, including ILA's quarterly publication, Listening Post.

Improving Your Listening
http://www.scs.tamu.edu/selfhelp/elibrary/listening_skills.asp
Techniques and principles from the Student Counseling Service, Texas A&M University.

The Power of Listening
http://www.speaking.com/articles_html/TonyAlessandra,Ph.D.,CSP,CPAE_107.html
An interesting essay on the importance of listening skills, written by a professional speaker and applied behavioral scientist.

Listening and Negotiation Skills
http://www.healthyplace.com/communities/depression/wilkerson/listening_skills.html
An article on the role of listening in successful negotiating.

Normally, such listening is not an issue, unless you are trying to listen in a noisy environment or have a severe hearing impairment. The fact that some people can become superb listeners even though they can't hear very well is a monument to the human spirit. The life of Helen Keller, who overcame deafness to acquire speech and to become a great citizen of the world, is a story of such heroism.

Comprehensive Listening

The second rung on the listening ladder is **comprehensive listening**. This is the point of transition between being aware of sounds and finding meaning in them. Comprehensive listening involves focusing on the message, understanding the speaker's verbal and nonverbal language, and interpreting the message in terms of one's own knowledge and experience. Comprehensive listening is voluntary, because we can choose whether to listen this way. In our story of Marie, discriminative listening did not become comprehensive listening until she heard her name called. At that point it was too late! We will say more later in this chapter about motivating ourselves to listen comprehensively.

Empathic Listening

The Chinese symbol for the verb *to listen* has four basic elements: undivided attention, ears, eyes, and heart.[11] The heart in this symbol represents **empathic listening.** When we listen empathically, we try to see things from speakers' points of view, even though we may not agree with them. Empathic listening encourages speakers by suspending judgment

Figure 4.1
The Ladder of Listening

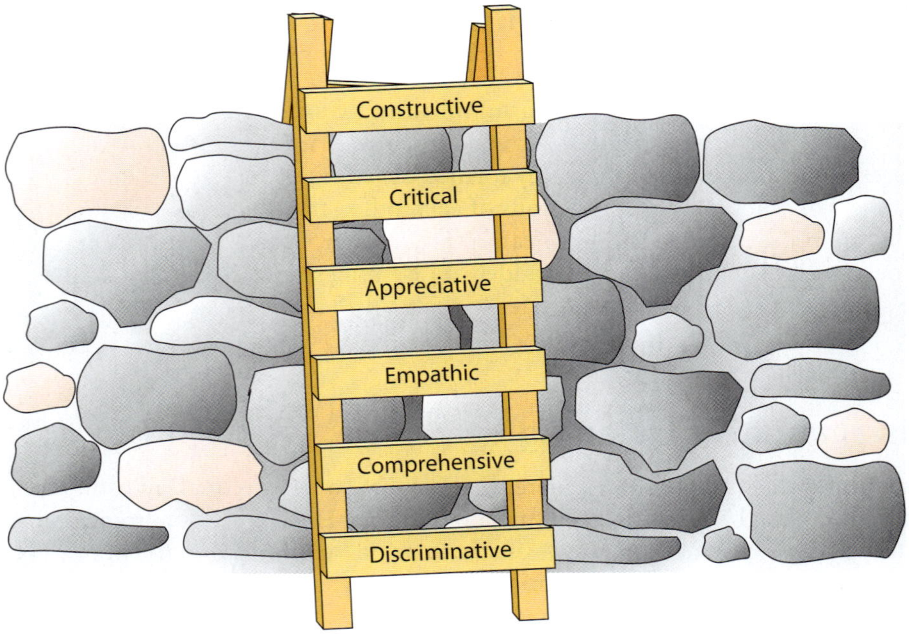

and allowing them to be heard.[12] It creates a receptive environment in the classroom, and it is especially important early in the term when beginning speakers are trying to cope with communication anxiety.

The Chinese symbol for listening suggests the complexity of the process.

Appreciative Listening

Appreciative listening, the next rung up the ladder, is the aesthetic phase of the listening process. It involves responding to the intrinsic beauty of a message. For example, we may enjoy the simplicity and balance of a speech, or the eloquence of a speaker's words. Although appreciative listening can add to the enjoyment of any speech, it is especially relevant to ceremonial speaking, when speakers often try to inspire listeners with colorful, vivid, even poetic language.

Critical Listening

Becoming adept at **critical listening** is a major goal of the educational process, as well as a sophisticated phase of the listening process. This large step up the Ladder of Listening adds "mind" to the Chinese symbol for listening. Critical listeners analyze and evaluate the content of a message. They inspect the reasoning process, weigh the value of evidence, decide whether points are really supported, and determine whether an overall message is successful. They are less influenced by the speaker's title, previous reputation, or charisma and are more resistant to emotional appeals. They know that much is at stake in public communication, and they are wary of what they hear. They accept nothing at face value. Cultivating a healthy skepticism and a critical listening orientation is a major goal of the public speaking class.

Constructive Listening

Constructive listening, the final rung of our ladder, involves an active search for the value that messages may have for our lives. It helps speakers grow by offering good feedback. It is motivated listening, in that it presumes that all messages may have value. Although they are alert to the possible defects of a message and wary of hidden agendas, constructive listeners go beyond critical listening. They ask themselves how they might use even flawed messages. Therefore, constructive listening is not passive, but quite active. Constructive listeners enter into the communication process and participate fully in the construction of meaning.

For example, after listening to a speech urging the importance of mathematics education in the public schools, constructive listeners in a recent class we taught asked about the importance of such education in developing logical thinking, and whether math education is adapted sufficiently to meet the local needs and life experiences of students. This excellent discussion focused and completed the meaning of a good speech, creating a dialogue in which the ultimate meaning of the message developed out of the interaction of the participants.[13] Developing a constructive listening orientation as the counterpart of a critical orientation is also high on the agenda of this chapter.

Overcoming Barriers to Effective Listening

Everyone faces certain challenges as a listener. Identify your listening problems by taking the **Listening Problems Inventory** under **Self-Assessments** in the **SpeechStudio.**

Go to: http//college.hmco.com/eduspace/

What keeps us from climbing to the top of the Ladder of Listening? And how can we remove or get around these barriers? Some barriers arise from problems in the speaking situation or with speakers. But the most troublesome barriers to effective listening are grounded in listeners themselves. Figure 4.2 will help you identify your own possible listening problems. Look through the list and place a check next to items that describe your listening attitudes and behaviors.

Listening Barriers Based on Situations and Speakers

Listening barriers based on the actual circumstances of speaking or on the inadequacies of speakers include physical noise, flawed messages, and presentation problems.

Physical Noise. You are working very hard listening to your English professor describing the contrasting rhyme schemes in the English and Italian sonnet forms. Suddenly his words are lost in the roar of a helicopter circling overhead. "Oh, no," you think, "what has happened now?" And while you are speculating about that and the professor talks on, you lose track of his message entirely and abandon the attempt to listen.

The victim in this case is discriminative listening. If we can't hear, we can't listen. It's as simple as that.

Speakers and listeners must work together to solve this problem. The speaker should talk louder to be heard. As a listener, you should provide feedback to let the speaker know there is a problem. Smile at the speaker, and cup your hand by your ear. Or lean forward, obviously straining to hear. If you still can't hear, move to a seat closer to the front of the room. If the noise comes from outside, get up and close the window or door.

Figure 4.2
Listening Problems Checklist

☐ *1.* I believe listening is automatic, not learned behavior.
☐ *2.* I stop listening when a speech is uninteresting.
☐ *3.* I find it hard to listen to ideas about which I have strong feelings.
☐ *4.* I react emotionally to certain words.
☐ *5.* I am easily distracted by noises when someone is speaking.
☐ *6.* I don't like to listen to speakers who are not experts.
☐ *7.* I find some people too objectionable to listen to.
☐ *8.* I nod off when someone talks in a monotone.
☐ *9.* I can be so dazzled by a glib presentation that I don't listen critically.
☐ *10.* I don't like to listen to messages that go against my values.
☐ *11.* I think up counterarguments when I disagree with a speaker.
☐ *12.* I know so much on some topics that I don't need to hear more.
☐ *13.* I believe a speaker—not the listener—is responsible for effective communication.
☐ *14.* I find it hard to listen when I have a lot on my mind.
☐ *15.* I stop listening when a subject is difficult.
☐ *16.* I can look like I'm listening when I am not.
☐ *17.* I listen for facts and ignore the rest of a message.
☐ *18.* I try to write down everything a lecturer says.
☐ *19.* I let a speaker's appearance determine how well I listen.
☐ *20.* I jump to conclusions before I have heard all of a message.

1. Study background material ahead of time.
2. Come prepared with paper and a pen or pencil.
3. Leave a 3-inch margin on the left, and take notes in outline form. Leave space between main points.
4. Don't try to write down everything you hear. Omit nonessential words.
5. Be alert for signal words such as:
   a. *for example* or *case in point,* which suggest that supporting material will follow.
   b. *the three causes* or *the four steps,* which suggest a list that you should number.
   c. *before* or *after,* which suggest that the order is important.
   d. *therefore* or *consequently,* which suggest a causal relationship.
   e. *similarly* or *on the other hand,* which suggest that a comparison or contrast will follow.
   f. *above all* or *keep in mind,* which mean that this is an important idea.
6. Summarize what you are hearing and jot questions in the left margin.
7. Review, correct, and complete your notes the same day that you take them.

Figure 4.3

Guidelines for Taking Notes

Message Problems. Before the helicopter mercifully intervened in the previous scene, your instructor had just enlightened you with this blockbuster: "The Petrarchan octave and sestet are replaced by the three Shakespearean quatrains and a rhyming couplet." "Uh huh," you think.

Messages that are full of unfamiliar words or that are poorly organized impede comprehensive listening. When speakers are insensitive to this problem or are ill prepared to deal with it, listeners must make a special effort to compensate. If you know that there may be unfamiliar words in a class lecture, read on the subject ahead of time. If a message is poorly organized, taking notes can help. Try to pick out the main points. See if you can identify key words, and look for a pattern among them. Differentiate these points and words from supporting materials such as examples or narratives. Figure 4.3 provides some helpful suggestions for taking notes.[14]

Presentation Problems. Speakers who talk too fast may be difficult to follow, posing yet another barrier to comprehensive listening. On the other hand, speakers who talk too slowly or too softly may lull you to sleep. Speakers also may have distracting habits, such as swaying to and fro or fiddling with their hair while they are talking. You may encounter speakers whose dress or hairstyle is so unusual that you find yourself concentrating more on how they look than on what they are saying.

Simply realizing you are responding to irrelevant cues may help you listen more attentively. If you find yourself drifting away because of such problems, remind yourself that what speakers say is the important thing.

Listening Barriers Based in Listeners Themselves

By far, the most formidable barriers to the listening process arise within listeners themselves. Chief among these barriers are inattention, bad listening habits, listener apprehension, attitudes, and reactions to words. Figure 4.4 shows how good and poor listeners respond differently to such problems.

Figure 4.4

Differences Between Good and Poor Listeners

Good Listeners	Poor Listeners
1. focus attention on the message.	1. allow their minds to wander.
2. control reactions to trigger words.	2. respond emotionally to trigger words.
3. set aside personal problems when listening.	3. let personal problems interfere when listening.
4. work to overcome distractions.	4. succumb easily to distractions.
5. don't let their biases interfere with listening.	5. let their biases interfere with listening.
6. don't let mannerisms interfere with listening.	6. allow mannerisms to interfere with listening.
7. listen for things they can use.	7. tune out dry topics.
8. recognize the role of the listener in communication.	8. hold the speaker responsible for communication.
9. listen actively.	9. listen passively.
10. reserve judgment until a speaker is finished.	10. jump to conclusions before a speaker is finished.
11. provide honest feedback to speakers.	11. feign attention, giving false feedback.
12. become familiar with difficult material ahead of time.	12. avoid listening to difficult material.
13. listen for main ideas.	13. listen only for facts.
14. don't demand all messages be entertaining.	14. want all messages to be entertaining.

Inattentiveness. One of the most common barriers affecting the lower rungs on the Ladder of Listening is simply *not paying attention.* How many times have you found yourself daydreaming when you know you should be listening? One cause of this problem is that our minds can process information faster than people speak. Most people talk at about 125 words per minute in public, but they can process information at about 500 words per minute.[15] This "communication gap" provides an opportunity for listeners to drift away to seemingly more interesting or demanding personal problems. Daydreamers may smile and nod encouragingly even though they haven't heard a word the speaker has said.

A second cause of inattention is *chance associations with words.* For example, a speaker mentions the word *desk*—which reminds you that you need a better place to study in your room—which reminds you that you have to buy a new lamp—which starts you thinking about going shopping—which gets you thinking about the fried mushrooms at the restaurant in the mall—which reminds you that you didn't eat breakfast and you're hungry. By the time your attention drifts back to the speaker, it's too late, the speech is over, and now your instructor is asking you to respond to it.

A third cause of inattention is *personal concerns.* When you are tired, hungry, angry, worried, or pressed for time, you may find it difficult to concentrate. Your personal problems may take precedence over listening to a speaker. Or you may have "listening burnout" from too much concentrated exposure to critical oral material.[16] If you've ever attended three lecture classes in a row, you will know what this is.

To overcome inattention, you must remind yourself of what is at stake when you are listening. Motivate yourself to look for the value in messages. Fill the communication gap by summarizing what the speaker has already said and by reflecting upon how you can use what you are hearing. Come to class well rested and well fed. Remind yourself that you can't do your homework for another class when someone is talking. Decide to do your worrying later. Sit near the front of the room, and clear your mind and your desk of everything except paper on which to take notes. Sit erect, leaning forward slightly, establish eye contact with the speaker, and consciously commit to listening.

To become effective listeners we may have to work to overcome boredom and fatigue.

Bad Habits. It is easy to acquire bad listening habits that interfere with comprehension. You may have watched so much television that you expect all messages to be fast moving and entertaining. You may have learned how to look like you are listening while tuning out dull or difficult material. Your experiences as a student may have conditioned you to listen just for facts. Such habits can interfere with effective listening.

William F. Buckley Jr. has commented that "the television audience . . . is not trained to listen . . . to 15 uninterrupted minutes."[17] Our television-viewing experiences may also lead us into "the entertainment syndrome," in which we demand that speakers be lively, interesting, funny, and charismatic to hold our attention. Unfortunately, not all subjects lend themselves to such treatment.

Although honest feedback is important to speech effectiveness, we all have learned how to *feign attention.* We sit erect, gaze at the speaker, nod or smile from time to time (although not always at the most appropriate times), and do not listen to one word that is being said! You are most likely to feign attention when a message is difficult. If the speaker asks, "Do you understand?" you may nod brightly, sending false feedback to be polite, or to avoid seeming dimwitted.

Your experiences as a student may contribute to another bad habit: *listening only for facts.* If you do this, you may miss the forest because you are so busy counting leaves. Placing too much emphasis on facts can keep you from attending to the nonverbal aspects of a message. Effective listening includes integrating what you hear and what you see. Gestures, facial expressions, and tone of voice communicate nuances that are vital to understanding a message.

Overcoming bad habits requires effort. When you find yourself feigning attention, remember that honest feedback helps speakers but that inappropriate feedback deceives them. Don't try to remember everything or write down all that you hear. Instead, listen to the main ideas and identify supporting materials. Try to build an overall picture of the meaning in your mind. Attend to the nonverbal cues as well. Does the speaker's tone of voice change the meaning of the words? Are the gestures and facial expressions consistent with the words? If not, what does this tell you?

Listening Apprehension. Is there really such a thing as fear of listening? For many people, the answer is a resounding "Yes!" This fear, which is similar to the communication anxiety experienced by speakers, can block both comprehension and access to the higher rungs of both critical and constructive listening.

Listener fear, which goes by the technical name **receiver apprehension** (RA), is defined as "the fear of misinterpreting, inadequately processing, and/or not being able to adjust psychologically to messages sent by others."[18] It is related to a fear of failure, motivation, evaluation, and message complexity.[19] We may experience listener apprehension when we believe a message is important, when we think we may be judged on how well we respond to it, or when it challenges our ability to understand things.

Our fear of failure may cause us to avoid listening to difficult material. If we are asked questions later, we can always say, "I wasn't really listening," instead of, "I didn't understand." Additionally, our desire to have things simplified so that we can understand them without much effort makes us susceptible to oversimplified remedies for everything from fallen arches to failing government policies.

Let's look at how the fear of failure and listening apprehension work.

> **Assume that the first speaker of the day announces that her speech will argue that government-funded student loans are unnecessary. You are attending school with the help of such a loan, so you feel threatened by her message and you don't look forward to what you are going to hear.**
>
> **Next, your instructor announces that he will name a respondent for each speech. In a critique following the speech, that student must demonstrate an understanding of the message, an appreciation for its qualities, and an awareness of the speaker's aims. The respondent also must discuss possible shortcomings of content or presentation and make constructive suggestions for improvement.**
>
> **Congratulations! You have just been named the respondent for the speech on government loan programs.**

How can you listen constructively to a speech on which you have a strong initial bias? As you think about this challenge, you may feel the faint stirrings of listener apprehension. The speech itself contains an incredible array of examples and statistics. The message is highly complex. As you try to follow the meaning of the speech, you feel your anxiety growing.

We hope we have made our point. Listener apprehension can be an important factor in communication. It can be positive if it makes us *want* to listen to messages, but this same anxiety can distract us and even cause us to distort what we hear.[20] To control your RA, we suggest that you try the techniques that work for speaker anxiety. Practice deep muscle relaxation, reword negative self-messages, and visualize successful outcomes.[21] Instead of telling yourself, "All these details are confusing," say, "I can see the overall meaning." Visualize yourself giving a critique that helps both speaker and other listeners see the strong points as well as possible problems in the message. Speaker's Notes 4.1, "Improving Your Listening Skills," summarizes how you might listen more effectively to messages.

Speaker's Notes 4.1

Improving Your Listening Skills

1. Identify your listening problems so that you can correct them.
2. Look for something of value in every speech.
3. Put problems and biases aside when listening.
4. Control reactions to trigger words and other distractions.
5. Delay judgments until you have heard a speech through to its conclusion.
6. Don't try to write down everything a speaker says.
7. Listen for the main ideas.

Emotional Reactions to Words. As you listen to a message, you react to more than just the objective meanings of words. Some words may set off such powerful emotional reactions that they dominate the meaning of a speech, derail your comprehension, and defeat critical listening. We call these **trigger words**. Trigger words can evoke either positive or negative reactions. Positive trigger words generally relate to values and traditions that we hold dear. Negative trigger words often relate to racial, ethnic, sexist, or religious slurs.

Positive trigger words can blind us to flawed or dangerous messages. Our reactions to them are usually subtle, and we may not realize that we are being influenced. How many times have people been deceived by such trigger words as *freedom, democracy,* or *progress* to justify certain courses of action?[22]

Negative trigger words often invoke extreme emotional reactions, and we are usually aware of these reactions. Although some words deserve condemnation, people should control words and not the other way around. We should not let trigger words prevent us from hearing and evaluating the entire message in which they are embedded. Consider this hypothetical case.

> **Assume that you consider the use of *girls* in reference to adult females to be demeaning. Now, suppose a recruiter visiting your campus is describing opportunities for advancement in his company. He talks about "one of the girls from the office" who was recently promoted to a management position. His use of the term *girls* leads you to think this is surely a sexist organization. As you sit there stewing over this, you miss his statement that two-thirds of all recent promotions have gone to women and that a program aimed at promoting more females is in effect.**

How can you lessen the power of trigger words? To gain control over them, Professor Richard Halley of Weber State University suggests that you observe your own behavior over a period of time and make a list of words that cause you to react emotionally.[23] You might then ask yourself the following questions:

- Do these words affect my responses to messages?
- Are speakers using these words to manipulate me?
- What can I do to gain control over my reactions?

Train yourself to look at the total message and analyze the situation. For example, would it make any difference if the recruiter in the previous example were a woman? Ask yourself, "Is this speaker really insensitive or is he testing me?" How can I determine whether this attitude is widespread in the company? By concentrating on such questions, you can help distance yourself from your emotions.

Attitudes. Our reactions to trigger words grow out of our underlying attitudes. Strong attitudes toward the speaker or the topic can block comprehension and warp critical listening. All of us have biases of one kind or another. Listening problems arise when we let our biases prevent us from receiving messages accurately. Some of the ways in which bias can distort messages are through filtering, assimilation, and contrast effects.[24]

Filtering means that you don't process all incoming information. You hear what you want to hear. You unconsciously screen the speaker's words so that only some of them reach your brain. Listeners who filter will hear only one side of "good news, bad news" speeches: the side that confirms their preconceived beliefs.

Assimilation means that you see positions similar to your own as being closer to it than they actually are. Assimilation occurs when listeners have a strong positive attitude toward a speaker or topic. For example, if you believe a person can do no wrong, you may assimilate everything she says so that it seems consistent with your beliefs.

A **contrast effect** occurs when you see positions different from yours as being more distant than they actually are. For example, if you are a staunch liberal, you may think anything conservatives say will differ from what you believe, even if that is not true. Biases can make you put words in a speaker's mouth, take them away, or distort them.

The attitudes that cause most listening problems are those related to the speaker or the topic. If you know speakers or have heard something about them, you may have developed attitudes toward them that cause listening problems. The more competent and interesting you expect a speaker to be, the more attentive you will be and the more likely you are to accept what the speaker says. If your positive feelings are extremely strong, you may accept anything you hear from the speaker without considering its merits. But if you anticipate an incompetent or uninteresting speaker, you may be less attentive and less likely to respect the message. You may dislike speakers because of positions they have previously defended or groups with which they are associated. Such biases can impair your listening ability.

For additional information, go to **VideoLab Lesson 3's Next Step: Strategies for Enhancing Listening.** VideoLab

Your attitudes toward certain topics also can affect how well you listen. If you believe that a topic is relevant to your life, you may listen more carefully than if you are indifferent to the topic. For example, speeches about retirement planning may fall on deaf ears with younger audiences. You may listen more attentively, although less critically, to speeches that support positions you already hold. If you feel strongly about a subject and oppose the speaker's position, you may find yourself rehashing counterarguments instead of listening. For example, if you have strong feelings concerning gun control, you may find yourself silently forming arguments against a speaker's position instead of listening to the actual message. Finally, you may think that you already know enough about a topic. In such cases, you are not likely to listen effectively and may miss potentially useful information.

Attitudes are not easy to control. The first step in overcoming a bias is to admit you have it. Next, decide that you will listen as objectively as you can and that you will delay judgment until you have heard the entire message. Being objective does not mean that you must agree with a message—it only means that you believe a speech deserves to be heard on its own terms. What you hear may help you see clearly the faults or the virtues of an opposing position. As a result, you may feel confirmed in what you already believe, or you may decide to reevaluate your position.

Finally, decide that you will find value in listening. Even if you are not interested in a topic, look for something in the speech that will benefit you personally. That consideration leads us on to the higher rungs on the Ladder of Listening.

Developing Critical Listening Skills

Put your critical listening skills to the test. View **Lesson 3's Screening Room** and answer the questions in **Drill 3.1: Critical Listening: Learning to Listen**. VideoLab

As we considered the barriers posed by trigger words and attitudes, we moved closer to the higher rung on the Ladder of Listening that we call *critical listening*. On the one hand, critical listening protects you from messages that wear a halo: speeches that rely on their high-charisma sources or that play upon your trigger words. On the other, critical listening bends over backward to give a fair hearing to messages that go against our attitudes or that come from unattractive sources.

Critical listening involves developing a questioning, skeptical orientation to what you hear.[25] This orientation centers on evaluating evidence and information, assessing the credibility of sources, analyzing language usage, and examining rhetorical strategies. We will introduce these topics here, and develop them further in later chapters.

Evaluating Evidence and Information

Ideas or claims should be supported with evidence in the form of facts and figures, testimony, examples, or narratives. Whenever speakers claim, "This statement is beyond dispute!" it is probably time to start a dispute. Listen for what is *not* said, as well as what *is* said. *No evidence equals no proof. No proof should equal no acceptance.* Don't hesitate to ask speakers challenging questions.

When evaluating evidence, remember the four R's: evidence should be **relevant**, **representative**, **recent**, and **reliable**. Relevant evidence relates directly to the issue in question. The speaker who shouts, "Television is destroying family values!" and then offers statistics that demonstrate a rising national divorce rate has not established the connection between television and family values. The evidence is not *relevant* to the claim.

Evidence also should be *representative* of the situation rather than an exception to the rule. The speaker who claims, "Young people have lost their sense of values," based on a study of juvenile delinquents in London, has violated this particular "R."

Facts and figures should be the most *recent* ones available. This is particularly important when knowledge about a topic is changing rapidly. Before the Iraqi war, the U.S. government often referred to a report from British intelligence to support its claim that Saddam Hussein possessed weapons of mass destruction. It turned out that part of the British evidence was over ten years old.[26]

Evidence should also be *reliable*—we must be able to depend on it. The more significant and controversial the claim, the more reliable should be the evidence. It turned out that the same report from British intelligence had been drawn not from confidential, professional sources of intelligence but from magazines and academic journals, including one article authored by a postgraduate student in California. These sources would not satisfy those who insist on a high standard of reliability in justifying decisions to go to war.

When you apply the standard of reliability, require

- that claims be confirmed by more than one source,
- that these sources be independent of each other, and
- that the sources possess expert credentials.

Even information that seems to meet these tests of evidence should be evaluated in terms of how well it fits with what you already know. Information that is inconsistent with what you know or believe should set off an alarm in your mind. You should always evaluate such material very carefully before you accept it. Keep an open mind, but ask yourself the tough questions in Speaker's Notes 4.2, "Questions for Critical Listening," before accepting what you hear.

InterConnections.LearnMore 4.2

Critical Thinking and Listening

The Critical Thinking Consortium
http://www.criticalthinking.org
The official web site of the Critical Thinking Consortium, an organization dedicated to promoting change in education and society through critical thinking. Affiliated with Sonoma State University, California. Contains numerous links to additional resources.

Critical Thinking: What It Is and Why It Counts
http://www.insightassessment.com/pdf_files/what&why98.pdf
An essay on the importance of critical thinking, prepared by Professor Peter A. Facione, former director of Critical Thinking Assessment and Consulting Services, California Academic Press.

Thinking
http://www.homestead.com/peoplelearn/criticalthinking.html
Web site of the Learning Domain, a repository of online resources about human learning. Provides links to many interesting articles on critical thinking.

Critical Thinking Across Cultures: What We Think We Know About Critical Thinking
http://www.asia-u.ac.jp/english/cele/articles/Connolly_Critical_Thinking.htm
An article discussing Eastern and Western perspectives on critical thinking, prepared by Professor Mark Connolly, Center for English Language Education, Asia University, Tokyo, Japan.

Critical Thinking on the Web
http://www.philosophy.unimelb.edu.au/reason/critical
A comprehensive directory of online resources on critical thinking, prepared by Dr. Tim van Gelder, Department of Philosophy, University of Melbourne, Australia.

Speaker's Notes 4.2

Questions for Critical Listening

1. Does the speaker support ideas or claims with evidence?
2. Is the evidence relevant, representative, recent, and reliable?
3. Does the information fit with what you already know?
4. Are the sources cited competent and trustworthy?
5. Does the speaker distinguish among facts, inferences, and opinions?
6. Is the language vague or incomprehensible?
7. Is there a balance between rational and emotional appeals?
8. Does the speaker promise too much?
9. Does the speaker acknowledge other perspectives?

When presenting evidence, speakers should make a clear distinction among facts, inferences, and opinions. **Facts** are verifiable units of information that can be confirmed by independent observation. **Inferences** are assumptions or projections based on incomplete data. **Opinions** add personal judgments to facts and inferences: they tell us what someone thinks about a subject. For example, "Mary was late for class today" is a fact. "Mary will probably be late for class again tomorrow" is an inference. "Mary is an irresponsible student" is an opinion. It may sound easy to make these distinctions among facts, inferences, and opinions, but often it is not. You must be alert to detect confusions among them as you listen to messages.

Just because an assertion or opinion is continually repeated in the media doesn't make it a fact. Kathleen Hall Jamieson, dean of the Annenberg School of Communication, calls this the "echo-chamber" effect. The echo-chamber works this way: an unconfirmed rumor is initially published or aired by a news source, and then it is repeated by others as though it had been substantiated.[27] After the rumor has been repeated many times, people tend to accept it as fact without any verification.

Assessing the Credibility of Sources

Evidence and supporting material should come from sources that are trustworthy and competent in the subject area. Ethical speakers cite their sources of information. It is also wise to specify the credentials of sources unless they are widely known. If credentials are left out or described in vague terms, the testimony may be questionable. We recently found an advertisement for a health food product that contained "statements by doctors." A quick check of the current directory of the American Medical Association revealed that only one of the six "doctors" cited was a member of AMA and that his credentials were misrepresented. Always ask yourself:"*Where does this information come from?*" and *"Are these sources qualified to speak on the topic?"*

Analyzing Language Use

When speakers want to hide something, they often use incomprehensible or vague language. Introducing people who are not physicians as "doctors" to enhance their testimony on health subjects is one form of vagueness. Another ruse is using pseudoscientific jargon, such as "This supplement contains a gonadotropic hormone similar to pituitary extract in terms of its complex B vitamin–methionine ratio." If it sounds impressive but you don't know what it means, be careful.

Examining Rhetorical Strategies

Critical listeners give close attention to the evidence and reasoning in a speech.

It is also important to look at the *way* a speaker uses evidence and supporting material. Vivid examples and compelling stories demonstrate a speaker's passion for a subject and invite the listener to share these feelings. An ethical speaker will also include sound information and good reasons to justify such feelings.

In politics, speakers who rely heavily on emotional appeals to promote their agendas, without regard to the accuracy or adequacy of their claims, are called **demagogues**. We should always ask: *"What are these speakers asking us to ignore?"* Republican leaders recently charged that the Democrats were asking voters to ignore the fact that without significant change the entire Medicare program would collapse. Democratic leaders countered that the Republicans were asking voters to ignore the fate of the poor and elderly who would be affected by their reforms. In the face of such conflicting claims, the critical listener will investigate carefully before reaching a conclusion.

Although we have just cautioned you to be wary of speakers who rely primarily on emotional appeals, you also should be wary of speakers who ignore the emotional aspects of a situation. You cannot fully understand an issue unless you understand how it affects others, how it makes them feel, how it colors the way they view the world. Suppose you were listening to a speech on environmental pollution that contained the following information:

> **The United States has 5 percent of the world's population but produces 22 percent of the world's carbon dioxide emissions, releases 26 percent of the world's nitrogen oxides, and disposes of 290 million tons of toxic waste.[28]**

Although these numbers are impressive, what do they tell you about the human problems of pollution? Consider how much more meaningful this material might be if accompanied by the story of Colette Chuda, a five-year-old California girl who died from cancer allegedly caused by her direct exposure to a polluted environment.[29]

The reasoning used in a speech should also be examined. The reasoning should be plausible, with conclusions following from the points and evidence that precede them. In other words, the reasoning should make good sense. The basic assumptions that support arguments should be those on which most rational, unbiased people agree. Whenever reasoning doesn't seem plausible, ask yourself why, and then question the speaker or consult with independent authorities before you commit yourself.

Exaggeration for effect is often used by speakers who wish to win you over to their position or sell you something you do not need. If an offer sounds too good to be true, it probably is. The health food advertisement previously described contained the following claims:

> **The healing, rejuvenating and disease-fighting effects of this total nutrient are hard to believe, yet are fully documented. Aging, digestive upsets, prostrate**

[sic] diseases, sore throats, acne, fatigue, sexual problems, allergies, and a host of other problems have been successfully treated. . . . [It] is the only super perfect food on this earth. This statement has been proven so many times in the laboratories around the world by a chemical analyst that it is not subject to debate nor [sic] challenge.

Maybe the product is also useful as a paint remover and gasoline additive. As you develop effective listening skills, you also develop resistance to persuasive scams from charlatans who try to mask a lack of substance or implausible reasoning with a glib presentation or irrelevant appeals.[30]

You should also consider whether a speaker acknowledges alternative perspectives on issues. Ask yourself, "How might people from a different cultural background see the problem?". "How might someone of the other gender see it?" "Might these people see it differently from the speaker?" "Would their solutions or suggestions be different?" Whenever a message addresses a serious topic, try to consider the issue from various points of view. New and better ideas often emerge when we look at the world through a new lens.

Evaluating Speeches

Use the **Evaluation Guides and Forms** in **SpeechStudio** when assessing your classmates' speeches.
Go to:
http//college.hmco.com/eduspace/

The final rung on the Ladder of Listening, constructive listening, invites you to become a creative, aggressive listener who meets the speaker more than halfway in finding meaning and value in messages. It also implies helping speakers become more effective communicators through the feedback you provide both during and after speeches. In this section we shall concentrate on the oral feedback provided by constructive listeners in the form of questions, appreciation of effective techniques, or suggestions for improvement.

To develop the capacity for such feedback, you must understand that there is an important difference between criticizing a speaker and offering a **critique** of a speech. "Criticism" suggests focusing on what someone did wrong. A "critique" is helpful and supportive, emphasizing strengths as well as weaknesses, showing consideration for the speaker's feelings, and focusing on how a speaker might improve.

VideoLab

Learn more about giving good feedback in **VideoLab Drill 3.3: Practicing Listening.** Watch the speech and constructively assess its strengths and weaknesses.

To provide constructive feedback, you need a set of standards to help you answer the question, "What makes a good speech?" The application of standards may vary with the assignment; for example, the critique of an informative speech might focus on the adequacy of statistics and examples, and that of a persuasive speech might emphasize evidence and reasoning. Nevertheless, there are four general areas of concern for evaluating all speeches: overall considerations, substance, structure, and presentation. Let's take a look at each.

Speaker's Notes 4.3

Guidelines for Oral Critiques

1. Be constructive and supportive.
2. Begin with a positive statement.
3. Be specific; don't just say, "I didn't like that speech."
4. Don't criticize the speaker; analyze the speech.
5. If you point out a problem, offer suggestions for improvement.
6. Word criticisms tactfully, such as, "Did you considering doing. . . ?"
7. End with a positive statement.

Overall Considerations

Overall considerations include issues that apply to the speech as a whole: commitment, adaptation, purpose, freshness, and ethics.

Commitment. Commitment means caring. You must sense that the speaker truly cares about the subject and about listeners. Committed speakers invest the time and effort needed to gain responsible knowledge of their subject. Commitment also shows up in how well a speech is organized and whether it has been carefully rehearsed. Finally, commitment reveals itself in the energy, enthusiasm, and sincerity the speaker projects. Commitment is the spark in the speaker that can touch off fire in the audience.

Karen Lovelace became a model of commitment in her class at Vanderbilt University by developing a series of informative, persuasive, and ceremonial speeches on the fate of disabled people in our society. By the end of the term many of us were ready to join her crusade for reform of laws and customs.

Adaptation. For a speech to be effective, it must meet the requirements of the assignment and be adapted to listeners' needs. An informative speech should extend our understanding of a topic, a persuasive speech should influence attitudes or actions, and a ceremonial speech should celebrate shared values on special occasions. The speech should also conform to specified time limits, have at least the minimum number of references required, and be presented in the style required for that assignment (such as using a presentation aid or extemporaneous delivery).

Effective speakers are listener-centered. They weigh each technique and each piece of evidence in terms of its appropriateness for the audience. Will this example interest listeners? Is this information important for them? How can I best involve the audience? The close involvement of subject, speaker, and listener is vital for effective speaking. One way speakers can invite such identification is to ask involving questions: "Have you ever thought about what it would mean not to have electricity?" Also, the pronoun *we* used artfully throughout a speech may draw audience and speaker closer together around a subject.

Purpose. Speeches should have a clear purpose, such as increasing listeners' knowledge of the causes of the greenhouse effect. The purpose of a speech will usually be evident by the time the speaker finishes the introduction and must be unmistakably clear by the time the speaker begins the conclusion.

A speech that lacks a clear purpose will drift and wander like a boat without a rudder, blown this way and that by whatever thoughts occur to the speaker. Developing a clear purpose begins with a consideration of audience needs. Speakers must determine exactly what they want to accomplish: what they want listeners to learn, think, or do as a result of their speeches.

Freshness. Any speech worth listening to brings something new to listeners. The topic should be fresh. A speech on an overused topic must be handled innovatively to sustain attention. One frequently overused topic for persuasive speeches is drinking and driving. When speakers choose such a topic, they can't simply reiterate the common advice "If you drink, don't drive" and expect to be effective. The audience will have heard that hundreds of times. To get through to listeners on such a subject, speakers must find a new way to present the material. One of our students gave a speech on "responsible drinking and driving" that stressed the importance of understanding the effects of alcohol and of knowing one's tolerance limits. Her fresh approach and important information gave us a new perspective on an old problem.

Ethics. Perhaps the most important measure of a speech is whether it is good or bad for listeners. *An ethical speech demonstrates respect for the audience, responsible* *knowledge, and concern for the consequences of exposure to the message.*

Respect for the audience means that speakers are sensitive to the cultural diversity of their audience and realize that well-meaning people may hold varying positions on an issue. Ethical speakers are considerate of others even as they refute their arguments or question their information. Ethical speakers base their messages on responsible knowledge. They evaluate their sources of information and watch for potential bias. They acknowledge their own prejudices and strive to be objective in their presentation of information. Ethical speakers do not pass off opinions and inferences as facts. Nor do they fabricate data or present the ideas or words of others without acknowledging their contributions.

Finally, ethical speakers are aware that words have consequences. Inflammatory language can arouse strong feelings in audience members that may impede critical listening. Ethical speakers think through the possible ramifications of their messages before they present them. The greater the possible consequences, the more carefully speakers must assess the potential effects of their messages, support what they say with credible evidence, and temper their conclusions with regard for listener sensitivities. Ethics Alert 4.1 lists these ideas.

Evaluating Substance

A speech has substance when it has a worthwhile message supported by facts and figures, testimony, examples, and/or narratives. The starting point for a substantive presentation is a topic that interests both speaker and listeners. When speakers already know something about the topics they select, their knowledge serves as the foundation for further research that enables them to speak responsibly. Although personal experience gives a good start to speech preparation, speakers should always expand such experience with research.

Skillful speakers combine different types of supporting material to demonstrate their points. Combining statistics with an example will make ideas clearer. For instance, a speaker might say, "The base of the Great Pyramid at Giza measures 756 feet on each side." Although precise, this information may be difficult for listeners to visualize. But by adding, "More than eleven football fields could fit in its base," the speaker has made the material more understandable by grounding the figures in an example that most listeners might relate to.

Evaluating Structure

A good speech carries listeners through an orderly progression of ideas that makes it easy to follow. Without a clear design, a speech may seem to be a random collection of thoughts, and the message can get lost in the confusion.

The introduction may begin with an example, a quotation, or a challenging question that draws you into the topic: "So you think there's no need in Idaho to worry about California's monetary crisis?" Once speakers gain attention, they can prepare listeners for what will come by previewing the main points.

Ethics Alert! 4.1

Determining the Ethical Quotient (EQ) of a Speech

1. Does the speaker have responsible knowledge of the topic?
2. Does the speaker show respect for the audience?
3. Does the speaker show concern about the impact of the speech on listeners?
4. Does the speaker document sources of information?
5. Does the speaker avoid inflammatory language that might impede critical listening?

The way the body of a speech is organized will vary with its subject and purpose. A speech that tells you how to do something—like how to plan a budget—should follow the order of the steps in the process it describes. If the subject breaks naturally into parts, such as the three major causes of California's monetary crisis, speakers may use a categorical design.

The conclusion of a speech should summarize the points that have been made and offer a final statement that helps listeners remember the essence of the message.

Effective speeches also contain transitions that link together the various parts. Transitions bridge ideas and aid understanding. During the speech they signal listeners when one thought is ending and a new one is beginning. Thus they help the speech flow better. Transitions are especially vital between the introduction and body of a speech, between the body and conclusion, and among main points within the body.

Evaluating Presentation Skills

No speech can be effective unless it is presented well. Both the actual words speakers use and the way they convey these words are important factors in presentation.

The Language of Speaking. The oral language of speeches must be instantly intelligible. This means that speakers' sentences should be simple and direct. Compare the following examples:

> **Working for a temporary employment service is a good way to put yourself through school because there are always jobs to be found and the places you get to work are interesting—besides, the people you work for treat you well, and you don't have to do the same thing day after day—plus, you can tailor the hours to fit your free time.**
>
> or
>
> **Working for a temporary employment service is a good way to put yourself through school. Jobs are readily available. You can schedule your work to fit in with your classes. You don't stay at any one place long enough to get bored. And, you meet a lot of interesting people who are glad to have your services.**

Which is easier to follow? The first example rambles with the speaker pausing only to catch a breath. The second example uses short sentences, inviting the use of pauses to separate ideas. As a result, the meaning is clearer.

Concrete words are generally preferable to abstract ones because they create vivid pictures for listeners and clarify meaning. Consider the following levels of abstraction:

most abstract	my pet
	my dog
	my puppy
	my eight-week-old puppy
	my eight-week-old black puppy
most concrete	my eight-week-old black Labrador puppy

As the language becomes more concrete, it is easier to visualize what is being said and there is less chance of misunderstanding.

The Speaker's Presentation. An effective presentation sounds natural and enthusiastic. There are few, if any, distracting mannerisms. Most class assignments call for an extemporaneous presentation, in which the speech is carefully prepared and practiced but *not* written out or memorized. Speakers follow an outline of ideas that is imprinted in their minds rather than a written script. Extemporaneous speaking helps speakers make instant adaptations. If listeners look confused, speakers can rephrase what they have just said or provide an example.

Practice may not make perfect, but it certainly improves a speaker's chances. While rehearsing, a speaker may discover that what *looked* good on paper doesn't *sound* as good when spoken. The more speakers practice, the better the speech should flow when presented to the class.

Speakers should talk loud enough to be heard easily in the back of the room. Their posture should be relaxed but not sloppy, tuned to the importance of the message being uttered. Movements should seem free, natural, and spontaneous as speakers gesture in response to their own ideas and to emphasize the points they are making.

Keep these points in mind as you prepare to offer constructive feedback. Figure 4.5 summarizes these guidelines. You may use it as a checklist for critiquing the speeches that you hear in class and in everyday life.

Figure 4.5
Guidelines for Evaluating Speeches

Overall Considerations
Was the speaker committed to the topic?
Did the speech meet the requirements of the assignment?
Was the speech adapted to the audience?
Did the speech promote identification among topic, audience, and speaker?
Was the purpose of the speech clear?
Was the topic handled with imagination and freshness?
Did the speech meet high ethical standards?
Substance
Was the topic worthwhile?
Had the speaker done sufficient research?
Were main ideas supported with information?
Was testimony used appropriately?
Were the sources documented adequately?
Were examples or narratives used effectively?
Was the reasoning clear and correct?
Structure
Did the introduction arouse interest?
Did the introduction preview the message?
Was the speech easy to follow?
Were the main points of the speech evident?
Were transitions used to tie the speech together?
Did the conclusion summarize the message?
Did the conclusion help you remember the speech?
Presentation
Was the language clear, simple, and direct?
Was the language colorful?
Were grammar and pronunciations correct?
Was the speech presented extemporaneously?
Were notes used unobtrusively?
Was the speaker appropriately enthusiastic?
Did the speaker maintain good eye contact?
Did body language complement ideas?
Was the speaker expressive?
Were the rate and loudness appropriate?
Did the speaker use pauses?
Did presentation aids enhance the message?
Were presentation aids integrated into the speech?
Was the presentation free from distracting mannerisms?

Ethical Listening

Ethics Alert! 4.2

1. Give the speaker your undivided attention.
2. Keep your mind open to new ideas.
3. Park your biases outside the door.
4. Provide honest feedback to the speaker.
5. Look for what is good or useful in the message.
6. Consider how the speech might affect others.
7. Listen to others as you would have them listen to you.

Ethical Responsibilities of a Listener

The concept of constructive listening is incomplete unless we acknowledge the importance of ethics. Listeners who would stand at the top of the Ladder of Listening must meet high ethical standards. Ethical listeners do not prejudge a speech, but keep an open mind. John Milton, a great seventeenth-century English intellectual, observed that listening to our opponents can be beneficial. We may learn from them, thus gaining a new perspective on an issue. Or, as we argue with them, we may discover *why* we believe as we do.

Just as we should be open to ideas, we should also be open to speakers representing different lifestyles and cultural backgrounds. We should not deprive ourselves of the chance to explore other worlds. In comparing and contrasting our ways with those of others, we learn more about ourselves.

Finally, keep in mind the impact of your listening on others. Good listeners help develop good speakers. Good listeners are also concerned about the ethical impact of messages on others who may not be present. In the sense that they represent all who might be affected by the message, they are the **universal listener**. Such listeners practice their own version of the Golden Rule: "Listen to others as you would have them listen to you." All sides benefit when speakers and listeners take their ethical roles seriously.

In Summary

Go to **VideoLab Lesson 3's Coach: Tips to Remember** for a list of the "Do's" and "Don'ts" of listening. VideoLab

The Benefits of Listening. Effective listening benefits both listeners and speakers. Improved listening skills can enhance both your academic performance and your chances for a successful career. Better listeners are less vulnerable to unethical advertising or to dishonest public communication. Feedback from good listeners can help communication work better. Supportive listeners help relieve communication apprehension and can boost a speaker's self-esteem. Despite this obvious importance, education in listening is often neglected.

The Process of Listening. Listening is a process that extends from the most primitive kind of awareness through the most sophisticated forms of reception. To climb the Ladder of Listening, we must first be able to hear a message, the *discriminative phase.* Next, we must master the skills of focusing, understanding, and interpreting, the *comprehensive phase.* In the *empathic phase,* we try to see things from the speaker's point of view, and in the *appreciative phase* we enjoy the speaker's ability to structure messages skillfully and to word ideas attractively. *Critical listening* requires that we test messages for the soundness of their content, and *constructive listening,* the final rung of the ladder, challenges us to become helpful listeners who find the value in messages for our lives.

Overcoming Listening Problems. Some listening problems arise from the speaking situation or from speakers. These problems may include noisy surroundings, flawed messages, or poor presentations.

The most serious listening problems are grounded in listeners themselves. These problems include inattention caused by the communication gap between the normal rate of speaking and what you are capable of comprehending, chance associations with words, or personal concerns crowding out everything else. Bad habits, such as pretending we are listening when we are not or listening only for facts, are another. Fear of listening, or *receiver apprehension*, can also block effective listening. We can become fearful listeners when we know that a message will be important for us personally, when we will be held responsible for it, and when it is difficult to understand.

Another listener-oriented listening problem is personal reactions to *trigger words* that set off strong positive or negative emotions. Trigger words are symptoms of biased attitudes that can distort messages. Other symptoms are *filtering*, a form of message distortion in which you hear only what you want to. *Assimilation* occurs when you interpret some favored person's views as identical with your own when actually there is a significant distance between the two positions. A *contrast effect* occurs when you see a position only slightly different from yours as quite different because you have a negative bias toward the source.

Such listener-oriented problems can be overcome. The first step is to identify your listening problems. Concentrate on the main ideas and the overall pattern of meaning in the speech. Strive to be as objective as you can, and withhold judgment until you are certain you understand the message.

Developing Critical Listening Skills. Critical listening helps protect you from messages that wear a "halo" and ensures that you give a fair hearing to messages that go against your attitudes. Critical listeners question what they hear, require support for assertions and claims, and evaluate the credentials of sources. They impose the four *R*'s: evidence should be *relevant, representative, recent*, and *reliable*. Critical listeners differentiate among *facts, inferences*, and *opinions*. They become wary when language seems overly vague or incomprehensible, when inflammatory speech takes the place of reasoning, or when a message promises too much. When what they hear does not fit with what they know, critical listeners start asking tough questions.

Evaluating Speeches. Speech evaluation in the classroom takes the form of a *critique*, a positive and constructive effort to help speakers improve. Criteria for speech evaluation include overall considerations, substance, structure, and presentation skills. Overall considerations encompass the speaker's commitment, adaptation to the audience and occasion, clarity of purpose, freshness of perspective, and ethical standards. Substance involves the value of the topic, the sufficiency of research, the adequacy of supporting material, and the speaker's ability to reason. Structural criteria include the presence of an effective introduction, a clearly organized body that includes the main points and supporting materials, and a conclusion that provides closure. Presentation questions touch on how well speakers use words and their ability to convey their messages through voice and gesture.

Ethical Responsibilities of Listeners. Ethical listeners do not prejudge a speech but are open to ideas and receptive to different perspectives. They are receptive to speakers representing different lifestyles and cultural backgrounds. Ethical listeners are also sensitive to the impact of ideas on others. They are the *universal listener* in the sense that they represent all who might be affected by the message.

Terms to Know

hearing
discriminative listening
comprehensive listening
empathic listening
appreciative listening
critical listening
constructive listening
receiver apprehension
trigger words
filtering
assimilation
contrast effect
relevant
representative
recent
reliable
facts
inferences
opinions
demagogues
critique
universal listener

Discussion

1. Complete the listening problems checklist on page 82 of this chapter. Working in small groups, discuss your listening problems with the other members of your group. Develop a listening improvement plan for the three most common listening problems in your group. Report this plan to the rest of the class.
2. List three positive and three negative trigger words that provoke a strong emotional reaction when you hear them. Have someone write these words on the chalkboard. Try to group the words into categories, such as sexist or ethnic slurs, political terms, ideals, and so on. Discuss why these words have such a strong impact and how listeners might control their reactions to them.
3. Identify a speaker (outside your class) you find difficult to listen to attentively. Identify the sources of interference in yourself that make it hard for you to listen. Design a plan to overcome this problem.

Application

1. Review your class notes from one of your lecture courses. Were you able to identify the main points, or did you try to write down everything that was said? Compare your note-taking skills before and after studying listening behavior. Can you see any differences?
2. Read the following paragraph carefully:

   Dirty Dick has been killed. The police have rounded up six suspects, all of whom are known criminals. All of them were near the scene of the crime at the approximate time that the murder took place. All had good motives for wanting Dirty Dick killed. However, Larcenous Lenny has been completely cleared of guilt.

   Now determine whether each of the following statements is true (T), False (F), or an inference (?).

T F ? 1. Larcenous Lenny is known to have been near the scene of the crime.

T F ? 2. All of the rounded-up criminals were at the scene of the murder.

T F ? 3. Only Larcenous Lenny has been cleared of guilt.

T F ? 4. The police do not know who killed Dirty Dick.

T F ? 5. Dirty Dick's murderer did not confess of his own free will.

T F ? 6. It is known that the six suspects were in the vicinity of the cold-blooded assassination.

T F ? 7. Larcenous Lenny did not kill Dirty Dick.

T F ? 8. Dirty Dick is dead.

You can find the answers at the end of the chapter notes.[31] Were you able to distinguish between inferences and facts?

Notes

1. Cited in Clifton Fadiman, ed., *The Little, Brown Book of Anecdotes* (Boston: Little, Brown, 1985), pp. 475–476.

2. Thomas L. Means and Gary S. Klein, "A Short Classroom Unit, but a Significant Improvement, in Listening Ability," *Bulletin of the Association for Business Communication* 57 (1994): 13.

3. Dan B. Curtis, Jerry L. Winsor, and Ronald D. Stephens, "National Preferences in Business and Communication Education," *Communication Education* 38 (1989): 7–14.

4. Gary T. Hunt and Louis P. Cusella, "A Field Study of Listening Needs in Organizations," *Communication Education* 32 (1983): 399.

5. W. B. Legge, "Listening, Intelligence, and School Achievement," in *Listening: Readings,* ed. S. Duker (Metuchen, N.J.: Scarecrow Press, 1971), pp. 121–133.

6. Some material for this section was synthesized from William B. Gudykunst, Stella Ting-Toomey, Sandra Sudweeks, and Lea P. Stewart, *Building Bridges: Interpersonal Skills for a Changing World* (Boston: Houghton Mifflin, 1995), pp. 228–229.

7. L. Barker et al., "An Investigation of Proportional Time Spent in Various Communication Activities by College Students," *Journal of Applied Communication Research* 8 (1980): 101–109; and Walter Pauk, *How to Study in College,* 4th ed. (Boston: Houghton Mifflin, 1989), pp. 121–133.

8. Richard Bruce Hyde, "Council: Using a Talking Stick to Teach Listening," *Speech Communication Teacher* (Winter 1993): 1–2.

9. Donal Carbaugh, "'Just Listen': 'Listening' and Landscape Among the Blackfeet," *Western Journal of Communication* 63 (1999): 250–270.

10. Luther Standing Bear, Oglala Sioux chief, cited in *Native American Wisdom: Photographs by Edward S. Curtis* (Philadelphia: Running Press, 1993), pp. 58–59.

11. Ronald B. Adler and George Rodman, *Understanding Human* Communication, 5th ed. (Fort Worth, Tex.: Harcourt Brace, 1994), p. 130.

12. C. Glenn Pearce, "Learning How to Listen Empathically," *Supervisory Management* 36 (1991): 11.

13. John Stewart and Carole Logan, "Empathic and Dialogic Listening," in *Bridges Not Walls: A Book About Interpersonal Communication,* ed. John Stewart, 7th ed. (New York: McGraw-Hill, 1999), p. 227.

14. Adapted from Dave Ellis, *Becoming a Master Student,* 7th ed. (Boston: Houghton Mifflin, 1994), pp. 136–150: and Pauk, pp. 136–161.

15. Andrew D. Wolvin and Carolyn Gwynn Coakley, *Listening,* 2nd ed. (Dubuque, Iowa: William C. Brown, 1985), p. 177.

16. Larry Barker and Kittie Watson, *Listen Up* (New York: St. Martin's Press, 2000), p. 33.

17. William F. Buckley Jr., "Has TV Killed Off Great Oratory?" *TV Guide,* 12 Feb. 1983, p. 38.

18. L. R. Wheeless, "An Investigation of Receiver Apprehension and Social Context Dimensions of Communication Apprehension," *Speech Teacher* 24 (1975): 263.

19. Joe Ayres, A. Kathleen Wilcox, and Debbie M. Ayres, "Receiver Apprehension: An Explanatory Model and Accompanying Research," *Communication Education* 44 (1995): 223–235. Also see Michael J. Beatty, "Receiver Apprehension as a Function of Cognitive Backlog," *Western Journal of Speech Communication* 45 (1981): 277–281; Michael J. Beatty and Steven K. Payne, "Receiver Apprehension and Cognitive Complexity," *Western Journal of Speech Communication* 45 (1981): 363–369; and Raymond W. Preiss, Lawrence R. Wheeless, and Mike Allen, "Potential Cognitive Processes and Consequences of Receiver Apprehension: A Meta-analytic Review," *Journal of Social Behavior and Personality* 5 (1990): 155–172.

20. C. V. Roberts, "A Validation of the Watson-Barker Listening Test," *Communication Research Reports* 3 (1986): 115–119.

21. Anthony J. Clark may have indicated indirectly the value of such exercises when he demonstrated a positive relationship between communication confidence and listening comprehension in "Communication Confidence and Listening Competence: An Investigation of the Relationships of Willingness to Communicate, Communication Apprehension, and Receiver Apprehension to Comprehension of Content and Emotional Meaning in Spoken Messages," *Communication Education* 38 (1989): 237–248.

22. Richard M. Weaver, "Ultimate Terms in Contemporary Rhetoric," in *Language Is Sermonic: Richard M. Weaver on the Nature of Rhetoric,* ed. Richard L. Johannesen, Rennard Strickland, and Ralph T. Eubanks (Baton Rouge: Louisiana State University Press, 1970), p. 95.

23. Professor Halley discussed this "Triggering Stimuli Assignment" on the web site of the International Listening Association, www.listen.org, (4 Aug. 1998)

24. J. J. Makay and W. R. Brown, *The Rhetorical Dialogue: Contemporary Concepts and Cases* (Dubuque, Iowa: William C. Brown, 1972), pp. 125–145.

25. John Chaffee, *Thinking Critically,* 2nd ed. (Boston: Houghton Mifflin, 1988), p. 59.

26. "Britain Admits That Much of Its Report on Iraq Came from Magazines," New York Times (International), 8 Feb. 2003. http://www.nytimes.com/2003/02/08/international/europe/08BRIT.html?th. (21 Aug. 2003).

27. "Investigating the President: Media Madness?" transcript of a special report on CNN, 28 Jan. 1998.

28. *Time,* 18 Dec. 1989, cover.

29. Jim Motavalli, "In Memory of Colette," *E: The Environmental Magazine,* May/June 1994, pp. 30–31.

30. Waldo Braden, "The Available Means of Persuasion: What Shall We Do About the Demand for Snake Oil?" in *The Rhetoric of Our Times,* ed. J. Jeffery Auer (New York: Appleton-Century-Crofts, 1969), pp. 178–184.

31. Answers to application item #2: 1-?, 2-T, 3-?, 4-?, 5-?, 6-?, 7-?, 8-T.

Preparation for Public Speaking

PART II

5 Adapting to Your Audience and Situation

This chapter will help you

- understand audience dynamics
- adapt your message to fit your audience
- meet the challenges of audience diversity
- adjust your message to the speaking situation

OUTLINE

Orators have to learn the differences of human souls.

PLATO

It's the beginning of the fall term, and the president of Students for Environmental Action (SEA) has a busy day ahead. At eight o'clock in the morning she will address students assembled in the field house in hopes of recruiting new members. That same afternoon, she will speak to the Decatur County Industrial Development Board to tell them about SEA's plans for the year. She wants to reassure them that the group's work will help and not hurt businesses in the area.

The general topic of this student's speeches will not change, but the two audiences and situations will require different approaches. Her listeners must be at the center of her thinking as she plans and develops her speeches. Moreover, the setting for these speeches can make a big difference in how she presents them. Her manner of presentation, as well as the language she chooses, will vary from the field house to the boardroom.

This chapter begins with a basic assumption: *The more you know about your audience and speaking situation, the more effective your speech will be.* As a public speaker, you become a serious student of audiences. A good audience analysis will help you determine what your listeners may already know about your topic, what they need to know, and how they feel about it. Your audience analysis can also help you select the most effective supporting materials, decide on the design and structure of your speech, and choose the best techniques to help listeners understand and relate to your topic.

You may question the ethics of adapting a message to fit a particular audience. Many of us have encountered speakers who "waffled"—taking one position with one audience and a different position with another. Such maneuvering is clearly unethical. But you can adapt to your audience without changing the essence of your message or surrendering your convictions. You can ethically adapt your message to a given audience in terms of the language you use, the examples you provide, the stories you tell, the authorities you cite, and your manner of presentation. Ask yourself: "*How can I tailor my message so that I can reach my audience without compromising my convictions?*" This chapter should help you answer this question.

To help you better understand your audience, we will first consider *audience dynamics,* the motivations, attitudes, and values of listeners. Second, we cover the potential impact of *demographic factors,* such as age, political and religious preferences, and gender. Next, we will discuss some of the major challenges speakers face when addressing a *diverse audience.* Finally, we will consider those aspects of the *communication situation* that may call for adaptations in your presentation.

Adapting to Audience Dynamics

Go to **Lesson 2's Screening Room.** Watch the student speech and answer the questions in **Drill 2.1: Identifying Audience Centeredness.** VideoLab

Audience dynamics are the motivations, attitudes, beliefs, and values that affect how listeners receive a message. An understanding of how these dynamics work is central to understanding your audience. The more you understand what makes people tick, the better you can tailor your message so that it serves their interests and needs.

Motivation

Our needs and wants make up our **motivation,** the force that draws our attention to certain things and makes us act in certain ways. Motivation helps explain *why* people behave as they do.[1] Therefore, motivation is important to both persuasive and informative speeches. *People will listen, learn, and remember a message only if it relates to their needs, wants, or wishes.* Understanding what motivates people can also help a speaker appeal to the common humanity in listeners that crosses cultural boundaries.

Motives can vary in importance according to the person, situation, and culture. *People are motivated by what they don't have that they need or want.* If you have recently moved to a new town, your need to make friends may attract you to places where you can meet others. Even when needs are satisfied, people still respond to wants. Suppose you have just eaten a very filling meal. You're not hungry, but if someone enters the room with a tray of freshly baked brownies, the sight and smell can make you want some.

The study of human motivation has an interesting history in twentieth-century psychology. Social scientists first concentrated on identifying different types of human motivation. In a pioneering study published during the 1930s, Henry A. Murray and his associates at the Harvard Psychological Clinic identified more than twenty-five different human needs.[2]

To understand more about your audience and their needs, go to **VideoLab Next Step: Identifying Universal Listener Needs** and complete the exercises. VideoLab

The late psychologist Abraham Maslow popularized the study of human needs by arranging them in a five-tiered hierarchy of potency (see Figure 5.1).[3] According to Maslow the lower-level needs (physiological and safety/security) must be satisfied to

Figure 5.1
Maslow's Hierarchy of Needs

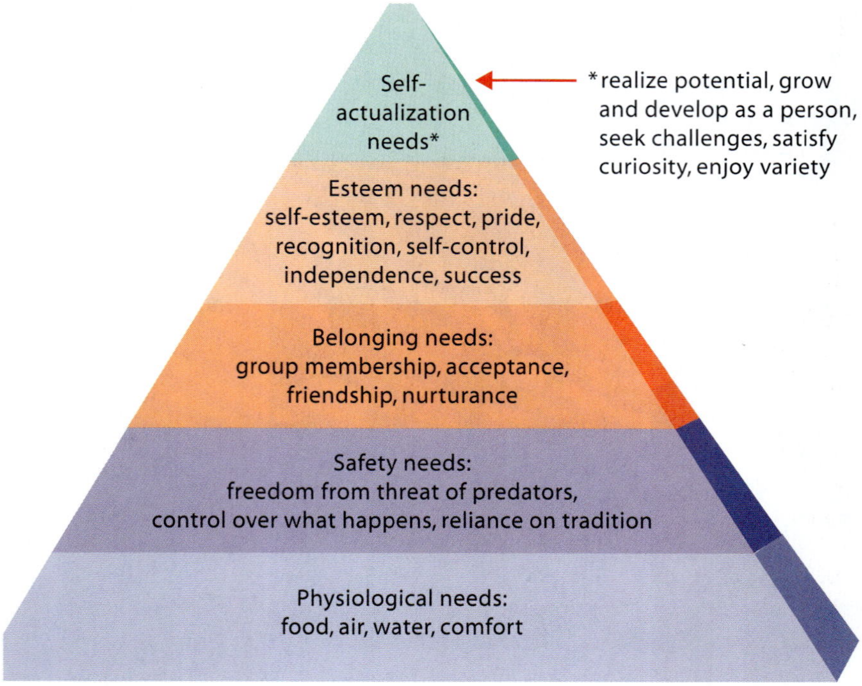

some reasonable degree before the higher-level needs (belonging, esteem, and self-actualization) come into play.

Physiological Needs. Maslow's most basic level contains our **physiological needs** for food, water, air, and comfort. When these needs are aroused, they can dominate behavior. This explains why speeches about healthy food to eat, clear air to breathe, and pure water to drink usually get the attention of listeners. In a class that met right before lunchtime, Hannah Johnston opened her speech in the following way:

> **What would you say if I asked you if you've ever eaten spinal cord? You'd probably think I was crazy, wouldn't you? But what if I asked you, "Have you ever eaten a fast food hamburger?" What's really crazy is that those two questions may be interchangeable.**

Hannah Johnston's introduction to her speech on fast foods tied her topic to the physical well-being of her listeners.

Hannah's descriptions of how meat is processed for the fast food industry had quite an impact. In fact, when she previewed her ideas for her informative speech during a topic briefing (see the text at the end of Chapter 6), one of her classmates asked to be excused from listening to it. "I eat this stuff all the time and I don't want to hear more about it!" he complained. Hannah's message had obviously gotten to him. If you can show listeners that your topic affects their physical well-being or will help satisfy their need for comfort, you'll have most of them listening closely.

Speech topics such as "Global Warming, or, Who Turned Up the World's Thermostat?" or "Is Our Water Really Safe to Drink?" would also work at this level of motivation.

Safety Needs. At the second level in Maslow's hierarchy are our **safety needs**. We need to feel protected from harm, and we like some measure of order and predictability in our lives. This perhaps explains why Amanda Miller's audience listened so intently to her informative speech on Alzheimer's disease. Because this disease is so damaging and mysterious, it constitutes a grave threat to our safety. Although most of her listeners were not at the age of personal risk from this disease, they did have parents and grandparents who might be or become affected. Thus, Amanda's speech also crossed over onto the level of family concerns as well.

Although physical safety often dominates this need level, our need for psychological security is also an integral part of such motivation. When the terrorist threat level in our country is elevated, when we sense that crime is running rampant, or when we feel we have lost control over our lives, our safety needs come to the forefront. Speeches that appeal to such needs often arouse fear in the audience, and fear-arousing appeals can be very effective. But if the fear appeals you use are too obvious or heavy-handed, listeners may feel that they are being manipulated, and they may reject both you and your message. Listeners can also resent it if you arouse fear without showing them how they can avoid the danger. If you develop fear appeals, be sure to show listeners how they can protect themselves from the threat you describe.

Providing protection ties our needs for safety and security into our needs for understanding and control. Understanding something helps us control it. We feel less vulnerable if we know what we can do to prevent a disaster or if there are steps we can take to counteract its effects. For example, understanding the relationship between smoking and lung cancer and knowing the steps one can take to help smokers quit gives us a sense that we can control this serious health hazard.

There is a negative side to our need for control. We often resist attempts from others to manipulate us. In the classes we teach, we often hear speeches warning us about controllers. Cloning and genetic testing, as well as other forms of technology, could have dire as well as favorable consequences. The powerful forces of advertising, in the hands of the tobacco, firearms, or insurance industries, can turn control against us. Thus, the fear of control by others is often a powerful motivational appeal.

Belonging Needs. Most people are strongly moved to give and receive affection, companionship, approval, and support from others. All of these factors come together in our **belonging needs**. People value friendship and family ties. Friends and family help define who we are, warm us with affection, and make the world a less lonely place. The importance of these needs is demonstrated by the intense homesickness that many people develop when they move away from the support of family and friends. They may feel isolated, diminished, or uprooted and may even develop physical illnesses.

The need for close ties with others may explain our desire to affiliate with groups and take pride in memberships. We like being with those who share our backgrounds and values. This almost sacred sense of group values may explain the power of such speeches as Amanda Miller's attack on the School of the Americas, a training camp for military personnel from Central and South America. Amanda charged that our government's support for this school, which she described as "the biggest base for destabilization in Latin America," is a repudiation of our country's basic beliefs. By the end of her speech, many listeners shared her strong indignation over a policy that contradicted national values. This same sense of righteous indignation animates many speakers today who criticize the legality of our country's treatment of suspects in the war on terrorism. In a more positive sense, this dynamic of group membership may also explain the underlying appeal of a form of proof we call *mythos*, which justifies plans of action by grounding them in the traditions and rituals of group membership. We will say more about mythos in Chapter 16.

In an era that advocates strengthening "family values," it is not surprising to hear speeches like Marie D'Aniello's tribute to her family (see text of speech at the end of Chapter 3). Our families give us a sense of roots—of cultural and personal history. It can be comforting to know that some things don't change. In many families, Thanksgiving dinner is always turkey and dressing, sweet potatoes, cranberries, and pumpkin pie, and woe be unto to anyone who would change that routine!

In addition to friendship and support, we also have strong feelings about fairness, whether it is directed to us or to those around us. We envision an ideal moral balance in the world in which we deserve whatever happens to us, both good and bad. This can be a compelling theme in speeches that argue that homosexuals are not treated fairly in our society, that the disabled don't get a fair break, and that affirmative action ensures (or denies) fairness. Speakers may express outrage over human rights abuses around the world, over sexism in the workplace, or over our treatment of Native Americans. While these speeches often portray fairness as a dream denied, abused, or repudiated, they also highlight the importance of fairness in our lives.

Our strong feelings about fairness are linked to the powerful sense of **identification** we may feel with others. At its most idealistic, that sense of sharing the fate of others may link us to all other members of the human family, and also to other life forms. Thus, speakers can ask for reform by appealing to our sense of identification with women in Afghanistan, or with baby seals in Alaska.

Our needs for belonging are also related to our needs for nurturance and altruism. Although we may seem concerned primarily with ourselves, we also have strong needs to care for others. Protecting and comforting the helpless or those in need can make us feel good. Speeches describing the plight of the homeless, pointing out the problems faced by the disabled, urging listeners to become volunteers, or exhorting them to support the rights of marginalized groups all relate to this need. Helping others is a basic tenet of most religious groups, reflected, for example, in the Christian parable of the good Samaritan and in the Islamic injunction to help the needy.

Appeals to these motives can be especially strong when speakers discuss the problems of children. Toni Meredith's speech describing the effects of child abuse that she witnessed while working as a paramedic held the attention of her classroom audience. Other student speakers also engaged this strong impulse to nurture children by advocating educational reforms, promoting arts education, or describing programs for children at risk. In such speeches the central issue was always "Will this program help children develop into productive adults?" Figure 5.2 lists many of the motivational appeals that can be used in speeches.

Esteem Needs. Our **esteem needs** for self-respect, prestige, pride, success, and the respect of others are usually satisfied through accomplishments, praise, and recognition. The need for success or achievement is one of the most thoroughly studied human motives.[4] Although winning may not be everything, most of us feel that losing doesn't have much to recommend it. Self-help books glut the market. Speeches that show your audience how they can improve themselves and enhance their chances for success touch on this important need.

Ceremonial speeches that hold up a model of success for listeners to emulate can be quite inspiring. They can challenge audiences to set high goals for themselves, to work hard to achieve these goals, and to enjoy the fruits of their success. Ashlie McMillan inspired her classmates by her tribute to her cousin Tina, who is a diastrophic dwarf. Ashlie painted a picture of her cousin as a very short person with a very large personality. Tina, she said, is fiercely independent and has received undergraduate and graduate degrees from Texas Christian University. She is planning her wedding and enrolling in the University of Texas Law School. The implication was that if Tina, against all odds, can achieve her personal goals, then so could Ashlie's listeners.

The use of esteem needs in speeches often involves appeals to pride. Sometimes these appeals are cast in a positive sense, as when listeners are told that if they do what the speaker suggests they can be proud of themselves. Marie D'Aniello expressed her personal sense of self-esteem as she paid tribute to her father: "Because of him, I take pride in my work and I take pride in myself." As you achieve success in public speaking and develop confidence in your communication skills, you may notice an increase in your own self-esteem.

If we harbor any doubts about our esteem, recognition from others can reassure us. The need for recognition may lead us to place great value on awards and compliments as tangible symbols of success. Speakers utilize the need for esteem when they begin their speeches with positive comments about the audience in the introductions to their speeches. "It's always good to speak in Livingston," begins the guest speaker, "where artists and ranchers sit down together at Cattleman's bar." This technique is especially helpful when the speaker is not well known or is uncertain of acceptance. We discuss the use of this technique in greater detail in Chapter 9.

Self-Actualization Needs. The highest level of needs in the Maslow hierarchy are our **self-actualization needs** to develop our identities and realize our potential. When we self-actualize, we strive to fulfill our potential for growth. As she described

Figure 5.2

Motivational Appeals for Use in Speeches

Comfort	Having enough to eat and drink; keeping warm when it's cold and cool when it's hot; being free from pain
Safety/Security	Feeling safe in your surroundings; protected from crime, pollution, accidents, natural disasters, and terrorism; having a sense of stability and order in your life
Control	Determining your own destiny; planning for the future; fixing things; influencing others; resisting control and manipulation; controlling your environment
Tradition	Having a sense of roots; having a feeling of continuity with the past; doing things as they have always been done; honoring your forebears; appreciating your history
Friendship	Establishing warm relations with others; being a member of a group or organization; being accepted by others; having someone to love and be loved by
Nurturance	Taking care of others; comforting those in distress; aiding the helpless; caring for animals; giving to charities; providing volunteer service; promoting the well-being of others
Fairness	Trying to establish or restore moral balance in the world so that people get the treatment they deserve
Recognition	Being treated as valuable and important; having your achievements praised by others; receiving trophies or awards; being the center of attention
Achievement	Accomplishing something of significance; overcoming obstacles to achieve your goals; doing better than expected; reaching the pinnacle of your profession
Independence	Being able to stand on your own; being self-sufficient; making your own decisions on important matters; being your own person
Variety	Longing for adventure; visiting new and unusual places; trying different things; changing majors; changing jobs; moving to a new location; meeting new people
Curiosity	Understanding the world around you; understanding yourself; understanding others; questioning why things happen or why people act as they do; exploring the unusual
Enjoyment	Doing something just for the fun of it; taking a vacation; pampering yourself; pursuing a hobby

the long journey of her development from a novice shooter on her high school rifle team to an Olympic hopeful on the U.S. National team, Beth Tidmore revealed her own self-actualization:

> **There's a bumper sticker that says, "A Lady with a Gun Has More Fun." Well, I have had so much fun. I've been all over the U.S., I've been to matches everywhere, I've won medals, I've been to World Cups and met people from all over the world. And I've experienced so much through my participation in shooting sports. My mother, who bought me my first tournament-grade rifle, once told me: "When you picked up that gun, you just looked like you belonged**

together. I knew there was a sparkle in your eye, and I knew that you were meant to do great things with that rifle."

Her audience listened avidly, because self-actualizing people often become models for others. We can apply lessons that worked for them to the challenges of our own lives. Moreover, whenever speakers indicate how their messages might enrich our lives and help us fulfill our potential, they enjoy our total attention. Self-actualization needs often manifest themselves when speakers tap into our attraction to independence, change, curiosity, and enjoyment.

Independence. Although we need other people, we also need independence. This desire to feel that we are masters of our own fate is strongly embedded in the American culture. For example, the idea that we can pull ourselves up by our own hard work is deeply engrained in our mythology. Ours is the land of opportunity, but to grasp our chance we need to assert our independence.

This need is especially strong in young adults who are in the process of finding themselves. The quest for independence allows young people to develop into fully functioning adults, to make decisions on their own, and to take responsibility for their own lives. Consequently, college audiences may be especially responsive to the need for freedom from arbitrary constraints on their ideas, actions, or lifestyles.

Change. One way that people discover their personal identities is through experimenting and exploring their options. Our need for change or variety may manifest itself as a longing for adventure, a desire to do something different and exciting, or a yen to travel to exotic places or to meet new and interesting people. Offer listeners something different, a topic out of the ordinary or a different point of view on a familiar subject, and you will be rewarded with their attention.

One of the more interesting such speeches we have heard in class recently was offered by Brandon Rader on gender bending, that is, public dress and behavior that appears more appropriate to the opposite sex. Brandon's argument was that gender is a social construct that has been subject to great variation over time and culture. Our expectations for how men and women are supposed to behave are not engraved somewhere in stone. The overall effect of his argument was to create more space for gender benders to explore the potential of their lives without earning social disdain.

Curiosity. One of the most popular series of children's books chronicles the exploits of Curious George, who sets out to explore the world around him. People are by nature curious. They want to know, "What is it?" "How does it work?" "Why is this happening?" When we satisfy curiosity, we increase our understanding of the world and the people around us. Expanding knowledge is an important part of self-actualization.

According to a group of prominent psychologists, we are likely to seek the causes of highly unusual or unpleasant events or anything that creates doubt about the future.[5] We may be drawn to the scene of a fire or to television coverage of catastrophes, not because we enjoy seeing people suffer, but because we are curious about such events. Speech topics that are unusual or that explain the causes of important events or behaviors may appeal to this need.

Enjoyment. There is an important "play instinct" in humans that may fuel our need to enjoy ourselves. For Hannah Johnston, constantly striving to improve while depriving herself of enjoyment had become a tiresome obsession. As she introduced herself, Hannah shared the theme of her life with listeners:

I thought about all the years I'd spent trying to please other people and how it never really made me happy. . . . You don't have to be the best just to enjoy yourself. . . . *As long as I'm happy*—that's my motto.

InterConnections.LearnMore 5.1

Audience Dynamics

Motivation
http://psychclassics.yorku.ca/Maslow/motivation.htm
A reprint of Maslow's original article, "A Theory of Human Motivation," setting forth his theory of motivation. The essay was originally published in Psychology Review *in 1943.*

Values
http://www.zetterberg.org/Papers/ppr1997b.htm
"The Study of Values," an article that covers a variety of approaches to the study of human values, by Professor Hans L. Zetterberg, sociologist and director of the Social Research Consulting Group in Stockholm, Sweden.

Attitudes
http://www.mdcc.edu/users/jmcnair/Joe5pages/-Attitude.htm
A basic discussion of how attitudes are formed and how they function. Developed and maintained by Professor Joseph D. McNair, School of Education, Miami-Dade Community College.

As Hannah had discovered, all work and no play will make Jill about as dull as Jack. College students who find themselves inundated with tests and papers and speeches to prepare, not to mention full-time or part-time jobs, are particularly aware of the need for enjoyment. If you can show listeners how to put some fun into their lives, you can gain and hold their attention.

Attitude Systems

The following was overheard at a nearby table at the student union:

"Where are you going this summer?"

"Back to New Mexico. I just love the Navajo and the Four Corners area."

"Really? What makes them so special?"

"They've just got it all together. Take the weavers, for example. They don't just make rugs. In Navajo weaving, the souls of the weavers enter into their rugs."

"Wow! That's heavy."

"Yes, I like their whole outlook. Navajo want to live a life dedicated to harmony and inner peace. The way they put it: they want to 'walk in beauty' among all the disruptive forces of life."

"Walk in beauty . . ."

"Yes. What an affirmation!"

This conversation illustrates that the motives driving our behavior often express themselves in three important ways: through *attitudes*, beliefs, and *values*. These three elements, which form our **attitude system**, incline us to act in certain ways unless the system changes. Therefore, speakers must deal with attitude systems: informative speakers operate within their boundaries, ceremonial speakers celebrate and reinforce them, and persuasive speakers try to change or adjust them, or apply them to controversial subjects. To be effective speakers, we must understand attitude systems better.

Attitudes. **Attitudes** are based on our feelings—whether we like or dislike, approve or disapprove of objects, people, events, or ideas—and how we are inclined to act toward them.[6] "I just love the Navajo and the Four Corners area" illustrates an attitude. Attitudes tend to be concrete and specific. They may be quite intense, but they can fade as our interests and concerns change. They can be unreflective: sometimes we know we have them, but we're not quite sure why. Perhaps we adopted them because most of our family or friends have them. They can express positive feelings, as the previous example illustrates, but they can also express racial, gender, or ethnic prejudice.

The good news is that of beliefs, attitudes, and values, attitudes are most susceptible to change. Speakers can sometimes refute and correct them, if they present a case built on sufficient evidence and sound reasoning. Moreover, if speakers can demonstrate that attitudes are inconsistent with beliefs and values, they may convince listeners to change. All of us seek *balance* within our attitude systems: we want our attitudes, beliefs, and values to be consistent with one another.

Beliefs. **Beliefs** are what we know or think we know about subjects, and reflect what we think is true about our experiences We often express them when we are

Figure 5.3

Attitude System

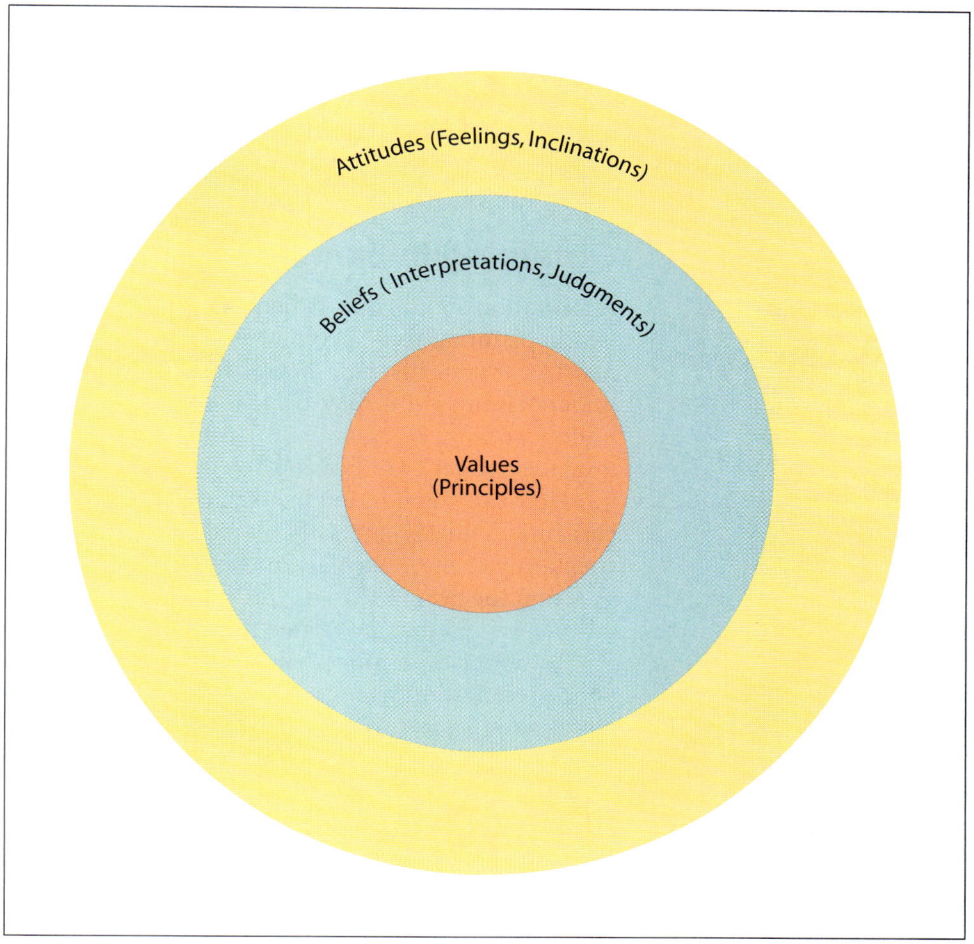

asked to explain our attitudes. In the overheard conversation, the expressed belief supports the speaker's attitude toward Navajos: "Weavers don't just make rugs. In Navajo weaving, the souls of the weavers enter into their rugs." Although more stable and enduring than attitudes, beliefs are still susceptible to change and accessible to influence. They can be influenced if we can show that they are inconsistent with audience values. For example, appeals to people to give up their prejudices about certain groups of "others" might work if we can show that such beliefs are not consistent with deeper political or religious values.

Values. Our more important attitudes and beliefs are anchored by our **values**, how we think we should behave or what we regard as an ideal state of being. Our values influence the attitudes we form and the beliefs we develop. Often values rise to the surface when audience members question the basis of our beliefs. In the overheard conversation, the explanation that Navajos "live a life dedicated to harmony and inner peace" and that they seek "to walk in beauty" are value statements that justify the speaker's admiration for a way of life.

Values are at the core of our identity. As principles that govern our behavior and our way of seeing the world, they are the most stable element in the system, the most resistant to change. Speakers don't normally try to change values; rather, they try to show how values relate to a topic in order to justify certain interpretations and recommendations.

With young people, who may be in the process of exploring and forming their identities, values themselves may be more amenable to influence. Part of the benefit of your college experience is that you can explore value options and select among them as you construct your self-identity. When people have not yet formed a clear set of values, their beliefs and attitudes will also be less stable and more susceptible to change. But these people will also be more vulnerable to counterpersuaders, speakers who present the other sides of issues. These three elements of the Attitude System are shown in Figure 5.3.

Obtaining Information About Attitude Systems

Go to **VideoLab Lesson 2's Next Step: Building an Audience Survey** and complete the exercise to learn more about creating your own audience survey.

Information about your audience's attitudes, beliefs, and values is obviously important in planning your speeches, especially your persuasive speeches (see Chapters 15 and 16). If your listeners' beliefs are based on incomplete information or a lack of understanding, you may be able to provide new information to improve their understanding. Being aware of audience attitudes can suggest what strategies you might use to get a fair hearing.

How can you find out in advance about your audience's attitude systems? In the classroom, this is not difficult because people reveal this kind of information constantly as they take part in class discussions. Outside the classroom, you might question the person who invites you to speak about those aspects of the audience's attitude system that are related to your topic.

To understand more fully how your audience's attitude systems may relate to your presentation, you can conduct a survey to explore what your listeners know about your topic, how they feel about it, and how they might respond to different sources of information. Figure 5.4 shows a sample audience survey questionnaire on the subject of capital punishment that may be used as a guide to developing a questionnaire on your subject.

When preparing an attitude survey questionnaire, you should use the following guidelines:

- Use simple sentences with a single idea.
- Use clear, concrete language.
- Keep questions short.
- Avoid words such as *all, always, none,* and *never.*
- Keep your own biases out of the questions.
- Keep the questionnaire short
- Provide room for comments.

After you conduct your audience analysis, go to the **Assessing your Audience** worksheet under **Audience Analysis** in the Online Speech-Studio.

Go to http://college.hmco.com/eduspace/

Finally, you should keep in mind that any questionnaire results you get, either from one you conduct yourself or from one that is professionally administered, provide only a general idea of where your audience stands on a topic. Compare what you learn from a questionnaire with what you hear as you listen to others talking about the issue in question.

Adjusting to Audience Demographics

How people feel about subjects is often affected by their age, gender, education, group affiliations, and sociocultural background. Such factors are called **audience demographics**. Demographic analyses are often used in marketing and political campaigns to identify important attitudes, preferences, or concerns across a general population or a particular target audience for a product. In the classroom, demographic information can help you estimate interest in your topic and how much

For each question, please circle the number that most clearly represents your position.

1. How interested are you in the topic of capital punishment?

Very Interested			Unconcerned			Not Interested
7	**6**	**5**	**4**	**3**	**2**	**1**

2. How important do you think the issue of capital punishment is?

Very Important			No Opinion			Very Unimportant
7	**6**	**5**	**4**	**3**	**2**	**1**

3. How much do you know about capital punishment?

Very Little			Average Amount			Very Much
7	**6**	**5**	**4**	**3**	**2**	**1**

4. How would you describe your attitude toward capital punishment?

Total Opposition			"On the Fence"			Total Support
7	**6**	**5**	**4**	**3**	**2**	**1**

5. Please place a check beside the sources of information on capital punishment that you would find the most acceptable.

_____ Attorney general's office
_____ FBI
_____ Local police department
_____ Criminal justice department of the university
_____ American Civil Liberties Union
_____ Local religious leaders
_____ Conference of Christians and Jews
_____ NAACP
_____ Other (please specify) ______________________________

Comments:

Figure 5.4

Sample Attitude Questionnaire

For another sample survey questionnaire, go to the **Sample Audience Attitude Questionnaire** under **Audience Analysis** in the Online SpeechStudio.

Go to http://college.hmco.com/eduspace/

listeners may already know about it. Outside the classroom, the person who invites you to speak may be able to supply such information. When you combine knowledge about audience demographics with an understanding of audience dynamics, you can better understand how your listeners may feel about your subject, and how you might best motivate them.

The insights you can get from a demographic analysis of your audience can help you tailor an effective message. But where and how should you start such an analysis? We suggest that you begin with material from the Internet. InterConnections. LearnMore 5.2 contains a list of public opinion web sites that may be helpful as you plan your speeches. Most of these sites contain data from recent surveys across a wide variety of topics. Many of the sites include searchable archives of previous surveys, useful for tracing trends and drawing comparisons across time.

Public opinion information is also available in many popular print periodicals: *Harper's* magazine regularly includes "Harper's Index," a compilation of unusual and interesting statistics; *USA Today* provides tidbits of poll results on a daily basis. *U.S.*

To learn more about adapting your message to your audience, go to **VideoLab Drill 2.3: Personalizing Your Message for Your Audience.**

News & World Report publishes a page of vital statistics in each issue. During political campaigns, the network news shows mention poll results regularly. With a little effort and ingenuity, you can usually find the complete text of the poll either in hard copy or on the Internet.

Of special interest is that each winter the Higher Education Research Institute at UCLA releases the results of a national survey of first-year college student attitudes, available on the Internet at http://www.gseis.ucla.edu/heri/heri.html. Follow-up information on changes during the first year in college is also available through links on that site.

Several words of caution are needed when interpreting demographic data from such sources. First, most information on audience demographics—as well as information on attitudes and values—is gathered through surveys that rely on self-reports. In such surveys people tend to give "socially appropriate" responses to questions. This doesn't necessarily mean people are lying, just that they sometimes report what they "think they ought to say," or how they "think they ought to feel." Also be cautious about using information from "polls" that local television stations or Internet sites conduct. Such material is often not scientifically gathered and may simply reflect the feelings of those prompted to reply.

Finally, generic sources produce generic data. *Don't assume that what is true in general about a population will automatically be true about the particular twenty-five or so people who will be listening to your speeches.* Demographic analyses can supply you with a list of tendencies, but you must confirm whether this list applies to your listeners. We turn now to the various elements of audience demographics: age, gender, educational level, group affiliation, and sociocultural background.

Age

Age has been used to predict audience reactions since the time of Aristotle, who suggested that young listeners are pleasure loving, optimistic, impulsive, trusting, idealistic, and easily persuaded. Older people, he said, are more set in their ways, more skeptical, cynical, and concerned with maintaining a comfortable existence. Those in the prime of life, Aristotle argued, present a balance between youth and age, being confident yet cautious, judging cases by the facts, and taking all things in moderation.[7]

Contemporary communication research supports the relationship between age and persuasibility that Aristotle identified. Maximum susceptibility to persuasion occurs during childhood and declines as people grow older. Most research also suggests that younger people are more flexible and open to new ideas and that older people tend to be more conservative and less receptive to change. Some recent research, however, suggests that older adults may be more willing to change than previously thought.[8] You can change the minds of older adults, but you'll have to work harder to do it.

Age can be an important factor in the selection of speech topics. For example, an audience consisting mainly of eighteen- and nineteen-year-olds might be interested in a speech on campus social activities. To an older audience, this topic could seem trivial or uninteresting. Age can also be important in terms of the language you use and the people, places, things, or events you refer to in your speeches.

Gender

In the 1950s, *Life* magazine interviewed five male psychiatrists, who suggested that women's ambitions were the "root of mental illness in wives, emotional upset in husbands, and homosexuality in boys."[9] Needless to say, we have come a long way from that era!

In our time, ideas about gender differences continue to change rapidly. The changes are especially marked in the areas of "gender appropriate" roles and interests, where the lines are becoming blurred. Some of the greatest changes in gender roles have come in the areas of education and work. In 1950, only 24 percent of all college degrees went to women; in 2001 women earned 57 percent of all degrees awarded.[10] In 1960, 38 percent of females between the ages of twenty-five and fifty-four were in the labor force; by 1998, this was up to 60 percent.[11] Between 1995 and 2000, the number of females in corporate officer positions of *Fortune* 500 companies rose from 5 percent to 10 percent.[12]

Given such changes, we would suggest great caution in making any adjustments based on the gender of your listeners.[13] Be certain that any assumptions you make are based on the most current data available, because the differences are often a matter of "now you see them, now you don't." Differences that seem true even as we write may be outdated by the time you read this text. Finally, be especially careful to avoid sexism and gender stereotyping. These two topics are covered in detail later in this chapter.

Educational Level

You can better estimate your listeners' knowledge of and interest in a topic from their educational level than from their age or gender. The more educated your audience, the more you can assume they know about general topics and current affairs, and the broader their range of interests is apt to be. Research suggests that better-educated audiences are more interested in social, consumer, political, and environmental issues. They are more curious, and they enjoy learning about new ideas, new things, and new places. If your speech presents a fresh perspective on a problem, they should be avid listeners. Finally, better-educated audiences tend to be more open-minded. They are more accepting of social and technological changes, and more supportive of women's rights and alternative lifestyles than are less educated listeners.[14]

Educational differences can also affect the strategies you use in a speech. For example, if there are several positions on an issue, you should assume that a better-educated audience will be aware of them. Therefore, you should be especially careful to acknowledge alternative viewpoints and to explain why you have selected your position.[15] Although you should always speak from responsible knowledge, knowing that your listeners are highly educated places even more pressure on you to prepare carefully. A well-educated audience will require that you supply evidence and examples that can stand up under close scrutiny. If you are not well prepared, such listeners will question your credibility.

InterConnections.LearnMore 5.2

Demographics on the Web

VALS
http://www.sric-bi.com/VALS/
A marketing research site that combines demographic and values data to classify people into clusters or types. Take the online survey and get immediate feedback on where you fit into the VALS typology.

Pew Research Center
http://www.people-press.org
A reputable political ideology research group that is often cited during political campaigns. Current poll results and commentary available online.

Gallup Organization
http://www.gallup.com
One of the oldest and most well known of the polling organizations. Gallup's web site contains an archive of past polls. You can sign up for a weekly briefing via your email.

National Opinion Research Center
http://www.norc.uchicago.edu
NORC is a nonprofit organization affiliated with the University of Chicago that conducts survey research to help policymakers, researchers, educators, and others address crucial public issues. Summary reports of major studies are available online.

American Demographics
http://www.demographics.com
The online edition of a major marketing magazine, containing a variety of articles and other interesting information useful to marketers and speechmakers.

The Roper Center for Public Opinion Research
http://www.ropercenter.uconn.edu/
This nonprofit, nonpartisan public opinion data archive affiliated with the University of Connecticut houses what they claim is the largest public opinion library available to researchers and others interested in the public voice. It also contains polls conducted in seventy foreign countries.

The Polling Report
http://www.pollingreport.com
This online service provides copies of polling reports from a variety of American public opinion polls.

Group Affiliations

The groups people belong to reflect their interests, attitudes, and values. Knowing the occupations, political preferences, religious affiliations, and social group memberships of an audience can provide useful information. This knowledge can help you design a speech that better fits the interests and needs of your listeners. It can make your message more relevant, and can help promote identification between listeners and your ideas.

Occupational Groups. Knowing your listeners' occupational affiliations, or perhaps in the case of your classmates their career aspirations, can provide insight into how much your listeners know about a topic, what type of vocabulary you should use, and which aspects of a topic should be most interesting to them. For example, speeches on tax-saving techniques given to professional writers and then to certified public accountants should not have the same focus or use the same language. With the writers, you might stress record keeping and business deductions and avoid using technical jargon. With the CPAs, you might concentrate on factors that invite audits by the IRS, and you would not have to be so concerned about translating technical terms into lay language. Knowledge of listeners' occupations also suggests the kinds of examples you may wish to provide and the authorities listeners will find most credible. If many of your classmates are business majors, for instance, they may place more credence in information drawn from the *Wall Street Journal* than from *USA Today.*

Political Groups. Members of organized political groups tend to be interested in problems of public life. Knowing how interested in politics your listeners are and their political party preferences can be useful in planning and preparing your speech.[16]

As she planned her speech attacking the U.S.-sponsored School of the Americas as a hotbed of ultra-right subversion in the Western hemisphere, Amanda Miller faced a considerable problem. Her audience analysis revealed that many of her listeners described themselves as conservative Republicans. If they sensed that she spoke as a left-oriented critic, they might dismiss her arguments as exaggerated and unwarranted. Therefore, Amanda decided on the following opening to her speech:

"If any government sponsors the outlaws and killers of innocents, they have become outlaws and murderers themselves, and they will take that lonely path at their own peril." President Bush spoke these words to the world, shortly after the attacks on the World Trade Towers.

By citing a person who was revered by many of her listeners, Amanda

Amanda Miller's speech attacking the School for the Americas was adapted to the political affiliations of her audience.

invited them to look into an ironic mirror: once they knew what many graduates of the School of the Americas had actually done, they could only conclude that the United States was the kind of rogue government the president had described. Her speech had a powerful impact that day because of the way she adapted it to the political affiliations of her audience.

People with strong political ties usually make their feelings known. Some of your classmates may be members of the Young Democrats or Young Republicans. Your college may conduct mock elections or take straw votes on issues of political interest, reporting the results in the campus newspaper. Be on the alert for such information.

Religious Groups. Knowing the religious affiliations of listeners can provide useful information, because religious training often underlies many of our social and cultural attitudes and values. Members of fundamentalist religious groups are likely to have conservative social and political attitudes. Baptists tend to be more conservative than Episcopalians, who in turn are often more conservative than Unitarians. In addition, a denomination may advocate specific beliefs that many of its members accept as a part of their religious heritage.

A word of caution needs to be added here. You can't always assume that because an individual is a member of a particular religious group he or she will embrace all of the teachings of that group. One thing you can count on, however, is that audiences are usually quite sensitive concerning topics related to their religious convictions. As a speaker, you should be aware of this sensitivity and be attuned to the religious makeup of your audience. Appealing to "Christian" values before an audience that includes members of other religious groups may offend listeners and diminish the effectiveness of your message. The classroom audience of today is likely to be made up of students from different religious backgrounds. Since religious affiliation may be a strong indicator of values, it is wise not to ignore its potential importance.

Knowing the group affiliations of your listeners could help you adapt your message to their interests, concerns, and needs.

Social Groups. Typically, we are born into a religious group, raised in a certain political environment, and end up in an occupation as much by chance as by design. But we choose our social groups on the basis of our interests. Membership in social groups can be as important to people as any other kind of affiliation. Photographers join the Film Club, businesspeople become involved with the Chamber of Commerce, and environmentalists may be members of the Sierra Club.

Knowing which social groups are represented in your audience and what they stand for is important for effective audience adaptation. A speech favoring pollution control measures might take a different focus, depending on whether it is presented to the Chamber of Commerce or to the Audubon Society. With the Chamber of Commerce, you might stress the importance of a clean environment in inducing businesses to relocate in your community; with the Audubon Society, you might emphasize the effects of pollution on wildlife. People tend to make their important group memberships known to others around them. Be alert to such information from your classmates, and consider it in planning and preparing your speeches.

Sociocultural Background. People often are grouped by sociocultural background, a broad category that can include everything from the section of the country in which they live to their racial or ethnic identity. The web sites listed at the end of this chapter provide access to a wide array of resources and information relevant to a variety of sociocultural groups. Although such material may be fascinating, it is *your* audience for *your* speech that is important.

People from different sociocultural backgrounds often have different experiences, interests, and ways of looking at things. Consider, for example, the different perspectives that urban and rural audiences may have on gun control. Urban audiences may associate guns with crime and violence in the streets, and rural audiences may associate guns with hunting and recreation. A white, middle-class audience might have difficulty understanding what it means to grow up as a member of a minority. Midwesterners and Southerners may have misconceptions about each other.

With diverse audiences, your appeals and examples should relate to those experiences, feelings, values, and motivations that people hold in common. It also may be helpful to envision smaller audiences within the larger group. You may even want to direct specific remarks to these smaller groups. You might say, for example, "Those of you majoring in the liberal arts will find computer skills just as important in your work as they are for business majors," or "Those of you majoring in business may discover that large corporations are looking for employees with the breadth of perspective that comes from a liberal arts education." Direct references to specific subgroups within the audience can keep your speech from seeming too general.

The "Average" College Audience

Given the incredible diversity we have described among those who come to the nation's colleges and universities each year, you may well question whether there is such a thing as an "average" audience for your speeches. Although this skepticism is understandable, a generic portrait of today's college student nevertheless emerges from the various demographic databases we have surveyed. Apply this portrait as a template to your particular listeners, and then correct it accordingly.

The most striking feature of today's college student is that he or she may be from one of various ethnic groups. The U.S. population in 2000 was 72 percent Caucasian, 12 percent African American, 11 percent Hispanic, 4 percent Asian American, and 1 percent Native American.[17] If you live on the East or West Coast or in the South, there is a high probability that your classmates will be ethnically very diverse.[18]

The average college student is also older than you might expect. In 2002, 39 percent of college students were over twenty-five.[19] If your classroom is typical, there will probably be more females than males in the class. In 2002, 8.7 million females were enrolled in college, compared with only 6.6 million males.[20]

What else do we know about today's college students? For starters, 75 percent of them live off campus, and 80 percent of them have paying jobs. In 2003, first-year students expressed more interest in political affairs than those in the recent past.[21] The annual survey of more than 275,000 first-year students conducted by the Higher Education Research Institute at UCLA also indicated that they describe themselves as politically moderate, liberal, and conservative in that order. Furthermore, reversing the trend of years of declining political involvement, the students feel that they can and should influence politics in this country.

The surveys also reveal that college students seem to go through a period of "culture shock" as they strike out on their own.[22] Many students, after receiving good grades in high school and expecting that trend to continue in college, are unpleasantly surprised to find that they are not doing as well as they had hoped. One reason may be that students are less engaged with their course work than they should be. Over a third of the students admitted to having turned in assignments that did not reflect their best work, and less than a third of the students spent more than ten hours a week studying or doing homework. Many of them spent more time socializing and partying in college than they did in high school.

Over one-third of first-year students also reported that they are frequently overwhelmed by all they have to do and feel lonely or homesick in their new environment. They are not volunteering or attending religious services as frequently as typical students from the past, even though they say that helping others who are in difficulty and integrating spirituality into their lives are important personal goals.

If your classmates gave introductory speeches or responded to one another in class, you should have a good idea of whether this template fits and how it should be adjusted. This will help you adapt your message to your listeners.

Meeting the Challenges of Audience Diversity

Learning to communicate with others from different backgrounds and cultures can be one of the most rewarding experiences of your public speaking class. To find out more about your own sociocultural background or about those of others, consult the relevant web sites listed at the end of this chapter. Again, keep in mind that the information you access relates to groups in general and not necessarily to your particular classmates.

To make the most of the opportunities of addressing diverse audiences, you must avoid certain pitfalls. You should understand the power of stereotypes and bias, and of the problematic "isms"—ethnocentrism, sexism, and racism. Finally, you should learn how to find and build common ground with your listeners.

Stereotypes and Bias

All of us use our past experiences to make sense of new information and to guide our interactions with others. To use our experiences efficiently, we react in terms of categories.[23] For example, having heard stories about poisonous reptiles, we may be leery of all snakes. Severe problems may arise, however, when we start categorizing people. The categories can harden into **stereotypes,** rigid sets of beliefs and expectations about people in a certain group that reflect our attitudes or biases toward the group.[24] When stereotypes dominate our thinking, we react more to them than to the people they represent. Wilma Mankiller, who served as principal chief of the Cherokee nation, offers a good idea of the practical problems posed by stereotypes:

> **Sometimes in Oklahoma, it's really discouraging to sit down with a group of people from different backgrounds and cultures and try to work on a common problem, whether it's education or economic development or whatever the problem is, because everybody's sitting around this table, and they're all looking at each other with stereotypes, and they can't get past that. It's like everybody's sitting there and they have some kind of veil over their face, and they look at each other through this veil that makes them see each other through some stereotypical kind of viewpoint. If we're ever gonna collectively begin to**

grapple with the problems that we have collectively, we're gonna have to move back the veil and deal with each other on a more human level.[25]

People often form stereotypes based on easily visible characteristics, such as gender, race, or age.[26] Stereotypes also may be related to ethnic identity, religion, occupation, or place of residence. We can form them from direct experiences with a few individuals who we assume are representative of a group. Most stereotypes, however, are learned indirectly from our families and friends, schools and churches, or media exposure. For example, our stereotype of Native Americans may come from exposure to Western movies, or our stereotype of West Virginians may be shaped by TV shows like *The Beverly Hillbillies.*

Whatever their origin, stereotypes can have a powerful influence on our thinking. We may judge people on the basis of stereotypes rather than on their merits as individuals. Stereotypes are also persistent: we are reluctant to give them up, especially when they agree with the stereotypes held by our friends and families. When we encounter people who do not fit our stereotypes, we may simply discount them as "exceptions to the rule." Beyond their obvious unfairness, stereotypes can also lead to disastrous consequences, such as the genocide that took place in Hitler's Germany.

Ethnocentrism, Sexism, and Racism

Ethnocentrism, sexism, and racism represent the most common types of problems that impede effective communication with a diverse audience.

Ethnocentrism. As we noted in Chapter 1, **ethnocentrism** is the belief that our way of life is the "right" and superior way. Actually, ethnocentrism is not always bad. In its milder form, ethnocentrism expresses itself in patriotism and national pride. It helps people unite and work toward common goals. It encourages immigrants to assimilate into a new national identity that provides common ground for living and getting along with one another.

But ethnocentrism has a darker side. Charles de Gaulle, who led the French people during the mid-twentieth century, once noted: "Patriotism is when love of your own people comes first; nationalism, when hate for people other than your own comes first."[27] When ethnocentrism goes beyond pride in one's own group and comes to include the rejection or derogation of others, it becomes a real problem in human relations and a barrier to communication.

The first step in controlling ethnocentrism is to recognize any tendencies you may have to overestimate your own and underestimate other cultures. For example, most Americans believe that over half of the world's population speak English, when actually only about 20 percent do so.[28] Our tendency to overvalue our own culture and ways of doing things, and then try to impose them on others, is one form of **imperialism**. An aggressive form of ethnocentrism, imperialism is usually resented by others. Its assumptions of superiority complicate the problems of communication, especially cross-cultural communication.

To overcome ethnocentrism and imperialism, *the language we use must respect the humanity in all people and recognize that this humanity transcends race and culture.* Former President Jimmy Carter, as he addressed the people of Cuba on Cuban state TV and radio during a visit to that country, put to rest the ghost of American imperialism as he offered these words:

I did not come here to interfere in Cuba's internal affairs, but to extend a hand of friendship to the Cuban people and to offer a vision of the future for our two countries and for all the Americas. That vision includes a Cuba

> **fully integrated into a democratic hemisphere, participating in a Free Trade Area of the Americas and with our citizens traveling without restraint to visit each other. I want a massive student exchange between our universities. I want the people of the United States and Cuba to share more than a love of baseball and wonderful music. I want us to be friends, and to respect each other.[29]**

Carter's vision expresses a wish for respectful equality to remedy the ills of ethnocentrism.

Sexism. **Sexism** occurs when we allow gender stereotypes to control our interactions with members of the opposite sex. **Gender stereotyping** involves making broad generalizations about men or women based on outmoded assumptions, such as, "Men don't know how to take care of children," or, "Women don't understand finances." Such attitudes transcend national boundaries and have been reported in over thirty countries in North and South America, Europe, Africa, Asia, and Australia.[30] Gender stereotyping is especially problematic when it implies that the differences between men and women justify discrimination.

As you plan and prepare your message, try to be aware of any gender stereotypes you might have that could interfere with effective communication. Be careful not to portray gender roles in ways suggesting superiority or inferiority. For instance, when you use examples or stories to illustrate a point, don't make all your authority figures male.

Gender stereotyping often reveals itself in the use of **sexist language**, which involves making gender references in situations in which the gender is unknown or irrelevant. It may involve the generic use of masculine nouns or pronouns, such as referring to "man's advances in science" or using *he* when the intended reference is to both sexes. You can avoid this problem simply by saying "she or he" or by using the plural *they.*

Some people have criticized this practice, saying that it makes the wording of messages awkward. They scoff at the seriousness of the problem. In her book on gender and communication, Julia Wood quotes the experience of a skeptical male student who suddenly found the situation reversed:

> **For a long time I thought all this stuff about generic *he* was a bunch of junk. I mean it seemed really clear to me that a word like *mankind* obviously includes women or that *chairman* can refer to a girl or a guy who chairs something. I thought it was pretty stupid to hassle about this. Then last semester, I had a woman teacher who taught the whole class using *she* or *her* or *woman* whenever she was referring to people as well as when she meant just women. I realized how confusing it is. I had to figure out each time whether she meant women only or women and men. And when she meant women to be general, I guess you'd say generic for all people, it still made me feel left out. A lot of the guys in the class got pretty hostile about what she was doing, but I kind of think it was a good way to make the point.[31]**

Such "reluctant testimony" seems conclusive: avoid the social disease of sexist language.

Racism. Just as gender stereotyping and sexist language can block communication, so also can racism. Although blatant racism and discrimination are no longer socially acceptable in most circles, a subtle form of such prejudice can still infect our thinking. Although we may pay lip service to the principles of racial equality, we may still engage in **symbolic racism**, which is expressed subtly or covertly.[32] For example, if we say, "In *our* neighborhood *we* believe in family values," the unspoken message may be, "*You* don't, and therefore *we* are superior." Or we might say, "*We* believe in hard work and earning *our* way," when we really mean, "Why don't *you* get off welfare?" Thus we may excuse the vestiges of racial stereotypes by appeals to values like family stability or the work ethic. In such cases, our underlying message may be, "*We* honor such values and *you* don't."

It may be helpful to view the impact that symbolic racism can have from the perspective of someone on the receiving end. Television commentator Bryant Gumbel described how it feels:

> **It is very hard for any white person to appreciate the depth of what it means to be black in America. . . . Racism isn't only being called a nigger and spit on. It's being flipped the bird when you're driving, or walking into a store and being asked to check your bag, or being ignored at the checkout counter, or entering a fine restaurant and being stared at.[33]**

As you take the factor of race into consideration in your audience analysis, examine your thinking for biases and stereotypes that you may rationalize as value or lifestyle differences. Be sensitive about the language you use. When you are referring to a different racial or ethnic group, use the terms members of that group prefer. Stay away from examples that cast members of a particular ethnic group into stereotypical roles that imply inferiority. And of course, avoid racist humor.

One language problem that relates to all three of these negative "isms" is **marking**, adding an irrelevant reference to gender, ethnicity, race, or sexual preference when none is needed. For example, if you referred to "Thompson, the Hispanic engineer," you might be trivializing her contribution by drawing attention to her ethnic backkground when it is irrelevant. Some audience members may interpret your remarks as suggesting that "Thompson fills our quota for Hispanic engineers," or "Thompson is a pretty good engineer for a minority person," whether you intend such implications or not. The following excerpt from a speech by Martina Navratilova, who was named the world's top-rated female tennis player for seven years, shows how marking affects people:

> **Labels, labels, labels—now, I don't know about you, but I hate labels. Martina Navratilova, the lesbian tennis player. They don't say Joe Montana, the heterosexual football player. One's sexuality should not be an issue. . . . I did not spend over 30 years of my life working my butt off trying to become the very best tennis player that I can be, to then be called Martina, the lesbian tennis player. Labels are for filing. Labels are for bookkeeping. Labels are for clothing. Labels are not for people.[34]**

Speaker's Notes 5.1

Avoiding Racist and Sexist Innuendos in Speeches

1. Do not use slang terms to refer to racial, ethnic, religious, or gender groups.
2. Avoid using the generic *he* and gender-specific titles such as *chairman*.
3. Avoid "markers" that introduce irrelevant references to race, gender, or ethnicity.
4. Avoid stereotypic references that imply inferiority or superiority.
5. Do not use sexist, racist, ethnic, or religious humor.

Finding Common Ground

Common values and interests can help bring groups together despite differences of age, gender, race, or ethnicity.

An ongoing study sponsored by the National Conference for Community and Justice (originally the National Conference of Christians and Jews) demonstrates that stereotypes and prejudice are present in all groups in our culture. Stereotypes of African, Asian, and Latino Americans are an obvious problem, but the survey also reveals that people of color see whites as "bigoted, bossy, and unwilling to share power."[35] Although each of the minority groups surveyed also demonstrates negative stereotypes of other people of color, they are united by a sense of being victims of discrimination. Some 80 percent of African Americans, 60 percent of Latino Americans, and 57 percent of Asian Americans are convinced that their opportunities in work, housing, and education are not equal to those enjoyed by whites. On the other hand, over 50 percent of all whites believe that people of color enjoy equal opportunities. The survey concluded that "most whites simply do not acknowledge the tangible effects that discrimination has on the daily lives of minorities."

Lest you think the situation is hopeless, we should also point out that there are some positive results in this research. More than 80 percent of all groups polled express admiration of Asian Americans for the value they presumably place on intellectual and professional achievement and for having strong family ties and respecting their elders. Similarly large majorities feel that Latino Americans take pride in their culture, work hard to attain a better life, and have deep religious and family ties. Equally sizable majorities agree that African Americans work hard when given a chance, believe strongly in American ideals and the American Dream, are deeply religious, and have made valuable contributions to American society. Over 90 percent of all groups surveyed also agree that learning to understand and appreciate the lifestyles, tastes, and contributions of other groups is either "very important" or "important." *The most encouraging finding is that nine out of ten Americans from all groups are willing to work with one another to solve the most pressing problems in their neighborhoods and communities.* They express a willingness to work together to protect each other's children from gangs and violence, to help improve schools, including teaching understanding and respect for the cultural heritage of all groups, and to look for ways to ease racial, religious, and ethnic tensions.

InterConnections.LearnMore 5.3

Seeking Common Ground

National Conference for Community and Justice
http://www.nccj.org
Formerly known as the National Conference of Christians and Jews, this organization promotes understanding among all races, religions, and cultures.

Anti-Defamation League
http://www.adl.org
Founded in 1913, this organization has been in the forefront in fighting anti-Semitism and other forms of bigotry and discrimination against groups of citizens.

Stop the Hate
www.stop-the-hate.org
An antiviolence web site aimed at creating an awareness of intercultural hate problems with links to a variety of antihate resources.

Institute for Cultural Partnerships
http://www.culturalpartnerships.org.
The web site of a nonprofit organization dedicated to bringing people and communities together so that individuals may successfully live, learn, and work in our increasingly diverse society.

Ethics Alert! 5.1

The Ethics of Audience Adaptation

1. When speaking before different audiences, change your tactics, not your convictions.
2. Appealing to shared needs can help bridge cultural differences that divide listeners.
3. Respect individual differences; demographic similarities do not mean that all members of your audience are alike.
4. Resist stereotypes that lead you to derogate or misjudge others.
5. Avoid irrelevant references to gender, ethnicity, race, or sexual preference.
6. When addressing people from other nations and cultures, use the language of respectful equality, and suppress any impulse toward ethnocentrism and imperialism.
7. When addressing diverse audiences, unify listeners by developing appeals based on universal human values.

In Chapter 1 we noted that the Institute for Global Ethics identified eight **universal human values** that transcend cultural differences: love, truthfulness, fairness, freedom, unity, tolerance, responsibility, and respect for life.[36] Contemporary social scientific research has also demonstrated the existence of transcendent social values. Shalom Schwartz and his associates at the Hebrew University of Jerusalem conducted a study of values in twenty different countries. They identified ten universal values: power, achievement, tradition, enjoyment, self-direction, security, unity, benevolence, conformity, and stimulation.[37] Figure 5.5 lists these universal values.

Figure 5.5
Universal Values

Power	Social power, authority, recognition from others, wealth
Achievement	Success, ambition, influence
Tradition	Acceptance of one's fate, devoutness, humility, respect for cultural heritage
Enjoyment	Pleasure
Self-Direction	Freedom, independence, choice of own goals, self-respect, curiosity, creativity
Security	National security, social order, family security, sense of belonging, personal health, reciprocity in personal relationships
Unity	Unity with nature, protecting the environment, inner harmony, social justice, equality, tolerance, a world at peace
Benevolence	Honesty, helpfulness, forgiveness, loyalty, responsibility, friendship, love, spiritual life, meaning in life
Conformity	Politeness, obedience, self-discipline, honoring parents and elders
Stimulation	Variety, excitement, daring

If you can appeal to these common values in your speeches to a diverse audience, you can often unite your listeners behind your ideas or suggestions.

Adjusting to the Communication Situation

Finally, we come to the setting for your speech. You must consider the time, place, occasion, size of the audience, and overall context of recent topic-related events to make final adjustments in your presentation.

Time

The time of day, day of the week, time of the year, and amount of time allotted for speaking can all be significant factors. If you are speaking early in the morning, you may need to be more forceful to awaken listeners. The energy in your voice must assert the importance of your message. Since we tend to grow drowsy after we eat, after-dinner speeches (discussed in Chapter 17) need lively examples and humor. Speeches presented in the evening also present a problem. Most listeners will have completed a day's work and will have left the comforts of home to hear you. You must justify their attendance with good ideas well presented.

If your speech is scheduled for a Monday, when people have not yet adjusted to the weekend's being over, or a Friday, when they are thinking of the weekend ahead, you need especially interesting material to hold attention. Similarly, gloomy winter days or balmy spring weather can put people in a different frame of mind, and their mood can color how they receive your speech.[38] Your materials and presentation style will have to be bright and engaging to overcome the blahs or to ward off daydreaming.

The amount of time allotted for your presentation is also critical. *A short speech does not necessarily mean shorter preparation time.* Actually, shorter speeches often require longer preparation. Short speeches require you to focus and streamline your topic so that it can be handled in the time allotted. You must limit the number of main points and use supporting materials selectively. Choose the most relevant and impressive facts, statistics, and testimony, the most striking examples and stories. Plan your speech so that you begin with a burst and end with a bang.

Place

The place where you will be speaking should also be considered in your planning. When speaking outside, you may have to cope with unpredictable distractions. When speaking inside, you need to know the size and layout of the room and whether a lectern or any needed electronic equipment may be available.

Speaker's Notes 5.2

Checklist for Analyzing the Communication Situation

1. Will the time or timing of my speech present any challenges?
2. Will room arrangements be adequate?
3. Will I have the equipment I need to use presentation aids?
4. What does the audience expect on this occasion?
5. Is there any late-breaking news on my topic that I should include in my speech?
6. Will I possibly have to adjust to previous speakers?
7. How large will my audience be?

Even in the classroom, speakers must learn to cope with distractions—noises may filter in from outside, or people in the hall may be raucous. How can you handle such problems? If the noise is temporary, you should pause and wait until it stops, then repeat your last words and go on with your message. If the noise is constant, you may have to speak louder to be heard. You may even have to pause and close a window or door. The important thing is to take such problems in stride and not let them distract you or your audience from your message.

Occasion

As you plan your message, you need to take into account *why* people have gathered to listen. When an audience is required to attend a presentation, such as a mandatory employee meeting, you may have to work hard to arouse interest and sustain attention. When audience members voluntarily attend a presentation, they usually are more motivated to listen. This is especially important for speeches given outside the classroom setting. If your topic has been publicized and you have factored in audience dynamics and demographics, you should have a good idea of why listeners are present and the needs they expect you to meet. When a speaker does not offer the kind of message listeners expect, they may be annoyed. For example, if they are expecting an informative presentation on investment strategies and instead get a sales pitch for a particular mutual fund, they may feel exploited. This could result more in irritation than in persuasion.

Size of Audience

The size of your audience can affect how you speak. A small audience provides feedback and an opportunity for interaction. Generally, a small group of listeners invites a more casual presentation. You could easily overwhelm them with a formal oratorical style, too loud a voice, or exaggerated gestures.

On the other hand, large audiences offer less feedback. Because you cannot make or sustain eye contact with everyone, you should choose representative listeners in various sections of the audience and change your visual focus from time to time. Establishing eye contact with listeners in all sections of the room helps more people feel included. With large audiences you also should speak more deliberately and distinctly. Your gestures should be more emphatic so that everyone can see them, and any presentation aids used must be large enough for those in the back of the audience to see without strain.

Speaking before a large audience requires adjustments in presentation style.

Context

Anything that happens near the time of your presentation becomes part of the context of your speech. Both recent speeches and recent events can influence how the audience responds to you.

Recent Speeches. Any speeches presented immediately before yours create an atmosphere in which you must work. This atmosphere has a **preliminary tuning effect** on listeners, preparing them to respond in certain ways to you and your message.[39] At political rallies, patriotic music and introductions prepare the audience for the appearance of the featured speaker. At concerts, warm-up groups put listeners in the mood for the star.

Preliminary tuning may also affect classroom presentations. Earlier speeches may affect the mood of the audience. If the speech right before yours aroused strong emotions, you may need to ease the tension in the introduction to your speech. You can do this by acknowledging listeners' feelings and using them as a springboard into your own speech:

> **Obviously, many of us feel very strongly about the legalization of same-sex marriages. What I'm going to talk about is also very important—but it is something I think we can all agree on—the challenge of finding a way to stop children from killing other children in our community.**

Another technique might be to begin with a story that involves listeners and refocuses their attention. At times, humor can help relieve tension, but people who are upset may be in no mood for laughter. Your decision on whether to use humor must be based on your reading of the situation: the mood of listeners, the subject under discussion, and your own ability to use the technique effectively.

In addition to dealing with the mood created by earlier speeches, you may also have to adapt to their content. Suppose you have spent the past week preparing a speech on the *importance* of extending endangered species legislation. Then the speaker before you makes a convincing presentation on the *problems* of extending endangered species legislation. What can you do? Try to turn this to your advantage. Point out that the earlier speech established the importance of the topic but that—as good as that effort was—it did not give the total picture: "Now you will hear the *other* side of the story."

Recent Events. When listeners enter the room the day of your speech, they bring with them information about recent events. They will use this knowledge to evaluate what you say. If you are not up on the latest news on your topic, your credibility can suffer. A student in one of our classes once presented an interesting and well-documented speech comparing public housing in Germany with that in the United States. Unfortunately, she was unaware of a local scandal involving public housing. For three days before her presentation, the story had made the front page of the local newspaper and had been the lead story in area newscasts. Everyone expected her to mention it. Her failure to discuss this important local problem weakened her credibility.

At times, the context of events to which you must adjust your speech may be totally unexpected. When that happens, you must make on-the-spot adjustments so that things work in your favor. During a graduation ceremony at Loyola Marymount University, the school's president fell off the platform immediately before the commencement address. Although the only thing injured was his dignity, the fall certainly distracted the audience. The speaker, Peter Ueberroth, organizer of the 1984 Los Angeles summer Olympic Games, recaptured their attention and brought down the house by awarding the president a 4.5 in gymnastics.[40]

Figure 5.6 provides an Audience Analysis Worksheet that will help you consider all the factors we have discussed in this chapter as you plan for the audience and situation of your speech. When you have sized up the situation, adding this knowledge to your analysis of audience dynamics and demographics, you will be ready for your next challenge—choosing a suitable topic for speaking.

Figure 5.6

Audience Analysis Worksheet

Topic: ______________________________

Audience: ______________________________

	Factor Description	Adaptations Needed
Audience Dynamics	Audience Attitude: ________	________
	Relevant Values: ________	________
	Motivational Appeals: ________	________
Audience Demographics	Age: ________	________
	Gender: ________	________
	Education: ________	________
	Group Affiliations: ________	________
	Sociocultural Background: ________	________
	Interest in Topic: ________	________
	Knowledge of Topic: ________	________
Speaking Situation	Time: ________	________
	Place: ________	________
	Occasion: ________	________
	Audience Size: ________	________
	Context: ________	________

In Summary

Both the audience you anticipate and the setting of your speech are critical to your planning. Successful audience adaptation requires that you understand *audience dynamics,* have relevant information concerning audience demographics, be sensitive to the challenges of audience diversity, and be able to adjust to situational factors.

Adapting to Audience Dynamics. *Motivation* explains why people behave as they do. People will listen, learn, and retain your message only if you can relate it to their needs, wants, or wishes. Some motives you may call on include understanding, control, health and safety, nurturance and altruism, friends and family, self-actualization, and the desire for fairness. Your *audience's attitudes, beliefs,* and *values* will also affect the way they receive and interpret your message. If your listeners are initially negative toward your topic, you will have to adjust your presentation to receive a fair hearing.

Adjusting to Audience Demographics. *Audience demographics* include information about the specific characteristics of your listeners, such as their age, gender, educational level, group membership, and sociocultural makeup (race, social class, and so forth).

The more you know about such factors, the better you can tailor your speech so that it serves your listeners' interests and needs.

Meeting the Challenges of Audience Diversity. Today we live in a global village composed of many diverse groups. Learning to understand and adapt to diversity will help you prepare more effective messages. Examine your thinking to identify any *stereotypes* that might categorize people inflexibly and attribute positive or negative traits to them. Be on guard against *ethnocentrism, sexism,* and *racism* as you plan and prepare your presentations. When speaking to a diverse audience, search for common ground based on *universal human values.*

Adjusting to the Communication Situation. You must be flexible enough to adjust to particular features of the speaking situation. The time when you speak, the place of your speech, the constraints of the occasion, and the size of your audience can all pose challenges. In addition, you will be speaking in a context of other speeches and recent events: these can have a *preliminary tuning effect* to which you must adjust as you make your presentation.

Terms to Know

audience dynamics
motivation
physiological needs
safety needs
belonging needs
identification
esteem needs
self-actualization needs
attitude system
attitudes
beliefs
values
audience demographics
stereotypes
ethnocentrism
imperialism
sexism
gender stereotyping
sexist language
symbolic racism
marking
universal human values
preliminary tuning effect

DISCUSSION

1. How might the following situations affect a speech you are about to give, and how would you adapt to them?
    a. You are the last speaker during the last class period before spring break.
    b. A lost student walks into the class right in the middle of your speech, looks around, says, "Oops! Wrong room," and walks out.
    c. The speaker right before you gives an incredibly successful speech which brings spontaneous applause from the class and high praise from the instructor.
    d. The speaker right before you bombs badly. The speech is poorly prepared, the speaker is very nervous and simply stops in the middle and sits down, visibly upset.
    e. (It rarely happens, but. . .) The speaker right before you gives a speech on the same topic, taking the same general approach.
2. Rank the ten universal values in Figure 5.5 in terms of their importance to you. Discuss how the three values you ranked highest might make you susceptible to certain speech topics and approaches.
3. Construct a demographic portrait of the average student at your school with respect to age, gender, educational background, group affiliations, and sociocultural background. What speech topics might this listener find most interesting? What motivations, values, and attitudes might she or he bring to these topics?

APPLICATION

1. Explain how you would tailor a speech on the general topic of recycling for an audience composed of
   a. middle school girl scouts
   b. the local Chamber of Commerce
   c. your classmates
   d. your college administration
2. If you were to speak on the general topic of recycling, what kinds of examples might you develop to appeal to the following audience needs:
   a. safety
   b. nurturance
   c. comfort
   d. recognition
3. Imagine that you are the speaker mentioned at the beginning of this chapter. You are the president of Students for Environmental Action. To refresh your memory, you have been asked to address a meeting of new students at the soccer field at eight o'clock in the morning to introduce them to SEA. Your major goals will be to inform them about SEA's projects for the coming year and to recruit new members. That evening, you have been invited to address the Decatur County Industrial Development Board on "what you students are up to." Your task is to reassure them that SEA's work will help, not hinder the business climate in the area.

   Like every good speaker, you have carefully constructed a demographic analysis of both groups and have also identified some pertinent situational factors. Your task is to analyze the data that follows in light of what you have learned from this chapter in order to plan an overall speech strategy. Develop a one page written report for each speech that will outline a plan for adaptation to each audience and situation.

   The audience for the morning speech consists of students attending the college for the first time. There are 2,225 first-year students and 426 transfer students, but not all of them will be at this student activities program. Most of them are from out of town and know very little about SEA. The average first year student is nineteen years old. Fifty-five percent of the students are female and 45 percent are male. They come mainly from the small towns and rural areas within a 200 mile radius of the campus. Seventy percent of the students are white, 12 percent are African-Americans, 8 percent are Latinos, and 6 percent are Asian Americans. Most have been raised in blue-collar homes with traditional values and moderate political beliefs. About half are Democrats and half are Republicans. Over 60 percent of the students will be working to help pay for their education. You will be the seventh speaker on the program. You have been asked to hold your remarks to under five minutes.

   The audience for the second speech is the fifteen member Industrial Development Board. All of them plan to attend the presentation in the executive board room of a local chemical manufacturing plant at seven-thirty in the evening. You will make a fifteen minute presentation, then answer questions. The board members represent a broad spectrum of business interests from service organizations to manufacturing. Thirteen members of the board are white, one is a Latino-American, and one is an Asian American. They are politically conservative and active in local politics. Nine are Republicans, four are Democrats, and two consider themselves Independents. Eight are members of the Junior Chamber of Commerce, four belong to the National Rifle Association, one is president of the local Bass Masters group, and one is active in the Sierra Club. Hunting and fishing are the major recreational activities in the area. You are the only person scheduled to speak at the meeting. Last week the local paper printed an article outlining SEA's plans for the year which include efforts to ban the dumping of industrial wastes into the Coahoma River and to lobby the state legislature to designate 300 acres of land owned by the college as a wildlife preserve.

   This is the third year that SEA has been active on campus. The first year the group had twenty members. They assessed campus environmental problems, and started a successful campus recycling effort. Last year SEA had over fifty members. They continued the recycling program and assessed environmental problems in the county. SEA's major project last year was to stop the poisoning of pigeons on campus. To call attention to the problem, the group had to take drastic action. They found out from someone in the grounds department when the poison was going to be set out. At five o'clock the next morning thirty SEA members collected the carcasses of dead pigeons and dumped them on the steps of the Administration Building, where they held a demonstration. The campus and local newspapers published pictures of the demonstrating students. The Associated Press picked up the story and called SEA a "junior Greenpeace."

You, the speaker, are a twenty-five-year-old junior prelaw major who served six years in the Navy. Your high school record was "undistinguished" and your successes in the military surprised you. While in the service you completed three courses at a junior college. You are a member of the African-American Student's Association and the Pre-Law Club in addition to being president of SEA. A picture of you leading last year's demonstration was on the front page of the local paper. You care very strongly about this year's SEA projects. Although you are a hunter, you don't think campus land should be used for that purpose. You also believe the dumping of wastes in the river can cause health problems in addition to spoiling recreational opportunities.

Notes

1. Barbara Engler, *Personality Theories: An Introduction,* 4th ed. (Boston: Houghton Mifflin, 1995), pp. 273–280, 340–363; and Thane S. Pittman, "Motivation," in *The Handbook of Social Psychology,* ed. Daniel T. Gilbert, Susan T. Fiske, and Gardener Lindzey, 4th ed., vol. 1 (Boston: McGraw-Hill, 1998), pp. 549–590.
2. Henry A. Murray, *Explorations in Personality* (New York: Oxford University Press, 1938). Interest in Murray's research continues, and the Radcliffe Institute for Advanced Study maintains a web site for the Murray Research Center at http://www.radcliffe.edu/.
3. Abraham H. Maslow, *Motivation and Personality*, 2nd ed. (New York: Harper & Row, 1970).
4. The study of achievement motivation began with the work of the Murray group and was extended by D. C. McClelland, *Human Motivation* (Glenview, Ill.: Scott, Foresman, 1985).
5. B. Weiner, "A Cognitive Attribution-Emotion-Action Model of Motivated Behavior," *Journal of Personality and Social Psychology* 39 (1980): 186–200.
6. Alice A. Eagly and Shelly Chaiken, "Attitude Structure and Function," in *The Handbook of Social Psychology*, vol. 1, pp. 323–390; and James M. Olson and Mark P. Zanna, "Attitudes and Attitude Change," *Annual Review of Psychology* 44 (1993): 117–154.
7. *The Rhetoric of Aristotle,* trans. George Kennedy (New York: Oxford University Press, 1992), Book 2, Chs. 11–14, pp. 163–169.
8. S. J. Ceci and M. Bruck, "Suggestibility of the Child Witness: A Historical Review and Synthesis," *Psychological Bulletin* 113 (1993): 403–439; J. A. Krosnick and D. F. Alwin, "Aging and Susceptibility to Attitude Change," *Journal of Personality and Social Psychology* 57 (1989): 416–425; Richard E. Petty and Duane T. Wegener, "Attitude Change: Multiple Roles for Persuasion Variables," in *Handbook of Social Psychology,* ed. Daniel T. Gilbert, Susan T. Fiske, and Gardener Lindzey, 4th ed., vol. 1 (Boston: McGraw-Hill, 1998), p. 358; Milton Rokeach, *The Open and Closed Mind* (New York: Basic Books, 1960); and T. R. Tyler and R. A. Schuller, "Aging and Attitude Change," *Journal of Personality and Social Psychology* 61 (1991): 689–697.
9. Cited in Allison Adato and Melissa G. Stanton, "If Women Ran America," *Life*, June 1992, p. 40.
10. "High School and College Graduates" (©2000, 2004 The Learning Network Inc.). http://www.infoplease.com/ipa/A0112596.html (19 Feb. 2004).
11. "Women in the Civilian Labor Force, 1900–2002" (© 2000, 2004 The Learning Network Inc.). http://www.infoplease.com/ipa/A0104673.html (19 Feb. 2004).
12. John Gettings and David Johnson, "Wonder Women: Profiles of Leading Female CEOs and Business Executives" (©2000, 2001 The Learning Network Inc.). http://www.infoplease.com/spot/womenceo1.html (19 Feb. 2004).
13. Daniel J. Canary and Kimberley S. Hause, "Is There Any Reason to Research Sex Differences in Communication?" *Communication Quarterly* 41 (1993): 129–144.
14. P. Schonback, *Education and Intergroup Attitudes* (London: Academic Press, 1981).
15. William McGuire, "Attitudes and Attitude Change," in *Handbook of Social Psychology*, ed. Gardner Lindzey and Eliot Aronson, vol. 2 (New York: Random House, 1985), pp. 271–272.
16. For a detailed analysis of this topic, see Donald R. Kinder, "Opinion and Action in the Realm of Politics," in *Handbook of Social Psychology,* vol. 2, pp. 778–867.
17. "Demographics . . . It's All the Rage!" *American Demographics*, June 2000, p. 72.
18. Alison Stein Wellner, "Diversity in America," *Supplement to American Demographics*, November 2002, p. S3.
19. Rebecca Gardyn, "Educated Consumers," *American Demographics*, November 2002, p. 18.

20. Ibid., p. 18.

21. "Political Interest on the Rebound Among the Nation's Freshmen, UCLA Survey Reveals" (26 Jan. 2004). http://www.gseis.ucla.edu/heri/03_press_release.pdf. (1 Feb. 2004).

22. "Your First College Year Findings." http://www.gseis.ucla.edu/heri/yfcy.yfcy_finding.html (15 Feb. 2004).

23. Sharon S. Brehm and Saul M. Kassin, *Social Psychology,* 3rd ed. (Boston: Houghton Mifflin, 1996), pp. 120–161; Susan T. Fiske, "Stereotyping, Prejudice, and Discrimination," in *Handbook of Social Psychology,* vol. 2, pp. 357–414; and Annie Murphy Paul, "Where Bias Begins: The Truth About Stereotypes," *Psychology Today,* May/June 1998, pp. 52–55, 82.

24. R. C. Gardner, "Stereotypes as Consensual Beliefs," in *The Psychology of Prejudice: The Ontario Symposium,* ed. Mark P. Zanna and James M. Olson, vol. 7 (Hillsdale, N.J.: Erlbaum, 1994), pp. 1–32.

25. Wilma Mankiller, "Rebuilding the Cherokee Nation," paper presented at Sweet Briar College, 2 April 1993. http://gos.sbc.edu/index.html (18 Sept. 1998). Reprinted by permission of the author.

26. Susan T. Fiske, "Social Cognition and Social Perception," *Annual Review of Psychology* 44 (1993): 155–194.

27. Cited in *The Merriam-Webster Dictionary of Quotations* (Springfield, Mass.: Merriam-Webster Inc., 1992), p. 309.

28. Humphrey Taylor, "Americans Believe That Over Half the World's Population Speaks English," Harris Poll November 1998. http://www.harrisinteractive.com/harris_poll/index.asp?PID+146 (19 Feb. 2004).

29. Jimmy Carter, speech in Havana, delivered 14 May 2002. Text available at http://www.cubadata.com/chronology/052002-Jimmy_Carter_Speech-English.htm (20 April 2004). Reprinted with permission of The Associated Press.

30. Brehm and Kassin, p. 164.

31. Julia T. Wood, *Gendered Lives: Communication, Gender, and Culture* (Belmont, Calif.: Wadsworth, 1994), p. 126.

32. Fiske, "Stereotyping, Prejudice, and Discrimination," pp. 357–414.

33. G. Plaskin, "Bryant Gumbel," *Us,* 5 Sept. 1988, pp. 29–35.

34. From a speech presented 4 April 1993; reprinted in Lisa DiMona and Constance Herndon, *The 1995 Information Please Women's Source Book* (Boston: Houghton Mifflin), pp. 344–345.

35. The data in this section come from the National Conference of Christians and Jews, "Taking America's Pulse: A Summary Report of the National Conference Survey on Inter-Group Relations," undated, available from The National Conference, 71 Fifth Avenue, New York, NY 10003. Information available on the Internet at http://www.nccj.org.

36. Rushworth M. Kidder, *Shared Values for a Troubled World* (San Francisco: Jossey-Bass, 1994), pp. 1–19.

37. Shalom H. Schwartz, Sonia Roccas, and Lilach Sagiv, "Universals in the Content and Structure of Values: Theoretical Advances and Empirical Tests in Twenty Countries," *Advances in Experimental Social Psychology* 25 (1992): 1–65.

38. N. Schwarz, H. Bless, and G. Bohner, "Mood and Persuasion: Affective States Influence the Processing of Persuasive Communications," *Advances in Experimental Social Psychology* 24 (1991): 161–199.

39. For more about preliminary tuning, see Theodore Clevenger Jr., *Audience Analysis* (Indianapolis: Bobbs-Merrill, 1966), pp. 11–12.

40. Reported in *Time,* 17 June 1985, p. 68.

Human Rights

Human Rights Watch **http://www.hrw.org/** The official web site of Human Rights Watch, a nonprofit nongovernmental organization dedicated to protecting the human rights of people around the world.

Human Rights Interactive Network **http://www.webcom.com/hrin/** An extensive directory of web sites related to human rights organizations and activities around the world.

Humanitarian Affairs **http://www.reliefweb.int/ocha_ol/index.html** The web site of the United Nations Office for the Coordination of Humanitarian Affairs, which deals with humanitarian policies, advocacy, and action worldwide.

Civil Liberties and Civil Rights **http://www.priweb.com/internetlawlib/93.HTM** An Internet Law Library directory to legal documents from a variety of sources.

Amnesty International **http://amnestyusa.org** The official web site of Amnesty International, a humanitarian advocacy group concerned with promoting human rights throughout the world.

Ethnic/Racial/ Cultural Diversity

General

In Motion **http://www.inmotionmagazine.com** A multicultural online U.S. publication covering a variety of topics relevant to cultural diversity. Also available in Spanish.

Diversity Web **http://www.diversityweb.org** An Association of American Colleges and Universities web site providing materials relevant to diversity in higher education.

Race and Ethnicity Database **http://eserver.org/race/** A University of Washington web site containing a compilation of reference materials, essays, and literary collections pertinent to race and ethnicity in the United States.

ESL Magazine **http://www.eslmag.com** An online magazine for educators and others interested in understanding the challenges of learning English as a second language.

African American

Black History **http://www.blackhistory.com** A web site offering articles on the contributions and problems of African Americans.

NAACP **http://www.naacp.org** The official web site of the National Association for the Advancement of Colored People, containing current information on problems relating to justice for African Americans.

National Civil Rights Museum **http://www.civilrightsmuseum.org** This site features an interactive tour documenting the struggle for civil rights in America.

Latino/Chicano/Hispanic

Hispanic.com **http://www.hispanic.com/** A web site containing information, services, and technology access to the Hispanic community in the United States.

HispanicOnline.com **http://www.hispaniconline.com/** A web site covering arts and entertainment, politics, lifestyles, and news of importance to the Hispanic community.

Andanzas al Web Latino **http://lib.nmsu.edu/subject/bord/latino.html** A comprehensive and annotated web directory covering social, cultural, political, and economic aspects of Latino culture. Includes links to Latino discussion groups.

Mexico Connect **http://ww.mexconnect.com/** An online magazine with news and feature articles, plus a directory of web sites.

Cuba Free Press **http://www.cubafreepress.org/** The web site of a nonprofit organization offering news and feature articles published in English and Spanish.

Asian American

China Today **http://www.chinatoday.com** A web site containing general information on the culture, history, and traditions of China.

The Japan Window **http://globalcompassion.com/japan.htm** An information source on Japanese business practices, culture, and education.

Korean Historical Connection **http://www.hongik.ac.kr/;khc/khc-eng.htm** A web site from the Department of History Education at Hong-Ik University, Seoul, Korea, that maintains an extensive database of articles on history, arts, and culture.

Hmong Homepage **http://www.hmongnet.org/** A web site offering links of interest on the history, culture, and traditions of the Hmong people in Vietnam, Laos, and Thailand.

Native American

Native American Nations **http://www.nativeculture.com/lisamitten/nations.html** A directory of links to the major American tribes.

Native Peoples **http://www.nativepeoples.com/** The online version of *Native Peoples* magazine, with current issues and archives.

Indian Country Today **http://www.indiancountry.com** The online version of a Native American newspaper distributed across the United States, containing current news and perspectives.

Native Web **http://www.nativeweb.com** A web site containing news and an extensive directory of over 3,000 links to other sources of information relevant to indigenous cultures around the world.

National Museum of the American Indian **http://www.si.edu/nmai** The web site of a branch of the Smithsonian Institution, containing material and information documenting the arts and culture of Native Americans.

Middle-Eastern/Eastern

Middle-Eastern Culture **http://www.reemcreations.com/culture/** A source of information on current news, travel, and social issues relevant to the Middle East.

Arab Net **http://www.arab.net** A news and opinion resource with information from an Arab perspective.

Macher's Gateway to Israel **http://www.machers.com/directory/Israel/index.html** A directory of links to Israeli politics, culture, arts, and history.

India Culture **http://www.indiaculture.net** A source of articles and links on the arts, culture, religion, and history of India.

European American

The following web sites contain information on the history and culture of the designated country plus links to other relevant web sites.

Italy **http://www.italian-american.com/main.htm**
France **http://www.france.com**
Germany **http://www.germany-info.org/**
Scotland **http://www.geo.ed.ac.uk/home/scotland/scotland.html**
Spain **http://www.cyberspain.com**
Ireland **http://www.local.ie/**
Poland **http://www.polish.org/**
Russia **http://www.amherst.edu/;acrc/**
Greece **http://www.greekvillage.com**

Gender

Women's Resources

Women's Studies Database **http://www.inform.umd.edu/EdRes/Topic/Women'sStudies/** A large directory of links to web sites for and about women.
NOW **http://www.now.org** The official web site of the National Organization for Women.
Advancing Women **http://www.advancingwomen.com** Information and links to sites relevant to women in the work force.
Women Leaders Online **http://www.wlo.org/** A networking web site for women in politics, the media, the work force, and cyberspace.

Men's Resources

Menstuff **http://www.menstuff.org** The web site of the National Men's Resource Center, with information for men on fatherhood, health, and relationships.
National Coalition of Free Men **http://www.ncfm.org** A web site devoted to examining how sexual discrimination affects men and boys.
Backlash **http://www.backlash.com** An equalitarian web site with articles and links on gender issues, parenting, divorce, and employment from the male perspective.
MenWeb **http://www.vix.com/menmag** An online magazine with articles about battered men, male sex abuse survivors, friendship, and male health and employment issues.

Gay and Lesbian News and Views

OUT.com **http://www.out.com** An online magazine with an emphasis on media, arts, and fashion.
The Advocate **http://www.advocate.com** An online magazine focusing on news, health, family, and homophobia issues.
National Gay and Lesbian Taskforce **http://www.ngltf.org** The official web site of the National Gay and Lesbian Taskforce, an activist organization working to extend civil rights to those with alternative lifestyles.
Lifestyle Resources **http://www.inform.umd.edu/EdRes/Topic/Diversity/Specific/Sexual_Orientation/Bibliographies** An online directory and bibliography pertaining to alternative lifestyles.

Political Diversity

General

Political Information **http://www.politicalinformation.com** A directory and specialized search engine with over 5,000 links to web sites on campaigns, grassroots movements, political issues, and political organizations.

Campaign Finance **http://www.opensecrets.org** A Center for Responsive Politics web site containing information on who's giving and who's getting political contributions.

Politics1 **http://www.politics1.com** A nonpartisan web site with directories for parties and issues.

Political Parties

Republican **http://www.rnc.org/** News and information on the official Republican National Committee web site.

Young Republicans **http://www.youngrepublicans.com** News and information of interest to Republicans between the ages of eighteen and forty.

Democratic **http://www.democrats.org** News and information on the official Democratic National Committee web site.

Young Democrats **http://www.yda.org/** News and information of interest to Democrats under thirty-six.

Libertarian **http://www.lp.org/** News and information on the official Libertarian Party web site.

Conservative

Town Hall **http://www.townhall.com** Conservative news, information, and issues with a library categorized by topics.

Media Research Center **http://www.mediaresearch.org** An exposé of the "liberal" media bias in American politics.

Young Americans for Freedom **http://www.yaf.com** News and information on issues of interest to young conservatives.

Liberal

TurnLeft **http://www.turnleft.com/liberal.html** The home of liberalism on the Web: information and links.

People for the American Way **http://www.pfaw.org** Political news and issues from the liberal perspective.

Brookings Institution **http://www.brookings.org** Foreign policy and domestic issues presented from a liberal viewpoint.

Religious Diversity

General

Finding God in Cyberspace **http://sim74.kenrickparish.com/** A directory of print and Internet resources on religious traditions.

American Religious Experience **http://are.as.wvu.edu** Articles and images of American religious history on the Web.

Theology and Religion **http://www.wabashcenter.wabash.edu/Internet/front.htm** An annotated guide to sources relevant to religious education.

Religious Traditions

The following web sites contain information on some of the major religious organizations active in the United States.

Orthodox Judaism **http://www.jewfaq.org/**
Reform Judaism **http://www.uahc.org/**
Buddhism **http://www.dharmanet.org/**
Islam **http://www.usc.edu/dept/MSA/introduction/woi_toc.html**
Hinduism **http://www.hindunet.org**
Roman Catholic **http://www.catholic.net**
Latter Day Saints **http://www.lds.org**
Anglicans **http://www.anglican.org**
Episcopal **http://ecusa.anglican.org/**
Lutheran **http://www.lcms.org**
Presbyterian **http://www.pcusa.org**
Methodist **http://www.umc.org**
Friends **http://www.quaker.org**
Unitarian **http://www.uua.org**
Baptist **http://www.baptist.org**
Church of Christ **http://www.church-of-christ.org**
United Church of Christ **http://www.ucc.org**
Christian Scientist **http://www.tfccs.com**
Church of God in Christ **http://www.cogic.org**

Finding Your Topic

6

OUTLINE

This chapter will help you

- discover a promising topic
- explore your topic productively
- refine your topic for speaking
- test your topic before your audience

The life of our city is rich in poetic and marvelous subjects . . . but we do not notice it.

BAUDELAIRE

"I have to speak for five whole minutes? That's an eternity! How can I speak that long when I know so little about anything? I've got nothing to talk about, and even if I did, no one would be interested." Your instructor has just given you your assignment. You are to prepare an informative speech on a subject of your choice. And right now, you are sitting on the edge of panic.

Preparing to speak before an audience can seem overwhelming, especially if you've never done it before. Simply getting started may be the most difficult part of speech preparation. If the task before you seems formidable, take it in small steps, advises Robert J. Kriegel, a performance psychologist who has counseled many professional athletes. While working as a ski instructor, Kriegel found that beginners would look all the way to the bottom of a slope. The hill would seem too steep and the challenge too difficult, and the skiers would back away. However, if he told them to think only of making the first turn, this would change their focus to something they knew they could do.[1]

On the "first turn" in speech preparation, you will decide on a topic that is right for you, your listeners, and the occasion and that fits the assignment and the time you have to speak. Surprisingly, you will find that five minutes goes by in the wink of an eye when you are talking about something that really interests and concerns you and the audience. Fortunately, there are some good ways to help you find the ideal topic. On the "second turn," you will focus your topic and develop a clear sense of purpose for your speech. On the "third turn," you will expand your knowledge so that you can make a responsible presentation. This chapter will help you negotiate the first two of these turns. Chapter 7 will guide you around the third turn, showing you how to research your topic.

What Is a Good Topic?

A good topic is one that involves you and that you care about. It allows you to express something that is important to you or to explore something that fascinates you. In fact, a good topic involves you so much that you forget to be frightened as you speak. It should also enrich the lives of your listeners. Finally, a good topic is one that you can speak about responsibly, given the time allowed for your speech and the preparation time available.

A Good Topic Involves You

Imagine yourself speaking successfully:

> **You're enthusiastic about what you're saying. Your face shows your involvement in your topic. Your voice expresses your feelings. Your gestures reinforce your meaning. Everything about you says, "This is important!" "This is interesting!" or "This will make a difference in your lives!"**

Go to the **Self-Awareness Worksheet** under **Selecting a Topic** in the **SpeechStudio** to further explore your interests and experiences.
Go to http://college.hmco.com/eduspace/

Once you can identify a subject that makes you feel this way, you know that's the topic you want. The enthusiasm you generate when you speak on it will be infectious, engaging listeners as well.

A Good Topic Involves Your Listeners

Visualize an audience of ideal listeners:

> **Their faces are alive with interest. They lean forward in their seats, intent on what you are saying. They nod or smile appropriately. You enjoy their attention. At the end of your speech, they break out in applause. They want to ask you questions about your ideas or to voice their own reactions. They really don't want you to sit down!**

What are your audience's interests and experiences? Fill out the **Audience Interests Worksheet** under **Selecting a Topic** in the **SpeechStudio** to organize your ideas.
Go to http://college.hmco.com/eduspace/

What topic will help you create this kind of audience response? By now, you probably have heard the first speeches in your class, and you are already learning about your listeners. Ask yourself, "What are my audience's interests? What do they care about? What do they need to know more about?"

Perhaps one of your classmates gave a speech honoring his family doctor while criticizing overall trends in modern medical practice. It sparked a lively classroom discussion and got you thinking about your own experiences with doctors. The lights come on in your mind. You could present an informative speech on the extent of medical malpractice in your state or a persuasive speech attacking (or defending) attorneys who specialize in malpractice lawsuits. Add these ideas to your list of promising topic possibilities. Before this chapter is completed, you should have an extensive list from which to select your speech topics.

A Good Topic Is One You Can Manage

The final test of a good topic is whether you can acquire the knowledge you need to speak responsibly on it. The time you have for the preparation and presentation of your speech is limited. Consequently, you should select a topic area you already know something about and then concentrate on developing a *manageable part* of it

Deciding When You've Found the Right Topic

Speaker's Notes 6.1

1. Do I really care about this subject?
2. Does the topic satisfy the assignment?
3. Can I help my listeners see my topic's importance?
4. Do I know enough, and can I learn enough, to speak responsibly on it?
5. Can I do this topic justice in the time I have available?
6. Have I found this topic after conducting carefully the discovery, exploration, and refinement phases of a search process?

for your presentation. Instead of trying to cover all the problems involved in the disposal of nuclear waste, it would be better to limit your discussion to your state's role in waste disposal, or to whether your community has an adequate plan to cope with the problem. The limited topic would be more manageable, could be better adapted to your audience, and should allow for responsible preparation.

The Process of Finding a Good Topic

Now that we understand what makes a good topic, the larger question rises: *How do we find one?* You should think of your search for the right topic as a process that goes through phases of discovery, exploration, and refinement. The **discovery phase** involves identifying large topic areas that seem promising. The **exploration phase** involves examining these areas closely to identify specific speech topics that might be pursued in connection with them. The **refinement phase** involves identifying the general and specific purposes of the speeches you could give on these topics and framing their thesis statements or central ideas. This chapter will guide you through this quest for the right topic.

What is important from the outset is that you recognize that *this process takes time to complete responsibly*. Give yourself at least a week to select your topic, do your research, outline your speech, and practice your presentation. You will find that this time is well invested. Nothing comforts you more on the eve of an important speech than knowing that you are well prepared.

Discovering Your Topic

If you are wondering—"What should I talk about? I don't know anything. I'm not even that interested in anything. Am I hopeless?"—take comfort in the fact that many students share such topic selection anxiety. The only thing really worrisome about topic anxiety is that it builds on itself. As topic anxiety rises within you, you become less and less able to undergo a really positive experience of discovery. To counter this effect, you can use three techniques that have long proved their worth in discovering speech topics: brainstorming, interest charts, and media prompts.

Brainstorming

Brainstorming is a technique that encourages and harnesses free associations. Ask yourself: "If I had to pick one topic area to explore for my next speech, what would it be?" Write down the first idea that occurs to you at the top of a legal pad or computer

Personal experiences, such as building houses for Habitat for Humanity, can be a useful source of examples or narratives for use in speeches.

page. Now write down in descending order at least six additional ideas that spontaneously occur to you in association with this topic. Do not try to edit or reflect critically on these associations until you have a sizeable list. Take your time and let your mind wander. You may discover, like a student of ours, that such "daydreaming" can be productive and creative.

Zachary came to our office one day early in the term with a serious case of topic anxiety. After we convinced him that his symptoms were not terminal, he accepted our invitation to participate in a brainstorming exercise. Zachary wrote down "flyfishing" at the top of his legal pad. He then wrote down the following associations: "trout," "Yellowstone," "Montana," "fire," "drought," "George Anderson" (a well-known fly fisherman), "catch and release," and "wolves." He paused for a moment and studied this list closely. "You know," he said, "I could speak on 'Fire and Water in Yellowstone: Too Much of One, Too Little of the Other.'" And eventually he did.

Brainstorming is a *nondirective* technique of topic discovery that works well for people like Zachary. Others require a more disciplined, directive approach to topic discovery, as in our next technique.

Interest Charts

The classical writers on rhetoric were the first to discover that the mind follows certain habitual paths that are often productive in creative as well as critical thinking. They called these paths "topoi": we have already used topoi when we developed the "Self-Awareness Inventory" in Chapter 3 to find topics for speeches of introduction. The productive paths we explored in that chapter can be easily adapted and enlarged here into **topoi of topic discovery**. They appear in the form of questions that stimulate and guide the mind; therefore, they provide a *directive* technique:

Fill out the **Personal Interests Worksheet** under **Selecting a Topic** in the **SpeechStudio** to further expand your topic possibilities.

Go to http://college.hmco.com/eduspace/

1. What *places* do you find interesting?
2. What *people* do you find fascinating?
3. What *activities* do you enjoy?
4. What *things* do you find interesting?
5. What *events* are foremost in your mind?
6. Which *ideas* do you find intriguing?
7. What *values* are important to you?
8. What *problems* concern you most?
9. What *campus concerns* do you have?

Figure 6.1

Your Interest Chart

Places	People	Activities
Livingston, MT	Osama Bin Laden	hiking
Okefenokee Swamp	Sammy Sosa	skiing
New Orleans	Wilma Mankiller	watching basketball
Route 66	Charles Lindbergh	cooking
New York City	Sojourner Truth	traveling
Objects	**Events**	**Ideas**
Kachinas	Olympics	objectivity in journalism
movie posters	World Trade Center	hedonism
antique fishing lures	canoeing the Colorado	anarchy
political cartoons	Mardi Gras	freedom of expression
graffiti	Cody Rodeo	creation myths
Values	**Problems**	**Campus Concerns**
close family ties	air and water pollution	race relations
tolerance	pre-emptive war	off-campus housing
physical fitness	substance abuse	date rape
respect	Internet censorship	campus security
world peace	coping with terrorism	escalating tuition costs

You can use the topoi of topic discovery to develop an **interest chart** that projects a comprehensive visual display of your interests. To create such a chart, write out brief responses to the probe questions. Try to come up with at least five alternatives for each question, letting your mind roam freely. Your interest chart might then look like that in Figure 6.1.

Once you have completed your personal interest chart, make a similar chart of audience interests as revealed by class discussion and your audience analysis. What places, people, events, activities, objects, ideas, values, problems, and campus concerns seem to spark discussions in class? Study the two charts together, looking for shared interests. To do this systematically, make a three-column **topic area inventory chart.** In the first column (your interests), list the subjects you find most appealing. In the second column (audience interests), list the subjects that seem foremost in the minds of your listeners. In the third column, match columns one and two to find the most promising areas of speech topics. Figure 6.2 shows a sample topic area inventory chart.

Compare your interests with the audience's interests on the **Personal and Audience Interests Worksheet** under **Selecting a Topic** in the **SpeechStudio.**
Go to http://college.hmco.com/eduspace/

In this example, your interests in travel and hiking match with the audience's interest in unusual places and suggest a possible topic area: "Weekend Adventures Close to Campus." Similarly, your concern for physical fitness pairs with the audience's interest in deceptive advertising to generate another possibility: "Exercise Spa Rip-offs." Your interest in air and water pollution combines with audience interests in leisure activities to lead to "Limit Cars in National Parks?" Finally, your concern over preemptive war resonates with audience fear of terrorism to suggest a provocative topic area: "Is PreEmptive War the Answer to Terrorism?"

Media Prompts

If brainstorming and interest charts don't produce enough promising topic discoveries (an unlikely possibility), you still have an ace up your sleeve. When using **media prompts,** you jump-start the creative process by scanning newspapers, magazines, and the electronic media for ideas. Go through the Sunday paper, scan *Time* and *Newsweek* or quality periodicals such as the *Atlantic* or *Smithsonian*, or read the daily headlines of the *New York Times* online. Also, if you type in the words *Speech Topics* on a search engine, you will find among the considerable piles of garbage on

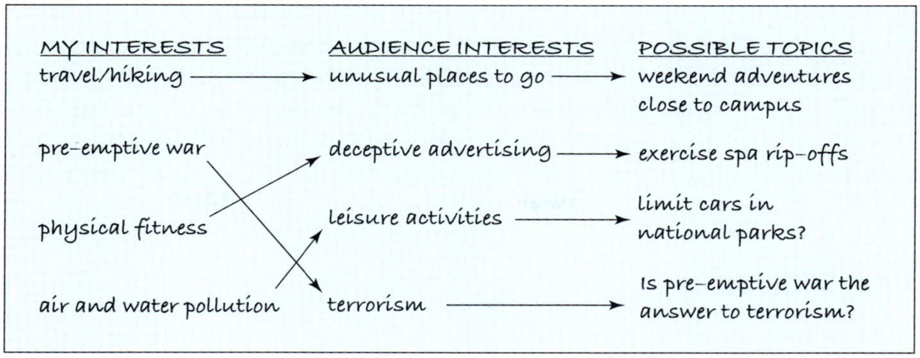

Figure 6.2
Topic Area Inventory Chart

the Internet a few gems. See InterConnections.LearnMore 6.1 for a few of these helpful lists of possible speech topics. As you scan the media, consider the headlines, advertisements, and pictures. What catches your attention? An item that interests you can grow into the topic for your next speech.

One student developed an idea for a topic after seeing an advertisement for bank services. The ad stirred some unpleasant memories of having written a bad check. This suggested an informative speech on keeping better personal financial records. His problem was getting listeners to see the importance of this topic to their lives. His solution was to develop an introduction that startled the audience into attention.

> **Last month I committed a crime! I wrote a bad check, and it bounced. The check was for $4.67 to a local grocery store where I bought the makings of a spaghetti supper. The bank charged me $25.00 for the overdraft, and the store charged me $10.00 to retrieve my bad check. That was the most expensive spaghetti I've ever eaten!**

Similarly, the headline "Travel Money Tips Offered" might inspire you to speak on "Champagne Travel on a Beer Budget." Or the personals section in the classified ads might prompt a speech on "The Dangers of Computer Dating Services."

The "media prompts" technique has one great advantage: The topics it generates are usually quite timely. But be careful not to misuse this technique. The media can suggest ideas for speeches, but you can't simply summarize an article and use it as a speech. The article should be only a starting point for your thinking. *Your* speech must be *your* message, designed to appeal to *your* specific audience. You should always bring something new to your topic—a fresh insight or a special application for your listeners.

InterConnections.LearnMore 6.1

Speech Topics

Research Questions: Persuasion
http://valencia.cc.fl.us/lrcwest/kaysmith.html
Suggestive list of controversial topics, prepared by Professor Kay Smith of Valencia Community College, Orlando, Florida.

Help with Speech Topics
http://faculty.cinstate.cc.oh.us/gesellsc/publicspeaking/topicsl.html
Thorough list of topics prepared by Carla Gesell-Streeter, instructor at Cincinnati State Technical and Community College.

Speech Topics on Public Policy Issues
http://www.libraries.psu.edu/socialsciences/speechtopics/topics.htm
Topic areas inviting persuasive policy speeches, prepared by librarians at Pennsylvania State University.

Sample Topics for Informative/Expository/Demonstrative Speeches
http://www.angelfire.com/ca3/phsspeech/topics.html
List of topic prompts for informative speeches.

Speech and Oral Topics
http://library.hilton.kzn.school.za/English/speech.htm
Lists a wide range of "starting points" for topic searches.

Exploring Your Topic Area

What you typically discover as you brainstorm, develop interest charts, and employ media prompts are not actual topics for speeches, but rather topic areas. Topic areas are promising but broad subjects that often cover too much ground for typical classroom speeches. You must explore topic areas carefully and narrow and focus them until they become specific and concrete enough to develop in the limited time allotted for your speech. The importance of focusing your topic cannot be overemphasized. As Winston Churchill once noted, "A speech is like a spotlight; the more focused it is, the more intense the light."[2] The two primary techniques available to you as you explore promising topic areas are the nondirective technique of mind mapping and the directive technique of topic analysis.

Mind Mapping

Mind mapping changes certain basic patterns of expression we take for granted in order to free our minds for creative exploration.[3] As we wrote the first draft of these words, we were composing on a legal pad. We started at the top of the sheet and wrote from left to right, moving down the page as we wrote. We have done it this way for so long that one might believe that this is the way thought naturally develops—in linear horizontal and vertical patterns.

These habitual patterns can produce what communication theorist Kenneth Burke once called a "trained incapacity" to think fully about subjects. Mind mapping disrupts these patterns for the sake of greater possible creativity. Mind mappers start with a sheet of unlined paper, which they turn on its side to emphasize width rather than length. Instead of starting at the top of the page, they start at the center. Instead of flowing down the page, thinking radiates out from the center so that it forms a coherent system.

Let us assume that you have carefully completed the interest charts. You have discovered your own keen interest in American popular music, an interest you think will be shared by many of your listeners. This convergence of interests has produced a promising topic area, the innovative music that flowed during the last half-century out of Sun Studio in Memphis, Tennessee. To explore this topic area using mind mapping, you would place it at the center of your page, as indicated in Figure 6.3. Before proceeding further, let's consider how this technique works and how we will adapt it for our purpose of topic exploration.

Mind mapping taps into the creative power of metaphorical thinking. It starts with a concept of our minds as uncharted territories waiting to be explored. We may think of this uncharted territory as intellectual space.[4] The central concept in this spacescape functions like a star, and the major ideas that circle it are its associated satellites. These satellites can be circled by even more particular associations that belong to them. Figure 6.3 illustrates this way of thinking.

Returning to our illustration, our minds have roamed freely around this central idea, and we have come up with five major satellite ideas: "Early Artists," "Later Artists," "Business Practices," "Musical Significance: Birth of Rock-and-Roll," and "Cultural Significance." Circling each of these is a second group of satellite subjects. Note how these subjects grow more and more concrete as we mind map the topic area.

Now as we study this system of ideas in space, we can see any number of speech topic possibilities. One might be a topic that would connect three of the major satellite ideas. We could focus on those early artists who performed the first significant rock-and-roll hits of Sun Studio and show how these hits blended elements of blues, country, and gospel music into rock-and-roll. We might title this speech "Sun Studio: Birthplace of an American Musical Form." We could develop presentation aids using photographs and excerpts from the music to make the speech truly colorful, enjoyable, and informative.

Mind mapping is an interesting but unpredictable technique of topic area exploration. It can result in striking discoveries. But because it is nondirective, there is no assurance that it will produce useful results. Rather than proceeding in productive directions, the mapping mind can simply wander aimlessly through a topic area. If you are convinced that mind mapping is not working well for you, you should use the more directive technique we call "topic analysis."

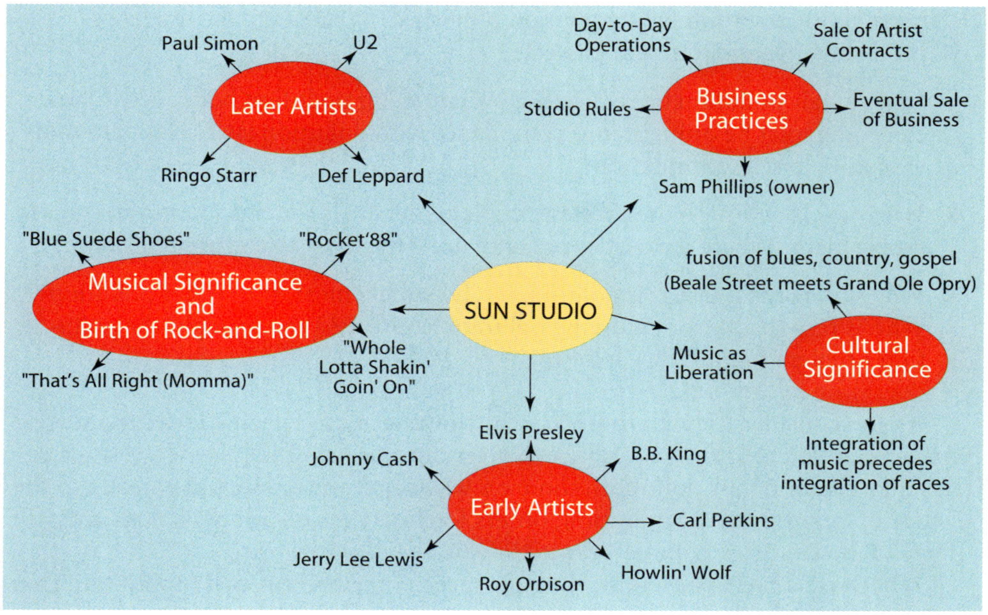

Figure 6.3
Mind Map of Sun Studio

Topic Analysis

Topic analysis uses a system of questions similar to that used by news writers. The beginning college course in journalism introduces fledgling reporters to the topoi of their craft: *what? why? when? how? where?* and *who*? The author Rudyard Kipling once described these probe questions as follows:

> **I keep six honest serving-men**
>
> **(They taught me all I knew):**
>
> **Their names are What and Why and When**
>
> **And How and Where and Who.**[5]

The idea is that if reporters ask these questions as they explore any story, the odds are better that they will do a competent job of reporting the news.

The respected literary scholar Wayne Booth also advises fledgling academic researchers to deploy the same system of questions as they seek promising topics: "Decide which questions stop you for a moment, challenge you, spark some special interest."[6] Such moments can produce good topics.

These same "honest serving-men" can also work for the public speaker who is exploring the possibilities of a topic area. Let's take "Environmental Pollution" as a topic area and see where these questions lead us:

- *What* is environmental pollution? What are the major air pollutants? What are the major water pollutants? What causes environmental pollution? What are the effects of such pollution? What can we do to control this pollution? What can individuals do to reduce environmental pollution? What is the greatest pollution problem in our area?
- *Why* do we have environmental pollution? Why are some companies reluctant to stop polluting? Why are some rural areas polluted? Why do some cities have more environmental pollution than others?
- *When* did environmental pollution first become a problem? When did people first become concerned about such pollution? When was the first important

book about environmental pollution published? When were the first laws protecting the environment passed?

- *How* can air pollution be reduced? How can water pollution be reduced? How can companies be brought into compliance with pollution laws? How can individuals help reduce pollution?
- *Where* is air pollution the greatest problem? Where is water pollution the greatest problem? Where have cities or states done the most to control pollution?
- *Who* suffers most from air pollution? Who suffers most from water pollution? Who is responsible for enforcing pollution controls? Who brought the pollution problem to public awareness?

As you consider the six prompts, write down as many specific ideas about your topic area as you can. You may notice that certain clusters of ideas emerge: some entries may center on air pollution, some on water pollution; some may relate to the history of environmental pollution, others to efforts to control pollution, and still others to the effects of pollution on wildlife or business interests.

What would be the best topic for your speech on environmental pollution? That depends a great deal on your audience and locale. If you live in an area with a major pollution problem, a speech describing the pollution might offer little new information. However, your audience might be interested in the history of environmental legislation or in local efforts to solve the problem. On the other hand, if you live in an area where pollution is not an immediate or apparent problem, you may need to work hard to convince listeners that they should be concerned about the situation.

Our example of topic analysis has related to an informative speech topic. The same type of analysis also can be used to find topics for persuasive speeches. Because persuasion often addresses problems, you simply change the focus of the questions and add a few that are specific to persuasive situations:

Who is affected by this problem?
What are the most important issues?
Why did the problem arise?
Where is this problem happening?
When did the problem begin?
How is this problem like or unlike previous problems?
How extensive is the problem?
What options are available for dealing with the problem?

Selecting Your Topic

Take ethics into consideration early in the speech preparation process. Go to **VideoLab Lesson 1's Next Step: Ethical Considerations in Topic Selection** and complete the exercises. VideoLab

After you have discovered topic areas and explored their potential for your speaking, two or three specific topics should emerge as especially promising possibilities. Now you should ask of each:

Does this topic fit the assignment?
Could I give a speech on this topic in the time available?
Can I learn enough about this topic to give a responsible speech?
Why would I want to speak on this topic?
Would a speech on this topic be good and useful for my audience to hear?

As you consider your options in light of these questions, you should be able to make a final choice.

Refining Your Topic

Having discovered and explored promising topic areas, you have finally decided on a topic. Now you move to the next phase of topic selection: refining and focusing your topic in preparation for speaking. To complete this phase, you must consider the general purpose of your speech, decide on your specific purpose, and develop a clearly worded thesis statement. These three steps elaborate the general concept of "message" that we discussed in Chapter 3. For the relatively simple first speeches, it is enough to have a clear idea of the message you wish to communicate. More complex informative and persuasive speeches require the more precise understandings we now consider.

General Purpose

Invitations to speak outside class will usually indicate the **general purpose** for your speech. Such an invitation may be, "Could you help us understand changes in the tax code?" or "Would you tell us why you are opposed to changes in the tax code?" or "Will you help us thank the president for his leadership in changing the tax code?" Speeches that would address such questions seek understanding, encourage taking a position on a controversial issue, or invite participation in a ritual of appreciation.

In class, the general purpose of your speech is usually assigned. For example, the three questions on the tax code correspond to the general purposes of *informing*, *persuading*, and *celebrating*.

- *The general purpose of a speech to inform is to share knowledge with listeners.* As Booth and his colleagues have written, "[Such communicators] . . . use information to answer a question that their topic inspired them to ask."[7]
- *If your general purpose is to persuade, you will advise listeners how to believe or act and give them sound reasons to accept your position.* Booth notes that persuasion often proceeds "by posing and solving a problem that . . . others should also recognize as worth solving."[8]
- *A speech of celebration emphasizes the importance of an occasion, event, or person, often with the intention of amusing or inspiring listeners.* Speeches of celebration include tributes, eulogies, toasts, after-dinner speeches, and inspirational messages.

Although it is easy to separate these purposes on paper, they often overlap in practice. For example, Marge Anderson, chief executive of the Mille Lacs Band of the Ojibwe, informed her mainstream Minnesota audience of her people's contributions to the larger community, celebrated the values of her culture, and urged listeners to begin a dialogue of learning, understanding, and appreciation—all in the same speech (reprinted in Appendix B).

As we noted earlier, people who invite you to speak outside the classroom will usually suggest the general purpose for your speech. One of your authors was recently invited to speak to a county historical society on the work of Humanities Tennessee, the state affiliate of the National Endowment for the Humanities. He knew that this audience would be most interested in the organization's grants to encourage local initiatives in the humanities. His speech would be mainly informative, but he would also need to introduce himself and encourage the group to think creatively about humanities programs and to prepare grant applications to support them. Had he used the occasion to launch an attack on politicians who want to reduce the government's financial support for the arts and humanities, he would

A speech about hiking in Shenandoah National Park presents a clearer focus than a speech about the park itself.

have violated the audience's expectations. That would have been his last invitation to address the historical society.

Specific Purpose

Becoming aware of your **specific purpose** helps you narrow your topic until it comes into sharp focus. It states precisely what you want your listeners to understand, believe, feel, or do. Having a specific purpose clearly in mind helps direct your research so that you don't waste valuable time wandering around the library or surfing the Internet for irrelevant material. You should be able to state your specific purpose clearly in a single phrase. Let's look at how a specific purpose statement can give focus to a speech:

Topic:	Explore Shenandoah National Park next summer
General purpose:	To inform

Here the discovery and exploration phases of topic selection have produced what appears to be a promising topic. However, as stated, the topic is still too general for a five- to six-minute speech. If you tried to cover the entire range of possible subjects in the time allotted, you would be stretched too thin. As you attempted to touch upon camping, fishing, driving the Skyline Drive, hiking down the Appalachian Trail, going horseback riding, seeing wild animals, and encountering environmental problems–to name just a few of the possible subtopics–you would find yourself in an impossible bind. You would not have time to produce any colorful details, concrete examples, or fascinating stories; instead, you would give only a vague sketch that would leave your listeners disappointed or (even worse) bored. So after confirming the general purpose of your speech (to inform), you decide on a specific purpose that will will narrow the focus of your speech so that it points in one precise direction (hiking trails):

Specific purpose:	To inform my audience about exciting hiking trails in Shenandoah National Park

You have just made a major move in refining your topic. Now you can test and improve this specific purpose statement.

Testing Your Specific Purpose Statement. Developing a successful specific purpose statement is one of the most important moves in topic refinement. But how do you know when you have made this move successfully? Applying the following tests can help you decide whether you have succeeded.

1. *Does the specific purpose really promise new information or fresh advice?* If you propose "to inform listeners that drunk driving is dangerous," you may well be greeted with yawns. You will have tied yourself to a tired topic. When you tell listeners something they have already heard many times, you simply waste their time.

2. *Can you fulfill your specific purpose statement in the time allotted?* If you propose "to persuade listeners that clean air standards in the United States are too lax," you may have bitten off more than you can chew. Remember, in a five-minute speech you have only about seven hundred words to get your message across. You may need to focus your remarks on air quality in your community so that you can meet your time restrictions. That strategy also would offer the benefit of addressing the specific interests of your listeners.

3. *Have you avoided the trap of double focus?* Sometimes it is difficult to make that final decision to narrow your topic to a single point of focus. It may be tempting to fall into the trap of double focus: "to inform my listeners of hiking and horseback riding opportunities in Shenendoah National Park." If you attempt to address both these subjects in any meaningful way, you may go beyond your time limits. The "and" in such statements is a red flag that you may have a double-focus problem.

4. *Have you avoided the trap of triviality?* When you speak to twenty-four people for five minutes, you will be occupying two hours' worth of their collective time. What are you offering them in return? If you promise "to inform them about how to mix a martini" or "how to punt a football" or "why I love my fraternity," you may well leave your listeners feeling cheated and violated. "So what?" may be their blunt reaction. You must convince listeners that you have a worthwhile specific purpose that promises them vital information, insights, and/or advice so that by the end of the speech they feel they have invested their time wisely.

5. *Have you avoided the trap of technicality?* Sometimes speakers forget that their listeners may not share their background of knowledge and technical language. They are hurt when listeners respond to their speeches with dazed, bewildered looks and the question, "Huh?" Speakers who promise "to inform listeners of the principles of thermonuclear energy" or "to inform my audience concerning the intellectual evolution of Kant's meta-ethics" are stepping directly into this trap. They have neglected to factor audience background and interests into the process of topic selection, and this failure becomes evident when they phrase their specific purpose statements.

Improving Your Specific Purpose Statement. Let's look at some examples of flawed specific purpose statements and see how they might be improved:

Flawed:	To inform my audience about Yellowstone National Park
Improved:	To inform my audience of three often overlooked attractions in Yellowstone Park
Flawed:	To persuade my audience that driving while distracted is dangerous
Improved:	To persuade my audience not to talk on a cell phone while driving

In the first example, the specific purpose is flawed because it is too general. It does not narrow the topic sufficiently. With this nonspecific purpose you could prepare a

Speaker's Notes 6.2

Testing Your Specific Purpose Statement

1. Can I offer fresh ideas or advice?
2. Can I accomplish my purpose in the time allowed?
3. Have I avoided the trap of double focus?
4. Have I avoided the trap of triviality?
5. Have I avoided the trap of technicality?

speech on the history of Yellowstone Park, on the wildlife of Yellowstone Park, on artists who have been inspired by Yellowstone Park, on the reasons why Old Faithful is so faithful, or on a multitude of other subjects. The improved version limits the topic so that it can be handled within the time permitted. This helps you concentrate your research on those materials most useful to your speech.

The second flawed specific purpose is also too vague and general, and it tells the audience nothing new. Who would argue that driving while distracted is not dangerous? The improved version focuses more precisely on a contemporary problem.

Thesis Statement

Framing the **thesis statement** is the final refinement you make in preparing a topic for presentation. Sometimes called the "central idea" of the speech, the thesis statement summarizes in a single sentence the essential meaning or message of your speech. For example, your thesis statement might read, "*Terrorism* has acquired multiple meanings in the speeches of our leaders" (informative speech) or "We need to define *terrorism* more precisely to avoid damaging the Constitution" (persuasive speech). Such a sentence, notes Booth, "states a potential claim"[9] that the speech itself must demonstrate or prove. It is often offered in your introduction so that listeners will understand your intentions from the outset.

Most of the time (but not always), your specific purpose will reveal itself in your thesis statement, but the two are not identical. The specific purpose expresses what you hope to accomplish; the thesis statement summarizes what you intend to say. The emphasis shifts from stating your intention to engaging your listeners in your message. Being able to write out your thesis statement implies that you know how your speech is going to develop; therefore, you may need to revise your thesis statement as you do research and learn more about your topic. The final version of your thesis statement may not develop until your research is completed. A recent student speech developed a relationship between the specific purpose and thesis statement as follows:

Specific purpose:	To persuade listeners that date rape is a serious problem on our campus
Thesis statement:	Today I want to discuss a moral blight on our campus—the problem of date rape—and what we can do about it.

In ethical speaking, the thesis statement will usually reveal the speaker's specific purpose; at the very least it will not disguise it. *But let the listener beware!* Not all speakers are totally candid. Although a speaker's specific purpose may be to sell listeners an encyclopedia, the thesis statement may suggest a different intention altogether:

> **I want to help you by offering—free of charge—this wonderful encyclopedia set [thesis statement]. Your only obligation is to let us mention you as a satisfied customer when we are selling encyclopedias in this community.**

Only toward the end of the speech does the real purpose come out: "And of course we ask that you do keep your set up to date for the next ten years by purchasing the annual supplements at a special discount rate."

Such disguised intentions may seem fairly trivial (unless you find yourself responsible for purchasing the set in ten installments). But if you substitute the hidden motives of religious cult leaders or even respectable leaders of nations, who sometimes make statements that disguise their actual purposes, you can understand how serious this problem can become. *The greater the distance between the hidden specific purpose and the thesis statement actually expressed in the speech, the larger the ethical problem.*

Ethics Alert! 6.1

The Ethics of Topic Selection

1. Do not select a topic that could be hurtful, such as "How to Make a Pipe Bomb."
2. Do not select a topic that invites illegal activity, such as "How to Get Forbidden Objects Through Airline Security Checks."
3. Do not select a topic that you don't understand yourself.
4. Do not select a topic on which you cannot obtain responsible knowledge.
5. Do not purposely obscure your thesis statement in order to hide your specific purpose.

At times, ethical speakers may omit the thesis statement from their presentations, leaving it to be constructed by listeners from cues within the speech. Cecile Larson left the thesis statement implicit in her speech "The 'Monument' at Wounded Knee," which appears in Appendix B. Speakers may leave the thesis statement unstated to create a dramatic effect as listeners discover it for themselves. Although it has some artistic merit, this technique also entails considerable risk. Listeners may miss the point! In most cases, speakers should integrate the thesis statement into the introduction of their speeches.

Within a speech, the thesis statement should adapt your specific purpose to listeners in a way calculated to gain their attention. Note how the language grows more colorful and personal as one moves from specific purpose to thesis statement in the following examples:

Specific purpose:	To inform my audience about three often overlooked attractions in Yellowstone Park
Thesis statement:	Today I want to introduce you to three remarkable features of Yellowstone Park that are often missing from your guidebook: the Fountain Paint Pots, the Grand Canyon of the Yellowstone, and the Firehole River.
Specific purpose:	To persuade listeners to lobby state representatives to support the bill limiting cell phone use by drivers
Thesis statement:	"Driving while distracted," using the cell phone while one is driving a car, should be prohibited by state law.

Qualities Vital to Thesis Statements. Because crafting the thesis statement is the climax of the process of topic selection, it is critical that the statement should possess two qualities that the preceding examples illustrate:

1. *Sharp, clear focus.* The speech that lacks a sharp, clear thesis statement is likely to ramble about in a disorganized way and leave no lasting impression on listeners. Speeches are structured to develop an idea. When that idea is obscure, there is no central focus to hold the structure of thoughts together. When there is no clear thesis statement, the specific purpose usually also will be vague. When listeners ask, "What exactly are you trying to say?" or "What would you like us to do?" you know the thesis statement has not been carefully stated.

2. *Colorful, engaging language.* The language of thesis statements should be colorful and concrete. Such language evokes pictures in listeners' minds and encourages constructive listening. Although some may advise students not to use figurative language in their thesis statements, these statements need not be plain and literal to be effective. Indeed, a little reflection on the actual practice of famous speeches like Martin Luther King's "I Have a Dream" or Franklin Delano Roosevelt's "First

Inaugural Address" ("We have nothing to fear but fear itself") should convince us that figurative speech can help make thesis statements both eloquent and memorable. The real enemy of thesis statements is, rather, vacuous expressions like "I want to show you that camping in the Rockies is really awesome." Such expressions are too vague and overused to be meaningful.

The only problem with using colorful, vivid language in a thesis statement might come if your words indicate that your mind has closed prematurely on a conclusion that ought to require further proof before careful listeners would be willing to accept it. "Today I want to show you that bloodthirsty, cold-blooded killers are waiting too long to die on death row" may tune out some listeners immediately. They might wonder, "Who is bloodthirsty here?"

An Overview of the Topic Selection Process

Let us now look at the entire process of moving from general topic area to thesis statement to see how these steps may evolve in speech preparation:

Topic area:	Vacations in the United States
Topic:	Camping in the Rockies
General function:	To inform
Specific purpose:	To inform my audience that there are beautiful, uncrowded places to camp in the Rockies
Thesis statement:	Three beautiful yet uncrowded camping areas in the Rockies are Bridger-Teton National Forest in Wyoming, St. Charles Canyon in Idaho, and Dinosaur National Monument in Utah.

It becomes clear that the entire refinement phase of topic selection is rather like looking at a topic through the lenses of a microscope. First, you see the topic as it emerges in rough form from the processes of discovery and exploration. Then you view the topic through the general purpose lens to test its appropriateness for the assignment. Next you view the topic through the much finer lens of the specific purpose as it converges with your interests and intentions. Finally, you view the topic as it might actually appear in the thesis statement. From the initial phase of discovery through the final phase of refinement, the process of topic selection is an intellectual adventure that is critical to successful speaking.

As our metaphor of the microscope suggests, when you identify the general purpose, specific purpose, and thesis statement of a speech topic, you bring the topic into sharper and sharper focus. The structure of the potential speech comes into view, and you can see how the speech might develop. You also get a clearer idea of the kind of research you will need to acquire and communicate responsible knowledge of your topic. How to acquire such research is covered in the next chapter.

Testing Your Topic Selection: An Application

In business settings executives often make short presentations called briefings. Briefings may include both reports on ongoing projects and proposals for approval. They can be both informative and persuasive, especially when they present a plan of action. The persuasive briefing, often called a "prospectus," is an occasion for both testing and "selling" an idea before a group of decision makers.

In like manner, a similar speaking or writing assignment on topic selection is called a **topic briefing**. The topic briefing is a prospectus for a speech or series of speeches you propose to give. In it you explain why you want to speak on this topic and why others should want to listen. You anticipate problems you might have and reassure listeners that you can deal with them. In short, you report the results of the discovery and exploration phases of topic selection. You also anticipate the refinement process by suggesting how one or more later speech topics might develop out of the topic area. The object of the assignment—and the special advantage of giving it orally—is to get feedback from the audience that will either encourage or discourage you from proceeding further.The audience can even make specific suggestions on how you might develop your speeches.

For example, when one of our students made her topic briefing proposing a set of speeches on mathematics education, she received a great deal of helpful feedback. First, the sheer volume of such feedback (at least six members of the audience made comments, asked questions, or offered suggestions) indicated that she had touched on an area rich with potential interest. But one of the questions ("What are your speeches going to be on?") indicated that she had a great deal of work to do in focusing and refining her topic. Still another person challenged her to "show how this applies to me," indicating that the speaker would have to give more attention to adapting her speech to her audience. Still another asked, "Why do Asian students often excel in mathematics?"—an invitation for her to consider a comparative-cultures approach. She emerged from her presentation both encouraged by this intense interest and aware that she had a great deal of work to do.

Topic briefings offer other advantages. They help you avoid the traps of trivial, overly technical, double-focused, and tired topics. If you propose a trivial topic, look for signs of audience contempt and lack of interest. If you offer an overly technical subject, expect to find confusion and bafflement reflected on the faces in front of you. If you drift into double-focus as you identify specific speech topics, expect someone to ask: "How are you going to do all that?" If you present a topic area that is simply stale from overuse, expect signs of boredom. Topic briefings offer a way to monitor the results of the topic selection process to ensure that it is free of such problems. It encourages you to think less about personal anxieties and more about the strategies of topic refinement. Finally, it encourages the research necessary for you to strengthen and justify your speeches with responsible knowledge.

Developing the Topic Briefing

How do you develop a topic briefing speech? First, as in any speech, *you have to gain the attention of your listeners and engage their interest*. David Zaborowski began his speech on educational reform by making a statement that aroused intense curiosity: "Children are not hamburgers." Of course not, we thought. Whoever would say that they were? What could they possibly mean if they made such an assertion? We were primed to listen intently to the rest of his topic briefing proposing speeches on educational reform.

Second, *you should explain why you are drawn to the topic area*. Erin Bourg opened her speech on medical malpractice by telling the story of how her mother had been victimized by a doctor's bad diagnosis. When you establish such a personal connection with a topic, you become a more *authentic* voice. You suggest that you can bring personal knowledge to bear.

Third, and even more important, *you must show what your listeners have to gain by listening to you speak on the topic*. Erin Evans proposed speeches that would inform her listeners about the abuse of prescription and over-the-counter drugs. On a humorous note, Erin asked. "Did you know that birth control pills can be canceled by antibiotics? My cousin found that out the hard way–her daughter is now two years old." On a more somber note, Erin quoted a recent story in the campus newspaper about a student who had died by overdosing on antidepressant and other prescription drugs. Erin's conclusion seemed self-evident: "Don't you think we should learn a little bit more about what we're putting in our bodies?"

Fourth, *you should point out how you might develop specific speech topics out of your topic area.* In her topic briefing, Leslie Eason proposed to explore racial identity in American life, based on her personal experience with and resentment over what she felt was an overemphasis on race. This was such an all-consuming passion for her that she planned to devote all her speeches to this topic. In her informative speech, she would examine the extent of the problem and explain its consequences for society. For her persuasive speech, she would advocate specific changes in government policies and practices. For her ceremonial speech, she would offer tribute to a public figure who had resisted being placed in a racial box. Her tribute to golfer Tiger Woods appears at the end of Chapter 17.

Fifth, *you should be able to assure listeners that sufficient resources are available to develop "responsible knowledge" for your speeches.* Erin Evans was able to offer such assurance to her listeners—not only that the resources existed but that she was aware of them:

> **There are government agencies that conduct research on drug usage and side effects. Agencies like the National Institute of Health, the Food and Drug Administration, and the Substance Abuse and Mental Health Administration are all wonderful resources. Additionally, public organizations like the National Council on Patient Information and Education offer a very good resource. They want to alert patients and physicians that they need to be aware of symptoms and side effects. Also, WebMD—a commercial group—gathers articles from newspapers and posts them on their web site. It offers a concentrated area of information.**

Sixth, *you should identify any special problems you think you might have, and explain how you intend to cope with them.* Leslie Eason was convinced that many in her audience might think that her topic had been overused or exaggerated, that she might be "beating a dead horse." To overcome this possible objection, she presented powerful personal evidence suggesting that the problem had simply been neglected rather than solved and that it remained serious. The imaginative development of her briefing indicated that she would bring a fresh, insightful point of view to the problem of racial identity. Therefore, her creativity became an implicit argument against the objection that there was little to be learned about the topic area.

Following a topic briefing a speaker must respond to questions from the audience.

Speaker's Notes 6.3

How to Develop a Topic Briefing

1. Engage audience interest on a subject.
2. Explain your attraction to the topic area.
3. Convince listeners they need to learn more about the subject.
4. Show how specific topics can be drawn out of the topic area.
5. Assure listeners that you can build responsible knowledge for your speech(es).
6. Anticipate problems and show how you will handle them.
7. Conclude by reinforcing the importance of the subject.

Seventh, *you should conclude by reminding listeners of the importance of your topic both to you and to them.* Ashley Roberson ended her proposal to develop speeches on Native American themes in the following way:

> **Through my mission trip experiences with the Navajos, I have learned a lot about Native American culture. Through these experiences, I have gained a love and respect for the Native American people. I hope through my upcoming speeches about the Navajo code talkers and about social injustices on the Reservation, that you will develop a love for them as well.**

Listening Constructively to Topic Briefings

Topic briefings place a burden of responsibility on the listener. Your constructive reactions as a listener can help the speaker focus later speeches or even change directions before it is too late. Indeed, much of the assignment's value comes after the briefing itself, when you have a chance to help speakers pursue promising opportunities or avoid pitfalls. If the briefing is not very interesting, you should find a tactful way to alert the speaker. Reporting your reactions honestly may encourage the speaker to explore other, better options. To provide helpful feedback, audiences should keep these questions in mind:

- Would you like to hear more about this topic? Why or why not?
- What suggestions do you have for developing the topic?
- Are you convinced this topic could generate successful speeches?
- Do you have any reservations about the topic? What might the speaker do to avoid or minimize them?

In Summary

To give a successful speech, you must discover promising topic areas, explore the specific topics they might offer, and refine the topic you select into sharply focused statements of purpose and theme. A good topic is one that involves and fascinates both you and your audience. It will be limited so that you can research it adequately and develop a speech that will fit within the allotted time.

Discovering Topic Areas. Three techniques can help you discover promising topic areas. The first, *brainstorming*, is a nondirective technique that encourages the free play of the mind in quest of topics. The second, the *interest chart*, is a directive technique that uses probe questions based on the *topoi of topic discovery*. These questions guide the mind in a systematic discovery process. As you record your interests and those of your listeners in a *topic area inventory chart*, you can often find points where these interests converge. These points often suggest promising topic areas. When you use the third technique, *media prompts*, you scan newspapers, magazines, electronic media, and the Internet to generate ideas. As you move toward your selection, consider whether a given topic fits the assignment, whether you can speak on it within the time limits, and why you would want to speak on it.

Exploring Topic Areas. Two techniques help you explore topic areas to determine specific topic possibilities. The first, *mind mapping*, is a nondirective exploratory technique that imagines a topic area as at the center of a system of ideas. You are encouraged to explore the ideas that surround and associate with the topic area. This exercise helps translate the topic area into more specific topic possibilities. The second, *topic analysis*, is a directive system that features the questions *who? what? where? when? how?* and *why?* Asking this list of questions, modified slightly in searches for persuasive topics, can lead you into a productive exploration of a topic area.

Refining Your Topic. As you seek to refine, polish, and focus a topic to complete the topic selection process, you need to go through three phases of preparation. The first phase confirms the *general purpose* of the speech: whether it is to inform, to persuade, or to celebrate. Speeches that inform share knowledge with listeners. Speeches that persuade advise listeners how to believe or act. Speeches that celebrate emphasize the importance of some occasion, event, or person, often with the intention of amusing or inspiring listeners.

The second phase of refinement pinpoints the *specific purpose* of the speech. The specific purpose states precisely what you want your listeners to understand, believe, feel, or do. It should promise fresh information or advice, should be realizable within the time allotted, and should avoid the traps of double focus, triviality, and technicality.

In the third phase of refinement, framing the *thesis statement*, one summarizes in a single sentence the meaning or message of the speech. The distance between the unstated specific purpose and the stated thesis statement is often a measure of the ethics of a speech. Qualities important to the thesis statement include clarity, focus, color, and concreteness.

Testing Your Topic. A speech or written exercise in which you "sell" your listeners on the importance of a topic you propose to develop is called the *topic briefing*. To develop a successful topic briefing, you must gain your listeners' attention, establish the importance of your topic both to you and to them, show how you might pinpoint your purpose and thematic statement, assure listeners that sufficient resources are available to develop responsible knowledge, identify any problems you must counter to speak successfully, and conclude by reinforcing the topic's value. The assignment emphasizes the importance of constructive listening to help speakers plan and develop their topics for presentation.

Terms to Know

discovery phase
exploration phase
refinement phase
brainstorming
topoi of topic discovery
interest chart
topic area inventory chart
media prompts
mind mapping
topic analysis
general purpose
specific purpose
thesis statement
briefing
topic briefing

Discussion

1. Make a list of trivial topics. What makes them trivial? Is there any way one might make them nontrivial?
2. Make a list of tired topics. Can you think of any way to put new life in them?
3. List some topics that might be too technical for public speaking before general audiences, such as animal cloning. Can you think of any way to transform these topics to make them acceptable?
4. Prepare a topic briefing (either a speech or written report) in which you propose speeches for the topic you rank first in application 3.

Application

1. Use brainstorming, interest charts, and media prompts to discover a minimum of five promising topic areas on which you might speak. Now rank these in order of preference. Explain in class or in a brief paper how you discovered these areas and why you have ranked them in this order.

2. Use mind mapping and topic analysis to narrow and focus the top three topic areas indicated in application 1. List five promising speech topics that emerge from this exploration, in order of preference. Explain in class or in a brief paper how and why these topics emerged and why you ranked them in the order selected.

3. Choose the top three speech topic possibilities indicated in application 2. Refine these topics until you have determined the general purposes, specific purposes, and thesis statements. Report on this process either in class or in a brief paper. Also, indicate your final order of preference among these topics and why you have ranked them in this way. Be sure to take into account the assignment, your time limits, and audience needs and interests, as well as the intrinsic value of the topics.

Notes

1. Robert J. Kriegel, *If It Ain't Broke . . . Break It!* (New York: Warner, 1991), pp. 167–168.

2. Cited in Judith Humphrey, "Executive Eloquence," *Vital Speeches of the Day,* 15 May 1998, p. 469.

3. The concept of mind mapping takes a different direction in books by those who sponsor seminars featuring the technique as the answer to many personal and corporate problems. See, for example, Joyce Wycoff, Steve Cook, and Michael J. Gelb, *Mindmapping: Your Personal Guide to Exploring Creativity and Problem-Solving* (New York: Berkley Publishing Group, 1991), and especially, Tony Buzan and Barry Buzan, *The Mind Map Book: How to Use Radiant Thinking to Maximize Your Brain's Untapped Potential* (New York: Plume Books, 1996).

4. Corporate mind mappers often refer to this space as "landscape." They think of the central concept as a tree, and its associated ideas as "branches."

5. Rudyard Kipling, *Just So Stories* (Garden City, N.Y.: Doubleday, 1921), p. 85.

6. Wayne C. Booth, Gregory G. Colomb, and Joseph M. Williams, *The Craft of Research* (Chicago: University of Chicago Press, 1995), p. 42.

7. Ibid., p. 35.

8. Ibid.

9. Ibid., p. 38.

Fast Food Nation

Hannah Johnston

■ ***Hannah's topic briefing followed David Zaborowski's on "Children Are Not Hamburgers." She connected her speech to David's in her opening, and then she gained attention by asking a startling question. Hannah never stated her thesis statement explicitly. She left listeners to infer it by referring to the interchangeability of "eating spinal cord" and "eating a fast food hamburger."***

Speaking of hamburgers and McDonald's, what would you say if I asked you if you've ever eaten spinal cord? You'd probably think I was crazy, wouldn't you? But what if I asked you, "Have you ever eaten a fast food hamburger?" What's really crazy is the fact that those two questions may be interchangeable.

There's been a lot of controversy lately on what can really be defined as *meat*, and technically, now that's anything that can be separated from the skeleton by AMR—or Advanced Meat Recovery systems. The problem with this is most AMR meat samples contain either bits of spinal cord, brain, and/or nervous tissues. And aside from being really gross, there are serious health risks involved in this: one of the most obvious and most dangerous would be Mad Cow Disease.

What led to the outbreaks of Mad Cow Disease? It began in the eighties when the British were looking for a cheap bone and meat supplement to fatten their cattle with. And they made the supplement from, among other things, road-kill, dead pets from animal shelters, and slaughterhouse waste. This is what they were feeding their cows. Some of those animals became diseased, contracting BSE—Bovine Spongiform Encephalopathy, or Mad Cow Disease.

BSE can be transmitted to humans when they ingest the beef from such cattle. The tissues that most easily transmit this disease are the brain and spinal cord tissue—the same tissues which were being labeled as *meat* and put inside our hamburgers.

People began to die from this in Britain, which prompted investigations and inspections of the slaughterhouses. And this led in turn to several sensational books—exposés of what was really going on behind the slaughterhouse scenes.

■ ***Fast food hamburgers are so widely consumed in this and other countries that Hannah does not need to establish her listeners' connections to the topic. Instead she spends her time defining the problem area she wishes to deal with.***

These books were in the tradition of Upton Sinclair's *The Jungle*—which, when he wrote it in 1906, led to a revolution in the meat packing industry and opened people's eyes. One in particular—a book called *Fast Food Nation: The Dark Side of the All-American Meal*—began to turn heads nationwide as Americans became aware of what they'd really been putting in their stomachs.

■ ***As Hannah moves into her discussion of resources, she reassures listeners that good information exists. She indicates that the real issue is whether the problem remains timely.***

This topic can easily be developed into an informative speech. I found so much information from newspapers of documented cases of food poisoning, mad cow disease, that sort of thing, to online journals and books like the one I mentioned that describe all the gory details of what's really being put in our food.

I don't know yet whether I'm going to carry it into a persuasive speech. I will have to do some more research before I decide one way or another, because most of the outbreaks of Mad Cow and things like that in people were in the mid- to late nineties. So, I need to confirm where we stand now: whether there have been any real changes in how we retrieve meat, whether there have been new laws reforming the safety procedures—things like that.

The only major problems I've come into researching this problem are following supposedly legitimate links to websites that turn out to be just anti-meat sites by crazy vegetarians, and that sort of thing. But there's enough real information from journals and books and offshoots of the U.S.D.A. food inspection website that I've got a lot to investigate.

So you can look forward to a real queaser of a speech. Sorry for ruining lunch!

■ ***Hannah ends rather abruptly. She might have developed the lunch idea further by talking about fast food houses near campus, and suggesting alternative eating plans.***

Researching Your Topic

7

OUTLINE

This chapter will help you

- acquire responsible knowledge
- evaluate research materials
- conduct a strategic search in the library and on the Internet
- plan interviews to acquire special information
- develop a system for recording research

I use not only all the brains I have, but all I can borrow.

PRESIDENT WOODROW WILSON

Jeremy couldn't understand why he was expected to do research for his speech. After all, he knew what he wanted to talk about—cell phone etiquette—and felt he could speak from firsthand experience. He tried to reason with his instructor, telling her he had some wonderful examples and stories about the misuse of cell phones and was sure the audience would find them very interesting. He added, "I know what good manners are. I was brought up to be polite."

Nevertheless, Jeremy's instructor insisted that he expand his knowledge beyond personal experience, and for all the right reasons. Even though personal experience adds authenticity to a speech, it is seldom adequate as the basis for public speaking. And although we have covered selecting your topic before taking up research, you will probably have to explore the topic before you can focus it precisely and frame your main points. Once you have begun reading what others have to say, you may even wish to reconsider your specific purpose. In short, to prepare an effective and ethical speech, you must gain responsible knowledge of your topic.

Acquiring Responsible Knowledge

Responsible knowledge is the most comprehensive understanding of your topic that you can develop in the time available for preparation. It includes information on

- the main issues concerning your topic.
- what respected authorities say about it.
- the latest developments relevant to it.
- related local applications of special interest to your audience.

To secure responsible knowledge, you should enter the research phase of preparation with an open, inquiring mind. Even if you are convinced that one side is correct on a controversial topic, try to understand why others might feel differently. This will help you develop arguments that reach out to more people.

When you ask listeners for their time and attention, you must give them something of value in return. Having responsible knowledge earns you the right to speak.[1] It allows you to enrich the lives of listeners with good information or advice. Whenever you speak, you put your mind and character on display. If you haven't made an effort to acquire responsible knowledge, you are saying, in effect, "I don't have much to offer, and I really don't care." On the other hand, having responsible knowledge may enhance your ethos in terms of both competence and character.[2]

Although you cannot become an authority on most topics with ten hours or even ten days of research, you can certainly learn enough to speak responsibly. The major sources of information available to you are your own knowledge and experience, library resources, Internet resources, and interviews. Each of these sources can provide you with facts, testimony, examples, or narratives to use as supporting materials in your speech.

As you pursue your quest for responsible knowledge, keep in mind the checklist offered in the Speaker's Notes 7.1, "Checklist for Acquiring Responsible Knowledge." It offers an overview of possible resources. Not every source will be appropriate for every speech, and some sources will be much more appropriate than others for a particular speech. By checking off the items one by one as they apply in your situation, you can be sure you have conducted your research thoroughly and systematically.

Go to the **Research Strategy Worksheet** under **Conducting Research and Gathering Support Materials** in the **SpeechStudio** to help with developing a strategy for maximum research efficiency.
Go to http://college.hmco.com/eduspace/

Speaker's Notes 7.1

Checklist for Acquiring Responsible Knowledge

1. _____ I have explored my personal knowledge of the topic.
2. _____ I have expanded my knowledge by consulting general and/or specialized dictionaries or encyclopedias.
3. _____ I have checked newspaper indexes and recent newsmagazines to ensure that my information is up to date.
4. _____ I have used library and Internet search services to identify books and articles on my subject.
5. _____ I have looked for materials in periodicals to enrich my speech.
6. _____ I have considered the usefulness of the following sources:
   _____ atlases
   _____ biographical resources
   _____ books of quotations
   _____ almanacs
   _____ government documents
7. _____ I have looked for local applications of my topic, using the indexing services and searching local newspaper indexes and abstracts.
8. _____ I have interviewed experts about my topic.

Because your preparation time will be limited, you should develop a strategic research plan. This will help you use your time more efficiently and also help you locate and evaluate your materials. You should

- assess your personal knowledge and experience to determine what additional information you need to make a responsible presentation.
- obtain this information by accessing library resources, using the Internet, and/or interviewing people for information and opinions.
- take notes to use in preparing your speech.

Personal Knowledge and Experience

Personal knowledge and experience add credibility, authenticity, and interest to a speech. You may not be an acknowledged authority on a subject, but personal stories may suggest that you have special insights on your subject. They also make it easier for an audience to identify with you and the topic.[3]

If you lack direct experience with a topic, you can always try to arrange some. Suppose you are planning a speech on how local television stations prepare newscasts. You have gathered information from books and periodicals, but it seems rather dry and lifeless. Call a local television station and ask the news director if you might spend an afternoon in the newsroom of the station, so that you can get a feel for what goes on during that hectic time right before a newscast. Take in the noise, the action, and the excitement that occur before and during a show. All of this can help enrich your speech. You might also schedule an interview with the news director while you are at the station (see the "Interviewing for Information" section later in this chapter).

As valuable as it is, personal experience is seldom sufficient to provide all the information, facts and figures, and testimony that you will need for your speech. Your personal knowledge may be limited, the sources from which you learned may have been biased, or your experiences may not have been typical. Even people who are acknowledged authorities on a subject look to other experts to give added authority to their messages. Use your personal knowledge and experience as a starting point and expand it through research.

Prepare a personal knowledge and experience summary sheet similar to the one shown in Figure 7.1. Include on your summary sheet what you know (or think you know) about the topic, where or how you learned it, and what additional information you might need to find. Also, jot down any brief references to examples or narratives from your experience so that you can remember them as you put your speech together. Use your summary sheet to give direction to your research.

Current periodicals can provide up-to-date information and opinions.

Doing Research in the Library

Although knowledge obtained from the library may lack the excitement and immediacy that personal experience provides, it

Figure 7.1
Personal Knowledge Summary

What I Know (or Think I Know)	Where/How I Learned It	What I Need to Find Out
Not many grizzly bears in park	Worked there 2 summers. Heard rangers talk about it, only saw 1 and I was looking	Approximately how many bears are in the park
Go to back country to see the grizzlies	Same as above/personal experience	Where in park they are most likely to be seen; specify trails and areas
Grizzly attacks are rare	Same as above	When was first attack recorded? Last? # of attacks relative to # of tourists; relative to other types of injuries
Camping precautions	See above, brochure, personal experience	Information probably sufficient

Examples/Narratives I Might Use in Speech:

For the past two summers I've worked waiting tables at Mammoth Springs Lodge in Yellowstone Park. We got two days a week off, and I spent nearly all my free time hiking and camping in the back country, far away from the tourists and crowds in the park. I counted up the number of hours I spent that way and discovered that I had logged in more than 350 hours in these remote locations—in the grizzly bear habitat of the park—hoping to see one. Only once, in all those hours, did I see a grizzly bear, and that was from a distance of about half a mile. If I hadn't been sitting quietly with my binoculars focused on a watering area, I probably would have missed seeing that one!

has definite advantages. Library research can give you a broad perspective and a sound basis for speaking responsibly. It can extend, correct, and enrich your experience by acquainting you with the experience and knowledge of others.

Because college and university libraries vary widely in the resources they offer and the means of accessing those resources, we strongly suggest that you take the guided tour usually offered at the beginning of each term at your library. Even if you took the tour last year, take it again. You may have missed some important information the first time through, or your library may have changed. If a hands-on tour is not available, access your library's web site through your college's home page. There may be an online guided tour or a tutorial that will help you use the resources most effectively. You may even be able to access their catalogues and databases from a personal computer.

As a general rule, most college and large municipal libraries have the following major research resources:

- *Reference or research librarian*: The most valuable resource in the library. This person can make your research easier and quicker by steering you to the most helpful materials in the library's collections.
- *Online catalog*: Lists the books and periodicals available in the library (and often available for use off-site). The catalog will also tell you the immediate status of an item: whether it has been checked out, placed on reserve, or is accessible at the moment.
- *General periodical databases*: These databases search a variety of periodicals and may provide abstracts or direct access to the full text of articles. Examples include FirstSearch, Infotrac, LexisNexis Academic, and ProQuest. Many of these databases are available through personal computer access, as well as in the library.

- *Special area databases*: These databases include such resources as BusManagement (Business Management), AskERIC (Education), ComAbstracts (Communication), and Humanities Abstracts (Humanities). Most provide abstracts, and some provide full texts of articles.
- *News resources*: Indexes to local and state newspapers, plus computerized databases that access many news sources, such as Newsbank Infoweb, World News Connection, and Ethnic Newswatch.
- *Reference area*: A special section of the library that contains encyclopedias, yearbooks, dictionaries, almanacs, atlases, and print indexes to periodicals.
- *Government documents area*: The repository for federal, state, and local government publications.
- *Nonprint media archives*: Collections of films, videos, CDs, recordings, and microfilms.
- *Special collections area:* Contains clippings and other materials that can help you adapt your topic to local needs and interests.

Many of these resources are described in greater detail in the "Guide to Library and Internet Resources" following this chapter.

Doing Research on the Internet

The Internet offers a wealth of information. It is an excellent source of breaking news, contemporary speech texts, and other time-sensitive material. It is also a helpful source of local news, with area newspapers and television station web sites that are automatically refreshed as information becomes available. Finally, the Internet is available 24/7, so that when your library is not open you can still find material for your speeches or update them at the last minute. This section aims to help you become an adept and critical Internet user. At the end of the chapter you will also find a list of recommended Internet research sites.

As you read through this material, keep in mind that the Internet is constantly changing. According to Bruce Clay, an Internet search consultant, "The search results you get today may not be the search results you'll see in January."[4] If a URL provided in this chapter doesn't open for you, try running the name of that web site through a general search engine to see if it has moved, or wait awhile and try the site again.

If you are a novice at using the Internet, the following books and web sites might be helpful:

> John R. Levine, Carol Baroudi, and Margaret Levine Young, *The Internet for Dummies* (IDG Books, latest edition)
>
> Joe Kraynak, *The Absolute Beginners Guide to Computers and the Internet* (Que Corp., 2001)
>
> *Microsoft Internet Tutorial*: http://www.microsoft.com/insider/internet/default.htm

The first step in learning to do Internet research is determining which search engine to use. You have probably used one of the more popular search engines such as Yahoo! (http://www.yahoo.com), but you may not know that there are various types of search sites available. The major types useful for research include general search engines, meta-search engines, subject directories, and gateways to the "invisible web."

General Search Engines. A **general search engine** allows you to enter a key word or phrase, then search the World Wide Web for sites containing that word or phrase. The searches are conducted by computer robots. The results may be organized in terms of relevance, popularity, or date of placement on the Web. The references cited are not screened for quality, so you may find links to everything from scholarly reports to Bubba's Homepage. You should know that many general search engines start their lists of sites with "sponsored" links, links to web sites that pay the search engine for optimal placement. Although the results from general search engines may contain a lot of useless links, they can be a good starting point for your research. Three of the more useful general search engines are Google (http://www.google.com), Teoma (http://www.teoma.com), and Alltheweb (http://www.alltheweb.com).

Meta-Search Engines. A **meta-search engine** engages several general search engines at the same time, thereby expanding the scope of your research. Meta-search engines work in much the same manner as general search engines, but they provide a broader base of information. Many of the meta-search engines cluster their results into subareas of the topic searched. Some offer suggestions for refining your search to get more topic-specific results. Three of the more useful meta-search engines are Vivisimo (http://vivisimo.com), Ixquick (http://www.ixquick.com), and SurfWax (http://www.surfwax.com).

InterConnections.LearnMore 7.1

Conducting Internet Research

Research-Quality Web Research
http://www.lib.berkeley.edu/TeachingLib/Guides/Internet/About.html#New
This online tutorial, developed and maintained by Joe Barker, the teaching library Internet instruction program coordinator of the University of California-Berkeley Library, provides a detailed, guided step-by-step approach to Internet research.

Teaching Internet Research Skills
http://www.virtualchase.com/researchskills/
This online seminar was developed by Genie Tyburski as part of the Drexel University College of Information Science and Technology's Continuing Professional Education Program. The site contains much interesting information not found in other online tutorials.

Deep Content: Guide to Effective Searching of the Internet
http://brightplanet.com/deepcontent/tutorials/search/index.aspn
This online tutorial provides detailed instruction on searching the invisible (deep) web. It was developed by BrightPlanet, a provider of business solutions for researching, monitoring, and indexing both surface and deep web content. This same group also sponsors the CompletePlanet search tool mentioned in this chapter.

Subject Directories. A **subject directory** organizes links on topic-specific materials. For example, a subject directory may contain links to categories such as "humanities," "education," "entertainment," and "sports" as some of their options. Many of the subject directories contain subdirectories within their major groupings: "education," for example, may be broken down into "K-12 resources," "bilingual education," and the like. The subject directories are compiled by humans, the web pages are handpicked, and the entries tend to be well annotated. Three of the more useful subject directories are Infomine (http://infomine.ucr.edu/Main.html), Librarians' Index to the Internet (www.lii.org), and Profusion (http://www.profusion.com).

Invisible Web Gateways. The term ***invisible web***, or *deep web*, as it is sometimes called, refers to a multitude of databases on the Internet that are not included in the searches of the more popular general search or meta-search engines. The invisible web contains much high-quality information from reputable sources. Search tools to uncover resources in the invisible web often provide subject directories with links to these otherwise difficult-to-find databases. For example, a search of the "United States history" category in the Invisible Web Directory yields links to such databases as History and Politics Out Loud (http://www.hpol.org), Lewis and Clark Journals Database (http://www.pbs.org/lewisandclark), and the Suffragists Oral History Project (http://bancroft.berkeley.edu/ROHO/ohonline/suffragists.html). Three major gateways to the invisible web are Invisible Web (http://www.invisible-web.net), Direct Search (http://www.freepint.com/gary/direct.htm), and Complete Planet (http://www.completeplanet.com). Figure 7.2, "Searching the Invisible Web,"

Figure 7.2

Searching the Invisible Web

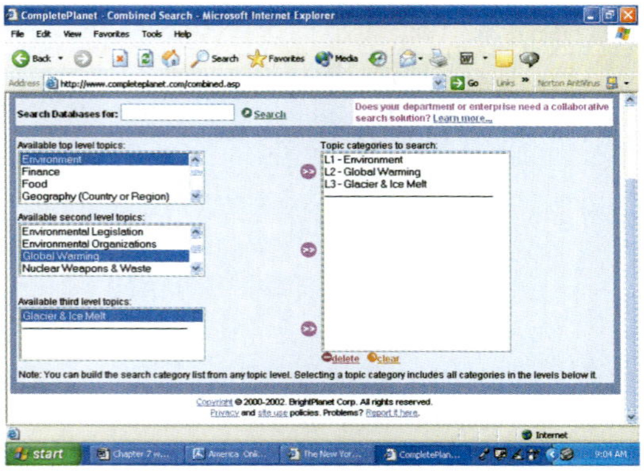

illustrates a web site that helps you make your search more specific. The box labeled "Available top level topics" contains key words similar to the "topic areas" we discussed in Chapter 6. Once you select one of the topic areas, a group of related subtopic areas appears in the second-level box. When you select a subtopic, more specific sub-subtopics appear in the third-level box.

Additional Suggestions. As you may have guessed from this information, there is often little overlap among the various search engines, meta-search engines, directories, and invisible web gateways. Therefore, *you should always try at least three search techniques to get the best results.* Most search tools will contain an "advanced search" option that instructs you how to limit or expand your inquiry. Running a Boolean search can also help limit or expand your research (see Speaker's Notes 7.2, "Tips for Conducting a Boolean Search").

When you access an article on the Internet, take careful notes on the specific information needed to document the source before you save the information on your computer: note the author's name and credentials if stated, the sponsoring source, the date of publication, the date you accessed the material, and the URL (Universal Resource Locator) or web address, which may be lost when you download the material to your desktop. Better still, save the link with your "Favorites" or "Bookmark" command so that you can easily return to the site.

Remember, you must be careful when you "cut and paste" material from Internet documents to your research notes. Unless you specify the source of the material and indicate in some way that a passage is a direct quotation, you could find yourself inadvertently committing plagiarism.

Speaker's Notes 7.2

Tips for Conducting a Boolean Search

1. Use AND or a plus sign to focus your search:
   mammogram AND ultrasound or mammogram+ultrasound.
2. Use OR or a slash mark to broaden your search:
   mammogram OR ultrasound or mammogram/ultrasound.
3. Use NOT or a minus sign to restrict or narrow your search:
   Lions NOT NFL or Lions-NFL.
4. Use NEAR when words should be close to each other in the document:
   moon NEAR river.
5. Use quotation marks to be more specific in your search:
   Baltimore Preparatory School gives 2,765 hits.
   "Baltimore Preparatory School" gives 275 hits.
6. When all else fails, read the instructions under "Advanced Search Tips" on the search engine home page.

One final caution: Be careful when typing in the web address of an Internet site you wish to reach. Once, when trying to access a popular computer magazine online, one of your authors inadvertently typed in ".net" rather than ".com," and she ended up at a porn site. To see what such a seemingly minor difference in a URL can mean, access and compare the http://www.whitehouse web sites from the following domains: .gov, .org, .net, and .com.

Evaluating Research Materials

When you find material that you think might be usable in your speeches, you must test it carefully. As you research your topic, ask yourself:

- Does this article contain relevant and useful information?
- Does this article cite experts that I can quote in my speech?
- Are there interesting examples I can use to make ideas clearer?
- Are there stories that can bring my topic to life?

Beyond these simple questions, it is important that the material you use in your speech meets the basic criteria we suggested for critical listening and critical thinking: it must be relevant, representative, recent, and reliable. As we noted in Chapter 4:

- Relevant material applies directly to your topic and specific purpose.
- Representative material depicts a situation as it typically exists.
- Recent material contains the latest knowledge.
- Reliable material comes from credible sources and can be confirmed by other authorities.

We cover the application of these criteria to each type of supporting material in Chapter 8.

Evaluating Material from Library Resources

As you do research in the library, be alert to two potential problems. First, you must consider the credibility of your sources in terms of the ethos of both the author and the publication. Second, you must remember that the timeliness of information is critical for some topics; on these, you must seek out the most up-to-date information available.

As you assess the credibility of an author, ask yourself: "Does this source qualify as an expert on my topic?" If the author is not well known or not associated with a prestigious organization or institution, check out his or her credentials in one of the biographical indexes. Some of the material you find may be written by professional journalists. In such cases you should consider the credibility of the "experts" cited in the articles.

You must also consider the ethos of the publication in which the material appears. Professional journals are often seen as more credible than popular periodicals such as magazines and newspapers. In turn, popular periodicals themselves vary in terms of their credibility. For most audiences, mainline newspapers will be deemed more credible than tabloids, and upscale magazines such as *Atlantic Monthly* will be seen as more credible than *Reader's Digest*. Popular periodicals may also reflect political or social biases. For example, the *New Republic* offers a more liberal perspective on contemporary issues and the *National Review* presents a more conservative outlook. Consequently, as you select authors and publications to cite in your speeches, you should consider how their reputation might affect the way your listeners receive your message.

The more sensitive or controversial the topic of your speech, the more important the credibility of your sources becomes. For example, let us assume that you wish to present a speech supporting the doctrine of preemptive war. From previous class discussions, you suspect that many in your audience may not be friendly to that point of view. For these listeners, citing information or opinions that support your case from more liberal sources such as the *New Republic* might surprise them and get them to listen more sympathetically. Such citations would function as "reluctant testimony" in which sources speak against their apparent self-interest. We discuss this often powerful use of citations in more detail in the next chapter.

Evaluating Material from the Internet

You must be especially careful while evaluating information you find on the Internet. Remember, anyone can put anything on the Internet. Internet material is subject to few—if any—legal, financial, or editorial constraints. How can you determine whether the information you find there satisfies the requirements of responsible knowledge?

First, you need to determine the kind of web site you have accessed. Then you need to apply an especially rigorous set of standards as you evaluate what you find. The basic types of web sites you will encounter on the Internet are advocacy sites, information sites, and personal sites.

Advocacy Web Sites. The purpose of an **advocacy web site** is to change attitudes or behaviors. An advocacy site might ask for contributions, try to influence voting, or simply strive to promote a cause. The URL of a nonprofit advocacy site often ends with .org. Some examples of advocacy sites include Greenpeace (http://www.greenpeaceusa.org), the National Rifle Association (http://www.nra.org), the Democratic National Committee (http://www.democrats.org), and the Republican National Committee (http://www.rnc.org).

The Greenpeace home page shown in Figure 7.3 illustrates many of the features that should alert you to the intent of an advocacy web site. For example, at the top there is a button to click to make a donation to the group. Also near the top of the page is a frame containing links to the various campaigns the group is conducting. Another place near the top provides a "Get Active" link that connects you to information on volunteering for the causes the group espouses.

Most nonprofit advocacy group web sites contain credible information, although they typically will present only one side of an issue. Knowing that the group has an agenda they want to promote, you should evaluate the material on advocacy sites very carefully. Additionally, when you access a web site that champions one side of an issue, try to find another web site that represents the other side. For example, if you look up something on the National Rifle Association web site, also check out the Brady Campaign to Prevent Gun Violence web site (http://www.handguncontrol.org).

Information Web Sites. The purpose of an **information web site** is to provide factual information on a specific topic. Information web sites may include research reports; current world, national, or local news; government statistics; or simply general information like you might find in an encyclopedia or almanac. The URLs of information web sites may have a variety of endings, such as .edu, .gov, or .com. For example, both the Mayo Clinic web site (http://www.mayoclinic.com) and the MEDLINEplus web site (http://www.medlineplus.gov) are excellent sources of

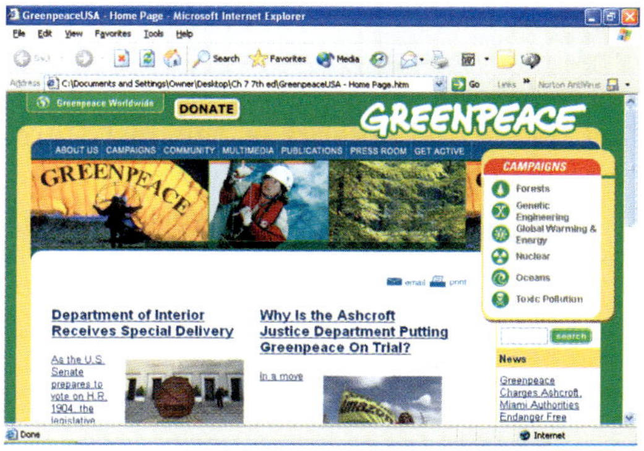

Figure 7.3
Advocacy Website Homepage

information about health issues. The material on the Mayo Clinic web site has been prepared by physicians and scientists affiliated with the clinic; the material on the MEDLINEplus web site comes from the government-sponsored National Library of Medicine.

Figure 7.4 shows the Mayo Clinic home page. Even though this web site is registered in the commercial domain (.com), the only thing it seems to be selling is good health practices. Note some of the differences between this information home page and the advocacy home page shown in Figure 7.3. You are not asked for a donation, and the only thing you can sign up for is a free electronic newsletter on health information.

It is not always so easy to differentiate between advocacy web sites and information web sites. Some advocacy web sites may deliberately downplay their true role so that they appear to be presenting straightforward information that is unbiased and free from persuasive intent. Caution should be the rule that guides you through such web sites. A reputable information web site will typically designate the author of the information and specify that person's credentials. It may also include the date that information was posted, and it may provide links to other related sources of information. When such a web site does include commercial advertising, it will separate such entries clearly from informational copy so that there is little chance for confusion.

Personal Web Sites. The purposes of a **personal web site** are many and varied. They represent the work or opinion of a single individual who may or may not be affiliated with an official organization. They can contain anything from a list of a person's favorite restaurants in Nashville, Tennessee (http://eller.arizona.edu/~reiley/home.html), to the scholarly musing of a highly regarded rhetorician (http://www.mcgees.net/fragments) to incoherent ramblings about conspiracy theories.[5] The home page of David Reiley Jr., an associate professor of economics at the University of Arizona, contains material on topics ranging from his teaching and professional interests to his thoughts and opinions on music, astronomy, food, and

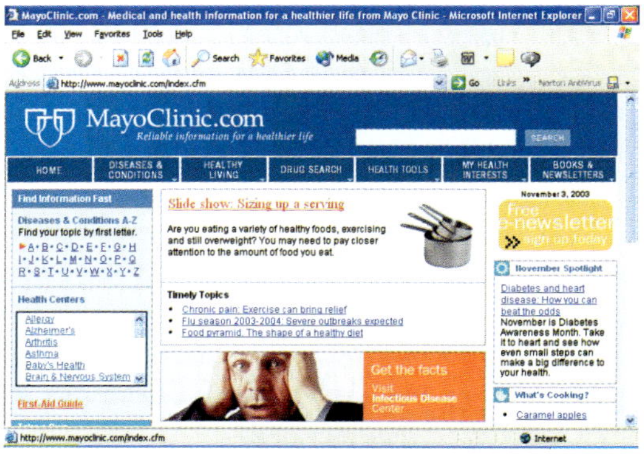

Figure 7.4
Information Website Homepage

wine. The Fragments site of the late University of Iowa professor Michael Calvin McGee contains everything from essays in critical rhetoric, to links to primary documents in rhetoric and public address, to a rogue's gallery of photos of people in the field, including one of the authors of this text (http://www.mcgees.net/fragments/gallery/images/BigO_Osborn-Gina.jpg).

Because there are absolutely no controls over what can be published on personal home pages, you should be careful about evaluating and using material from them.

Criteria for Internet Evaluation

Janet E. Alexander and Marsha Ann Tate, information specialists at the Wolfgram Memorial Library of Widener University, suggest five criteria for evaluating Internet research:

- authority
- accuracy
- objectivity
- currency
- coverage[6]

These criteria are also useful for evaluating material from any source.

Authority. To determine the **authority** of information you find on the Internet, you must evaluate the credentials of both the source and the sponsor of the information. Most reputable web sites will provide information regarding the source or author of the material and the sponsoring agency. If no one takes credit for what is on the site, don't trust it.

Even when the source or author of material is listed, you should investigate the person's credentials. Does the web site provide contact information? Is a URL or email address provided? Is a postal address included? Such information should help you verify any claims of competence that may be found on the site. You might contact the person via email, or, if a mailing address is provided, you might look for a phone number in an online telephone directory (http://www.switchboard.com) and call the author. If authors seem defensive when you contact them, you might want to consider not using their material.

To ensure responsible knowledge in your speeches, carefully evaluate materials you find on the Internet.

You also can often verify an author's credentials by running an Internet search with the person's name enclosed in quotation marks. If the author claims an academic affiliation, go to that institution's web site and look in the faculty directory. Many educational institutions also include faculty resumés on their web sites. If the author claims a medical affiliation, run the name through the Medline Index on the National Institutes of Health web site (http://www.nlm.nih.gov) and

Questions to Ask About Internet Materials

Speaker's Notes 7.3

1. What type of a web site have I accessed? Advocacy? Information? Personal?
2. Is the author or sponsoring agency identified?
3. Does the author or sponsoring agency have appropriate credentials to address the issue?
4. Does the material contain links to other information on the subject or citations of available print resources?
5. Is the material objective, or does it seem tainted by bias?
6. Is the material up-to-date on time-sensitive topics?
7. Is the material covered with enough breadth and depth?

see what comes up. If the author claims a hospital or clinic affiliation, check that source as well. If the author claims to have written books on the subject, check the Library of Congress catalog (http://www.loc.gov) or access Amazon.com (http://www.amazon.com) to check for a listing of books by that person and for biographical data that is often provided on the site.

You should also evaluate the sponsorship of a web site in a similar manner. Most reputable web sites will have an "About Us" or "About This Website" link on their home page. Check this out before doing anything else. If it is not immediately obvious, you can determine the sponsor of the material by deleting parts of the URL, starting at the right and moving toward the left. A tilde (˜) suggests a personal home page. The information immediately to the left of the domain (right before .com, .gov, etc.) suggests the sponsoring organization. For example, a URL with "nih.gov" indicates that the National Institutes of Health is the sponsoring agency. Run a search with the name of the organization or association enclosed in quotation marks for additional information and news about the group. You can also check out an organization or association using the Scholarly Societies Project web site (http://www.lib.uwaterloo.ca/society/overview.html).

Once you have verified the credentials of the author and sponsoring agency, ask yourself if the person's or group's expertise is appropriate to the material in question. For example, a lawyer could provide credible information on legal issues, but she might not be considered an expert on medical questions. Also consider how your audience might evaluate any controversial sources of information. If listeners would not accept them as authorities because of their reputation, it will not help you to cite them in your speech.

Accuracy. One way to evaluate the **accuracy** of information is to look for additional links to other web sites or citations of print documents that relate to the topic. Check these out to confirm the correctness of the information. Material that is accurate and reliable should be verifiable through other sources. If the site claims that this is "exclusive" information that is so "new" or "revolutionary" that no one else has access to it, beware!

The sources of statistical information should be identified, and the originating reports should either be available online or as print materials accessible in libraries. The results of proprietary research that has been done for compensation may not be available to the general public. This does not mean that such information is not reliable, only that it should be subject to intense critical scrutiny. If you cannot ascertain the accuracy and reliability of the information you find, don't use it in your speeches.

Caution lights should turn on in your head if Internet materials are filled with spelling and grammatical errors. These problems could indicate incompetence, a lack of quality control, and/or carelessness on the part of those posting the material. At the very least, such problems raise significant questions concerning the accuracy and reliability of the material offered.

Finally, evaluate the accessibility of the information to an average, educated consumer. If the writing seems purposely obscure, exercise caution when using it. Most reputable information web sites present material in a way that is understandable to a lay audience. One excellent web site guide for evaluating the overall accuracy of online materials may be found at Virtual Chase (http://www.virtualchase.com/quality/index.html), a web site devoted to teaching legal professionals and legal librarians how to do quality research online.

Objectivity. The **objectivity** of information on a web site measures its freedom from bias or personal feelings and the degree to which you can trust it. It goes without saying that advocacy web sites and many commercial web sites contain elements of bias. Advocacy web sites try to "sell" you a particular point of view; most commercial web sites try to "sell" you a product line. Many advocacy and commercial web sites are up-front with their intentions. This does not necessarily mean that you cannot find reliable or accurate information on their sites. In fact, these web pages may use "unimpeachable data to influence readers."[7] However, knowing that a source of information is not objective should be a cue to look for additional information from differing perspectives.

The biased web sites that try to hide their objectives are the ones you really must be wary of. The lack of an "About Us" or "Mission Statement" link should be a clear indication that the site may be peddling something other than what seems evident. Disreputable web sites may provide misleading medical information or dispense hatred while seeming benign.[8] For example, one web site, Bamboo Delight Company (http://www.bamboo-delight.com/), offers links to anti-Semitic and racist web sites along with information on "Chinese medicinal exercises." Also be wary of sites that dazzle you with stunning graphics or special effects, where the sizzle may cover up a lack of substance or malicious intent. Verify any information from such sites from reputable sources such as those listed following this chapter.

Currency. The **currency** of information on the Internet relates to the date of posting or revising material. Currency is particularly important on time-sensitive topics such as medical research and foreign relations. The most timely materials on the Internet may be found on newspaper web sites. The NewsDirectory.com web site (http://www.ecola.com) contains links to daily and weekly newspapers, television stations, magazines, and other media outlets throughout the world. Many of the online newspapers, such as the *New York Times* (http://www.nytimes.com), have searchable archives of past issues, allowing you to trace the evolution of news on a specific topic up to the present.

Coverage. The **coverage** of material concerns the breadth and depth of information provided. No single article can provide all the information you need on a topic. Reputable, ethical web sites will contain links to additional information or research that should be useful. When you are visiting an advocacy site on a controversial topic, you should realize that other opposed positions may not even be mentioned there. You should seek additional resources for other perspectives. In general, you should assume that any single source offers only a partial view. Check other sites to ensure that you are getting a larger, more complete, and less distorted picture.

For example, if you researched drilling for oil in the Arctic National Wildlife Refuge, you would encounter advocacy sites as diametrically opposed as Arctic Power ("Take Action! Help Pass the Energy Bill") and Defenders of Wildlife ("Save the Arctic Refuge from Big Oil"). You would have to read these opposed perspectives carefully to understand the background of the dispute, the major interests in conflict, what each had to gain or lose, what each proposed or opposed, and the major arguments each offered. Only then could you meet the standard of responsible knowledge needed to develop informative or persuasive speeches on the topic.

The depth of information needed to acquire responsible knowledge varies with the topic you are researching and the audience for whom the material is intended. For example, the more important a topic is to the well-being of your audience, the greater the depth of information you need. It may be acceptable to cite a public periodical such as the *Reader's Digest* on a topic that has benign consequences for your audience, such as cell phone etiquette. However, if the topic is a more important one, such as the effects of air pollution on the health of listeners, you should search for material from sources that are more scientifically oriented. To find this deeper information, run your topic through a search engine that accesses the invisible web.

Conducting Strategic Research

Begin your research by developing a strategic plan. The "Research Strategy Worksheet" shown in Figure 7.5, should help you conduct this work efficiently. Fill in this form and accumulate research notes until you are satisfied that you have acquired responsible knowledge. As you move from top to bottom of the form, you will be following these steps:

1. Developing an overview of your subject
2. Building a bibliography on your topic
3. Acquiring in-depth knowledge
4. Checking to see that your information is up to date
5. Focusing your discussion on local applications

We discuss each of these steps in the following sections.

Develop an Overview

You should begin developing a comprehensive picture of your subject by consulting sources of background information about it. Even if you have extensive personal experience, you may find that your knowledge is incomplete, or you may discover areas of the topic that you had overlooked. The reviews also can help you focus your speech by pointing out the most important ideas concerning your topic.

InterConnections.LearnMore 7.2

Evaluating Internet Resources

Bibliography on Evaluating Internet Resources
http://www.lib.vt.edu/research/libinst/evalbiblio.html
A directory of web sites that address the problem of using critical thinking skills to evaluate Internet resources; sponsored by the University Libraries at Virginia Tech.

Evaluating Web Resources
http://www2.widener.edu/Wolfgram-Memorial-Library/webevaluation/webeval.htm
One of the first and best web sites offering information on evaluating Internet resources, with checklists for evaluating advocacy, information, and personal web sites; prepared by Jan Alexander and Marsha Ann Tate and sponsored by the Widener University Library.

Internet Detective
http://sosig-ac.uk./desire/internet-detective.html
An online tutorial on evaluating Internet research, with excellent models for applying critical thinking skills to the analysis of Internet information; sponsored by the Institute for Learning and Research Technology at Bristol University, Bristol, England.

The Virtual Chase
http://www.virtualchase.com/quality/index/html
This online guide for evaluating Internet resources is part of a public service web site sponsored by Ballard, Spahr, Andrews, & Ingersoll, LLP. Also included are articles about conducting Internet research. The materials are prepared and maintained by Genie Tyburski, author of a law office computing column on electronic research strategies, and Greg Kaplan, Internet services librarian from Drexel University.

Review articles are found mainly in encyclopedias and specialized dictionaries, housed in the reference section of the library. On the Internet, go to the Library Spot (http://www.libraryspot.com) for links to most of the major encyclopedias online. General encyclopedias, such as *Encyclopaedia Britannica* (http://www.eb.com), contain background information, specify key words to use in your search for in-depth information, and often list references for additional research. The articles are brief and written in lay language.

Specialized encyclopedias, such as the *International Encyclopedia of the Social and Behavioral Sciences* (http://www.iesbs.com), cover specific topics in greater detail. Specialized dictionaries, available on diverse subjects ranging from American

Figure 7.5
Research Strategy Worksheet

Topic: ______________________________

Specific Purpose: ______________________________

General Information Sources: (List sources of general information applicable to your topic) ______________________________

Key Terms and Access to Information Sources: (List the key terms you will use andŁ 2 sources of access to information you will use to identify specific and/or in-depth references)

Key Terms *1.* ______________ *2.* ______________

3. ______________ *4.* ______________

Access *1.* ______________ *2.* ______________

Specific and/or In-Depth Information References: (List 3 or 4 references to specific and/or in-depth information applicable to your topic of which at least 2 must be from periodicals or books)

1. ______________________________

2. ______________________________

3. ______________________________

4. ______________________________

Current Information References: (List 1 or 2 sources of current information if applicable to your topic)

1. ______________________________

2. ______________________________

Local Applications Sources: (List 1 or 2 sources for local applications material if applicable to your topic)

1. ______________________________

2. ______________________________

slang to zoology, provide more than definitions and pronunciations. For example, the *Oxford English Dictionary* presents the origin, meaning, and history of English words. A directory of dictionaries on the Internet is located at the Open Directory Project (http://dmoz.org/Reference/Dictionaries).

Once you have found sources of general information that are relevant to your topic, read the background material, take notes on what you find, and identify at least four key terms you can use to access in-depth information (see Figure 7.5).

Build a Bibliography

Since your preparation time for speeches is limited, you must know how to access information quickly. The major sources of access to information in the library include periodical indexes, newspaper indexes, and the card or online catalog. Some of the periodical indexes, such as the *Reader's Guide to Periodical Literature,* cover publications of general interest. Others, such as the *Business Periodicals Index,* are specific to a subject area. Many indexes are now available on computers in the library, which saves research time. To access information from an index, you must enter the key terms you have identified for your topic. As noted earlier, most encyclopedia entries list relevant key terms.

On the Internet, the major sources of access to information are the search engines discussed in detail earlier in this chapter. Use all these materials to build a bibliography on your topic. From your bibliography, identify those articles or books that seem most relevant to your specific purpose.

Acquire In-Depth Knowledge

Most of the facts and figures, testimony, examples, ideas for narratives, and materials for presentation aids will come from in-depth sources of information, such as periodicals and books. The "Guide to Library and Internet Resources" at the end of this chapter contains a list of periodicals that may be useful in speech preparation. As you research your speech, try to use a variety of sources representing different perspectives on your topic. As we mentioned earlier, periodicals have a reputation of their own. Some periodicals, such as *Scientific American,* will be perceived as highly credible and objective, whereas others may be less acceptable to critical listeners. Even highly credible sources may be tinged with bias on certain topics. For example, the American Cancer Society might be an excellent source of information about the relationship between cancer and smoking, but may be biased by self-interest on the question of government funding for medical research. As you read in-depth material, you may discover that one book is frequently mentioned. Read it, and check the *Book Review Index* for summaries of reviews of it.

When you need facts and figures, consult an almanac, yearbook, or atlas. Almanacs and yearbooks provide accurate, up-to-date compilations of information on a wide range of topics. Such materials go beyond simple lists, often including short articles and graphics that you can adapt for presentation aids. Atlases are useful when your topic calls for geographic information. They include data on such things as population density or industrial production and are a good source of materials for presentation aids. Biographical resources can provide information about the qualifications of experts you might cite in a speech. Books of quotations can offer material for the introductions and conclusions of speeches. Most such books are indexed by topic and author, making it easy for you to find what others have had to say about your subject. Most of these resources are available on the Internet as well as in the library.

Ethics Alert! 7.1

Doing Ethical Research

1. Allow enough research time to gain responsible knowledge.
2. Investigate differing perspectives on your topic.
3. Access credible sources of information.
4. Never fabricate or distort information.
5. Take careful notes on what you read to minimize error.
6. Cite your sources in your presentation.

A word of caution: *The articles you find do not provide you with a speech;* rather, they provide ideas, information, opinions, examples, and narratives for use in the speech that *you* prepare for *your* particular audience. If you simply summarize an article and present it as though it were your own, you are committing plagiarism. Although we discussed plagiarism in Chapter 1, these guidelines bear repeating:

- Introduce authors of quotations.
- Identify sources of information.
- Give credit to the originators of ideas.

Be Sure Your Information Is Up-to-Date

As we noted earlier, the timeliness of information is important for topics that change rapidly, such as medical research or computer technology. In addition, if you are not aware of current happenings related to your topic, your credibility will suffer. The best source of timely information is the Internet. By logging on to local newspapers and television stations throughout the world, you can keep abreast of what is happening during crisis situations. One of the best library sources for current information is *Facts on File,* a weekly publication that reports on current events by topics. Additional sources of current information include the most recent issues of weekly newsmagazines and newspapers.

Include Local Applications

To involve listeners with your subject, you should show them how it relates to them and their community. For example, if you were discussing methods of disposing hazardous waste, it would be especially effective to talk about how that problem affects the local area. Your library may index local newspapers and may subscribe to regional magazines. Local newspapers may have archives that you can search online.

Many libraries maintain a vertical file that contains newspaper clippings, pamphlets, and other materials about important local people or issues. These materials may contain names of people you could interview to hear the kind of personal stories and inside information that might really make your speech come to life.

Interviewing for Information

Personal interviews can be an excellent source of local applications. Material from interviews can become another form of personal experience that adds credibility both to you and your speech. Citing material from an interview makes you seem

Material from face-to-face interviews can add much to a speech.

committed to creating a speech with value for your audience. If you can say, "Carolyn Jenkins, the director of research and development at Richardson Electronics, told me . . . ," your audience will sit up and listen.

However, interviews are not without problems. Finding the right person to interview can be difficult. Once you find the person and are granted an interview, you may feel so grateful that you simply accept what the person says without critical evaluation. If you don't know a great deal about the subject, it may be hard for you to judge what you hear. However, the potential benefits of a good interview far outweigh any possible shortcomings.

To minimize problems, make interviews the final phase of your research preparation. Check your library's local clipping service or local newspaper archives to help you identify nearby prospects for face-to-face interviews. Through your general readings, identify widely recognized experts for possible telephone or email interviews. Although it is generally preferable to conduct an interview face to face, email and telephone interviews can be used to verify information, acquire a brief quotation, or discover a person's opinion.[9] Don't overlook the most obvious source available to you–your own campus. Every college and university has faculty members with expertise on a wide array of topics, and they are often willing to grant interviews to students.

Once you have identified prospects for interviews, you must establish contact, prepare for the interview, conduct the interview, and record what you learn so that it is readily accessible for speech preparation.

Establish Contact

The best way to initiate contact with interviewing prospects is to write them a letter in which you explain why you would like to interview them. You might even include a list of the questions you would like to ask. Such a letter helps the prospects evaluate your motives, builds your credibility, and sets the agenda for the interview. It also gives the experts, who probably are busy people, some idea of how much time you will need.[10] Express your sincere interest in the subject, and explain the significance of your request: you are preparing a public speech on a topic that is important to both them and you. Follow up the letter with a telephone call to schedule the interview. If time is short, initiate contact directly through a telephone call or email. Don't be shy. A request for an interview is a compliment because it suggests that you value the person's information.

Prepare for the Interview

Complete most of your library and Internet research before you conduct the interview so that you know what questions to ask and can talk intelligently on the subject.

Write out your interview questions so that the responses will be relevant to your specific purpose.

Plan open questions that invite discussion, not "yes" or "no" answers.[11] Never supply the answer you want in your question, as in "Don't you think that global warming is a crisis that demands our attention?" Design your questions in a sequence so that the answers should form a coherent line of thought:

> What are the causes of air pollution in Silver City?
>
> What is the impact of air pollution on the citizens of our area?
>
> Is there a serious effort under way to minimize air pollution?
>
> Are polluters cooperating in this campaign? Why or why not?
>
> What can students do to help the effort?

Plan your wording so that your questions don't sound abrasive. Questions such as "When are you intellectuals going to climb down from the ivory tower and get involved in the campaign for a better environment?" may seem argumentative and offensive. Save any controversial questions for late in the interview, after you have established rapport. Ask such questions tactfully: "Some people say that experts like you need to 'dirty their hands more' in the day-by-day effort to improve the environment. How do you respond to such criticism?" If asked with sincerity rather than hostility, this type of question can produce the most interesting part of your interview. Also, learn as much as you can about the person you will interview. This will help you develop rapport at the beginning of your interview.

Should you tape-record your interview? A tape recorder can free you from having to take notes to get down the exact wording of answers. However, many people dislike being tape-recorded. Never attempt to record an interview without securing the prior consent of your expert. A good time to seek such consent is during your initial contact. If the expert seems reluctant, don't press the point.

Conduct the Interview

Arrive for the interview on time. Dress nicely to show that you take the interview seriously and as a sign of respect for the person you are interviewing. When you meet your expert, take time for a little small talk before you get into your prepared questions. Talk about things you may have in common. This might include such things as where the person lived, where he or she went to school, or simply your mutual interest in the topic.

Let the expert do most of the talking while you do the listening. Allow the person you are interviewing to complete the answer to one question before you ask another. Don't interrupt and jump in with another question every time your expert pauses. Your expert may go from one point to another and may even answer a question before you ask it. You should adapt to the flow of conversation.

Be alert for opportunities to follow up on answers by using probes, mirror questions, verifiers, or reinforcers.[12] **Probes** are questions that ask a person to elaborate on a response: "Could you tell me more about the part played by auto emissions?" **Mirror questions** reflect part of a response to encourage additional discussion. The sequence might go as follows:

> **"So I told Joan, 'If we want people to change their attitudes, we're going to have to start marching in the front of the movement.'"**
>
> **"You felt you were moving toward a leadership role?"**

Speaker's Notes 7.4

Interviewing for Information

1. Locate and contact an expert on your topic.
2. Research your topic before the interview.
3. Plan a series of questions that relate to your specific purpose.
4. Be on time.
5. Be courteous and tactful
6. Don't ask leading questions.
7. Let your expert do most of the talking.
8. Summarize what you hear so your expert can verify it.

A **verifier** confirms the meaning of something that has been said, such as "If I understand you correctly, you're saying . . ." A **reinforcer** provides encouragement for the person to communicate further. Smiles, nods, or comments such as "I see" are reinforcers that can keep the interview moving.

If you feel the interview beginning to drift off course, you can often steer it back with a transition. As your expert pauses, you can say, "I believe I understand now the causes of air pollution. But can you tell me more about how this level of pollution affects our lives?"

Do not overstay your welcome. As the interview draws to a close, summarize the main points you have heard and how you think they may be useful in your speech. A summary allows you to verify what you have heard and reassures the expert that you intend to use the information fairly and accurately. Thank your expert for his or her time, and follow up with a telephone call or thank-you note in which you report the successful results of your speech.

Record What You Learn

If you plan to take notes during an interview, tell your expert you want to be sure to quote him or her correctly in your speech. If you are not certain you wrote down an answer correctly, read it back for confirmation. After you have completed the interview, find a quiet place to go over your notes and write out the answers to important questions while your expert's wording is still fresh in your mind.

VideoLab

View how the speakers in **VideoLab Lesson 4's Next Step: Citing Sources Correctly** use note cards to cite their sources.

Taking Notes on Your Research

The best research in the world will not do you any good unless you take notes to help you prepare your speech. Take notes on anything you read or hear that might be usable in your speech. It is better to have too much material to work with than to remember that you read something important about a point, but you can't remember where. Even if you download material, you may find it is useful to prepare research cards because they are easy to handle and sort by categories. The 4 × 6 index cards often work best because they provide adequate space for any information you want to record.

Preparing research cards also may help you avoid "cut and paste" plagiarism. You should prepare both source and information cards for each article or book you might use.

A **source card** should contain standard bibliographical information: the author's name, the title of the article or book, the title and volume number of the periodical for an article, the place and date of publication for a book, the date of publication for an article, and the page references (see Figure 7.6). To make source

Figure 7.6
Source Card

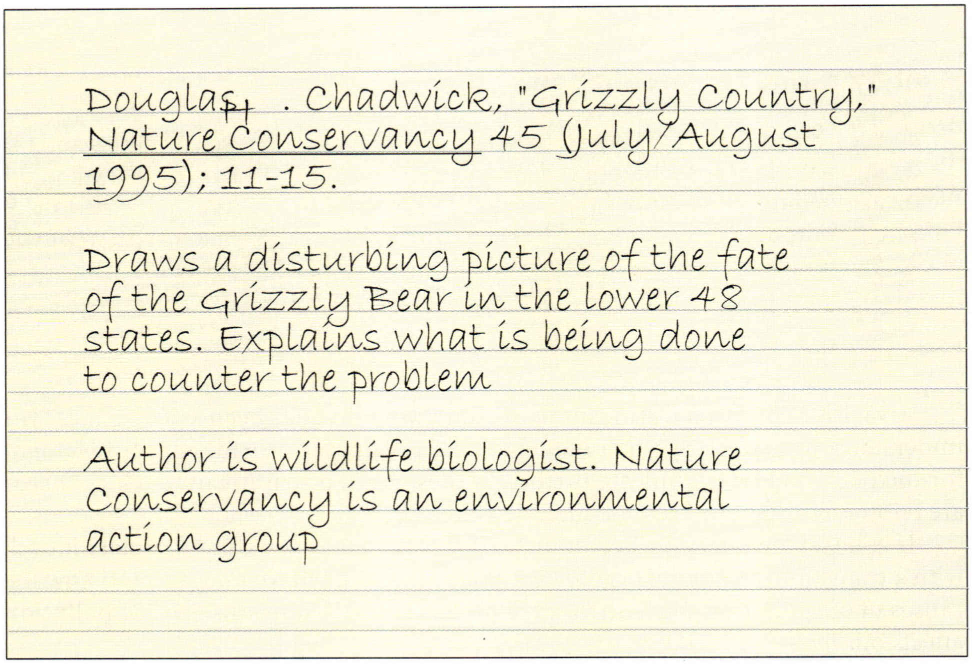

Go to the **SpeechStudio** and complete the **Research Overview Worksheet** under **Conducting Research and Gathering Support Materials** to help you structure your note taking.
Go to http://college.hmco.com/eduspace/

cards on your online materials, note all the previously mentioned information, including the URL and the date you accessed the material. If your instructor requires a formal outline for your speech, be sure to follow the format that is assigned for the "Works Cited" or "Works Consulted" listing at the end of the outline (see Chapter 10, page 276–277). You also may wish to include a short summary of the material, information about the author's credentials, and any of your own comments or reactions to the material.

Use an **information card** to record facts and figures, examples, or quotations (See Figure 7.7). Use a different card for each item of information you think you might use in your speech. Each card should have a heading that describes the information it contains, an abbreviated identification of the source from which the material was taken, and the information itself.

Figure 7.7
Information Card

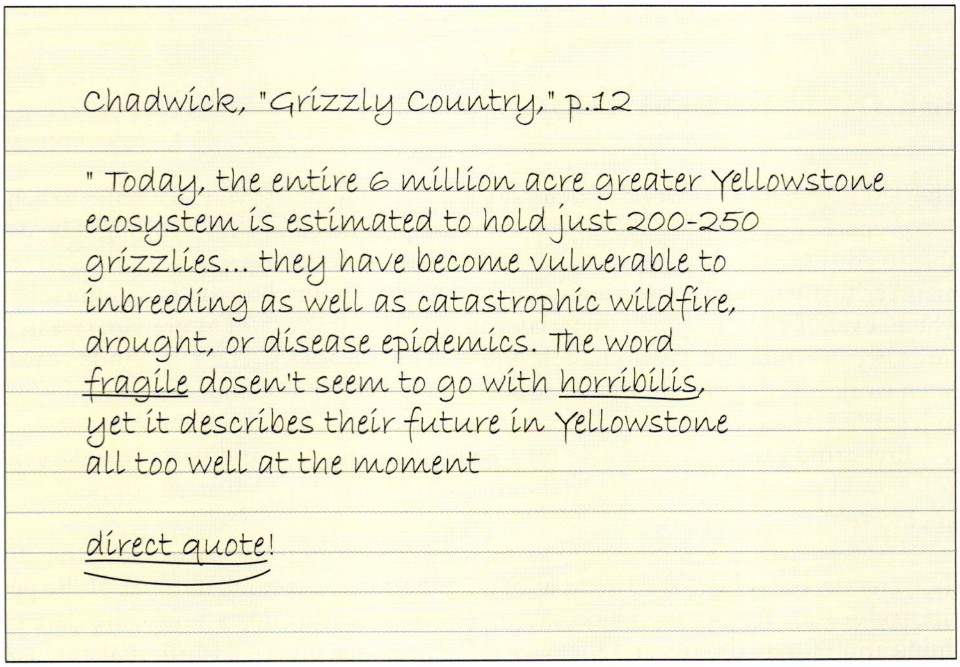

In Summary

Acquiring Responsible Knowledge. To give a successful speech, you must expand your knowledge so that you can speak responsibly. *Responsible knowledge* implies that you have a good grasp of the main issues surrounding a topic, what experts say about it, the most recent developments, and how it applies specifically to your listeners. You can acquire responsible knowledge from personal experience, Internet and library research, and interviews.

Personal knowledge and experience add credibility, authenticity, and interest to a speech, but they should be supplemented with library and/or Internet research. Try to arrange a tour of your campus library and learn to use the Internet effectively.

In the library use the online catalogs of books and periodicals to locate materials. Start with the general periodicals databases, and then move on to specialized databases as needed.

The Internet offers a wealth of information, including late-breaking news. It can be searched using a *general search engine*, a *meta-search engine*, or *subject directories*. Specialized search engines allow you to find scholarly materials from databases in the *invisible web*. Since there is little overlap in the materials covered, search for information on the Internet using at least three different search engines.

Evaluating Research Materials. It is important to evaluate articles and information from both the library and the Internet. When using the Internet for research, differentiate between *advocacy web sites*, *information web sites*, and *personal web sites*. Advocacy web sites try to influence attitudes and behaviors. Information web sites offer factual reports on specific topics. Personal web sites present the work and/or opinions of individuals. Evaluate all material you plan to use in terms of its *authority, accuracy, objectivity, currency*, and breadth and depth of *coverage*.

Go to **VideoLab Lesson 4's Coach: Tips to Remember** for "Do's" and "Don'ts" of researching your topic.

VideoLab

Conducting Strategic Research. Develop a research plan that steers you systematically through developing an overview of your topic, building a bibliography, acquiring in-depth knowledge, checking to see that information is current, and developing local applications. Interviewing for information can especially add freshness, vitality, and local relevance to your speeches.

Taking Notes on Research. Take careful notes so that you can incorporate what you learn into your speeches. Prepare *source cards* with publication information for each article, book, or Internet entry. Prepare *information cards* to preserve quotations or precise bits of information.

Terms to Know

responsible knowledge
general search engine
meta-search engine
subject directory
invisible web
advocacy web site
information web site
personal web site
authority
accuracy
objectivity
currency
coverage
probes
mirror questions
verifier
reinforcer
source card
information card

Discussion

1. Access an advocacy web site on a controversial issue such as gun control, abortion, or smoker's rights. Select an article from the web site and analyze it in terms of its authority, accuracy, objectivity, currency, and coverage. Report your findings to the class.

2. Access an information web site on the same issue used for discussion exercise 1. Select an article from the web site and analyze it in terms of its authority, accuracy, objectivity, currency, and coverage. Report your findings to the class. Compare the results of this analysis with those of the advocacy web site analysis.
3. Using a topic you are considering for your informative speech, search the topic in the library using one of their online periodical indexes. Print out the results of this search. Using the same topic, run a search on an Internet general search engine. Print out the results of this search. Compare the results of the two searches and share them with your classmates, discussing the pros and cons of both types of research tools.

Application

1. Take a walking tour of your library and locate the various resources described in this chapter. While you are there, try to find the answers to the following questions. Do not ask the librarian for assistance. Keep track of how long it takes you to find the information, and record the source of each answer.
   a. What was the population of the city in which you were born in the year of your birth?
   b. What television show had the highest Nielson rating when you were ten years old?
   c. Select the contemporary figure that you admire most. When was he or she born? What awards has he or she received?
   d. Who won the Pulitzer Prize for literature in the year your most admired public figure was born? For what work was this awarded? For what other works is the author noted?
   e. What actress won the Academy Award for best supporting actress in the year of your birth? What movie was she in?
   f. What noteworthy event took place during the month and year of your birth? When and where did this happen?
2. In the questions above, substitute your mother for yourself. Then use the Internet to locate the answers to these questions. Keep track of how long it takes you to find the information, and record the source of each answer. Compare the results obtained from the Internet with those you found in the library.

Notes

1. In his classic textbook *Speech: Its Techniques and Disciplines in a Free Society* (New York: Appleton-Century-Crofts, 1952), William Norwood Brigance gave his chapter on researching a speech the following title: "Earning the Right to Speak."
2. James C. McCroskey, *An Introduction to Rhetorical Communication*, 5th ed. (Englewood Cliffs, N.J.: Prentice Hall, 1986), p. 72.
3. Study by J. Berger and R. Vartabedian, originally published in *Journal of Applied Social Psychology*, vol. 15, no. 2, cited in Jeff Meer, "Political Intimacies: Better Left Unsaid," *Psychology Today*, January 1986, pp.19–20.
4. Byron Acohido, "Simplifying the Info Hunt: Search Engines Explore New Ways to Help Dig for Answers," *USA Today*, 17 Nov. 2003, p. 11E.
5. Because of the insidious nature of many of these web sites, we have refrained from providing URLs for them. For specific web sites and detailed information on misinformation on the Internet, see Anne P. Mintz et al., *Web of Deception* (Medford, N.J.: Cyberage Books, 2002).
6. Janet E. Alexander and Marsha Ann Tate, *Web Wisdom: How to Evaluate and Create Information Quality on the Web* (Mahwah, N.J.: Lawrence Erlbaum, 1999).
7. Alan M. Schlein, *Find It Online* (Tempe, Ariz.: Facts on Demand Press, 2003), p. 381.
8. See Mintz et al. See also Anti-Defamation League, "Hate on Display: A Visual Database of Extremist Symbols, Logos and Tatoos," 2000. http://www.adl.org/hate_symbols/default.asp (2 Nov. 2003).

9. Michael Schumacher, "The Interview and Its Uses," in *1992 Writer's Market,* ed. Mark Kissling and Roseann Shaughnessy (Cincinnati: F & W Publications, 1991), p. 9.

10. "Expert Advice: Five Rules for Working with Subject Matter Experts," *Online Learning Magazine,* April 2001, pp. 44–48. http://www.onlinelearningmag.com.

11. See the discussion in Jeanne Tessier Barone and Jo Young Switzer, *Interviewing Art and Skill* (Boston: Allyn and Bacon, 1995), pp. 89–99.

12. Lois J. Einhorn, Patricia Hayes Bradley, and John E. Baird Jr., *Effective Employment Interviewing: Unlocking Human Potential* (Glenview, Ill.: Scott, Foresman, 1982), pp. 135–139.

Library Resources

General Information and Background

GENERAL ENCYCLOPEDIAS AND DICTIONARIES

American Heritage Dictionary
Collier's Encyclopedia
Encyclopedia Americana
Encyclopaedia Britannica
Oxford English Dictionary

SPECIALIZED ENCYCLOPEDIAS AND DICTIONARIES

Black's Law Dictionary
Dictionary of American History
Dictionary of Americanisms
Dictionary of the History of Ideas
Dictionary of Psychology
Dictionary of Science
Dictionary of Word and Phrase Origins
Encyclopedia of Associations
Encyclopedia of Education
Encyclopedia of Philosophy
Encyclopedia of Religion and Ethics
Encyclopedia of Science and Technology
Encyclopedia of World Art
Harper's Bible Dictionary
International Encyclopedia of the Social Sciences
Safire's Political Dictionary
Scientific Encyclopedia
Webster's New World Dictionary of Business Terms

Sources for Access to Information

PERIODICAL INDEXES AND ABSTRACTS

American Statistics Index A master guide to government statistical publications.
Art Index Covers photography, films, architecture, fine arts, graphic arts, and design.
Biography Index Lists current articles and books containing biographical information.
Business Index Covers business and industry periodicals.
Business Periodicals Index Covers management, economics, computers, advertising, and other business subjects.
Congressional Information Service: Index and Abstracts Two volumes covering congressional working papers, hearings, reports, and special publications of congressional committees.
Education Index Covers articles relating to children and/or education.
Engineering Index Covers international journals and special technical reports.
Environment: Index and Abstracts Covers articles relating to environmental issues.
Federal Index Covers *Congressional Record, Weekly Compilation of Presidential Documents, Federal Register, Code of Federal Regulations, United States Code,* and other government publications.
General Science Index Covers fields such as astronomy, botany, genetics, mathematics, physics, and oceanography.

Humanities Index Covers fields such as archaeology, folklore, history, language and literature, performing arts, and philosophy.
Index Medicus Covers journal articles, editorials, and biographies related to medicine.
MLA International Bibliography Covers modern languages, literatures, and linguistics.
Music Index Covers popular music, dance, jazz, and classical music.
Psychology Abstracts Covers articles in psychology and related journals.
Reader's Guide to Periodical Literature Covers popular periodicals.
Social Sciences Index Covers anthropology, psychology, sociology, and related areas.
United Nations Document Index (UNDEX) Covers publications of the United Nations.
Women's Studies Abstracts Covers books and periodicals on topics relevant to women.

NEWSPAPER INDEXES

Christian Science Monitor Index
Newspaper Index Includes a variety of regional and major market newspapers.
New York Times Index
Wall Street Journal Index

COMPUTERIZED INDEXES

Business Index Covers business periodicals, books, the *New York Times* financial section, and the *Wall Street Journal.*
Educational Resources Information Center (ERIC) Covers all aspects of education.
General Periodicals Index Covers 1,100 general, business, and academic publications since 1987.
Infotrac Covers general periodicals and government documents from 1985 to the present.
Magazine Index Covers 350 popular magazines going back to the 1940s.
National Newspaper Index Covers the *New York Times, Christian Science Monitor, Wall Street Journal, Washington Post,* and *Los Angeles Times.*
Reader's Guide to Periodical Literature Covers popular periodicals going back to 1983.

Sources for Specific and/or In-Depth Information

ALMANACS, YEARBOOKS, REGISTERS

Annual Register of World Events
Book of Lists
Canadian Almanac and Directory
Economic Almanac
Information Please Almanac
Statistical Abstract of the United States
Whitaker's Almanack: Great Britain
World Almanac and Book of Facts

ATLASES

Rand McNally World Atlas
The Times Atlas of the World
Township Atlas of the United States
Webster's New Geographic Dictionary

BIOGRAPHICAL INFORMATION

American Men and Women of Science
Current Biography
Dictionary of American Biography
Dictionary of Canadian Biography

Directory of American Scholars
International Who's Who Since 1935.
Notable American Women
Who's Who
Who's Who in America
Who's Who of American Women

QUOTATIONS

Bartlett's Familiar Quotations
Beyond Bartlett: Quotations by and About Women
Oxford Dictionary of Quotations
Peter's Quotations: Ideas for Our Time
Quotable Woman
Simpson's Contemporary Quotations

SELECTED PERIODICALS

American Demographics Focuses on demographic trends and changing demographics.
American Heritage An interesting history magazine.
Americana A contemporary approach to American history; focuses on preservation.
Business Week Concentrates on business news; patterned after weekly newsmagazines.
Changing Times Kiplinger's monthly report on personal finance.
Columbia Journalism Review A critical analysis of media issues.
Consumer Reports A good source of information on consumer goods and services.
Discover A popular science magazine.
Ebony Articles for and about black readers.
Equinox In-depth profiles of Canadian people, places, and wildlife.
Foreign Affairs An establishment quarterly, very influential in government circles.
Gray's Sporting Journal An upscale outdoor magazine.
Harper's A high-quality general issue magazine.
Harvard Business Review Upscale articles on business and management.
Harvard Medical School Health Letter Reliable, up-to-date medical information written so the lay reader can understand it.
Inquiry A libertarian publication (pro–free enterprise, anti–big government).
Modern Maturity A publication of the American Association of Retired Persons.
Money Covers personal finance and consumer issues.
Mother Jones A radical left-wing publication; occasionally has good exposés.
Nation A liberal perspective on contemporary political issues.
National Parks A publication of the National Parks and Conservation Association.
National Review A conservative perspective on contemporary issues.
Natural History Published by the American Museum of Natural History.
New Republic A liberal perspective on contemporary issues.
Newsletter on Intellectual Freedom Published by the American Library Association; contains lists of censored books.
Nucleus The quarterly report of the Union of Concerned Scientists.
Omni Science for nonscientists.
Quarterly Review of Doublespeak An excellent exposé on how language is used to con the public.
Science News A good weekly on what's new in science.
Scientific American A good science monthly; difficult reading for the lay audience.
Sierra Published by the Sierra Club; emphasizes conservation and environmental politics.
Smithsonian Published by the Smithsonian Institution; articles on popular culture and the fine arts, history, and natural science.
Today's Health Published by the American Medical Association.
Village Voice A left-oriented publication; good political exposés.

Wilderness The quarterly publication of the Wilderness Society, a nonprofit organization devoted to conservation and preservation.

Wilson Quarterly Summaries of articles in other magazines plus original articles on many contemporary subjects.

Sources for Current Information

Facts on File: A Weekly Digest of World Events with Cumulative Index

Recent issues of newspapers

Recent issues of periodicals, especially newsweeklies

Sources for Local Applications

City or state magazines from your area

Index to major local or area newspapers

Vertical File Index

Internet Resources

Search Engines, Directories, and Libraries

Academic Info http://academicinfo.net/ An educational subject directory with gateways to material on a variety of academic disciplines.

BUBL Link http://bubl.ac.uk/link A subject directory of selected Internet resources covering all academic subject areas. Searchable through general subject areas or by an alphabetical listing.

ERIC http://www.eric.ed.gov The online search engine of the Educational Resources InformationCenter (ERIC); large collection of resources on educational issues.

Internet Public Library http://www.ipl.org/ An easy-to-access cyberlibrary maintained as a public service by the University of Michigan School of Information.

iTools Research It http://www.itools.com/research-it/ Tools for tracking down quotations; retrieving biographical, geographical, and financial information; translating terms from language to language; etc.

Librarian's Index to the Internet Recommended Search Tools http://infopeople.berkeley.edu/search/file/searchtools A variety of search engines that can be accessed directly from the site. Includes library-based search tools as well as general and meta-search engines.

Libraries Online http://library.usask.ca/hytelnet/usa/usall.html A directory of links to libraries in the United States.

New York Times Navigator http://www.nytimes.com/library/tech/reference/cynavi.html Annotated links to interesting web sites; frequently updated.

The Reference Desk http://www.refdesk.com A combination subject directory and search engine, Refdesk indexes and reviews quality, credible, and current information-based sites and assists readers in navigating them.

Scoop http://scoop.evansville.net A subject directory designed for journalists; links to an interesting assortment of web sites, classified by topic.

Health Issues

Centers for Disease Control and Prevention http://www.cdc.gov An online digest of information on current public health issues, including news, statistics, and reports.

Merck Manual http://www.merckhomeedition.com/home.html A guide to diseases, disorders, and prescription medications.

National Library of Medicine http://www.nlm.nih.gov/ Health information, publications, research reports, and news in medicine; maintained by the National Institutes of Health.

Prevention http://www.prevention.com/ The online version of the popular medical magazine.

World Health Organization http://www.who.int/home-page/ News, information, and updates on humanitarian relief by a consortium of medical personnel from around the world.

Museums and Art Galleries

Museums Online http://www.museumstuff.com/museums/index.html A gateway to links to the major online museums throughout the world.

American Museum of Natural History http://www.amnh.org/home/index.html Information on exhibits, history, and an online edition of this New York City museum's magazine.

Louvre http://www.louvre.fr/louvrea.htm The official web site of the Louvre; information on collections, special exhibits, and virtual tours.

Smithsonian http://www.si.edu/ The web site of the Smithsonian, with articles and information on the various museums in the system.

Environmental Concerns

EnviroLink http://www.envirolink.org An environmental and animal concerns web site with news and links to educational and government resources.

Greenpeace http://www.greenpeace.org/ An activist environmental web site; news on ongoing campaigns involving climate, toxics, nuclear power, oceans, genetic engineering, and forests.

National Environmental Information Service http://www.eco-web.com A practical reference source for government departments, companies, development agencies, educational organizations, and individuals engaged in environmental activities. Information indexed by problem areas.

Sierra Club http://www.sierraclub.org/ The official web site of the Sierra Club; news, feature articles, and an energy saving guide.

Books and Literature

Online Books http://digital.library.upenn.edu/books/ Over 20,000 links to full-text manuscripts of classics and other titles that are not under copyright or that have been given reprint permission. Also contains other information about literature and links to banned books. This site was founded and is edited by John Mark Ockerbloom, digital library planner and researcher at the University of Pennsylvania.

The Oxford Shakespeare http://www.bartleby.com/70/index.html Links to full-text versions of the works of William Shakespeare from the 1914 Oxford edition.

Project Gutenberg http://www.promo.net/pg/ A large full-text book repository of material no longer under copyright, including major classics; searchable by author or title.

News

News Directory http://www.newsdirectory.com A directory of worldwide links to more than 17,000 English-language newspapers and TV stations searchable by country, state, and region, plus a magazine database of links searchable by type and topic.

Newslink http://newslink.org This subject directory contains links to newspapers, magazines, radio and television stations, and news services.

TV News Archive http://tvnews.vanderbilt.edu/ A searchable database of newscasts from ABC, CBS, and NBC, plus news specials; online abstracts and transcripts back to 1968; videotapes of newscasts available; maintained by Vanderbilt University.

Major U.S. Newsmagazines and Newspapers

Los Angeles Times http://www.latimes.com/
New York Times http://www.nytimes.com
Newsweek http://www.newsweek.com
Time http://www.time.com/time/index.html
U.S. News & World Report http://www.usnews.com
USA Today http://www.usatoday.com
Washington Post http://www.washingtonpost.com/

Communication—General

Archives of American Public Address http://www.douglassarchives.org/ An electronic archive of American oratory; developed and maintained by Northwestern University.

Gifts of Speech http://ripley.wo.sbc.edu/departmental/library/gos/ Texts of women's speeches presented from around the world, including texts of lectures given by female Nobel laureates; maintained by Sweet Briar College.

Historic Radio Archives http://www.webcorp.com/sounds/index.htm An audio archive of clips from famous contemporary speeches.

National Communication Association http://www.natcom.org The official web site of the major American professional association serving communication instructors and students.

Science—General

Discovery http://www.discovery.com The online accompaniment to the TV channel; interactive, in-depth coverage of topics from current programs.

Science Frontiers http://www.knowledge.co.uk/frontiers/ Articles on scientific anomalies that challenge prevailing scientific thinking.

Scientific American http://www.sciam.com/ The online edition; science news, articles, and archives of past issues.

Humanities—General

Biography.com http://www.biography.com Biographical information and articles on over 25,000 people, past and present, with an emphasis on contemporary celebrities and people in the news. Contains a section on classroom activities. Sponsored and maintained by A&E Television networks.

EDSITEment http://edsitement.neh.fed.us Learning activities in literature and language arts, foreign languages, art and culture, and history and social studies; sponsored and maintained by the National Endowment for the Humanities.

HistoryNet http://www.thehistorynet.com/ Online articles and information on world and American history, the Civil War, and World War II; archived with a site search tool. Sponsored and maintained by the Primedia History Group, publishers of ten history magazines.

H-Net http://www.h-net.org Articles and discussions on the humanities and social sciences hosted by Michigan State University.

Matrix http://matrix.msu.edu The web site of the Center for the Humane Arts, Letters, and Social Sciences Organization Online at Michigan State University. Contains articles and links to a variety of resources, including the *National Gallery of the Spoken Word* and *Civics Online.*

Philanthropies and Charities

Global Impact http://www.charity.org A not-for-profit umbrella organization of U.S.-based international service agencies offering humanitarian and disaster relief for families and children. Includes links to such organizations as Doctors Without Borders, CARE, Save the Children, and Project HOPE.

Nonprofit Organizations on the Internet http://www.fiu.edu/~time4chg/nonprofit.html A directory with links to a variety of social and political advocacy nonprofit organizations; sponsored and maintained by the Volunteer Action Center at Florida International University.

United Way http://www.unitedway.org A gateway web site with links to local chapters and information on health and human services activities and issues.

Government and Politics

Central Intelligence Agency http://www.cia.gov Interesting unclassified information about the workings of this agency; detailed almanac-type information on the countries of the world available in site's *World Fact Book.*

FirstGov http://www.firstgov.gov/ The official web portal for the U.S. government; contains links to all government web sites–federal, state, local, and tribal–with a comprehensive search engine.

Library of Congress http://www.loc.gov Online catalogues with special sections on legislative information, exhibits, collections, and services; excellent "American Memory" archive of words, sounds, and pictures of American history.

U.S. Census Bureau http://www.census.gov Immediate online access to the most recent census information as it becomes available.

U.S. House of Representatives http://www.house.gov The official web site of the U.S. House of Representatives; information on legislation and a source of contact with your representatives.

U.S. Senate http://www.senate.gov The official web site of the U.S. Senate; information on legislation and a source of contact with your senators.

White House http://www.whitehouse.gov The official web site of the presidency; links to full texts of speeches and press conferences.

Business and Commerce

Business Connections http://www.nytimes.com/library/cyber/reference/busconn.html An extensive directory to business, financial, and investing links on the Internet; maintained and updated by the *New York Times.*

Business Week http://www.businessweek.com The online version of the magazine; continuously updated with business news from Reuters and stock market reports.

Business Women's Network http://www.bwni.com An interactive web site with news and articles of interest to women in the workplace.

Forbes http://www.forbes.com The online version of the financial magazine; articles on investing and other financial topics.

Fortune http://www.fortune.com The online version of the magazine; articles of interest on financial and investment topics.

Inc. http://www.inc.com An extensive assortment of articles and advice on starting up and running a business.

Language

AmeriSpeak http://www.rootsweb.com/~genepool/amerispeak.htm Phrases and idioms no longer in use, with their contemporary equivalents.

Guide to Grammar and Style http://andromeda.rutgers.edu/~jlynch/Writing A guide to grammar and style with rules, explanations, common errors, and usage suggestions; developed and maintained by Jack Lynch, English Department, Rutgers University.

The Linguistic Fun Page http://www.ojohaven.com/fun/ An interesting assortment of English-language trivia links, including the *Hellatine Dictionary of Bureaucratese* and *A List of Oxymora*. Developed and maintained by Phillip Miller Eberz, a programmer with interests in mathematics, linguistics, and technology.

Slanguage http://www.slanguage.com A fun site cataloging regional and foreign slang; developed and maintained by Michael Lawrence Ellis III.

Legal Concerns

Findlaw http://www.findlaw.com A comprehensive directory of online legal resources for professionals, students, and the public, with daily news updates and a site search tool. Includes a web search engine that targets legal information, cases and codes, and legal news. Developed by attorneys Timothy Stanley and Stacy Stern as part of a workshop for law librarians; posted as a web site for general access in 1996.

Internet Legal Resource Guide http://www.ilrg.com An index of more than 4,000 select legal web sites in 238 nations, islands, and territories. Includes access to free legal forms, law school course outlines, and legal research tools. Developed and maintained by Maximillan Ventures LLC, a provider of online services for business and legal consumers.

Law.Com http://www.law.com Legal news and articles of interest, updated daily. Site provides access to national and regional legal publications and case and decision databases.

Supreme Court Collection http://supct.law.cornell.edu/supct/index.html This web site contains links to the texts of Supreme Court decisions, information about Supreme Court justices (past and present), Supreme Court rules, and a glossary of legalese. Developed and maintained by the Legal Information Institute, an outreach program of Cornell University Law School.

Supporting Your Ideas

8

OUTLINE

This chapter will help you

- use facts and statistics to substantiate ideas
- use expert, lay, and prestige testimony to make your speech credible
- use examples to bring your speech to life
- use narratives to involve your audience
- select the most appropriate supporting material for your speech

The universe is made up of stories, not of atoms

MURIEL RUKEYSER

Our home stands atop a high ridgeline in Tennessee. The land slopes at about a 45-degree angle, so that the front of the house rests on solid ground and the back of the house (which is about thirty feet above the ground) is supported by posts. You might think the house would be flimsy, but actually it is quite strong. Our builders selected good-quality wood, concrete, and steel and fashioned these materials into strong supports for the house.

Throughout the next several chapters, picture yourself as a builder—a builder of ideas. Think of your speeches as thought-structures built on solid pillars of supporting materials. Like a good builder, you must know your materials and what they can support. You need to know how to select and use them wisely. Just as our home is built to withstand storms and high winds, your speech must withstand doubt and controversy. When you rise to present your speech, you must be confident of its structural integrity.

Facts and statistics, testimony, examples, and narratives are the major forms of **supporting materials** used in building speeches. Facts and statistics are the most basic type of supporting material and should underpin almost every informative or persuasive speech. Their function is to bring reality to listeners. They are especially important when you need to verify controversial statements or claims. Testimony, examples, and narratives add credibility and human interest to speeches. They help arouse and sustain interest, explain the meaning of ideas, make interpretations more credible, and underscore the importance of ideas to listeners.

Your personal experience, Internet and library research, and interviews with experts (described in Chapter 7) should have provided you with a good stockpile of supporting materials to use in your speeches. We will discuss each type of supporting material, explaining how to identify its good and defective forms, how to know when it can be most useful, and how to put it to work in your speeches.

Facts and Statistics

Facts and statistics are the most objective forms of supporting material, so they are vital to responsible informative or persuasive speaking. **Facts** are statements that can be verified by independent observers. **Statistics** are facts expressed in numbers. Neither facts nor statistics depend upon the experience of a single person or group; rather, they are confirmed repeatedly in human experience. This means that they add credibility to your ideas. If "the facts are in your favor," this creates a presumption that what you are saying is true. Therefore, facts and statistics are especially important when your topic is unfamiliar or your ideas are controversial.

Remember to support each main idea with high-quality evidence. Go to the **Speech-Studio** and complete the **Online Worksheet for Supporting an Idea** under **Conducting Research and Gathering Supporting Materials.**
Go to http://college.hmco.com/eduspace/

Facts

The factual value of a speech is the extent to which it is grounded in reality. The more an issue means to us, the more any speech addressing that issue—be that speech informative or persuasive—must be grounded in reality. Richard Weaver, a noted communication critic writing in the 1950s, suggested that Americans honor facts and numbers as the highest form of knowledge, much as some other societies respect divine revelations.[1] This is especially true when the facts are based on science. In a more recent Gallup survey, 86 percent of those polled agreed that "references to scientific research in a story increased its credibility."[2]

The following statements are factual because they can be shown to be either true or false:

> Ford Explorer is an American-made sports utility vehicle.
> Most students at our college take five years to earn their degree.
> Television ads often rely on emotional appeals.

Although factual statements can stand by themselves, speakers rarely use them without interpreting them. Interpretations typically contain value terms that change factual statements into judgments, claims, or opinions:

> Ford Explorer is a *superior* American-made utility vehicle.
> Most *hard-working* students at our college take five years to earn their degree.
> Television ads often rely on *unethical* emotional appeals.

There is nothing inherently wrong with making interpretations or voicing opinions. We often want to present factual information so that it reflects our point of view. The problem comes when speakers or audiences confuse facts and opinions. Factual statements normally require only minimal demonstration or support. The addition of such words as *superior, hard-working,* or *unethical* means that speakers must assume a further burden of support. They now must produce additional facts or statistics, examples, expert testimony, or stories to prove that their claims are justified—that they are more than just expressions of personal feeling.

We usually cannot directly demonstrate the accuracy of judgments or opinions. There is no way on our own that we can verify that Ford Explorers actually are "superior." We have to look for additional support from independent experts who have no vested personal or financial interest in what they report. For example, we might say, "According to the latest issue of *Consumer Reports,* which did extensive tests on many SUVs, the Ford Explorer is superior." This type of support is called expert testimony, which we discuss later in this chapter. Incidentally, note also how this statement further reassures listeners: the source is the "latest," and *Consumer Reports* was responsible in its work ("did extensive tests").

Sources of information have ethos just as speakers do. For example, *Consumer Reports* is known for responsible, objective testing of products. On social or political issues, the ideological position of the source may be important. If you cited William F. Buckley's *National Review* in support of a claim, skeptical listeners might respond, "Well, that's a conservative magazine. Of course Buckley will support this right-wing claim!" On the other hand, if you also cite the *New Republic,* a more liberal publication, then skeptical listeners might think, "Well, if both left and right agree, then maybe what she's saying is true."[3]

Even seemingly neutral sources present "factual" information that is colored by its cultural environment. Compare the following excerpts from the same encyclopedia in its 1960 hard copy and 2004 online editions:

> **1960: Kiowa Indians hunted buffalo on the southwestern plains of the United States. The Kiowa and their allies, the Comanche, raided many Texas ranches. They probably killed more whites than any other Indian tribe. . . . By [a] treaty signed in 1868, the Kiowa agreed to go with the Comanche to a reservation in Indian territory (now Oklahoma). But only the Kiowa chiefs had signed the treaty, and no chiefs could force their young men to make such a sacrifice. Many struggles and arrests occurred before the Kiowa finally went to live on the reservation. When trouble broke out in 1874, Satanta, one of the most daring Kiowa leaders, was arrested and sentenced to prison. There he committed suicide. The Kiowa then "put their hands to the plow." They now live peacefully as farmers. Several have become well-known artists.**
>
> **2004: Kiowa Indians are a tribe that lives largely in Oklahoma and elsewhere in the Southwestern United States. According to the 2000 U.S. census, there are about 8,600 Kiowa. Most of them live in rural communities near Anadarko, Carnegie, and Mountain View, Oklahoma. Other tribal members live in urban areas and work in law, medicine, teaching, and other professions. . . . The tribe is governed by the Kiowa Indian Council, which consists of all members who are at least 18 years old. The Kiowa Business Committee, an elected group, manages tribal programs in such fields as business, education, and health.[4]**

The 1960 encyclopedia entry stressed the warlike qualities of the Kiowa.

Both of these accounts are "factual," but the first dwells upon past conflicts, portraying the Kiowas as historically warlike, and the second emphasizes their present government and business programs. The contrast reminds us that even relatively objective descriptions are selective and incomplete. We should always ask ourselves what any given description leaves out and whether that omission might be critical. In short, we should try to determine what is information and what is **disinformation**: "misplaced, fragmented, irrelevant, or superficial information . . . that creates the illusion of knowing something but which, in fact, leads one away from knowing."[5]

Statistics

Statistics are numerical facts that can describe the size of something, make predictions, illustrate trends, or show relationships. Americans are almost as much in awe of numbers as they are of science. In the same Gallup study cited earlier, 82 percent of those surveyed said that statistics increased an example's credibility.[6] Statistics are a very powerful form of supporting material, especially in persuasive speeches.

The following example from a student speech demonstrates how statistical information can appear in speeches:

> **The Environmental Protection Agency is saying that secondhand smoke causes 3,000 lung cancer deaths a year and 35,000 heart disease deaths a year, and contributes to 150,00 to 300,000 respiratory infections in babies, mainly bronchitis and pneumonia, resulting in 7,500 to 15,000 hospitalizations. It triggers 8,000 to 26,000 new cases of asthma in previously unaffected children and exacerbates symptoms in 400,000 to 1 million asthmatic children.**

Note that in this example the speaker rounds off the numbers. This is typical practice, especially when the central point is not really in dispute. Very few people still argue that secondhand smoke is harmless: what is not so well known is the *magnitude* of the problem. The statistics in this example create in the minds of listeners a general and lasting impression of the enormity of this problem and of its special threat to children.

On more controversial issues, when listeners may disagree about the central point, precise figures may make the statistical evidence seem more credible and difficult to dismiss. The prevalence of guns in our society, as well as how, whether, and how much to control them, is an ongoing issue that profoundly concerns many people. Dr. Richard Corlin, president of the American Medical Association, used exact numbers to confront his listeners with what he called the "epidemic" of gun violence in America:

> **Since 1962, more than a million Americans have died in firearm suicides, homicides, and unintentional injuries. In 1998 alone, 30,708 Americans died by gunfire. . . .**
>
> **This is a uniquely American epidemic. In the same year that more than 30,000 people were killed by guns in America, the number in Germany was 1,164. In Canada, it was 1,034. In Australia 391. In England and Wales 211. And in Japan the number for the entire year was 83.[7]**

Dr. Corlin's precise statistics suggested to his listeners that his facts were authoritative and that he knew what he was talking about. The exact numbers also made his comparisons among nations far more compelling, making it all the more difficult for some listeners simply to ignore his argument. To determine which of these techniques you should use—rounded-off or precise numbers—you will have to decide what work you want your statistics to accomplish: whether you need to impress listeners with the magnitude of an issue they may have ignored or the validity of an issue they may have repressed.

When presented orally, statistics can be overwhelming. Don't simply drown your listeners in a bath of numbers. If you make listening too difficult, your audience may simply give up the effort and escape into daydreams. To counteract this problem, speakers often use additional supporting techniques. In the former example, the student speaking about secondhand smoke used a series of presentation aids—brief charts that gave visual representation to the figures—to help listeners keep track of her statistics. As she presented each figure, she also pointed to a chart that illustrated it. In the latter example, Dr. Corlin used the comparison and contrast technique to lend impact and clarity to his numbers. Brief explanations and examples can also help numbers come to life.

The 2004 encyclopedia entry focuses on the activities of contemporary Kiowas, such as the award-winning author N. Scott Momaday.

View **VideoLab Lesson 3's Screening Room.** How does this speaker use statistics as evidence? VideoLab

InterConnections.LearnMore 8.1

Understanding Statistics

MeanDeviation
http://www.meandeviation.com/tutorials/stats/
This online tutorial helps students understand and interpret the meaning of statistics. Compiled and maintained by Dr. Alan Dix, professor, Computer Department, Lancaster University, UK.

Statistics Every Writer Should Know
http://www.robertniles.com/stats/
This engrossing website explains basic statistical concepts in lay language and offers guidelines for how not to get duped by numbers. Provides really interesting articles on detecting statistical scams. Compiled and maintained by Robert Niles, former financial management consultant turned journalist.

Statistical Concepts and Controversies
http://www.whfreeman.com/scc/con_index.htm?99esr
Offers case studies demonstrating the questionable use of statistics. Compiled and maintained by the Department of Statistics, Ohio State University.

Evaluating Facts and Statistics

For almost any speech topic, your research notes should contain a wide assortment of facts and statistics. Before you decide which of these materials you will actually use in your speech, apply the critical evaluation skills we discussed in Chapters 4 and 7. The information you use should be relevant, representative, current, and come from credible, objective sources. It should also be consistent with what other reputable sources report. Finally, the information you use should be complete. It should not leave out important material that could alter its interpretation.

As you review your research notes, you may discover much interesting information about your topic that does not relate directly to your specific purpose. As we noted earlier in Chapter 7, no matter how fascinating it seems, if the information does not fit, don't use it. A speech that is cluttered with interesting digressions is hard for listeners to follow. You should also be certain that any statistics you cite are relevant to your locale. If you talk about the "crisis of unemployment" in your area, basing your claim on a national average of 7 percent, you could have a problem if someone points out that the local rate is only 4 percent.

You must also consider how current the information is, especially when your topic is one on which information changes rapidly. On certain fast-breaking subjects, yesterday's news may be obsolete. When you speak on such topics, be sure you are up to date. Save yourself the embarrassment of having a listener point out that your claims are invalid because of what happened this morning!

It is also important that you evaluate the sources of your information. Test even "factual" material for potential bias, distortions, or omissions. Don't be taken in by scientific-sounding names, especially if the information contradicts common sense. Cynthia Crossen, a reporter and editor with the *Wall Street Journal,* exposes many instances of such deception in her book *Tainted Truth.* For example, she points to a claim made by "the Cooper Institute for Aerobic Research" that "white bread will not make you gain weight." It turns out that the study that produced this amazing conclusion was funded by the makers of Wonder Bread.[8]

To guard against deceptive information, do not rely too heavily on any one source. Compare what different expert sources have to say. The more controversial your topic, the more important it is that your information be sound. In your speech, tell listeners how you have tested vital pieces of information, especially if they run counter to what listeners may believe.

As you weigh your facts and statistics, be careful not to read into information what you want to find or to exaggerate the results. Be on guard against the tendency to distort facts and statistics by the way you word them. Don't ignore information that contradicts your claims by simply rejecting it as atypical or irrelevant.

Be especially careful when using statistics. Keep in mind that statistical predictions are based on probability, not certainty, and that they are subject to misuse and abuse. Peter Francese, founder and president of *American Demographics,* has pointed out that although statistics are supposed to represent reality, they may also be used to *create* reality:

> **Politicians and lobbyists carefully select the numbers they use to talk about crime (it's always rampant) or immigration (it's always out of control). The**

Figure 8.1

Checklist for Evaluating Facts and Statistics

____	Is this information relevant to my purpose?
____	Is this information the most recently available?
____	Is this information truly representative of the subject?
____	Is this information from a credible source?
____	Is this information consistent with what other reputable sources report?
____	Is this information free from bias?
____	Is this information complete?

numbers are typically used to prove there is a "big" problem. It's like rounding up vicious dogs to prove that all dogs bite. . . . No number can represent truth perfectly. Every survey has some error or bias. Data from public records, such as crime reports, can be underreported or misclassified. And even perfectly collected data are open to different interpretations.[9]

Chapter 16's discussion of other misuses of facts and statistics as evidence in persuasive speaking will give you additional help in evaluating information and using it ethically.

Using Facts and Statistics

Obviously, you can't just stand up and rattle off facts and numbers and expect your speech to be effective. You must artfully integrate this material into your message. Three effective techniques for presenting facts and statistics in a speech are definitions, explanations, and descriptions.

Definitions. A **definition** translates unfamiliar or technical terms into words your listeners will understand. Definitions help ensure that the speaker and listeners will be talking and thinking about the same things. As a general rule, you should provide definitions for unfamiliar terms the first time you use them. In her informative speech on genetic testing, Ashlie McMillan first offered a technical definition: "According to 'The Genetic Revolution,' an article in *Scientific* magazine, genetic testing 'is co-relating the inheritance of a distinctive segment of DNA, a marker localizing the mutant gene on a DNA strand which composes our chromosomes.'" Noting the puzzled looks on her listeners' faces, Ashlie then said, "I found that a little confusing too, so I tried to put it in my own words: genetic testing looks at people's DNA to see if they have a genetic condition or disease, or are likely to get the disease. That's basically what it is."

Definitions can be persuasive as well as informative. A persuasive definition reflects your way of looking at a controversial subject, presenting your perspective in such a way that your listeners will want to share it. Usually it puts the subject in an emotional context. In a speech on domestic violence against women, Donna Shalala, then U.S. secretary of Health and Human Services, provided the following persuasive definition of domestic violence: "Domestic violence is terrorism. Terrorism in the home. And that is what we should call it."[10]

Speaker's Notes 8.1

Using Facts and Statistics

1. Check several sources to verify important information.
2. Use information from sources with no vested interest in what they report.
3. Do not distort the meaning of information.
4. Use the most recent facts and figures.
5. Make statistics more understandable with examples or presentation aids.

Explanations. Longer and more detailed than a definition, an **explanation** helps clarify a topic or demonstrates how it works. John F. Smith Jr., chairman of the board of General Motors Corporation, used an explanation to both define and clarify the OnStar system:

> **Basically, the OnStar system combines the Global Positioning System (GPS) satellite network with wireless technology to link the driver and vehicle to the OnStar Center. There are currently two centers, in Michigan and North Carolina. Each is staffed by real human beings, 24 hours a day, 7 days a week, 365 days a year. . . . They are there to offer immediate, real-time, personalized help to any query.**
>
> **OnStar has been used to assist subscribers in everything from emergency services to tracking stolen vehicles; getting the doors opened when the keys are accidentally locked inside; finding the nearest ATM machine; guiding the driver to the local zoo or gasoline station; and arranging dinner reservations and theater ticket purchases. If an OnStar-equipped vehicle is in a crash that deploys an airbag, the car itself automatically "calls" the Center and an advisor immediately calls the vehicle to see what kind of assistance is needed.[11]**

It is important to offer such explanations early in your speech to help listeners grasp your meaning.

Descriptions. A **description** is a "word picture" that helps listeners visualize what you are talking about. The best descriptions evoke vivid images in the minds of the audience. The great Roman rhetorician Longinus once said that images occur when, "carried away by enthusiasm and passion, you think you see what you describe, and you place it before the eyes of your hearers."[12] Images not only increase understanding, they also color information with the speaker's feelings and establish a mood that affects how listeners perceive a subject. Note how the following description of the monument at Wounded Knee, which commemorates the massacre of hundreds of Sioux men, women, and children, both paints a picture and establishes a mood:

Word pictures can help listeners visualize what you are talking about and capture the mood you want to convey.

> **Two red brick columns topped with a wrought iron arch and a small metal cross form the entrance to the grave site. The column to the right is in bad shape: Cinder blocks from the base are missing; the brickwork near the top has deteriorated and tumbled to the ground; graffiti on the columns proclaim an attitude we found repeatedly expressed about the Bureau of Indian Affairs: "The BIA sucks!" Crumbling concrete steps lead you to the mass grave. The top of the grave is covered with gravel, interrupted by unruly patches of chickweed and crabgrass.**

Descriptions help bring information to life. But a word of caution is in order. The description just given works well because it is *understated*. Be wary of emotional overkill in descriptions that could result in a perception of manipulation. If a speaker had added too many emotional adjectives, if "grave site" was "lonely grave site," if "attitude" was "angry attitude," and if "mass grave" was "abandoned mass grave," the description would have been less effective. You should let listeners provide the adjectives in their minds. That way, they participate in creating images and will feel engaged by the speech rather than manipulated by it.

Testimony

Testimony, citing the words or ideas of others, can reinforce or interpret the facts and figures in your message. Testimony can also bring witnesses to support your message, add a touch of humanity to it, or bless your speech with the eloquent words of admired leaders. Three types of testimony are useful as supporting material. Expert testimony comes from sources who are authorities on the topic. Lay testimony involves citing ordinary citizens, who may have firsthand experience with the topic or strong feelings about it. Prestige testimony comes from people who are highly regarded but not necessarily experts on the specific topic.

Expert Testimony

Expert testimony comes from people who are qualified by training or experience to speak as authorities on a subject. As you review your research notes, you will probably discover statements by experts offering opinions, information, examples, or stories. When you cite experts in your speeches, you are calling on them as qualified witnesses to support your case. Using expert testimony allows you to borrow their credibility to make your own message more convincing. Expert testimony is especially important when your topic is innovative, unfamiliar, highly technical, or controversial.

When you use expert testimony, remember that competence is area-specific: your experts can speak as authorities only within their area of expertise. For example, emergency room physicians could provide expert testimony on the physical effects of gunshot wounds but may not qualify as experts on the treatment of cancer. As you introduce expert testimony, be sure to establish that your source is an authority on the specific topic of your speech. If the testimony is recent, emphasize that fact. If the testimony appears in a prestigious journal, book, or newspaper, report that as well. Note how the speaker in the following example presents the credentials of his expert:

> **Dr. Lee Gonzales, chair of our Criminal Justice Department and former member of the Presidential Task Force on Inner-City Violence, said last week in the *Washington Post* that a law requiring the licensing of handguns would . . .**

Expert testimony from people qualified by training or experience can make your message more credible.

Obviously, knowing the exact source of information is vital for critically evaluating information and opinions. This can be a problem when citing sources from newspapers, newsmagazines, or television in which the original sources are not identified. Kathleen Hall Jamieson, dean of the Annenberg School at the University of Pennsylvania, has noted:

> **Journalists, in many cases, aren't telling us anything about the source to let us judge whether or not there might be a bias. . . . Where [for example] did *Newsweek* get the [secret] tape? Is it a reliable source or a biased source? Can we trust that this wasn't a selective leak for partisan advantage?"[13]**

Both speakers and listeners need to be cautious about such information. Ethical speakers should warn listeners when sources are not disclosed, and careful listeners should factor this into their reception of messages.

Bias is a major consideration in assessing expert testimony. Sources who are passionately invested in a topic put critical listeners on guard. However, there is one situation in which bias enhances the usefulness of a source. This occurs in the case of **reluctant testimony**, in which people speak *against* their apparent self-interest. Listeners give high marks for character and honesty to those who feel compelled to tell the truth, *despite* their own agendas.[14] Therefore, reluctant testimony is highly valued by persuaders. In his speech on the epidemic of gun violence mentioned earlier in this chapter, Dr. Richard Corlin cites the words of a respected conservative chief justice of the Supreme Court, the late Warren Burger:

> **"The Second Amendment has been the subject of one of the greatest pieces of fraud, I repeat the word fraud, on the American people by special interest groups that I have ever seen in my lifetime. The very language of the Second Amendment refutes any argument that it was intended to guarantee every citizen an unfettered right to any kind of weapon. Surely the Second Amendment does not remotely guarantee every person the constitutional right to have a Saturday night special or a machine gun."[15]**

The late Christopher Reeve's testimony in support of stem cell research demonstrates that when a celebrity has actual experience with an issue, his testimony becomes more powerful.

Lay Testimony

Lay testimony represents the wisdom of ordinary people. It is highly regarded, especially in societies in which popular elections are the source of political power. In these societies "the people" often become a symbol of almost mystical power, frequently invoked to justify policy.[16] Why should we have (or not have) gun control, or educational reform, or lower taxation? Because "the people" demand (or reject) it. Most of our information about how "the people" feel about issues comes from public opinion polls. As we noted in Chapter 5, professional pollsters have elevated the art of prediction to a science. Much valuable information is available from polls conducted by reputable organizations such as the Gallup Organization and the Pew Foundation. However, not all of the information on public opinion floating around in the media comes from such sources. Be wary of the "unscientific" polls conducted by major Internet service providers or local newscasters—"Log on to www.wgn5.com and let us know how you feel on this important issue."

Lay testimony is very useful for providing an understanding of the real-life consequences of issues. As he addressed the annual meeting of the Public Broadcasting System, Bill Moyers used lay testimony to emphasize the value of public radio and television:

> **There was a cabbie [in New York City] named Youssef Jada. He came here from Morocco six years ago. . . . Youssef kept his car radio tuned to National Public Radio all day and his television set at home on Channel Thirteen. He said—and this is a direct quote—"I am blessed by these stations." He pointed me to a picture on the dashboard of his 13-month-old son, and he said: "My son was born in this country. I will let him watch Channel Thirteen so he can learn how to be an American."**
>
> **Think about that. . . . Why shouldn't public television be the core curriculum of the American experience?[17]**

Lay testimony that is used in support of a person, practice, product, or institution is called a **testimonial**. Testimonials often reflect personal experiences and appeals to feelings. Use such testimony when it is appropriate to point out the relevance of your topic to the lives of ordinary people. It is not appropriate to use lay testimony to establish the objective validity of ideas. That is the job of expert testimony.

Prestige Testimony

Prestige testimony associates your message with the words of a respected public figure. This person is usually an eloquent writer or cultural icon who, although not necessarily an expert on your particular topic, has voiced some timeless truth that supports, illuminates, and elevates your ideas. Citing such testimony can add distinction to your speech. It allows you to associate your ideas with the ethos of the revered person. Because of these qualities, prestige testimony is often the source of inspiration in ceremonial speaking. Colin Powell used prestige testimony to dramatize his inspirational speech at the National Volunteer Summit in Philadelphia:

> **The great American poet Langston Hughes talked about a dream deferred, and he said, "What happens to a dream deferred? Does it dry up like a raisin in the sun, or fester like a sore and then run? Does it stink like rotten meat or crust and sugar over like a syrupy sweet? Maybe it just sags, like a heavy load. Or, does it explode?"**
>
> **For too many young Americans, that dream deferred does sag like a heavy load that's pushing them down into the ground. . . . As we see too often, it does explode in violence, in youngsters falling dead, shot by other youngsters. . . . And it has the potential to explode our society.**
>
> **So today, we . . . pledge that the dream must no longer be deferred, and [that] it will never, as long as we can do anything about it, become a dream denied.[18]**

Prestige testimony is also one source of mythos, a form of proof discussed in Chapter 16 that summons the power of tradition in support of your message. In a speech on the "giveaway of our public lands," Brock Evans, vice president of the Audubon Society, used prestige testimony to emphasize the depth of the problem and to place it in cultural perspective:

If there ever was a crisis for all our public lands and wildlife heritage, it is now. The words that keep running through my head, over and over again these terrible times, come from President Abraham Lincoln, who, in another time of crisis 130 years ago, said: "Fellow countrymen, we cannot escape history. . . . The dogmas of the quiet past will no longer suffice for the stormy present. . . . As the occasion now before us is piled high with difficulties, so we must rise to that occasion. . . . History will judge us if we fail."

And that is how I feel about these times now. . . . These are frightening times for anyone who loves the American land and its biological treasures, for anyone who believes in that great tradition of public lands ownership, for anyone who shares the opinion of our forefathers that some lands should belong to all the people.[19]

In this example, Evans used Lincoln's exact words so that he would not lose the elegance and force of the language. If you must paraphrase a lengthy passage, be sure that you reflect fairly the spirit and meaning of the words you summarize.

Evaluating Testimony

As you review your research notes, you should find a variety of information and opinions credited to others that you might cite in your speech. As with any form of supporting material, consider its relevance and whether it is appropriate for your purpose. Also consider if you are accurately quoting or paraphrasing the testimony. Beyond these basic considerations, the questions you should ask will vary with the type of testimony involved.

If you are using expert testimony, evaluate the credentials of your source, making certain they are accurate. If you have any doubt, check them out, using the websites suggested in Chapter 7. Determine if the source is an expert in the area of your topic, and consider whether the source is free from bias. You should also compare the information from this source with that of other authorities on the topic and check the date to be sure it reflects the latest thinking on the subject. Finally, decide if this testimony helps to further verify other information in your speech.

If you are using lay testimony, you should consider whether it will help sensitize listeners to the human aspects of your topic. Also evaluate how well this testimony might enhance identification among the speaker, the topic, and the audience. The source should be someone the audience would find likeable and attractive. If your lay testimony comes in the form of survey data, check to be sure that it comes from a reputable polling organization and that the survey was conducted recently. Finally, determine whether you are using the testimony appropriately. Remember, lay testimony cannot be used to verify facts.

If you are using prestige testimony, consider whether your listeners will think highly of the person you are citing and whether this testimony will add grace or dignity to your speech. You should also determine if associating with this person will increase your credibility as a speaker and the credibility of your message. You don't have to worry about the recency of prestige testimony: in contrast with expert or lay testimony, where "*latest is best*," the rule for prestige testimony is often, "*the older the better*." Wisdom ages well. Finally, be sure you are us-

InterConnections.LearnMore 8.2

Sources of Prestige Testimony

Quoteland.com
http://www.quoteland.com
A compilation of quotations from literature, accessible by topic or author.

Bartleby.com
http://www.bartleby.com/quotations/
A collection of quotations from contemporary and classic sources with a search tool.

PhilosophyQuotes
http://www.philosophyquotes.com
A free daily ezine, plus archives, with an assortment of quotations by philosophers. Searchable by philosopher or key words.

Dictionary of Scientific Quotations
http://www.naturalscience.com/dsqhome.html
A short collection of interesting quotations from scientists.

Figure 8.2

Checklist for Evaluating Testimony

General
- ____ Is this testimony relevant to my purpose?
- ____ Am I quoting or paraphrasing accurately?
- ____ Am I using the appropriate type of testimony for my purpose?

Expert Testimony
- ____ Have I verified the credentials of my source?
- ____ Are my expert's credentials appropriate for my topic?
- ____ Will this expert be acceptable to my listeners?
- ____ Is my expert free from vested interest?
- ____ Is this testimony consistent with that of other authorities?
- ____ Does this testimony reflect the latest knowledge on my topic?

Lay Testimony
- ____ Does this testimony demonstrate the human applications of my topic?
- ____ Does this testimony enhance identification with my topic?
- ____ Are the people cited likeable and attractive?
- ____ Is polling data from a reputable organization?
- ____ Is polling data recent?

Prestige Testimony
- ____ Do my listeners believe this person is prestigious?
- ____ Does this testimony add grace and dignity to my speech?
- ____ Does associating with this person enhance my credibility as a speaker?
- ____ Does associating with this person enhance the credibility of my speech?

ing this type of testimony appropriately. Like lay testimony, prestige testimony cannot be used to verify facts.

Using Testimony

When you repeat the exact words of others, you are using a **direct quotation**. Direct quotations are useful when the material is brief, the exact wording is important, or the language is especially eloquent. When points are controversial, a direct quotation can seem especially authoritative and conclusive. Former senator Sam Nunn underscored the threat of the spread of nuclear and biological weapons by citing the exact words of an archenemy of the West: "In 1999, terrorist Osama Bin Laden said: 'To seek to possess the weapons that could counter those of the infidels is a religious duty.'"[20]

You also may **paraphrase**, or restate in your own words, what others have said, especially when repeating the exact words would be too long for your speech. When you paraphrase testimony, you must cite the source, identifying who said it, his or her credentials on the subject, and when it was said.

As you use testimony, be sure that the quotation you select reflects the overall meaning and intent of its author. Never twist the meaning of testimony to make it fit your purposes—this unethical practice is called **quoting out of context**. Because political candidates try to put a positive spin on their image, political advertising is often rife with this abuse. For example, during a political campaign in Illinois, one state representative sent out a fundraising letter that claimed he'd been singled out for "special recognition" by *Chicago* magazine—and, indeed, he had. He had been cited as "one of the state's ten worst legislators."[21]

To ensure accuracy, have quotations written out on note cards so that you can read them, rather than relying on your memory. A transition, such as "According to . . ." or "In the latest issue of . . .," leads gracefully into such material. To discover useful information about the credentials of your sources, check the biographical resources mentioned in the list following Chapter 7.

Speaker's Notes 8.2

Using Testimony

1. Select sources your audience will respect.
2. Quote or paraphrase material accurately.
3. Point out the qualifications of sources as you cite them.
4. Use expert testimony to validate information.
5. Use lay testimony to build identification and add authenticity.
6. Use prestige testimony to enhance the general credibility of your message.

Finally, don't simply accept what experts say uncritically. Experts have been known to be wrong. In 1903, the president of the Michigan Savings Bank advised Henry Ford's lawyer not to invest in the Ford Motor Company, saying, "The horse is here to stay, but the automobile is only a novelty—a fad." In 1943 Thomas Watson, chair of IBM, reached the following brilliant conclusion: "I think there is a world market for maybe five computers."[22] And in 1946 Darryl F. Zanuck, head of 20th Century Fox studios, predicted: "Television won't be able to hold on to any market it captures after the first six months. People will soon get tired of staring at a plywood box every night."[23]

Examples

Examples bring a speech to life. Just as pictures serve as graphic illustrations for a printed text, **examples** serve as verbal illustrations for an oral message. In fact, some scholars prefer the term *illustration* to *example.* This term derives from the Latin *illustrare,* which means "to shed light" or "to make bright." Good examples illuminate the message of your speech, making it clearer and more vivid for your audience.

In addition to clarifying ideas, examples also arouse attention and sustain interest. They demonstrate that what you have said either has happened or could happen. Examples may also be used to personalize your topic, especially when you draw them from your own experience. Speakers acknowledge their importance when they say, "Let me give you an example." Sue Suter, speaking before the Dallas conference of the National Industries for the Severely Handicapped, used a series of brief examples to point up the challenges she had experienced as a disabled person:

> **I contracted polio when I was two years old. I don't remember it. But I do remember my parents telling me about the advice the doctor gave when it was time for me to leave the hospital. He told them, "Just put her in bed, she's going to be staying there the rest of her life." I had a college counselor who advised me that going after more education might hurt me. He warned that it was hard enough for a woman with a disability to get married; a master's degree would only intimidate a man more.**
>
> **And I remember when I went after my first job as a secretary. The boss nearly didn't hire me because he worried that I couldn't carry coffee to him every morning. Talk about a double barrel insult—being doubted whether you could do something that you really shouldn't have to do in the first place! . . . I never spilled coffee on the boss's lap, although the temptation was real.[24]**

Examples about people give the audience someone with whom they can identify, thus involving them in the speech. Shared personal examples help the audience to *experience* your ideas, not simply to understand them. Examples that point out common experiences, beliefs, or values also help to bridge gaps in cultural understanding. When Senator Hillary Rodham Clinton spoke at the United Nations Fourth World Conference on Women in Beijing, China, she used many brief examples to demonstrate that all women share common problems and face a common destiny:

> **Over the past two-and-a-half years, I have had the opportunity to learn more about the challenges facing women in my own country and around the world. I have met new mothers in Jojakarta, Indonesia, who come together regularly in the village to discuss nutrition, family planning, and baby care. . . . I have met women in South Africa who helped lead the struggle to end apartheid and are now helping build a new democracy. . . . I have met women in India and Bangladesh who are taking out small loans to buy milk cows, rickshaws, thread and other materials to create a livelihood for themselves and their families. I have met doctors and nurses in Belarus and Ukraine who are trying to keep children alive in the aftermath of Chernobyl. The great challenge of this conference is to give voice to women everywhere whose experiences go unnoticed, whose words go unheard.[25]**

Examples also provide emphasis. When you make a statement and follow it with an example, you are pointing out that what you have just said is IMPORTANT. Examples amplify your ideas. They say to the audience, "This bears repeating." Examples are especially helpful when you introduce new, complex, or abstract material. Not only can they make such information clearer, but they also allow time for the audience to process what you have said before you move on to your next point.

Types of Examples

Examples take different forms, and these forms have different functions. An example may be brief or extended and may be based either on an actual event or on something that might have happened.

Brief Examples. A **brief example** mentions a specific instance to demonstrate a more general statement. Brief examples are concise and to the point. To explain the work of the Navajo Code Talkers during World War II, Ashley Roberson used a series of brief examples in her classroom speech:

> **The code talkers assigned Navajo words for approximately four hundred and fifty frequently used military terms. For example, the Navajo word for "iron fish" or "beschlow" was used to symbolize "submarine." The Navajo word for "hummingbird"—"dahaitahi"—was used to symbolize "fighter plane." This unique code baffled the Japanese code breakers, and they were never able to crack it.**

Extended Examples. An **extended example** contains more detail and allows you to dwell more fully on an illustration. Jane Goodall, the noted naturalist and UN Messenger of Peace, made good use of the technique to explain how she maintained her optimism following 9/11:

> **A lot of people have said to me, "But, Dr. Jane, surely after 9/11 that damaged your optimism for the future." I was in New York when the World Trade Towers were destroyed, and I felt with everyone in New York the shock, the numbness, the terrible grief, the mounting anger of the city as it struggled in**

the aftermath of 9/11. That one day, I think we saw the sort of ultimate in human evil, using innocent people to kill innocent people.

But we also saw this amazing heroism, the people who risked and lost their lives to rescue those trapped in the rubble. . . . And there was this outpouring of generosity; people gave whatever they had to give. . . . They opened their homes, they gave clothes, they gave blood, they gave what they could. And for a while people questioned their values: Were we spending too much time searching for more and more wealth and not enough time with our families? And even today . . . there are still people who tell me that they have much more contact with their families than they did before.[26]

Extended examples give us more details. They allow speakers to develop the message of their speeches as they develop the examples.

Factual Examples. A **factual example** is based on an actual event or the experiences of a real person. Factual examples provide strong support for your ideas because they actually did happen: they authenticate the point you are trying to make. University of Memphis student Alfred Montesi used the following factual example to define the meaning of generosity:

Generosity? I'll tell you what it means. Last week, tennis champion Arthur Ashe died—one more innocent victim of AIDS. Yesterday, a retired secretary and grandmother who is dying of lung cancer in Brooklyn gave $400,000 to St. Jude Children's Research Hospital to help create the Arthur Ashe Chair for Pediatric AIDS Research. She wanted his name remembered, not hers. We know only that she is a person "of very modest means" who received the money in a malpractice suit. She wanted to reach out to children who, like her, are fighting a terminal illness. While she remains anonymous, this woman is a champion—a champion of the human spirit. She has given us a gift far more precious than her money.

Hypothetical Examples. Examples need not be real to be effective. A **hypothetical example** is a composite of actual people, situations, or events. Although created by the speaker, a hypothetical example claims to represent reality and therefore must be plausible. The following hypothetical example was used by University of New Mexico student Susan Romero to illustrate the meaning of *cabin fever*:

Picture the following: you're in a room with five other people—four of them under ten years old, brimming with energy. It's been raining for six days—a cold, heavy rain. No one can go outside. The kids run in circles and fight with one another. The other adult nags at you when awake, and snores when asleep. Would you feel the walls closing in on you? Would you have an irresistible impulse to go somewhere, anywhere, to escape? That, my friends, is cabin fever.

You should use hypothetical examples when the factual examples you find don't adequately represent the truth of a situation or when a factual example might embarrass the people involved. Be especially careful that your hypothetical examples are truly representative and that they don't distort the truth just to make your point. Always alert your listeners to the hypothetical nature of your example: such introductory phrases as "Imagine yourself . . ." or "Picture the following . . ." should caution audiences that they will be hearing a hypothetical example. The standards of ethical speech require that you never present a hypothetical example as though it were factual.

____	Is this example relevant to my topic and purpose?
____	Does this example fairly represent the reality of a situation?
____	Will this example make my ideas more understandable?
____	Will this example make my point more memorable?
____	Will my listeners find this example believable?
____	Is this example appropriate for this audience?
____	Is this example in good taste?
____	Is this example interesting?

Figure 8.3
Checklist for Evaluating Examples

Evaluating Examples

You should evaluate examples in terms of their relevance. If an example does not advance your specific purpose, leave it out. Check to be sure that any examples you use help to clarify the point you wish to illustrate. If they don't make your message more understandable or more memorable, don't use them. Be certain that your examples fairly represent a situation as it actually exists. Examples based on exceptions to the rule present an unfair picture of a situation. You should also consider if the example you want to use is believable. If it is too far-fetched, your listeners will sense this, and it could damage your position and your credibility.

Keep in mind that what works well with one audience may seem out of place with another. Ask yourself if this example will connect with the motives, attitudes, or values of your listeners. Examples should further the mood and spirit of the occasion and must meet the tests of good taste and propriety. You should risk offending listeners only when they must be shocked into attention before they can be informed or persuaded. Last, but not least, be sure any example you use is interesting. Dull examples will not further your purpose or enhance your ethos.

Using Examples

Examples often make the difference between a speech that is humdrum and one that is outstanding. Highlight the authenticity of your examples by providing concrete details—the names of the people, places, times, and institutions involved in them. It is much easier for a listener to relate to Matt Dunn of the local General Motors plant than to some anonymous worker in an unnamed company. Use factual examples whenever possible. Let listeners know when you are using hypothetical examples.

Keep examples as brief as possible and to the point, even when you are using extended examples. Cut out all extraneous detail: one of the great lessons Ernest Hemingway learned as a developing writer was that the more selective he was in describing scenes, the more effective they were. Readers (in this case, listeners) are stimulated to provide details on their own, and their imaginations are engaged more closely with the text (or speech). Also, you should be selective as you supply examples. Use them only when they will reinforce the key ideas in your speech. Too many examples can distract listeners from your central meaning. Finally, use transitions to move smoothly from statement to example and from example to statement. Phrases such as "For instance . . ." or "As you can see . . ." work nicely.

Speaker's Notes 8.3

Using Examples

1. Use examples to emphasize major points.
2. Use examples to attract and hold attention.
3. Use examples to clarify abstract ideas.
4. Name the people and places in your examples.
5. Use factual examples whenever possible.
6. Keep examples brief and to the point.

Narratives

A **narrative** goes beyond an extended example by *telling a story*. Humans have been storytellers from the dawn of time. Most children are brought up on narratives—stories that entertain, fables that warn of dangers, and parables that teach virtues. Narratives help us recall the past and envision the future. They allow us to express emotions vicariously, and they set a mood that permeates the speech. They give voice to our ideals and transmit cultural traditions, and they help define who we are and what we are about.

People organize their experiences and memories in terms of the stories they tell.[27] Moreover, when information seems odd (for example, a Harvard-educated plumber), people look for stories that will explain the phenomenon and satisfy their curiosity.[28] The power of narratives, however, goes beyond simply explaining unusual phenomena. The author Norman Mailer has noted:

> **We tell stories in order to make sense of life. Narrative is reassuring. There are days when life is so absurd, it's crippling—nothing makes sense, but stories bring order to the absurdity. Relief is provided by the narrative's beginning, middle, and end.[29]**

Perhaps for all these reasons, Walter R. Fisher, who introduced the importance of narrative to communication studies, actually defines humans as storytelling animals (*homo narrans*).[30]

Certainly narratives can do important practical work in speeches. Stories are effective because they draw listeners into the action. They give listeners a chance to rehearse or enact certain roles, guided by the models of good and bad behavior they provide. Thus, narratives can influence changes in identity and action. Moreover, they stimulate the process of constructive listening that we discussed in Chapter 4. Because stories prompt listeners to create meaning from what they hear, the audience becomes involved in the creation of the message. It becomes *their* discovery, *their* truth.

Personal narratives also increase identification between speakers and audiences. They can help bridge the cultural differences that separate people of diverse backgrounds. According to Al Gore, storytelling can even help old enemies make peace. On one occasion, when Palestinian, Israeli, Jordanian, and Syrian leaders met to discuss a peace treaty, Gore saw the negotiations coming to a standstill. The situation looked unpromising until, in Gore's words, "the breakthroughs came when they told stories about their families. I have seen time and time again how storytelling brings people together."[31]

Successful narratives serve many of the same functions as examples. They make a speech more interesting, help sustain attention, clarify abstract or technical ideas, and emphasize a point. A narrative functions as a speech within a speech—it begins with an attention-getting introduction, continues with a body in which the story develops, and ends with a conclusion that reinforces the meaning. Facts and statistics fade with time, but narratives leave the audience with something to remember.

For all these good reasons, the ability to tell stories effectively has become one of the most sought-after skills among candidates for top entry-level positions in American business. More than fifty corporate recruiters surveyed by the Owen Graduate School of Management at Vanderbilt University identified communication skills in general, and storytelling ability in particular, as key to successful interviewing for top positions. Peter Veruki, director of career planning at Owen, concluded:

> **It is becoming increasingly important for candidates to be adept at the art of storytelling. The more the candidate can make his or her experience vivid and memorable for the recruiter, the greater the odds are of advancing to the next**

stage of the interview process. M.B.A.s should engage the interviewer by adding rich, visual detail to what they relate about their work and personal histories.[32]

Because they can be so effective at involving the audience, narratives are often used in the introductions of speeches. Heather Rouston Ettinger, an executive with Roulston & Company, told a story to illustrate the emerging status of women:

Last summer, Buffalo Bills quarterback, Doug Flutie, was watching the final game of the Women's World Cup soccer match on TV with his 12-year-old soccer-playing daughter, Alexa. During the soccer match between the USA and China teams, the hugely successful advertisement for Gatorade featuring Michael Jordan and Mia Hamm came on. As most of you well know, Michael Jordan, formerly of NBA fame, is the most influential athlete of the last century. Mia Hamm was the star forward of the USA national team. You might remember the theme to this was "Anything you can do I can do better." As Doug Flutie tells the story, when the ad came on, Alexa asked, "Dad, who's the guy with Mia?"[33]

Narratives that are humorous also help make the audience comfortable.[34] Bob Newhart opened a commencement speech at Catholic University of America with the following story:

When I was asked to be the commencement speaker I was reminded of a story about Jascha Heifetz, the famed violinist, who was asked to play in Grange Hall in Minot, North Dakota. He agreed to do it sometime in December. As December came around the weather turned terrible in New York and he called up and said, "I'm sorry, I won't be able to make it." The man who arranged for him to appear there said, "We have 3,000 people in Grange Hall here in Minot, could you try to?" And he said, "I will." So he finally got out of New York and flew to Denver, caught a small plane, and finally got into Minot at about 11 o'clock at night and walked into Grange Hall and there were 12 people waiting.

He said, "I'm sorry I can't appear in front of such a small audience. You said there were 3,000 people here." And he said, "Well there were, but they were afraid you wouldn't show up." He said, "I've never appeared in front of such a small audience." And the man who had arranged for him to be there said, "Jascha, if you could just sing one or two songs, that would be . . ."

So I feel somewhat like that. . . . I'm not sure you have the right man, but I'm very honored.[35]

Concluding narratives leave the audience with something to remember and extend the impact of a message. They can establish a mood that will last long after the closing words have been spoken. In a speech presented to the Economic Club in Chicago, Newton Minow, former chair of the Federal Communications Commission, concluded his plea for campaign finance reform with the following:

I leave you with a story President Kennedy told a week before he was killed. The story was about

InterConnections.LearnMore 8.3

Storytelling

International Storytelling Center
http://www.storytellingfoundation.com/
Organization dedicated to enriching the human experience through the power of storytelling; sponsors the annual National Storytelling Festival in Jonesborough, Tennessee. Provides links to information on activities and articles on storytelling.

Storytelling Resources
http://www.timsheppard.co.uk/story/index.html
A comprehensive collection of links for storytellers with a focus on skill development. Also contains links to full texts of stories. Compiled and maintained by Tim Sheppard, founder of Wordweavers, an innovative storytelling group in England.

Effective Storytelling
http://www.eldrbarry.net/roos/eest.htm
A short, well-written, engaging manual on the art of storytelling. Developed by Barry McWilliams, pastor, stimulating speaker, and gifted storyteller.

French Marshal Louis Lyautey, who walked one morning through his garden with his gardener. He stopped at a certain point and asked the gardener to plant a tree there the next morning. The gardener said, "But the tree will not bloom for one hundred years!" The Marshal looked at the gardener and replied, "In that case, you had better plant it this afternoon."[36]

Evaluating Narratives

As with all other forms of supporting materials, narratives must meet the test of relevance. Speakers sometimes "borrow" a narrative from an anthology of stories or jokes and then strain to connect it with their topic. Narratives should not be used simply to amuse listeners—they must also help you make your point. An irrelevant narrative distracts listeners.

Narratives should illustrate a situation as it actually exists. They should help listeners better understand your message and create identification among the speaker, topic, and audience.

Narratives must also meet the test of propriety. Audiences can be turned off by stories that foster negative stereotypes or that contain offensive language. Ask yourself further whether the narrative will seem fresh and original. If listeners have already heard your story, they may decide you have nothing new to say in the rest of your speech.

Finally, Professor Fisher suggests that we evaluate narratives in terms of what he calls their "narrative coherence" and "narrative fidelity." **Narrative coherence** means that the story fits together well. Events must seem to flow within the proper order from beginning to end, and the characters must seem to fit the actions they perform. **Narrative fidelity** means that the story resonates with what you already know about the world. It rings true and makes sense.

Using Narratives

You may think that storytelling is a natural and easy skill to acquire, but that is not always true. We recently had a student who "teased" his listeners with vague promises of stories that never materialized in his speech. He would say, "There's a really funny story here. . .," and then he would ramble on without pausing to tell us the story. At best, he would simply paraphrase the story or present a punch line without any preparation. Listening to him was a truly frustrating experience.

Figure 8.4
Evaluating Narratives

____ Is the narrative relevant to my topic and purpose?
____ Does the narrative fairly represent the situation?
____ Will the story help listeners make sense of things?
____ Will the narrative draw listeners into the action?
____ Is the narrative appropriate for this audience?
____ Will the story provide appropriate role models?
____ Will the story enhance identification among listeners, topic, and speaker?
____ Will the narrative make my speech more memorable?
____ Does the story set an appropriate mood for my message?
____ Is the narrative fresh and interesting?
____ Does the story flow well?
____ Is the narrative believable?
____ Is the narrative in good taste?

It takes time to tell a story well. Beyond having a beginning, middle, and end, a story must have a scene, characters, and plot. Remember how the fairy tales of your youth started—"Once upon a time in the land of . . ."—and built up from there. In a similar manner, narratives within a speech must present a sequence of details in the order in which they might occur and build up to a climax or punch line. The characters in your narrative must seem to come alive through the use of vivid language. You must let listeners see things as you describe them by using language that is colorful and rich in imagery.

As you tell your story, let yourself get caught up in it. Enjoy yourself! If telling the story is fun for you, your listeners will probably enjoy it too. Set the narrative off from the rest of your speech by pausing before you begin and after you end the story. Narratives are to be savored, and these pauses help an audience prepare for and reflect upon the listening experience. Use voice and dialect changes to signal that a "character" is speaking. Since storytelling is an intimate form of communication, reduce the distance between yourself and your listeners and move closer to your audience. You can also be less formal than in the rest of your speech. If your story evokes laughter, wait for it to subside before going on. It will help to practice telling your story so that you can get the wording and timing just right. Polish and memorize the punch line: the story exists for it. It is the gem at the center, the capstone at the top.

Use dialogue in a narrative rather than paraphrasing what someone says. When speakers use dialogue, they reproduce conversation directly. Paraphrasing can save time, but it robs a narrative of power and immediacy. Let people speak for themselves! The late senator Sam Ervin of North Carolina was a master storyteller. Note how he used dialogue in the following narrative, which opened a speech on the Constitution and our judicial system:

> **Jim's administrator was suing the railroad for his wrongful death. The first witness he called to the stand testified as follows: "I saw Jim walking up the track. A fast train passed, going up the track. After it passed, I didn't see Jim. I walked up the track a little way and discovered Jim's severed head lying on one side of the track, and the rest of his body on the other." The witness was asked how he reacted to his gruesome discovery. He responded: "I said to myself, 'Something serious must have happened to Jim.'"**
>
> **Something serious has been happening to constitutional government in America. I want to talk to you about it.[37]**

Had "Mr. Sam" paraphrased the punch line by saying, "The witness reported that he knew instantly that the victim had had a serious accident," he would have destroyed its effect. Dialogue makes a narrative come alive by bringing listeners close to the action. Paraphrase distances the audience.

Avoid stories that are funny at the expense of others. If you poke fun at anyone, let it be yourself. Speakers who tell amusing stories about themselves sometimes rise in the esteem of listeners. When this technique is effective, the stories that seem to put the speakers down are actually building them up. Former Memphis mayor Wyeth Chandler loves to tell a story at his own expense that probably has this effect for most audiences. The local newspaper summarized this story as follows:

> **As mayor, he had dispatched a city helicopter to Arkansas in hopes of rescuing a Memphis hunter. The mission failed and the hunter drowned. Chandler says the man's widow later telephoned to thank him for the city's heroic effort. As the call ended, the woman apologized for taking up his time. "I know you must be busy," he recalls her saying.**
>
> **"Yeah, I can barely keep my head above water," Chandler said. One of Chandler's staff members . . . remembers Chandler's grimace even as the words were still coming out of the mayor's mouth.[38]**

Speaker's Notes 8.4

Using Narratives

1. Use stories to involve the audience with your topic.
2. Practice telling your stories so that they flow smoothly.
3. Develop the characters in your stories so they seem to come to life.
4. Use voice and dialect changes for characters.
5. Use dialogue rather than paraphrase.
6. Use colorful, vivid language.

A well-told narrative can add much to a speech, but too many stories can turn a speech into a rambling string of tales without a clear focus. Save narratives for special occasions. Use them to arouse or sustain attention, to create a special mood for your message, or to demonstrate some important truth.

Three Techniques for Using Supporting Materials

The best materials for building homes on hilltops are only as good as the builders who use them. Similarly, the best supporting materials for speeches depend for their effectiveness on the skill of speechmakers. Much of the art of building speeches depends on the wise use of three major techniques—comparison, contrast, and analogy.

Comparison

A **comparison** helps an audience grasp a subject by pointing out its similarities to something else. These similarities provide a context or frame in which the subject can be understood. In this way comparison can make an unfamiliar or controversial idea seem clearer or acceptable by connecting it with something the audience already understands or accepts. Comparisons can also help the audience see the significance of supporting materials. Consider how Maurice Johnson used comparison in a classroom speech to point up the meaning of a statistic:

> **Let's suppose that you have a job offer here in Memphis that pays $40,000 per year. You're not really sure you want to stay in Memphis, and you know salaries are higher in other cities. But how do these salaries really compare? Will that higher salary in Boston, or Chicago, or New York City actually be higher than what you could earn in Memphis? *Money Magazine*'s web site has a "Salary Comparator" that lets you see how things stack up. For example, in 2004, to equal the purchasing power of the Memphis $40,000 salary, you'd have to make $63,000 in Boston; in Chicago, you'd have to make $66,000; and, in New York City you'd have to make a whopping $98,000.**

Here the comparisons make the meaning of the hypothetical salary offer stand out in bold relief. Before you decide to use a comparison, ask yourself these questions:

- *Are there enough similarities to justify the comparison?* The similarities among four places that are all large urban cities in the United States might be enough to justify a comparison.

Tidmore wanted to explain the significance of her mother's gift of an Olympic-grade rifle. A brief analogy served her well:

> **Someone outside of the sport might think, "Eh, minor upgrade. A gun is a gun, right? No. Imagine a 15-year-old who has been driving a used Toyota and who suddenly gets a new Mercedes for her sixteenth birthday. That's how I felt.**

M. George Allen, senior vice president of research and development for the 3M Company, combined comparison, contrast, and analogy as he established a perspective for his speech, "Succeeding in Japan":

> **I think of doing business in Japan as being like a game of football. But first, you need to know which game of football it is you are playing. Is it the American gridiron sport—or what the rest of the world calls football and what we call soccer?**
>
> **American football is a bruising battle. The players are huge and strong. They have nicknames like "Refrigerator." And the game is played in short bursts of intense energy. In soccer football, the players are smaller, but faster. Play is continuous. And a soccer fullback weighs less than lunch for a gridiron fullback.**
>
> **In a nutshell, gridiron football is trench warfare: soccer football is the cavalry. Likewise, when it comes to business, the Japanese play a different game than we do.[41]**

In this example Mr. Allen first draws a *comparison* with football, perhaps to emphasize the aggressive, competitive qualities of international business. Next he develops a *contrast* between the sports of football and soccer, to establish the basis for a *figurative analogy:* just as similar forms of sport can be quite different, so can styles of business reflect the fundamentally different lifestyles of nations.

As you weigh the use of an analogy, ask yourself the following:

- *Will the analogy help me make some fundamental point about my subject?*
- *Will the analogy distract my listeners?* In the above example, the speaker risked losing some listeners who would rather think about soccer and football than about international business practices.
- *Does the analogy establish a beneficial association for my subject?* Some critics complain that the analogy between sports and politics, so popular among American journalists who describe the "horserace" of political campaigning, both trivializes politics and dehumanizes politicians. The above example could illustrate a similar problem in talking about international business.

Ethics Alert! 8.1

The Ethical Use of Supporting Material

1. Provide the date, source, and context of information cited in your speech.
2. Don't present a claim or opinion as though it were a fact.
3. Remember that statistics are open to differing interpretations.
4. Protect your listeners from biased information.
5. Tell listeners if you can't identify the exact sources of your information.
6. Don't "quote out of context" to misrepresent a person's position.
7. Be sure examples reflect reality.
8. Don't present hypothetical examples as though they were factual.

Deciding What Support Material You Should Use

VideoLab

Critique the speaker's use of supporting materials in **VideoLab Lesson 4.3: Assessing the Use of Supporting Materials.**

Every main point in your speech should be supported with a variety of materials. Adjust these materials according to the challenge of your speech.

1. If your ideas are *controversial,* rely primarily on facts, statistics, factual examples, or expert testimony from sources the audience will respect and accept.
2. If your ideas or concepts are *abstract,* bring them to life with examples and narratives.
3. If a point is highly *technical,* supplement facts and statistics with expert testimony.
4. If you need to *excite emotions,* use lay or prestige testimony, examples, or narratives. Sharpen both understanding and feelings by using contrast and analogy.
5. If you need to *defuse emotions,* emphasize facts and statistics and expert testimony. Keep the focus on definitions and explanations.
6. If your topic is *distant* from the lives of listeners, draw it closer to them through information, examples, and narratives, activated by descriptions, comparisons, and analogies.
7. If your ideas are *novel,* use comparisons, contrasts, or analogies to help your listeners better comprehend them. Use definitions, explanations, and descriptions to aid understanding. Examples, comparisons, contrasts, and analogies will help listeners integrate information.

To guide you through the evidence-gathering process for your main ideas, go to the **SpeechStudio** and complete the **Checklist for Supporting an Idea** under **Conducting Research and Gathering Supporting Materials.**

Go to http://college.hmco.com/eduspace/

Although the need for particular types of supporting material may vary with different topics and audiences, *you should always support each main point with the most important and relevant facts and statistics available.* For additional clarity, use testimony, definitions, explanations, and descriptions. *Support each main point with at least one interesting example or narrative.* To make your presentation more memorable, emphasize examples and narratives, brought to life through striking comparisons, contrasts, or analogies.

In Summary

Facts and statistics, testimony, examples, and narratives are the major forms of supporting materials. They provide the substance, strength, credibility, and appeal a speech must have before listeners will place their faith in it.

Facts and Statistics. Information in the form of facts and statistics is the most objective form of supporting material, especially useful for unfamiliar or controversial topics. *Facts* are verifiable, which means that independent observers see and report them consistently. *Statistics* are numerical facts that describe the size of something, make predictions, illustrate trends, or show relationships. Be careful not to confuse factual statements with interpretations and claims. Be sure that your information meets the tests of relevance, recency, credibility, and reliability.

Use definitions, explanations, and descriptions to frame facts and statistics into powerful supports. A *definition* states the meaning of an unfamiliar term concisely in words the audience can understand. An *explanation* more fully expands on what something is or how it works. *Descriptions* are word pictures that help the audience visualize what you are talking about.

Testimony. *Testimony* cites the ideas or words of others in support of your message. When you repeat the exact words of others, you make use of *direct quotation.* When you summarize what others say, you *paraphrase* them. *Expert testimony* comes from recognized authorities who support the validity of your claims. *Lay testimony* represents "the voice of the people" on a topic; sometimes it takes the form of a *testimonial. Prestige testimony* connects your message with the general wisdom of some revered figure.

Be sure that the sources you cite are free from bias. State their credentials as you introduce their testimony, and never quote them out of context.

Examples. *Examples* serve as verbal illustrations. They help arouse interest, clarify ideas, sustain attention, personalize a topic, emphasize your major points, demonstrate how your ideas can be applied, and make it easier for listeners to remember your message. *Brief examples* mention specific instances. *Extended examples* contain more detail and give the speaker more time to build impressions. *Factual examples* are based on actual events and persons. *Hypothetical examples* are invented by the speaker to represent reality. Use people's names to personalize examples and magnify their power.

Narratives. A *narrative* tells a story that illustrates some truth about the topic. Good narratives draw listeners into the action and help establish a mood. They should be told in colorful, concrete language, using dialogue and characterization. A lively and informal style of presentation can enhance narration. Avoid narratives that demean others or reinforce negative stereotypes.

Three Techniques for Using Supporting Materials. Comparison, contrast, and analogy are general techniques used to make the most of supporting materials. *Comparison* points out the similarities of an unfamiliar or controversial topic to something the audience already understands or accepts. *Contrast* emphasizes the differences among things to make some important point. *Analogy* combines the principles of comparison and contrast to heighten awareness. *Figurative analogy* especially can help listeners see a topic in a new way by pointing out previously unexpected relationships.

Terms to Know

supporting materials
facts
statistics
disinformation
definitions
explanations
descriptions
testimony
expert testimony
reluctant testimony
lay testimony
testimonial
prestige testimony
direct quotation
paraphrase
quoting out of context
examples
brief example
extended example
factual example
hypothetical example
narrative
narrative coherence
narrative fidelity
comparison
contrast
analogy
literal analogy
figurative analogy

Discussion

1. Find the text of a recent speech in *Vital Speeches of the Day* that contains statistical information. Were you convinced by the statistics? Did the speaker use examples to make the statistics more meaningful? Was the source of the statistics clearly identified? How did this affect your perception of the credibility of the speech?
2. Evaluate the use of supporting materials in one of the student speeches in Appendix B. Consider the following: What types of supporting material are used? Is there sufficient supporting material? Are the types of supporting material appropriate to the purpose? Do they make the speech more effective for you? How and why?
3. Look in newspapers or magazines for recent statements by public officials that purport to be factual but that may actually contain distortions. What tips you off to the distortion? In your judgment, would most readers be likely to detect this bias?

Application

1. Think back to your childhood and remember your favorite bedtime story. Prepare a brief (less than three minutes) presentation of this story. Practice presenting it as if you were telling it to a group of first-graders. Working in small groups, share your story with other group members. Listen to theirs. What storytelling techniques seemed most effective? What made some of the stories less effective?
2. Determine which types of testimony might best support the following statements:
   a. Native Americans don't get a square deal in the United States.
   b. Campus security measures are inadequate.
   c. America should lift the embargo on Cuba.
   d. Asian American children are outperforming Anglo-American children in our public schools.
3. Develop a hypothetical example or narrative to illustrate one of the following abstract concepts: love, compassion, charity, peace, justice.

Notes

1. Richard Weaver, "Ultimate Terms in Contemporary Rhetoric," in *The Ethics of Rhetoric* (Chicago: Henry Regnery, 1953), pp. 211–232.
2. Cynthia Crossen, *Tainted Truth: The Manipulation of Fact in America* (New York: Simon and Schuster, 1994), p. 36.
3. For similar commentary on other periodicals, see Howard Kahane, *Logic and Contemporary Rhetoric: The Use of Reason in Everyday Life* (Belmont, Calif.: Wadsworth, 1984), pp. 337–338.
4. Reprinted by permission of *World Book Encyclopedia.* This material was brought to our attention by Professor Gray Matthews of the University of Memphis.
5. Neil Postman, "Critical Thinking in the Electronic Era," *Phi Kappa Phi Journal* 65 (1985): 7.
6. Crossen, p. 36.
7. Richard F. Corlin, "The Secrets of Gun Violence in America," *Vital Speeches of the Day*, 1 Aug. 2001, pp. 610–615.
8. Crossen, p. 42.
9. Peter Francese, "Editorial: Lies, Damned Lies . . .," *American Demographics,* Nov. 1994, p. 2.
10. Donna E. Shalala, "Domestic Terrorism: An Unacknowledged Epidemic," *Vital Speeches of the Day,* 15 May 1994, p. 451.
11. John F. Smith Jr., "Eyes on the Road, Hands on the Wheel," *Vital Speeches of the Day,* 15 Nov. 2000, pp. 67–68.
12. Longinus, *On the Sublime,* trans. W. Rhys Roberts, in *The Great Critics: An Anthology of Literary Criticism,* 3rd ed., ed. James Harry Smith and Edd Winfield Parks (New York: W. W. Norton, 1951), p. 82.
13. Kathleen Hall Jamieson appeared as a panelist on the CNN special report "Investigating the President: Media Madness?" aired on 28 Jan. 1998.
14. William L. Benoit and Kimberly A. Kennedy, "On Reluctant Testimony," *Communication Quarterly* 47 (1999): 376–387.
15. Corlin, p. 613.
16. The power of lay testimony is one possible implication of Michael Calvin McGee's "In Search of the People: A Rhetorical Alternative," *Quarterly Journal of Speech* 61 (1975): 235–249.
17. Bill Moyers, "Best of Jobs: To Have and Serve the Public's Trust," keynote address at the PBS Annual Meeting, 23 June 1996, reprinted in *Current,* 8 July 1996.
18. Colin Powell, "Sharing in the American Dream," *Vital Speeches of the Day,* 1 June 1997, p. 484; from *Collected Poems of Langston Hughes* by Langston Hughes, copyright ©1994 by the Estate of Langston Hughes. Used by permission of Alfred A. Knopf, a division of Random House, Inc.
19. Brock Evans, "A Time of Crisis: The Giveaway of Our Public Lands," *Vital Speeches of the Day,* 1 Sept. 1995, p. 691.
20. Sam Nunn, "A New Way of Thinking," *Vital Speeches of the Day,* 1 May 2001, p. 425.
21. "On the Campaign Trail," *Reader's Digest,* March 1992, p. 116.
22. Chester Burger, "Sooner Than You Think: Technology Pulling the World Together," *Vital Speeches of the Day,* 15 Sept. 2000, p. 715.
23. *Newsweek,* 27 Jan. 1997, p. 86.

24. Excerpt from Sue Suter, "Disability Is No Big Deal: Seeing People as They Really Are," *Vital Speeches of the Day,* 15 Aug. 1997, pp. 650–651. Reprinted by permission of the author.

25. Hillary Rodham Clinton, "Women's Rights are Human Rights," *Vital Speeches of the Day,* 1 Oct. 1995, p. 739.

26. Jane Goodall, "Dangers to the Environment," *Vital Speeches of the Day*, 15 Nov. 2003, p. 77.

27. Jerome S. Bruner, *Acts of Meaning* (Cambridge: Harvard University Press, 1990), and "The Narrative Construction of Reality," *Critical Inquiry* 18 (1991): 1–21.

28. Z. Kunda, D. T. Miller, and T. Claire, "Combining Social Concepts: The Role of Causal Reasoning," *Cognitive Science* 14 (1990): 551–577.

29. From Norman Mailer, *The Spooky Art*, excerpted in *Newsweek*, 27 Jan. 2003, p. 64.

30. Walter R. Fisher, *Human Communication as Narration: Toward a Philosophy of Reason, Value, and Action* (Columbia: University of South Carolina Press, 1987).

31. Associated Press, "Gore Promotes Benefits of Good Storytelling," *Memphis Commercial Appeal,* 8 Oct. 1995, p. B2.

32. "M.B.A.s Who Tell Stories Get a Jump on the Job Search," excerpted from *Spotlight,* 15 Sept. 1995.

33. Heather Rouston Ettinger, "Shattering the Glass Floor: Women Donors as Leaders of Fundamental Change," *Vital Speeches of the Day,* 15 Sept. 2000, p. 727.

34. Roger Ailes, *You Are the Message* (New York: Doubleday, 1988), pp. 70–74.

35. Bob Newhart, "Humor Makes Us Free: Laughter Gives Us Distance," *Vital Speeches of the Day,* 15 July 1997, p. 607.

36. Newton Minow, "Campaign Finance Reform: We Have Failed to Solve the Problem," *Vital Speeches of the Day,* 1 July 1997, p. 558.

37. Sam J. Ervin Jr., "Judicial Verbicide: An Affront to the Constitution," presented at Herbert Law Center, Louisiana State University, Baton Rouge, 22 Oct. 1980, in *Representative American Speeches 1980–1981,* ed. Owen Peterson (New York: H. W. Wilson, 1981), p. 62.

38. Michael Lollar, "Dean's Scream Wasn't First Political Howler," *The Commercial Appeal*, 1 Feb. 2004, p. 1A.

39. Marge Anderson, "Looking Through Our Window: The Value of Indian Culture," *Vital Speeches of the Day,* 1 Aug. 1999, p. 633.

40. Minow, pp. 555–556.

41. M. George Allen, "Succeeding in Japan: One Company's Perspective," *Vital Speeches of the Day,* 1 May 1994, p. 430.

Structuring Your Speech

9

OUTLINE

This chapter will help you

- develop a simple, balanced, and orderly speech design
- select and arrange your main points
- plan transitions to make your speech flow smoothly
- prepare effective introductions for your speeches
- design memorable conclusions for your speeches

Every discourse ought to be a living creature; having a body of its own and head and feet; there should be a middle, beginning, and end, adapted to one another and to the whole.

PLATO

Global warming is a gradual warming of the earth caused by human activities that dump carbon dioxide and other gases into the atmosphere. August 1998 was the hottest month since weather records have been kept. Fossil fuel use has more than doubled since 1950. One cause of global warming is industrial emissions. The ten hottest years in recorded history have occurred since 1970. Skin cancers could increase as much as 26 percent if the ozone level drops another 10 percent. Global warming endangers our world.

How much of this randomly scrambled information would you remember if you heard it presented this way? There seems to be important news here, but it gets lost because it is poorly organized. A well-organized presentation makes it easier for listeners to learn and remember your message.[1]

Suppose you must take a course in basic physics next semester, and you get the following material from Students for Better Teaching about the instructors who teach the course:

> JOHNSON, DENNIS: **Professor Johnson is very entertaining. He tells a lot of funny stories and puts on demonstrations that seem like a "magic show." But he doesn't explain difficult material in any systematic fashion, so it's hard to take notes. When it's time for departmental examinations, you often don't know how or what to study.**
>
> MARTINEZ, MARIA: **Professor Martinez is very businesslike. Don't expect to be entertained in her class. She starts each lecture by reviewing the material covered in the last session and asks if anyone has questions. Her lectures are easy to follow. She points out what is most important for students to know and uses clear examples that make difficult ideas easier to understand and apply.**

Which instructor would you choose? When a message is important, most of us would choose the well-organized person over the entertainer. In fact, a recent study indicated that students dislike instructors who go off on tangents, jump from one idea to another, ramble, or are generally disorganized.[2]

How well your presentation is organized affects your ethos.[3] As we noted in Chapter 3, competence is an important part of credibility. It is hard for listeners to think of you as competent when your speech is poorly organized. They may conclude either that you lack the capacity to organize or that you did not care enough to prepare carefully.

In this chapter we look at the principles that underlie well-organized messages to explain how to structure the body of your speech. Next, we consider the important role of transitions in making a speech flow smoothly. Finally, we discuss how to prepare effective introductions and conclusions.

Principles of Good Form

The structure of a speech should follow the ways people naturally arrange things in their minds. People rarely store information in individual bits. Instead they "chunk" material for easy recall. For example, people recall telephone numbers as two or three chunks of numbers, such as 219-647-2830, not 2-1-9-6-4-7-2-8-3-0.[4] Well-organized speeches should follow a few simple principles of **good form**.[5] To develop good form, a concept that comes from the work of the Gestalt psychologists, you should keep your presentation simple, balance the parts of your speech, and arrange your main points so that they develop in a meaningful pattern. In other words, good form depends on simplicity, balance, and order.

VideoLab

Organizational patterns for persuasive speeches often differ from those used in informative speaking. Watch the student persuasive speech about Olestra and answer the questions in **Drill 5.2: Identifying Keys to Good Persuasive Organization.**

Simplicity

A simple design makes it easy for listeners to follow, understand, and remember your message.[6] Simplicity is important because listeners usually do not have manuscripts to refer to if what they hear is confusing. To achieve **simplicity** in your speeches, you should limit the number of your main ideas and keep your wording direct and to the point.

Evaluate the structure of your speech by going to the **Worksheet for Structural Analysis** under **Organizing Your Speech** in the **Online SpeechStudio**.

Go to http://college.hmco.com/eduspace/

Number of Main Points. The fewer main points in a speech the better, because each main point must be developed with supporting material.[7] It takes time to present information, examples, narratives, and testimony effectively. Short speeches like those you will present in class should have no more than four main points. Look at what happens when a speech becomes overburdened with main points:

Thesis statement:	Government welfare programs aren't working.	
Main points:	I.	There are too many programs.
	II.	The programs often duplicate coverage.
	III.	Some people who need help are left out.
	IV.	The programs are poorly funded.
	V.	The programs waste money.
	VI.	Recipients have no input into what is needed.
	VII.	The programs create dependence.
	VIII.	The programs stifle initiative.
	IX.	The programs rob the poor of self-respect.

Each of these points may be important, but presented this way they could be confusing. It would be hard for listeners to remember them because they are not organized into meaningful chunks. Let's see how these ideas might be clustered into a simpler structural pattern:

Thesis statement:	Our approach to welfare in America is inadequate, inefficient, and insensitive.	
Main point:	I.	Our approach is inadequate.
Subpoints:		A. We don't fund it sufficiently.
		B. Some people who need help get left out.

Main point:	II.	Our approach is inefficient.
Subpoints:		A. There are too many programs.
		B. There is too much duplication.
		C. There is too much waste of money.
Main point:	III.	Our approach is insensitive.
Subpoints:		A. It creates dependence.
		B. It stifles initiative.
		C. It robs people of self-respect.

This simple structure makes the speech easier to follow. The thesis statement offers an overview of the speech. Each main point elaborates a dimension of the thesis statement. The subpoints organize and focus the secondary ideas so that they support the major ideas. Overlapping ideas have been combined, and unnecessary ideas have been omitted. The new structure answers systematically the questions raised in the minds of thoughtful listeners in response to the thesis statement: "Is welfare indeed 'inadequate, inefficient, and insensitive'? What do these claims mean?" The overall result is a design that satisfies such listeners and helps them remember what they have heard.[8]

Phrasing Main Points. You should state your main points simply. In our revised example, the wording of main points is clear and direct. The repeated phrase ("Our approach is . . .") suggests that these are *main* points and helps listeners remember them. It allows the speaker to refer to the "Three I's" of welfare (Inadequate, Inefficient, and Insensitive) in the introduction and conclusion, a strategy that ties the speech together.

Balance

Speeches that use sequential design follow a step-by-step pattern of development.

Balance means that the major parts of your speech–the introduction, the body, and the conclusion–receive appropriate development. Instructors typically specify time limits for speeches, so keep these in mind as you plan your message. It can be very upsetting to finish the first main point of your speech and find that you have only one minute left and two more main points plus your conclusion to present. Time yourself as you practice your speech to be sure it fits within the time limits. The following suggestions will help you plan a balanced presentation:

1. *The body should be the longest part of your speech.* It contains your major ideas. If you spend three minutes on your introduction, a minute and a half on the body, and thirty seconds on the conclusion, your speech will be out of balance.

2. *Balance the development of each main point.* If your main points seem equally important, you should give each point *equal emphasis.* This strategy might be appropriate for the speech on the "Three I's" of welfare policy, in which each point merits equal attention. If your main points vary in importance, however, you must adjust this strategy. You might start with the most important point, spending more of your time on it, and then present the other points with a *descending* emphasis, according to their importance. For example, in a speech that follows the problem-solution design, you may need to convince listeners first that there actually is a problem. Thus you would devote most of your time to meeting the challenge of establishing this first main point. Such a speech appears at the end of Chapter 15. Alternatively, you might wish to develop your main points with an *ascending* emphasis. If listeners agree there is a problem but don't know what to do about it, then you should devote most of your time to your solution, the second main point. Such a speech appears at the end of Chapter 16. Figure 9.1 illustrates these variations of emphasis.

3. *The introduction and conclusion should be approximately equal in length.* Your introduction may be slightly longer than your conclusion, but the total amount of time spent on your introduction and conclusion should be less than the amount spent on the body of your speech. As a general rule, in a five-minute presentation, the combined length of the introduction and conclusion should require about a minute. This leaves four minutes to develop the main points of the message.

Order

A speech that demonstrates **order** follows a consistent pattern of development from beginning to end. It starts by introducing its subject and purpose, continues by developing the main ideas in the body of the speech, and ends by summarizing and reflecting on the meaning of what has been said. To build an orderly speech, you should follow the advice implied by Plato in our chapter-opening epigram: design the body of the speech first, because that is where you will do the work of presenting, illustrating, and proving your message. Once you have structured the body of your speech, you can prepare an introduction and a conclusion that are custom-tailored for your message.

Figure 9.1

Balanced Speech Designs

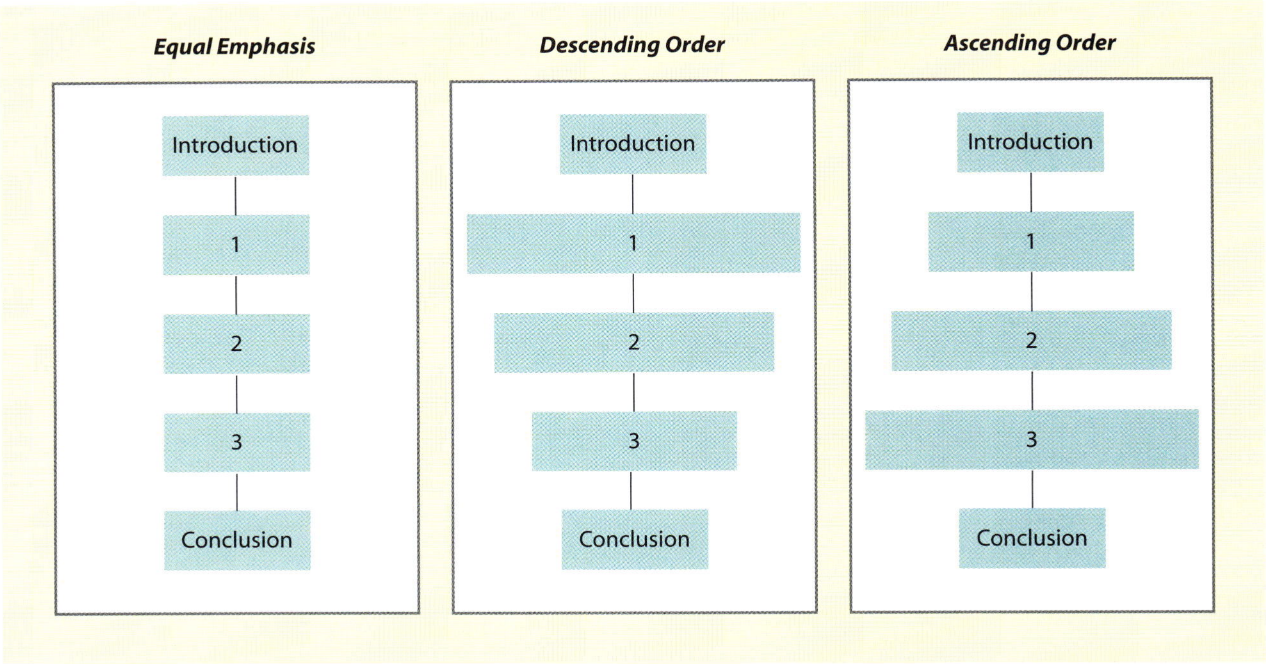

Order also applies to the way you arrange your main points. If you propose a solution, you should first present the problem, because that is how our minds work. We don't normally come up with solutions and then look for problems to fit them. An orderly arrangement is also important when you are demonstrating the steps in a process or describing the events in a historical perspective. These arrangements are at the heart of what we call the sequential and the chronological designs. When structuring your speech according to these patterns, begin with the first step or the first event, and then cover the rest of the steps and events in the order in which they occur. If you jump around, the audience may get lost, decide that you are unprepared, or conclude that the disorderly speech reflects a disorderly mind.

Structuring the Body of Your Speech

The body of your speech should highlight your main points and develop them effectively. As you structure the body, you have three major tasks to accomplish:

1. Selecting your main points
2. Arranging these points appropriately
3. Deciding on supporting materials

Selecting Your Main Points

The **main points** are the most important ideas of your message, the points of focus that will advance your specific purpose. How do you identify and construct your main points? As you research your topic, you should discover some repeated themes. These are the most important issues connected with your topic. Consider how they relate to your specific purpose, your thesis statement, and the needs and interests of your listeners. Your main points will come from these repeated themes and your analysis of their relevance.

Let's look at how you might select the main points for a speech on global warming. Begin by preparing a **research overview**, listing your main sources of information and a summary of the major ideas from each. Figure 9.2 presents a sample research overview based on four sources of information: a *Time* magazine special issue, summary reports from the Intergovernmental Panel on Climate

Figure 9.2
Sample Research Overview

Environment News Service	Time	U.S. News	Intergovernmental Panel on Climate Change
1. Increase in Earth's temperature	1. Use less energy	1. CO_2 problems	1. Climate changes
2. Build-up of greenhouse gases	2. Drive efficient vehicles	2. Climate changes	2. U.S. largest polluter
3. Flooding and climate changes	3. Go with solar or gas energy	3. What we can do A. Learn more about it B. Save energy C. Drive less	3. Energy and global warming
4. Attributed to human influences	4. Geoengineering ideas		4. Transportation and global warming

Change, an article from *U.S. News & World Report*, and research reports from the Environment News Service. Scanning the overview, you might come up with the following repeated themes:

- Increased temperatures are evidence of global warming.
- Human activities cause global warming.
- Global warming will cause climate changes.
- Global warming will cause health, environmental, and economic problems.

Once you have identified the main themes from the research, you need to determine how these relate to your specific purpose and your audience. In this example, let us assume that your specific purpose is "to inform my audience about the problem of global warming." You anticipate that the audience's knowledge of the subject may be limited and possibly even confused. Therefore, you decide that your first major challenge will be to define global warming in terms these listeners can understand, using simple, everyday comparisons and explanations. After that, you want to increase audience understanding; because global warming appears to be an effect, you decide to develop a *causation design* that will describe the causes and consequences of the problem. In light of the repeated themes revealed by your research overview, you might come up with the following main points:

Decide the best way to organize your speech by going to the What Design to Use When document under Selecting a Speech Design.
Go to http://college.hmco.com/eduspace/

1. Global warming is a gradual warming of the earth's surface.
2. The major causes of global warming are industrial emissions, deforestation, and personal energy use.
3. Global warming may cause climate changes and health problems.

Arranging Your Main Points

Once you have determined your main points, you must decide how to arrange them. (We already began to do that with the global warming example.) You need to come up with a way of ordering them that is appropriate for your audience, that fits your material, and that serves your specific purpose.

As we noted earlier in this chapter, people mentally organize information into patterns that are easy to remember. These patterns set up expectations that are used to process further experiences. They function like mental templates through which we see and experience the world. The way we arrange material in our speeches must be in harmony with these expectations. Drawing again on gestalt psychology, *these templates are based on the principles of similarity, proximity, and closure.* In this section, we provide a brief overview of some basic speech designs that relate to each of these principles. More detailed examples of speech designs, complete with skeleton outlines, are provided as they become appropriate for informative, persuasive, and ceremonial speeches in Chapters 14, 16, and 17.

InterConnections.LearnMore 9.1

Principles of Perception

Gestalt and the Principles of Design in Art
http://daphne.palomar.edu/design/gestalt.html
An article covering the concepts of closure, continuance, similarity, proximity, and alignment, including how they apply to the graphic arts. Prepared by Professor James T. Saw of the Art Department at Palomar College, San Marcos, California.

Gestalt Psychology Today
http://www.psych.yorku.ca/classics/Kohler/today.htm
The text of the 1959 Presidential Address to the American Psychological Association, presented by Wolfgang Kohler, one of the founders of gestalt psychology. Site developed and maintained by Professor Christopher D. Green, Department of Psychology, York University, Toronto, Canada.

Gestalt Psychology
http://www.cultsock.ndirect.co.uk/MUHome/cshtml/index.html
Well-written article explaining the major principles of gestalt psychology. Included in the Communication, Culture and Media Studies Infobase (http://www.ccms-infobase.com) site developed and maintained by Michael Underwood, an educator in Great Britain.

Similarity. The **principle of similarity** leads people to group things together that seem alike. This tendency underlies the *categorical design* for speeches. Speakers use categories when they discuss "three major causes of global warming" or "the four basic components of a good stereo system." Categories can be based on the actual divisions of a topic, such as the symptoms of a disease. They also may represent customary ways of thinking about a subject, such as the four basic food groups. Such factors go together because they seem alike in some important way.

The principle of similarity also applies to the *comparative design* in which speakers show how things are similar (or different). For example, an informative speaker might compare the New Madrid and major California earthquakes, and persuasive speakers might compare the Republican and Democratic Party positions on key issues. The *refutative design*, in which persuasive speakers attempt to discredit opposing positions, might also apply the principle of similarity. For example, a speaker might develop a speech refuting the three main arguments defending (or attacking) the United States boycott on trade with Cuba. These three arguments would be similar because they would all work together to support a certain position.

Proximity. The **principle of proximity** suggests that things that usually occur together in time or space should be presented in the order in which they naturally occur. For example, a "how-to" speech should have a *sequential design* that presents the steps in the order in which they should be taken. If you want to show listeners "how to" make origami cranes, you should use a sequential design.

If you want to discuss the events that led up to a present-day problem, you might use the *chronological design* to present a historical perspective on the situation. Your research might show that the major events occurred in 1955, 1970, and 1987. If you follow this chronological pattern, your speech will be easy to understand. But if you start talking about 1970, then jump back to 1955, then leap ahead to the present before doubling back to 1987, you will probably lose most of your listeners by violating the principle of proximity.

If you were preparing a speech on the wineries in California's Napa Valley, you might well use a *spatial design.* Such a design is based on physical relationships, such as east-west, north-south, or points around a circle. You could begin at Domaine Chandon at the southernmost end of the valley, take listeners north visiting the wineries along the Silverado Trail, and end up at the north end of the valley with the cable ride to the top of the hill at the Sterling Winery. This way, your audience gets a verbal map to follow as well as a picture of the major wineries in the valley.

Closure. The **principle of closure** is based on people's natural tendency to seek completion.[9] We like to have patterns completed so that we feel we have the whole story. Have you ever started reading a magazine article in a waiting room, only to find that someone had torn out the last page of the story? Do you remember how frustrated you felt? Your need for closure had been violated.

The principle of closure applies to several speech designs. As already noted, the *narrative design* is based on the principle of closure. If you don't finish a story, listeners will be frustrated. Similarly, if you omit an important category when developing your topic, listeners may notice its omission. If you leave out a necessary step in a sequence, audiences may sense the flaw. Although all speeches should satisfy this need, there are two speech patterns for which closure is absolutely essential. These are *causation* and *problem-solution designs.* The *motivated sequence design*, a variation of the problem-solution pattern, also belongs to this category. Let's look at each of these speech patterns.

Because we want the world to seem purposeful and controllable, we want all events to have clear causes and all problems to have satisfactory solutions. A cause-effect speech can go in two directions: it can begin by focusing on some present situation as an effect and then seek its causes, or it can look at the present as a potential cause of future effects. Sometimes these variations can be combined. You might take a current situation, such as a budget shortfall on campus, and develop a speech tracing its origins. If you had enough time, you might predict the future effects of the deficit, such as tuition increases. Understanding the causes could help your listeners see what needs to be done to reduce the deficit. Predicting future effects might make your listeners want to take steps to prevent these from happening.

The problem-solution design focuses attention on a problem and then provides a solution for it. Such speeches often seek to arouse strong feelings in order to motivate listeners. Once you have aroused emotions, your solutions must show listeners a way out of the problem, or they will feel frustrated. After Joshua Logan had informed his listeners about global warming (speech at the end of Chapter 10) and convinced them that it was a dangerous problem (speech at the end of Chapter 15), he had to tell them what to do to resolve it (speech at the end of Chapter 16).

The motivated sequence design develops through five steps, in which you

1. arouse attention,
2. demonstrate a need,
3. show how the need might be satisfied,
4. visualize the results, and
5. call for action.

Check the organization of your speech in the Online Speech Studio under **Selecting a Speech Design.**
Go to http://college.hmco.com/eduspace/

Beth Tidmore had already walked her audience through the first three steps in her informative speech explaining the Special Olympics program and the unique services it provides. In her persuasive speech recruiting volunteers for Special Olympics, she emphasized steps 4 and 5 of the motivated sequence as she helped her listeners visualize themselves participating in the program and asked for their commitment. Both the motivated sequence and the closely related problem-solution design are patterns that are often used in persuasive speeches.

Apply the principles of similarity, proximity, and closure to develop the most effective designs for your speeches. Figure 9.3 lists the major designs used to structure the bodies of speeches and directs you to the chapters where these designs are covered in additional detail.

Adding Supporting Materials

Once you have selected and arranged your main points, you must support them with facts and figures, testimony, examples, or narratives. As you develop your main points, also consider whether you need to divide them into subpoints. The subpoints should contain information or ideas that listeners must understand before they will accept the main point. For example, let us assume that you are presenting a speech on the topic "New Weapons in the War on Cancer." As you design the speech, you frame the following main point: "Scientists have developed productive new ways of thinking in cancer research." To develop this main point, you realize that you must establish two subpoints: "Scientists no longer seek to *cure* cancer" and "Scientists now seek to *control* cancer."

You strengthen both main points and subpoints by providing supporting materials. In the instance just mentioned, you could support your first subpoint by presenting facts, testimony, and narratives that show how scientists were at first frustrated by their inability to find a magic bullet–the master cure for cancer. To support your second subpoint, you might explain how scientists now approach the research problem of controlling cancer. You might use examples to show how powerful new drugs successfully stop the growth of cancer cells in specific forms of the disease.

Figure 9.3

Speech Designs

Spatial	A pattern that arranges main points as they occur in physical space. Takes listeners on an orderly tour of your topic. Based on the principle of proximity. Additional information and skeleton outline in Chapter 14.
Sequential	A pattern that arranges main points in terms of their order of occurrence. Useful for explaining the steps in a process. Based on the principle of proximity. Additional information and skeleton outline in Chapter 14.
Chronological	A pattern that arranges main points in terms of their development in time. Useful for providing a historical perspective on a topic. Based on the principle of proximity. Additional information and skeleton outline in Chapter 14.
Categorical	A pattern that arranges main points in terms of natural or customary divisions. Useful for organizing large amounts of material. Based on the principle of similarity. Additional information and skeleton outline in Chapter 14.
Comparative	A pattern that juxtaposes two different things so that their similarities and differences become apparent. Useful when a topic is novel and difficult to understand. Based on the principle of similarity. Additional information and skeleton outline in Chapter 14.
Causation	A pattern that presents the causes and/or consequences of a situation. Useful when you wish to account for the present or predict the future. Based on the principle of closure. Additional information and skeleton outline in Chapter 14.
Problem-solution	A pattern that first presents a problem and then advances a solution. Useful when your topic presents a situation that needs to be corrected. Based on the principle of closure. Additional information and skeleton outline in Chapter 16.
Motivated sequence	A variation on the problem-solution pattern that ends with a call for action. Useful for important topics that require audience commitment. Based on the principle of closure. Additional information and skeleton outline in Chapter 16.
Refutative	A persuasive pattern that attacks the arguments against your position. Useful when you must discredit the opposition. Based on the principle of similarity (and contrast). Additional information and skeleton outline in Chapter 16.
Narrative	A pattern that is arranged in the form of a story with a beginning, middle, and end. Useful as an indirect form of information or persuasion. Based on the principle of closure. Additional information and skeleton outline in Chapter 17.

In this example you have used two of the special techniques discussed in Chapter 8. The first is *contrast,* drawn between past and present, cure and control. These dramatic contrasts should interest listeners and help them to see your point clearly. The second technique is *analogy,* especially the figurative analogy between scientific research and war (such as, new "weapons," "war on cancer," the researcher as heroic "warrior," etc.). This technique heightens the drama and can aid understanding, especially when subjects are complex and abstract. Note how Dr. Leonard Saltz, a colon cancer specialist at Memorial Sloan-Kettering, used another figurative analogy to illustrate the significance of such contrast in research approaches: "I don't think we're going to hit home runs, but if we can get a series of line-drive singles going and put enough singles back to back, we can score runs."[10] The example shows how both contrast and analogy can make supporting materials more effective.

Speaker's Notes 9.1

Determining and Arranging Your Main Points

1. Prepare a research overview to identify repeated ideas.
2. Create main points that fit your purpose and the needs of your audience.
3. Limit your main points to four or fewer for a short speech.
4. Apply the principle of similarity to develop categorical and comparative designs or to refute opposition.
5. Apply the principle of proximity to arrange main points in spatial, sequential, and chronological patterns.
6. Apply the principle of closure to provide completeness in causation, problem-solution, and narrative designs.

In Chapter 8 we provided general guidelines for selecting supporting materials. Here we show you how to work supporting materials into the structure of your speech. Supporting materials help to fortify a message against the doubts or disagreements of reasonable listeners. They answer four basic questions that listeners often ask:

1. *What is the basis of this idea?* (Supply facts or statistics.)
2. *How do we know this? Who else says so?* (Supply expert testimony.)
3. *How does this work? Where is this true?* (Supply an example.)
4. *So what? Why should anyone care?* (Supply a narrative that explains why.)

Although the situation will vary from topic to topic, speaker to speaker, and audience to audience, it is possible to set up an ideal model for the support of any main point or important subpoint. This model includes the point plus the following supporting materials:

- The most relevant facts and statistics
- The most authoritative testimony from respected sources
- At least one story or example that clarifies the idea and brings it to life

Figure 9.4 provides a format for applying this model to support a point. Assume that you want to demonstrate the main point that suntans are not a sign of good health. Here is one way you could follow this format to support the point:

Statement:	Suntans are not as "good" *for* you as they look *on* you.
Transition:	Let's examine some of the evidence.
Facts/statistics:	According to a 2002 report by the American Cancer Society, prolonged exposure without protection is responsible for about 90 percent of all skin cancers.
Transition:	Moreover, exposure without protection also accelerates the aging process.

Figure 9.4

Format for Supporting a Point

Statement: ______________________________

____

Transition into facts or statistics: ______________________________

1. Factual information or statistics that support statement: ______________

____

____

Transition into testimony: ______________________________

2. Testimony that supports statement: ______________________________

____

____

Transition into example or narrative: ______________________________

3. Example or narrative that supports statement: ______________________

____

____

____

Transition into restatement: ______________________________

Restatement of original assertion: ______________________________

____

Expert testimony:	In the words of Dr. John M. Knox, head of dermatology at the Baylor University College of Medicine, "If you do biopsies on the buttocks of people ages seventy-five and thirty-five, you won't see any differences under the microscope. . . . Protected skin stays youthful much longer."
Transition:	Let's look at one person who suffered from overexposure.
Example:	Jane was a fair-skinned blond-haired girl who loved swimming and sunbathing. She often sunburned but didn't think there would be any effects other than the short-term pain. Having a good tan seemed so healthy, she didn't dream it could harm her. Now at forty-five, she knows better. She couldn't believe it when her doctor told her she had skin cancer. Now she can't go out into the sun, even for a few minutes, without using a sunscreen and wearing a hat, a long-sleeved shirt, and long pants.
Transition:	What does all this mean?
Restatement:	A suntan may make you look healthy, but it is not healthy. Overexposure to the sun causes cancer and premature aging. Are you willing to take that risk just to look good for a brief time?

In this example, three forms of supporting material–statistical information, expert testimony, and example–work together to establish the main point. Each contributes its special strength. If each of your main points is well supported, your message should stand up even if challenged.

Using Transitions

Our example of using supporting materials also illustrates the way **transitions** work in a speech. Transitions show your listeners how your ideas connect with one another. They help your listeners focus on the meaning of what you have already discussed and prepare them for what is still to come. They serve as signposts that help listeners see the overall pattern of your message. Transitions connect your main points and tie the body of a speech to its introduction and conclusion.

Some transitions are simple, short phrases such as "Another point that must be made is . . ." More often, however, transitions are worded as phrases that link ideas. For example, the sentence, "Having looked at why people don't pay compliments more often, let's consider some ways to offer them" summarizes what you have just said and directs listeners to your next point.

Certain stock words or phrases can be used to signal changes in a speech. Words and phrases like *until now* or *just last week* point out time changes. Transitions such as *in addition* show that you are expanding on what you have already said. The use of the word *similarly* indicates that a comparison will follow. Phrases such as *on the other hand* cue listeners to a contrast. Cause-and-effect relationships can be suggested with words like *as a result* or *consequently.* Introductory phrases like *traveling north* can indicate spatial relationships. Phrases or words like *in short, finally,* or *in conclusion* signal that the speech is coming to an end. Figure 9.5 contains a list of some commonly used transitions.

An **internal summary** is a special type of transition that reminds listeners of the points you have covered before you move on to the next part of your message. Internal summaries are especially useful in cause-effect and problem-solution

Figure 9.5
Common Transitions

To Indicate	Use
Time Changes	until, now, since, previously, later, earlier, in the past, in the future, meanwhile, five years ago, just last month, tomorrow, following, before, at present, eventually
Additions	moreover, in addition, furthermore, besides
Comparison	compared with, both are, likewise, in comparison, similarly, of equal importance, another type of, like, alike, just as
Contrast	but, yet, however, on the other hand, conversely, still, otherwise, in contrast, unfortunately, despite, rather than, on the contrary
Cause-Effect	therefore, consequently, thus, accordingly, so, as a result, hence, since, because of, due to, for this reason
Numerical Order	first, second, third, in the first place, to begin with, initially, next, eventually, finally
Spatial Relations	to the north, alongside, to the left, above, moving eastward, in front of, in back of, behind, next to, below, nearby, in the distance
Explanation	to illustrate, for example, for instance, case in point, in other words, to simplify, to clarify
Importance	most importantly, above all, keep this in mind, remember, listen carefully, take note of, indeed
The Speech Is Ending	in short, finally, in conclusion, to summarize

speeches, where they signal that you have finished your discussion of the causes or problem and are now going to describe the effects or solution. In addition, by condensing and repeating your ideas, an internal summary can help your listeners remember your message. If listeners have somehow missed the point, this type of transition helps get them back on track. Consider the following example:

> **So now we see what the problem is. We know the cost in human suffering. We know the terrible political consequences and the enormous economic burden. The question is, What are we going to do about it? Let me tell you about a plan that experts agree may turn things around.**

Internal summaries should be brief and to the point so that they highlight only the major ideas in your message.

Not having planned transitions may cause beginning speakers to overuse words and vocalized pauses such as *well, you know, okay*, or *er* . . . . Plan a variety of transitions to help your speech flow smoothly. If you have trouble developing effective transitions, rethink the structure of your message. Outline your thoughts to be sure that they move in a clear direction and an orderly sequence. We cover outlining in Chapter 10.

Once you have organized the body of your speech—identified and arranged your main points, decided how to develop them with supporting materials, and planned how to connect them with transitions—you should prepare an introduction and conclusion to begin and end your speech effectively. Introductions and conclusions are important because listeners tend to be most affected by what they hear at the beginning and end of a message.[11] The introduction allows you to make a good first impression and to set the stage for how your audience will respond. The conclusion gives you a final opportunity to make a lasting impression.

Introducing Your Message

When you first begin to speak, the audience will have three basic questions in mind: *Why should I listen to this speech?, Why should I listen to this* speaker?, and *What must I understand?* These questions relate to the three basic functions of an introduction:

- It should capture attention and arouse interest so that your audience wants to listen to your message.
- It should help establish your ethos as a competent, strong, and trustworthy person of goodwill with whom the audience can identify.
- It should focus and preview your message to make it easier for the audience to follow.

A successful introduction also helps get you ready to present the rest of your speech. When you get off to a good start, you have less performance anxiety. Therefore, you should prepare your introduction carefully. Practice until you are confident and comfortable with your opening words. Establish good eye contact with listeners. *Do not read your introduction!*

Capturing Attention

All too often, speakers open their presentations with something like "Good evening. My speech today is on . . . ," and then jump right into their message. Needless to say, this is not a good way to begin a speech because it does not make the audience want to listen.

There are several ways to attract, build, and hold the interest of your audience. You may

- acknowledge the audience, location, or occasion.
- involve the audience.
- ask questions.
- relate a personal experience.
- tell a story.
- use humor.
- develop suspense.
- begin with a quotation.
- use a presentation aid.
- startle the audience.

Let's take a look at each of these strategies.

The introduction of your speech must immediately engage your audience. If you don't get their attention within the first minute of speaking, they may be lost to you forever.

Acknowledge the Audience, Location, or Occasion.

When you speak outside a classroom, it is customary to make some brief opening remarks that acknowledge your audience, the location, or the occasion. People like to hear good things about themselves and their community. Note how Jerry Daniels, president of Boeing Military Aircraft and Missile Systems, opened a speech before the Dayton, Ohio, Chamber of Commerce:

> **It's a pleasure to be here at the cradle of aviation—two years and two weeks before the 100th anniversary of the "Miracle at Kitty Hawk." In paying tribute to Orville and Wilbur, historian Darrel Collins noted: "Before the Wright brothers, no one in aviation did anything fundamentally right: since the Wright brothers, no one has done anything fundamentally wrong."[12]**

These introductory remarks can be very brief, but they should also contain a touch of eloquence, as illustrated by the opening words of President John F. Kennedy in a speech given at a White House dinner honoring Nobel Prize winners:

> **I think this is the most extraordinary collection of talent, of human knowledge, that has ever been gathered together at the White House, with the possible exception of when Thomas Jefferson dined alone.[13]**

With this elegant tribute, Kennedy was able to honor his guests without embarrassing them or going overboard with praise. His witty reference to the genius of Thomas Jefferson also paid tribute to the past, as did Daniel's reference to the Wright brothers.

Involve the Audience. You involve listeners when you connect them with your message. Involvement is especially important when you know you are going to ask something of your audience. Getting them to do something with you becomes an important first step. Note how Beth Tidmore involved her classroom audience at the start of her persuasive speech:

> **Please repeat after me: "Let me win, but if I cannot win, let me be brave in the attempt." [Audience repeats the words.] This is the Special Olympics oath, and this is something that the Special Olympians take every year before they are allowed to compete.**
>
> **Now, a lot of you have heard what I have to say about Special Olympics. You know the philosophy, you know the history. But what you might not know is what it's like to be a volunteer. I've been volunteering for over fourteen years: I've been a chaperone, a fundraiser, a cheerleader, and a county board member. And this summer I hope to compete as an athlete on a unified swim team.**
>
> **I've had so many great experiences, but these are hard to describe without overworking words like "fulfilling" and "rewarding." So I'm going to help you experience it for yourself. I want everybody to pack your bags—we're going to the Special Olympics summer games in Georgia!**

Beth then took her listeners through an imaginary weekend at the Special Olympics. After her introduction, it was easy for them to get caught up in her message.

Involving your audience is also important if your topic seems distant from the audience's immediate concerns or experiences. A student at Kutztown University wanted to give an informative speech on the Black Plague of the Middle Ages. He knew that he had to do something dramatic to involve his audience from the outset and make the topic interesting and relevant. Here is how he handled it:[14]

> **As the students entered the classroom, a friend of the speaker gave each student a card containing the name of a profession, such as clergyman, sailor, farmer, or merchant. The number of cards for each profession was proportional to its representation in European society at the time of the plague. When the student's name was called to speak, he entered from the back of the room wearing an oversized black sweatshirt, hood up, cinched around the waist with a length of sash cord. He opened with a rhetorical question, "If the Black Plague were to strike Kutztown today, given the same medical limitations, how many do you think would survive?" He then asked everyone to stand, and after a pause, continued as follows: "Will all of you with a card reading 'physician' please sit down. In tending the sick, you have come in contact with the disease and have become one of its victims." A student took her seat. He followed with "Will all of those identified as 'sailor' or 'merchant' please be seated. You have traveled about the country or the world and so have also come close to other victims and have sealed your fate." Five more students sat down. He then called out the clergy, city dwellers, dockworkers, soldiers, and others who would have been exposed to the disease.**
>
> **By the time he finished reading the list of those most susceptible to the disease, only three of his twenty-five classmates were left standing. He then explained that if the plague were to strike Kutztown the way it did many cities during the Middle Ages, those three would have the awesome task of rebuilding society.**

Your introduction need not be this dramatic to involve the audience. If you can demonstrate that what you are talking about matters to listeners, your speech will be more effective.[15] You also can involve them by relating your topic to their motivations or attitudes and by using inclusive pronouns such as *we* and *our.*

Ask Questions. Speakers will often open a presentation with a question or series of questions. Questions start the audience thinking about a topic and also get them actively involved. Sometimes the questions will call for a direct answer. For example, Holly Carlson, a student at Vanderbilt, opened a speech on censorship by reading a list of banned books. As she read off the title of each book, she asked listeners to raise their hands if they had read it.

Not all questions used in speeches call for direct answers, however. **Rhetorical questions** such as "Have you ever thought about what your life would be like if you were a different color?" arouse curiosity and start listeners thinking about the topic. Erin Bourne opened her classroom speech with the following rhetorical question:

> **How would you feel if you were a perfect driver—never had a car wreck, never had a speeding ticket—and you got your car insurance bill one day, and it had gone up so high that you could no longer afford to drive? So, you call your insurance company, thinking that there must be some mistake, and they tell you that they had to raise your rates to compensate for all of the not-so-good drivers out there on the road, and the claims that they had to pay out for those.**
>
> **This is analogous to a healthcare problem that is widespread in the United States right now. A few bad doctors are driving malpractice insurance rates up so high in some areas that good doctors are having to either quit practicing medicine or move out of their states.**

By posing this rhetorical question and framing the analogy between automobile insurance and medical insurance, Erin gained the attention of her listeners for a topic that otherwise might have seemed distant from them.

Calling on personal experience at the beginning of a speech can gain interest and create high credibility for the message.

Relate a Personal Experience. An old adage suggests that people are interested first in themselves, next in other people, then in things, and finally in ideas. This may explain why relating a topic to personal experience heightens audience interest. When speakers have been personally involved with a topic, they gain credibility. We are more willing to listen to others and take their advice if we know they have traveled the road themselves. Jason Shafer, a Dean's List student at Vanderbilt University, related the following personal experience as he began his self-introductory speech:

> **With a lot of hard work, your son might make it through a trade school. That was what my parents heard when I was in third grade. You see, I was a terrible student. I was the worst. I'm sure most of you just flew through grade school, getting A's and B's. No problem whatsoever. Me, on the other hand, not at all. I got C's and D's, and I had to work hard to get them. My teachers tried different techniques, but nothing really seemed to work. I guess the point of crisis came in third grade when my teacher realized that I couldn't even read yet. It just about killed my parents. Then they had some testing done and discovered I had a learning disability.**

Relating your subject to personal experience can be very important if you face an unfriendly audience. Brock Evans, vice president of the Audubon Society, once addressed the Seattle Rotary Club on the Endangered Species Act amid controversy over logging restrictions in the Northwest. Because of the possible hostility of this group to some of his ideas, the introduction to his speech would be especially critical. In his introduction Evans both involved the audience and related the topic to personal experience:

> **It is always a distinct honor to be invited to speak before a prestigious group like the Rotary Club of Seattle. I thank you for inviting me to be here today, and not just because of the opportunity to share a few thoughts about this very important subject. Those of you who know me know that my roots here run very deep. It was 30 years ago that I moved here from the Midwest, because I wanted to live in what I thought then–and still do now–was the most beautiful part of the country.**
>
> **And those of you who know me know that my passion for this special Northwest land, its unique blend of mountain and forest and sea, goes even deeper. It caused me to leave a law practice here, in order to devote my life to fight to help keep our way of life, to keep the Northwest the special place it is. It has now become a life's work that has taken me many places, first all across the Northwest, and finally into "exile" as I now believe–in the nation's capital–that other Washington, where for better or worse, so many of the great issues of our time are finally resolved.[16]**

In this example, the love of the area and its beauty unites the speaker and his listeners. The fact that the speaker had "adopted" the area lends special credence to his passion for it.

Tell a Story. We humans began our love affair with stories around the campfires of ancient times. It is through stories that we remember the past and pass on our heritage to future generations. Stories also entertain and educate us because they depict abstract problems in human terms. In introductions, stories help capture audience attention and involve listeners in creating the meaning of the message. Marie D'Aniello opened a speech on the nature of friendship with the following story:

> **It's nine o'clock at night. I'm curled up in the back seat of a new truck and my friends, Cammy and Joe, are in the front singing along with the radio. As I listen to them sing, and I'm lying there, I start to think about my life and all the changes that have occurred in the past year. A year ago I didn't even know who Cammy and Joe were. And now they're two of my dearest friends. It made me think about friendship and its meaning.**

Narratives are also good for establishing the mood of your message. In a self-introductory speech, Ashlie McMillan began with the following sensory narrative:

> **Imagine you're sitting aboard a dive boat. It's rocking back and forth, you can feel the sun beating down on you. You can feel the wind blowing on you. You smell the ocean, the salt water. You can hear the waves crashing up against the boat. You put on your dive pack with your heavy oxygen tank and you walk unsteadily across the deck of the rocking boat. And all of a sudden you plunge into a completely different environment. All around you is vast blueness and infinite space, a world completely different from the one you left above. But all you have to do is turn on your back and look above you and you see the sunlight streaming in through the top of the water. And you can see the world that you left behind.**

An opening narrative may also be based on a historical event. Sandra Baltz, a premed major, opened a speech on setting priorities for organ transplants with the following narrative:

> **On a cold and stormy night in 1841 the ship *William Brown* struck an iceberg in the North Atlantic. Passengers and crew members frantically scrambled into the lifeboats. To make a bad disaster even worse, one of the lifeboats began to sink because it was overcrowded. Fourteen men were thrown overboard that horrible night. After the survivors were rescued, a crew member was tried for the murders of those thrown overboard.**
>
> **Fortunately, situations like this have been few in history, but today we face a similar problem in the medical establishment: deciding who will live as we allocate scarce medical resources for transplants. Someday, your fate—or the fate of someone you love—could depend on how we resolve this dilemma.**

In the preceding example, the story sets a somber mood for the serious message that follows. Stories can also be used to establish a lighter mood through the use of humor.

Use Humor. Humor can enliven an introduction and can put your audience in a receptive mood for your message. But humor may also be the most misused technique for introducing speeches. Because someone once told them that starting with a joke will ensure success, beginning speakers often search through anthologies of humor to find something that will make people laugh. Unless it is carefully adapted, however, such material often sounds canned, inappropriate, or only remotely relevant to the topic or occasion. If you wish to use humor in your introduction, be certain the material is fresh and pertinent to your topic.

Be especially careful when using humor to open a speech. It can be grossly inappropriate for some topics and occasions. Also, don't let a humorous introduction "upstage" the rest of your speech. We once heard a student open a speech with a rather risqué quotation from Mae West, "Is that a gun in your pocket, or are you happy to see me?" It drew an initial gasp followed by some hearty laughter. Unfortunately, as the speech continued, one student would chuckle over the remembered joke, and then the audience would start laughing all over again even when nothing funny had been said. After the speaker finished, we questioned the audience about their "inappropriate" responses. They said, "We kept remembering that Mae West line. We just couldn't help it." And to this day, neither of your authors can remember the topic of the speech, either.

Develop Suspense. You can attract and hold your listeners' attention by arousing their curiosity and then making them wait before you satisfy it. The following introduction creates curiosity and anticipation:

> **Getting knocked down is no disgrace. Champions are made by getting up just one more time than the opponent! The results are a matter of record about a man who suffered many defeats: Lost his job in 1832, defeated for legislature**

Speaker's Notes 9.2

Using Humor

1. Don't use humor just to be funny. Keep it relevant to your topic.
2. Use humor to put the audience at ease and make them receptive to your ideas.
3. Avoid religious, ethnic, racist, or sexist humor that speaks poorly of you.
4. If you must poke fun at someone, let it be yourself.
5. Don't use humor that might trivialize a serious topic.

> **in 1832, failed in business in 1833, sweetheart died in 1835, had nervous breakdown in 1836, defeated for nomination for Congress in 1843, elected to Congress in 1846, lost renomination in 1848, rejected for land officer in 1849, defeated for Senate in 1854, defeated for nomination for Vice-President in 1856, defeated for Senate in 1858. In 1860 Abraham Lincoln was elected President of the United States. Lincoln proved that a big shot is just a little shot who keeps shooting. The greatest failures in the world are those who fail by not doing anything.[17]**

Reciting the list of failures aroused the audience's curiosity: Who was this loser? Many were surprised when they discovered his identity. This effective introduction set the stage for the speaker's message that perseverance is the key to success.

Begin with a Quotation. Starting your speech with a striking quotation or paraphrase from a well-known person or respected authority (with the possible exception of one from Mae West) can both arouse interest and give you borrowed ethos. The person you cite should be someone the audience knows, respects, or can identify with. Historical figures are especially apt, particularly in ceremonial speeches, where they evoke a sense of cultural heritage. Elissa Scadron opened her speech celebrating the United States as a sanctuary of human rights by saying: "We are, in the words of Abraham Lincoln, 'the last best hope of earth.'"

Most effective opening quotations are short and to the point. They are used to lead into the message. One student used a very brief quote from folklore as a lead-in to an informative speech on cystic fibrosis:

> **"Woe to the child who when kissed on the forehead tastes salty. He is bewitched and he soon will die." This northern European folk adage is a reference to the genetic disorder cystic fibrosis. Well, we know today that children with cystic fibrosis aren't bewitched. And we have a lot better ways to test for cystic fibrosis than to kiss them on the forehead.**

Most books of quotations are indexed by key words and subjects, as well as by authors. Collections of quotations are also available on the Internet. They are an excellent source of statements you might use to introduce your topic. InterConnections.LearnMore 9.2 will guide you to some of these sources.

Use a Presentation Aid. Sometimes using a presentation aid at the beginning of a speech can help to establish a mood or set a theme that carries on throughout the message. One of our students placed a photograph face down on each seat in the audience. At the beginning of her speech she had listeners turn over the photos, and then she asked them, "Do you think the girl in the photo is at risk?" Her speech on volunteer services for at-risk teenagers presented the stories of the girls pictured in the photos.

InterConnections.LearnMore 9.2

Online Sources of Quotations

Quoteland
http://www.quoteland.com
An Internet directory of quotations categorized by topic and browsable by author. Contains resources for identifying a quote and user forums for additional help, such as "Who said it?" and "I need a quote!"

Simpson's Contemporary Quotations
http://www.bartleby.com/63/
A searchable database of "The Most Notable Quotations: 1950–1988." Originally published in hard copy in 1988 by James B. Simpson.

Creative Quotations
http://creativequotations.com
An excellent source of quotes from over 3,000 famous people. Also contains biographical information on the sources of the quotes. Searchable by key words and such unique categories as "creative women," "creative wit," and "quotational poetry."

Advertising Quotations
http://advertising.utexas.edu/research/quotes/
A directory of links to quotations about advertising and marketing. Indexed by topic. Compiled and maintained by the Department of Advertising, University of Texas at Austin.

Good Quotations by Famous People
http://www.cs.virginia.edu/;robins/quotes.html
A compilation of pithy epigrams, such as "Not everything that can be counted counts, and not everything that counts can be counted" (Albert Einstein). Much material that might be useful in introductions and conclusions of speeches. Not categorized by topic or author, but well worth reading through for that special gem you might find! Compiled and maintained by Professor Gabriel Robins, University of Virginia.

A Short Dictionary of Scientific Quotations
http://naturalscience.com/dsqhome.html
A compilation of interesting but offbeat quotations arranged alphabetically by author. Not easily searchable but worth perusing if you are planning a speech on a scientific topic.

The use of presentation aids is not confined to the classroom. Let's look at how Carol Quinn, director of human resources for Argonne National Laboratory, integrated a novel visual aid into a speech presented at a Secretary's Day breakfast in Chicago:

> **Good morning, everyone. I am delighted to be here and am honored that you have selected me as your keynote speaker for Secretary's Day. Most of you have coffee or juice, or perhaps tea. What I have here in this glass is Kool–Aid. But I'm not going to drink it.**
>
> **Why I have this Kool-Aid and why I'm not going to drink it are in a sense what I want to talk about this Secretary's Day. What I would like to share with you today are six suggestions for maximizing your career success by playing to your strengths.**
>
> **This glass of Kool-Aid represents the worst job I've ever had. Yes, you are looking at a former "Kool-Aid tester" for General Foods. There really is—or at least "was"—such a job. When we weren't testing Kool-Aid, we were expected to taste daiquiri mixes, or nibble potato chips, or smell soap, or otherwise play the role of "average consumer." I came away from that with a longstanding aversion to Kool-Aid, which is why I'm not going to drink this.[18]**

Additional references to the Kool-Aid were artfully woven into the speech.

Startle the Audience. Anything out of the ordinary draws attention to itself and arouses curiosity. Consider the headlines from the sensationalist tabloids: "BIGFOOT SPOTTED IN NORTHWEST ARKANSAS!" "WOMAN PREDICTS EARTHQUAKES WITH HER TOES!"

One of our students at Vanderbilt opened with the following narrative:

> **Imagine a warm, sunny June day. A bride stands at the back of the church. It is beautifully decorated with fresh flowers, and the music of a pipe organ fills the sanctuary. There is not a dry eye as the father gives the bride away. The couple recites their vows, and upon pronouncing the couple married, the minister proclaims, "Katie, you may kiss the bride."**
>
> **The surprise that many of you just experienced is the reaction gay rights activists have been trying to eliminate since 1969. This fight simply to be accepted as part of everyday life is one that continues today.**

Another student combined the use of a presentation aid with the "shock and startle" technique to open his speech:

> **[Sound of cell phone ringing: speaker takes phone from pocket and speaks into it.]**
>
> **"Hey!" (pause)**
>
> **"Nah, That's okay. What's up?"**
>
> **"Cool!"(short pause, light laugh)**
>
> **"Yeah! Well, hey, uh—Can I call you back after a while? I'm in my speech class right now—getting ready to give my speech." (pause)**
>
> **"Okay—just a minute."**
>
> **[Speaker leaves podium, goes to classmate in front row.]**
>
> **"Can I borrow your pen? I've got to write down her cell phone number."**
>
> **[Speaker returns to podium, writes something on speaking outline.]**
>
> **"Gotta go. Catch you later."**
>
> **[Speaker pushes phone button, puts cell phone in pocket: long pause, speaker looks around at audience.]**
>
> **"Sorry 'bout that. Was that rude of me?" (long pause)**
>
> **Today I want to talk with you about cell phone etiquette, about what annoys other people, and about the polite way to use your phone.**

Speaker's Notes 9.3

Capturing Attention

1. Acknowledge the audience, location, or occasion.
2. Show listeners how the topic involves them.
3. Call on personal experience with the topic.
4. Ask questions to make listeners think.
5. Build suspense and create anticipation to get listeners involved.
6. Open with a story that relates to your topic
7. Engage your listeners with humor.
8. Begin with a quotation from a well-known person.
9. Use a presentation aid to establish a mood or framework for the speech.
10. Startle the audience with unusual information.

This unusual introduction was so artfully handled that the students thought the student actually had received a call during class. Fortunately, the instructor had been prepped on what to expect, so she didn't stop the speaker before he got started.

The startle technique must always be used with care. You don't want your introduction to arouse more interest than the body of your speech can satisfy. If your opening is too sensational, it will upstage the rest of your speech. Similarly, be careful not to go beyond the bounds of propriety. You want to startle your listeners, not offend them.

Establishing Your Credibility

The second major function of an effective introduction is to establish yourself as a competent, trustworthy, likeable, and strong person. People tend to form first impressions of speakers that color their later perceptions.[19] In Chapter 3 we discussed the importance of the impressions you make on listeners in terms of your competence, integrity, goodwill, and dynamism—your ethos. As you make later presentations, you will carry over some of the initial ethos you established with your first presentation and with your interactions in class. You must confirm this initial ethos in the introduction of each speech.

Establishing qualifications to speak on a subject is often difficult for beginning speakers. As we noted in Chapter 3, you can seem competent only if you know what you are talking about. People listen more respectfully to those who speak both from knowledge and from personal experience.[20] You will seem more competent if you select a topic you already know something about and do sufficient research to speak responsibly on it. In your introduction, you can allude to your research to reinforce your credibility:

> **I was amazed to learn in my psychology classes that research does not support a strong link between exposure to persuasive communications and behavior. This discovery led me to do more reading on the relationship between advertising and consumer activity. What I found was even more surprising, especially when you consider that, according to *American Demographics,* advertisers routinely paid over $550,000 for a half minute of air time on *ER*.**

In this example, the reference to a respected source of information suggests that you have done the research needed to make a responsible speech. It would not be effective, however, to simply announce at the beginning of your speech:

> **The information for my speech comes from my psychology textbook, two articles from the *Journal of Applied Psychology,* and an article in *American Demographics.***

That would seem forced, awkward, and artificial. It would interrupt the natural flow of your introduction. Your perceived competence will be further strengthened if your speech is well organized, if you use language ably and correctly, and if you have practiced so that your presentation flows smoothly.

To create a perception of integrity, you must come across to listeners as an ethical and honest person. Audiences are more receptive to speakers who strike them as straightforward, sincere, and concerned about the consequences of their words.[21] You can enhance your integrity by showing respect for those who hold different opinions while still maintaining your personal commitment to your topic and position.

You should also present yourself as a likeable and confident speaker, someone who is pleasant and tactful. Likeable speakers treat listeners as friends, inspiring affection in return.[22] They share their feelings and are able to laugh at themselves. To come across as a confident speaker, you must appear in control of the situation from the outset. Your introduction should reflect your enthusiasm for your message. A smile and eye contact signal listeners that you want to communicate. These qualities build an overall impression of dynamism that should make you more effective.

When you establish favorable ethos in the introduction of your speech, you also lay the foundation for one of the most powerful effects of communication: identification between yourself and listeners. **Identification** occurs when people overcome the personal and cultural differences that separate them and share thoughts and feelings as though they were one.[23] When you seem likeable, sincere, competent, and forceful, your listeners want to identify with you, and you are more effective as a communicator.

Previewing Your Message

The final function of an introduction is to preview the body of your speech. The **preview** indicates the main points you will cover and offers your listeners an overview of the speech to come. Previews are very useful for speeches on unfamiliar, complicated, or technical subjects. They help listeners follow what you are saying.

Hannah Johnston provided a preview in the introduction to her speech on the perils of fast food:

> **I'm sure most of you saw the famous old movie *Soylent Green*. Or, you've heard about the ending, where Charlton Heston finds out what he's really been eating for so long and screams, "Soylent Green is people!"**
>
> **Well, I'm not saying we need to run around shouting, "MacDonald's is feeding us spinal cords," or anything of the sort, but we do need to be aware of a few important things.**
>
> **First of all, exactly what ends up in our fast food that shouldn't be there? Secondly, what conditions in slaughterhouses can lead to mistakes in food preparation? And finally, what are the global health consequences of increased fast food consumption?**

By informing her listeners of her intentions and letting them know how her speech would develop, Hannah helped her audience listen intelligently to her message. Previews are most essential for informative and persuasive speeches. In ceremonial speeches that tell a story rather than develop a topic by logical design, the preview may take the form of a prologue using a **foreshadowing** technique: "I never expected that my life would be forever changed by what would happen that day." When speakers foreshadow their stories, they don't tell their listeners what will happen, but they do alert them that something important will happen. Thus they prepare them to listen intently to the story.

Selecting and Using Introductory Techniques

There are no hard and fast rules for determining exactly how you should open a speech. As you review your research notes, look for material that would make an effective introduction. The following guidelines may help you make a wise selection:

- Consider your audience. Use your introduction to tie your topic to their needs, interests, or well-being.
- Consider the mood you want to establish. Some topics call for a light touch. Others may require you to be more solemn.
- Consider your time constraints. If you are to speak for seven minutes, you can't use a five-minute introduction.
- Consider what you do best. Some people are effective storytellers, and others are better using striking statistics or quotations. Go with your strength!

VideoLab

Go to **VideoLab Drill 5.3: Creating Powerful Introductions**. Watch the clips of three speech introductions and assess their effectiveness.

Developing an Effective Conclusion

Many beginning speakers end their presentations awkwardly. The conclusion of your speech should not be that point at which you just got tired of talking or ran out of time. "That's all, folks!" may be an effective ending for a cartoon, but in a speech such a conclusion violates the audience's need for closure. Saying, "That's it, I guess," or, "Well, I'm done," and then giving a sigh of relief, suggests that you have not planned your speech carefully. The final words of your speech should stay with listeners, remind them of your message, and, when appropriate, move them to action.

Summarizing Your Message

Your conclusion will normally include a summary and final remarks. Generally, you should begin your conclusion with a brief **summary statement** of the main points made in your speech. The more complicated your topic, the more important this summary becomes. The summary statement functions as a transition between the body of your speech and your final remarks. It signals the audience that you are about to finish.

Note how Benjamin Ola Akande, dean of the School of Business and Technology at Webster University, provided a summary as he concluded his speech to the scholarship winners of the National Association of Black Accountants:

> **As you continue to grow and learn, please remember:**
>
> - **A road without potholes is not worth traveling–expect challenges, expect obstacles, but expect to overcome them.**
> - **Set and achieve goals that are not within easy reach.**
> - **Don't believe in conventional wisdom because conventional wisdom says you should continue to do the same thing and hope for better results. Conventional wisdom is about tradition: it's about not trying new ways or embracing new initiatives.**
> - **We are all born originals, but spend the rest of our lives trying to be copies. I appeal to you, stay original.[24]**

This summary encapsulated the meaning of his speech.

Concluding Remarks

Although a summary statement can offer listeners a sense of closure, to seal that effect you need to provide some concluding remarks that stay with your listeners. Many of the techniques that create effective introductions can also be used to develop memorable conclusions.

Echo the Introduction. A conclusion that echoes the introduction can provide a nice sense of closure for the audience. Note that we said "echoes," not "repeats." A conclusion that echoes the introduction may employ the same technique you used in the introduction. For example, if you began with a story, you might end with a different story that reinforces the meaning. You could also finish a story that you started in the introduction. The speaker who recited the long list of Lincoln's failures waited until the end before satisfying audience curiosity as to who this "loser" actually was. Carol Quinn came back to her glass of Kool-Aid for the conclusion of her speech:

> If I really wanted to end this speech with flair, I would now drink this glass of Kool-Aid. But there being no power on the planet which could force me to drink another glass of Kool-Aid, I will instead wish you health, happiness, a wonderful day, and—you know what?—strawberry Kool-Aid is really the best. Thanks for inviting me.[25]

Involve the Audience. At the beginning of a speech, you involve the audience by showing them how your message relates directly to their lives. At the conclusion of your speech, you should remind them of what they personally have at stake. In the speech on global warming mentioned earlier, the summary statement was followed immediately by remarks that brought the message close to the lives of listeners:

> Global warming is a monster we are making. If we don't stop now, we, our children, and our children's children will have to pay the price: sky-high temperatures, rising seas, violent storms, and a host of dangerous health problems that will make future generations wonder why we sacrificed the quality of their lives.

Call for Action. In persuasive speeches, concluding remarks often urge listeners to take the first step to confirm their commitment to action and change. This call for action is the characteristic concluding technique for speeches that follow the motivated sequence design. The call for action should make it easy for listeners to comply. Note how Beth Tidmore used this technique to conclude her speech urging her classmates to volunteer for Special Olympics:

> Becoming a volunteer is the best way that you can help. If you can't give a weekend, give a

Many persuasive speeches end with a call for action.

> **couple of hours. If you can't become a leader, just become a cheerleader. Show up. Be a happy, smiling face. It's the best way to give to charity, because you can see the results right in front of you. You can see the shiny medals, the triumphant finishes, the happy faces, the screaming fans. And you know that you're helping someone else and giving of yourself to them. The benefits are truly rewarding, even if the only thing you get out of it is the satisfaction of knowing you've made a difference.**
>
> **Can drives need cans. Blood drives need blood. And, the Special Olympics need volunteers. They need smiling faces, warm hearts, and open minds. In Special Olympics, everyone is a winner—especially the volunteers.**

At the end of her speech Beth distributed sign-up forms that helped her listeners make their commitment.

Ask Rhetorical Questions. When used in an introduction, rhetorical questions help arouse attention and curiosity. When used in a conclusion, such questions give your audience something to think about after you have finished. Elinor Fraser opened a speech attacking the use of cell phones while driving in the following way: "How many of you had a nice little cell phone chat while driving to class this morning?" After a speech that proved the danger of such behavior in graphic terms, her final words were: "Now that you know the risk you are running, are you going to talk again on the way home? If so, tell me so I can travel in a different direction."

When used at the end of a persuasive speech, concluding questions may be more than rhetorical. They can serve as a call for action that requires a response from the audience. Evangelists frequently use this technique during revivals when they issue a call to "come forth and be saved." During political campaigns, Jesse Jackson often used this technique to register voters. He would end a speech by asking:

> **How many of you are not registered to vote? Raise your hands. No, stand up so we can see you! Is that all of you who aren't registered? Stand up! Let me see you!**

Such questioning and cajoling would be followed by on-site voter registration. To be effective, this technique must be the climax of a speech that has prepared its audience for action.

End with a Story. Stories are remembered long after facts and figures are forgotten. A concluding narrative can help your audience *experience* the meaning of your message. To end a speech on domestic terrorism, which she opened with a narrative, Donna E. Shalala, then secretary of Health and Human Services, told the following story:

> **Let me conclude by telling you about a child psychologist named Sandra Graham-Berman who took responsibility for doing even more [about the problem of domestic abuse]. Several years ago she became aware of a support group for battered women. But she heard that there was no professional support for their children. On her own time and with her own money she began a support group for the children of these battered women. She began to see the girls and boys act out, talk out, and draw out their fears and their frustrations. She helped them learn they are not alone in their pain. And she taught them that when mommy is in trouble—when she is being hurt by daddy—it's possible to get help by dialing 9-1-1.**
>
> **A few years later, a shy 8-year-old girl walked in on a fight. Her father—if you can believe it, a child psychiatrist—was beating her mother on the head with a hammer. Try to imagine that. Try to imagine what you would do. Well, that little girl knew what to do. She remembered the lesson taught to her by a**

> **caring adult. And so she went to that phone, picked it up, pressed 9-1-1, and saved her mother's life. The father is in prison now and the family's trying its best to build a new life. If that little girl can have the courage to pick up the telephone, surely we can have the courage to prevent such stories from happening.[26]**

Close with a Quotation. Brief quotations that capture the essence of your message make effective conclusions. For example, if one historic quotation opens a speech, another on the same theme or from the same person can provide an elegant sense of closure. Be certain that the person you choose to quote is someone the audience respects. Note how Benjamin Ola Akande followed up his concluding summary with the following quotation:

> **I end with a prayer I heard the great civil rights icon, Rev. Andrew Young, deliver earlier this week at the United Nations Dinner in New York City in honor of the Presidents of Uganda and Kenya. "We ain't what we were. We ain't what we wanna be. Thank you Lord for who we are. Amen."[27]**

End with a Metaphor. A striking metaphor can end your speech effectively.[28] As we will discuss at greater length in Chapter 12, **metaphors** combine things that are apparently unlike so that we see unexpected relationships. In the conclusion of a speech, an effective metaphor may reveal hidden truths about the speaker's subject in a memorable way. Melodie Lancaster, president of Lancaster Resources, used such a metaphor, developed within a narrative, as she concluded a speech to the Houston Council of the American Business Women's Association:

> **We recall the story of the three stonemasons who were asked what they were doing. The first said, "I am laying brick." The second replied, "I am making a foundation." And the third said: "I am building a cathedral." Let's you and I set our sights that high. Let's build cathedrals of success today, tomorrow, and the day after tomorrow.[29]**

Consider the many meanings this parable might evoke in the minds of listeners. First, the speaker suggests listeners must work hard. Second, she suggests they must work with specific goals in mind. Third, she suggests they must work with a vision that gives significance to what they do. All these meanings are packed into the metaphor, "cathedrals of success," making it memorable for her audience.

Use Strategic Repetition. Repetition helps implant ideas in the minds of your listeners. When repetition is combined with parallel construction, in which certain phrases are repeated in close succession for added emphasis, the results can be both elegant and dramatic. Note how Spenser Abraham, then U.S. secretary of energy, used this technique to conclude a speech presented as part of a Carnegie Foundation conference on international nonproliferation:

> **Working together we can make the world safer. We owe our people, our children and their children, nothing less.**
>
> **We owe them a world where nuclear and radiological materials are secure, not just in Russia, but elsewhere throughout the world.**
>
> **We owe them a world where terrorists have little chance of getting their hands on these materials—which might just discourage them from trying in the first place.**
>
> **We owe them a world where our borders are secure, and there is little risk of dangerous materials being shuttled about.**
>
> **And we owe them a world where nations work together to achieve these lofty objectives.[30]**

Speaker's Notes 9.4

Ending Your Speech

1. Summarize your message to remind listeners of what is important.
2. Echo your introduction to provide a sense of closure.
3. Involve the audience to remind them of the importance of the message to them.
4. Issue a call for action to get listeners to confirm their commitment.
5. Ask questions that give your audience something to consider after your speech.
6. End with a memorable story that helps listeners experience your message.
7. Close with a quotation that captures the essence of your ideas.
8. Reveal some hidden truth about your subject by using a metaphor.
9. Use strategic repetition to implant your ideas in the minds of your listeners.

Selecting and Using Concluding Techniques

Whatever closing technique you select, be certain that it satisfies your audience that what was promised in the beginning has now been delivered. Plan your summary statement and concluding remarks carefully, just as you did with your introduction. Practice them until you are confident you will end your speech impressively. After your final words, pause a moment to let them sink in, then take your seat.

There are no absolute criteria for deciding what concluding techniques you should use. Here we provide some general guidelines for their selection as we did with selecting introductory techniques:

- Think about what will work best for your audience.
- Consider the message you want your listeners to take with them.
- Use your conclusion to reinforce feelings about your topic that you want listeners to have.
- Remember time constraints. Your conclusion should be brief. Make every word count.
- Play to your strengths as a presenter. Do what you do best.

In Summary

A carefully structured speech helps the audience understand the message and enhances the speaker's ethos.

Good Form. A well-structured speech has *good form:* it is simple, balanced, and orderly. *Simplicity* occurs when you limit the number of main points and use clear, direct language. A speech has *balance* when the major parts receive proper emphasis and work together. An *orderly* speech follows a consistent pattern of development.

Structuring the Body of Your Speech. You should structure the body first, so that you can build an introduction and conclusion that fit your message. To develop the body, determine your *main points,* decide how to arrange them, and then select effective supporting materials. To discover your main points, prepare a *research overview* of the information you have collected. This summary can help you spot major themes that can develop into main points.

Arrange your main points so that they follow natural mental patterns based on the principles of similarity, proximity, and closure. The *similarity* of objects or events may suggest a categorical, comparative, or refutative design for structuring main points. *Proximity* suggests that things should be discussed as they happen together in space or time. If steps need to follow in a specific order, use a sequential design for your speech. If the ideas trace a historical development, a chronological design should be used. If they occur in physical relationship to one another, a spatial design might be appropriate. The structure of the body satisfies the principle of *closure* when it completes the design it begins. Narrative, causation, and problem-solution designs require closure to be effective.

Supporting materials fill out the speech and buttress ideas. In an ideal arrangement, you should support each point with information, testimony, and an example or story that emphasizes its human aspects.

Using Transitions. Effective *transitions* point up the relationships among ideas in your speech and tie the speech together. *Internal summaries* remind listeners of the points you have made in one part of your speech before you move on to another.

Preparing an Effective Introduction. The introduction to a speech should arouse your listeners' interest, establish your credibility, and focus and preview your message. Some useful ways to introduce a speech include acknowledging the audience, location, or occasion, involving your listeners, relating your subject to personal experience, asking *rhetorical questions,* creating suspense, telling a story, using humor, beginning with a quotation, using a presentation aid, and startling the audience. As you build credibility, you also make possible *identification* between yourself and the audience. When you *preview* your message, you give your readers the blueprints of the speech that will follow. In a narrative design, the preview *foreshadows* the meaning of your story.

Developing an Effective Conclusion. An effective conclusion should review the meaning of your speech in a *summary statement,* provide a sense of closure, leave the audience with final reflections on the significance of the speech, and, if appropriate, motivate listeners to act. Techniques that are useful for conclusions include echoing the introduction, calling for action, involving the audience, asking questions, closing with a quotation, telling a story, ending with a metaphor, and using strategic repetition. Your speech will seem more symmetrical and satisfying if your conclusion ties into your introduction.

Terms to Know

good form
simplicity
balance
order
main points
research overview
principle of similarity
principle of proximity
principle of closure
transitions
internal summary
rhetorical question
identification
preview
foreshadowing
summary statement
metaphor

Discussion

1. Working in small groups, share your research overviews for your next speeches. What major themes emerge, and how might these be developed into main points in light of the specific purpose of your speech and your listeners' needs? Encourage input from group members to help you select the main points for your speech.
2. Share the organizational plan for your next speech with a classmate so that you become consultants for each other. Help each other come up with alternative patterns for your main points. After the speeches are presented, each consulting team should explain the options it considered and why it chose the particular structure used for each speech.

Application

1. Select a speech from Appendix B and write a thorough critique of its structure. Consider the following questions:
   A. Did this speech satisfy the requirements of "good form"? Did it meet the needs of simplicity, balance, and order?
   B. What kind of arrangement of main ideas did the speech use? Did this arrangement satisfy the principle of similarity, proximity, or closure?
   C. Did transitions keep the message in focus for listeners?
2. Select a speech from Appendix B and write an alternative introduction and conclusion for the speech, using a different technique. What techniques did the speaker use? Do you think the speaker's introduction and conclusion were effective? Do you think different techniques would be more or less effective? Why?
3. What type of introductory and concluding techniques might be most effective for speeches based on the following specific purpose statements?
   A. To inform my audience of the steps to follow to get financial assistance.
   B. To persuade my audience that it is better to marry than to live together.
   C. To inform my audience of the signs of child abuse.
   D. To persuade my audience to begin recycling.

Notes

1. Patricia R. Palmerton, "Teaching Skills or Teaching Thinking," *Journal of Applied Communication Research* 20 (1992): 335–341; and Robert G. Powell, "Critical Thinking and Speech Communication: Our Teaching Strategies Are Warranted—Not!" *Journal of Applied Communication Research* 20 (1992): 342–347. Most of the research on the effects of structure was conducted in the 1960s and 1970s. Notable among these studies are Christopher Spicer and Ronald E. Bassett, "The Effect of Organization on Learning from an Informative Message," *Southern Speech Communication Journal* 41 (1976): 290–299; Ernest Thompson, "Some Effects of Message Structure on Listeners' Comprehension," *Speech Monographs* 34 (1967): 51–57; and Arlee Johnson, "A Preliminary Investigation of the Relationship Between Organization and Listener Comprehension," *Central States Speech Journal* 21 (1970): 104–107.
2. Patricia Kearney, Timothy G. Plax, Ellis R. Hayes, and Marily J. Ivey, "College Teacher Misbehaviors: What Students Don't Like About What Teachers Say and Do," *Communication Quarterly* 39 (1991): 309–324.
3. J. C. McCroskey and R. S. Mehrley, "The Effects of Disorganization and Nonfluency on Attitude Change and Source Credibility," *Communication Monographs* 36 (1969): 13–21.
4. Saul Kassin, *Psychology* (Boston: Houghton Mifflin, 1995), pp. 208–251.
5. Material in this section is based on the work of the Gestalt psychologists as summarized in Kassin, pp. 78–129.
6. Scott E. Caplan and John O. Green, "Acquisition of Message-Production Skill by Younger and Older Adults: Effects of Age, Task Complexity, and Practice," *Communication Monographs* 66 (1999): 31–48.
7. Charles Hulme, Steven Roodenrys, Gordon Brown, and Robin Mercer, "The Role of Long-Term Memory Mechanisms in Memory Span," *British Journal of Psychology* 86 (1995): 527–536.
8. Douglas A. Bernstein, Edward J. Roy, Thomas K. Srull, and Christopher D. Wickens, *Psychology,* 2nd ed. (Boston: Houghton Mifflin, 1991), p. 308.
9. Kassin, p. 111.
10. Michael D. Lemonick and Alice Park, "New Hope for Cancer," *Time,* 28 May 2001, p. 65.
11. Loren J. Anderson, "A Summary of Research on Order Effects in Communication," in *Concepts in Communication,* ed. Jimmie D. Trent, Judith S. Trent, and Daniel J. O'Neill (Boston: Allyn and Bacon, 1973), pp. 129–130.
12. Jerry Daniels, "Transforming Aerospace: A Submariner's View," *Vital Speeches of the Day*, 4 Feb. 2002, pp. 249–252.
13. Cited in Arthur M. Schlesinger Jr., *A Thousand Days: John F. Kennedy in the White House* (Boston: Houghton Mifflin, 1965), p. 733.
14. Our thanks for this example go to Professor Reno Unger, Kutztown University.

15. James Price Dillard, "Persuasion Past and Present: Attitudes Aren't What They Used to Be," *Communication Monographs* 60 (1993): 91.

16. Brock Evans, "The Endangered Species Act: Implications for the Future," *Vital Speeches of the Day,* 15 Mar. 1993, p. 339.

17. Bob Lannom, "Patience, Persistence, and Perspiration," *Parsons (Tenn.) News Leader,* 20 Sept. 1989, p. 9.

18. Carol Quinn, "Playing to Your Strengths," *Vital Speeches of the Day,* 1 June 1998, p. 508. Reprinted by permission.

19. Sharon S. Brehm and Saul M. Kassin, *Social Psychology,* 2nd ed. (Boston: Houghton Mifflin, 1993), pp. 127–128.

20. R. G. Hass, "Effects of Source Characteristics on the Cognitive Processing of Persuasive Messages and Attitude Change," in *Cognitive Responses in Persuasion,* ed. R. Petty, T. Ostrom, and T. Brock (Hillsdale, N.J.: Erlbaum, 1981), pp. 141–172; M. Heesacker, R. E. Petty, and J. T. Cacioppo, "Field Dependence and Attitude Change: Source Credibility Can Alter Persuasion by Affecting Message-Relevant Thinking," *Journal of Personality* 51 (1983): 653–666; and J. E. Maddux and R. W. Rogers, "Effects of Source Expertness, Physical Attractiveness, and Supporting Arguments on Persuasion: A Case of Brains over Beauty," *Journal of Personality and Social Psychology* 39 (1980): 235–244.

21. A. H. Eagly, W. Wood, and S. Chaiken, "An Attribution Analysis of Persuasion," in *New Directions in Attribution Research,* ed. J. Harvey, W. Ickes, and R. Kidd (Hillsdale, N.J.: Erlbaum, 1981), pp. 37–62.

22. Brehm and Kassin, pp. 220–221.

23. Kenneth Burke, *A Rhetoric of Motives* (Berkeley and Los Angeles: University of California Press, 1969), pp. 20–23.

24. Benjamin Ola Akande, "Crossroads Are Just Crossroads" *Vital Speeches of the Day*, 15 Jan. 2004, p. 224. Reprinted with permission of the author.

25. Quinn, p. 510.

26. Donna E. Shalala, "Domestic Terrorism: An Unacknowledged Epidemic," *Vital Speeches of the Day,* 15 May 1994, p. 453.

27. Akande, p. 226.

28. John Waite Bowers and Michael Osborn, "Attitudinal Effects of Selected Types of Concluding Metaphors in Persuasive Speeches," *Speech Monographs* 33 (1966): 148–155.

29. Melodie Lancaster, "The Future We Predict Isn't Inevitable: Refraining Our Success in the Modern World," *Vital Speeches of the Day,* 1 Aug. 1992, p. 638.

30. Spenser Abraham, "Ten Principles for Nuclear and Radiological Materials Security," *Vital Speeches of the Day*, 15 Dec. 2002, p. 134.

Outlining Your Speech

10

OUTLINE

This chapter will help you

- understand why outlining is important
- learn how to develop a working outline
- prepare a formal outline
- prepare a key-word outline to use as you speak

Our plans miscarry because they have no aim. When a man does not know what harbor he is making for, no wind is the right wind.

SENECA

As we planned our home on the Tennessee River, we often met with our builders to make decisions. We knew what materials we had to work with, and we knew our options for constructing the home. But before the construction could begin, we had to make commitments. As we made our choices, the builders would revise their projections. Eventually, they developed a set of blueprints that represented the final detailed plans of the home that would rise on the hilltop above the river.

Like a home, a speech must be planned. As you prepare your speeches, you first conduct research (Chapter 7) to find your supporting materials (Chapter 8). Then, you consider various ways of structuring your speech (Chapter 9). As a plan for your speech begins to form in your mind, you record it in a series of working outlines. Finally, you prepare a formal outline, the blueprint of the speech you will present.

Outlining is a process that helps you structure your speech. You need to develop an outline because:

- It objectifies your thinking: it takes ideas out of your head, where they can get all tangled up, and puts them down on paper, where you can see them and work with them.[1]
- It is both a creative and a corrective process: as you think about the relationships among your ideas, you may come up with new ones. You can see what ideas need more research, whether a point is really relevant, and whether the overall structure is well balanced.[2] You may need to add something here, subtract something there.
- It helps you find and correct problems before they become mistakes.
- It points out where you need transitions.
- It helps you see whether your planned introduction and conclusion actually fit your speech.

In this chapter, we provide you with sample outline formats that can be adapted for general use. In Chapter 14, we provide abbreviated sample outlines for specific designs that are especially useful in informative speeches: spatial, sequential, chronological, categorical, comparative, and causation. In Chapter 16, we provide abbreviated outlines for the major persuasive speech designs: problem-solution, motivated sequence, and refutative. In Chapter 17, we provide a brief sample outline for the narrative design, which is especially useful in ceremonial speaking.

As you prepare your speech, you will probably develop several working outlines, a formal outline, and a key-word outline to use as a prompt during presentation.

Developing a Working Outline

A **working outline** is a *tentative* plan for your speech. It displays the relationships among ideas and allows you to identify potential trouble spots. Assume that you plan to present an informative speech on "the greenhouse effect." You have done some research, but you are not completely sure how your speech should develop. Your working outline is a tool that can help reduce your uncertainty. It is also a discipline: merely following the format of an outline helps you think clearly about the design of your speech. Figure 10.1 provides a format for developing a working outline.

You should not think of this format as a rigid structure. Adapt it so that it works for you. In this early stage of developing your speech, don't worry about the formalities of outlining.[3] Your working outline is simply a tool to help you arrange your ideas. You will probably prepare and discard several working outlines before you find the right approach.

A good starting point for your working outline is to write out your specific purpose and thesis statement (discussed in Chapter 6). Having these statements in front of you in writing helps you check to see how well your main points fit with them.

Go to the **Speech Outliner** in the **Online SpeechStudio** for step-by-step help in creating your outline.

Go to http://college.hmco.com/eduspace/

Specific purpose:	To inform my audience of the significance of the greenhouse effect.
Thesis statement:	We must understand the greenhouse effect before we can hope to counter global warming.

Developing Your Main Points

The second step in preparing a working outline is to sketch the body of your speech. Following the process discussed in Chapter 9, write out your main points. Remember that your research overview will help you select these points. Consider the major themes from your overview in light of the purpose of your speech, your audience's needs, and the amount of time available for you to speak. In our ongoing example of preparing a speech on the greenhouse effect, the first working outline contained the following main points:

First main point:	Harmful agricultural and industrial emissions accelerate the greenhouse effect.
Second main point:	Personal energy consumption magnifies the greenhouse effect.
Third main point:	The loss of woodlands adds to the greenhouse effect.

InterConnections.LearnMore 10.1

Outlining Aids

Basic Outlining
http://www.lib.jjay.cuny.edu/research/outlining.html
A brief online guide to outlining with suggestions for further reading. Developed and maintained by the Lloyd Sealy Library, John Jay College of Criminal Justice.

Developing an Outline
http://owl.english.purdue.edu/handouts/general/gl_outlin.html
An online guide to developing an outline with links to sample outlines and other tools. Developed and maintained by the Purdue University Online Writing Lab.

Outlining
http://www.ceap.wcu.edu/Houghton/EDELCompEduc/Themes/Outlining/outlining.html
An overview of electronic outlining with links to electronic outlining tutorials. Developed and maintained by Professor Robert S. Houghton, College of Education and Allied Professions, Western Carolina University.

Organizing Information
http://www.ipl.org/div/aplus/linksorganizing.htm
An online directory of links to Internet sites on outlining and organizing information by cubing, mapping, and more. Developed and maintained by Kathryn L. Schwartz, School of Information, University of Michigan, in conjunction with the Internet Public Library.

Figure 10.1

Format for a Working Outline

Topic: ______

Specific purpose: ______

Thesis statement: ______

INTRODUCTION

Attention material: ______

Thesis statement: ______

Preview: ______

(**Transition** to body of speech)

BODY

First main point: ______

- Subpoint: ______
  - Sub-subpoint: ______
  - Sub-subpoint: ______
- Subpoint: ______

(**Transition** to second main point)

Second main point: ______

- Subpoint: ______
- Subpoint: ______
  - Sub-subpoint: ______
  - Sub-subpoint: ______

(**Transition** to third main point)

Third main point: ______

- Subpoint: ______
- Subpoint: ______

(**Transition** to conclusion)

CONCLUSION

Summary statement: ______

Concluding remarks: ______

The main points of a speech are the columns that support its structure.

Once you have the main points written out, ask yourself the following questions:

- Will these points make my message clear to my audience?
- Is this the right order in which to develop them?
- Have I left out anything important?

As you consider these questions, you realize that you have left something out. You remember that all of your sources explained what the greenhouse effect was before discussing its causes. You note that your original list of main points neither explains the greenhouse effect nor gives the audience a reason to be interested in it. You also see another potential trouble spot: There is no clear, logical order in your arrangement of main points. But if you explained what the greenhouse effect is and why we should worry about it in your first main point, and then ordered the remaining points from less destructive causes to most destructive causes, you would discuss, in order, lost woodlands, agricultural and industrial emissions, and personal consumption. This way you would both involve and inform listeners and establish an order of increasing importance among the remaining points. Your speech could build toward its conclusion. You decide to toss out your first working outline and to revise the main points as follows:

First main point:	The greenhouse effect is a process by which certain gases in the atmosphere retain the heat of the sun.
Second main point:	The loss of woodlands adds to the greenhouse effect.
Third main point:	Agricultural and industrial emissions accelerate the greenhouse effect.
Fourth main point:	Personal energy consumption magnifies the greenhouse effect.

Developing Subpoints

Once you have determined and arranged your main points, you can break them down into more specific statements that explain and support the main ideas. These more specific statements are the **subpoint** level of your outline. Each main point will be buttressed by two or more subpoints that make it more understandable, believable, or compelling.[4]

To identify the subpoints for each of your main points, imagine a critical listener in front of you. When you state the main point, this listener will want to know:

- What do you mean?
- Why should I care?
- How do I know this is true?

The subpoints for each main point should answer these questions. If the main points are columns built on the foundation of your purpose and thesis statement, the subpoints reinforce these columns so that they will stand up under critical scrutiny. For example, as you develop your working outline, you might list the following subpoints for your first main point:

First main point: The greenhouse effect is a process by which certain gases in the atmosphere retain the heat of the sun.

Subpoints:

A. Among these gases are carbon dioxide and methane.

B. They form a window that holds the heat.

C. This natural process has been unbalanced by human activities.

D. Too many gases are holding too much heat.

E. Heat waves are breaking all records.

F. This situation causes climate and health problems.

You notice that you have listed six subpoints. Recalling the principles of good form learned in Chapter 7, you conclude rightly that you have *too many* subpoints for your speech to be simple, balanced, and orderly.

At this point, you examine how your subpoints relate to one another. Can you combine any of them? Do you need to break out the material to a more detailed level of **sub-subpoints**? For example, you might develop the first main point in this working outline as follows:

First main point: The greenhouse effect is a process by which certain gases in the atmosphere retain the heat of the sun.

Subpoint A: This natural process makes the earth livable.

Subpoint B: Process now unbalanced by human activities.

Sub-subpoints:

1. High concentrations of carbon dioxide and methane in the atmosphere.
2. Heat waves are breaking all temperature records.
3. This threatens many living things.

Follow this same procedure as you develop each main point. When you finish, review the working outline of the body of your speech and ask yourself:

- Will a speech based on this outline satisfy my thesis statement?
- Will I be able to do all of this in the time available?

Be honest with yourself. It's better to be frustrated now than disappointed during your presentation. In addition, be sure your ideas are arranged in an orderly manner that is easy to follow. Make certain that each subpoint relates directly to the main point above it and that you have enough supporting material to build a strong, responsible structure of ideas. If you are lacking in any of these respects, now is the time to discover and correct the problem.

Completing Your Working Outline

To complete your working outline, prepare an introduction that gains attention, enhances your credibility, and focuses and previews your speech, as we discussed in Chapter 9. Next, develop a conclusion that includes a summary and concluding remarks. Finally, add transitions to tie your speech together. Transitions should connect the introduction to the body, tie each point to the next point as you develop the body, and move the speech from the body to the conclusion.

Now, take a final look at your working outline. (Figure 10.2 is a sample working outline for a speech on global warming.)

Review your outline using the "Checklist for a Working Outline" in Speaker's Notes 10.1. Go over the outline with someone whose judgment you respect. Another person sometimes can see problems you might miss because you are too close to the material.

Speaker's Notes 10.1

Checklist for a Working Outline

_____ 1. My topic, specific purpose, and thesis statement are clearly stated.

_____ 2. My introduction contains attention-getting material, establishes my credibility, and focuses and previews my message.

_____ 3. My main points represent the most important ideas on my topic.

_____ 4. I have an appropriate number of main points to cover my material in the time allotted.

_____ 5. Each subpoint breaks its main point into more specific detail.

_____ 6. My conclusion contains a summary statement and concluding remarks that reinforce and reflect on the meaning of my speech.

_____ 7. I have planned transitions to use between the introduction and body, between each of my main points, and between the body and conclusion of my speech.

As you review your working outline, keep the audience at the center of your thinking. Remember the advice given to beginning journalists: *Never overestimate your audience's information, and never underestimate their intelligence!* Ask yourself the following questions:

- Are my main points arranged so they are easy to follow?
- Do I have enough supporting material for each main point?
- Do I have different types of supporting materials for each main point?

Speech preparation proceeds in fits and starts, periods of frustration followed by moments of inspiration and revision. You may find yourself making and revising several working outlines before you are satisfied.

Topic: The Greenhouse Effect
Specific purpose: To inform my audience of the significance of the greenhouse effect.
Thesis statement: We must understand the greenhouse effect before we can hope to counter global warming.

INTRODUCTION

Attention material: Antarctic icebergs breaking loose: ominous signs of global warming. Nero fiddled while Rome burned: we're fiddling while the Earth burns.
Thesis statement: We must understand the greenhouse effect before we can hope to counter global warming.
Preview: We need to be concerned especially about the loss of woodlands, harmful agricultural and industrial emissions, and our own energy consumption.

(**Transition** to body of speech: "Let's begin by understanding the greenhouse effect.")

BODY

First main point: The greenhouse effect is a process by which certain gases in the atmosphere retain the heat of the sun.
Subpoint A: This natural process makes the Earth livable.
Subpoint B: Process now unbalanced by human activities.
Sub-subpoints: 1. High concentrations of carbon dioxide and methane in the atmosphere.
2. Artificial heat wave is breaking all temperature records.
3. This threatens Earth's climate and many living things.

(**Transition** to second main point: "Let's examine the causes, one by one.")

Second main point: The loss of woodlands adds to the greenhouse effect.
Subpoint A: Loss from cutting.
Subpoint B: Loss from clearing.
Subpoint C: Loss from burning.

(**Transition** to third main point: "An even greater cause is harmful agricultural and industrial emissions.")

Third main point: Agricultural and industrial emissions accelerate the greenhouse effect.
Subpoint A: Farming an important part of problem.
Sub-subpoints: 1. Frequent tilling and massive CO_2.
2. Rice farms and methane.
3. Cattle ranches and more methane.
Subpoint B: Industrial emissions from burning fossil fuels another big source of problem.

(continued)

Figure 10.2
Sample Working Outline

- *Begin by writing down your topic, specific purpose, and thesis statement so that you have them clearly in mind as you work.*
- *Sketch your introduction, including short notes on attention materials. Notice that this tentative plan omits any direct effort to build credibility. A credibility strategy should emerge by the formal outline. As planning proceeds, revise any of these elements as needed.*
- *Labeling the body of the speech points out its importance. Remember to develop the body of the speech before you develop the introduction or conclusion.*
- *Include transitions to remind yourself to tie material together and make it flow smoothly.*
- *Note that the working outline does not follow the numbering and lettering system of a formal outline. The purpose of the working outline is to allow you to organize ideas and see how they work together.*

Figure 10.2
(Continued)

■ *The working outline serves as your guide and provides a check on the structure of the speech and the adequacy of your preparation.*

■ *Like the introduction, the conclusion is merely sketched in the working outline. Specific techniques are worked out as planning proceeds.*

(**Transition** to fourth main point: "Finally, let's consider the most important cause of the runaway greenhouse effect—ourselves.")

Fourth main point: Our personal energy consumption magnifies the greenhouse effect
- **Subpoint A:** Both population and prosperity fuel the problem.
  - **Sub-subpoints:** 1. More people = more energy consumption.
  - 2. Improved living standards add to the problem.
- **Subpoint B:** Personal energy consumption single largest cause of greenhouse effect.
  - **Sub-subpoints:** 1. Fossil fuels account for 90% of U.S. personal energy consumption.
  - 2. Personal cars tripled since 1950.

(**Transition:** "In conclusion . . .")

CONCLUSION

Summary statement: The greenhouse effect is the key to understanding global warming. Major causes are loss of woodlands, agricultural and industrial emissions, and increased personal consumption.

Concluding remarks: Future generations will ask why we did this to the quality of their lives.

Developing a Formal Outline

Once you are pleased with your working outline, you can prepare your formal outline. The **formal outline** is the final step in planning the structure of your speech. It imposes a discipline on your preparation and demonstrates to your instructor that the research and planning phase of your work is completed. The formal outline for a speech follows many of the established conventions of outlining. Figure 10.3 shows a formal speech outline format illustrating these conventions:

1. Identification of speech topic, specific purpose, and thesis statement
2. Separation of speech parts: introduction, body, and conclusion
3. Use of numbering and lettering to display coordination and subordination
4. Wording of main points and subpoints as simple declarative sentences
5. A title
6. A list of major sources consulted

Topic, Specific Purpose, and Thesis Statement

Some student speakers recite their topic, specific purpose, and thesis statement at the beginnings of each speech as though they had been programmed: "My topic is. . . , My specific purpose is . . . , My thesis statement is . . . ." This is not a good way

Figure 10.3
Format for a Formal Outline

TITLE

Topic: ______
Specific purpose: ______
Thesis statement: ______

INTRODUCTION

Attention material: ______

Thesis statement: ______

Preview: ______

(**Transition** into body of speech)

BODY

I. First main point: ______
- **A.** Subpoint or supporting material: ______
- **B.** Subpoint or supporting material: ______
  - **1.** Sub-subpoint or supporting material: ______
  - **2.** Sub-subpoint or supporting material: ______

(**Transition** into next main point)

II. Second main point: ______
- **A.** Subpoint or supporting material: ______
  - **1.** Sub-subpoint or supporting material: ______
  - **2.** Sub-subpoint or supporting material: ______
- **B.** Subpoint or supporting material: ______

(**Transition** into next main point)

III. Third main point: ______
- **A.** Subpoint or supporting material: ______
- **B.** Subpoint or supporting material: ______
  - **1.** Sub-subpoint or supporting material: ______
  - **2.** Sub-subpoint or supporting material: ______
    - **a.** Sub-sub-subpoint or supporting material: ______
    - **b.** Sub-sub-subpoint or supporting material: ______

(**Transition** into conclusion)

CONCLUSION

Summary statement: ______

Concluding remarks: ______

WORKS CONSULTED

to begin a speech! Nevertheless, you should write these headings out at the top of your outline because they help you focus your message.

Separation of Speech Parts

As you did in the working outline, separate the introduction, body, and conclusion of the speech so that you give each section the careful attention it requires.

Your outline transfers your ideas for your speech from your head onto a piece of paper.

Note that in Figure 10.3 only the body of the speech follows an outlining format.[5] In contrast, the introduction and conclusion are presented exactly as you will say them. As we suggested in Chapter 3, it is better to write out and commit to memory your introduction and conclusion to ensure that you get into and out of your speech gracefully and effectively. Although there may be times when you must adapt and change your introduction in light of the situation (we discussed these moments in relation to "Context" in Chapter 5), as a general rule a carefully worded beginning works best. Knowing *exactly* what you want to say and how you want to say it gets you off to a good start and helps build the confidence you need to make your presentation effective. At the end of your speech, the exact wording of your concluding remarks can determine whether you make a lasting impression.

Numbering and Lettering Your Outline

Figure 10.3 shows you how to use letters, numbers, and indentation to set up a formal outline that follows the principles of coordination and subordination. The actual number of main points and levels of subpoints may vary, but the basic format remains the same. Roman numerals (I, II, III) identify the main points of your speech. Capital letters (A, B, C) identify the subpoints under each main point. Arabic numbers (1, 2, 3) identify the sub-subpoints under any subpoint. Lowercase letters (a, b, c) identify any sub-sub-subpoints in your outline.

The principle of **coordination** suggests that all statements at a given level (your *I*'s and *II*'s, *A*'s and *B*'s, and so forth) should be of similar importance. In the sample formal outline shown later in this chapter, the main points include an explanation of the greenhouse effect and its three major causes arranged in ascending order of importance (see Figure 9.1 in the previous chapter). Think how strange it would seem if a fifth main point, "The greenhouse effect will decrease our recreational opportunities," were added to this outline. This statement would not be coordinate in importance with the other main points. Nor would it fit within the pattern of relationships. Adding such a main point would violate the principle of coordination.

The principle of **subordination** requires that material descend in importance from the general and abstract main points to the concrete and specific subpoints, and sub-subpoints related to them as shown below:

More important	I. Main point	more general
	A. Subpoint	
	1. Sub-subpoint	
Less important	a. Sub-sub-subpoint	more specific

The more important a statement is, the farther to the left it is positioned. If you rotate an outline clockwise so that it rests on its right margin, the "peaks" will represent the main points, the most important ideas in your speech, with the height of the other points representing their relative significance.

The easiest way to demonstrate the importance of coordination and subordination is to look at an abbreviated sample outline that violates these principles:

I. Computers can help you develop writing skills.
  A. Using PCs can improve your schoolwork.
  B. PCs can be useful for organizing class notes.
II. Computers can help you keep better financial records.
  A. They can help you plan personal time more effectively.
  B. They can be useful in your personal life.
  C. They can help organize your research notes for class projects.

This collection of ideas may look like an outline, but it isn't. It violates the principles of coordination and subordination. The points at each level are not equal in importance, nor are they logically related to one another. To straighten out this problem, look at points I and II. They are neither the most important nor the most general statements. The main points are actually I-A and II-B: the ideas that PCs can improve your schoolwork and can be useful in your personal life. Once we put the main points where they belong, we can see where the subpoints go:

I. Computers can improve your schoolwork.
  A. PCs can help you develop writing skills.
  B. PCs can be useful for organizing class notes.
  C. PCs can help organize your research notes for class projects.
II. Computers can be useful in your personal life.
  A. PCs can help you keep better financial records.
  B. PCs can help you plan personal time more effectively.

Wording Your Outline

Each main point and subpoint in your outline should be worded as a simple declarative sentence containing only one idea. As the name suggests, such a sentence makes a simple declaration, such as "Computers can be useful in your personal life." It is not weighted down with qualifying, dependent clauses, as in "*Even though they are expensive,* computers can be useful in your personal life." If the points in your outline start sprouting such clauses, you should simplify the structure of your speech. You may need to break down complex main points into subpoints or complex subpoints into sub-subpoints. For example, the following does not make a good main point sentence: "Bad eating habits endanger health and lower feelings of self-worth, reducing life span and causing personal anguish." The sentence works better in an outline if it is simplified in the following way:

I. Bad eating habits are a threat to our well-being.
  A. Bad eating habits endanger health.
    1. They can result in increased heart disease.
    2. They can shorten the life span.
  B. Bad eating habits can damage self-image.
    1. Obese people sometimes dislike themselves.
    2. They can feel that they have nothing to offer others.

Breaking the complex sentence down into outline form helps you to focus what you are going to say. It simplifies and clarifies both the structure and the logic of your speech.

Try to use **parallel construction** when wording the main points of your speech. In parallel construction, *successive sentences or phrases follow the same pattern of wording in order to emphasize an idea.* If you were developing a speech on the need for reforms in political campaign financing, you might word your main points as follows:

I. We need reform at the national level.

II. We need reform at the state level.

III. We need reform at the local level.

IV. But first, we need to reform ourselves.

If you used these words in the introduction of your speech, the parallel construction would give listeners a guide to the structure of your speech. You could also repeat the parallel pattern as you summarize your speech, further imprinting its message on the minds of your listeners.

Parallel construction has many advantages. Because each sentence has the same basic structure, any variations stand out sharply. Thus, parallel construction emphasizes important points. In this example, the parallel structure helps the speech narrow its focus like a zoom lens as it moves from a national to an individual perspective.

Using parallel construction for your main points can also help you sharpen internal summaries: "Having looked at reform at the national, state, and local levels, we come to the most important part of the problem—ourselves." Since it involves repetition, it makes your message easy to remember. It satisfies the principles of good form and closure discussed in Chapter 9.

Supporting Your Main Points

Your formal outline should show how your supporting material fits into your speech. As we noted in Chapter 8, supporting materials strengthen the points you make. For example, a subpoint that states, "Global warming is causing climate changes" might need a factual example and expert testimony to substantiate that claim: "According to climatologist Allen Myerson, writing in the *New York Times,* the summer of 1998 was the hottest on record." In particular, be sure that each main point receives the type and amount of supporting material it needs to be effective. In Chapter 8 we offered guidelines for deciding what supporting materials you should use if your ideas are controversial, abstract, technical, or distant from the lives of your listeners. In Chapter 9 we described how to work supporting materials into your speech. You should go back and review this material as you prepare your outline.

Title

For speeches given outside the classroom, a title may help attract listeners to a presentation. A good title arouses curiosity. It makes people want to hear the message. You may wish to mention your title in your introduction and then refer to it throughout the speech as a reminder of your thesis statement. However, you don't want to begin your speech by simply stating your title. Rather, find some artful way to weave the title into your introduction in order to focus attention. The following provides a model:

As I reflect upon the meaning of my speech today, I am drawn to my title, "Life in the Greenhouse." How is "Life in the Greenhouse"? I can tell you in

B. Industrial emissions from fossil fuels are a major part of the problem.
   1. Smokestacks strain to produce more energy.
   2. Fleets of trucks crowd the nation's highways.
   3. Flocks of airplanes crisscross the skies.

(**Transition** to fourth main point: "Finally, let's consider the most important cause of the runaway greenhouse effect—ourselves.")

IV. Our personal energy consumption magnifies the greenhouse effect (Shute).
   A. Both population and prosperity fuel the problem (Kluger).
      1. More people means more energy consumption.
      2. Improved living standards around the world add to the problem.
   B. Personal energy consumption is the single largest cause of the greenhouse effect (Myerson).
      1. Fossil fuels account for 90 percent of America's personal energy consumption.
      2. The number of personal cars has more than tripled since 1950.

(**Transition:** "In conclusion")

CONCLUSION

Summary statement: Step outside into the greenhouse. Listen for the falling trees, watch the smokestacks darkening the sky, smell the rich bouquet of fumes.

Concluding remarks: Future generations will ask: "why did we carelessly, willfully, ignorantly allow this to happen to their world? Why did we poison planet Earth?"

WORKS CONSULTED

Begley, Sharon. "Ice Cubes for Penguins." Newsweek 3 Apr. 1995: 56.
"Feeling the Heat." Time 9 Apr. 2001: 22–39.
Kluger, Jeffrey. "A Climate of Despair." Time 9 Apr. 2001: 30–36.
Lemonick, Michael D. "One Big, Bad Iceberg." Time 20 Mar.1995: 65.
Myerson, Allen R. "U.S. Splurging on Energy After Falling Off Its Diet," New York Times Online 22 Oct. 1998. 24 April 2001 <http://www.nytimes.com/library/financial/>.
Petit, Charles W."Polar Meltdown." U.S. News & World Report 28 Feb. 2000: 65–74.
Schneider, David. "Global Warming Is Still a Hot Topic." Scientific American Feb. 1995: 13–14.
Shute, Nancy. "The Weather Turns Wild." U.S. News & World Report 5 Feb. 2001: 44–52.
Summary for Policymakers: A Report of Working Group 1 of the [United Nations] Intergovernmental Panel on Climate Change. Jan. 2001. 17 Apr.2001 <http://www.usgcrp.gov/ipcc/wg/wg1spm.pdf>.
Thompson, Dick. "Sprawl." Time April-May 2000: 50–51.
Union of Concerned Scientists, "The Causes of Global Warming." Undated posting. 19 Apr. 2001 <http://www.ucsusa.org/warming/gw.causes.html>.

Figure 10.4

(Continued)

■ *The third main point is more fully developed than the second. It appears rich in facts and figures but will be more interesting if examples, vivid language, and/or presentation aids are used.*

■ *Again the transition signals a change of focus.*

■ *The conclusion creates a startling image as it also summarizes the message. It uses rhetorical questions arranged according to the principle of parallel construction for the concluding remarks.*

■ *The references in the works consulted follow the format recommended by the Modern Language Association of America. The speaker has used a variety of sources of information to acquire responsible knowledge for the development of the speech.*

- If the "author" is a group, list the name: (Union); if the author is not provided, list the first word of the title (*Summary*).

Remember: Documenting your sources in your outline does not satisfy the need for oral documentation as you present your speech. Your listeners are not privy to the full written citations at the end of your formal outline. Nor would listeners really want or need to know every detail offered there. Oral documentation is actually selective documentation. Note how Joshua Logan, who presented the informative

VideoLab

Watch the video and answer the questions in **Lesson 4's VideoLab Next Step: Citing Sources Correctly**. Did this speaker cite her sources correctly?

Your key word outline should fit onto a single sheet of paper or a few note cards.

speech we have been studying, handles oral documentation near the beginning of his speech:

> **Right on cue, during the winter of 1995, *Time* magazine reported that a gigantic iceberg—23 miles wide and 48 miles long, almost as large as the state of Rhode Island—broke off the Larsen Ice Shelf in the Antarctic Peninsula. More than this, the whole Ice Shelf is crumbling. Rudolfo Del Valle, director of geoscience at the Argentine Antarctic Institute, told *Newsweek* that it "looked liked polystyrene that had been broken by a little boy." The elephant seals that once thrived nearby have now vanished, reports *U.S. News & World Report* in its February 2000 issue.**

Joshua's oral citations offer the source, the general time frame in which the publication appeared, relevant credentials for the experts he cites, and a brief quotation that underscores the urgency of his message. He touches the highlights of the written citations given at the end of his formal outline, but he avoids the pedantic repetition of every detail there. That, he realizes, would quickly become tiresome.

Oral documentation in your presentation allows you to give credit where credit is due and to enjoy some well-deserved credit for your careful research. Citing expert sources as you speak also enhances your ethos and helps forestall any suspicion of plagiarism.

Listing Your References

A list of your major sources of information should appear at the end of your formal outline as "Works Cited" or "Works Consulted." The former lists just those sources you actually cite in your speech; the latter lists all works you consulted during research preparation. Ask your teacher which of these procedures she or he prefers.

Such lists indicate the range of sources from which you draw supporting materials. They are evidence for your claim to responsible knowledge of your subject. Should any of your sources be challenged, the list provides precise information to authenticate what you have said. The Modern Language Association (MLA) and the American Psychological Association (APA) have published extensive guidelines for constructing such lists. Other protocols include the *Chicago Manual of Style* and the

Speaker's Notes 10.2

Guidelines for Oral Citations

1. Identify the publication in which evidence appears.
2. Identify the general time frame of the publication.
3. Offer "highlight" credentials for the experts you cite.
4. Select direct quotations from experts that are brief, colorful, and dramatic; use words that constitute "impact statements."
5. Avoid the pedantry of citing every detail found in written citations: that would quickly become tedious, tiresome, and even ludicrous.
6. The more controversial and time-sensitive the citation, the more full and precise your oral documentation must be.

InterConnections.LearnMore 10.2

Online Guides to Citation Style

Citing Sources and Avoiding Plagiarism: Documentation Guides
http://www.lib.duke.edu/libguide/citing.htm
A comprehensive resource that can help you find examples of all types of citations rendered side by side in APA, Chicago, MLA, and Turabian formats. Developed and maintained by Kelley A. Lawton and Laura Cousineau, Duke University Libraries, and Van E. Hillard, The University Writing Program, Duke University.

Columbia Guide to Online Style
http://www.columbia.edu/cu/cup/cgos/idx_basic.html
This well-developed site includes material excerpted from their hard-copy style guide covering the elements of citation and the preparation of bibliographic material. Contains abundant examples. Developed and maintained by Columbia University Press.

Citing Electronic Documentation: APA, Chicago, and MLA Styles
http://www.rhetoric.umn.edu/Student/Graduate/%7Emstewart/citations
An up-to-date guide for citing electronic resources using three major style manuals. Contains separate links for the guidelines of each style. Developed and maintained by Professor Mark D. Stewart, Department of Rhetoric, University of Minnesota.

Electronic References
http://www.apastyle.org/elecref.html
This website contains material excerpted from the APA publication manual. You can sign up for automatic email updates and hints issued weekly.

Turabian Manual for Writers of Term Papers, Theses, and Dissertations. Ask your instructor which style he or she prefers. For your convenience, Figure 10.5 provides an abridged compilation of the MLA and APA citation formats for the kinds of sources most frequently used in speeches.

After you have completed your formal outline, review it using the "Checklist for a Formal Outline" in Speaker's Notes 10.2.

Speaker's Notes 10.3

Checklist for a Formal Outline

_____ 1. My topic and specific purpose are clearly stated.
_____ 2. My thesis statement is written as a declarative sentence.
_____ 3. My introduction contains material to create attention, establish my credibility, and preview my message.
_____ 4. My main points represent the most important ideas on my topic.
_____ 5. My main points are similar in importance.
_____ 6. My main points are stated as declarative sentences.
_____ 7. Each main point is supported by facts, statistics, testimony, examples, or narratives.
_____ 8. My subpoints are divisions of the main points they follow and are also written in simple sentences.
_____ 9. My subpoints are more specific than the main points they follow.
_____ 10. My conclusion contains a summary statement that repeats my message and concluding remarks that reflect on its meaning and significance.
_____ 11. I have provided transitions where they are needed to make my speech flow smoothly.
_____ 12. I have compiled a list of works cited or consulted in the preparation of my speech.

Figure 10.5

MLA and APA Citation Styles

Book: Single Author

MLA Mann, Thomas. The Oxford Guide to Library Research. New York: Oxford UP, 1998.

APA Mann, T. (1998) The Oxford Guide to Library Research. New York: Oxford University Press.

Book: Two or More Authors

MLA Alexander, Janet E., and Marsha Anne Tate. Web Wisdom: How to Evaluate and Create Information Quality on the Web. Mahwah, NJ: Lawrence Erlbaum, 1999.

APA Alexander, J. E., & Tate, M. A. (1999) Web Wisdom: How to Evaluate and Create Information Quality on the Web. Mahwah, NJ: Lawrence Erlbaum.

Book: Second or Later Edition

MLA Schlein, Alan M. Find It Online: The Complete Guide to Online Research. 3rd ed. Tempe, AZ: Facts on Demand Press, 2003.

APA Schlein, A. M. (2003). Find It Online: The Complete Guide to Online Research (3rd ed.). Tempe, AZ: Facts on Demand Press.

Book: Corporate Authors

MLA American Association of Cereal Chemists. Sweeteners. St. Paul, MN: American Association of Cereal Chemists, 1998.

APA American Association of Cereal Chemists. (1998). Sweeteners. St. Paul, MN: American Association of Cereal Chemists.

Signed Article in Reference Work

MLA Richardson, Brenda L. "Heart Health." Everywoman's Encyclopedia. New York: Wellness Press, 2003.

APA Richardson, B. L. (2003) Heart health. In Everywoman's Encyclopedia (pp. 202-206). New York: Wellness Press.

Unsigned Article in Reference Work

MLA "Musik, Melody." Who's Who in the South, 2003-2004. Mentone, AL: Southern Who's Who, 2004.

APA Musik, Melody (2004). In Who's who in the south, 2003-2004 (p. 146). Mentone, AL: Southern Who's Who.

Signed Magazine Article

MLA Stix, Gary. "Ultimate Self-Improvement." Scientific American Sept. 2003: 44-45.

APA Stix, G. (2003 September) Ultimate Self-Improvement. Scientific American, pp. 44-45.

Unsigned Magazine Article

MLA "Primary Sources." Atlantic Monthly Nov. 2003: 54-55.

APA Primary Sources (2003 October). Atlantic Monthly, pp. 54-55.

Developing a Key-Word Outline

Your formal outline is a blueprint of your speech, not the speech itself. *Do not use your formal outline as you present your speech.* If you do, you will be tempted to read it. You will lose eye contact with listeners and miss feedback from them. Your speech will lack the sense of spontaneity that is important for an effective presentation. Instead, prepare a **key-word outline** that reduces your formal outline to those essential words or phrases that will jog your memory and remind you of the order of your main points.

Your key-word outline should fit on a few sheets of paper or index cards. Number the pages or cards to help keep them in order. If you are preparing your

Figure 10.5
(Continued)

Journal Article

MLA Barge, J. Kevin. "Hope, Communication, and Community Building." Southern Communication Journal 69 (2003): 63-81.

APA Barge, J. K. (2003). Hope, Communication, and Community Building. Southern Communication Journal, 69, 63-81.

Signed Newspaper Article

MLA Beifuss, John. "Who's Hoping for an Oscar?" Memphis Register 14 Feb. 2004: E6.

APA Beifuss, J. (2004, Feb. 14). Who's hoping for an Oscar? Memphis Register, p. E6.

Unsigned Newspaper Article

MLA "It's Gut-check Time," Louisville Chronicle, 23 February 2004: C1.

APA It's gut-check time. (2004, Feb. 23). Louisville Chronicle, p. C1.

Government Publication

MLA United States. Environmental Protection Agency. New Motor Vehicles and New Motor Vehicle Engines Air Pollution Control: Voluntary Standards for Light-Duty Vehicles. Washington, D.C. : Government Printing Office, 1998.

APA U.S. Environmental Protection Agency. (1998). New Motor Vehicles and New Motor Vehicle Engines Air Pollution Control: Voluntary Standards for Light-Duty Vehicles. Washington, D.C. : Government Printing Office.

Personal Interview

MLA Hogan, Michael. Personal interview. 19 Feb. 2004.

APA Hogan, M. (2004, February 19). [Personal interview].

Letter or E-Mail Communication

MLA McGee, Michael Calvin. E-mail to the author. 9 July 2002.

APA McGee, M. C. (mmcgee@dreammail.net). (2002, July 9). Reply to Questions for Book. E-mail to S. Osborn (sso@mailmyth.net).

Speech or Lecture

MLA Vidulic, Robert. Lecture on dogmatism. Psychology 4231: Social Psychology. University of Memphis, 15 March 2004.

APA Vidulic, R. (2004, March 15). Dogmatism [Lecture]. In Psychology 4231: Social Psychology. University of Memphis.

World Wide Web Document

MLA Today: Health. "Can You Spot a Liar?" 29 Jan. 2004. <http://www.msnbc.msn.com/id/4072816/> 29 Jan. 2004.

APA Today: Health. (2004, January 29). Can you spot a liar? [Online]. Available: http://www.msnbc.msn.com/id/4072816/. [2004, 29 January].

key-word outline by hand, use a dark felt marker and print in letters large enough to read without straining. If you are preparing it on a computer, choose a large font size (14 points or larger). Also choose the "Bold" command on your toolbar to enhance readability as you glance quickly at the outline during presentation.

You should follow the same format for lettering, numbering, and indentation that you used in your formal outline. If you are preparing your outlines by hand, go through a copy of your formal outline and highlight the numbers, letters, and key words. Copy these onto another piece of paper or note cards for use as a key-word outline. If you are working on a computer, make a copy of your formal outline. On the copy, select the numbers, letters, and key words, change them to **bold**, delete the rest of the material, and save. With a few stylistic changes, you will create your key-word outline.

Be sure to include major source citations to help you remember to use them as oral footnotes during your presentation. However, the format of the source citation may change slightly. Instead of referring to a list of Works Cited or Works Consulted, as they do in the formal outline, key-word citations should point you directly to the source you wish to cite in the speech. For example, in place of a source citation such as (Kluger), which might refer in the formal outline to a title in the Works Consulted list, you instead might identify the source as (*Time* 2001), because you are going to mention both the magazine title and the date in your presentation.

If you will be using verbatim quotations in your speech, print these on index cards so that you can read them during your presentation. Keep your quotations short, number the cards, and include a note to yourself on your key-word outline that will help you retrieve them easily, such as (*Time* 2001: Card 1). Arrange your quotation cards in the order in which you will use them in the speech.

Let's return to the third main point of the formal outline for the greenhouse speech to see how it might be turned into a key-word outline format:

III. Agricultural and industrial emissions accelerate the greenhouse effect (Union).

- A. Farming is an important part of problem.
  1. Frequent tilling releases massive CO_2.
  2. Rice farms add methane.
  3. Cattle ranches add more methane.
- B. Industrial emissions from fossil fuels are a major part of problem.
  1. Smokestacks strain to produce more energy.
  2. Fleets of trucks crowd the nation's highways.
  3. Flocks of airplanes crisscross the skies.

In this example we have highlighted the key words for the main point, each subpoint, and each sub-subpoint. These then convert into the following key-word format:

III. Cause 2: Emissions (Union: Card 2)

- **A. Farming**
  1. **Tilling**
  2. **Rice farms**
  3. **Cattle**
- **B. Industrial**
  1. **Smokestacks**
  2. **Trucks**
  3. **Airplanes (pause for emphasis)**

As you practice your speech, you may be able to reduce your key-word outline even further. *Remember, the more the speech is outlined in your head rather than on paper, the better.* Begin practicing using your formal outline. Go through the speech two or three times until you feel comfortable with what you are going to say and how you are going to say it. Then practice from your key-word outline until your speech flows smoothly. As you practice, you may want to write brief presentation notes, such as "pause" or "slow down," on your key-word outline. Make these notes in a different color so that you don't confuse them with the outline during presentation. Put your outline aside for a while, and then rehearse again, using the key-word outline. If the key words still jog your memory, your preparation has been effective. We provide more suggestions for rehearsing your speech in Chapter 13. Figure 10.6 shows a key-word outline for the speech on the greenhouse effect.

INTRODUCTION

Symptoms of global warming (Hit these hard!)
The "Greenhouse Effect" (Need good eye contact)
Must understand the second to control the first

BODY

I. Greenhouse effect a natural process
  A. Makes earth livable
  B. Now unbalanced by us (Summary; Schneider)
    1. Too much CO_2 and methane
    2. Record temperatures
      a. 1990s warmest decade
      b. 1998 hottest year of millennium! (Be dramatic)
    3. Threatens all living things—including us! (Be emphatic!)

II. Cause 1: loss of trees (*Time* 2001)
  A. Cutting
  B. Clearing (*Time* 2000)
  C. Burning (Pause for effect)

III. Cause 2: Emissions (Union: Card 1)
  A. Farming
    1. Tilling
    2. Rice farms
    3. Cattle
  B. Industrial
    1. Smokestacks
    2. Trucks
    3. Airplanes (Pause for emphasis)

IV. Cause 3: Personal Consumption (*U.S. News* 2001)
  A. Population and prosperity
    1. More people = More consumption
    2. Higher standards = More consumption
  B. Single largest cause (*NY Times* Oct. 98) (Emphasize strongly)
    1. Fossil fuels 90% of personal energy use
    2. Cars on road tripled since 1950 (Repeat for emphasis)

CONCLUSION

Listen, Watch, Smell (Slow down and emphasize)
Questions from the future (Really hit them with these)

Figure 10.6

Sample Key-Word Outline

■ *The speaker has added prompts for presentation.*

■ *This key-word outline follows the same format of indenting used in the formal outline. It makes it easier for the speaker to check at a glance. The outline contains just enough information to keep the speaker focused on the planned sequence of points and subpoints. The single words and short phrases prevent the speaker from being tempted to read the speech.*

VideoLab

To test your skills and expand your understanding of organizing and outlining your speech, go to **Lesson 5: Organizing and Outlining Your Speech** and go through the videos, exercises, and tips provided.

In Summary

An outline provides an overview of what you want to say and how you want to say it. It can sharpen and improve the structure of your speech.

Developing a Working Outline. Your *working outline* is a tentative plan of your speech. It helps you clarify the relationships among your ideas, shows the relative importance of your points, and depicts how they fit together. As working outlines for a speech evolve, they indicate how and where you will use supporting materials. By developing working outlines, you can judge the effectiveness of your research and determine if you need additional material.

Developing a Formal Outline. The *formal outline* is the final product of the research and planning phase of your speech. It follows a number of conventions, including coordination and subordination. *Coordination* requires that statements that are alike in kind and importance be placed on the same level in the outline. *Subordination* requires that statements descend in importance from main points through *subpoints* and *sub-subpoints,* and that each level logically include the level below it. As you descend through the outline, points become more specific and concrete.

The main points in a formal outline should be worded as simple declarative sentences containing only one idea. *Parallel construction*, in which successive sentences or phrases follow the same pattern of wording in order to emphasize an idea, helps the audience remember your message. *Source citations* provide documentation. They show how you have integrated your research into your speech. Do not forget to provide oral documentation for major evidence and ideas gleaned from your research as you present your speech.

A formal outline concludes with a list of *works cited* or *works consulted.* The most frequently used formats for such lists are those issued by the Modern Language Association and the American Psychological Association.

Developing a Key-Word Outline. A *key-word outline* can aid you as you present your speech. It reduces the formal outline to a few essential words or phrases that remind you of the content and design of your speech, as well as your sources of supporting materials. Notes on the key-word outline can also remind you of presentation strategies. Put quotations you must read on numbered index cards to use along with your key-word outline during presentation.

Terms to Know

working outline
subpoint
sub-subpoints
formal outline
coordination
subordination
parallel construction
source citation
works cited
works consulted
key-word outline

Discussion

1. Working in small groups, share a working outline for your next speech. Explain your strategy for structure, and show how your outline satisfies the principles of coordination and subordination. Demonstrate that you have adequate supporting materials for each main point in your speech. Revise your outline as appropriate in light of the discussion that follows.
2. Select one of the speeches from Appendix B and prepare a formal outline of it. Does this outline clarify the structure of the speech? Does it reveal any structural flaws? Can you see any different ways the speaker might have developed the speech? Present your thoughts on these questions in class discussion.

Application

1. Thinking back to the last round of speeches you heard in your class, come up with titles for three of them that could be used in advance advertising to attract an audience.
2. See if you can "unjumble" the following outline of the body of a speech using the principles of coordination and subordination. What title would you suggest for this speech?

   Thesis statement: Deer hunting with a camera can be an exciting sport.

I. There is a profound quiet, a sense of mystery.
   A. The woods in late fall are enchanting.
      1. The film-hunter becomes part of a beautiful scene.
      2. Dawn is especially lovely.
   B. Time that a big doe walked under my tree stand.
      1. When they appear, deer always surprise you.
      2. How a big buck surprised me after a long stalk.

II. Hunting from a stand can be a good way to capture a deer on film.
    A. The stalk method on the ground is another way to hunt with a camera.
        1. Learn to recognize deer tracks and droppings.
            a. Learn to recognize deer signs
            b. Learn to recognize rubs and scrapes.
        2. Hunt into the wind and move slowly.
    B. There are two main ways to hunt with a camera.
        1. Stands offer elevation above the deer's line of sight.
        2. Portable stands are also available.
        3. Locating and building your permanent stand.

III. The right camera can be no more expensive than a rifle.
    A. Selecting the right camera for film-hunting is important.
    B. Certain features, such as a zoom lens, are necessary.

IV. Display slide of doe.
    A. You can collect "trophies" you can enjoy forever.
    B. Display slide of buck.
    C. You can also use a camcorder.
    D. Not all hunters are killers.
    E. The film-hunter celebrates life, not death.

Notes

1. Robert DiYanni and Pat C. Hoy II, *The Scribner Handbook for Writers* (Needham Heights, Mass.: Allyn and Bacon, 1995), p. 14.
2. Douglas Hunt, *The Riverside Guide to Writing,* 2nd ed. (Boston: Houghton Mifflin, 1995), pp. 503–504.
3. Ibid., p. 503.
4. Robert T. Oliver, Harold P. Zelko, and Paul D. Holtzman, *Communicative Speaking and Listening* (New York: Holt, Rinehart and Winston, 1968), p. 125.
5. This suggestion is consistent with DiYanni and Hoy's advice that the "outline is used primarily to organize the difficult middle portion of an essay" (p. 14).

Life in the Greenhouse

Joshua Logan

■ ***Note how the source citations become "oral footnotes," which make the speech authoritative and strengthen the speaker's ethos, which is important when the topic is technical. They are especially numerous near the beginning of the speech, where they help establish credibility.***

■ ***Note that Joshua does not provide a preview. He was concerned that such a statement might sound mechanical. His strategy was to hope that the speech would be clear if he identified the three causes of the greenhouse effect as his speech developed.***

■ ***To keep his speech from becoming too technical, Joshua uses brief comparisons to help listeners understand and create vivid word-pictures, like "a huge iceball suspended in space."***

■ ***Note how the speech uses repetition to emphasize the importance of a critical fact. In his actual presentation, Joshua varied his vocal pattern so that he presented the italicized sentence slowly and forcefully.***

Since you have watched the "greenhouse effect" speech develop from its beginnings, we thought you might like to see the final product. Here is a text of the speech as it was presented by Joshua Logan, a student at the University of Memphis. Note how the outlined body of Josh's speech transformed into a text that reached out to its listeners.

Almost twenty years ago, environmentalists urged scientists to look to Antarctica for signs of what they called the runaway "greenhouse effect"—the rapid warming of the earth because of human activity. Right on cue, during the winter of 1995, *Time* magazine reported that a gigantic iceberg—23 miles wide and 48 miles long, almost as large as the state of Rhode Island—broke off the Larsen Ice Shelf in the Antarctic Peninsula. More than this, the whole Ice Shelf is crumbling. Rudolfo Del Valle, director of geoscience at the Argentine Antarctic Institute, told *Newsweek* that it "looked liked polystyrene that had been broken by a little boy." The elephant seals that once thrived nearby have now vanished, reports *U.S. News & World Report* in its February 2000 issue.

These are ominous signs for our future. They are symptoms of global warming—that great calamity that now threatens to turn the whole Earth into one gigantic hothouse. According to the authoritative *Summary for Policymakers,* provided by the United Nations Intergovernmental Panel on Climate Change, the 1990s were the warmest decade of the past thousand years, and 1998 in particular was the hottest year of the millennium. Reporting the views of hundreds of the world's foremost environmental scientists, the IPCC warns of a world in which rising temperatures will transform green places into deserts, displace great masses of people, destroy coastal areas with rising seas, cause massive epidemics of disease, eliminate many species of plants and animals—and generally raise hell with all living things.

If we want to rein in global warming—and I can't imagine us not wanting to—we must first understand this runaway "greenhouse effect." That's my purpose today—I want to pass along what I've learned about "Life in the Greenhouse," and hopefully add to your knowledge of how we might cope with it.

So what is this greenhouse effect? First of all, there's nothing wrong with a healthy dose of it. As a matter of fact, it makes our planet livable. Certain gases that collect naturally in the atmosphere trap the sun's heat: this natural "greenhouse effect" helps keep the Earth's average temperature at a comfortable average of 59° Fahrenheit. Without these natural greenhouse gases, the Earth would be about 0° Fahrenheit—like a huge iceball suspended in space.

So how did the greenhouse effect become such a problem? That's where *we* enter the picture. Much of what we do, especially those of us in the highly industrialized nations, changes the order of nature. We are responsible for adding enormous amounts of carbon dioxide, methane, and nitrous oxides to this natural canopy of gases. Each year, according to *Science News,* five tons of carbon are pumped into the atmosphere for each man, woman, and child in the United States. You heard me right: *that's five tons for each and every one of us!* It's no accident that the 1990s were the hottest decade on record!

So just what has thrown nature out of balance? Let's examine the major causes, one by one. The first is the loss of woodlands that convert carbon dioxide into oxygen. One football field sized area of forest is lost every second from cutting, clearing, or burning. Significant forest loss occurs in the rain forests in Central and South America, where teak and mahogany are logged for furniture and houses. But it also occurs in this country and elsewhere as developers clear more and more land for more and more people. The wide-scale burning of these forests in places like Indonesia to clear land for farming and housing further compounds the problem. From these vast burning fields huge clouds of smoke choked with carbon dioxide rise into our atmosphere. Altogether, according to *Time*'s "Earth Day" special edition, deforestation accounts for about 20 percent of the problem we face with runaway greenhouse gases.

■ ***Stylistic devices are important here: the comparison to a "football field" helps bring the magnitude of the problem into focus. "Vast burning fields," "huge clouds of smoke," and descriptions of cattle as "living, belching methane factories" touch off ugly pictures in listeners' minds.***

An even greater cause of the greenhouse effect—according to *Time*'s special report on global warming—is agricultural and industrial emissions. They occur on farms, where frequent tilling of the earth releases carbon dioxide into the atmosphere. They occur on rice farms, where frequent flooding and the wrong uses of fertilizer add methane to the noxious mix. They occur on cattle ranches, where feeding cows the wrong food can transform them into living, belching methane factories.

The picture for industrial emissions is just as ugly. The smokestack has become the icon of our times. As we burn more and more fossil fuels in our desperate quest for energy, we release larger and larger amounts of carbon dioxide into the atmosphere. Fleets of trucks and flocks of airplanes swell the canopy of gas and magnify the heat.

And the greenhouse effect continues to grow! Every day, more and more third world nations become more and more industrialized, and use more and more fuel. But, guess what? We Americans are the worst offenders. We have only 5 percent of the world's population, but we use 26 percent of the world's oil, release 26 percent of the world's nitrogen oxide, and produce 22 percent of the world's carbon dioxide emissions. We are the world's greatest energy hogs!

■ ***Here Joshua uses striking statistics leading to an even more striking conclusion. Better documentation of these facts would have made them even more effective.***

The good news in all this is that we could do much better. Better agricultural and industrial practices are available to us, if only we have the will—personally and as a nation.

All of this leads us to the last and greatest cause of the runaway greenhouse effect—ourselves! *Personal energy consumption is the single most important cause of the greenhouse effect.* The more of us there are, especially in industrialized countries, the more energy we consume. And here's another point: as populations grow and as living standards rise around the world, more people develop greater expectations—they want to live the good life. If you multiply more people times rising expectations, you can see what this means for energy consumption—and for the greenhouse effect!

According to the U.S. Department of Energy, 90 percent of America's personal energy consumption comes from fossil fuels. In 1950 there were 40 million cars in the U.S. Today there are more than three times that many cars on our roads, many of them SUVs. Too many gas guzzlers, too many energy hogs! We are paying a big environmental price by driving too much and keeping our houses too hot in the winter and too cold in the summer.

In conclusion, if you want to understand why global warming has become one of the great crises of our time, you've simply got to step outside into the greenhouse. Listen for the falling trees, watch the industrial smokestacks darkening the sky, and smell that rich bouquet of exhaust fumes that we are constantly pumping into the air. The greenhouse effect is a monster we all are creating. And if we don't stop, we, our children, and their children face an ominous future. Generations to come may well ask of us: "Why did they carelessly, willfully, ignorantly allow this to happen to our world? Why did they poison planet Earth?"

■ ***Instead of a bare summary, such as "Today I've shown you three causes of the greenhouse effect . . . ," Joshua concludes by inviting his audience to "listen," "watch," and "smell,"—reminding them of the major causes while challenging them to use their senses to verify the problem.***

Developing Presentation Skills

PART III

11 Presentation Aids

This chapter will help you

- appreciate how presentation aids can benefit you
- understand which presentation aids work best in different situations
- plan, design, and prepare presentation aids
- make PowerPoint presentations

OUTLINE

Seeing . . . most of all the senses, makes us know and brings to light many differences between things.

ARISTOTLE

Imagine that during your summer vacations you run a small landscaping business. Most of your work has come from neighbors who want you to mow their grass and carry off trash. To attract new business, you posted notices on a community bulletin board. You have just gotten a call from a small company asking you to present a landscaping plan for its property next week. You will be competing against other, better-established landscaping companies.

If you want to have a shot at the contract, you will need some well-designed presentation aids to use as you introduce your plan. You could construct a model that shows the building and proposed landscaping. If that isn't feasible, you could draw sketches that show your plan and have these made into slides or transparencies. If the proper equipment is available, you could make a computer-assisted presentation. Regardless of the method you choose, without some type of presentation aids you won't stand a chance against the competition.

With the advent of computer technologies, the types and uses of presentation aids are multiplying rapidly. In this chapter, we describe both the traditional and new kinds of presentation aids, identify the ways they can be used in speeches, offer suggestions for preparing them, and present guidelines for their use.

You should use presentation aids only when they increase the clarity and effectiveness of your speech. As you read this chapter, you will notice that certain suggestions are repeated time and again: Keep things simple and be consistent! These considerations are primary to whatever type of presentation aid you use.

Go to **Video-Lab Drill 5.3** and watch the student speech. Is the use of a presentation aid in the introduction effective?

VideoLab

The Pros and Cons of Presentation Aids

Presentation aids give your audience direct sensory contact with your message. When properly prepared and used, they can help speeches in many different ways. But if they are used improperly, they can become a liability. Figure 11.1 summarizes the advantages and disadvantages of using presentation aids.

Advantages of Presentation Aids

The strength of presentation aids results from a certain weakness of words as communication tools. As powerful as words can be, they are essentially abstract. They represent objects and ideas, but they are not the objects and ideas they represent. Thus, words can create a barrier of abstraction between listeners and reality. Imagine how hard it would be through words alone to describe the carburetor system of a car. Even with models or charts, such a speech would still be difficult for many of us to comprehend. It can require both words and presentation aids, skillfully used together, to explain some topics to some audiences. The concreteness of presentation aids makes possible certain specific advantages:

- *Presentation aids enhance understanding.* As we noted, words are abstractions that listeners transform into mental images. Different listeners may conjure up different mental images for the same words. Some of these images may not be consistent with what you intend. As a speaker, you have less control over these images through words alone than you do when you present both words and visuals that augment them. Moreover, it is easier to give directions to someone when there is a map that both of you can see. It is easier to explain the steps in a process when listeners are shown the steps on a numbered list or in a flow chart.
- *Good presentation aids make your presentation memorable.* Recent research suggests that audiences recall an informative presentation better when visuals are used and that recall is even better when the visuals are in high-quality color.[1] Other research suggests that we typically remember only 20 percent of what we hear, but if we *both hear and see* something, we remember more than 50 percent.[2] Presentation aids are easier to remember than words, again because of their concreteness. A photograph of a hungry child may linger in our memories, increasing the influence of a speech urging charitable contributions. Similarly, we may remember the bright red markings on a map that indicate dangerous places.
- *Presentation aids help establish the authenticity of your words.* When you show listeners what you are talking about, you demonstrate that it actually exists. This type of evidence is important in both informative and persuasive mes-

Figure 11.1

Major Advantages and Disadvantages of Presentation Aids

Advantages	Disadvantages
1. Enhance understanding	*1.* Distract listeners
2. Make message memorable	*2.* Distract speaker
3. Establish authenticity	*3.* Reduce eye contact
4. Improve your credibility	*4.* Damage credibility if sloppy
5. Improve delivery	*5.* Take time to prepare
6. Add variety and interest	*6.* Depend on equipment availability

sages. If your audience can actually see the differences between videotapes and DVDs, they are more likely to be convinced that one is better than the other.

- *Neat, attractively designed presentation aids enhance your credibility as a speaker.* They tell the audience that you put extra effort into preparing your speech. Speakers who use presentation aids are judged to be more professional, better prepared, more credible, more interesting, more concrete, and more persuasive than speakers who do not use such aids.[3] In some organizational settings, audiences expect speakers to use presentation aids, such as PowerPoint. If you don't have them, the audience may be disappointed, and your credibility may suffer.
- *Presentation aids can also help improve your delivery skills,* which in turn can further enhance your credibility. Using a presentation aid in a speech encourages movement as you point out the specific features of an aid. Movement energizes a speech. It gets you away from the "stand behind the lectern/talking head" mode of delivery that many audiences find boring. If you have problems with communication apprehension, purposeful movement—such as pointing to something on an aid—provides a constructive outlet for nervous energy. It directs your attention away from yourself and away from your problem.
- Finally, *presentation aids add variety and interest to a speech.* Too much of a good thing, even a well-fashioned fabric of words, can seem tedious. Just as pictures and boxed materials may be used to break up long stretches of text in a book, presentation aids can be used to break up long stretches of words in a speech. Variety creates interest and helps sustain or recapture attention.

When using a presentation aid, try not to turn your back to the audience or you will lose eye contact and be less effective as a speaker.

Disadvantages of Presentation Aids

Occasionally, presentation aids can do your speech more harm than good. It is important to recognize these potential problems so that you can plan to avoid them or lessen their impact.

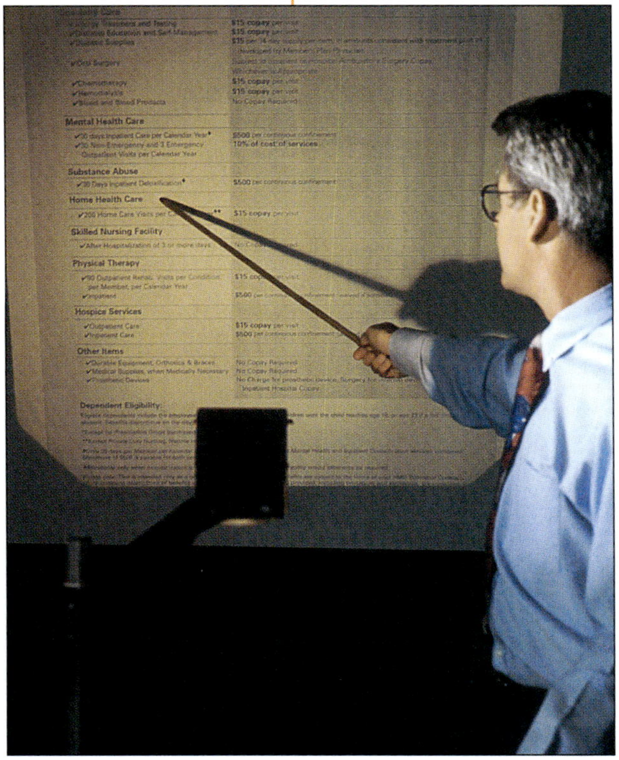

- *Presentation aids can distract listeners.* They can divert attention from your message if they are not used properly, or if you use too many presentation aids in a speech. For example, if an aid is difficult for listeners to read, they may strain to see it and not listen to what you are saying. You may encounter similar problems of distraction if you pass around objects or pictures during a speech, or if you distribute handouts before speaking. Listeners may become so engrossed in your presentation aids that they ignore your real message.

  An especially unusual presentation aid can upstage a speaker completely. We once had a student who was a volunteer with the local rescue squad. He gave a persuasive speech urging his classmates to volunteer. After his introduction, he announced, "Now we are all going outside." When we got outside, we were greeted by the sight of an emergency vehicle. While the speaker tried to tell his audience about the equipment, they were climbing in and out of the vehicle. He lost their attention completely and was never able to complete his speech. Don't make this type of mistake. Keep the focus on the words of your message, not your presentation aid.

- *Presentation aids can also distract speakers.* If you haven't rehearsed your speech using your presentation aid, you may get so caught up worrying about how you are going to use it that you lose track of what you are saying. If you are not confident in your ability to use electronic equipment, this uneasiness may show up in your presentation. If something goes awry with the equipment, it might throw you off course.
- *Using presentation aids can inhibit eye contact between the speaker and the audience.* Remember, eye contact is very important to an effective presentation. If you talk to your charts, graphs, or pictures rather than to your listeners, you will lose effectiveness.
- Although a good presentation aid can improve ethos, the reverse is also true: *a bad presentation aid can damage your credibility.* If your aid is sloppy, poorly prepared, or inaccurate, your credibility will suffer. Listeners may think you did not care enough about your presentation to invest the time and effort needed to prepare an effective presentation aid. Worse still, they may think you are incapable of preparing one. Be careful. If you are artistically challenged, use all the tools available to put together an attractive and effective presentation aid.

Watch the speech and answer the questions in **VideoLab Lesson 6 Next Step: Evaluating the Use of Presentation Aids.** VideoLab

- *Presentation aids take time to prepare.* As you research your speech, be alert for material that you might use as a presentation aid. Allow yourself enough time to do a good job preparing these materials. Don't forget to practice using your aids until you can integrate them seamlessly into your presentation.
- *Presentation aids put you at the mercy of the available equipment.* If the speech site is not equipped to handle computerized presentation aids, then you must rely on other forms. Be sure you know in advance what kind of equipment is available. Also be sure you know how to use the equipment and have a plan to fall back on in case anything goes wrong.

InterConnections.LearnMore 11.1

Presentation Aids

Communicate Using Technology
http://www.communicateusingtechnology.com/presenting_using_technology_articles.htm
Contains a variety of how-to articles for technology-enhanced presentations. Presents good, practical advice for beginning or advanced speakers who wish to improve their presentations. Developed and maintained by Dave Paradi, communicating with technology specialist.

Designing Effective Visuals
http://www.kumc.edu/SAH/OTEd/jradel/Effective_visuals/VisStrt.html
An online tutorial designed to help medical personnel make better oral presentations. Contains guidelines for deciding which presentation aids to use and how to maximize their visual impact. Designed and maintained by Jeff Radel, professor in the Department of Occupational Therapy Education, University of Kansas Medical Center.

Virtual Presentation Assistant
http://www.ukans.edu/cwis/units/coms2/vpa/vpa7.htm
This website offers concise guidelines for developing and using visual aids in presentations. Developed and maintained by the Communication Studies Department of the University of Kansas.

Types of Presentation Aids

The number and types of presentation aids are limited only by your imagination. We shall examine some of the more frequently used kinds and the situations in which they are most helpful.

People

As a speaker, you cannot avoid being a presentation aid for your own speech. Your body, grooming, actions, gestures, voice, facial expressions, and demeanor provide an added dimension to your speech. It follows also that what you wear for a presentation can be important. If you will be speaking about camping and wilderness adventures, blue jeans and a flannel shirt might be appropriate. If you are a nurse discussing a medical topic, your uniform might enhance your credibility. If you are talking about how to dress for an employment interview, your professional attire should illustrate your recommendations. We discuss the importance of personal appearance in more detail in Chapter 13.

You can also use other people as presentation aids. John Kache was a freshman in college when he contracted meningococcal meningitis, a life-threatening disease for which immunizations are available. John survived his illness, but he lost his right leg and all of the fingers on his hands. After he recovered, he spoke often at high schools, urging students to get their shots before they went off to college. Typically, he would use a volunteer from the audience to demonstrate what life without fingers was like for him. As he put it, "I'd wrap up one of the student's hands in an Ace bandage, then throw him a bag of candy and tell him to open it and pass the candies around."[4] This dramatic demonstration brought home to listeners the seriousness of this disease and the importance of being immunized.

Your use of people as a presentation aid need not be this dramatic to be effective. One of our students, Neomal Abyskera, used two of his classmates to illustrate the lineup positions in the game of rugger, as played in his native Sri Lanka. At the appropriate moment, Neomal said, "Pete and Jeff will show you how the opposing players line up." While his classmates demonstrated the shoulder grip position, Neomal explained when and why the position was assumed. The demonstration was more understandable than if he had simply tried to describe the positioning verbally.

The people you ask to function as a presentation aid should be willing to do so. They should understand that their role is to illustrate your message, not draw attention away from it, and should also agree to meet with you to rehearse the presentation. They should sit in the front row so that as you stand to speak they can come forward, participate in the demonstration, and then sit down quickly.

Objects and Models

Presenting the actual objects you are discussing can magnify your listeners' attention and understanding and add a great deal of authenticity to your speech. However, if using actual objects presents difficulties, models may be a better option.

Objects. If you are speaking about something portable that all listeners can see without straining, then you can use the object itself as a presentation aid. You should also be able to keep the object out of sight until it is time to use it. If you display the object throughout your speech, listeners may focus on it rather than on your message. If you plan to use more than one object, display them one at a time, and then conceal them as you finish using them. A student of ours once brought in six different types of materials used in a Montessori preschool. She lined them up across the front of the desk before she began to speak. One classmate in the front row was so intrigued with the objects that he actually scooted his chair closer to the desk and picked up one of them to examine it. She then had to stop and ask him to put it back. Had she concealed the objects until she was ready to use them, this problem would have been averted.

Living things used as presentation aids can present certain problems.

Inanimate objects work better than living things, which you can't always control. We once had a student bring a six-week-old puppy to use in a speech on caring for young animals. At the beginning of her speech, she removed the lectern from the speaker's table, spread out some newspapers, and placed the puppy on the table. We are sure you have already guessed what happened. The first thing the puppy did was wet on the papers (including her note cards, which she laid on the table while trying to control the puppy). The first thing the audience did was giggle. From there it was all downhill. The puppy squirmed and tried to jump on the speaker while yipping and barking throughout the speech. The speaker was totally upstaged by her presentation aid. When this fiasco was over, we asked her why she had brought the puppy to class. She said she thought that because she was talking about animals, it would be nice to bring one along.

Problems also can arise when presentation aids are used to shock the audience into attention. *Objects that are dangerous, illegal, or potentially offensive, such as guns, drugs, or pornography, must not be used in classroom speeches.* Even replicas of such materials can cause problems. One of our students brandished a very realistic-looking "toy" semiautomatic weapon that he pulled from beneath the lectern during the introduction of a speech on gun control. Several audience members became so upset that they could not concentrate on his message.

Another student was more successful at shocking the audience into attention with a presentation aid. At the beginning of a speech on regulating the sale of tobacco products to minors, Allison McIntyre held up a gallon jar of cigarette butts that she had collected on the Vanderbilt campus right outside her classroom building. Although the spectacle was rather gross, it did grab our attention and reinforced the meaning of her message. The lesson here is, be careful. If you have questions about the propriety of an object, check with your instructor.

Objects are often used in "how-to" speeches. Indeed, such speeches often cannot succeed without presentation aids that help instruct listeners on procedures. An engaging example of this type of usage occurred near Halloween in a speech on jack-o'-lanterns, both how to make them and the folklore behind them. The speaker demonstrated how to draw the face on a pumpkin with a felt marker and how to make a beveled cut around the stem so that the top wouldn't fall in. As she was showing her listeners how to do these things, she was also telling stories of the ancient myths surrounding jack-o'-lanterns. Her presentation aid and her words helped each other: the demonstration enlivened her speech, and the stories gave the demonstration depth and meaning. As she came to her closing remarks, she reached inside the lectern and produced a finished jack-o'-lantern complete with a lighted candle. The effect was memorable.

Models. When an object is too large to carry, too small to be easily seen, very rare, expensive, or fragile, or simply unavailable, a replica of the object can work well as a presentation aid. George Stacey brought a slightly smaller-than-life-sized model of a person to demonstrate cardiopulmonary resuscitation (CPR). The model folded into a suitcase so that it could be kept out of sight when not in use.

When using a model as a presentation aid, be sure that it is truly representative. It should be constructed to scale, maintaining the proper proportions among parts. The model should also be large enough for all listeners to see from their seats. Any presentation aid that the audience must strain to see will be more of a distraction than a help.

Graphics

Graphics are visual representations of information and include sketches, maps, graphs, charts, and textual materials. Because graphics will be displayed for only a short time during your speech, they must be instantly clear. They must be simpler than graphics designed for print, which readers can study at their leisure. Each graphic should focus on one idea. Because they will be viewed from a distance, the colors should be intense and should contrast sharply with the background. We will cover such considerations more fully under "Preparing Presentation Aids" later in this chapter. Graphics may be prepared on poster board or on computers for use as overhead projections or slide presentations.

Graphs and charts are often used as presentation aids in speeches.

Sketches. Sketches are simplified representations of what you are talking about. If you don't draw well, search children's coloring books for drawings that you can trace. Make the sketch first on paper; then enlarge it or transfer it onto a transparency with a copier. You can also make sketches using clip art or the drawing program on a computer. One of our students, Mark Peterson, used a sketch that he had transferred to a transparency to illustrate the measurements one should take before buying a bicycle. While talking about making bar-to-pedal and seat-to-handlebar measurements, he pointed to them as he said, "Let me show you how to take some basic measurements."

Maps. Commercially prepared maps contain too much detail to use as presentation aids. The best maps are those that you make specifically for your speech so that they are simple, relevant to your purpose, and uncluttered. Maps are particularly useful for speeches based on spatial relationships.

The map in Figure 11.2 was used in a classroom speech to show the route between major attractions at Yellowstone National Park. Seeing such a map helps the audience put locations and distances into perspective. Student speaker Stephen Huff

Figure 11.2
Map of Yellowstone Park

used a simplified map to help his listeners see where a series of earthquakes occurred along the New Madrid fault and to understand how a recurrence of such earthquakes might endanger his Memphis classmates.

Whether a map works well as a presentation aid depends on how effectively you integrate it into your presentation. Student speaker Elizabeth Walling used a map of the wilderness canoe area in northern Minnesota to familiarize her Memphis audience with that area. She made a double-sided poster that she was able to keep hidden behind the speaker's table until she was ready for it. On one side she highlighted the wilderness canoe area on an outline map of northern Minnesota, pointing out various places of interest. To illustrate how large the area is, Elizabeth said, "Let me put this in a more familiar context for you." She then turned the poster over, revealing an outline map of western Tennessee on which she had superimposed the wilderness area. At a glance, we could see that the area would extend from Memphis to past Jackson, Tennessee, some eighty miles away. Elizabeth's artful use of the two maps had created a striking visual comparison. The same type of effect can be obtained by overlaying transparencies.

Graphs. Mrs. Robert A. Taft, wife of a prominent senator and lioness of Washington society, once commented, "I always find that statistics are hard to swallow and impossible to digest. The only one I can ever remember is that if all the people who go to sleep in church were laid end to end, they would be a lot more comfortable."[5] Many people share Mrs. Taft's feelings about statistics. As we noted in Chapter 8, masses of numbers presented orally can be overwhelming. But a well-designed graph can make statistical information easier for listeners to understand.

A **pie graph** shows the size of a subject's parts in relation to one another and to the whole. The "pie" represents the whole, and the "slices" represent the parts. The segments or slices are percentages of the whole and must add up to 100. The most effective pie graphs have six or less segments. Too many segments make the graph difficult to read. The pie graph in Figure 11.3 shows Internet users' perceptions of the reliability of information from Internet websites.

A **bar graph** shows comparisons and contrasts between two or more items or groups. Bar graphs are easy to understand because each item can be readily compared with every other item on the graph. Bar graphs can also have a dramatic visual impact, especially when they make use of **pictographs** (symbolic representations) in place of the bars. Figure 11.4 is a bar graph that uses police hats to present the results of a Gallup poll comparing how confident Americans are in law enforcement agencies, ranging from local police to the CIA.

Figure 11.3

Sample Pie Graph: Perceptions of Internet Information Reliability

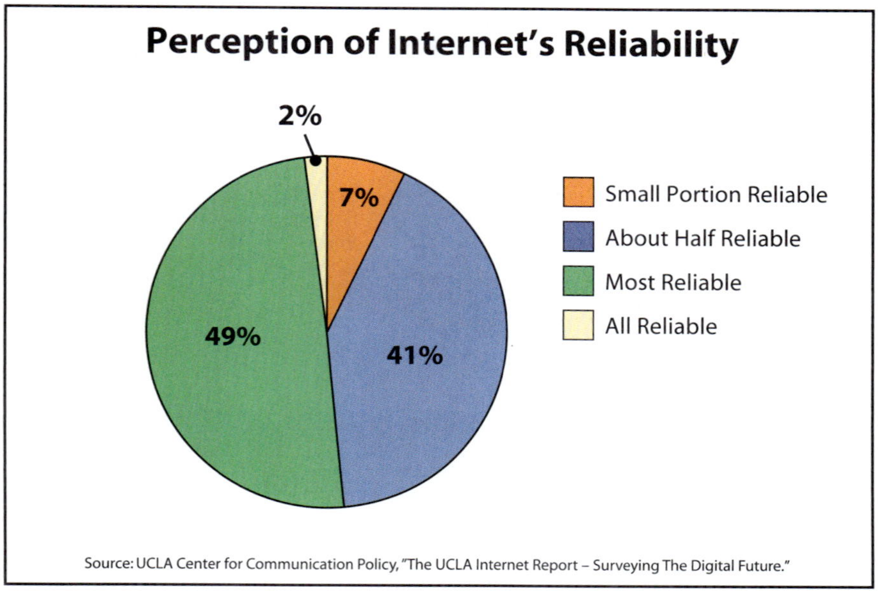

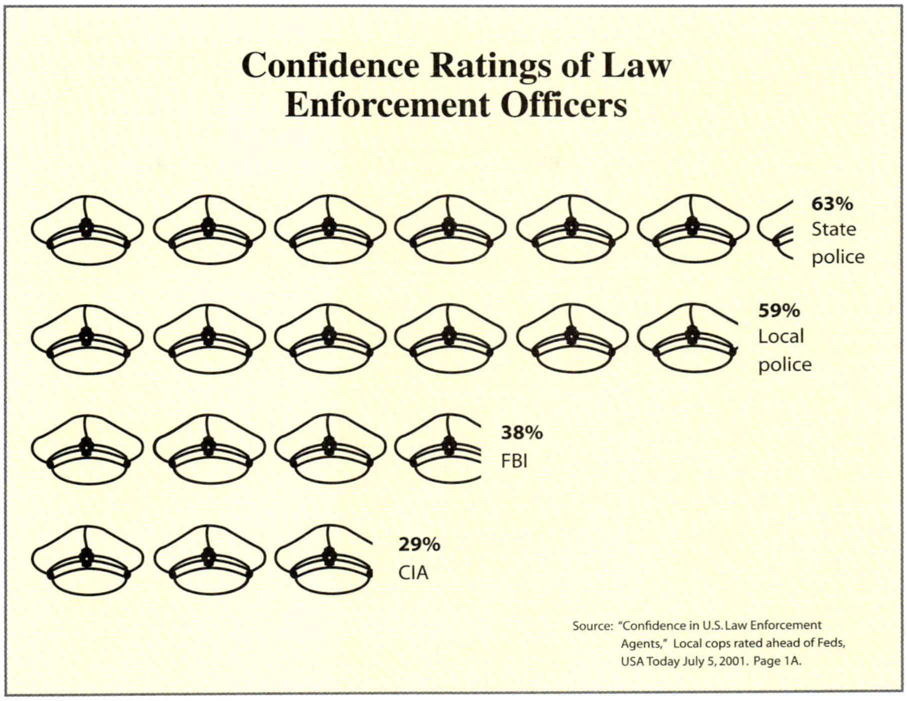

Figure 11.4

Sample Bar Graph: Confidence in U.S. Law Enforcement Agents

A **line graph** demonstrates changes across time, and it is especially useful for indicating trends in growth or decline. Figure 11.5 shows the number of college graduates by gender from 1950 through 2000. The upward-sloping lines confirm the dramatic increases in the numbers of both male and female graduates across this span of time. When you plot more than one line on a graph, use different colors. To avoid confusing listeners, never try to plot more than three lines on a graph.

Charts. Charts provide visual summaries of processes and relationships that are not in themselves visible. In print communications charts can be quite complex: the challenge to the speaker is to simplify them without distorting their meaning, so that they meet the needs of oral communication. The listener must be able to understand them instantly and to read them from a distance.

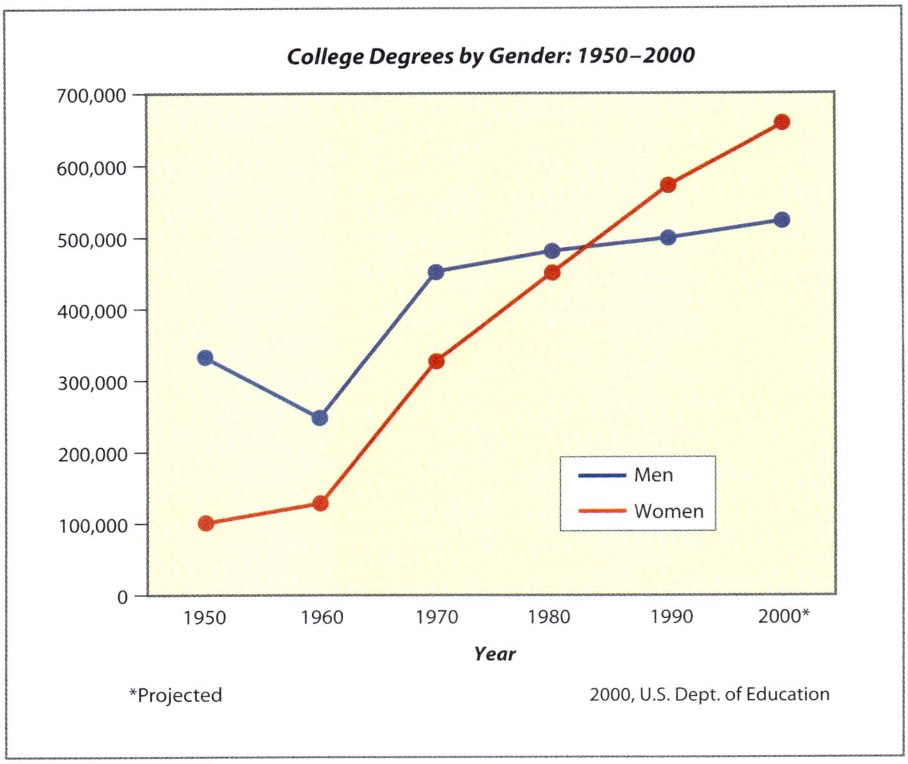

Figure 11.5

Sample Line Graph: College Graduation by Gender 1950–2000

Figure 11.6

Flow Chart: Major Steps in the Preparation of a Speech

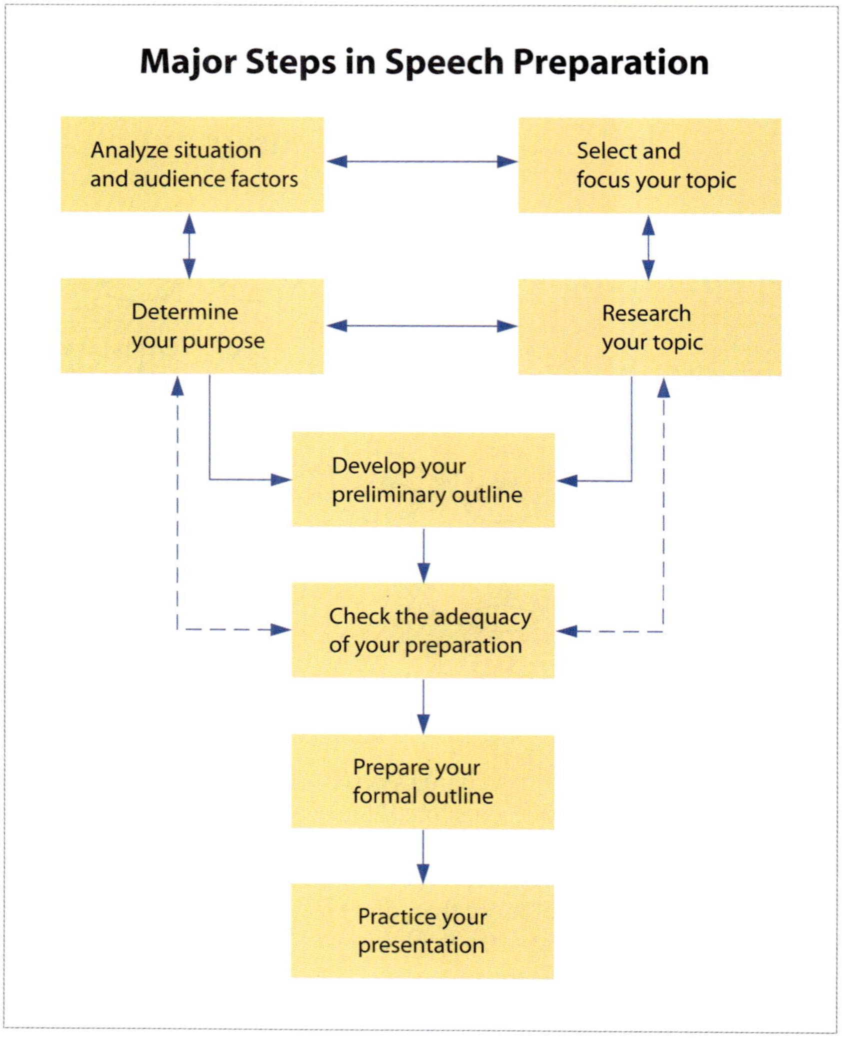

One frequently used type of chart is a flow chart. A **flow chart** can show the steps in a process, the hierarchy and accountability in an organization, or the genealogy of a family tree. In a flow chart that explains a process, the lines and arrows indicate what steps occur simultaneously and what steps occur sequentially. Figure 11.6 is a flow chart that illustrates the major steps in the preparation of a speech. Notice the double-ended arrows in this chart, which suggest that a speaker works back and forth between the steps.

A problem that often arises when charts are used in oral communication is that speakers may be tempted to load them with too much information. Too much material on a chart invites the audience to read rather than listen. If charts are "busy" or complicated, they compete with the speaker for attention and may confuse instead of enlighten listeners. One way around this problem is to use **sequence charts**, which are presented in succession. For example, you might choose to illustrate information on the awarding of college degrees by gender in a series of charts. Figure 11.7 reveals the first and last charts in a series showing degrees by gender across the years. It is a different way of illustrating the same information shown in the line graph (Figure 11.5). In the first chart, the pictograph of a man is three times larger than that of a woman, representing the 3:1 ratio in earned degrees during 1950. The second chart uses the pictographs to underscore the dramatic reversal of this ratio: in 2000 women actually received more degrees than did men. Intermediate charts for decade years could show the more gradual changes in the relative sizes of these figures as the trend developed.

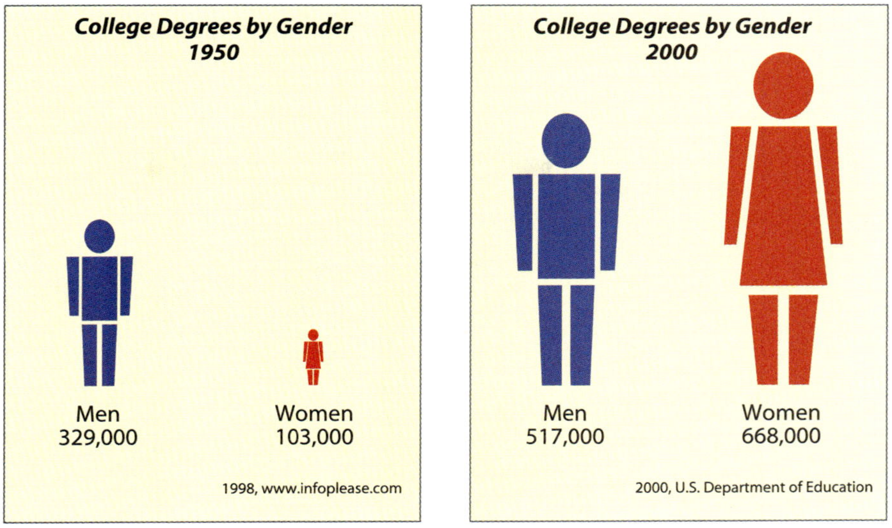

Figure 11.7
Sample Sequence Charts

Textual Graphics. **Textual graphics** are lists of words, phrases, or numbers. Unfamiliar material is clearer and easier for listeners to remember when they can both hear and see the message. Presenting the key words in a message visually can help an audience follow complicated ideas more easily. For example, in an informative speech that describes a process, you might show a sequence of posters or slides identifying each step in the process, with a number identifying the step and a key word or phrase that describes what happens in the particular step. That way you could guide your audience through the main points of your speech.

The most frequently used textual graphics contain **bulleted lists** of information such as that shown in the computer-generated slide in Figure 11.8. When you make a bulleted list, begin with a title, and then place the material under it. Keep the graphic simple. Use intense colors with good contrast. To adapt this technique to the speaking situation, have no more than six lines of information and no more than six words to a line.

Another frequently used type of textual graphic presents an **acronym** composed of the initial letters of words to help your audience remember your message. The transparency in Figure 11.9 used the acronym EMILY in a persuasive speech urging students to begin saving early for retirement. When preparing such a graphic, use the acronym as a title; then list the words under it. Use size and/or color to make the first letters of the words stand out.

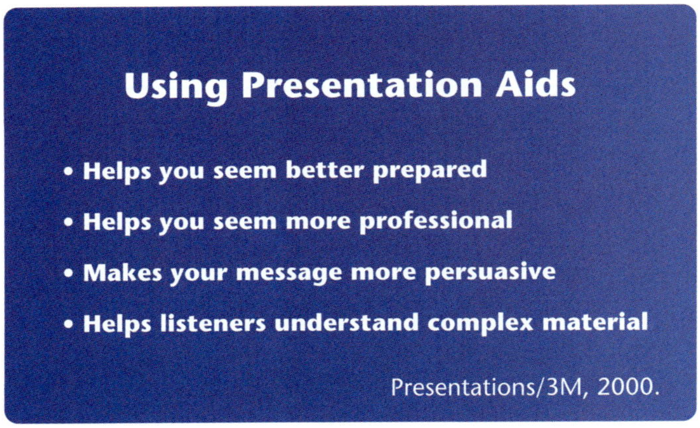

Figure 11.8
Sample Bulleted List

Figure 11.9
Acronym Graphic

EMILY

EARLY
MONEY
IS
LIKE
YEAST

IT MAKES DOUGH GROW!

Textual graphics may also be used to present numerical information. When you use a textual graphic to present numbers, you should keep it very simple. Have no more than three columns and five rows. Textual graphics designed for handouts can contain more information, but not so much that they compete with your words for attention. Figure 11.10 illustrates a simple numerical graphic.

Pictures

Although pictures may indeed be "worth more than a thousand words" in some situations, it is also true that pictures and photographs are difficult to use effectively in speeches unless you have the proper projection equipment. Small photographs will be difficult for anyone beyond the first row to see, and passing them around during

Figure 11.10
Numerical Graphic

INVESTMENT GROWTH
$1,000 – 8%

5 years	$1,469
10 years	$2,159
15 years	$3,172
20 years	$4,666

Berger, *Feathering Your Nest*, 1995.

Figure 11.11

Photos of Glacier National Park

These two photos illustrate the dramatic reduction in size of the glacier at Glacier National Park between 1910 and 1997.

a presentation can be a major distraction. Moreover, speakers may rely too heavily on the pictures, forgetting that words are the primary means of communication in a speech. Pictures that are disturbing can also be distracting. One student who was a paramedic showed pictures of child abuse victims taken in a local emergency room. Some members of the audience became so upset that they were not able to concentrate on her message.

Despite these problems, a good photograph can authenticate a point in a way that words alone cannot. It can make a situation seem more vivid and realistic. For instance, suppose a speaker said, "If present climate conditions continue, the glaciers in Glacier National Park will be gone in thirty years." Would this not be more dramatic and convincing if the speaker showed the photographs in Figure 11.11 to reveal the changes that have already taken place?

Pictures should be selected for their relevance to your speech. They should be controlled just as you control charts and graphs—revealed only to illustrate a point and then put out of sight. Color copiers can make inexpensive eleven-by-seventeen-inch enlargements from snapshots. This is probably the minimally acceptable size for most classroom speeches. Mount pictures on poster board for ease of presentation. Digital photographs can be used as PowerPoint projections or be made into transparencies on most computer printers.

Although running slides of pictures while you are speaking can be a distraction, one student did use this technique very effectively as the background for a speech on capital punishment.[6] The slides were a series of individual color photos of children and adults with the simple caption "Murder Victim" across the bottom. In his speech, the student did not directly refer to the photos as he presented his substantive arguments. They simply served to provide a sense of pathos that framed the logical dimension of his message and demonstrated the authenticity of the problem.

Computerized slide presentations and flip charts are frequently used as presentation aids in business meetings.

Presentation Media

There are many different types of presentation media. Traditional media include flip charts, posters, handouts, chalk or marker boards, transparencies, videotapes, and audiotapes. Newer presentation media use computer programs, such as PowerPoint, that can incorporate slides, films, and sound. These are rapidly becoming the standard for presentations in organizational and educational settings. Let's take a look at the various types of presentation aids.

Flip Charts

A flip chart is a large, unlined tablet. Most flip charts are newsprint pads that measure about two feet wide by three feet high. They are placed on an easel so that each page can be flipped over the top when you are done with it. Flip charts are convenient, inexpensive, and adaptable to many settings. Business meetings, decision-making groups, and organizational training sessions often use flip charts, in addition to more sophisticated types of presentation tools.

Flip charts are designed to be used spontaneously. This makes them especially useful when subjects come up in a meeting that should be written out so that they can be analyzed and understood. When using flip charts, keep each page as simple as possible. Use wide-point felt markers in strong colors, and print or write legibly in large letters.

Although flip charts can be effective in some group communication settings, they seldom work as well in classroom speeches. They often look sloppy, suggesting that the speaker did not care enough to prepare a more polished presentation aid. Writing on a flip chart also forces speakers either to stop speaking or to speak with their backs to the audience. This loss of direct audience contact can offset any gain from using the charts.

Posters

Posters can be used to display sketches, maps, charts, graphs, or textual graphics. In an average-size room with a small audience, posters about fourteen by seventeen inches may work best, because they are easier to handle than larger posters, and easier to see than smaller posters. They can be used for sequence charts with one idea or graphic per board. You can place them face down on the lectern or table and display them as you refer to them. You can also use the back of a poster as a "cheat sheet" that cues you to the next point in your presentation. Be sure to number the posters on the back so that they don't get out of sequence. Keep your posters simple and neat. Use large letters in strong colors that are easy to read. Have a lot of white space. Rehearse your speech using the posters so that you can integrate them smoothly into your presentation.

Handouts

Handouts are useful when your subject is complex or your message contains much statistical information. When the speech is over, listeners have something to remind them of your message.

There is one serious drawback to using handouts: they can distract listeners from what you are saying. If you distribute a handout before you speak, it will compete with you for attention. The audience may decide to read the handout instead of listening to you. Therefore, you should distribute handouts before your speech *only* when it is necessary for listeners to refer to them as you speak. Never distribute handouts during your speech; this is a sure-fire way to divert, confuse, and lose listeners. Multipaged handouts are multidistracting.

Student speaker Dwight Davidson distributed a one-page handout at the beginning of his speech on job trends. His audience was able to follow along with him as he explained the statistical table in the handout. Without this material, his listeners would have been lost. George Stacey distributed a handout listing the steps required for administering CPR *after* his speech on that subject. By waiting until he was finished, he avoided distracting listeners but still helped his audience remember the procedure. Your decision on whether to distribute a handout before or after a speech should be based on the nature of the subject, how confident you are in your ability to control attention, and what you would like your handout to accomplish.

Chalk and Marker Boards

A chalk or marker board is a presentation medium that is available in almost every classroom or corporate conference room. Like flip charts, these boards are best used for spontaneous, unpredictable illustrations and demonstrations. Despite careful preparation, there may be times when you look at your listeners and realize that some of them have not understood what you have just said. One way you can respond to such feedback is by writing a few words on the board or by drawing a simple diagram to help reduce audience confusion.

When you write on a board, use large letters so that people in the back of the room can read them without straining. Write or print legibly. Clear the board before you begin, and, as a courtesy to later speakers, erase the board when you are finished. Because you inevitably lose eye contact with listeners while writing on a board, do not use this medium for anything that will take more than a few seconds to write or draw. Never use chalk or marker boards simply because you did not want to take the time to prepare a polished presentation aid.

Transparencies and Slides

Transparencies and slides allow audiences to see graphics or photographs more easily, especially when audiences are large or spread out in a large room. Business speakers often prefer them to posters or flip charts, because they look more professional.

Transparencies are easier to use than slides, because you don't have to darken the room when you show them. They are simple to make, inexpensive, and adaptable. Another advantage is that you can write on a transparency while it is being shown, thereby adding flexibility and spontaneity to your presentation. You can also use a pencil as a pointer to direct listeners' attention to features you want to emphasize.

When using photographic slides and a traditional carousel projector, the room usually has to be darkened. Unfortunately, this means that the illuminated screen becomes the center of attention instead of you. The major disadvantage of using either transparencies or slides is that often you must speak from where your equipment is located. You may have to stand behind or in the middle of the audience to run the projector. This means you will be talking to someone's back. If you do not have remote-control equipment, your best solution may be to have a classmate change the projections or slides on cue. You will need to practice with your assistant to coordinate the slides with your words.

Most transparencies and slides are now prepared on personal computers. You can purchase transparency sheets for use with most printers. You also can draw or print your material onto plain paper and convert it to a transparency on a copying machine. If you have access to only a black-and-white copier or printer, you can add color with opaque markers.

To prepare materials for use as transparencies, follow the general guidelines presented earlier for the use of graphics. You should frame your transparencies to avoid glare from light showing around the outside edges of the projection. Frames can be purchased at most copy shops or made from construction paper.

When you arrange slides in a carousel, be sure they are in the proper order and that none of them are upside down. Today, most personal computers are packaged with software that allows you to prepare and present slides without a carousel projector. We will discuss this in greater detail in our section on computer-assisted presentations, which follows this chapter.

If you decide to use transparencies or slides, check the equipment ahead of time and become familiar with its operation. You may need a long extension cord to position the equipment where you want it. Practice using the equipment as you rehearse your speech. One final caution: Don't use too many slides or transparencies in a short speech. A presentation aid should do just that—*aid* your speech, not compete with or replace it.

Videotapes, Audiotapes, and Compact Disks

Videotapes, audiotapes, and material on compact disks (CDs, CD-ROMs, DVDs, and MP3s) can authenticate and add variety to your presentation. Be sure in advance that the place where you will be making your presentation has the proper type of equipment to work with your materials.

Videos are especially useful for transporting the audience to distant, dangerous, or otherwise unavailable locations. Although you could verbally describe the beauty of the Montana Rockies, your word-pictures might come to life if reinforced with actual scenes projected electronically.

Using videos on tape or disks can present some special problems. Moving images attract more attention than the spoken word, so they can easily upstage you. Moreover, a videotape segment must be edited so that splices blend without annoying static. Such editing takes special skill and equipment. Transferring this material onto CDs is simpler, easier to handle, and can be done on most personal computers with a DVD/CD burner. Finally, video clips can be difficult to work into a short

Speaker's Notes 11.1

Deciding What Presentation Media to Use

1. Use flip charts and chalk or marker boards as an audience adaptation tool.
2. Use posters to display maps, charts, graphs, or textual graphics.
3. Use handouts to present complex information or statistical data.
4. Use transparencies or slides to show graphics or photos to a large audience.
5. Use audios (tapes, CDs, MP3s) and videos (CDs, CD-ROMs, DVDs) to authenticate a point.
6. Use computerized materials to make your presentation appear more professional.

speech without consuming all of your time. In a short speech, a video clip should be no more than thirty seconds long.

For certain topics, however, carefully prepared videos can be more effective than any other type of presentation aid. One student at Northwest Mississippi Community College, who was a firefighter, used videotape in an informative speech on fire hazards in the home. By customizing the video to fit the precise needs of his speech, he was able to show long shots of a room and then zoom in on various hazards.[7] He prepared the video without sound so that his speech provided the commentary needed to interpret and explain the pictures. Using this technique, he made his subject much more meaningful for listeners.

Audiotapes, audio on CDs, or MP3 files may also be useful as presentation aids. If you wanted to describe the alarm cries of various animals or the songs of different birds, an audiotape could be essential. When in doubt about the wisdom or practicality of using such aids, consult your instructor.

Computer-Assisted Presentations

Most personal computers can generate a wide variety of presentation aids, including sketches, maps, graphs, charts, and textual graphics for handouts, slides, and transparencies. The materials produced on computers are usually much neater and more accurate than those drawn by hand. Presentation software programs, such as PowerPoint, are readily available. Specialized publications sponsored by computer and software manufacturers, such as *Presentations* (http://www.presentations.com/), are available both online and in hard-copy versions. Your campus computer lab may have training programs to help you learn how to use these materials. You may also consult the tutorial that follows this chapter.

Computer-assisted presentations can bring together text, numbers, pictures, music, video clips, and artwork made into slides, videos, animations, and audio materials. Materials such as graphs and charts that are generated with the computer can be changed at any time, even during a presentation. The programs come with a variety of templates to assist you in designing your presentation aids. The templates can be adapted to suit your particular needs.

When using a computer for developing presentation aids, be careful not to get so caught up with the glitz and glitter that you lose sight of the fact that *it is your message that is most important.* In cautioning against the misuse or overuse of such technology, Rebecca Ganzel in *Presentations* magazine pictured the following scenario:

> **It's that nightmare again—the one in which you're trapped in the Electronic Presentation from Hell. The familiar darkness presses in, periodically sliced in half by a fiendish light. Bullet points, about 18 to a slide, careen in all directions. You cringe, but the slides keep coming, too fast to read, each with a new template you half-remember seeing a hundred times before: Dad's Tie! Sixties Swirls! Infinite Double-Helixes! A typewriter clatters; brakes squeal. Somewhere in the shadows, a voice drones on. Strange stick people shake hands and dance around a flowchart. Typefaces morph into Word Art.**
>
> **But the worst is yet to come. As though you're watching a train wreck in slow motion, you look down at your hand—and *you're holding the remote.*[8]**

Using technology in your presentation does not excuse you from the usual requirements for speaking. In fact, if your presentation aids draw more attention than your ideas, they may be a hindrance more than a help. Be especially careful not to get caught up with swirling backgrounds and flashy transitions. *Remember, it is*

InterConnections.LearnMore 11.2

PowerPoint Presentations

Microsoft PowerPoint
http://office.microsoft.com/home/office.aspx?assetid=FX01085797
Microsoft PowerPoint home page; contains links to tips, tricks, how-to articles, and other online course materials.

PowerPoint in the Classroom
http://www.actden.com/pp/
A simple online tutorial that walks you through the basics of preparing a PowerPoint presentation, incorporating all the bells and whistles. A good resource for the technophobic student.

PowerPointers
http://www.powerpointers.com/
A lot of good tips and pointers on using PowerPoint and other presentation software.

PowerPoint Answers
http://www.powerpointanswers.com
A weekly online newsletter with articles, solutions to problems, and resources for PowerPoint users.

better to be subtle than sensational. Follow the general guidelines for developing and using presentation aids put forth in this chapter.

PowerPoint Presentations. More than 90 percent of all computerized presentations in the United States are created by using the PowerPoint program, which is widely distributed as part of the Microsoft Office software.[9] Why is PowerPoint so popular? For starters, it is the most widely available software of its type and is prepackaged on many computers sold to businesses and educational institutions. As we noted earlier, computer-generated presentation aids are neater and more professional looking than those prepared using other materials. PowerPoint is also fairly easy to use. The software contains templates and comes with a step-by-step tutorial. Once you have mastered the basic process, you can generate materials on a moment's notice. If changing situations require altering a presentation aid, you can insert new material quickly and easily. You can even revise a slide or transparency during an actual presentation.

PowerPoint may also be the most frequently misused type of presentation aid. We have all been subject to poor PowerPoint presentations—or will be in the near future, since they are so hard to avoid. Their ease of usage is a double-edged sword. It is too easy to put together a poor PowerPoint presentation that actually annoys an audience and does little to enhance the understanding of a message or the credibility of the presenter. A recent survey conducted by technology specialist Dave Paradi has identified the most annoying elements of PowerPoint presentations:

1. Reading slides to the audience
2. Using text too small to be easily read
3. Writing full sentences instead of bulleted points
4. Making poor color choices that make slides hard to see
5. Using moving or flying text or graphics
6. Interjecting annoying sounds
7. Projecting complex diagrams or charts[10]

Clearly, these are all things a speaker can control. Never let a PowerPoint slide show substitute for your speech. Don't put your speech outline on PowerPoint slides and then read it to the audience. Be sure your material is easy to read. Use a large, plain font and select colors that provide good contrast, such as light on dark or dark on light. Avoid shaded backgrounds that might make some of your print illegible. Keep your materials simple. Limit the amount of information on any slide. Use bulleted points, not full sentences. Don't try to project complex charts or graphs; simplify them or find another format for providing them. Avoid overly dramatic techniques such as flying text and startling sound effects. Figure 11.12 displays a good and a bad PowerPoint slide.

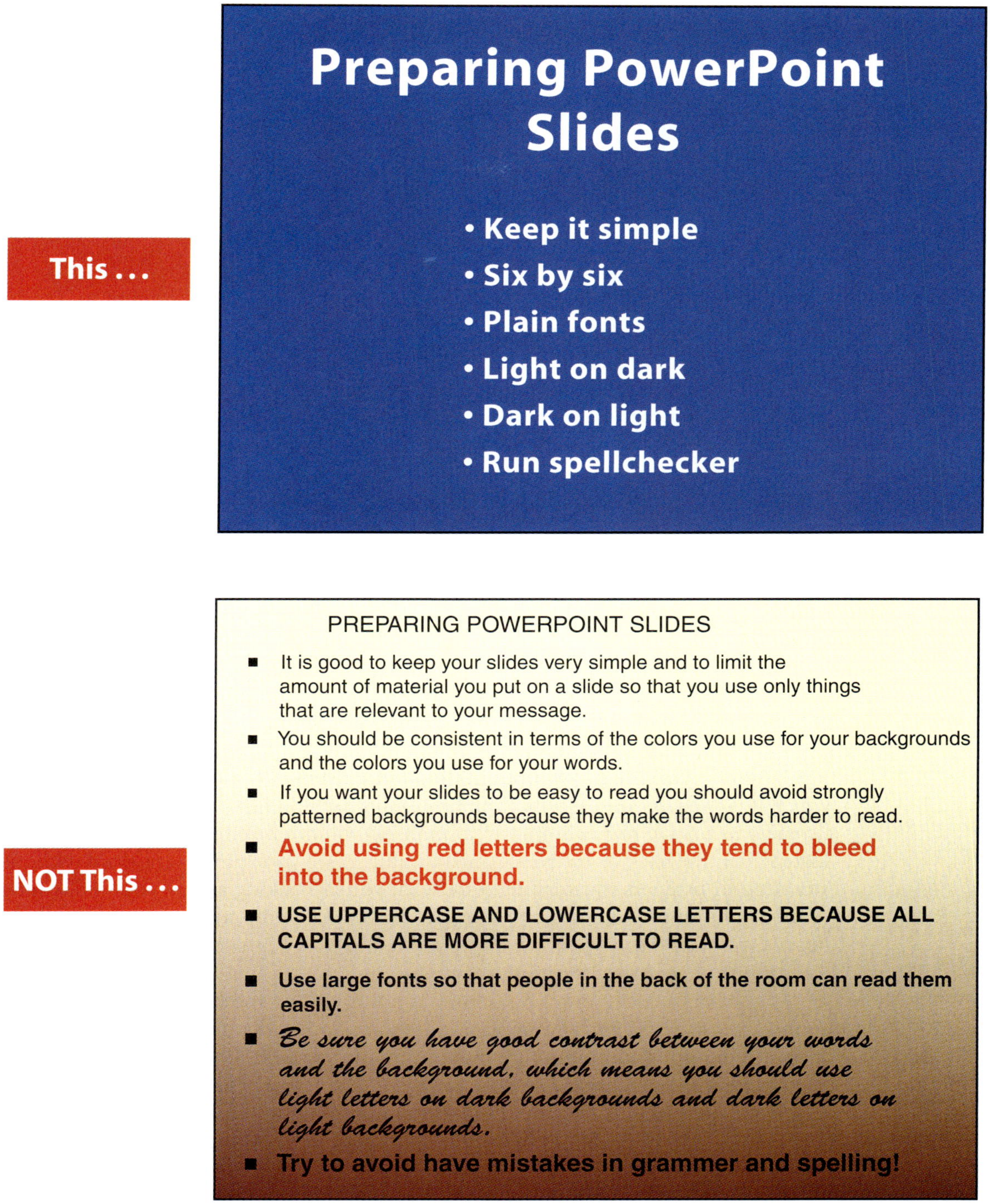

Figure 11.12

Good Versus Poor PowerPoint Slides

Preparing Presentation Aids

Good presentation aids should be carefully thought out and planned to fit your message. Regardless of the type of media you will use to produce them, they should follow accepted principles of design and color. You should always rehearse your speech using your presentation aids so that you don't end up fumbling around when you are actually making your presentation.

Principles of Design

A good presentation aid is simple and easy to see, emphasizes what is important, and is well-balanced. Consider the basic principles of simplicity, visibility, emphasis, and balance as you plan and prepare your materials. Look at your aids from the perspective of an audience member and see if they meet these criteria, which we shall discuss below.

Simplicity. Beginning speakers often try to cram too much information into a single presentation aid. Such aids are distracting as listeners try to figure out what everything is and what it means. We have seen a student divide a standard two-by-three-foot poster board into twelve segments, glue samples of medicinal herbs in each box, and then print its name and use under each sample. Needless to say, only listeners in the front row could actually read any of the print, and the aid created more confusion than illumination.

Each aid should focus on a single idea that you want to illustrate. Apply the so-called KISS principle (Keep It Simple, Stupid!) as you design your presentation aids.

Visibility. The size of any presentation aid must be appropriate to the setting in which it is used. A very large aid will be cumbersome to handle and can overwhelm listeners in a small room. Similarly, a small aid will not be effective in a large room. Listeners in the back of the room must be able to see your presentation aid without straining. If listeners must labor to see what you are talking about, your aid will be more of a hindrance than a help. In classrooms that hold up to forty students, poster boards will work fairly well. In a larger room and with a larger audience, you should use some type of projection equipment.

When preparing a poster board presentation aid for speeches in standard classrooms, follow these minimum size guidelines: your titles should be about three inches high and other text at least an inch and a half high. If you generate slides or transparencies on a computer, use a large font. Computer print is typically sized in terms of points (pt). Such presentation aids should use the following sizes of letters:

	Transparencies	Slides	Handouts
Title	36 pt	24 pt	18 pt
Subtitles	24 pt	18 pt	14 pt
Other text	18 pt	14 pt	12 pt

Use a plain font that is easy to read. For example, which of the following styles do you think would work better?

How Easy Is This to Read?
compared with
How Easy Is This to Read?

Emphasis. Focus your presentation aids so that they emphasize what your speech emphasizes. Your listeners' eyes should be drawn immediately to what you want to illustrate. On the acronym chart (Figure 11.9), the first letters of each word stand out. The map of Yellowstone Park (Figure 11.2) eliminates all information except what the speaker wishes to stress. Had the speaker added pictures of bears to indicate grizzly habitats and drawings of fish to show trout streams, the presentation aid would have been decorative but distracting. Avoid cuteness! Graphics prepared for handouts may be more detailed than those used for posters, slides, or transparencies, but they should not contain extraneous material. When in doubt, leave the details out. Let your words provide the elaboration.

Balance. Presentation aids that are balanced are pleasing to the eye. You achieve balance when you position textual materials in such a way that they form a consistent pattern that helps listeners focus on the message. Don't try to use every square inch of a poster board or overload a slide. White space is important! You should have a margin of about two inches at the top and bottom of a poster board. Side margins should be about one and a half inches wide. On computer-generated slides, you should leave blank space at both the top and bottom and have equal side margins. In the computer-generated slides in Figure 11.12, the first illustrates a balanced design. The second is unbalanced and cluttered and violates all of the principles of design.

Principles of Color

As many of the illustrations in this chapter show, color adds impact to presentation aids. Most colored presentation aids attract and hold attention better than black-and-white ones. Color also can convey or enhance meaning. For example, a speech about crop damage from a drought might use an enlarged outline map showing the least affected areas in green, moderately damaged areas in orange, and severely affected areas in brown. The natural colors would reinforce the message.

Color can also be used to create moods and impressions. Blue suggests power, authority, and stability (blue chip, blue ribbon, royal blue). Using blue in your graphics can invest them with these qualities. Red signals excitement and sometimes crisis (in the red, red ink, "I saw red"). Line graphs tracing the rise in cases of AIDS could be portrayed in red to convey the urgency of the problem. You should avoid using red when presenting financial data unless you want to focus on debts or losses. In our American culture, green is associated with both money (greenbacks) and environmental concerns (Greenpeace). The green in Figures 11.9 and 11.10 resonates with the green of U.S. currency. When selecting colors, you should also be aware of cultural differences. For example, in the United States, white is associated with weddings, baptisms, confirmations, and other joyous ritual occasions. In Japan, white has an entirely different connotation. There it is a funeral color, associated with sadness.[11]

Combining colors in different ways can convey subtle nuances of meaning. An **analogous color scheme** uses colors that are adjacent on the color wheel, such as green, blue green, and blue. At the same time that this type of color scheme shows the differences among the elements represented, it also suggests their connection and compatibility. For example, a pie graph could use analogous colors to represent the students, faculty, and administration of a university. The different colors suggest that although these parts are separate, they belong together. In this subtle way, the presentation aid itself makes the statement that the components of a university ought to work together.

A **complementary color scheme** uses colors that are opposites on the color wheel, such as red and green. Complementary color schemes suggest tension and opposition among elements in a speech. Because they heighten the sense of drama, they may enliven informative speaking and encourage change in persuasive speaking. Figure 11.13 illustrates an analogous and a complementary color scheme.

Figure 11.13

Analogous and Complementary Color Schemes

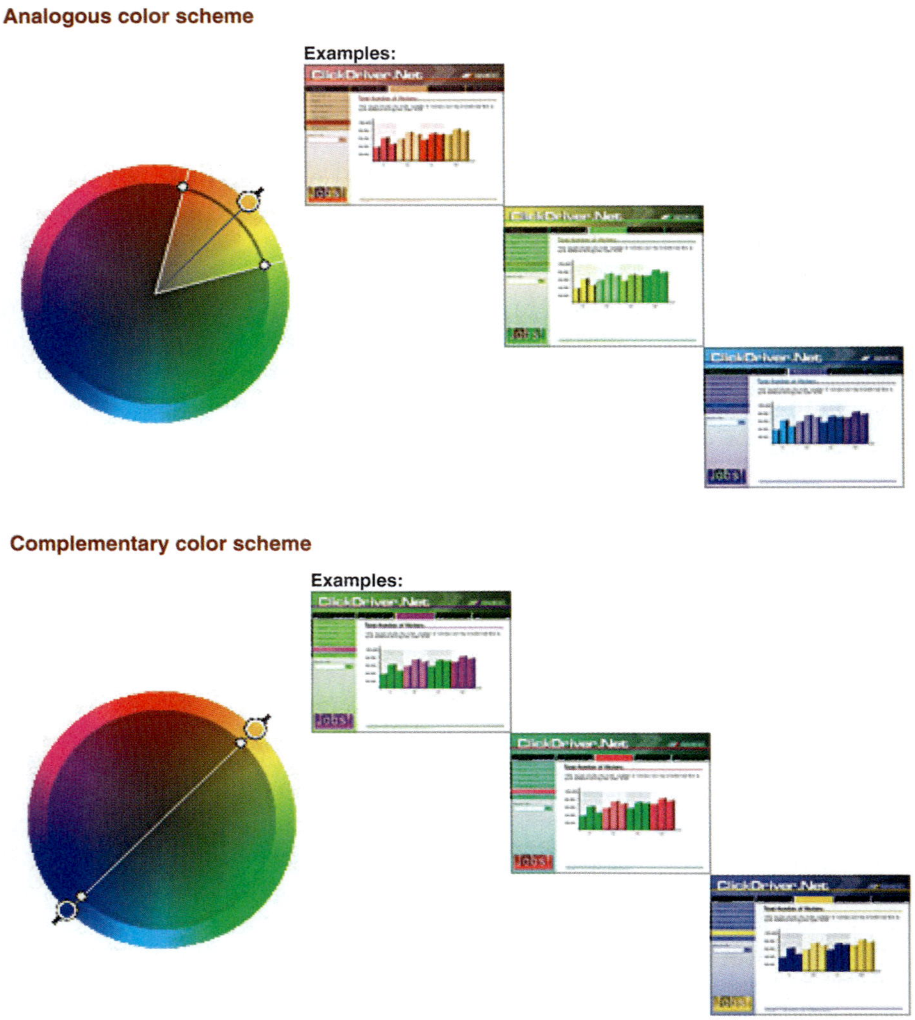

A **monochromatic color scheme** uses intense variations of a single color. Both the acronym graphic (Figure 11.9) and the numerical graphic (Figure 11.10) use a monochromatic color scheme. These schemes suggest variety within unity. A monochromatic color scheme would be inappropriate for bar graphs or line graphs, because these require more contrast to be effective.

The colors you use for text should always contrast with the background of your aid. Patterned backgrounds make words difficult to read. With poster board, it is best to use a white- or cream-colored board and strong primary colors such as red, blue, and green for contrast. However, don't use red letters against a light background on transparencies or slides, because red tends to bleed, making the words blurry and difficult to read, and a light background can create glare. Therefore, you might want to use a strong primary color for the background and have the text or other graphic elements printed in white.

Color contrast is especially important for computer-generated slides and transparencies, because the colors will appear less distinct when projected than they do when seen on a computer monitor. Colors like pastel pink, light blue, and pale yellow, or those with a grayish tinge, may not be strong enough for good graphic emphasis in any type of presentation aid.

A final word of caution concerning color: When you prepare presentation aids on a computer, the colors on your monitor will differ from the final colors when they are printed on a transparency or slide. Run a sample and project it to see how

Speaker's Notes 11.2

Checklist for Preparing Presentation Aids

_____ 1. My presentation aid is as simple as I can make it.
_____ 2. I have limited myself to one major idea per aid.
_____ 3. I have ample margins at the top, bottom, and sides of my aid.
_____ 4. My print is large enough to be read from the back of the room.
_____ 5. My aid emphasizes what I want to emphasize.
_____ 6. I have good color contrast on my aid.
_____ 7. I use colors and lettering consistently.
_____ 8. I have checked for spelling errors.

the final colors will actually look to an audience. If the results are not what you expected, try other colors until you are satisfied.

Making Presentation Aids

To make handmade charts, graphs, or other poster aids, begin with a rough draft that allows you to see how your aid will look when it is finished. If you are making a poster, prepare your draft on newsprint or butcher paper of the same size. With a light pencil, mark off the margins to frame your aid. Divide your planning sheet into four equal sections to help you balance the placement of material. Use a wide-tipped felt marker to sketch in your design and words.

Now step back and inspect your presentation aid from about the same distance as the back row of your audience. Can you read it without straining? Is everything spelled correctly? Is your eye drawn to what is most important? Have you positioned your material so that it looks good? Does the poster look balanced?

Remember, keep your presentation aid simple! Be sure your margins and borders are large enough to provide ample white space. See if there is anything you can cut. If your draft looks "busy," make a series of presentation aids instead of just one. Once you have completed a rough draft of the aid, construct the final product. If you are artistically challenged, use stencils or stick-on letters and numbers.

If you use computer-generated graphics to produce slides, transparencies, or handouts, experiment with several different designs. Limit the amount of information on slides and transparencies to a maximum of six lines per slide and six words per line. Limit the number of slides or transparencies you use. You should probably have *no more than four aids for a six-minute presentation, and no more than six aids for a ten-minute presentation.* If you use more than this, your speech may become just a voice-over for a slide show. At the end of this chapter, we provide step-by-step instructions for preparing simple PowerPoint slides.

Using Presentation Aids

As we discussed each kind of presentation aid, we offered suggestions on how to use it in presentation. Here, we review these suggestions and extract some general guidelines.

Figure 11.14

Using Presentation Aids (PAs): Dos and Don'ts

Do	Don't
1. Practice your speech using PAs.	1. Try to "wing it" using PAs.
2. Display PAs only when using them.	2. Leave PAs in full view during speech.
3. Stand to side of PA when using it.	3. Stand in front of PA.
4. Point to what is important as you refer to it.	4. Deliver your speech to your PA.
5. Maintain eye contact with your audience.	5. Distribute handouts during speech.
6. Limit the number of PAs in your speech.	6. Pass around objects when speaking.
7. Have a backup plan for electronic PAs.	7. Talk over sound from PAs.

Practice using your presentation aids as you rehearse your speech. Plan to use transitions such as "As we can see on this chart . . ." to integrate the material into your message. Well in advance of your speech, check out the room where you will be speaking to decide where you will place your aid both before and after you use it in your speech, as well as how you will display it. Be sure it can be seen well from all points in the room. Also determine if you will have what you need to display your presentation aid. Is there an easel you can use for a poster board or flip chart? Might you need to bring masking tape or push pins to display your aid? Will you need something to conceal it until you are ready to use it? Check out any electronic equipment you will use (slide projector, overhead projector, VCR, computer, etc.) in advance of your presentation, and be certain that you can operate it and that it is working properly. If you are bringing in computerized materials on a floppy disk or CD, be sure that they are compatible with the equipment in the room.

Do not display your presentation aid until you are ready to use it; it will distract your audience. When you have finished using the aid, cover or conceal it. Never stand directly in front of your presentation aid; stand to the side of it and maintain eye contact with listeners. You want them to see both you and your presentation aid. As you refer to something on the presentation aid, point to what you are talking about; don't leave your audience searching for what you are describing. Never deliver your speech to your presentation aid; maintain eye contact with your audience.

Do not distribute materials during your speech. If you have prepared handouts, the best time to distribute them may be after you speak. Don't pass around pictures or objects for listeners to examine. You want them to focus on your message, not on your presentation aid.

Do not use too many presentation aids in one speech. Remember, they should enhance your verbal message, not replace it.

Ethical Considerations for Using Presentation Aids

Presentation aids can enlighten a message, but they can also mislead. Tempted by their power, speakers can use presentation aids to deceive listeners. Thus, using presentation aids can raise challenging ethical questions.[12]

Graphs and charts, for example, can be rigged so that they misrepresent reality.[13] Figure 11.15 shows how a recent decade's growth in the percentage of women partners in major accounting firms might be misrepresented in bar graph A to make a small gain look like a large gain. Bar graph B in the same figure puts these slight

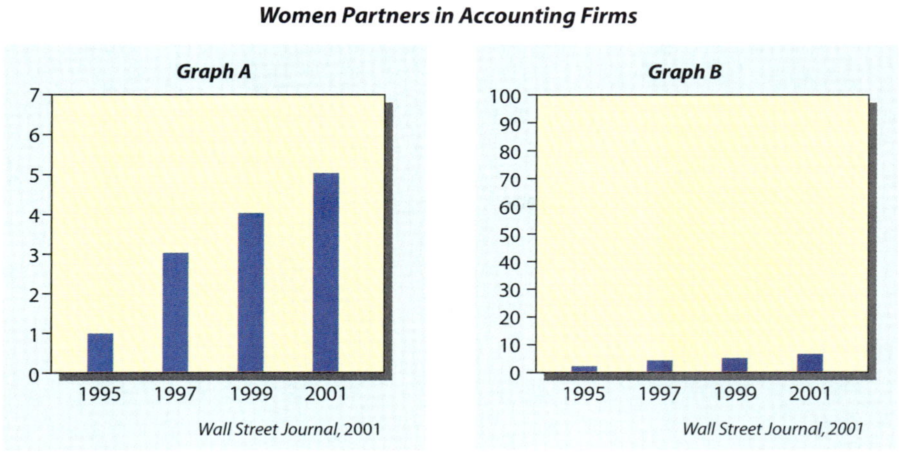

Figure 11.15

Misleading Bar Graph and Same Material Presented So It Is Not Misleading

gains into the proper perspective.[14] Be careful to prepare graphs so that they honestly represent a situation.

You must also remember to credit your sources on your presentation aids. Be sure to include this information in smaller (but still visible) letters at the bottom of any material you plan to display (see how this is done in Figure 11.8). Citing your source in this fashion both verifies the data presented and reminds you to mention the source in your oral presentation.

Probably the most interesting ethical questions involve the use of film and tape materials. For example, the most famous photographer of the Civil War, Matthew Brady, rearranged bodies on the battlefield to enhance the impact of his pictures. Eighty years later, another American war photographer carefully staged the now celebrated photograph of marines planting the flag at Iwo Jima.[15] Fifty years after that, *Time* magazine electronically manipulated a cover photograph of O. J. Simpson to "darken it and achieve a brooding, menacing quality."[16] On the one hand, these famous images are fabrications: they pretend to be what they are not. On the other, they bring home reality more forcefully. In other words, the form of the photos may be a lie, but the lie may reveal a deeper truth. So are these photographs unethical, or are they simply artistic?

With today's technology, the potential for abuse looms ever larger. Video and audio editing easily produces illusions of reality. Consider how moviemakers depicted Forrest Gump shaking hands with Presidents Kennedy, Johnson, and Nixon. Call to mind the image of the late Fred Astaire dancing with a vacuum cleaner in a television commercial. In movies and ads, such distortions can be amusing. In real life, they can be dangerous. When they purportedly convey actual objects or events, as when television networks or newspapers "stage" crashes to make their stories more dramatic without letting us in on the artifice, they can be quite deceptive.[17] All

Ethics Alert! 11.1

The Ethical Use of Presentation Aids

1. Be certain charts or graphs do not distort information.
2. Never manipulate visual images to deceive your audience.
3. If you alter an image to reveal some deeper truth, let the audience know you have done so.
4. Cite the source of any data you present in a graph.
5. As a listener, be on guard against the power of presentation aids to trick you.

these practices relate to the ancient adage "Seeing is believing." We have been conditioned by experience and taught by tradition to trust the "reality" revealed by our eyes and ears.

To be an ethical communicator, you should alert your listeners to the illusion whenever you manipulate images so that they reveal your message more forcefully. You should also be prepared to defend your creation as a "better representation" of the truth. As a listener, you should develop a skeptical attitude about images and seek additional evidence if there is any question concerning their validity.

In Summary

Presentation aids are tools to enhance the effectiveness of speeches. They can increase comprehension, improve retention of information, authenticate a point, add variety, increase your credibility, and help your speech have lasting impact.

Kinds of Presentation Aids. Every speech has at least one presentation aid: the speaker. Your appearance, clothing, and body language must all be in concert with your message and appropriate to the audience and situation. Another form of presentation aid is an object. Unless it is large enough to be seen, small enough to be portable, and strictly under your control, you may have to use a model or a sketch instead.

Visual representations of information, or *graphics,* provide a number of options for presentation aids. Maps can be useful in speeches based on spatial designs. Draw them specifically for your speech so that they contain only the material you wish to emphasize. Graphs can help make complex numerical data more understandable to an audience. *Pie graphs* illustrate the relationships between parts and a whole. *Bar graphs* highlight comparisons and contrasts. *Line graphs* show changes over time.

Charts are visual representations that give form to abstract relationships. *Flow charts* may be used to outline the steps in a process or to show power and authority relationships within an organization. *Sequence charts* that are presented in succession can be especially effective in speeches to emphasize and illustrate various stages in a process. *Textual graphics* are lists of phrases, words, or numbers. They are often presented as *bulleted lists, acronyms,* or *columns of data.*

Photographs and pictures can add authenticity to a speech. Photographs provide slice-of-life realism but can also include irrelevant detail. Any photograph used in a speech should be enlarged so that everyone in the audience can see it.

Presentation Media. Speakers may use flip charts, posters, handouts, chalk or marker boards, transparencies, slides, videos, audios, and computerized programs to develop presentation aids. Flip charts may be used as spontaneous presentation aids. Handouts can be effective for explaining complex or unfamiliar material but should be distributed either before or after a speech. Chalk and marker boards should be used sparingly to emphasize points or to clarify questions that can arise during the presentation of a speech.

Transparencies and slides help audiences see graphics or pictures more clearly. Transparencies are popular because they are easy to make, inexpensive, and adaptable. Videos and audiotapes add variety to a message. They should be used sparingly in presentations because they can easily upstage the speaker.

Most personal computers have the capacity to generate effective, professional-looking presentation aids, such as transparencies, handouts, or slides.

Preparing Presentation Aids. As you plan your presentation aids, follow the basic principles of design and color. The presentation aid must be easy for listeners to see. It should emphasize what the speech emphasizes, excluding all extraneous material. It should seem balanced and pleasing to the eye. Use strong colors to add interest and impact.

Using Presentation Aids. Practice using the presentation aid until it seems a natural part of your presentation. Always talk to your audience, not to your presentation aid, and keep the aid out of sight when it is not in use.

As you consider the use of presentation aids, be sensitive to their potential ethical impact. Be certain that your presentation aid represents its subject without distortion.

Terms to Know

presentation aids
graphics
pie graph
bar graph
pictographs
line graph
flow chart
sequence charts
textual graphics
bulleted lists
acronym
computer-assisted presentations
analogous color scheme
complementary color scheme
monochromatic color scheme

Discussion

1. Recall classes in which your instructors used presentation aids. Which of the following functions discussed in this chapter did these aids serve?
   a. Did they aid your understanding of the material?
   b. Did they authenticate a point in the lecture?
   c. Did they enhance your instructor's presentation skills?
   d. Did they enhance your instructor's credibility?
   e. Did they add variety or make the lecture more interesting?
   f. Did they make the material easier to remember?

   Why or why not?
2. Describe a situation you witnessed in which a speaker was or was not an effective presentation aid for his or her own speech? How did the speaker's appearance enhance or detract from the speech?
3. Look through a recent magazine and analyze the advertisements according to the principles of design discussed in this chapter. Do the presentation aspects of the ads work in concert with the words to emphasize the message? Which of the ads seem most balanced and pleasing to the eye? Do any of the ads violate the rules of simplicity and ease of understanding? Which ads used color most and least effectively? Bring copies of the most interesting ads to class and discuss your findings.

Application

1. Select a speech from Appendix B and prepare the rough draft of a presentation aid that might have been used with it. Would the aid have helped the speech? What other options did you consider?
2. What kinds of presentation aids might be most useful for the following speech topics?
   a. Nuclear waste disposal sites in the United States
   b. Surviving a tornado
   c. History of the stock market over the past decade
   d. How your state's budget is divided into major categories
   e. Administering your college: who has the power to do what to whom?
   f. How we got laptop computers: the growth of an invention
   g. The sounds of navigation and what they mean

Notes

1. Cheryl Hamilton and Cordell Parker, *Communicating for Results,* 6th ed. (Belmont, Calif.: Wadsworth, 2001), p. 396.
2. Robert Heinich, Michael Molenda, and James D. Russell, *Instructional Media and the New Technologies of Instruction,* 4th ed. (New York: Macmillan, 1993), p. 66.
3. See studies conducted by Wharton Business School's Applied Research Center and the Management Information Services Department of the University of Arizona, cited by Robert L. Lindstrom, "The Presentation Power of Multimedia," *Sales and Marketing Management* (Sept. 1994): 51, and by Donal Meilachl, "Even the Odds with Visual Presentations," *Inc. Annual* (1994): 1–7.
4. Lisa Collier Cool, "Danger in the Dorm," *Family Circle,* 17 Feb. 2004, p. 15.
5. Cited in Laurence J. Peter, *Peter's Quotations: Ideas for Our Time* (New York: Bantam, 1979), p. 478.
6. Our thanks for this example go to Professor Dave Klope of Trinity Christian College. CRTNET posting #5618, December 12, 2000.
7. Our thanks for this example go to Professor Mary Katherine McHenry, Northwest Mississippi Community College, Senatobia, Mississippi.
8. Rebecca Ganzel, "Power Pointless," *Presentations,* February 2000, pp. 53–58.
9. Ricky Telg and Tracy Irani, "Getting the Most Out of PowerPoint," *Agricultural Education Magazine,* April 2001, p. 11.
10. Dave Paradi, "Survey Shows How to Stop Annoying Audiences with Bad PowerPoint," survey conducted September 2003.http://www.comunicateusingtechnology.com/articles/pptsurvey_article.htm (14 Mar. 2004).
11. Richard Kern, "Making Visual Aids Work for You," *Sales and Marketing Management* (February 1989): 45.
12. Kenneth Brower, "Photography in the Age of Falsification," *Atlantic Monthly,* May 1998, pp. 92–111.
13. Gerald Everett Jones, *How to Lie with Charts* (Lincoln, Nebr.: Authors Choice Press, 2000).
14. Lee Berton, "Deloitte Wants More Women for Top Posts in Accounting," *Wall Street Journal,* 28 Feb. 1993, p. B1.
15. Cornelia Brunner, "Teaching Visual Literacy," *Electronic Learning* (November–December 1994): p. 16.
16. Arthur Goldsmith, "Digitally Altered Photography: The New Image Makers," *Britannica Book of the Year: 1995* (Chicago: Encyclopaedia Britannica, 1995), p. 135.
17. Gloria Borger, "The Story the Pictures Didn't Tell," *U.S. News & World Report,* 22 Feb. 1993, pp. 6–7; and John Leo, "Lapse or TV News Preview?" *Washington Times,* 3 Mar. 1993, p. G3.

This tutorial will help you prepare a simple slide or series of slides for use in your speeches using Microsoft's software for PowerPoint 2000 or PowerPoint 2002. Because of the planned obsolescence of software programs, the materials that follow may not be exactly the same as what you will see on your computer screen. But while programs change from version to version, the general directions remain similar.

We begin with a series of cautions. First, don't develop your slide(s) until after you have prepared your speech. Second, include information and material on your slide(s) only when it adds to your oral message. Third, don't simply copy your speech outline onto slides and then read them to the audience.

Begin preparing your slide(s) by opening the PowerPoint program on your computer. You can access this by using the "Start" button in the bottom left corner of the screen, then opening Programs, and clicking on PowerPoint. The first screen that will be displayed contains three options for creating a PowerPoint presentation: an AutoContent Wizard, a Design Template format, and a Blank Presentation option.

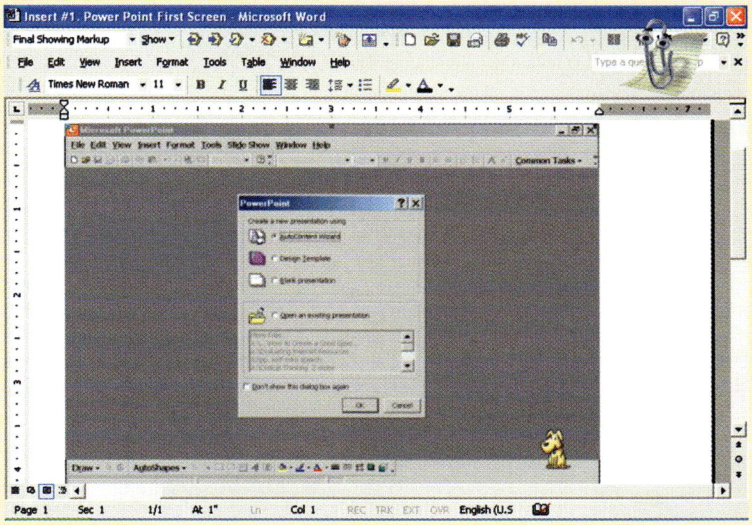

The AutoContent Wizard provides a fixed set of templates and formats. It guides you through the process by asking questions about the type of presentation you plan to make. Although this may sound like an easy way to develop your slide(s), it is probably not the best approach for learning the basics of preparing such materials. Most of the presentation options in the AutoContent Wizard do not match the typical public speaking class assignments. They are designed to prepare "slide shows"—often with sound and animated graphics—not to prepare presentation aids for speeches.

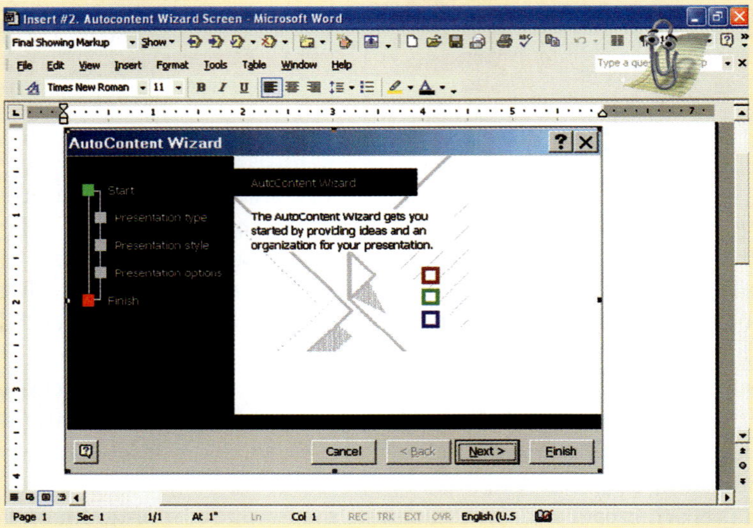

The Design Template format provides a large selection of slide backgrounds on which you can type your text. Each template can be viewed on the right of your screen by clicking the button next to the template name. Many of these backgrounds are attractive, but some of them are "busy." Busy backgrounds can distract listeners. Slides with shaded backgrounds often make some of the text difficult to read.

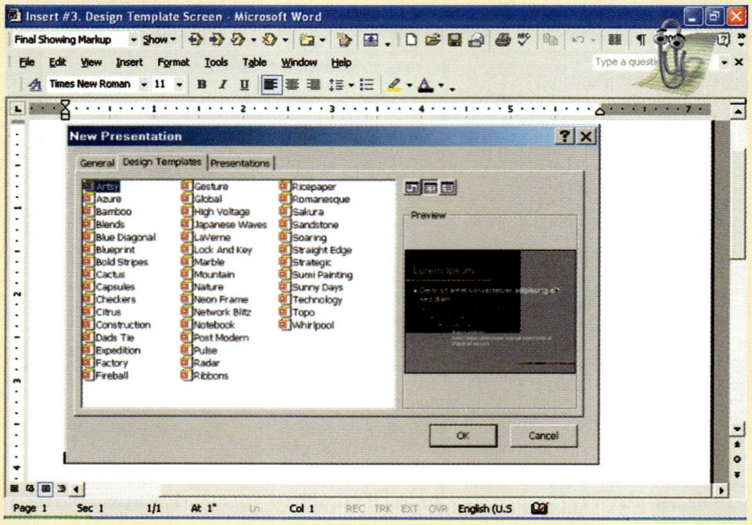

The Blank Presentation option allows you to control everything that goes on your slide(s). Consequently, you should prepare your slide(s) using either a very simple background from the Design Template format or build them from scratch using the Blank Presentation option. Our instructions will take you through working with the Blank Presentation option, but they are applicable to the Design Template format as well.

No matter which option you choose, the Office Assistant will appear as an icon (usually an animated paper clip) on your screen. If you get confused or can't remember how to do something, simply click on the icon and a box will appear. Type a question in the space provided, click the "Search" command, and the Office Assistant will provide an answer.

When you choose the Blank Presentation option, the next screen that comes up on your monitor will provide slide layout options.

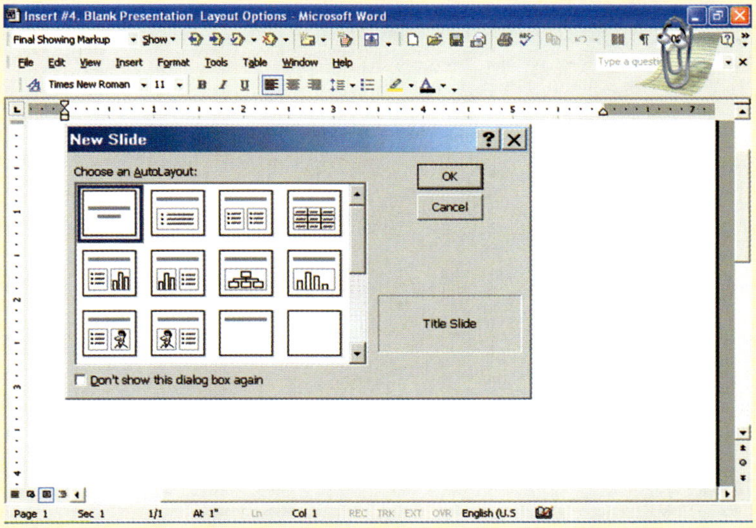

On this screen, you can choose from a title page, a bulleted list, and a variety of chart, graph, and clip art options. Select the bulleted list by clicking on the icon showing a bulleted list. Now the working box on your screen will show a slide with the appropriate layout.

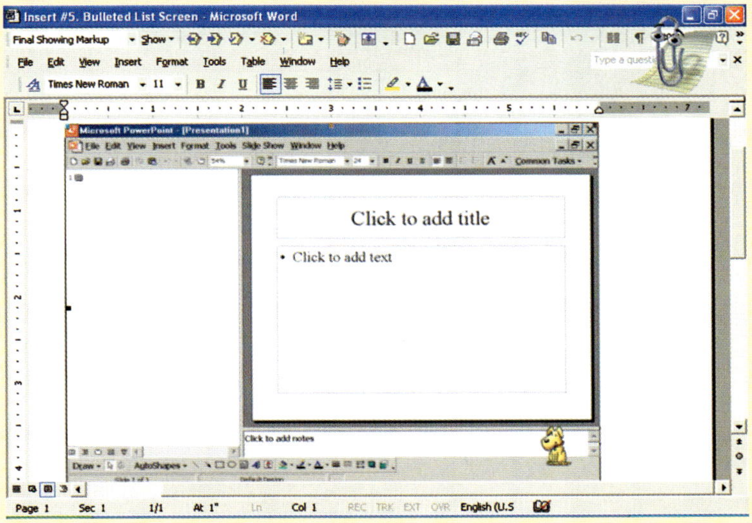

Decide what background color you want for your slides. Remember, if you choose a light background, you must use dark text to provide the contrast necessary for your slide(s) to be easily read. Also keep in mind that white backgrounds are prone to glare. If you want a light background for your slide(s), choose a pale cream or ivory. If you choose a dark background, you will need to use a light text color for clear definition. To add background color to your slide, pull down the Format menu from your top toolbar, and click on Background.

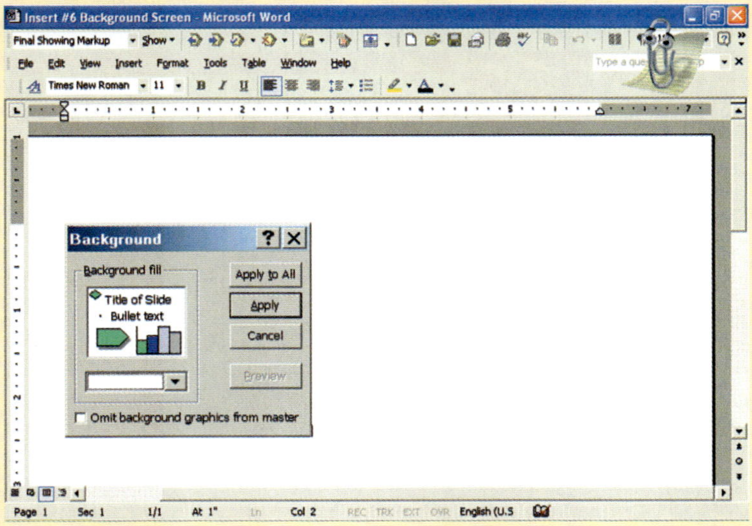

To find the color you want to use as the background for your slide(s), click the arrow for the blank pull-down box at the bottom of the menu. Select the "More Colors" command, which will display the entire color spectrum available.

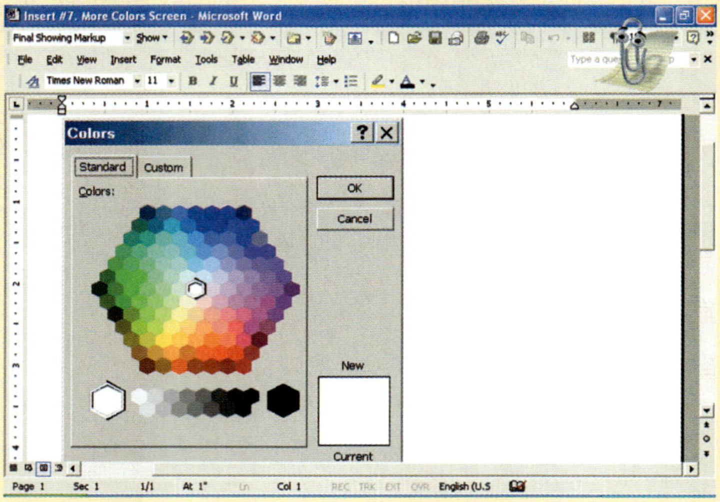

Choose your background color, then click "Apply to All." Each slide you prepare for this presentation will have the same background. We have selected a rich royal blue as a background color.

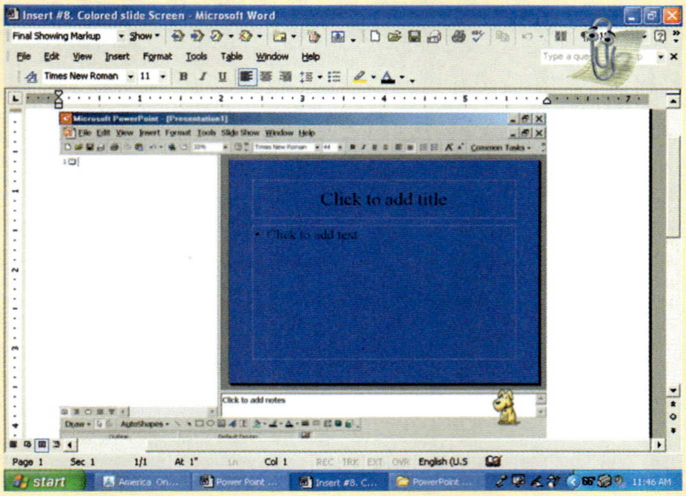

Before you begin typing material onto your slide, you must select the font style and color for the text on your slide. Return to the Format menu on your top toolbar. Open this and click Font. Choose a simple, easy-to-read font. Some good choices include Arial, Century Gothic, Courier, and Times New Roman. Avoid any font that has the word *narrow* in its name: it will be hard to read when projected in a slide. Don't use script or decorative fonts such as Dauphin and GoudyHandtooled, which are also difficult to read.

Next, select a font color that contrasts with the background of your slide. We have chosen white text for use on the blue background.

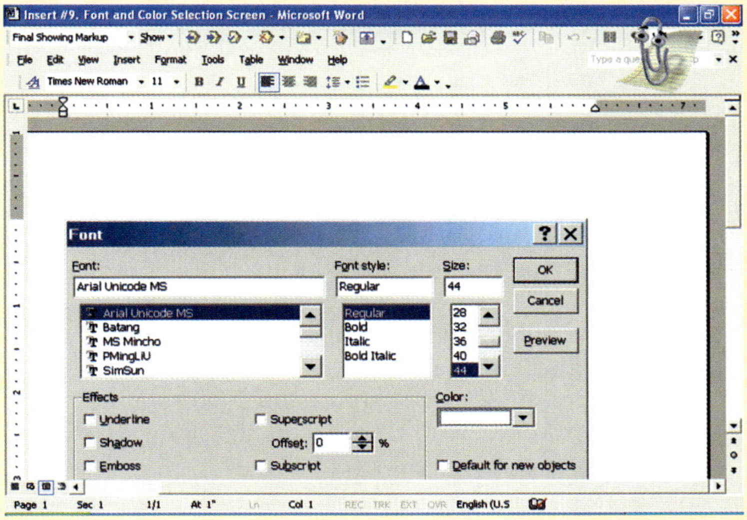

Now you can begin adding text to your slide. Type the title of your slide in the title box and the text in the text box.

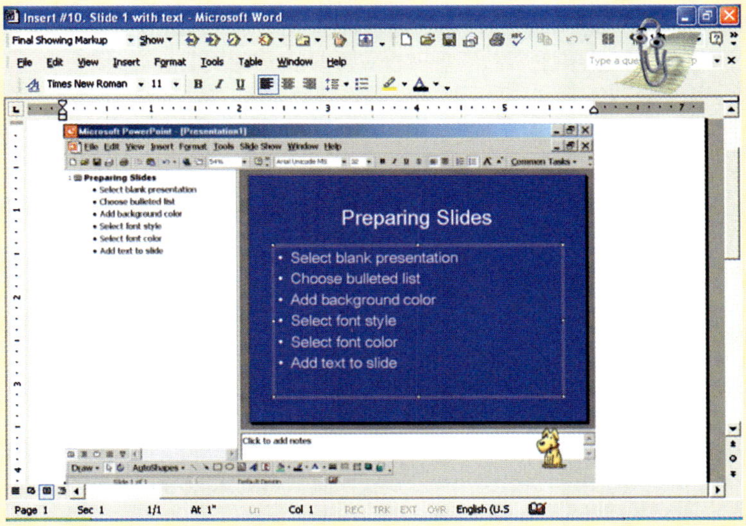

Don't try to cram too much material into a slide. For a bulleted list, you should have no more than six lines or bullets, and no more than six words to a line. Do not write out your bulleted points as full sentences. They will be too long and will draw attention away from your spoken words as listeners read them. If you have too much material to meet the six-by-six guidelines, consider making a series of slides.

To make additional slides for your presentation, go to the "New Slide" command on the top toolbar on your screen. The "Layout Options" box will open, and you can then choose the layout you want for this slide.

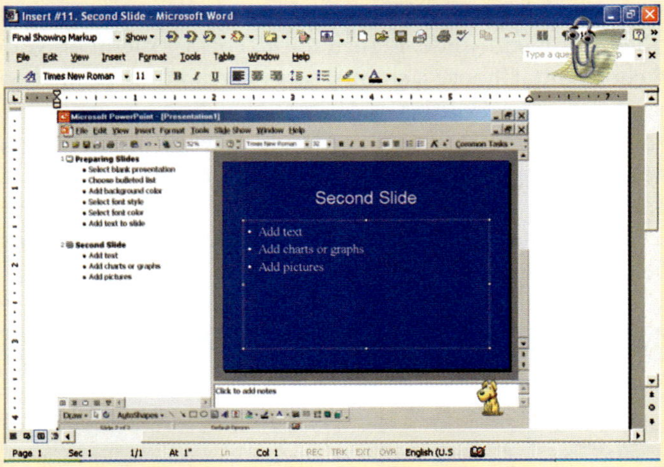

When you will use more than one slide in your presentation, be sure that the slides are visually consistent with one another. Each slide should have the same background and the same color scheme. The slides should use the same fonts, the same type of bullets for multiple bulleted lists, and the same type of spacing between words and lines.

If you prepare a slide and decide you want a different layout, open the Common Tasks menu, click on Slide Layout, and then select the layout you want. When you have completed all of your slides, save them in a folder on your desktop and make a backup copy on a disk. Once you have prepared the slides, you can open them from this folder and edit them by changing colors or text.

You can preview your complete presentation by using the Slide Sorter view from the View menu on the toolbar. This screen shows you all the slides in your presentation. Use the slide sorter to rearrange the order of your slides. To change the order of your slides, click on the slide, then drag it to where you want it positioned.

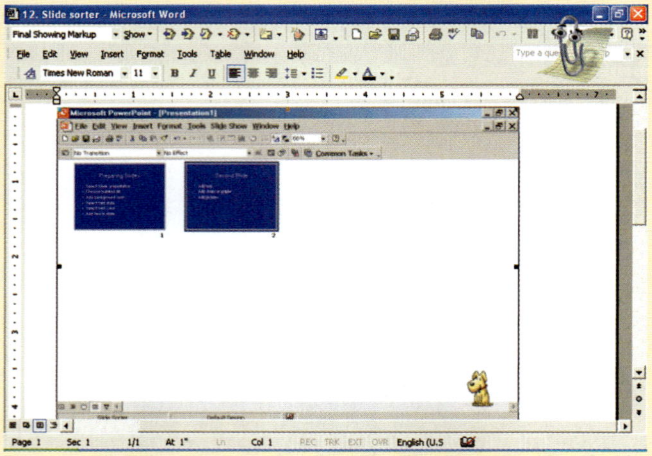

With Microsoft's Excel program, you can prepare charts and graphs on your computer and import them into your PowerPoint slides. You can also import clip art and pictures to add variety to your presentation.

Once you have prepared all of your materials, your next step is to open the Slide Show menu on your toolbar. This allows you to view your presentation on your computer monitor. For a speech before an audience, select the Manual Timing option so that you can control the appearance of slides by left-clicking your mouse. Show a slide only when you refer to it in a speech. You can make the screen go black between slides by hitting the "b" on your computer keyboard.

If you need immediate help while preparing and previewing your PowerPoint presentation, click on the Office Assistant. For additional information and instructions for more advanced presentations with clip art, transitions, and animation, consult one of the online resources listed in InterConnections 11.1, "PowerPoint Presentations."

Using Language Effectively

12

OUTLINE

This chapter will help you

- understand the power of language
- apply standards to use language effectively
- learn ways to magnify the power of language

Give me the right word and the right accent, and I will move the world.

JOSEPH CONRAD

A legislator was asked how he felt about whiskey. He replied, "If, when you say whiskey, you mean the Devil's brew, the poison scourge, the bloody monster that defiles innocence, dethrones reason, creates misery and poverty—yes, literally takes the bread from the mouths of little children; if you mean the drink that topples Christian man and woman from the pinnacle of righteous, gracious living into the bottomless pit of degradation, despair, shame and helplessness, then certainly I am against it with all my power.

"But if, when you say whiskey, you mean the oil of conversation, the philosophic wine, the ale that is consumed when good fellows get together, that puts a song in their hearts and the warm glow of contentment in their eyes; if you mean Christmas cheer; if you mean the stimulating drink that puts the spring in an old gentleman's step on a frosty morning; if you mean that drink, the sale of which pours into our treasury untold millions of dollars which are used to provide tender care for our crippled children, our blind, our deaf, our dumb, pitiful, aged and infirm, to build highways, hospitals, and schools, then certainly I am in favor of it.

"That is my stand, and I will not compromise."[1]

The "Whiskey Speech," a legend in southern politics, was originally presented some years ago by N. S. Sweat Jr. during a heated campaign to legalize the sale of liquor by the drink in Mississippi. Because about half of his constituents favored the question and the other half were vehemently opposed, Representative "Soggy" Sweat decided to handle the issue with humor. In the process, he provided an illustration of the magical power of words.

In this chapter we discuss this power, and explain six standards you must satisfy to make language work effectively in your speeches. We conclude by exploring some special techniques you can use to magnify the power of words.

The Power of the Spoken Word

To expand on your knowledge of language, watch the videos, complete the exercises, and read the tips in **VideoLab Lesson 7: Language Use**.

The ability to use language effectively is one of the most important skills you will ever acquire. There are three important reasons why this is so.

- *First, most of us think in words, and the words of our language shape the way we think.* For example, in most parts of the United States we have just one word for and one conception of snow. However, in the land of the Eskimos, where snow is a constant phenomenon, there are many words to describe it and many ways to think about it.
- *Second, language is the basis of all our social interactions.* Our choice of words can determine the success or failure of these interactions.
- *Finally, words are the essence of our being, of what and how we think about ourselves.* Our language is an integral part of our cultural identity. This becomes especially important when a language faces the possibility of extinction. D. Y. Begay, a prominent Navajo weaver and art curator, noted, "My father says when you stop speaking the language is when you stop being Navajo."[2]

Oral Language Versus Written Language

We begin our exploration of the power of the spoken word by considering the differences between oral and written language. The first difference is that oral language is more spontaneous and less formal than written language. For example, a journalist might write, "Eight thousand, three hundred twenty-three cases of measles have been reported in Shelby County." A speaker, communicating the same information, would more likely say, "More than eight thousand cases of measles have been reported in Shelby County." It's not really important that listeners remember the exact number of cases. What is important is that they see the magnitude of the problem. Rounding off numbers helps listeners focus on the large picture.

Oral language is also more colorful and intense than written language. Sentence fragments and slang expressions are more acceptable in speeches than in essays. Oral language also is more interactive. It depends on audience involvement for its effectiveness. Consider the following excerpt from a speech:

> **You want to know what we're going to do? I'll tell you what we're *not* going to do. We're *not* going to play along. This is a rule that deserves to be broken. Yes, broken! And we're going to do the breaking.**

This brief example illustrates the spontaneous, informal, intense, fragmentary, and interactive qualities of oral language. The speaker is keenly aware of her audience. Her words illustrate the conversational character of effective speeches that we discussed in Chapter 1. Moreover, as we discuss in detail in Chapter 13, oral language uses pauses, vocal emphasis, and pitch variations to clarify and reinforce meaning. Such resources are not available in written communication.

In oral communication, time is also important. Jerry Tarver, professor of speech communication at the University of Richmond, emphasizes three significant time differences between spoken and written language.[3] First, he offers "Tarver's Law of Conciseness: *It takes more words per square idea to say something than to write it.*" Because listeners cannot reread words that are spoken, oral language must be simple and speakers often must repeat themselves to be understood. Speakers may need to amplify ideas with examples to ensure that listeners get the point.

Tarver's second time difference concerns *the order in which spoken thoughts develop in a sentence.* His example is excellent:

> **I recently read in a newspaper column a spirited defense of a public figure. The last line of the column was, "For that he should be congratulated, not chastised." Well and good. The reader gobbles up the line in an instant and digests the contrast between congratulations and chastisement. But when we speak the line we feed it to a listener morsel by morsel. And the last two words prove to be rather bland. We need to *hear* "For that he should not be chastised, he should be congratulated." More words; but more important, a different order. . . . In the slower pace of speech, individual words stand out more, and thus *time* accords a special emphasis to the last idea, the climactic idea in the sentence.**
>
> **As a rule, then, the stronger, more impressive idea should be saved for the end. And it will often be the case that the punch comes from a positive rather than a negative thought.[4]**

Tarver's advice to *build up* to your most important point within a sentence repeats a structural principle discussed in Chapter 9—that the main points of a speech often work best when arranged in an order of ascending importance.

Tarver's third effect of time is that "*the rhythm of the syllables is even more important in words written to be heard than in words written to be seen.*" Spoken language can play on the senses like a drum. The beat of the words can embed them in memory and charge them with emotion. At a low point during World War II, when a German invasion of Great Britain seemed imminent, Prime Minister Winston Churchill spoke on radio to the British people in language that seemed to march in military formation. Read the following words aloud to savor their full oral power:

> **We shall not flag nor fail. We shall go on to the end. We shall fight in France and on the seas and oceans; we shall fight with growing confidence and growing strength in the air. We shall defend our island whatever the cost may be; we shall fight on beaches, landing grounds, in fields, in streets and on the hills. We shall never surrender. . . .[5]**

When used in such skillful ways, the spoken word can touch listeners in ways that the written word cannot. There are four ways that effective oral language can influence your audience:

1. It can influence how listeners see subjects.
2. It can influence how listeners feel about those subjects.
3. It can influence how listeners identify with one another.
4. It can influence how listeners act.[6]

Speaker's Notes 12.1

Characteristics of Oral Language

1. Oral language is personal.
2. Oral language is informal.
3. Oral language is colorful.
4. Oral language uses short, simple sentences.
5. Oral language repeats and amplifies ideas.
6. Oral language relies on examples and stories.
7. Oral language emphasizes rhythm.

Understanding these powers of oral language—and how they can be abused as well as used—is essential for both speaker and listener.

The Power to Make Listeners See

Speakers and listeners often see subjects in different ways. The artful use of language, however, can close the gap that separates them. Consider, for example, the problem that confronted one of our students, Scott Champlin. Scott wanted to share an experience he had had in the military so that others would understand what it meant to him. One option was to describe the experience matter-of-factly:

> **While I was parachuting into Panama as part of Operation "Just Cause," I was wounded by a tracer bullet.**

The more he considered that option, the less adequate it seemed. How could he use words to convey the *true sense* of that experience? The depiction he developed allowed listeners to share his leap into danger:

> **The darkness of two o'clock in the morning was penetrated by streaks of red light marking the paths of tracer rounds as they cut their way through the night. Suddenly, I felt something hit me in the right leg with a force that spun me around like a twisted yo-yo at the end of a string.**

Here the use of contrast—between "darkness" and "streaks of red light"—paints a vivid word picture. Action verbs such as *penetrated, cut,* and *spun* enliven the picture. The simile—"like a twisted yo-yo at the end of a string"—brings the picture into sharp focus. Through his artful word choice, Scott was able to share the meaning of his experience.

The power to influence how listeners see things is particularly important when a topic is unfamiliar or unusual. In such cases, your words can become windows that reveal the subject with startling clarity. There can, however, be a negative side to this power of depiction. When listeners don't have a picture of their own to compare with the one revealed by the speaker's words, they are susceptible to deception. Over four hundred years ago, the Renaissance scholar Francis Bacon suggested that the glass in the windows of depiction can be "enchanted": that is, the perspective may be distorted. Words can color or alter things, thus disguising or obscuring reality. The power to make listeners see can also be a power that blinds them.

The Power to Awaken Feelings

Language also can awaken powerful feelings. It can touch listeners and change their attitudes. Nowhere have we seen this power described more eloquently than by twelve-year-old Katherine Stout of Goodlettsville, Tennessee. In her entry in a junior-high school "Letters About Literature" competition sponsored by Humanities Tennessee, Katie wrote: "Words cannot break bones, but they can break hearts."[7] This power of words is used ethically when it *supplements* sound reasoning and credible evidence. It is abused if speakers *substitute* appeals to feelings for evidence or reasoning. To arouse emotions, language must overcome the barriers of time, distance, and apathy. Let's take a look at each of these.

Overcoming Time.

Listeners live in the present. This makes it difficult for speakers to awaken feelings about events that lie in the remote past or the distant future. To overcome this obstacle, speakers can use language to make the past and future come alive. Stories that recapture feelings from the past are often told at company meetings to re-create the human dimension of the business and to reestablish corporate heritage and culture. In the following story, the speaker reminds listeners of the legend of Federal Express, a pioneer in overnight delivery:

> **You know, we take a lot for granted. It's hard to remember that Federal Express was once just a fly-by-night dream, a crazy idea in which a few people had invested—not just their time and their money, but their lives and futures. I remember one time early on when things weren't going so well. We were really up against it. Couldn't even make the payroll that week. It looked like we were going to crash. Fred [Smith, founder of the company] was in a deep funk. Never saw him quite like that before or since. "What the hell," he said, and flew off to Las Vegas. The next day he flew back and his face was shining. "We're going to make it," he said. He had won $27,000 at the blackjack table! And we made it. We met the payroll. And then things began to turn around, and Federal Express grew into the giant it is today.[8]**

This story enlivens the past by emphasizing the contrast of emotions—the "deep funk" versus the "shining" face. The use of lively, colloquial dialogue—"What the hell," and "We're going to make it!"—re-creates the excitement and brings those feelings into the present. It would not have been as effective had the speaker simply said, "Fred was depressed, but after he got back from Las Vegas he was confident." Such a bare summary would have distanced the listener and diminished the emotional power of the scene.

Language can also bring the future close to listeners. Because words can cross the barrier of time, both tradition and a vision of tomorrow can guide us through the present.

Overcoming Distance. The closer anything is to us, the easier it is to develop feelings about it. But what if speakers must discuss faraway people and places? Words can telescope such subjects and bring them close to hand. Let's see how Martha Turnbow used language to reduce the distance between her urban classroom audience and her rural subject:

> **James Johnson has lived in Perry County for eighty-four years. He taught me some important things: why the mist rises on a lake at night, how to make the best wild blackberry jam you've ever put in your mouth, and how to take care of baby rabbits that are abandoned. Today, I want to tell you more about James—and about myself through him.**

By focusing on concrete details of sight, taste, and touch—the mist, the jam, the rabbits—the speaker overcame distance and aroused feelings about a subject that might have otherwise seemed remote. Similarly, when Beth Tidmore, our student who won the U.S. Junior Olympics air rifle event at Colorado Springs in 2003, wanted to share her feelings about her shooting experiences, she concentrated on sensory details. "My friends," she said, "don't know what it's like to feel the cold, smooth wood of the cheekpiece against your face. And they don't know the rich smell of Hoppe's No. 9 [oil] when you're cleaning your rifle."

Overcoming Apathy. We live in an age of communication overkill. Modern audiences are beset with an endless barrage of information, persuasion, and entertainment. Personal images, such as those used by Jesse Jackson at the 1988 Democratic National Convention, allow speakers to reach out and touch even jaded listeners:

> **America's not a blanket woven from one thread, one color, one cloth. When I was a child growing up in Greenville, South Carolina, and grandmother could not afford a blanket, she didn't complain and we did not freeze. Instead, she**

Vivid language can arouse emotions and bring people together in support of a cause.

took pieces of old cloth—patches, wool, silk, gabardine, croakersack on the patches—barely good enough to wipe off your shoes with. But they didn't stay that way very long. With sturdy hands and a strong cord, she sewed them together into a quilt, a thing of beauty and power and culture.

Now, Democrats, we must build such a quilt. Farmers, you seek fair prices and you are right, but you cannot stand alone. Your patch is not big enough. Workers, you fight for fair wages. You are right. But your patch, labor, is not big enough. Women, you seek comparable worth and pay equity. You are right. But your patch is not big enough. Women, mothers, who seek Head Start and day care and pre-natal care on the front side of life, rather than jail care and welfare on the back side of life, you're right, but your patch is not big enough. . . .

But don't despair. Be as wise as my grandmama. Pool the patches and the pieces together, bound by a common thread. When we form a great quilt of unity and common ground we'll have the power to bring about health care and housing and jobs and education and hope to our nation.[9]

Jackson's references to his grandmother's loving care aroused latent feelings. The image of a quilt—suggesting the warmth of home and the creation of beauty and value from lowly materials—gave the audience a vision of what they, too, might do.

When artfully used, language can overcome the barriers of time, distance, and apathy to make us care about a subject. The role of language in arousing feeling is also underscored by the contrast between denotative and connotative forms of meaning. The **denotative meaning** of a word is its dictionary definition or generally agreed-on objective usage. For example, the denotative definition of *alcohol* is "a colorless, volatile, flammable liquid, obtained by the fermentation of sugars or starches, which is widely used as a solvent, drug base, explosive, or intoxicating beverage."[10] How different this is from the two connotative definitions offered in this chapter's opening example! **Connotative meaning** invests a subject with the speaker's personal connections and emotions. Thus, the "intoxicating beverage" is no longer just a chemical substance but either "the poison scourge" or "the oil of conversation." Connotative language intensifies feelings: denotative language encourages detachment.

The Power to Bring Listeners Together

In many situations, individual action is not enough. It may take people working together to get things done. In addition to arousing strong feelings, Jesse Jackson also reminded listeners that they were part of an important larger group. Only if they acted together—as Democrats rather than as individual interest groups—would they have a chance to win the election.

InterConnections.LearnMore 12.1

Language Online

Verbivore
http://verbivore.com
Site devoted to "verbivores," who "feast on the English language." Written and maintained by Richard Lederer, author of Anguished English, it explores the uses and misuses of language; see especially its "Language Links on the Net," a comprehensive guide to classic sites focusing on style, grammar, and the ways of words.

Language: What We Speak
http://www.thymos.com/tat/language.html
An interesting essay exploring the relationship between language and thought; written by Piero Scaruffi, University of California lecturer and author in the area of artificial intelligence.

Power of Words
http://prisonsucks.com/scans/instead_of_prisons/index.shtml
Fascinating study of the power of words in the criminal justice system, especially as language functions as a semantic prison in support of the literal penal system; authors are activists who wish to abolish prisons.

Although words can unite people, they can also drive them apart. Name calling, exclusionary language, and unsupported accusations are invidious dividers. It may take their more positive counterparts to bring people back together. During a 1996 Republican Party primary debate, the contenders attacked and berated each other. Finally, one candidate, Representative Robert Dornan of California, reminded the others that their attacks on each other threatened party unity:

> **I wish the spirit of Ronald Reagan would descend on New Hampshire . . . and [remind us of] his eleventh commandment, that no Republican should speak ill of another. . . . We have to stop tearing at one another. . . . The target is Clinton . . . [and] the moral crisis in the White House. . . . Gentlemen, we're a family here. Let's unify ourselves and make sure we take the White House on November 5th.[11]**

Note that as Dornan pled for unity, he invoked a group hero, Ronald Reagan. He also used the "family" metaphor to counter the division, and he reminded listeners of a common enemy and shared goal: their desire to defeat President Clinton.

Heroes and enemies, common goals, shared values, and metaphors of inclusion—all can work together to heighten the value of group membership. We discuss these techniques more closely later in this chapter.

Vivid imagery and impassioned language can move people into action.

The Power to Encourage Action

Even if your listeners share an identity, they still may not be ready to act. What might stand in their way? For one thing, they may not be convinced of the soundness of your proposal. They may not trust you, or they may not think they can do anything about a problem. Finally, they may not be ready to invest the energy or take the risk that action demands.

Your language must convince listeners that action is necessary, that your ideas are sound, and that success is possible. In her speech urging students to act to improve off-campus housing conditions (see Appendix B), Anna Aley painted vivid word-pictures of deplorable off-campus housing. She supported these

Speaker's Notes 12.2

Uniting a Divided Group

1. Bring to life images of their heroes and enemies.
2. Describe group traditions they may have forgotten.
3. Depict in concrete terms the deeper values they share.
4. Picture common problems.
5. Illustrate goals they can share.
6. Define in simple terms the first step they can take together, and urge them to take it.
7. Speak the language of inclusion, such as using family or team metaphors.

with both factual examples and her personal experiences. She also reminded listeners that if they acted together, they could bring about change:

> **What can one student do to change the practices of numerous Manhattan landlords? Nothing, if that student is alone. But just think of what we could accomplish if we got all 13,600 off-campus students involved in this issue! Think what we could accomplish if we got even a fraction of those students involved!**

Anna then proposed specific actions that did not call for great effort or risk. In short, she made commitment as easy as possible. She concluded with an appeal to action:

> **Kansas State students have been putting up with substandard living conditions for too long. It's time we finally got together to do something about this problem. Join the Off-Campus Association. Sign my petition. Let's send a message to these slumlords that we're not going to put up with this any more. We don't have to live in slums.**

Anna's words expressed both her indignation and the urgency of the problem. Her references to time—"too long" and "it's time"—called for immediate action. Her final appeals to join the association and sign the petition were expressed in short sentences that packed a lot of punch. Her repetition of "slumlords" and "slums" motivated her listeners to transform their indignation into action.

Anna also illustrated another language strategy that is important when you want to move people to action: the ability to depict dramas showing what is at stake and what roles listeners should take.[12] Such scenarios draw clear lines between right and wrong. Be careful, however, not to go overboard with such techniques. Ethical communication requires that you maintain respect for all involved in conflict. As both speaker and listener, be wary of melodramas that offer stark contrasts between good and evil. Such depictions often distort reality.

The Six C's of Language Use

To harness the power of language in your speeches, your words must meet certain standards: clarity, color, concreteness, correctness, conciseness, and cultural sensitivity. We call these the six *C*'s of oral language.

Ethics Alert! 12.1

The Ethical Use of Powerful Language

1. Avoid depictions that distort reality: your words should illuminate the subject, not blind the listener.
2. Use words to support sound reasoning, not substitute for it.
3. Use language to empower both traditions and visions.
4. Use images to renew appreciation of shared values.
5. Use language to strengthen the ties of community, not divide people.
6. Use language to overcome inertia and inspire listeners to action.
7. Be cautious about melodramatic language that reduces complex issues and the people in disputes into good versus evil.

Clarity

VideoLab

To assess how well a particular speaker uses language to communicate information, go to **Next Step: Mastering the 6 *C*'s of Language Effectiveness** in **Lesson 7** and complete the quiz.

Clarity is the first standard, because if your words are not clear, listeners cannot understand your meaning. This may seem obvious, but it is often ignored! To be clear, you must yourself understand what you want to say. Next, you must find words that convey your ideas as precisely and as simply as possible. Your voice, face, and gestures should help to reinforce the idea as you present it, a process we shall discuss in the next chapter. Your listeners must be capable of interpreting your words and nonverbal cues. The standard of clarity is met when something closely approximating the idea you intend is reproduced in the minds of these listeners.

One factor that impairs clarity is the use of **jargon**, the technical language that is specific to a profession. Such language is often referred to with an *-ese* at the end, as in "speaking computerese." If you use jargon before an audience that doesn't share that technical vocabulary, you will not be understood. For example, "We expect a positive vorticity advective" may be perfectly understandable to a group of meteorologists, but for most audiences, simply saying, "It's going to rain" would be much clearer. Speakers who fall into the jargon trap are so used to using technical language that they forget that others may not grasp it. It does not occur to them that they must translate the jargon into lay language to be understood by general audiences. Adapting technical language so that nonspecialists can understand it can be challenging, but an example in Chapter 8 (page 206), explaining how the OnStar system works in cars, shows how this can be done effectively.

A similar problem is using words that are needlessly overblown. A notorious example occurred when signmakers wanted to tell tourists how to leave the Barnum museum. Rather than drawing an arrow with the word *Exit* above it, they wrote "To the Egress." There's no telling how many visitors left the museum by mistake, thinking that they were going to see that rare creature—a living, breathing "Egress."

Although such misunderstandings may result from innocent incompetence, at other times jargon seems to be purposely befuddling. One term for such jargon is **doublespeak**, in which words evade the responsibility of talking about the important meanings in a situation or even point in the direction opposite from the reality they should be describing. Some speakers like to satisfy their egos and intimidate others by preening their technical vocabularies. The parent of a student in Houston received a message from the high school principal regarding a special meeting on a proposed educational program. The message read:

> **Our school's cross-graded, multiethnic, individualized learning program is designed to enhance the concept of an open-ended learning program with emphasis on a continuum of multiethnic, academically enriched learning, using the identified intellectually gifted child as the agent or director of his own**

learning. Major emphasis is on cross-graded, multiethnic learning with the main objective being to learn respect for the uniqueness of a person.

The parent responded:

> **Dear Principal: I have a college degree, speak two foreign languages and know four Indian dialects. I've attended a number of county fairs and three goat ropings, but I haven't the faintest idea as to what you are talking about. Do you?[13]**

Some people seem to take a strange joy in *not* communicating, but others may try to hide the truth behind a smokescreen of technobabble and doublespeak. The former is mindless chatter that hides the lack of actual content: the latter disguises some awkward reality. The *New York Times* charged that the Bush administration developed what they call *ecospeak* (an apparent variation of *doublespeak*) to disguise probusiness and antienvironmental initiatives:

> **Mr. Bush . . . may fairly be said to have become the master of the ostensibly ecofriendly sound bite. . . . "Healthy Forests," for instance, describes an initiative aimed mainly at benefiting the timber industry rather than the communities threatened by fire. "Freedom Car" (to be powered by "Freedom Fuel") describes a program to develop a hydrogen-fueled car that, while beguiling in the long term, absolves automakers from making the near-term improvements in fuel economy necessary to reduce oil dependence and the threat of global warming. . . . [In another case] Mr. Bush's purpose was to defend his controversial decision in August to rewrite the Clean Air Act in ways that spared power companies the expense of making investments in pollution controls. . . . His basic argument was that the rules thwarted modernization and economic growth . . . and that his own initiative—dubbed "Clear Skies," in the come-hither nomenclature favored by the White House—would achieve equal results at lower cost.[14]**

Some time earlier, public television commentator Bill Moyers had warned his audience at the University of Texas against the dangers of such language:

> **If you would . . . serve democracy well, you must first save the language. Save it from the jargon of insiders who talk of the current budget debate in Washington as "megapolicy choices between freeze-feasible base lines." (Sounds more like a baseball game played in the Arctic Circle.) Save it from the smokescreen artists, who speak of "revenue enhancement" and "tax-base erosion control" when they really mean a tax increase. . . . Save it from . . . the official revisionists of reality, who say that the United States did not withdraw our troops from Lebanon, we merely "backloaded our augmentation personnel."[15]**

Fearing the reactions of listeners who actually understand their meaning, such speakers hide behind cloudy technical language.

One way to achieve clarity in oral language is through **amplification**, in which you rephrase ideas to bring them into focus. In effect, you tell listeners something and then expand and repeat what you said. Providing important bits of information or examples that compare and contrast the unfamiliar with the familiar is one way to amplify an idea. Note how amplification works in the following speech excerpt, in which each sentence expands and repeats the meaning of the sentence that comes before it:

> **The roadrunner is not just a cartoon character that makes a fool of Wile E. Coyote. It is a member of the cuckoo family and state bird of New Mexico.**

Figure 12.1
Doublespeak

When they say:	What they often mean is:
Marital discord	Spouse beating
Department of human biodynamics	Department of physical education
Downsizing	Firing
Making a salary adjustment	Cutting your pay
Failed to fulfill wellness potential	Died
Chronologically experienced citizen	Old codger
Initial and pass on	Let's spread the blame
Friendly fire	We killed our own people
Collateral damage	We killed innocent people

> **Still, the cartoon roadrunner and the real roadrunner have much in common. Both are incredibly fast, real roadrunners having been tracked at ground speeds up to 17 miles per hour. Neither takes to the air to chase prey or escape a predator. Both look rather awkward as they run, with strides up to 20 inches long—a real feat for a bird that is only 24 inches long with over half its length in its tail.**

Color

Color refers to the emotional intensity or vividness of language. Colorful words are memorable because they stand out in our minds. Speakers who use them also are remembered.

In political campaigns, colorful language often gives one candidate an edge over others. During the 1996 presidential primaries, Pat Buchanan became a leading contender, at least partially because of his skill with words. Early in the campaign, another candidate had gained a great deal of attention by proposing tax reform. A third contender, Senator Phil Gramm, criticized this proposal as follows: "I reject the idea that income derived from labor should be taxed and that income derived from capital should not."[16] Nice contrast, but about as flat as the tax he was talking about. Now look at how Buchanan expressed the same idea: "Under Forbes's plan, lounge lizards in Palm Beach would pay a lower tax rate than steelworkers in Youngstown." Whereas Gramm's words were abstract, Buchanan's were colorful. "Lounge lizards" is striking. So is the use of contrast, setting the "lounge lizards" against steelworkers, Palm Beach against Youngstown. It's sloth and privilege against character and virtue, and we know which side Buchanan is on. Colorful language paints striking pictures for listeners. Notice how Leslie Eason made Tiger Wood come alive in her speech of tribute:

> **Mothers with daughters of a certain age (mine included) describe him as the son-in-law they'd like to have. Six foot two, a hundred fifty-five pounds, smart—Stanford, remember. Clean cut in his creased khakis, curly hair, gorgeous teeth. Skin the color of what they used to call "suntan" in the Crayola box. And rich. Very rich.**
>
> **He's the very opposite of the gangsta boys in the hood. Boys who wear their pants hanging below their belt as though they were already in the penitentiary. Next to them he's prep school and Pepsodent.**

One very special type of colorful language is **slang**. You've probably been told most of your life not to use slang, that it is a mark of illiteracy and coarseness, that it is vulgar, that it epitomizes "bad" English. But according to general semanticist S. I. Hayakawa, slang is also "the poetry of everyday life." Or, as the poet Carl Sandburg noted, slang is "language that rolls up its sleeves, spits on its hands, and goes to work." Sometimes slang becomes incorporated into the more formal language of a culture. For example, you may have heard of Kill Devil Hill, the site of the Wright brothers' first powered flight. But did you know that this name derived from the slang term *kill-devil,* meaning "strong West Indian rum," which was brought in at a nearby harbor?[17]

Slang has its use in speeches: it can add vigor to your message and be a source of identification between you and listeners. But use it with caution. Slang is inappropriate on formal occasions when a high level of decorum is called for. Moreover, you must be certain that your audience will understand your slang. If you have to stop and define your words, they will lose their punch. In such cases, slang will distance you from your listeners, not create identification. You must also be careful about using ethnic slang or other words that your audience might find offensive. Finally, slang should be used sparingly—to emphasize a point or add a dash of humor and color. It should supplement Standard English usage in your speech, not replace it.

Using colorful language makes a speech interesting. It enhances your ethos by increasing your attractiveness. For all these reasons, color is an important standard for the effective use of language.

InterConnections.LearnMore 12.2

Language Usage

The American Heritage Book of English Usage
http://www.bartleby.com/64/
A practical guide to contemporary English, with sections on grammar, style, word choice, gender, and pronunciation challenges.

Dr. NAD's Prig Page
http://www.geocities.com/CapeCanaveral/5229/p_.htm
A website for prigs who "cling tightly to the rules of English grammar" and for others interested in sounding articulate and intelligent; includes a Pet Peeves page and a Prig Test; developed and maintained by Neil Anthony Durso III.

Paul Brians' Common Errors in English
http://www.wsu.edu/~brians/errors/index.html
A useful website designed to help students keep from sounding unintelligent or ignorant; concentrates mainly on errors of usage in American English; developed and maintained by Professor Paul Brians, Department of English, Washington State University.

World Wide Words
http://www.worldwidewords.org
An interesting site presenting English from a British viewpoint; focuses on word usage, turns of phrase, weird words, and other vagaries of language; developed and maintained by Michael B. Quinion of the editorial staff of the Oxford English Dictionary.

Concreteness

It is almost impossible to discuss any significant topic without using some abstract words. However, if you use language that is overly abstract, your audience may lose interest. Moreover, because abstract language is more ambiguous than concrete language, a speech full of abstractions invites misunderstanding. Consider this continuum of terms describing a cat.

Mehitabel is a/an

creature   animal   mammal   cat   Persian cat   gray Persian cat

abstract >————————————————>**concrete**

A similar continuum can be applied to active verbs. If we wanted to describe how a person moves, we could use any of the following terms:

Jennifer

moves   walks   strides

abstract >————————————————>**concrete**

The more concrete your language, the more pictorial and precise the information you convey. Concrete words are also easier for listeners to remember. Your language should be as concrete as the subject permits.

Correctness

Nothing can damage your credibility more than the misuse of language. Glaring mistakes in grammar can make you seem uneducated, and even ignorant. While touting his education plan, one prominent politician told listeners that the most important consideration should be, "Is your children learning?" Other common grammatical errors that make listeners cringe are listed in Figure 12.2.

Mistakes in word selection can be as damaging as mistakes in grammar. Occasionally beginning speakers, wanting to impress people with the size of their vocabulary, get caught up in the "thesaurus syndrome." They will look up a simple word to find a synonym that sounds more impressive or sophisticated. What they may not realize is that the words shown as synonyms often have slightly different meanings. For example, the words *disorganize* and *derange* are sometimes listed as synonyms. But if you refer to a disorganized person as "deranged," you will see what we mean.

People often err when using words that sound similar. Such confusions are called **malapropisms,** after Mrs. Malaprop, a character in an eighteenth-century play by Richard Sheridan. She would say, "He is the very *pineapple* of politeness," when she meant *pinnacle*. Thus a prominent baseball player, trying to explain why he had forgotten an appointment for an interview, said, "I must have had *ambrosia*" (which probably caused his *amnesia,* which is what he apparently meant). Archie Bunker in the classic TV show *All in the Family* was prone to malapropisms, such as "Don't let your imagination run *rancid*" when he meant *rampant.* William J. Crocker of Armidale College in New South Wales, Australia, collected the following malapropisms from his students:

> A speaker can add interest to his talk with an *antidote.* [anecdote]
>
> Disagreements can arise from an unintended *conception.* [Indeed they can!]

Figure 12.2
Grammatical Errors

1. Using the wrong tense or verb form:
   Wrong: He *done* us a big favor.
   Right: He *did* us a big favor.
2. Lack of agreement between subject and verb:
   Wrong: *Is* your students giving speeches?
   Right: *Are* your students giving speeches?
3. Using the wrong word
   Wrong: *Caricature* is the most important factor in choosing a mate.
   Right: *Character* is the most important factor in choosing a mate.
4. Lack of agreement between a pronoun and its antecedent:
   Wrong: A hyperactive *person* will work *themselves* to death.
   Right: Hyperactive *people* will work *themselves* to death.
   or
   A hyperactive *woman* will work *herself* to death.
5. Improper type of pronoun used as subject:
   Wrong: *Him* and *me* decided to go to the library.
   Right: *He* and *I* decided to go to the library.
6. Improper type of pronoun used as object:
   Wrong: The speaker's lack of information dismayed my students and *I.*
   Right: The speaker's lack of information dismayed my students and *me.*
7. Double negative:
   Wrong: I *don't never* get good grades on my speeches.
   Right: I *never* get good grades on my speeches.

The speaker hopes to arouse *apathy* in his audience. [sympathy? empathy?]

Good language can be reinforced by good *gestation*. [gestures]

The speaker can use either an inductive or a *seductive* approach. [deductive][18]

Students, ballplayers, and fictional characters are not the only ones who make such blunders. Elected officials are also not above an occasional malapropism. One former United States senator declared that he would oppose to his last ounce of energy any effort to build a "nuclear waste *suppository*" [repository] in his state. A long gone but not forgotten Chicago mayor once commented that he did not believe "in casting *asparagus* [aspersions] on his opponents." And the Speaker of the Texas legislature once acknowledged an award by saying, "I am filled with *humidity*" (perhaps he meant moist hot air as well as humility).

The lesson is clear. To avoid being unintentionally humorous, use a current dictionary to check the meaning of any word you feel uncertain about.

Conciseness

In discussing clarity, we talked about the importance of amplification in speeches. Although it may seem contradictory, you must also be concise, even while you are amplifying your ideas. You must make your points quickly and efficiently. Follow the advice on speaking given by President Franklin Delano Roosevelt to his son James: "Be sincere . . . be brief . . . be seated!"

Simplicity and directness help you be concise. Thomas Jefferson once said, "The most valuable of all talents is that of never using two words when one will do." Use the active voice rather than the passive in your verbs: "We want action!" is more concise—and more direct, colorful, and clear—than "Action is wanted by us."

You can also achieve conciseness by using **maxims**, those compact sayings that encapsulate beliefs. During the Chinese freedom demonstrations of 1989, a sign carried by students in Tiananmen Square adapted the maxim of Patrick Henry: "Give Me Democracy or Give Me Death." Sadly, the Chinese authorities took them at their word. To reinforce his point that we need to actively (and audibly) confront the problems of racism, sexism, and homophobia, Haven Cockerham, vice president of human resources for Detroit Edison, said: "Sometimes silence isn't golden—just yellow."[19]

As these examples suggest, maxims often attract mass-media attention. When printed on signs, they are picked up for visual messages. Their brevity and dramatic impact make them well suited to the time constraints of television news. Of even greater importance, maxims evoke cultural memories and invite identification. When the Chinese students adapted the Patrick Henry maxim, they were in effect both declaring that they shared American values and appealing for our assistance in their struggle. When their cause was crushed, many Americans felt the injustice in a personal way, and the resulting tension between the Chinese government and our own lingers to this day.

InterConnections.LearnMore 12.3

Language Resources for ESL Students

English as Second Language
http://esl.about.com/education/adulted/esl/
Articles and links to online materials, exercises, and quizzes for beginning, intermediate, and advanced ESL students; a very useful supplement to what is offered on your campus; developed and maintained by Kenneth Beare.

Dave's ESL Café
http://www.pacificnet.net/~sperling
A cyber meeting place for students and teachers from around the world. Includes a chat room, help center, slang translations, idioms of American English, and links to other ESL resources; developed and maintained by Professor Dave Sperling, ESL, California State University, Northridge.

Alta Books
http://www.altaesl.com/index_dave.cfm
Styles itself as the largest source of ESL books and materials in the world.

TEFL Skills
http://www.onestopenglish.com/tefl_skills/speaking.htm
Exercises designed to encourage English speaking practice in the classroom; sponsored by Onestop Magazine.

Chinese students who protested in Tiananmen Square carried an image of "Lady Liberty" along with signs that read, "Give me democracy or give me death."

A caution is in order about using maxims. They should not be substituted for a carefully designed and well-supported argument. However, once you have developed a responsible and substantive speech, consider using maxims to reinforce your message.

Cultural Sensitivity

Because words can both lift and unite or wound and hurt your audience, you must exercise **cultural sensitivity** in your choice of language. Looking back into the history of human communication, you will find little about cultural sensitivity. The ancient Greeks, for example, worried only about speaking to other male Athenians who were "free men" and citizens. Today, with the increasing emphasis on empowering diverse cultures, lifestyles, and races and the pursuit of gender equity, cultural sensitivity becomes an important standard for effective language usage.

As we noted in Chapter 5, your classroom audience may represent many different cultures. As listeners, they will be sensitive to clumsy efforts by speakers to identify with folkways that aren't their own. Campaigning for the presidential nomination in his native South in 1992, Bill Clinton could get away with using such folksy expressions as "my opponents are squealing like a pig caught under a gate." Senator Bob Kerrey of Nebraska, however, was less adept when speaking to southern audiences. At Atlanta's Spelman College during the same campaign, Kerrey declared that if Clinton got the nomination, President George H. Bush would open him up "like a soft peanut." Kerrey's listeners simply looked puzzled. Someone apparently spoke with his speechwriters, because in later speeches in that peanut-growing area Kerrey changed the expression to "boiled peanut."[20] Don't try to be what you're not, or you may look ridiculous.

A lack of cultural sensitivity almost always has negative consequences. At best, audience members may be mildly offended; at worst, they will be irate enough to reject both you and your message. Cultural sensitivity begins with being attuned to the diversity of your audience, respectful of the differences between cultural groups, and careful about the words you choose. Always think before you speak. Don't be like the politician who singled out some audience members in wheelchairs for special praise. After lauding their accomplishments, he said, "Now, will you all stand and be recognized?"

Although you must make some generalizations about your audience, avoid getting caught up in stereotypes that suggest that one group is inferior in any way to another. Stay away from racial, ethnic, religious, or gender-based humor, and avoid any expressions that might be interpreted as racist or sexist (see Speaker's Notes 5.1 on page 124 for guidelines on avoiding racist and sexist language).

VideoLab

Go to **Drill 7.2: Identifying Language Techniques** and view the video clips. Afterwards, take the quiz to assess your knowledge of the speakers' use of figures of speech and word choice.

Magnifying the Power of Language

There are critical moments in a speech—at the beginning, at the ending, or as arguments reach their conclusions—when you want your words to be most effective. At these moments you can call on special techniques that magnify the power of language.

The branch of communication study that deals with identifying and understanding these techniques is called *rhetorical style.* Over the centuries, many such techniques have been identified; they seem to be grounded in our nature, and to have evolved to meet our need for effective communication. Here we discuss three broad categories of techniques that seem especially useful for public speaking. These are various forms of *figurative language,* techniques that alter the customary *order* of words, and techniques that exploit the *sounds* of words for special effects. Let's look at each of these.

Cultural sensitivity requires that you be attuned to the diversity of your audience, respectful of the differences between cultural groups, and careful about the words you choose.

Using Figurative Language

Figurative language uses words in surprising and unusual ways. Although many kinds of such language have been identified, we shall focus on six forms that are especially useful: metaphors, enduring metaphors, similes, personifications, culturetypes, and ideographs.

Metaphors. As we noted in Chapter 8, drawing comparisons is a fundamental way in which our minds work to understand unfamiliar or abstract ideas. A **metaphor** offers a brief, concentrated form of comparison that is implied, unexpected, and sometimes even startling. It connects elements of experience that are not usually related. When you use a metaphor, you pull a rabbit out of a hat. Having read that, your first reaction might be, "Wait a minute, words are not rabbits and language is not a hat!" But when a metaphor works, the listener's next reaction is, "Oooh, I see what you mean!" Good metaphors reveal unexpected similarities in striking ways. They also can add color and concreteness to your message.

Metaphors may be our most useful and versatile stylistic tool. They can be especially helpful in introductions and conclusions. At the beginnings of speeches, metaphors can offer an overall frame of understanding in which a topic can develop. Note how Antoinette M. Bailey, president of the Boeing-McDonnell Foundation, used a wave metaphor to open a speech presented to the International Women in Aviation Conference:

> **Suppose we have gone down to the beach on a quiet day. We are standing in the water, admiring the view. Suddenly, a speedboat zooms by at full throttle. Seconds later, we are struck by a powerful wave. This is a bow wave, and it can**

Speaker's Notes 12.3

The Six C's of Effective Language Use

1. Clarity makes speeches understandable.
2. Color adds punch to your message.
3. Concreteness reduces misunderstandings.
4. Correctness enhances your credibility.
5. Conciseness keeps you from wasting your audience's time.
6. Cultural sensitivity is an ethical imperative.

Eloquent language can intensify our feelings about subjects.

knock you off your feet if you aren't prepared for it. A very large and fast-moving bow wave is just now beginning to hit the aerospace industry. This morning I want to talk about what we, as an industry, and we, as women, should do to prepare for it.[21]

In a similar vein, concluding metaphors can offer a final frame of understanding that interprets the meaning of a speech for its listeners. When Martin Luther King Jr. spoke to the striking sanitation workers in Memphis the night before he was assassinated, he talked of the "spiritual journey" that his listeners had traveled. He ended his speech by saying that he had climbed the mountain ahead of them—that he had "seen the Promised Land." These metaphors of the journey and the mountain lifted his listeners and allowed them to share his vision, just as he had earlier shared his "dream" with them in his famous "I Have a Dream" speech. More than just communicating in a superficial way, such metaphors may reveal the speaker's soul.

Because metaphors can be so powerful, you should select them carefully and use them with restraint. First, *the gravity of the metaphor must match the seriousness of your subject.* Just as you would not typically wear formal attire to a basketball game, you should not use certain metaphors to express certain subjects. If you used Dr. King's mountaintop image to express your overview of the can recycling industry, the effect might be more comic than persuasive.

Second, *mixing metaphors by combining images that don't fit together can confuse listeners and lower their estimation of your competence.* The politician who attacked an opponent saying, "You can't have it both ways in the political process. You can't take the high horse and then claim the low road," mixed his metaphors.

Third, *you also should avoid trite metaphors*, such as "that person [or idea or practice] is so cool" or "I was on an emotional roller coaster." Overuse has turned these metaphors into clichés that no longer affect people. Not only are they ineffective, but using them may again damage your ethos. Tired comparisons suggest a dull mind.

Enduring Metaphors. One special group of metaphors taps into shared experience that persists across time and that crosses many cultural boundaries. These **enduring metaphors** are especially popular in speeches, perhaps because they invoke experience that has great meaning and that can bring people together. They connect their particular, timebound subjects with timeless themes, such as light and darkness, storms, the sea, disease, and the family. A brief look at three of these metaphors demonstrates their potential power to magnify meaning.[22]

Light and Darkness. From the beginnings of time, people have made negative associations with darkness. The dark is cold, unfriendly, and dangerous. On the other hand, light brings warmth and safety. It restores control. When speakers use the light-darkness metaphor, they usually equate problems or bad times with darkness and solutions or recovery with light. The speaker's proposal may offer the "dawn," a "candle to light our way," or a "beacon of hope."

Storms and the Sea. The storm metaphor is often used when describing problems. Typically the storm occurs at sea—a dangerous place under the best of conditions. When political problems are the focus of the speech, the solution often comes from the "captain" steering the "ship of state." In his 2001 inaugural address, George W. Bush noted that "through much of the last century, America's faith in freedom and democracy was a rock in a raging sea."[23]

The Family. Family metaphors express the dream of a close, loving relationship among people through such images as "the family of humanity."[24] These can be especially useful when listeners may feel alienated from each other and from their surroundings. In such situations, family metaphors can be a powerful force to bring listeners together and to effect identification. Wade Steck demonstrated the potential of such metaphors as he was describing his experiences at the University of Memphis Frosh Camp Program, his introduction to college life:

> **As we were riding to camp, my heart was beating really fast. I guess I was kind of nervous—didn't know what I was getting into, wasn't sure I was ready to meet all these new people. But when I got to Frosh Camp, they made me feel at home. First thing they did was to break us into "families" of ten to twelve people who would share the same cabin for those few days. Each "family" had its counselors, carefully selected juniors and seniors who were really called your "mom" and "dad." Sounds corny, I guess, but it did put my mind at ease. . . .The thing I liked most were the Fireside Chats. At night under the stars, watching the logs burn and listening to the crickets chirp, people would just relax and talk about what was in their hearts. I found out those in my family shared my concerns and anxieties. Once we got those out in the open and talked about them, we were ready to go on to college and to start our new lives.**

Similarly, the *disease* metaphor pictures our problems as illness and offers solutions in the form of cures.[25] Metaphors of *war and peace* can frame conflict situations and our quest for their resolution.[26] The *building* metaphor, as when we talk about "laying the foundation" for the future, emphasizes our ancient impulse to shape and control the conditions of our lives. And *spatial* metaphors often reflect striving upward and moving forward toward goals.[27]

Perhaps the reason such metaphors are so powerful is that they express the motives we discussed in Chapter 5. Light and darkness, for example, may connect with safety needs (representing our fears as darkness) or esteem and self-actualization needs (representing our successes and growth in terms of light).

Similes. A **simile** is a variation of metaphor that tips its hand by warning listeners that a comparison is coming. Words such as *like* or *as* function as signals that soften the impact of the expression. The result is to offer a more controlled form of figuration in which the speaker guides the comparison. Remember Scott Champlin's words "a force that spun me around *like* a twisted yo-yo at the end of a string"? Most of us, we hope, will never be hit by a tracer bullet while parachuting, but helped by the simile, we can imagine the experience. Similarly, one critic used simile to express her feelings about the president's proposal to send astronauts on an expedition to Mars: "Spending billions in outer space is like buying a new Lexus when the fridge is empty and the roof is leaking."[28]

Although a simile is related to metaphor, it is certainly not the same thing. During the 2004 Democratic primary campaign for the presidency, Howard Dean complained about certain below-the-belt tactics being used against him. When his opponents responded that he himself was guilty of using dehumanizing metaphors, Dean responded in effect that what he had actually used was a simile. Here is how the exchange went, as recorded in *Newsweek:*

> **[Interviewer]: There are some people who would say that it takes a little bit of chutzpah for you to complain since at various times you've called the people inside Washington cockroaches—**
>
> **[Dean]: That actually is not true. What I said was that they'll be scurrying around in Washington just like cockroaches. That is not calling members of Congress cockroaches.[29]**

Dean at least believed that there was a substantial difference between metaphor and simile!

As the Dean example may indicate, you should be careful about what you select for comparison. Words as well as people are judged by the company they keep. An imprudent simile can make your subject seem trivial or repulsive and make you seem tasteless if not insensitive. Some critics thought former president Clinton also used poor judgment when he suggested that stalling action on health care reform "will make it just like a hangnail or an ingrown toenail. It's just going to get worse."[30] When they work well, however, similes can magnify the effect of comparison.

Personifications. One persistent form of figurative speech, **personification**, treats inanimate subjects, such as ideas or institutions, as though they had human form or feeling. The Chinese students who were demonstrating for freedom in Tiananmen Square also carried a statue they called the "Goddess of Liberty." They were borrowing a personification that has long been used in the Western world: the representation of liberty as a woman.[31] When those students then had to confront tanks, and their oppressors destroyed the symbol of liberty, it was easy for many, living thousands of miles away in another culture, to feel even more angry over their fate. Personification makes it easier to arouse feelings about people and values that might otherwise seem abstract and distant.

Culturetypes. **Culturetypes**, sometimes stated in the form of metaphor, express the values, identity, and goals of a particular group and time.[32] In 1960, John F. Kennedy dramatized his presidential campaign by inviting Americans to explore with him "new frontiers" of challenge and discovery. That metaphor worked well in American culture, but it probably would not have made much sense in other countries. For Americans, the frontier is a unique symbol that offers the promise of freedom and opportunity.

Some words that have culturetypal quality include what rhetorical critic Richard Weaver once described as "god and devil terms."[33] He suggested that *progress* has been a primary "god term" of American culture. People often seem willing to follow that word as though it were some kind of divine summons. Tell us to do something in the name of "progress," and many of us will feel obligated to respond. Other terms, such as *science, modern,* and *efficient,* are similarly powerful because they seem rooted in American values. If "science" tells us something, we are apt to listen respectfully. If something is "modern," many of us will think it is better, probably because it has benefited from "progress." If something is "efficient," many Americans will more often select it over options that are perhaps more ethical or beautiful. On the other hand, words like *communist* and *un-American* are "devil terms." Tie them to a subject, and it will seem repulsive.

Culturetypes can change over time: in recent years, words like *natural, communication,* and the *environment* have been emerging god terms; *liberal, pollution,* and especially *terrorist* are emerging devil terms.

Ideographs. Communication scholar Michael Calvin McGee identified an especially potent group of culturetypes that he called **ideographs**. These words express a country's basic political values.[34] McGee suggested that words like *freedom, liberty,* and *democracy* are important because they are shorthand expressions of political identity. It is inconceivable to us that other nations might not wish to have a "democratic" form of government or that they might not prize "liberty" over every other value. Expressions like "*freedom* fighters" or "*democracy* in action" have unusual power for us because they utilize ideographs.

As an audience we can be especially vulnerable to such language, and it can be dangerous. After all, one person's "freedom fighter" can be another person's "terrorist." We need to look behind such glittering generalities to inspect the agendas they may hide. You may recall that in Chapter 4 we discussed "trigger words," the idea that we as individuals may react unthinkingly to certain words that trigger emotional response and short-circuit reflection. Ideographs and culturetypes can function as widely shared, cultural trigger words. They are capable of honorable work: they can magnify the appeal of sound arguments, remind us of our heritage, and suggest that we must be true to our values. But the potential for abusing such words in unethical communication is considerable. You must prove that they apply correctly to your topic. As a speaker, use them sparingly, and as a listener, inspect them carefully.

To develop a healthy resistance to such words, we must learn to apply a system of critical questions whenever we encounter them:

1. *Is this really what it claims to be?* For example, does the development of increasingly more powerful weapons of mass destruction really represent "progress"? Are "freedom fighters" actually thugs?
2. *Are those who make these claims legitimate speakers?* For example, are those who advance the "science" of cryonics really "scientists"? Or do they simply exploit our fears of mortality?
3. *Do these claims reflect a proper hierarchy of values?* For example, lopping off the top of a mountain to strip-mine coal may be a highly "efficient" form of mining, but should we be thinking about efficiency here? Could protection of the environment be a more important value?
4. *What kinds of actions are these words urging me to endorse or undertake?* For example, should I be asked to support and even die for "democracy" in a nation whose citizens may prefer another form of government?

Changing the Order of Words

We grow accustomed to words falling into certain patterns in sentences. Strategic changes in the order of words violate these expectations and call attention to the meaning intended. *Antithesis, inversion,* and *parallel construction* all involve changes in the way that words are ordered in messages. Their primary functions are to magnify the speaker as a leader and to enhance appeals to action. Let's consider them briefly.

Antithesis. **Antithesis** arranges different or opposing ideas in the same or adjoining sentences to create a striking contrast. Beth Tidmore used the technique well in her speech on Special Olympics: "With the proper instruction, environment, and encouragement, Special Olympians can learn not only sport skills, but life skills." Antithesis also can suggest that the speaker has a clear, decisive grasp of options. It magnifies the speaker as a person of vision, leadership, and action.

Ethics Alert! 12.2

Questions for Resisting Culturetypes and Ideographs

1. *Is the substance of the claim* really what it purports to be?
2. Are there hidden motives beneath the glittering surface of words?
3. What values are *not* represented here that ought to be considered?
4. What am I being asked to support or do? Can I really defend that?

President John F. Kennedy often used antithesis in his speeches. Consider these famous words from his Inaugural Address:

> **Ask not what your country can do for you—ask what you can do for your country.**

You may have learned this quotation in high school and, prompted with the first few words, could probably recite it verbatim today. But Kennedy said essentially the same thing during a campaign speech in September of 1960:

> **The new frontier is not what I promise I am going to do for you. The new frontier is what I ask you to do for your country.**

Same message, different words. The first is memorable; the second is not. The difference is effective antithesis (as well as effective inversion and parallel construction).[35] In its entirety, the passage from the inaugural was as follows:

> **And so, my fellow Americans: Ask not what your country can do for you—ask what you can do for your country.**
>
> **My fellow citizens of the world: Ask not what America will do for you, but what together we can do for the freedom of man.**

Inversion. **Inversion** reverses the expected order of words in a phrase or sentence to make a statement more memorable and emphatic. Consider how the impact of Kennedy's statement would have been diminished had he used "Do not ask" instead of "Ask not." Paul El-Amin concluded his criticism of internment practices after the 9/11 disaster by adapting the same passage from the poem by John Donne: "Ask not for whom the bell tolls. It tolls for me. And it tolls for thee. For all of us who love the Bill of Rights, it tolls." The "ask not" that begins this statement and the final sentence are both inverted from their usual order. The unusual order of the words gains attention and makes the statement impressive. Moreover, the "thee" adds to the impression that this is old, even religious wisdom. Used in student speeches, inversion works best as a beginning or ending technique, where it can gain attention, add dignity to the effort, and/or frame a memorable conclusion.

Parallel Construction. **Parallel construction** repeats the same pattern of words in a sequence of phrases or sentences for the sake of impact. We discussed the use of parallel construction for framing the main points in a speech in Chapter 10, but parallel construction can occur at any critical moment in a speech. As the Kennedy example illustrates, the repetition of the pattern of words can stamp its message into the mind and make its statement memorable. Perhaps the most famous examples in American public address are Martin Luther King's repeated phrase "I have a dream . . ." in his classic March on Washington speech and Lincoln's "of the people, by the people, and for the people . . ." near the end of the Gettysburg Address. More recently, President George W. Bush also used the technique strikingly. As he announced that military strikes against the Taliban had begun in Afghanistan, the president sounded very much like Winston Churchill as he proclaimed:

> **The battle is now joined on many fronts. We will not waver; we will not tire; we will not falter; and we will not fail. Peace and freedom will prevail.**[36]

In her tribute to Tiger Woods (see the complete text at the end of Chapter 17), Leslie Eason also used parallel construction in her introduction:

> **You're at the Western Open, where Tiger Woods could be Elvis resurrected. People clap when he pulls out the club. They clap when he hits the ball. They clap no matter where that ball lands. They clap if he smiles. They clap because he is.**

Exploiting the Sounds of Words

As they are pronounced, words have distinctive sounds. Part of the appeal of parallel construction is that it repeats these sounds. As the Bush example also illustrates, the rhyming of these sounds can add a striking, pleasing effect. At least two other techniques, alliteration and onomatopoeia, also arrange these sounds in distinctive ways. Both techniques magnify the language of feeling.

Alliteration. **Alliteration** repeats the initial sounds in a closely connected pattern of words. One student speaker who criticized the lowering of educational standards paused near the end of her speech to draw the following conclusion: "We don't need the *d*octrine of *d*umbing *d*own." Her repetition of the *d* sound was distinctive and helped listeners remember her point. It expressed her strong feeling about practices she condemned.

Onomatopoeia. **Onomatopoeia** is the tendency of certain words to imitate the sounds of what they represent. For example, suppose you were trying to describe the scene of refugees fleeing from war and starvation. How could you bring that scene into focus for listeners who are far removed? One way would be to describe an old woman and her grandson as they *trudge* down a road to nowhere. The very sound of the word *trudge* suggests the weary, discouraged walk of the refugees. Hannah Johnston also used the technique when she described packing house workers as "literally drenched in a river of blood." By its very sound, *drenched* suggests the unpleasant idea of being soaked with blood as you work. Combined with the "river of blood" metaphor, the technique draws listeners close to what the language describes. Onomatopoeia has this quality of conveying listeners into a scene by allowing them to hear its noises, smell its odors, taste its flavors, or touch its surfaces. The technique awakens sensory experience.

As you contemplate using these various ways to magnify the power of language, remember that your words must not seem forced or artificial. For these techniques to work, they must seem to arise naturally and spontaneously in your speaking, and they must seem to fit both you and your subject. You should use them sparingly, so that they stand out from the rest of your speech. Used artfully, and in concurrence with the six standards discussed earlier, they can both increase and harness the power of language so that it works productively.

VideoLab

Go to **Lesson 7 Coach: Tips to Remember** and watch the speech clip. Read through the list of reminders concerning effective language use. How well does this speaker measure up?

In Summary

Many of us underestimate the power of our words. The language we select can determine whether we succeed or fail as communicators.

The Power of the Spoken Word. Oral language is more spontaneous, less formal, and more interactive than written communication. The spoken word can be more colorful and expansive; it alters the structure of sentences, and it depends more on the cadence or rhythm of language as it is voiced.

Words can shape our perceptions. They invite us to see and share the world from the speaker's point of view. Words can also distort reality and block certain ways of seeing. They can arouse intense feeling by overcoming the barriers of time, distance, and audience apathy. The spoken word can bring listeners together in a common identity. Finally, words can prompt us to action.

The Six C's of Language Use. As you speak, strive to meet the standards of *clarity, color, concreteness, correctness, conciseness,* and *cultural sensitivity.* Clear language is simple and direct: it draws its comparisons from everyday life and avoids *jargon*. Amplification promotes clarity by dwelling on important, difficult points.

Color refers to the emotional intensity and vividness of language and is especially vital to the sharing of feeling. The more concrete a word, the more specific the information it conveys. Correctness is vital to ethos because grammatical errors and improper word choices can lower perceptions of your competence. *Malapropisms,* confusions among words based on similarities of sound, can be quite damaging. Concise speakers strive for brevity, often using comparisons that reduce complex issues to the essentials. *Maxims* are the ultimate in conciseness. *Cultural sensitivity* demands

Using Figurative Language		
Technique	**Definition**	**Example**
Metaphors	An unexpected figurative comparison	An iron curtain has descended across the continent.
Enduring metaphors	Metaphors that transcend time and cultural boundaries	The development of the Internet marked the dawn of a new way of learning.
Similes	Figurative comparison using *like* or *as*	The jellyfish is like a living lava lamp.
Personifications	Attributing human characteristics to things or events	Liberty raises her flame as a beacon.
Culturetypes	Words that express the values, identity, and goals of a group	This company is devoted to the ideals of modern, efficient, progressive science.
Ideographs	Words that express a country's basic political beliefs	All we ask is liberty and justice.

Manipulating the Order of Words		
Technique	**Definition**	**Example**
Antithesis	Presenting contrasting ideas in parallel phrases	There is a time to sow and a time to reap.
Inversion	Changing the expected word order	This insult we did not deserve, and this result we will not accept.
Parallel construction	Repetition of words/phrases at beginning or end of sentences	It's a program that ... It's a program that ... It's a program that ...

Exploiting the Sounds of Words		
Technique	**Definition**	**Example**
Alliteration	Repetition of initial sounds in closely connected words	Beware the nattering nabobs of negativism.
Onomatopoeia	Words that imitate natural sounds	The creek gurgled and babbled downŁ to the river.

Figure 12.3

Magnifying the Power of Language

that a speaker be aware of the diversity within an audience and respectful of cultural differences.

Magnifying the Power of Language. Certain techniques can magnify the power of words at critical moments in your speeches. Figurative language, techniques that alter the natural order of words, and techniques that exploit the sounds of words are all devices of magnification.

Prominent forms of *figurative language* are *metaphors, enduring metaphors, similes, personifications, culturetypes,* and *ideographs.* Metaphor surprises us with implied, unusual comparisons. Enduring metaphors are rooted in basic human experience and appeal across time and culture. Similes signal and soften the comparison with words such as *like* or *as.* Personifications, as in "lady liberty," attribute human form and feeling to inanimate subjects. Culturetypes express the values of a particular people. Ideographs are compact expressions of political faith.

Techniques that alter the natural order of words include *antithesis, inversion,* and *parallel construction.* Antithesis arranges opposing ideas in the same or adjoining sentences to create a striking contrast. Inversion reverses the expected order of words in a phrase or sentence to make a statement distinctive. Parallel construction repeats the same pattern of words in a sequence of phrases or sentences for the sake of impact.

Alliteration and *onomatopoeia* are techniques that exploit the sounds of words. Alliteration repeats initial sounds in a closely connected pattern of words. Onomatopoeia is the tendency of certain words to imitate the sounds of what they represent. Both techniques magnify the language of feeling.

To be effective, all such techniques must seem natural.

Terms to Know

denotative meaning
connotative meaning
jargon
doublespeak
amplification
slang
malapropisms
maxims
cultural sensitivity
figurative language
metaphors
enduring metaphors
similes
personifications
culturetypes
ideographs
antithesis
inversion
parallel construction
alliteration
onomatopoeia

Discussion

1. In the 1950s, Richard Weaver suggested that *progress* was the primary culturetype of American society. What words would you nominate as culturetypes in contemporary society (remember, you should be looking for "devil" as well as "god" terms)? Find examples of how these words are used in public communication. Are there any ethical problems with the way these words are used?
2. Analyze how you used the power of language in your last speech. Did you have to overcome any barriers to perception or feeling among your listeners? What techniques did you use? Could you have done better?
3. The example that opens this chapter presents arguments for and against whiskey, using connotative language. Rephrase these arguments, using instead denotative language. What is lost and what is gained? Which situations might call more for denotative language, and which for more connotative speech?

Application

1. Look for examples of the use of enduring metaphor in contemporary public communication (speeches, editorials, advertising, visual, and televisual communication). Explain the power of these metaphors by connecting them to Maslow's hierarchy of motives, discussed in Chapter 5 (pages 106–107).
2. Study the language used in a contemporary political speech. How is the power of language exercised? What special techniques are used to magnify this power? Evaluate the effectiveness of this usage according to the six *C*'s discussed in this chapter: clarity, color, concreteness, correctness, conciseness, and cultural sensitivity.
3. Your instructor will assign different language techniques to members of the class and then present a subject. Your task will be to make a statement about this subject, using the technique you have been assigned. Share these statements in class. What does this exercise reveal about the power of the spoken word?

Notes

1. William Raspberry, "Any Candidate Will Drink to That," *Austin American Statesman,* 11 May 1984, p. A-10.
2. Ollie Reed, "Corsicans, Navajo Weave Ties," Scripps Howard News Service, 3 July 2001. *(Memphis) Commercial Appeal.* http://www.gomemphis.com (5 July 2001).
3. Jerry Tarver, "Words in Time: Some Reflections on the Language of Speech," *Vital Speeches of the Day,* 15 Apr. 1988, p. 410.
4. Ibid., pp. 410–412.

5. Winston Churchill, "Dunkirk," in *The World's Great Speeches,* ed. Lewis Copeland and Lawrence W. Lamm, 3rd ed. (New York: Dover, 1973), p. 439.

6. These powers of language were first explored in Michael Osborn, *Orientations to Rhetorical Style* (Chicago: Science Research Associates, 1976), and are developed further in Michael Osborn, "Rhetorical Depiction," in *Form, Genre, and the Study of Political Discourse,* ed. Herbert W. Simons and Aram A. Aghazarian (Columbia: University of South Carolina Press, 1986), pp. 79–107.

7. Katherine Stout, "Dear Ryan White," Letters About Literature competition, Level II, 2004, sponsored by Humanities Tennessee for the National Endowment for the Humanities.

8. Based on the account in Claire Perkins, "The Many Symbolic Faces of Fred Smith: Charismatic Leadership in the Bureaucracy," *Journal of the Tennessee Speech Communication Association* 11 (1985): 22.

9. Jesse Jackson, "Common Ground and Common Sense," *Vital Speeches of the Day,* 15 Aug. 1988, pp. 649–653.

10. Adapted from *The American Heritage Dictionary,* 2nd ed. (Boston: Houghton Mifflin, 1985), p. 92.

11. From a transcription of the debate, CNN, 15 Feb. 1996.

12. Listeners whose lives seem dull and unrewarding are especially susceptible to such dramas. See the discussion in Eric Hoffer, *The True Believer: Thoughts on the Nature of Mass Movements* (New York: Harper, 1951).

13. Ann Landers, "Translate Gobbledygook, Please," *Commercial Appeal*, 21 Aug. 1992, p. C3.

14. "Presidential Ecospeak," *New York Times,* Editorials/Op-Ed, 18 Oct. 2003. file://Documents%20and%20Settings/Owner/Desktop/For%207th%20ed/For%20Ch. . . .(29 Oct. 2003).

15. Bill Moyers, "Commencement Address," presented at the Lyndon B. Johnson School of Public Affairs, University of Texas, Austin. Cited in *Time,* 19 June 1985, p. 68.

16. All quotations are from *USA Today,* 18 Jan. 1996, p. 4A.

17. J. E. Lighter, *Random House Historical Dictionary of American Slang* (New York: Random House, 1994), p. xxv.

18. "Malapropisms Live!" *Spectra,* May 1986, p. 6.

19. Haven E. Cockerham, "Conquer the Isms That Stand in Our Way," *Vital Speeches of the Day,* 1 Feb. 1998, p. 240.

20. *Time,* 9 Mar. 1992, p. 19.

21. Antoinette M. Bailey, "Bow Wave," *Vital Speeches of the Day,* 1 June 2001, p. 502.

22. For additional discussion of such metaphors, see Michael Osborn, "Archetypal Metaphor in Rhetoric: The Light-Dark Family," *Quarterly Journal of Speech* 53 (1967): 115–126, and "The Evolution of the Archetypal Sea in Rhetoric and Poetic," *Quarterly Journal of Speech* 63 (1977): 347–363.

23. George W. Bush, "Inaugural Address," *Vital Speeches of the Day,* 1 Feb. 2001, p. 226.

24. See another side of this image in J. Vernon Jensen, "British Voices on the Eve of the American Revolution: Trapped by the Family Metaphor," *Quarterly Journal of Speech* 63 (1977): 43–50.

25. For an insightful discussion of the metaphors we use to construct our ideas about illness, see Susan Sontag, *Illness as Metaphor* (New York: Vintage Books, 1979), and *AIDS and Its Metaphors* (New York: Farrar, Straus and Giroux, 1988).

26. See Robert Ivie, "Images of Savagery in American Justifications for War," *Communication Monographs* 47 (1980): 279–294.

27. Michael Osborn, "Patterns of Metaphor Among Early Feminist Orators," in *Rhetoric and Community: Studies in Unity and Fragmentation,* ed. J. Michael Hogan (Columbia: University of South Carolina Press, 1998), pp. 10–11.

28. Wendi C. Thomas, "Spaced Out on Budget Priorities," *The Commercial Appeal,* 1 Jan. 2004. http://www.commercialappeal.com/mca/news_columnists/article/0,1426,MCA_646_2594495,00.html (22 Jan. 2004).

29. "I'm Feeling like Job," *Newsweek,* 12 Jan. 2004, p. 25.

30. "Southern-Speak: Clinton Uses It Well," *Norfolk Virginian-Pilot and the Ledger-Star,* 10 Apr. 1994, p. A6.

31. Michael Calvin McGee, "The Origins of Liberty: A Feminization of Power," *Communication Monographs* 47 (1980): 27–45.

32. Osborn, *Orientations to Rhetorical Style,* p. 16.

33. Richard Weaver, "Ultimate Terms in Contemporary Rhetoric," in *The Ethics of Rhetoric* (Chicago: Henry Regnery, 1953), pp. 211–232.

34. Michael Calvin McGee, "The Ideograph: A Link Between Rhetoric and Ideology," *Quarterly Journal of Speech* 66 (1980): 1–16.

35. This example is adapted from Ronald H. Carpenter, *Choosing Powerful Words: Eloquence That Works* (Boston: Allyn and Bacon, 1999), pp. 14–15.

36. Statement by the President, broadcast from the Treaty Room at the White House, 7 Oct. 2001.

Presenting Your Speech

13

OUTLINE

This chapter will help you

- understand the concept of integrated communication
- develop your voice for better communication
- develop more effective body language
- become versatile in using the various modes of presentation
- become flexible in adapting to special situations
- practice your presentation

There is no gesture that does not speak.

MONTAIGNE

At the end of Chapter 14, we present the text of a speech by Marie D'Aniello on the nature of friendship. As a printed text, it makes for mildly interesting reading and illustrates many important features of informative speaking. It also reveals the inadequacy of the printed word for conveying the rich totality of a living communication event.[1]

The actual speech event was much more exciting. As she presented her speech, Marie invested herself in it. At the beginning, she established eye contact, moved out from behind the lectern, and stepped toward her listeners as though inviting greater psychological closeness. Her words glowed with excitement about her subject, her face was alive with the meaning of her words, amplifying them in a striking way. Her gestures were abundant and expressive, and her voice was warm and inviting. She seemed to embody her subject: her listeners concluded that this friendly person must surely know something about the nature of friendship. Her entire speech had an electric quality that established a vital connection between her and her listeners.

Marie exemplified what we call **integrated communication**—the convergence of body, voice, and speech content to produce a larger-than-life communication experience for all who participate in it.

We have spent much of our time thus far helping you develop a plan for your speech. Planning, however, can take you only so far. Now you must actually present the speech to an audience of listeners, giving it a chance to influence their thinking and giving them a chance to respond to your ideas. This is the moment of **presentation**.

In this chapter, we help you prepare for this moment by discussing two major resources, your voice and your body. We also want to help you become more versatile in using the various modes of presentation and more flexible for special communication situations. Finally, we coach you through the vital moments of practicing your presentation.

Developing your ability to present speeches should help you in other settings, such as job interviews, meetings, and even social occasions. Learning how to present yourself and your ideas tends to stay with you over the years, providing what Francis Bacon once called "continual letters of recommendation."

The Goal of Integrated Communication

Integrated communication is both an ideal and a goal. It builds upon the etymology of the word *communication*, which stems from the Latin word *communis*, meaning "common." Integrated communication allows a speaker and the audience to hold ideas and feelings in common, even when they come from different cultural backgrounds. Such a presentation combines the power of words with the nonverbal power of voice and gesture to create shared meaning. Marie D'Aniello's presentation clearly illustrated the harmonious interplay of verbal and nonverbal symbols.

An ideal can also be defined by performance that falls far short of it. We remember another student speaker who described her childhood in these terms: "I was always getting into trouble." But as she said these words, she seemed listless; she slouched at the podium and avoided eye contact. Her passive manner did not reinforce her self-portrait as a boisterous child. Instead, *there was an incongruity between what she said and what she showed.* Law enforcement interviewers often refer to such moments as "discrepancies, places where words, facial expressions and body language do not jibe."[2]

Whenever verbal and nonverbal symbols seem out of sync, listeners typically assign more importance to the nonverbal message. One interesting explanation for this tendency is that nonverbal language is older and more biologically embedded than verbal language. Psychologist Paul Ekman argues that facial expressions

> **have their own evolutionary history. Smiling, for example, is probably our oldest natural expression. For humans, as for monkeys, smiling is a way to disarm and reassure those around us. . . . Some geneticists date the origin of language back as little as 50,000 years, and the richness of words actually seems to distract us from the older medium of faces.[3]**

Clearly, communication goes far beyond the mere exchange of words.

Requirements of Integrated Communication

What are the requirements of integrated communication? *First, there are certain technical standards that must be met.* For example, your voice must be loud enough to be heard easily in the back of the room. However, it should not call attention to itself or distract from your message. Thus, you should avoid pompous pronunciations, an artificial manner, and overly dramatic gestures.

Instead, *an effective presentation must sound natural and conversational*—as though you were talking *with* listeners, not *at* them. Your goal should be a speech characterized by an **expanded conversational style**, which we discussed in detail in Chapter 1. An expanded conversational style is direct, spontaneous, colorful, and tuned to the responses of listeners. Although it is a bit more formal than everyday conversation, it is still *natural.*

Even more important than surface, tangible requirements for an effective presentation are the deeper intangible requirements, the greatest of which is *attitude.* As a speaker, you must be committed to your topic and want to share this commitment. As a listener, you should meet the speaker's commitment with respect and receptivity, the conviction that you can learn and grow by sharing the spoken word. As both speaker and listener, *you should want to communicate.*

This may seem obvious, but we remember another student in whom this desire to communicate seemed oddly missing. She had done well in high school speaking contests, she told listeners in her

An effective presentation makes your ideas come alive while you are speaking.

first speech, and thought of herself as a good speaker. And in a technical sense, she was right. Her voice was pleasant and expressive, her manner direct and competent. But there was a false note, an overtone of artificiality. As a result, her listeners gave her a rather chilly reception. It was clear that, for her, speaking was an exhibition. *She* was more important than her ideas. Listeners sensed that she had her priorities wrong.

The proper communication attitude produces a sense of **immediacy,** a closeness between speaker and listeners.[4] Immediacy relates to the likeableness dimension of ethos, which we discussed in Chapter 3. It encourages listeners to open their minds to you and to be influenced by what you say.[5]

You can encourage immediacy by first reducing the actual distance between yourself and listeners. If possible, move closer to them. Smile at them when appropriate, maintain eye contact, use gestures to clarify and reinforce ideas, and let your voice express your feelings. Even if your heart is pumping, your hands are a little sweaty, and your knees feel wobbly, the self you show to listeners should be a person in control of the situation. Listeners admire and identify with speakers who maintain what Ernest Hemingway once called "grace under pressure."

To summarize, *an effective presentation realizes the goal of integrated communication: it makes your ideas come alive while you are speaking.* It blends nonverbal with verbal symbols so that reason and emotion, heart and head, mind and body all work together to advance your message. The remainder of this chapter will help you move closer to a presentation that reaches the goal of integrated communication.

Developing Your Voice

The first major resource you must develop to reach the goal of integrated communication is your own voice. Consider the following simple sentences:

> Watch the speech in the **VideoLab Lesson 6 Screening Room** and complete **Drill 6.1**. How does this speaker use her voice to convey her message? (VideoLab)

I don't believe it.
You did that.
Give me a break.

How many different meanings can you create as you speak these words, just by changing the rhythm, pace, emphasis, pitch, or inflection of your voice?

Your ethos as well as your message can be affected by the quality of your voice. A good speaking voice enhances your image in the ears of listeners. But if you sound tentative, people may think you are not very decisive, perhaps not even convinced by your own message. If you mumble, they may think you are trying to hide something. If you are overly loud or strident, they may conclude you are not very likeable.

How you talk is also part of your identity. Someone who talks in a soft, breathy voice may be thought of as "weak"; another, who speaks in a more forceful manner, may be considered "authoritative." For some speakers, a dialect is part of their ethnicity and a valued part of their personality.[6]

Although you may not want to make radical changes in your speaking voice, minor improvements can produce big dividends. As one voice specialist put it, "Though speech is a human endowment, how well we speak is an individual achievement."[7] With a little effort and practice, most of us can make positive changes. However, simple vocal exercises will not fix all voice impairments. If you have a serious problem, contact a speech pathology clinic for professional help.

The first step in learning to use your voice more effectively is to evaluate how you usually talk. Tape-record yourself while speaking and reading aloud. When you hear yourself, you may say, "Is that really me?" Most tape recorders will slightly distort the way you sound because they do not exactly replicate the spectrum of sounds made by the human voice. Nevertheless, a tape recording gives you an idea of how you may sound to others. As you listen, ask yourself:

- Does my voice convey the meaning I intend?
- Would I want to listen to me if I were in the audience?
- Does my voice present me at my best?

If your answers are negative, you may need to work on pitch, rate, loudness, variety, articulation, enunciation, pronunciation, or dialect. Save your original tape so that you can hear yourself improve as you practice.

Pitch

Pitch is the placement of your voice on the musical scale. Vocal pitches can range from low and deep to high and squeaky. For effective speaking, find a pitch level that is comfortable and that allows maximum flexibility and variety. Each of us has a **habitual pitch**, the level at which we speak most frequently. We also have an **optimum pitch**, the level that allows us to produce our strongest voice with minimal effort and that permits variation up and down the scale. You can use the following exercise to help determine your optimum pitch:

> **Sing the sound *la* down to the lowest pitch you can produce without feeling strain or having your voice break or become rough. Now count each note as you sing up the scale to the highest tone you can comfortably produce. Most people have a range of approximately sixteen notes. Your optimum pitch will be about one-fourth of the way up your range. For example, if your range extends twelve notes, your optimum pitch would be at the third note up the scale. Again, sing down to your lowest comfortable pitch, and then sing up to your optimum pitch level.[8]**

Tape-record this exercise, and compare your optimum pitch to the habitual pitch revealed during your first recording. If your optimum pitch is within one or two notes of your habitual pitch, then you should not experience vocal problems related to pitch level. If your habitual pitch is much higher or lower than your optimum pitch, you may not have sufficient flexibility to raise or lower the pitch of your voice to communicate changes in meaning and emphasis. You can change your habitual pitch by practicing speaking and reading at your optimum pitch.

Read the following paragraphs from N. Scott Momaday's *The Way to Rainy Mountain* at your optimum pitch level, using pitch changes to provide meaning and feeling. To make the most of your practice, tape-record yourself so you can observe both problems and progress.

> **A single knoll rises out of the plain in Oklahoma, north and west of the Wichita Range. For my people, the Kiowas, it is an old landmark, and they gave it the name Rainy Mountain. The hardest weather in the world is there. Winter brings blizzards, hot tornadic winds arise in the spring, and in the summer the prairie is an anvil's edge. The grass turns brittle and brown, and it cracks beneath your feet. There are green belts along the rivers and creeks, linear groves of hickory and pecan, willow, and witch hazel. At a distance in July or August the steaming foliage seems almost to writhe in fire. . . . Loneliness is an aspect of the land. All things in the plain are isolate: there is no confusion of objects in the eye, but one hill or one tree or one man. To look upon that landscape in the early morning, with the sun at your back, is to lose the sense of proportion. Your imagination comes to life, and this, you think, is where Creation was begun.[9]**

The purpose of this exercise is to explore the full range of variation around your optimum pitch and to make you conscious of the relationship between pitch and effective communication. Tape yourself reading the passage again, this time exaggerating the pitch variations as you read it. Play back both of the taped readings. If you have a problem with a narrow pitch range, you may discover that exaggerating makes you sound more effective.

When you speak before a group, don't be surprised if your pitch seems higher than usual. Pitch is sensitive to emotions and will usually go up when you are under pressure. If pitch is a serious problem for you, hum your optimum pitch softly to yourself before you begin to speak, so that you start out on the right note.

Rate

Your **rate**, or the speed at which you speak, helps set the mood of your speech. Serious material calls for a slow, deliberate rate; lighter topics need a faster pace. These variations may involve the duration of syllables, the use of pauses, and the overall speed of presentation.

The rate patterns within a speech produce its **rhythm,** an essential component of all communication.[10] With rhythmic variations, you point out what is important and make it easier for listeners to comprehend your message.

Beginners who feel intimidated by the speaking situation often speed up their presentations and run their words together. What this rapid-fire delivery communicates is the speaker's desire to get it over with and sit down! At the other extreme, some speakers become so deliberate and slow that they almost put themselves and their audiences to sleep. Neither extreme lends itself to effective communication.

As we noted in Chapter 3, the typical rate for extemporaneous speaking is approximately 125 words per minute. You can check your speed by timing your reading of the excerpt from *Rainy Mountain.* If you were reading at the average rate, you would have taken about sixty seconds to complete that material. If you allowed time for pauses between phrases, which is appropriate for such formal material, your reading may have run slightly longer. If you took less than fifty seconds, you were probably speaking too rapidly, or not using pauses effectively.

Pausing before or after a word or phrase highlights its importance. Pauses also give your listeners time to contemplate what you have said. They can help build suspense and maintain interest as listeners anticipate what you will say next. Moreover, pauses can clarify the relationships among ideas, phrases, and sentences. They are oral punctuation marks, taking the place of the commas and periods, underlinings and exclamation marks that occur in written communication. For all these good reasons, experienced speakers learn how to use pauses to maximum advantage. Humorist William Price Fox once wrote of Eugene Talmadge, a colorful Georgia governor and fabled stump-speaker, "That rascal knew how to wait. He had the longest pause in the state."[11] Be sure to use pause and vocal emphasis to state your main ideas forcefully.

Read the following passage aloud again, using pauses (where indicated by the slash marks) and rate changes (a faster pace is indicated by italic type and a slower pace by capital letters) to enhance its meaning and demonstrate mood changes. This exercise will give you an idea of how pausing and changing rate can emphasize and clarify the flow of ideas:

> **A single knoll rises out of the plain in Oklahoma / north and west of the Wichita Range // For my people / the Kiowas / it is an old landmark / and they gave it the name / Rainy Mountain /// The hardest weather in the world is there // *Winter brings blizzards / hot tornadic winds arise in the spring / and in the summer the prairie is an anvil's edge // The grass turns brittle and brown / and it cracks beneath your feet* // There are green belts along the rivers and creeks / linear groves of hickory and pecan, willow, and witch hazel // At a**

distance / in July or August / the steaming foliage seems almost to writhe in fire /// LONELINESS IS AN ASPECT OF THE LAND // ALL THINGS IN THE PLANE ARE ISOLATE /// THERE IS NO CONFUSION OF OBJECTS IN THE EYE // BUT ONE HILL // OR ONE TREE // OR ONE MAN /// To look upon that landscape in the early morning / with the sun at your back / is to lose the sense of proportion // Your imagination comes to life // AND THIS / YOU THINK / IS WHERE CREATION WAS BEGUN.

Just as pausing can work for you, the wrong use of silence within a speech can be harmful. *There is a considerable difference between a pause, which is deliberate, and a hesitation, which can signal confusion, uncertainty, and/or a lack of preparation.* Moreover, some speakers habitually use "ers" and "ums," "wells" and "okays," or "you knows" in the place of pauses, without being aware of it. These **vocal distractions** may fill in the silence while the speaker thinks about what to say next, or they may be signs of nervousness. They may also be signals that speakers lack confidence in themselves or their messages. To determine if you have such a habit, tape-record yourself speaking extemporaneously about one of the main points for your next speech. Often simply becoming aware of such vocal distractions is enough to help you control them. Also, don't use "okay," "well," or "you know" as transitions in your speech. Plan more effective transitions (see Chapter 9). Practice your presentation until the ideas flow smoothly. Finally, don't be afraid of the brief strategic silence that comes when you pause. Make silence work for you.

If your natural tendency is to speak too slowly, you can practice developing a faster rate by reading light material aloud. Read the following poem by Charlotte Perkins Gilman in a lively, expressive manner:

There was once an Anthropoidal Ape,
Far smarter than the rest,
And everything that they could do
He always did the best;
So they naturally disliked him,
And they gave him shoulders cool,
And when they had to mention him
They said he was a fool.

Cried this pretentious Ape one day,
"I'm going to be a Man!
And stand upright, and hunt, and fight
And conquer all I can!
I'm going to cut down forest trees,
To make my houses higher!
I'm going to kill the Mastodon!
I'm going to make a fire!"

Loud screamed the Anthropoidal Apes
With laughter wild and gay;
They tried to catch that boastful one,
But he always got away.
So they yelled at him in chorus,
Which he minded not a whit;
And they pelted him with cocoanuts,
Which didn't seem to hit.
And then they gave him reasons
Which they thought of much avail,
To prove how his preposterous
Attempt was sure to fail.
Said the sages, "In the first place
The thing cannot be done!

And, second, if it could be,
It would not be any fun!
And, third, and most conclusive,
And admitting no reply,
You would have to change your nature!
We should like to see you try!"
They chuckled then triumphantly,
These lean and hairy shapes,
For these things passed as arguments
With the Anthropoidal Apes.[12]

If you enjoy this exercise, try reading stories by Dr. Seuss to children. Such tales as *The Cat in the Hat* and *Green Eggs and Ham* should bring out the ham in you! Children normally provide an appreciative audience that encourages lively, colorful, dramatic uses of the voice.

Different cultures have different speech rhythms. In the United States, for example, northerners often speak more rapidly than southerners. These variations in the patterns of speech can create misunderstandings. Californians, who use longer pauses than New Yorkers, may perceive the latter as rude and aggressive. New Yorkers may see Californians as too laid back or as not having much to say.

Such problems can even go beyond simple misunderstanding. Sociologist Ron Scollon reports that Native American Alaskans show deference to authority by slowing their speech and pausing before responding to questions. Unfortunately, non-Native law enforcement and legal officials often interpret these speech customs as signs of antagonism or hostility, and the Native Americans typically receive longer jail sentences than non-Natives.[13] Guard against stereotyping individuals on the basis of what may be culturally based speech rate variations.

Loudness

No presentation can be effective if the audience can't hear you. Nor will your presentation be successful if you overwhelm listeners with a voice that is too loud. When you speak before a group, you usually need to speak louder than you do in general conversation. The size of the room, the presence or absence of a microphone, and background noise may also call for adjustments. Take your cues from audience feedback. If you are not loud enough, you may see listeners leaning forward, straining to hear. If you speak too loudly, they may unconsciously lean back, pulling away from the noise.

You should also be aware that different cultures have different norms and expectations concerning appropriate loudness. For example, in some Mediterranean cultures, a loud voice signifies strength and sincerity, whereas in some Asian and American Indian cultures, a soft voice is associated with good manners and education.[14] When members of your audience come from a variety of cultural and ethnic groups, be especially attentive to feedback on this point.

To speak at the proper loudness, you must have good breath control. If you are breathing improperly, you will not have enough force to project your voice so that you can be heard at the back of a room. Improper breathing can also cause you to run out of breath before you finish a phrase or come to an appropriate pause. To check whether you are breathing properly for speaking, do the following:

Stand with your feet approximately eight inches apart. Place your hands on your lower rib cage, thumbs to the front, fingers to the back. Take a deep breath—in through your nose and out through slightly parted lips. If you are breathing correctly, you should feel your ribs moving up and out as you inhale.

Improper breathing affects more than just the loudness of your speech. If you breathe by raising your shoulders, the muscles in your neck and throat will become tense. This can result in a harsh, strained vocal quality. Moreover, you probably will not take in enough air to sustain your phrasing, and the release of air will be difficult to control. The air and sound will all come out with a rush when you drop your shoulders, leading to unfortunate oral punctuation marks when you don't want or need them. To see if you have a problem, try this exercise:

Take a normal breath and see how long you can count while exhaling. If you cannot reach fifteen without losing volume or feeling the need to breathe, you need to work on extending your breath control. Begin by counting in one breath to a number comfortable for you, and then gradually increase the count over successive tries. Do not try to compensate by breathing too deeply. Deep breathing takes too much time and attracts too much attention while you are speaking. Use the longer pauses in your speech to breathe, and make note of your breathing pattern as you practice your speech.

You should vary the loudness of words and phrases in your speech, just as you vary your pitch and your rate of speaking. Changes in loudness are often used to express emotion. The more excited or angry we are, the louder we tend to become. But don't let yourself get caught in the trap of having only two options: loud and louder. Decreasing your volume, slowing your rate, pausing, or dropping your pitch can also express emotion quite effectively. Vanderbilt student speaker Leslie Eason illustrated this point dramatically as she introduced her speech on racism. As she read the concluding lines of her poem ("What if I go to Heaven, and then at me they yell, White Angels enter here, Black Angels go to Hell"), Leslie reduced her loudness, lowered her pitch, and slowed her rate. These vocal contrasts had a dramatic impact on listeners.

To acquire more variety in loudness, practice the following exercise recommended by Hillman and Jewell: "First, count to five at a soft volume, as if you were speaking to one person. Then, count to five at medium volume, as if speaking to ten or fifteen people. Finally, count to five, as if speaking to thirty or more people."[15] If you tape-record this exercise, you should be able to hear the clear progression in loudness.

Variety

The importance of vocal variety shows up most in speeches that lack it. Speakers who drone on in a monotone, never varying their pitch, rate, or loudness, send a clear message: They tell us that they have little interest in their topic or in their listeners, or that they fear the situation they are in. Variety can make speeches come to life by adding color and interest. One of the best ways to develop variety is to read aloud materials that demand it to express meaning and feeling. As you read the following selection from *the lives and times of archy and mehitabel,* strive for maximum variation of pitch, rate, and loudness. Incidentally, archy is a cockroach who aspires to be a writer. He leaves typewritten messages for his newspaper-editor mentor, but, because he is a cockroach, he can't type capital letters and never uses punctuation marks. His friend mehitabel, whom he quotes in this message, is an alley cat with grandiose dreams and a dubious reputation.

archy what in hell have i done
to deserve all these kittens
life seems to be just one damn litter after another
after all archy i am an artist
this constant parade of kittens

interferes with my career
its not that i am shy on mother love archy
why my heart would bleed if anything happened to them
and i found it out
a tender heart is the cross i bear
but archy the eternal struggle between life and art
is simply wearing me out[16]

Tape-record yourself while reading this and other favorite poems or dramatic scenes aloud. Compare these practice tapes with your initial self-evaluation tape to see if you have improved in the use of variety in your presentations.

Patterns of Speaking

People often make judgments about others based on their speech patterns. If you slur your words, mispronounce familiar words, or speak with a dialect that sounds unfamiliar to your audience, you may be seen as uneducated or socially inept. When you sound "odd" to your listeners, their attention will be distracted from what you are saying to the way you are saying it. In this section we cover articulation, enunciation, pronunciation, and dialect as they contribute to or detract from speaking effectiveness.

Articulation. **Articulation** refers to the way you produce individual speech sounds. Some people have trouble making certain sounds. For example, they may substitute a *d* for a *th,* saying "dem" instead of "them." Other sounds that are often misarticulated include *s, l,* and *r.* Severe articulation problems can interfere with effective communication, especially if the audience cannot understand the speaker or if the variations suggest low social or educational status. Such problems are best treated by a speech pathologist, who retrains the individual to produce the sound in a more acceptable manner.

Enunciation. **Enunciation** refers to the way you pronounce words in context. In casual conversation it is not unusual for people to slur their words—for example, saying "gimme" for "give me." However, careless enunciation causes credibility problems for public speakers. Do you say "Swatuh thought" for "That's what I thought"? "Harya?" for "How are you?" or "Howjado?" for "How did you do?" These lazy enunciation patterns are not acceptable in public speaking. Check your enunciation patterns on the tape recordings you have made to determine if you have such a problem. If you do, concentrate on careful enunciation as you practice your speech. Be careful, however, to avoid the opposite problem of inflated, pompous, and pretentious enunciation, which can make you sound phony. You should strive to be neither sloppy nor overly precise.

Pronunciation. **Pronunciation** involves saying words correctly. It includes both using the correct sounds and placing the proper accent on syllables. Because written English does not always indicate the correct pronunciation, we may not be sure how to pronounce words that we first encounter in print. For instance, does the word *chiropodist* begin with a *sh*, a *ch*, or a *k* sound?

If you are not certain how to pronounce a word, consult a dictionary. An especially useful reference is the *NBC Handbook of Pronunciation,* which contains 21,000 words and proper names that sometimes cause problems.[17] When international stories and new foreign leaders first appear in the news, newspapers frequently indicate the correct pronunciation of their names. Check front-page stories in the *New York Times* for guidance with such words.

In addition to problems pronouncing unfamiliar words, you may find that there are certain words you habitually mispronounce. For example, how do you pronounce the following words?

government	library
February	picture
ask	secretary
nuclear	just
athlete	get

Unless you are careful, you may find yourself slipping into these common mispronunciations:

goverment	liberry
Febuary	pitchur
axe	sekaterry
nuculer	jist
athalete	git

Mispronunciation of such common words can damage your ethos. Most of us know what words we chronically mispronounce and are able to pronounce them correctly when we think about it. The time to think about it is when you are practicing your speech.

Dialect. A **dialect** is a speech pattern typical of a geographic region or ethnic group. Your dialect usually reflects the area of the country where you were raised or lived for any length of time, or your cultural and ethnic identity.[18] In the United States there are three commonly recognized dialects: eastern, southern, and midwestern. Additionally, there are local variations within the broader dialects. For example, in South Carolina, one finds the Gullah dialect from the islands off the coast, the low-country or Charlestonian accent, the Piedmont variation, and the Appalachian twang.[19] And then there's always "*Bah-stahn*" [Boston], where you buy a "*lodge budded pup con*" [large, buttered popcorn] at the movies!

There is no such thing in nature as a superior or inferior dialect. However, there can be occasions when a distinct dialect is a definite disadvantage or advantage. Listeners prefer speech patterns that are familiar to their ears. Audiences may also have stereotyped preconceptions about people who speak with certain dialects. For example, those raised in the South often associate a northeastern dialect with brusqueness and abrasiveness, and midwesterners may associate a southern dialect with slowness of action and mind. Comedian Jeff Foxworthy has noted:

> **A lot of people think everyone in the South is a redneck. . . . I went to Georgia Tech. I was an engineer at IBM. I just sound stupid. I can't help this, because where I grew up everybody else talked this way. People hear the accent and they want to deduct 100 IQ points.[20]**

You may have to work to overcome such a prejudice against your dialect.

Your dialect should reflect the standard for educated people from your geographic area or ethnic group. You should be concerned about tempering it only if it creates barriers to understanding and identification between you and your audience. Then you may want to work toward softening your dialect so that you can lower these barriers for the sake of your message.

Developing Your Body Language

How do the speakers in **VideoLab Drill 6.2: The Importance of Nonverbal Communication** use nonverbal communication to convey their messages?

VideoLab

Communication with your audience begins before you ever open your mouth. Your facial expression, personal appearance, and air of confidence all convey a message. How do you walk to the front of the room to give your speech? Do you move with confidence and purpose, or do you stumble and shuffle? As you begin your speech, do you look listeners directly in the eye, or do you stare at the ceiling as though seeking divine inspiration?

Body language is the second great resource you must manage and develop to achieve integrated communication.[21] For public speaking to be effective, *your body language must reinforce your verbal language*. If your face is expressionless as you urge your listeners to action, you are sending inconsistent messages. Be sure that your body and words both "say" the same thing. Although we discuss separate types of body language in this section, in practice they all work together and are interpreted as a totality by listeners.[22]

Facial Expression and Eye Contact

I knew she was lying the minute she said it. There was guilt written all over her face!

He sure is shifty! Did you see how his eyes darted back and forth? He never did look us straight in the eye!

Most of us believe we can judge people's character, determine their true feelings, and tell whether they are honest from their facial expressions. If there is a conflict between what we see and what we hear, we will usually believe our eyes rather than our ears.

The eyes are the most important element of facial expressiveness. In the mainstream American culture, frequent and sustained eye contact suggests honesty, openness, and respect. We may think of a person's eyes as windows into the self. If you avoid looking at your audience while you are talking, you are drawing the shades on these windows of communication. A lack of eye contact suggests that you do not care about listeners, that you are putting something over on them, or that you are afraid of them. Other cultures view eye contact quite differently. In Japan, downcast eyes may signal attentiveness and agreement. In China, Indonesia, and rural Mexico, people may lower their eyes as a sign of deference. Some Native Americans may find direct eye contact offensive or aggressive.[23]

When you reach the podium or lectern, turn, pause, and look at your audience. This signals that you want to communicate and prepares people to listen. During your speech, try to make eye contact with all sectors of your audience. Don't just stare at one or two people. You will make them uncomfortable, and other members of the audience will feel left out. First, look at people at the front of the room, then shift your focus to the middle, and finally, look at those in the rear. You may find that those sitting in the rear of the room are the most difficult to reach. They may have taken a back seat because they don't want to listen or be involved. You may have to work harder to gain and hold their attention. Eye contact is one way you can reach them.

Start your speech with a smile, unless this is inappropriate to your message. A smile signals your good will toward listeners and your ease in the speaking situation—qualities that should help your ethos.[24] We noticed that several of our Vanderbilt students combined a smile, a pause, and a nod to certain of their listeners to acknowledge a connection between the point they were making and previous speeches by those listeners. This smile-pause-nod combination illustrates an implied **intertextual signifier**. Such signifiers connect and bridge the various speeches heard by a group. They demonstrate that speakers are aware of the overall communication context in which they are speaking, and they also help listeners make connections.

Beyond the initial moment of speaking, your face should reflect and reinforce the meanings of your words. An expressionless face suggests that the speaker is afraid or indifferent. The frozen face may be a mask behind which the speaker hides. The solution lies in selecting a topic that excites you, concentrating on sharing your message, and having the confidence that comes from being well prepared.

You can also try the following exercise. Utter these statements, using a dull monotone and keeping your face as expressionless as possible:

> I am absolutely delighted by your gift.
>
> I don't know when I've ever been this excited.
>
> We don't need to beg for change—we need to demand change.
>
> All this puts me in a very bad mood.

Now repeat them with *exaggerated* vocal variety and facial expression. You may find that your hands and body also want to get involved. Encourage such impulses so that you develop an integrated system of body language.

InterConnections.LearnMore 13.1

Nonverbal Communication

Essentials of Nonverbal Communication
http://www3.usal.es/~nonverbal/introduction.htm
An extensive directory of materials and websites devoted to the study of nonverbal communication; developed and maintained by Professor Jaume Masip, Department of Social Psychology and Anthropology, University of Salamanca, Spain.

Body Language
http://digilander.iol.it/linguaggiodelcorpo/nonverb
An interesting collection of information and links available in English, Italian, and Spanish; a useful online library of resources in proxemics, gestures, facial expressions, and paralinguistics; covers a range of topics from flirting behavior to subliminal advertising; developed and maintained by Professor Marco Pacori, University of Padova, Italy, and Professor Aleksandra Kostic, University of Nis, Serbia. Note: *Much, but not all, of the material linked on the home page has been translated into English.*

Controlling Nonverbal Symptoms of Fear
http://www.presentations.com/presentations/delivery/article_display.jsp?vnu_content_id=1000465046
Practical advice offered by Byron Kalies, management consultant, on how to control the symptoms of communication fear; published originally in February 2004 issue of Presentations *magazine.*

Movement and Gestures

Most actors learn—often the hard way—that if you want to steal a scene from someone, all you have to do is move around, develop a twitch, or swing a leg. Before long, all eyes will be focused on that movement. This theatrical trick shows that physical movement sometimes can attract more attention than words. All the more reason that your words and gestures should work in harmony and not at cross-purposes! This also means you should avoid random movements, such as pacing back and forth, twirling your hair, rubbing your eyes, or jingling change in your pockets. Once you are aware of such mannerisms, it is easy to control them.

Your gestures and movement should grow out of your response to your message.[25] They should always appear natural and spontaneous, prompted by your ideas and feelings. They should never look contrived and artificial. For example, you should avoid framing a gesture to fit each word or sequence of words you utter. Perhaps every speech instructor has encountered speakers like the one who stood with arms circled above him as he said, "We need to get *around* this problem." That's not a good way to gesture!

Effective gestures involve three phases: *readiness, execution,* and *return.* In the readiness phase, you must be prepared for movement. Your hands and body should be in a position that does not inhibit free action. For example, you cannot gesture if your hands are locked behind your back or jammed into your pockets, or if you are grasping the lectern as though it were a life preserver. Instead, let your hands rest in a relaxed position, at your sides, on the lectern, or in front of you, where they can obey easily the impulse to gesture in support of a point you are making. As you execute a gesture, let yourself move naturally and fully. Don't raise your hand halfway, and then stop with your arm frozen awkwardly in space. When you have completed a gesture, let your hands return to the relaxed readiness position, where they will be free to move again when the next impulse to gesture arises.

Do not assume that there is a universal language of gesture. A study of Rwandan culture reveals that Rwandans learn an elaborate code of gestures that is a direct extension of their spoken language.[26] In contrast, our "gesture language" is far less complex and sophisticated. Even more, assuming a universal language of gesture could get you in big trouble with a culturally diverse audience. For example, the American sign for A-OK (thumb and index finger joined in a circle) has an obscene meaning in some cultures, and nodding the head up and down may mean "no" instead of "yes."[27] Management consultant Marc Hequet provides additional insight:

> **The "Hook 'em, Horns!" hand signal beloved of fans who follow the fortunes of the University of Texas Longhorns college football team once started a brawl in a crowded Italian nightclub when Texans at separate tables merrily flashed each other the sign—hand raised, middle fingers held down by thumb, index and pinky extended. The innocents didn't know it but in Italy the gesture is referred to as cuckold horns. It means, "Your wife is being unfaithful."[28]**

The Factor of Distance. From **proxemics**, the study of how humans use space during communication, we can derive two additional principles that help explain the effective use of movement during speeches. The first of these principles suggests that *the actual* ***distance*** *between speakers and listeners affects their sense of closeness or immediacy.* Bill Clinton made effective use of this principle during the second of the televised debates of the 1992 presidential campaign. In the town meeting setting of that debate, Clinton actually rose from his seat after one question and approached the audience as he answered it. His movement toward his listeners suggested that he felt a special closeness for that problem and for them. Clinton's body language also enhanced his identification with the live audience and with the larger viewing audience they represented. In contrast, his opponents, President George H. Bush and Ross Perot, were made to seem distant from these audiences.

Reducing the physical distance between the speaker and audience can help increase identification.

It follows also that the greater the physical distance between speaker and audience, the harder it is to achieve identification. This problem gets worse when a lectern acts as a physical barrier. Short speakers can almost disappear behind it! If this is a problem, try speaking from either beside or in front of a lectern so that your body language can work for you.

A related (but quite different) problem arises if you move so close to listeners that you make them feel uncomfortable. If they pull back involuntarily in their chairs, you know you have violated their sense of personal space. A form of this problem occurred during the Bush-Gore presidential debates of 2000. In the third and last of these debates, Gore on several occasions moved aggressively toward Bush's side of the platform as he answered questions. Some viewers felt that Gore had come too close to his opponent; this behavior, they thought, was boorish and inappropriate. For these viewers, this behavior reinforced a related bad impression Gore had made during the first debate when he constantly interrupted Bush, sighed and rolled his eyes during Bush's statements, often went overtime during his own answers, and generally seemed not to respect either his opponent or the rules of the debate. Gore's lack of sensitivity to the first law of proxemics and to debate etiquette made him look bad to many, especially when he had been expected to dominate the debates. The lesson should be clear: To increase your effectiveness, you should seek the ideal physical distance—not too far and not too close—between yourself and listeners.

The Factor of Elevation. The second principle of proxemics suggests that ***elevation** will also affect the sense of closeness between speakers and listeners.* When you speak, you often stand above your seated listeners in a "power position." Because we tend to associate *above* us with power over us, speakers may find that this arrangement discourages identification with some listeners. Often they will sit on the edge of the desk in front of the lectern in a more relaxed and less elevated stance. If your message is informal and requires close identification, or if you are especially tall, you might try this approach.

Personal Appearance

Your clothing and grooming affect how you are perceived. General Norman Schwarzkopf, who became a familiar figure on American television as commander of operations for Desert Shield and Desert Storm during the Iraqi conflict of 1991, underscored how important dress can be as he spoke at the University of Richmond:

> **Now, first of all for those of you who don't recognize me, I am *the* General Schwarzkopf. I said that because for some reason people expect me to be wearing camouflage. If I am not wearing camouflage, I'm not General Schwarzkopf. . . . I work out every other day as you can tell from this magnificent body that stands before you, and at the end of my workout I always go into the steam bath. True story—last summer I walked into the steam bath. I was not wearing camouflage at the time, and there was a man in there, and he turned and looked at me and said, "Did anybody ever tell you that from a distance you look exactly like General Schwarzkopf?" And I thought I'd play along, and I said, "Yes, I hear that a lot." He said, "Yes, it's only when you get up close you realize you're not General Schwarzkopf."[29]**

Your clothing and grooming can affect how you are perceived.

Few of us have a public identity so closely associated with the way we dress, but nevertheless what we wear is important.[30] How we dress can even influence how we see ourselves and how we behave. A police officer out of uniform may not act as authoritatively as when dressed in blue. A doctor without a white jacket may behave like just another person. You may have a certain type of clothing that makes you feel comfortable and relaxed. You may even have a special "good luck" outfit that raises your confidence.

When you are scheduled to speak, dress in a way that makes you feel good about yourself. Think of your speech as a *professional* situation, and dress accordingly. By dressing a little more formally than you usually do, you emphasize both to yourself and to the audience that your message is important. As we noted in Chapter 11, your appearance can serve as a presentation aid that complements your message. Like any other aid, it should never compete with your words for attention or be distracting. Always dress in good taste for the situation you anticipate.

Developing Versatility in Presentation

VideoLab

Watch the student speeches in **VideoLab Drill 6.3: Assessing Delivery**. How do the speakers use each mode of speech presentation to their advantage?

As you work to develop your natural resources of voice and body language, you should also keep in mind the four modes of speech presentation: impromptu speaking, memorized text presentation, reading from a manuscript, and extemporaneous speaking. Your goal should be to develop competency in all these modes of presentation, because you may have to use all of them when presenting a speech. A versatile speaker is able to move easily among these modes of presentation as they become relevant in a communication situation.

Impromptu Speaking

Impromptu speaking is sometimes called "speaking off the cuff," a phrase that suggests you could put all your notes on the cuff of your shirt. Impromptu speaking is useful when you have little or no time for preparation or practice. Even in a carefully prepared speech, there may be moments of impromptu presentation—times when you must make on-the-spot adjustments to audience feedback or respond to questions at the end of your speech.

There are situations, however, in which impromptu speaking is the dominant mode. At work you might be asked to make a presentation "in fifteen minutes." Or in meetings, you may decide to "say a few words" about a new product. In both cases, you will make impromptu speeches. You can also use impromptu speaking skills in other classes—to answer a question or to comment on a point made by your professor.

Speakers in public meetings must adapt to the situations that confront them.

When you have just a few minutes to prepare, first *determine your purpose*. What do you want the audience to know? Why is this important? Next, *decide on your main points*. Limit yourself to no more than three main points. Don't try to cover too much. If you have access to any type of writing material—a note pad, a scrap of paper—jot down a memory-jogging word for each idea, either in the order of importance or as the ideas seem to flow naturally. This skeletal outline will keep you from rambling or forgetting something that is important. Stick to the main points, using simple transitions as you go: "My first point is . . . Second, it is important to . . . Finally, it is clear that . . ." Use the **PREP formula** to develop each point: state the *p*oint, give a *r*eason or *e*xample, then restate the *p*oint. Keep your presentation short, and end with a summary of your remarks.

*P*oint:	The proposal to allow John Clark to operate a helicopter port in the neighborhood is not sound.
*R*eason(s):	The noise generated by helicopters taking off and landing would
*E*xample(s):	destroy the tranquility of this quiet residential neighborhood. It would be especially disturbing to the residents of the nursing home one block from the proposed facility.
Restatement of *P*oint:	Therefore, this is not a good idea. It ought to be rejected.

An impromptu speech often is one of several such speeches as people express their ideas in meetings. The earlier speeches create the context for your presentation. If others stood at the front of the room to speak, you should do so as well. If earlier speakers remained seated, you may wish to do the same. However, you should consider whether earlier speakers have been successful. If these speakers offended listeners while making standing presentations, you may wish to remain seated to differentiate yourself from them. If seated speakers have made trivial presentations, you may wish to stand to signal that what you are going to say is important.

Fortunately, most impromptu speaking situations are relatively casual. No one expects a polished presentation on a moment's notice. However, the ability to organize your ideas quickly and effectively and to present them confidently puts you at a great advantage. The principles of preparing speeches that you are learning in this course can help you become a more effective impromptu speaker.

Memorized Text Presentation

Memorized text presentations are written out, committed to memory, and delivered word for word. There are moments in speechmaking that may call for memorization. Because the introduction and conclusion of a speech are especially important—the introduction for gaining audience attention and the conclusion for leaving a lasting impression—their wording should be carefully planned and rehearsed. You might also want to memorize short congratulatory remarks, a toast, or a brief award acceptance speech.

In general, you should avoid trying to memorize entire speeches because this method of presentation poses many problems. Beginning speakers who try to memorize their speeches usually get so caught up with *remembering* that they forget about *communicating*. The result often sounds stilted or sing-songy. Speaking from memory also inhibits adapting to feedback. It can keep you from clarifying points that the audience doesn't understand, or from following up on ideas that seem especially effective.

Another problem with memorized speeches is that they must be scripted word for word in advance. Most people do not write in a natural oral style. The major differences between oral and written language, covered in Chapter 12, bear repeating. Good oral style uses short, direct, conversational speech patterns. Even sentence fragments can be acceptable. Repetition, rephrasing, and amplification are more necessary in speaking than in writing. The sense of rhythm and saving the most forceful idea for the end of the sentence are more important in oral style. Imagery can be especially useful to help the audience visualize what you are talking about.

If you must memorize a speech, commit it so thoroughly to memory that you can concentrate on communicating with your audience. If you experience a "mental block," keep talking. Restate or rephrase your last point to put your mind back on track. If this doesn't work, you may find yourself forced into an extemporaneous style and discover that you can actually express your ideas better without the constraints of exact wording.

Reading from a Manuscript

When you make a **manuscript presentation**, you read to an audience from either a text or a teleprompter. Manuscript presentations have many of the same problems as memorized presentations. Because speakers must look at a script, they lose eye contact with listeners. This, in turn, causes a loss of immediacy and inhibits adapting to feedback. Moreover, as with memorized presentations, you may have trouble writing in an oral style.

Some problems are exclusive to manuscript presentations. Most people do not read aloud well. Their presentations lack variety. Also, when people plan to read a speech, they often do not practice enough. Unless speakers are comfortable with the material, they end up glued to their manuscript rather than communicating with listeners. Other problems may arise if your manuscript pages get out of order or if you pick up the wrong paper or teleprompter material on your way to a presentation.

Although this last predicament may sound improbable, it can happen, as it once did to President Clinton. In September of 1993 Clinton presented a speech on health care to a joint session of Congress. He had been working on the speech for some time and finished revising it on the ride to the Capitol. The final changes were entered onto computer disks immediately before he was to speak. Here is a report of what happened:

> **No one realized that a White House communications aide had already accidentally merged the new speech with an old file of the February 17 speech to Congress. . . . When Clinton took the podium minutes later, he was understandably alarmed to see a seven-month-old speech on the teleprompter's display screens. Clinton told the news to Gore. . . . Gore summoned Stephanopoulos, who scrambled to fix the mistake, eventually downloading the correct version. . . . But for seven minutes, Clinton vamped with just notes.[31]**

During the first seven minutes of his presentation, the president was forced into an extemporaneous style—the method of presentation most communication instructors recommend. The speech was received with high acclaim:

> **For a man reading the wrong speech off his teleprompter, Bill Clinton spoke with persuasive passion as he addressed Congress and the nation about health care last week. Gone was the Slick Willie. . . . Suddenly Clinton looked the leader millions of Americans hoped they were voting for: decisive, forceful, even visionary.[32]**

Manuscript presentations are most useful when the speaker seeks accuracy or eloquence, or when time constraints are severe, as in legal announcements, formal political speeches, or media presentations that must be timed within seconds. Extemporaneous presentations may also include quotations or technical information that must be read if they are to achieve their effect. Because you will need to read material from time to time, we offer the following suggestions:

- Use large print to prepare your manuscript so you can see it without straining.
- Use light pastel rather than white paper, to cut down on glare from lights.

- Double- or triple-space the manuscript.
- Mark pauses with slashes.
- Highlight material you want to emphasize.
- Practice speaking from your manuscript so that you can maintain as much eye contact as possible with your audience.

Figure 13.1 shows a sample manuscript prepared for presentation. Note that two or three slashes together indicate longer pauses. The speaker highlights emphasized material by underlining it.

As you make final preparations, ask a friend to videotape your rehearsal. Review the tape and ask yourself: Do I sound as though I'm *talking with* someone, or as if I'm reading a text? Do I maintain eye contact with my imaginary audience? Do I pause effectively to emphasize the most important points? Does the presentation flow smoothly? Revise and continue practicing until you are satisfied.

Extemporaneous Speaking

Extemporaneous speaking *is prepared and practiced, but not written out or memorized.* Rather than focusing upon the exact wording of the speech, the speaker

Figure 13.1
Sample Speech Script

We Americans are big on monuments. / We build monuments in memory of our heroes. // Washington, Jefferson, and Lincoln live on in our nation's capital. // We erect monuments to honor our martyrs. / The Minute Man still stands guard at Concord. / The flag is ever raised over Iwo Jima. / Sometimes we even construct monuments to commemorate victims. // In Ashburn Park downtown there is a monument to those who died in the yellow fever epidemics. /// However, there are some things in our history that we don't memorialize // Perhaps we would just as soon forget what happened. /// Last summer I visited such a place — // the massacre site at Wounded Knee.

concentrates instead on the sequence of ideas that will develop in the speech, on its underlying message, and on the final impression the speech should leave with listeners. Extemporaneous speaking features a spontaneous and natural-sounding presentation and makes it easier to establish immediacy with an audience. The speaker is not the prisoner of a text, and each presentation will vary according to the audience, occasion, and inspiration of the moment.

Another large advantage is that extemporaneous speaking encourages interaction with an audience. The Vanderbilt student speaker who distributed photographs and then instructed listeners on how to view them, and another student who asked listeners to close their eyes and to imagine themselves living as dwarfs, were playing up these advantages. Such interaction encourages the audience to participate in constructing the message of the speech. It becomes their creation as well, which is especially important when persuading listeners.

Because it requires speakers to master the overall pattern of thought within their speeches, extemporaneous speaking emphasizes the importance of preparation and practice. At its best, such speaking combines the advantages of the other modes of speaking, the spontaneity and immediacy of impromptu speech, and the careful preparation of manuscript and memorized presentations. *It is therefore the master mode of speaking*, the best for most speaking situations, and therefore preferred by most instructors for most classroom speeches. Its special advantage is that it encourages you to adapt to audience feedback in creative and constructive ways.

Responding to Feedback from Your Audience. As we saw in Chapter 1, **feedback** is the message listeners send back to you as you speak. Facial expressions, gestures, or sounds of agreement or disagreement let you know how you are coming across. Since most feedback is nonverbal, you should maintain eye contact with your audience so that you can respond to these signals. Use feedback to monitor whether listeners understand you, are interested, and agree with what you are saying. Negative feedback in particular can alert you that you need to make on-the-spot adjustments.

Feedback That Signals Misunderstanding. Listeners' puzzled expressions can signal that they don't understand what you are saying. You may need to define an unfamiliar word or rephrase an idea to make it simpler. You could add an example or story to make an abstract concept more concrete. It might help to compare or contrast an unfamiliar idea with something the audience already knows and understands. When you detect signs of misunderstanding, you can say, "Let me put it another way." Then provide a clearer explanation.

Feedback That Signals Loss of Interest. Bored listeners wiggle in their seats, drum their fingers, or develop a glazed look. Remind them of the importance of your topic. Provide an example or story that makes your message come to life. Involve listeners by asking a question that calls for a show of hands. Startle them with a bold statement. Keep in mind that enthusiasm is contagious: your interest can arouse theirs. Move from behind the lectern and come closer to them. Whatever happens, do not become disheartened or lose faith in your speech. In all likelihood, some people—probably more than you think—will have found the speech interesting.

Feedback That Signals Disagreement. Listeners who disagree with you may frown or shake their heads to indicate how they feel about what you are saying. A number of techniques can help you soften disagreement. If you anticipate resistance, work hard to establish your ethos in the introduction of your speech. Listeners should see you as a competent, trustworthy, strong, and likeable person who has their best interests at heart.

To be perceived as competent, you must *be* competent. Arm yourself with a surplus of information, examples, and testimony from sources your audience will re-

Method	Use	Advantages	Disadvantages
Impromptu	When you have no time for preparation or practice	Is spontaneous; can meet demands of the situation; is open to feedback.	Is less polished, less well-researched, less organized; allows less use of supporting material.
Memorized	When you will be making a brief remark, such as a toast or award acceptance, or when the wording of your introduction or conclusion is important	Allows planning of eloquent wording; can sound well polished.	Must be written out in advance; can make you forget to communicate; can sound sing-songy.
Manuscript	When exact wording is important, time constraints are strict, or your speech will be telecast	Allows planning of precise wording; can be timed down to seconds.	Requires practice and an ability to read well; inhibits response to feedback.
Extemporaneous	For most public speaking occasions	Is spontaneous; encourages responding to audience feedback; encourages focusing on the essence of your message.	Requires considerable preparation and practice; experience needed for excellence.

Figure 13.2

Methods of Presentation

spect. Practice your presentation until it is polished. Set an example of tolerance by respecting positions different from your own.

You may find that although you differ with listeners on methods, you agree with them on goals. Stress the values that you share. Appeal to their sense of fair play and their respect for your right to speak. You should be the model of civility in the situation. Avoid angry reactions and the use of inflammatory language. Think of these listeners as offering an opportunity for your ideas to have impact.

Developing Flexibility in Special Situations

To the versatility you develop as you master and integrate the various modes of speaking, you should add flexibility in special speaking situations. We shall address two such situations, question-and-answer sessions and video presentations.

Handling Questions and Answers

If you are successful in arousing interest and stimulating thinking, your listeners may want to ask questions at the end of your speech. You should welcome and encourage this sign of success, and certainly not be defensive about it. The following suggestions should make handling questions easier for you.[33]

Answering questions gives you a chance to extend and increase the influence of your speech.

First, *prepare for questions.* Try to anticipate what you might be asked, think about how you will answer these questions, and do the research required to answer them effectively. Practice your speech before friends, and urge them to ask you tough questions.

Second, *repeat or paraphrase the question.* This is especially important if the question was long or complicated and your audience is large. Paraphrasing ensures that everyone in the audience hears the question. It gives you time to plan your answer, and it helps verify that you have understood the question. Paraphrasing also enables you to steer the question to the type of answer you are prepared to give.

Third, *maintain eye contact with the audience as you answer.* Note that we say "with the audience," not just "with the questioner." Look first at the questioner, and then make eye contact with other audience members, returning your gaze to the questioner as you finish your answer. The purpose of a question-and-answer period should be to extend the understanding of the entire audience, not to carry on a private conversation with one person.

Fourth, *defuse hostile questions.* Reword emotional questions in more objective language. For example, if you are asked, "Why do you want to throw our money away on people who are too lazy to work?" you might respond with something like, "I understand your frustration and think what you really want to know is 'Why aren't our current programs helping people break out of the chains of unemployment?'"

Fifth, *don't be afraid to say, "I don't know."* Simply conceding a point or saying, "I don't know" can also help defuse a hostile questioner. Roger Ailes, a political media adviser for three U.S. presidents, described how former New York City mayor Ed Koch once used this technique. Koch had spent three hundred thousand dollars putting bike lanes in Manhattan. Cars were driving in the bike lanes. Cyclists were running over pedestrians. The money seemed wasted. Soon thereafter, when Koch was running for re-election, he appeared on a meet-the-press type of show. This is how the questioning went:

> **One reporter led off with "Mayor Koch, in light of the financial difficulties in New York City, how could you possibly justify wasting three hundred thousand dollars on bike lanes? . . ." Koch smiled and he said, "You're right. It was a terrible idea." He went on. "I thought it would work. It didn't. It was one of the worst mistakes I ever made." And he stopped. Now nobody knew what to do. They had another twenty-six minutes of the program left. They all had prepared questions about the bike lanes, and so the next person feebly asked, "But, Mayor Koch, how could you do this?" And Mayor Koch said, "I already told you, it was stupid. I did a dumb thing. It didn't work." And he stopped again. Now there were twenty-five minutes left and nothing to ask him. It was brilliant.[34]**

Sixth, *keep your answers short and direct.* Don't give another speech.

Speaker's Notes 13.1

Handling Questions and Answers

1. Practice answering tough questions on your topic before an audience of friends.
2. Repeat or paraphrase the question you are asked.
3. Maintain eye contact with the audience as you answer. Don't look at just the person who asks the question.
4. Defuse hostile questions by rewording them in unemotional language.
5. Don't be afraid to say, "I don't know."
6. Keep answers short and to the point.
7. Handle nonquestions politely.
8. Bring the question-and-answer session to a close by reemphasizing your message.

Seventh, *handle nonquestions politely.* If someone starts to give a speech rather than ask a question, wait until he or she pauses for breath and then intervene with something like, "Thank you for your comment" or "I appreciate your remarks. Your question, then, is . . ." or "That's an interesting perspective. Can we have another question?" Don't get caught up in a shouting match. Stay in command of the situation.

Finally, *bring the question-and-answer session to a close.* Call for a final question, and, as you complete the answer, summarize your message again to refocus listeners on your central points.

Making Video Presentations

It is quite likely that at some time in your life you will make a video presentation. You may find yourself speaking live on closed-circuit television, videotaping instructions or training materials at work, using community access cable channels to promote a cause, running for public office, or even appearing on commercial television. Many of these video presentations will utilize a manuscript printed on a teleprompter. At other times you may need to speak impromptu or extemporaneously. With some minor adaptations, the skills you are developing should serve you well in such situations.[35]

We live in a culture in which the mass media have changed audience expectations. Television especially seems to bring speakers into our homes, giving mass communication more the feeling of personal communication and encouraging a more intimate style of presentation.[36] Because television brings you close to viewers, it magnifies every aspect of your appearance. Therefore, you should dress conservatively, avoiding shiny fabrics, glittery or dangling jewelry, and flashy prints that might "swim" on the screen and distract viewers. You also should not wear white or light pastels because they reflect glare. Ask in advance about the color of the studio backdrop. If you have light hair or if the backdrop will be light, wear dark clothing for contrast. If you have a dark skin tone, request a light or neutral background and consider wearing light-colored clothes.

Both men and women need makeup to achieve a natural look on television. Have powder available to reduce skin shine or hide a five o'clock shadow. Women should use makeup conservatively, because the camera will intensify it. Avoid glasses with tinted lenses: they will appear even darker on the screen. Even untinted lenses may cause problems, as they reflect glare from the studio lights. Wear contact lenses if you have them. If you can see well enough to read the monitor without glasses, leave them off.

Television requires a conversational mode of presentation. Your audience may be single individuals or small groups assembled in their homes. Imagine yourself talking with another person in an informal setting. While intimate, however, television is also remote. Since you will have no immediate feedback to help you, your meaning must be instantly clear. Use language that is colorful and concrete so that your audience will remember your material. Use previews and internal summaries to keep viewers on track. You may use visual aids to enhance comprehension, but be sure to confer in advance with studio personnel to be certain your materials will work well in that setting. For example, large poster boards displayed on an easel are more difficult to handle in video presentations than smaller materials. (See related considerations in Chapter 11.)

Vocal variety and facial expressions will become your most important forms of body language. Remember that television will magnify all your movements and vocal changes. Slight head movements and underplayed facial expressions should be enough to reinforce your ideas. Avoid abrupt changes in loudness as a means of vocal emphasis. Rely instead on subtle changes in tempo, pitch, and inflection, and on pauses, to drive your point home.

For most televised presentations, timing is crucial. Five minutes of air time means five minutes, not five minutes and ten seconds. If you run overtime, you will be cut off in midsentence. For this reason, television favors manuscript presentations read from a teleprompter. The teleprompter controls timing and preserves a sense of direct eye contact between speakers and listeners. Ask studio personnel how to use the equipment.

Try to rehearse your presentation in the studio with the production personnel. Develop a positive relationship with studio technicians. Your success depends in large part on how well they do their jobs. Provide them with a manuscript marked to show when you will move around or use a visual aid. Practice speaking from the teleprompter if you will be using one. Also use the microphone correctly. Don't blow into it to see if it's working. Remember that the microphone will pick up *all* sounds, including shuffling papers or tapping on a lectern. If you use a stand or hand-held microphone, position it about 10 inches below your mouth. The closer the microphone is to your mouth, the more it will pick up unwanted noises like whistled *s* sounds or tongue clicks. Microphones with cords will restrict your movement. If you plan to move about during your presentation, know where the cord is so you won't trip over it.

Don't be put off by distractions as you practice and present your speech. Studio technicians may need to confer with one another while you are speaking. This is a necessary part of their business; they are not being rude or inattentive. Even though they are in the room with you, they are not your audience. Keep your mind on your ideas and your eyes on the camera. The camera may seem strange at first, but think of it as a friendly face waiting to hear what you have to say. Your eye contact with the camera becomes your eye contact with your audience. Be prepared for lighting and voice checks before the actual taping begins. You can use this time to run through your introduction. Before you begin your speech and after you finish, always assume that any microphone or camera near you is "live." Don't say or do anything you wouldn't want your audience to hear or see.

Even though the situation is strange, try to relax. If you are standing, stand at ease. If you are sitting, lean slightly forward as if you were talking to someone in the chair next to you. The floor director will give you a countdown before the camera starts to roll. Clear your throat and be ready to start on cue. Begin with a smile, if appropriate, as you make eye contact with the camera. If several cameras are used, a red light on top will tell you which camera is on. During your presentation, the studio personnel may communicate with you using special sign language. The director will tell you what cues they will use.[37]

If you are using a teleprompter script, it will appear directly below or on the lens of the camera. Practice your speech ahead of time until you *almost* have it memorized so that you can glance at the script as a whole. If you have to read it word for word, your eyes may be continually shifting (which will make you look suspicious). If you make a mistake, keep going. Sometimes "mistakes" are improvements. Do not stop unless the director says "cut." If appropriate, smile when you finish and continue looking at the camera to allow time for a fade-out.

Practicing for Presentation

It takes a lot of practice to sound natural. Although this statement may seem contradictory, it should not be surprising. Speaking before a group is not your typical way of communicating. Even though most people seem spontaneous and relaxed when talking with a small group of friends, something happens when they walk to the front of a room and face a larger audience of less familiar faces. They often freeze or become stilted and awkward. This blocks the natural flow of communication.

The key to overcoming this problem is to practice until you can respond fully to your ideas as you present them. Don't fall into the trap of avoiding practice because it reminds you that you are not confident about your upcoming speech: That makes you a prime candidate for a self-fulfilling prophecy![38] Instead, rehearse your speech until your voice, face, and body can express your feelings as well as your thoughts. On the day of your speech, you become a model for your listeners, showing them how they should respond in turn.

Go to the **VideoLab Coach: Tips to Remember** "do's" and "don'ts" of speech delivery. VideoLab

To develop an effective extemporaneous style, practice until you feel the speech is part of you. During practice you can actually hear what you have been preparing and try out the words and techniques you have been considering. What looked like a good idea in your outline may not seem to work as well when it comes to life in spoken words. It is better to discover this fact in rehearsal than before an actual audience.

You will probably want privacy the first two or three times you practice. Even then you should try to simulate the conditions under which the speech will be given. Stand up while you practice. Imagine your listeners in front of you. Picture them responding positively to what you have to say. Address your ideas to them, and visualize your ideas having impact.

If possible, go to your classroom to practice. If this is not possible, find another empty room where the speaking arrangements are similar. Such on-site rehearsal helps you get a better feel for the situation you will face, reducing its strangeness when you make your actual presentation. Begin practicing from your formal outline. Once you feel comfortable, switch to your key-word outline, and then practice until the outline transfers from the paper to your head.

It is important to keep material to be read to a minimum. Type or print quotations in large letters so you can see them easily, and put each quotation on a single index card or sheet of paper. If using a lectern, position this material so that you can maintain frequent eye contact while reading. If you will speak beside or in front of the lectern, hold your cards in your hand and raise them when it is time to read. Practice reading your quotation until you can present it naturally while only glancing at your notes. If your speech includes presentation aids, practice handling them until they are smoothly integrated into your presentation. They should seem a natural extension of your verbal message.

Speaker's Notes 13.2

Practicing for Presentation

1. Practice standing up and speaking aloud, if possible in the room where you will be making your presentation.
2. Practice first from your formal outline; then switch to your key-word outline when you feel you have mastered your material.
3. Work on maintaining eye contact with an imaginary audience.
4. Practice integrating your presentation aids into your message.
5. Check the timing of your speech. Add or cut if necessary.
6. Continue practicing until you feel comfortable and confident.
7. Present your speech in a "dress rehearsal" before friends. Make final changes in light of their suggestions.

During practice, you can serve as your own audience by recording your speech and playing it back. If videotaping equipment is available, arrange to record your speech so that you can see as well as hear yourself. Always try to be the toughest critic you will ever have, but also be a constructive critic. Never put yourself down or give up on yourself. Work on specific points of improvement.

In addition to evaluating yourself, you may find it helpful to ask a friend or friends to listen to your presentation. This outside opinion may be more objective than your self-evaluation, and you will get a feel for speaking to real people rather than to an imagined audience. Seek constructive feedback from your friends by asking them specific questions. Was it easy for them to follow you? Do you have any mannerisms (such as twisting your hair or saying "you know" after every other sentence) that distracted them? Were you speaking loudly and slowly enough? Did your ideas seem clear and soundly supported?

On the day that you are assigned to speak, get to class early enough to look over your outline one last time so that it is fresh in your mind. If you have devoted sufficient time and energy to your preparation and practice, you should feel confident about communicating with your audience. Speaker's Notes 13.2 summarizes our suggestions for practicing.

Taking the Stage

As you step to the front of the room at the moment you are asked to speak, you should do so with a certain panache. You should radiate the expectation that you have something worthy and important to say that listeners should consider carefully. This confidence, this air of leadership, is what communication consultant Judith Humphrey calls "taking the stage."[39] This theatrical metaphor summarizes much of what we have said to this point about preparing for public speaking. Although Humphrey directs her remarks at women in management roles, what she says applies to all public speakers who aspire to influence others in positive ways. Taking the stage, she says, implies six steps.

The first is to have the *attitude* that every public communication situation is an opportunity to influence, inspire, and motivate others. The second is to have the *conviction* that what you bring to others will have great value. The third is to create the *character of leadership* as you speak. Humphrey says: "A leader has vision. A leader has a point of view and is not afraid to express it. A leader must also be centered, totally authentic."[40]

Step four is to have a great *script.* You should have a simple, clear, positive message. That leads to step five, which is to use the *language* of leadership. Your words should be forceful and should avoid indirection and self-correction. Don't overuse phrases like "in my opinion" or "maybe I'm wrong but." Don't soften your point or subvert yourself.

Ethics Alert! 13.1

The "Dos" and "Don'ts" of Presentation

1. Don't use presentation skills to disguise faults of content.
2. Don't judge the character of others by how they sound.
3. Don't let culturally based variations in eye contact, loudness, or gesture control how you respond to speakers.
4. Don't speak unless you are convinced of the value of your message. Then let your entire body confirm that fact to listeners.

Finally, *believe in your views.* As you stand at the lectern, don't shrink into yourself. Expand. Throw an arm over the lectern and stand tall. Stand still and don't fidget. Establish firm eye contact and make strong gestures. Use pauses to make your points. "Taking the stage" is your invitation and opportunity to lead others.

In Summary

The goal of *integrated communication* is to combine the power of body language, voice, and speech content to produce a larger-than-life communication experience for those who participate in it. The moment of *presentation* represents the goal and climax of speech preparation. To help prepare for this moment, you must develop your natural resources of voice and body, become versatile in the various modes of speaking, and become flexible in special situations.

The Goal of Integrated Communication. Integrated communication allows speaker and listeners to share a special moment of meaning. To achieve this moment, tangible, technical requirements must be met: you must be heard, and you must sound natural and conversational. Even more important are the intangibles: you must want to communicate. *Immediacy* describes the closeness that develops when speaker and listeners share this attitude.

Developing Your Voice. A good speaking voice conveys your meaning fully and clearly. Vocal expressiveness depends on your ability to control your *pitch, rate, loudness*, and *variety*. Your *habitual pitch* is the level at which you usually speak. Your *optimum pitch* is the level at which you can produce a clear, strong voice with minimal effort. Speaking at your optimum pitch gives your voice flexibility. The rate at which you speak can affect the impression you make on listeners. You can control rate to your advantage by using pauses and by changing your pace to match the moods of your material. To speak loudly enough, you need proper breath control. Vary loudness for the sake of emphasis. Vocal variety adds color and interest to a speech, can make a speaker more likeable, and encourages identification between speaker and audience.

Articulation, enunciation, pronunciation, and dialect refer to the unique ways you give voice to words. *Articulation* concerns the manner in which you produce individual sounds. *Enunciation* refers to the way you utter words in context. Proper *pronunciation* means that you say words correctly. Your *dialect* may identify the area of the country in which you learned language or your cultural or ethnic background. Occasionally, dialect can create identification and comprehension problems between speaker and audience.

Developing Your Body Language. You communicate with *body language* as well as with your voice. Eye contact signals listeners that you want to communicate. Your facial expressions should project the meanings of your words. Movement attracts attention; therefore, your movements and gestures must complement your speech, not compete with it. *Proxemics* is the study of how humans use space during communication. Two proxemic principles, *distance* and *elevation*, can affect your identification with an audience as you speak. Be sure your grooming and dress are appropriate to the speech occasion and do not detract from your ability to communicate.

Developing Versatility in Presentation. You must also be a versatile speaker, adept in the different modes of presentation. The four methods of speech presentation are impromptu speaking, memorized presentation, reading from a manuscript, and extemporaneous speaking. In *impromptu speaking* you talk with minimal or no preparation and practice. To present an effective impromptu speech, follow the PREP formula: state your *p*oint, give a *r*eason or *e*xample, and then restate your *p*oint.

Both *memorized* and *manuscript presentations* require that your speech be written out word for word. Be sure that your speech is written in good oral style. An *extemporaneous presentation* requires careful planning, but the wording is spontaneous. Instructors usually require that you present speeches extemporaneously, but any given speech can require that you use all of these modes of presentation interchangeably. Extemporaneous speaking allows you to adapt to *feedback* from your audience. Be especially alert for signs that your audience doesn't understand, has lost interest, or disagrees with you, and then make adjustments to your message to cope with these problems.

Developing Flexibility in Special Situations. Two special situations, question-and-answer sessions and video presentations, require that you develop specialized presentation skills. Following any presentation, you may need to answer questions about your material and ideas. Although your responses will be impromptu, you should prepare for questions in advance and plan appropriate responses. Video presentations require a conversational manner in which vocal variety and facial expressions assume special importance. The television camera will magnify all movements and vocal changes. To cope with time restraints, video presentations often encourage manuscript speaking, using the teleprompter to create the sense of directness and immediacy.

Practicing for Presentation. You should practice your speech until you have the sequence of main points and supporting materials well established in your mind. It is best to practice your presentation in conditions similar to those in which you will give your speech. Keep citations or other materials that you must read to a minimum. You can evaluate your presentation as you practice by tape-recording or videotaping your rehearsals. All that you do should prepare you for the moment when you "take the stage."

Terms to Know

integrated communication
presentation
expanded conversational style
immediacy
pitch
habitual pitch
optimum pitch
rate
rhythm
vocal distractions
articulation
enunciation
pronunciation
dialect
body language
intertextual signifier
proxemics
distance
elevation
impromptu speaking
PREP formula
memorized text presentation
manuscript presentation
extemporaneous speaking
feedback

Discussion

1. Join an audience listening to a lecture or political speech. Evaluate the speech by applying the standards of integrated communication. Did the speaker read from a manuscript, make a memorized presentation, or speak extemporaneously? Was the speaker adept at moving from one mode of presentation to another? How flexible was the speaker in answering questions? Was the speaker's voice effective or ineffective? Why? How would you evaluate the speaker's body language? Report your observations in class.
2. Comedians often capture the personalities of public figures by exaggerating their verbal and gestural characteristics in comic impersonations. Be alert for such impersonations on late-night television. Which identifying characteristics do the comedians exaggerate? What might this indicate about the "real" speaker's presentation peculiarities? Contribute your observations to a class discussion.
3. You have been invited to present your most recent classroom speech on a community access television channel. How would you adapt your message to that medium? Report your ideas in class. What general conclusions can you draw about the impact of video presentations on public speaking?
4. Make a list of questions you think you might be asked following your next speech. Plan the answers you might make to these questions. Working in small groups, distribute your questions to group members to ask of you. Invite them to evaluate your responses.

Application

1. Exchange your self-evaluation tape with a classmate and write a critique of that person's voice and articulation. Emphasize the positive, but make specific recommendations for improvement. Work on your classmate's recommendations to you, and then make a second tape to share with your partner. Do you hear signs of improvement in each other's performance?
2. As you practice your next speech, deliberately try to speak in as dull a voice as possible. Stifle all impulses to gesture. Then practice speaking with as colorful a voice as possible, giving full freedom to movement and gesture. Notice how a colorful and expressive presentation makes your ideas seem more lively and vivid.
3. Form small groups and conduct an impromptu speaking contest. Each participant should supply two topics for impromptu speeches, and participants should then draw two topics (not their own). Participants have five minutes to prepare a three-minute speech on one of these topics. Each student then presents the speech to the group, which evaluates the speeches according to the criteria discussed in this chapter and selects a winner.

Notes

1. Janet Beavin Bavelas, "Redefining Language: Nonverbal Linguistic Acts in Face-to-Face Dialogue," 1992 Aubrey Fisher Memorial Lecture, presented at the University of Utah, October 1992.
2. Richard Conniff, "Reading Faces," *Smithsonian* 34 (January 2004): 49.
3. Quoted in ibid., p. 47.
4. James C. McCroskey, *An Introduction to Rhetorical Communication,* 3rd ed. (Englewood Cliffs, N.J.: Prentice Hall, 1993), pp. 263–264.
5. Virginia P. Richmond, James C. McCroskey, and S. K. Payne, *Nonverbal Behavior in Interpersonal Relations,* 2nd ed. (Englewood Cliffs, N.J.: Prentice Hall, 1991), pp. 208–228.
6. Howard Giles and Arlene Franklyn-Stokes, "Communicator Characteristics," in *Handbook of International and Intercultural Communication,* ed. Molefi Kete Asante and William B. Gudykunst (Newbury Park, Calif.: Sage, 1989), pp. 117–144.
7. Jon Eisenson, *Voice and Diction: A Program for Improvement* (New York: Macmillan, 1974), p. vii.
8. Adapted from Stewart W. Hyde, *Television and Radio Announcing,* 6th ed. (Boston: Houghton Mifflin, 1991), pp. 80–85.
9. N. Scott Momaday, *The Way to Rainy Mountain* (Albuquerque: University of New Mexico Press, 1969), p. 5.
10. Carole Douglis, "The Beat Goes On: Social Rhythms Underlie All Our Speech and Actions," *Psychology Today,* November 1987, p. 36–41
11. William Price Fox, "Eugene Talmadge and Sears Roebuck Co.," in *Southern Fried Plus Six* (New York: Ballantine Books, 1968), p. 36.
12. Charlotte Perkins Gilman, "Similar Cases," from *In This Our World,* reprinted in Wayland Maxfield Parrish, *Reading Aloud: A Technique in the Interpretation of Literature* (New York: Ronald, 1941), pp. 144–145.
13. Cited in Douglis, p. 36.
14. Michael L. Hecht, Peter A. Andersen, and Sidney A. Ribeau, "The Cultural Dimensions of Nonverbal Communication," in *Handbook of International and Intercultural Communication,* ed. Molefi Kete Asante and William B. Gudykunst (Newbury Park, Calif.: Sage, 1989), pp. 163–185; Larry A. Samovar and Richard E. Porter, *Communication Between Cultures* (Belmont, Calif.: Wadsworth, 1991), pp. 205–206.
15. Ralph Hillman and Delorah Lee Jewell, *Work for Your Voice* (Murfreesboro, Tenn.: Copymatte, 1986), p. 63.
16. Don Marquis, adapted from "mehitabel and her kittens," in *the lives and times of archy and mehitabel.* Copyright ©1927 by Doubleday and Company, Inc. Reprinted by permission of the publisher.
17. *NBC Handbook of Pronunciation,* 4th ed. (New York: Harper, 1991).
18. William B. Gudykunst et al., "Language and Intergroup Communication," in *Handbook of International and Intercultural Communication,* ed. Molefi Kete Asante and William B. Gudykunst (Newbury Park, Calif.: Sage, 1989), pp. 145–162.
19. Carolanne Griffith-Roberts, "Let's Talk Southern," *Southern Living,* February 1995, p. 82. For a detailed explication of regional dialect variances, see Charles K. Thomas, *An Introduction to the Phonetics of American English,* 2nd ed. (New York: Ronald, 1958), pp. 191–260.
20. "Jeff Foxworthy: From Hootenanny to Hoosier," *Satellite TV Week,* 28 July–3 August 1996, p. l.

21. Samovar and Porter, p. 177.

22. Peter A. Andersen, "Nonverbal Immediacy in Interpersonal Communication," in *Multichannel Integrations of Nonverbal Behavior,* ed. A. W. Siegman and S. Feldstein (Mahwah, N.J.: Erlbaum, 1985).

23. S. Ishii, "Characteristics of Japanese Nonverbal Communication Behavior," *Communication,* Summer 1973, pp. 163–180; Samovar and Porter, pp. 198–200; "Understanding Culture: Don't Stare at a Navajo," *Psychology Today,* June 1974, p. 107.

24. Research psychologist Carolyn Copper has found that newscasters influence voters when they smile while speaking of candidates, further evidence of the power of facial expression ("A Certain Smile," *Psychology Today,* January–February 1992, p. 20).

25. Charlotte I. Lee and Timothy Gura, *Oral Interpretation,* 8th ed. (Boston: Houghton Mifflin, 1992), pp. 118–119.

26. Edouard Gasarabwe-Laroche, "Meaningful Gestures: Nonverbal Communication in Rwandan Culture," *UNESCO Courier,* September 1993, pp. 31–33.

27. Mary Munter, "Cross Cultural Communication for Managers," *Business Horizons,* May–June 1993, pp. 69–78. For additional insights into cultural differences in nonverbal communication, see Roger Axtell, *Gestures: The Do's and Taboos of Body Language Around the World* (New York: Wiley, 1991); E. Hall, *Understanding Cultural Differences* (Yarmouth, Maine: Intercultural Press, 1990); J. Mole, *When in Rome . . . A Business Guide to Cultures and Customs in Twelve European Nations* (New York: AMACOM, 1991); D. Ricks, *Big Business Blunders* (Homewood, Ill.: Dow Jones-Irwin, 1983); and C. Storti, *The Art of Crossing Cultures* (Yarmouth, Maine: Intercultural Press, 1990).

28. Marc Hequet, "The Fine Art of Multicultural Meetings," *Training,* July 1993, p. 29.

29. Norman Schwarzkopf, "Leaders for the 21st Century," *Vital Speeches of the Day,* 15 June 1999, p. 519.

30. The literature supporting this conclusion is reviewed by Virginia Kidd, "Do Clothes Make the Officer? How Uniforms Impact Communication: A Review of Literature," presented at the Visual Communication Conference at Pray, Montana, 8 July 2000.

31. Michael Duffy, "Picture of Health," *Time,* 4 Oct. 1993, pp. 28+. *Time Almanac Reference Ed.* CD-ROM. Compact, 1994.

32. "A Letter to Our Readers," *Newsweek,* 4 Oct. 1993, p. 29.

33. These guidelines for handling questions and answers are a compendium of ideas from the following sources: Stephen D. Body, "Nine Steps to a Successful Question-and-Answer Session," *Management Solutions,* May 1988, pp. 16–17; Teresa Brady, "Fielding Abrasive Questions During Presentations," *Supervisory Management,* February 1993, p. 6; J. Donald Ragsdale and Alan L. Mikels, "Effects of Question Periods on a Speaker's Credibility with a Television Audience," *Southern States Communication Journal* 40 (1975): 302–312; Dorothy Sarnoff, *Never Be Nervous Again* (New York: Ballantine, 1987); Laurie Schloff and Marcia Yudkin, *Smart Speaking: Sixty-Second Strategies* (New York: Holt, 1991); and Alan Zaremba, "Q and A: The Other Part of Your Presentation," *Management World,* January–February 1989, pp. 8–10.

34. Roger Ailes, *You Are the Message: Getting What You Want by Being Who You Are* (New York: Doubleday, 1988), p. 170.

35. The authors are indebted to Professor Roxanne Gee of the television and film area in the Department of Communication at the University of Memphis for her assistance and suggestions in putting together this advice.

36. Ailes, pp. 15–19.

37. Illustrations of major video hand signals may be found in Stewart W. Hyde, *Television and Radio Announcing,* 6th ed. (Boston: Houghton Mifflin, 1991), pp. 80–85.

38. Ralph R. Behnke and Chris R. Sawyer, "Public Speaking Procrastination as a Correlate of Public Speaking Communication Apprehension and Self-Perceived Public Speaking Competence," *Communication Research Reports* 16 (1999): 40–47.

39. Judith Humphrey, "Taking the Stage," *Vital Speeches of the Day,* 1 May 2001, pp. 435–438.

40. Ibid., p. 436.

Types of Public Speaking

PART IV

14 Informative Speaking

This chapter will help you

- understand the functions of informative speaking
- learn the types of informative speeches and how to develop them
- apply psychological principles to help listeners learn
- arrange information for maximum effectiveness
- respond to the special challenge of informative speaking

OUTLINE

> *The improvement of understanding is for two ends: first our own increase of knowledge; secondly, to enable us to deliver that knowledge to others.*
>
> JOHN LOCKE

In ancient Greek mythology, Prometheus was punished by the other gods for teaching humans how to make fire. According to the myth, these jealous gods knew that people would now be able to keep warm, cook food, use the extended light, and share knowledge as they huddled around their campfires. Eventually they would build civilizations and challenge the gods themselves with the power of their new learning. These mythical gods had every right to be angry with Prometheus. He had given the first significant speech of demonstration.

This tale of Prometheus reminds us that information is power. Because we cannot personally experience everything that may be important or interesting to us, we must rely on the knowledge of others to expand our understanding and competence. *Sharing knowledge is the essence of informative speaking.*

Shared information can be important to survival. Early detection and warning systems alert us to storms, and news of medical breakthroughs tell us how to stay healthy. Beyond simply enabling us to live, information helps us to live *better*. It helps us deal with our world and the people in it. In this chapter, we look at the functions of informative communication, suggest ways to help your listeners learn, discuss the major types of informative speeches and how to develop them, present some basic informative speech designs, and discuss how you might use them. We also describe the special challenge posed by informative speaking and discuss how you might meet it. Our objective is to help you bring fire to your listeners.

Functions of Informative Speaking

Go to the **VideoLab Drill 8.3: Functions of Informative Speaking** and complete the exercises.

VideoLab

Informative speaking is defined by its function. Speeches don't always fall into neat categories. In the same speech you might introduce yourself, provide information, urge action, and celebrate values. *But if your main purpose is to share knowledge, then we call the speech informative.*

Informative speaking is important for four reasons.

1. It can empower listeners by giving them new ideas and skills.
2. It can shape listener perceptions.
3. It can help set the agenda of public concerns.
4. It can clarify options for action.

Let's take a look at each of these individually.

Sharing Information and Ideas

An informative speech *gives* to listeners rather than *asks* of them. The demands on the audience are relatively low. As an informative speaker, you want listeners to pay attention and understand, but you do not try to make them change their behavior. For example, Heide Norde presented an informative speech to her class on the dangers of prolonged exposure to ultraviolet radiation, but she did not urge listeners to boycott tanning salons. What they did in response to her speech was up to them. Similarly, in the speech reprinted at the end of this chapter, Marie D'Aniello deepened her audience's appreciation for the meaning of friendship, but she did not advocate that they go out and seek friends. Again, what they did with their new knowledge would be their decision.

Although informative speaking makes modest demands on the listener, the demands on the speaker are high. Good informative speakers must have a thorough understanding of their subject. It is one thing to know something well enough to satisfy yourself. It is quite another to know it well enough that you can justify making a public speech about it.

Shared information can be important to survival.

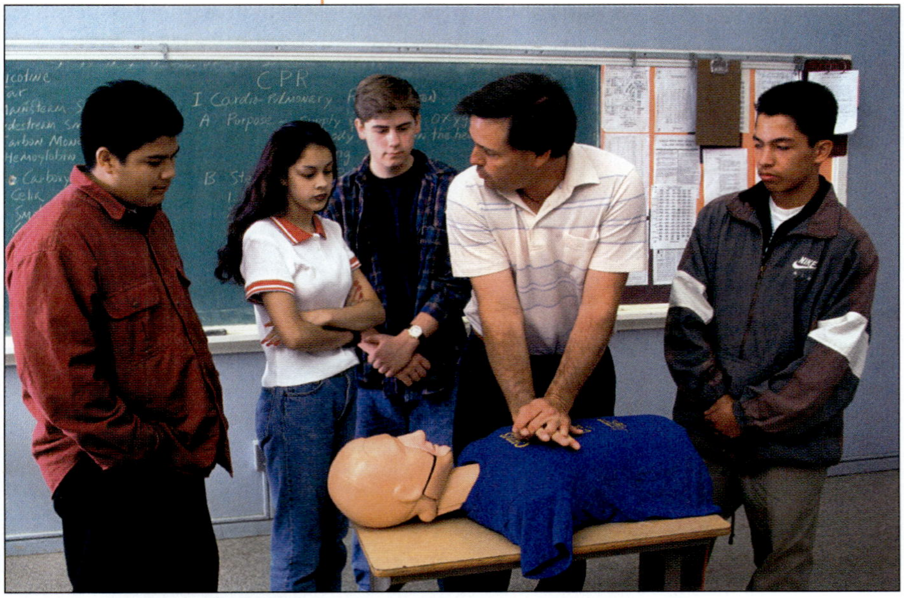

By sharing information, an informative speech reduces ignorance. It does not simply repeat something the audience already knows. Rather, *the* ***informative value*** *of a speech is measured by how much new and important information or understanding it provides the audience.* As you prepare your informative speech, ask yourself the following questions:

- Is my topic significant enough to merit an informative speech?
- What do my listeners already know about my topic?

- What more do they need to know?
- Do I understand my topic well enough to help others understand it?

The answers to these questions should help you plan a speech with high informative value.

In informative speaking, the speaker acts as a teacher. To teach effectively, you must arouse and sustain attention by adapting your message to listeners' interests and needs. You must make your audience aware of how important the new information is. When you have finished, they should feel they have benefited from your message.

Shaping Audience Perceptions

When speakers share information, they also share their points of view. It is virtually impossible to cover everything there is to know about any important subject in a short message. Speakers must be selective about the information they convey, and what they omit may be as important as what they include. When you present an informative speech, your business is not to advise listeners about what they should do or how they should feel about your topic. Nevertheless, when listeners see a subject through the speaker's eyes, they really see an interpretation of it. Moreover, the word-pictures painted by speakers are often colored in subtle, unconscious ways by their feelings. This selective exposure to a subject can influence the way we respond to it, especially if it is new to us.

This power of informative speaking to influence perceptions can serve a **prepersuasive function**, preparing listeners for later persuasive messages. Suppose that you hear one of two speeches reporting on personal experiences in teaching. The first, presented by an enthusiastic teacher, describes the personal rewards of teaching and stresses the joy of helping children learn. The other, offered by a teacher suffering from burnout, focuses on discipline problems and administrative red tape. Neither suggests that you should or should not become a teacher. Each provides what he or she *believes* to be an accurate picture. But each creates a totally different predisposition to respond. Depending on which message you hear, you will be primed quite differently for a later persuasive message urging you to become a teacher.

In his speech reprinted at the end of Chapter 10, Josh Logan offered a carefully researched report on the causes of the greenhouse effect. Although the speech is primarily informative, it is nevertheless colored by Josh's feelings: the greenhouse effect "changes the order of nature" and is the key to "the great calamity" of global warming. Josh had to work hard to maintain the overall objectivity of his speech so that listeners would feel they were receiving unbiased information. To counterbalance his own feelings, Josh kept the emphasis on "hard" information: supporting material in the form of facts, statistics, and an abundance of expert testimony. Only with such authoritative information could Josh's speech perform its *prepersuasive* function of preparing his audience for the persuasive speeches he would offer later in his public speaking course (see the speeches at the end of Chapters 15 and 16).

If you have strong feelings about a subject, you also will have to work hard *not* to present a distorted perspective. If listeners feel you are blurring the truth or displaying obvious bias, they may dismiss your message as unreliable and lower their estimation of your character and competence.

Setting an Agenda

The amount of information reaching people today can be overwhelming. This flood of information from the mass media serves an **agenda-setting function.**[1] As the media present the "news," they also tell us what we should be thinking about. By the

Figure 14.1

The Functions of Informative Speaking

Function	Important When You Are
Sharing information and ideas	Introducing new ideas or skills
Sharing perceptions	Preparing listeners for later persuasive messages
Setting an agenda	Establishing the importance of a topic
Clarifying options	Providing a balanced perspective on a subject

amount and kind of coverage allotted to a topic, the media establish the topic's importance in the public mind.

Informative speaking also performs an agenda-setting role. As it directs our attention to certain subjects, it influences what we feel is important. The informative speech "The 'Monument' at Wounded Knee," which appears in Appendix B, demonstrates this agenda-setting function because it shapes perceptions about our country's policy toward Native Americans. Hearing that speech could predispose listeners both to believe that the issue is important and to favor better treatment for this group. Similarly, Josh Logan's speech brought the greenhouse effect to the attention of his listeners. They were both alerted to that topic and prepared to give a favorable reception to his later persuasive speeches.

As you prepare an informative speech, remember the power you have to establish the importance of your topic in the minds of your listeners. Consider the ethical consequences of your words.

Clarifying Options

An informative speech also can reveal and clarify options for action. Information expands our awareness, opens new horizons, and suggests fresh possibilities. It can also help us discard unworkable options. The better we understand an issue, the more intelligent the choices we can make. For example, what should we know about obesity? Informative speeches may tell us about the consequences of doing something or nothing to correct this condition. They may teach us about the medical soundness of different diets. They may also inform us about the roles of exercise and counseling in weight control. Such information would expand our options for dealing with the problem.

As he discussed the causes of the greenhouse effect, Josh Logan identified three major causes: the loss of woodlands, agricultural and industrial emissions, and personal energy consumption. Implied in his analysis were a variety of options for dealing with this situation, ranging from changing personal habits to supporting a political agenda of local, national, and international policy solutions. Josh did not identify and discuss these options in this speech: that would be the business of later persuasive speeches. But he had widened the horizon of understanding, preparing listeners for the choices they might make among the alternatives available to them.

VideoLab

Evaluate how well the speaker in **VideoLab Lesson 8's Next Step** meets the guidelines for ethical informative speaking.

Informative speakers carry a large ethical burden to communicate responsible knowledge of their topics. A responsible informative speech should cover all major positions on a topic and present all vital information. Although speakers may have strong feelings on a subject, it is unethical to deliberately omit or distort information that is necessary for audience understanding. Similarly, speakers who are unaware of information because they have not done sufficient research are irresponsible. As you prepare your speech, you should seek out material from sources that present different perspectives on your subject. The two speeches on the teaching profession mentioned earlier demonstrate potential ethical abuses of the

The Ethics of Informative Speaking

Ethics Alert! 14.1

1. Be sure you can ethically defend your choice of a topic.
2. Mention all major positions on a topic when there are differing perspectives.
3. Present all information on a topic that is important for audience understanding.
4. Do not distort information that is necessary for audience understanding.
5. Do sufficient research to speak responsibly on your subject.
6. Do not omit relevant information because it is inconsistent with your perspective.
7. Strive to be as objective as possible.

option clarifying function of informative speaking. If the speeches are presented as *representative* of teaching as a career, then both speakers are guilty of overgeneralizing from limited personal experience.

Types of Informative Speeches

As we have noted, the major purpose of any informative speech is to share knowledge in order to expand your listeners' understanding or competence. To meet this challenge, an informative speech will typically *describe, demonstrate*, or *explain* its subject. These different procedures divide informative speaking into types, although a single speech can combine several of these purposes. After we discuss each of them, we will also consider briefings as an important subtype of informative speaking.

VideoLab

Watch the student speech in **VideoLab Lesson 8** and complete the accompanying exercises to learn more about types of informative speeches.

Speeches of Description

Often the specific purpose of a speech is to describe a particular activity, event, object, person, and/or place. A **speech of description** should give the audience a clear picture of your subject. Effective description relies heavily on the artful use of language. The words must be clear, concrete, and colorful to delineate the subject precisely and to convey the feeling of the message. The speech "The Monument at Wounded Knee" in Appendix B describes a *place* and *object* by providing vivid word-pictures. Thus, the landscape is not simply desolate; it is characterized by "flat, sun-baked fields and an occasional eroded gully." Cecile Larson goes on to describe the monument:

> **The monument itself rests on a concrete slab to the right of the grave. It's a typical, large, old-fashioned granite cemetery marker, a pillar about six feet high topped with an urn—the kind of gravestone you might see in any cemetery with graves from the turn of the century. The inscription tells us that it was erected by the families of those who were killed at Wounded Knee. Weeds grow through the cracks in the concrete at its base.**

While she describes a place and an object, Cecile's purpose is also to deepen historical understanding of an *event* that occurred there. The overtones of her description suggest that she wishes to cure her audience of cultural arrogance by reminding them of past cruel treatment of Natives Americans. The speech could serve a prepersuasive function of preparing listeners for later speeches advocating more humane policies on reservations.

In her speech exposing conditions in the fast food industry, student speaker Hannah Johnston used vivid language to describe an *activity*—what it's like to work in a slaughterhouse.

> **Slaughterhouse work conditions have not changed much over the past fifty to one hundred years. Now the work is done mostly by underpaid migrant workers who have virtually no other job options. But who would choose to work in a place like this if they did have options? Who, for example, would choose to become a "sticker," a person who, for about eight and a half hours a day, does nothing other than stand, literally drenched in a river of blood, slitting the throats of steers that pass every ten seconds or so?**

Hannah's speech clearly served agenda-setting and prepersuasive functions, as she prepared listeners for later speeches proposing reforms in the industry.

As these examples make clear, the art of verbal description comes down to one basic rule: *You must create in the minds of your listeners a sharp, pictorial realization of what your subject looks like.* Concrete, colorful, metaphorical language—the language of effective imagery—can obviously help. Such language will rely heavily on the principles of contrast, intensity, and activity, which we shall discuss further in the next section.

The topic, purpose, and strategy of your speech of description should suggest the appropriate design for it. The "Monument" speech follows a spatial pattern, in that it develops within a verbal map of the Pine Ridge reservation. Hannah's descriptions of slaughterhouse conditions occur within a categorical design, as she discusses the content of fast food, the conditions under which it is produced, and its increasingly global health consequences. We will discuss these and other design options later in this chapter.

Speeches of Demonstration

The **speech of demonstration** shows the audience how to do something. Dance instructors teach us the Texas two-step. Others may tell us how to do research on the Internet, or how to prepare for the Law School Admission Test, or even how to build a fire. The tip-off to the speech of demonstration is the phrase "*how to*." What these examples have in common is that they demonstrate a process.

The speech of demonstration shows the audience how to do something.

Successful speeches of demonstration empower listeners so that they can perform the process themselves. Jeffrey O'Connor showed his University of New Mexico classmates "how to" read a textbook efficiently. He guided them through five steps of effective reading, each step representing a main point of his speech. His presentation, outlined later in this chapter, follows a sequential design.

Suzanne Marchetti illustrated another form of the speech of demonstration when she took her classmates on a verbal tour of Yellowstone Park, showing them how to access major attractions there. Her speech, again outlined later in this chapter, employs a spatial design.

Most speeches of demonstration are helped by the use of presentation aids. The speaker can present and discuss objects that listeners must use to accomplish something, show slides that reveal the steps in a process, or actually demonstrate how to perform an activity. If you are preparing a speech of demonstration, review the materials on presentation aids in Chapter 11 to determine how you might help your audience understand. When you are demonstrating a process, "show and tell" is usually much more effective than just telling.

Speeches of Explanation

A **speech of explanation** offers information about subjects that are abstract or complicated. Because understanding is the object of such a speech, a speech of explanation should set forth the critical characteristics of a subject and offer abundant examples.[2] In her speech explaining Alzheimer's disease, student speaker Amanda Miller set forth the critical features of her subject in the following way:

1. She justified her speech by quoting a famous victim, Ronald Reagan, who asked for greater public awareness and understanding of the disease as he made his exit from public life.
2. She defined the disease.
3. She explained its significance for those afflicted with it, their families, and the nation (in terms of cost).
4. She described the process of the disease.
5. She identified the risk factors associated with it.
6. She explained how to minimize susceptibility to it.

Similarly, Marie D'Aniello, in her classroom speech "What Friends Are All About," defined the nature of friendship, explained its significance to her listeners, and traced the evolution (process) of friendship as people mature. Like Amanda, she offered examples and expert testimony at every step to clarify and authenticate her explanations.

As you set forth the critical features of your subject in your own speech of explanation, be sure you go through the essential phases of defining your subject, explaining its significance to the lives of your listeners, and describing any processes by which it develops. Include abundant examples and testimony.

Speeches of explanation face a considerable challenge when their information runs counter to generally accepted beliefs. Professor Katherine Rowan provides an example of how this can work in public service campaigns:

> **A particularly resilient obstacle to [seat] belt use is the erroneous but prevalent belief that hitting one's head on a windshield while traveling at 30 miles per hour is an experience much like doing so when a car is stationary. . . . If people understood that the experience would be much more similar to falling from a three-story building and hitting the pavement face first, one obstacle to the wearing of seat belts would be easier to overcome.[3]**

As her example indicates, dramatic analogies—such as comparing an auto accident at thirty miles per hour to falling from a building—can help break through our resistance to new ideas that defy folk wisdom. The use of such strategic comparisons and contrasts can help listeners accept new information and use it in their lives.

Briefings

A **briefing** is a short presentation offered in an organizational setting, often for informative purposes. It may involve description and demonstration, but more generally, it emphasizes explanation. Briefings often take place during meetings, as when employees gather at the beginning of a workday to learn about plans or policy changes.[4] At such a meeting, you might be asked to give a status report on a project. Briefings also take place in one-on-one situations, as when you report to your supervisor at work. They can occur as a press briefing after a crisis or major event occurs.[5] Often a question-and-answer period will follow the briefing.

Although briefings occur frequently in organizations, they are not often done well. Most how-to books on communicating in organizations deplore the lack of brevity, clarity, and directness in presentations.[6] When executives in eighteen organizations were asked, "What makes a poor presentation?" they responded with the following list of descriptions:

- It is poorly organized.
- It is not well delivered.
- It contains too much jargon.
- It is too long.
- It lacks examples or comparisons.[7]

This situation offers you quite an opportunity. Developing the art of the briefing will increase your value in an organization. The following rules should guide your preparation:

First, a briefing should be what its name suggests: brief. Cut out any material that is not related directly to your main points. Keep your introduction and conclusions short. Begin with a preview and end with a summary.

Second, organize your ideas before you open your mouth. How can you possibly be organized when you are called on without warning in a meeting to "tell us about your project"? The answer is simple: prepare in advance (also review our guidelines for making impromptu speeches in Chapter 13). *Never go into any meeting in which there is even the slightest possibility that you might be asked to report without a skeleton outline of a presentation.* Select a simple design and make a key-word outline of points you would cover and the order in which you would cover them. Put this outline on a note card and carry it in your pocket. Your supervisors and colleagues will be impressed with your foresight.

Third, rely heavily on facts and figures, expert testimony, and short examples for supporting materials. Don't drift off into long stories. Use comparison and contrast to make your points clearly and directly.

Fourth, adapt your language to your audience. If you are an engineer reporting on a project to a group of managers, use the language of management, not the language of engineering. Tell them what they need to know in language they can understand. Relate the subject to what they already know.

Fifth, present your message with confidence. Be sure everyone can see and hear you. Stand up, if necessary. Look listeners in the eye. Speak firmly with an air of assurance. After all, the project is yours, and you are the expert on it.

Finally, be prepared to answer tough questions. Respond forthrightly and honestly. No one likes bad news, but worse news will come if you don't deliver the bad

Rules for Effective Informative Speaking — Speaker's Notes 14.1

1. Speeches of description should come alive through colorful language.
2. Speeches of demonstration should follow a clear, orderly sequence of steps.
3. Speeches of demonstration are helped by presentation aids.
4. Speeches of explanation need clear definitions of important terms.
5. Speeches of explanation require good examples.
6. Briefings should be short and simply designed.

news to those who need to know it *when* they need to know it. Review our suggestions for handling question-and-answer sessions in Chapter 13.

Helping Listeners Learn

No matter what the function and type of your informative speech, its success will be measured in terms of whether and how much listeners learn from it. Preparation for a successful informative speech begins by considering how much listeners know initially about your topic, how interested they may be in it, what preconceptions they may have about it that might help or hinder your purpose, and how they regard you as a speaker. These basic audience considerations can help you select strategies for your presentation. Figure 14.2 charts these audience considerations and directs you to possible strategies you can use.

As an informative speaker, you need to apply basic principles of learning to make your speeches effective. To help your listeners learn and remember your message, you must motivate them by establishing its relevance to their lives, hold their attention throughout your message, and structure your speech so that it is easily understood.

You should also keep in mind that there are different types of intelligence and learning styles.[8] For example, some people are *aural learners* who learn well through the spoken word alone. Others are *print learners* who learn better when they see things in writing. These people respond well when you provide charts and textual graphics to illustrate your words. A third group, *visual learners*, need something to watch as they listen; they are helped especially by demonstrations, pictures, and models. Keep these various learning styles in mind as you design your speeches, so that you can better serve the needs of a wide population of listeners.

Motivation

To motivate listeners, especially those who are not initially interested in your subject, you must tell them why your message is important to them. In Chapter 5 we discussed motivation as a general factor in audience analysis. Now we consider motivation more precisely in terms of giving listeners a reason to learn. Ask yourself why listeners would want to know what you have to tell them.

- Will it help them understand and control the world around them?
- Will it satisfy their curiosity?
- Will it improve their health, safety, or general well-being?
- Will it give them a sense of making a contribution by caring for others?

Figure 14.2

Audience Considerations for Informative Speeches

Audience Type	Strategies
Interested but uninformed	• Provide basic information in clear, simple language. • Avoid jargon, define technical terms. • Use examples and narratives for amplification. • When communicating complicated information, use analogies, metaphors, and/or presentation aids. • Use voice, gestures, and eye contact to reinforce meaning.
Interested and knowledgeable	• Establish your credibility early in the speech. • Acknowledge diverse perspectives on topic. • Go into depth with information and expert testimony. • Offer engaging presentation that keeps focus on content.
Uninterested	• Show listeners what's in it for them. • Keep presentation short and to the point. • Use sufficient examples and narratives to arouse and sustain interest. • Use eye-catching presentation aids and colorful language. • Make a dynamic presentation.
Unsympathetic (toward topic)	• Show respect for listeners and their point of view. • Cite sources the audience will respect. • Present information to enlarge listeners' understanding. • Develop stories and examples to arouse favorable feeling. • Make a warm, engaging presentation.
Distrustful (of speaker)	• Establish your credibility early in the speech. • Rely heavily on factual examples and expert testimony. • Cite sources of information in your presentation. • Be straightforward, business-like, and personable. • Keep good eye-contact with listeners.

- Will it help them establish better relations with family and friends?
- Will it give them a sense of accomplishment and achievement, thus enhancing their personal growth, power, and independence?
- Will it contribute to the restoration of moral balance and fairness in the world?
- Will it provide them with enjoyment?

Visual learners are best served by demonstrations, pictures, and models.

Go back over the motivations discussed in Chapter 5 and determine which of these are most relevant to your topic and your audience. Then frame your speech so that it connects with these needs.

For example, you might relate a speech on how to interview for a job to the need for achievement. You could begin by talking about the problem of finding a good job in today's marketplace and provide an example that illustrates how a successful interview can make the difference in who gets hired and who does not. As you preview the body of your speech, you might say, "Today, I'm going to describe four factors that can determine whether you get the job of your dreams. First, . . ." In this case you have given your audience a reason for wanting to listen to the rest of your speech. You have begun the learning process by motivating your listeners.

Listeners must be motivated to learn new information. Organizational training programs must combine motivation and information to help employees become more effective.

Hannah Johnston began her speech on the fast food industry by appealing to health and safety motivations: "If you had a choice, I'm sure you wouldn't choose to eat some of the stuff that can end up in processed meat." Hannah ruined lunch for some of her classmates, but they could not help but listen closely. Marie D'Aniello opened her speech on the nature of friendship with a narrative that aroused curiosity: "It's nine o'clock at night. I'm curled up in the back seat of a new truck and my friends, Cammy and Joe, are in the front singing along with the radio." Hmmm, her listeners puzzled. What happened in the truck? Why were Cammy and Joe singing? They were ready to listen to the rest of her informative speech.

Attention

Once you have motivated your audience to listen, you must hold their attention throughout your speech. In Chapter 7, we discussed how to attract audience attention in the introduction of your speech. Here we focus on how to sustain that interest. You can do so by applying one or more of the six factors that affect attention: intensity, repetition, novelty, activity, contrast, and relevance.

Intensity. The **intensity** of an object is a function of how much it contrasts with its background. Merely printing the word "intensity" in boldface is an example of the principle at work: signaling that this term is especially important by making it stand out against the words that surround it. Our eyes are drawn to bright lights, and we are startled by loud noises. In speeches, intense language and vivid images can be used to attract and hold attention, especially when your audience may lack initial interest. You can further emphasize a point by using examples that magnify its importance. You can also achieve intensity through the use of presentation aids and by vocal emphasis and variety. Note how Stephen Huff held the attention of his classmates through the intensity of his descriptions of the New Madrid earthquakes that struck the southcentral United States in the early nineteenth century:

> **The Indians tell of the night that lasted for a week and the way the "Father of Waters"—the Mississippi River—ran backward. Waterfalls were formed on the river. Islands disappeared. Land that was once in Arkansas ended up in Tennessee. Cracks up to ten feet wide opened and closed in the earth. Geysers squirted sand high into the air. Whole forests sank into the earth as the land turned to quicksand.**

Repetition. Repeated sounds, words, or phrases attract and hold attention. Skillful speakers may use **repetition** to emphasize points, help listeners follow the flow of ideas, and embed their messages in audience memory. As we saw in Chapter 12, repetition underlies alliteration and parallel construction. Alliteration lends vividness to main ideas: "Today, I will discuss how the *M*ississippi River *m*eanders from *M*innesota to the sea." The repetition of the *m* sound catches attention and emphasizes the statement. Similarly, parallel construction establishes a pattern that sticks in the mind. Repeated questions and answers such as "What is our goal? It is to . . ." sustain attention.

Novelty. We are attracted to anything new or unusual: thus, the importance of **novelty**. If you have a fresh way of seeing and saying things, uninterested and distrustful listeners may increase both their respect for you and their interest in your subject. A novel phrase can fascinate listeners and hold their attention. In a speech on environmental stewardship, Jim Cardoza found a novel way to describe the magnitude of pollution. After reporting that nineteen million tons of garbage are picked up each year along the nation's beaches, he concluded: "And that's just the tip of the wasteberg." His invented word, *wasteberg,* reminded listeners of *iceberg* and suggested the vastness of the problem. Some famous novel expressions in American history that aroused attention for political programs and philosophies in their time are "New Deal," "the New Frontier," and "the Great Society."

Activity. As we noted in Chapter 13, anything that moves attracts attention. Gesturing, approaching the audience to add emphasis to a point, and referring to presentation aids can all add **activity**. An exciting story or example can also bring a speech to life and attract attention. Such techniques can be especially useful when listeners lack initial interest in the subject. You can further create a sense of activity by using vivid words, rhythm, and vocal variety. Stephen Huff used a clever stylistic technique near the beginning of his speech on "The New Madrid Earthquake Area" to create the sense of living presence:

> **How many of you can remember what you were doing around seven o'clock on the evening of October 17th? If you're a sports fan like me, you had probably set out the munchies, popped a cold one, and settled back to watch San Francisco and Oakland battle it out in the World Series. . . . You may not have been paying close attention to the TV—*until—until—until* both the sound and picture went out because of the Bay Area earthquake.**

Speakers who gesture sustain attention.

Here the repetition of "until" simulates the sense of trembling instability one experiences during an actual earthquake.

Josh Logan, on the other hand, used a graphic action picture to leave a vivid impression on his listeners as he concluded his speech, "Life in the

Greenhouse." In effect he invited his audience to experience what he had been talking about in his speech:

> **If you want to understand why global warming has become one of the great crises of our time, you've simply got to step outside into the greenhouse. Listen for the falling trees, watch the industrial smokestacks darkening the sky, and smell that rich bouquet of exhaust fumes that we are constantly pumping into the air. The greenhouse effect is a monster we all are creating.**

Whether you are beginning or concluding your speech, creating the sense of activity can earn favorable attention for your speech.

Contrast. The principle that *opposites attract attention* explains the importance of **contrast**. If you work in a noisy environment and it suddenly becomes quiet, the stillness can seem deafening. Similarly, abrupt changes in your pitch or rate of speaking will draw attention. Presenting the pros and cons of a situation creates a sense of conflict and drama that listeners often find arresting. You can also highlight contrasts by speaking of such opposites as life and death, light and dark, or the highs and lows of a situation.

In a speech dramatizing the need to learn more about AIDS, a speaker introduced two or three specific examples with the statement "Let me introduce you to *Death*." Then, as the speech moved to the promise of medical research, she said, "Now let me introduce you to *Life*." This usage combined repetition and contrast to create a dramatic effect.

Similarly, Cecile Larson used contrast between the grand monuments of American life—such as the heroes sculpted on Mount Rushmore—and the much more humble "monument" at Wounded Knee to arouse shame and indignation and to focus audience attention on a less proud incident in the nation's history.

When contrast works, it produces something of a surprise or shock effect. Once people become accustomed to an established pattern, they no longer think about it. But they notice any abrupt, dramatic change from the pattern.

Relevance. Things that relate to our specific needs, interests, or concerns hold our attention. Often listeners who might think that they are unsympathetic to a subject simply need to be shown how it relates to their lives. Allison McIntyre created **relevance** for her agenda-setting speech on smoking advertisements by placing a large jar of cigarette butts on the table by the lectern.

> **So you think the cigarette advertisers are losing their fight to recruit smokers at American colleges and universities? Here's what I collected myself in about 45 minutes at noon yesterday, right around the outside of this building. These are our butts. Vanderbilt student butts. Think of all the damaged lungs these represent, right here in this building.**

The striking relevance of her presentation aid made it hard to ignore her speech.

Stephen Huff created relevance for his earthquake speech by relating the San Francisco earthquake to the

InterConnections.LearnMore 14.1

Learning Styles

Index of Learning Styles
http://www2.ncsu.edu/unity/lockers/users/f/felder/public/ILSpage.html
Links to learning-style sites and a self-administered, computer-scored quiz that reflects four dimensions of learning: active versus reflective, sensing versus intuitive, visual versus verbal, and sequential versus global. Developed by Professor Emeritus Richard Felder of North Carolina State University.

Seven Perceptual Styles
http://www.learningstyles.org/menu.html
Overview of the seven ways people learn: print, aural, interactive, visual, haptic (touch), kinesthetic, and olfactory; sponsored by the Institute for Learning Styles Research.

Multiple Intelligence and Adult Learning
http://www.literacynet.org/mi/flash.html
Relates information on multiple intelligences to adult learning situations; includes explanatory articles and links to other sources and programs; developed by Leslie Shelton, director of Project Read: Multiple Intelligence for Adult Literacy and Adult Education.

New Madrid area in which he and his listeners lived. Then he dramatized this relevance through the use of contrast, pointing out that the energy level of the New Madrid quakes of the previous century "was over nine hundred times more powerful than the Hiroshima atomic bomb and more than thirty times more powerful than the 7.0 quake that hit San Francisco." Needless to say, Stephen had his listeners' attention as he talked about how to prepare for the next major quake in the area.

Retention

Even the best information is useless unless your listeners remember and use it. Repetition, relevance, and structural factors can all be used to facilitate audience **retention**. The more frequently we hear or see anything, the more likely we are to retain it. This is why advertisers bombard us with slogans to keep their product names in our consciousness. These slogans may be repeated in all of their advertisements, regardless of the visuals or narratives presented. The repetition of key words or phrases in a speech also helps the audience remember. In his famous civil rights speech in Washington, D.C., Martin Luther King's repetition of the phrase "I have a dream . . ." became the hallmark of the speech and is now used as its title.

Relevance is also important to retention. Our minds filter incoming information, associating it with things we already know and evaluating it for its potential usefulness. *If you want listeners to remember your message, tell them why and how it relates to their lives.*

Structural factors also affect how well a message is retained. Previews, summaries, and clear transitions can help your audience remember your message. The way you organize your material also affects retention. Suppose you were given the following list of words to memorize:

> **north, man, hat, daffodil, green, tulip, coat, boy, south, red, east, shoes, gardenia, woman, purple, marigold, gloves, girl, yellow, west**

It looks rather difficult, but look what happens when we rearrange the words:

> north, south, east, west
> man, boy, woman, girl
> daffodil, tulip, gardenia, marigold
> green, red, purple, yellow
> hat, coat, shoes, gloves

In the first example, you have what looks like a random list of words. In the second, the words have been organized by categories: now you have five groups of four related words to remember. Material that is presented in a consistent and orderly fashion is much easier for your audience to retain.

Speaker's Notes 14.2

Getting and Holding Attention

1. *Motivate* listeners by showing them how they can benefit from your message.
2. *Speak with intensity*—develop word-pictures that vividly depict your topic.
3. *Use strategic repetition* to amplify your message.
4. *Rely on novelty* to appeal to listeners' fascination for fresh expressions and new examples.
5. *Use active language* that makes your subject come to life.
6. *Present contrasts* to show what your topic is not.
7. *Highlight relevance* to connect your subject directly to the experience of listeners.

Speech Designs

Let us assume at this point that you have now gone through a careful process of preparing for your informative speech. You have selected a topic that promises important new information for your listeners. You know what you want to accomplish, and you understand the challenge posed by the type of speech you want to present. You have researched carefully, gathered responsible knowledge, and framed some striking ideas that should interest listeners. Our discussion of the learning process has suggested how you might motivate listeners and gain and hold their attention.

Still, your preparation will not be complete until you find the right design for your ideas, the overall structure that will focus the content of your speech into an effective pattern. Six design formats serve the needs of most informative speeches: spatial, sequential, chronological, categorical (topical), comparative, and causation. These designs may also be adapted for use in persuasive and ceremonial speeches.

VideoLab

Test your knowledge of speech designs in **VideoLab Drill 8.2: Identifying Informative Organizational Speaking Patterns.**

Spatial Design

A **spatial design** is appropriate for speeches that develop their topics within a physical setting. Because the order of discussion is based on the nearness of things to one another, the pattern follows the principle of proximity, discussed in Chapter 9. Suppose someone asked you to name the time zones in the United States. If you live in Washington, D.C., you would probably reply, "Eastern, Central, Mountain, and Pacific." If you live in Oregon, you might answer, "Pacific, Mountain, Central, and Eastern."[9] Either answer would follow a spatial pattern, taking where you are as the initial point of reference.

Most people are familiar with maps and can readily visualize directions. A speech using a spatial design provides listeners with an oral map, such as we see in Cecile Larson's "Wounded Knee" speech. Spatial designs are especially useful for speeches of description; they help listeners visualize the physical relationships of objects to one another. To develop a spatial design that is easy for listeners to follow, select a starting point and then take your audience on an orderly, systematic journey to a destination. Once you begin a pattern of movement, stay with it to the end of the speech. If you change directions in the middle, the audience may get lost. Be sure to complete the pattern so that you satisfy listeners' desire for closure.

Suzanne Marchetti's informative speech introducing Yellowstone Park developed within a spatial design:

> *Preview:* When you visit Yellowstone, stop first at the South Entrance Visitor's Center, then drive northwest to Old Faithful, north to Mammoth Hot Springs, and then southeast to the Grand Canyon of the Yellowstone.
>
> I. Your first stop should be at the South Entrance Visitor's Center.
>   A. Talk with a park ranger to help plan your trip.
>   B. Attend a lecture or film to orient yourself.
>   C. Pick up materials and maps to make your tour more meaningful.
>
> II. Drive northwest through Geyser Valley to Old Faithful.
>   A. Hike the boardwalks in the Upper Geyser Basin.
>   B. Join the crowds waiting for Old Faithful to erupt on schedule.
>   C. Have lunch at Old Faithful Inn.
>
> III. Continue north to Mammoth Hot Springs.

A. Plan to spend the night at the lodge or in one of the cabins.

B. Attend the evening lectures or films on the history of the park.

IV. Drive southeast to the Grand Canyon of the Yellowstone.

A. Take in the view from Inspiration Point.

B. Hike down the trail for a better view of the waterfalls.

Speeches that follow a spatial design often use maps to help people visualize directions.

Suzanne's speech design described an approximate circular pattern that was orderly and pleasing, leaving her listeners with a good sense of the location of important places within the park. Each of her main points received about the same amount of attention, so that her speech seemed well balanced as it traced this circle. Speakers using the spatial pattern often use a presentation aid, such as a map, to reinforce the sense of space created in their speeches.

Sequential Design

A **sequential design** moves listeners through time. Speeches built on a sequential design typically present the steps in a process. This design is especially appropriate for speeches of demonstration. You begin by identifying the necessary steps in the process and the order in which they must take place. These steps become the main points of your speech. In a short presentation, you should have no more than five steps as main points. Assign numbers to these steps as you make your presentation.

The following abbreviated outline, developed by Jeffrey O'Connor, illustrates a sequential design:

Preview: The five steps of efficient textbook reading include skimming, reading, rereading, reciting, and reviewing.

I. First, *skim* through the chapter to get the overall picture.

A. Identify the major ideas from the section headings.

B. Read any summary statements.

C. Read any boxed materials.

D. Make a key-word outline of major topics.

II. Second, *read* the chapter a section at a time.

A. Make notes in the margins on questions you have.

B. Look up definitions of unfamiliar words.

C. Go back and highlight the major ideas.

III. Third, *reread* the chapter.

A. Fill in your outline with more detail.

B. Try to answer the questions you wrote in the margin.

C. Frame questions for your instructor on anything you don't understand.

IV. Fourth, *recite* what you have read.

A. Use your outline to make an oral presentation to yourself.

B. Explain the material to someone else.

V. Finally, *review* the material within twenty-four hours.

A. Review your outline.

B. Reread the highlighted material.

Presenting the steps in this orderly, sequential way helped Jeffrey "walk and talk" his University of New Mexico classmates through the process.

Chronological Design

The **chronological design**, which is closely related to the sequential design, follows the sequence of important events in the history of a subject. However the sequential design works best for speeches of demonstration, and the chronological pattern is better suited to speeches of explanation. The first focuses on *how to do something*, the second on *how something happens.*

Using the chronological design, you may start with the beginnings of the subject and trace it up to the present through its defining moments. Or, you may start with the present and trace the subject back to its origins. To keep your listeners' attention and to meet time requirements, you must be selective. Choose landmark events as the main points in your message, and then arrange them in their natural order. D'Angelo Dartez presented a speech on the evolution of the T-shirt based upon the following chronological design:

Preview: The T-shirt began as an undergarment, developed into outerwear as a bearer of messages, and has emerged as high-fashion apparel.

I. The T-shirt originated as an undergarment early in the twentieth century.

A. The first undershirts with sleeves were designed for sailors, to spare sensitive people the sight of hairy armpits.

B. They were first sold commercially in the late 1930s.

C. During World War II, T-shirts were used as outerwear in the tropics.

II. After World War II, civilians began using T-shirts as outerwear.

A. They were comfortable and absorbent.

B. They were popularized in movies like *Rebel Without a Cause.*

C. They were easy to care for.

III. T-shirts soon became embellished with pictures and messages.

A. Children's T-shirts had pictures of cartoon characters.

B. Adult T-shirt designs were usually related to sports teams.

C. T-shirts soon were used for "political" statements.

IV. Today's T-shirts are unique.

A. You can customize a message.

B. You can put your picture on a T-shirt.

C. You can buy bejeweled T-shirts.

Speeches of explanation such as the T-shirt speech are generally the most complex types of informative speaking. Rather than indicating how to do things or describing objects or events, they develop ideas. Therefore, we should not be surprised to find that the designs for such speeches are also often more complex. The T-shirt speech actually illustrates what we might call a combination design. While it traces the chronology of events over time, it also discusses categories of development: in this case, the evolution of undergarments into outerwear. This example provides a convenient bridge into our next pattern, categorical design.

Categorical Design

Consider the **categorical design**—sometimes called the topical design—when you want to explain subjects that have natural or customary divisions. Natural divisions may exist within the subject itself, such as red, white, and blended wines. Customary divisions represent typical ways of thinking about a subject, such as the four food groups that are essential to a healthy diet or, as we just saw, undergarments and outerwear. Categories are the mind's way of ordering the world by seeking patterns within it or by supplying patterns to arrange it. Categories help us sort information so that we can make sense of it.

Each category in the design becomes a main point for development. For a short presentation, you should limit the number of categories to four or at most five: three is an ideal number. Remember, you must develop these points with supporting material that details, authenticates, and illustrates what you are talking about. That takes time! You don't want to go beyond the time limits set by your instructor. Nor do you want to overtax your listeners' ability to remember and their willingness to give you their attention.

Figure 14.3

What Speech Design to Use When

Design	Use When
Spatial	Your topic can be discussed by how it is positioned in a physical setting or natural environment. It allows you to take your audience on an orderly "oral tour" of your topic.
Sequential	Your topic can be arranged by time. It is useful for describing a process as a series of steps or explaining a subject as a series of developments.
Chronological	Your topic can be discussed as a historical development through certain defining moments.
Categorical	Your topic has natural or customary divisions. Each category becomes a main point for development. It is useful when you need to organize large amounts of material.
Comparative	Your topic is new to your audience, abstract, technical, or simply difficult to comprehend. It helps make material more meaningful by comparing or contrasting it with something the audience already knows and understands.
Causation	Your topic is best understood in terms of its underlying causes or consequences. May be used to account for the present or predict future possibilities.

In an informative speech to her class, Amanda Watkins discussed four major categories of child abuse. An abbreviated outline of the body of her speech follows:

> *Preview:* Four types of child abuse are neglect and mental, physical, and sexual abuse.
>
> I. Abusive neglect means failure to provide basic care.
> - A. Health care needs are often neglected.
> - B. Truancy represents educational neglect.
> - C. Emotional neglect occurs when child is ignored.
> - D. Symptoms of neglect are often evident.
>
> II. Mental abuse involves emotional, verbal, and psychological abuse.
> - A. This form can have serious behavioral or cognitive impact.
> - B. Sometimes it involves unusual forms of torment.
> - C. Symptoms of mental abuse may be less obvious.
>
> III. Physical abuse involves inflicting bodily harm on a child.
> - A. This may result from overdiscipline.
> - B. There may be no intent to harm the child.
> - C. Symptoms are often clear.
>
> IV. Sexual abuse can involve any form of sexual exploitation.
> - A. Sexual abuse may be committed by the caregiver.
> - B. Sexual abuse is typically underreported because of shame or threats.
> - C. Symptoms of sexual abuse may be less evident.

As we noted earlier, some speeches combine designs to accomplish their aims. Marie D'Aniello's speech on friendship at the end of this chapter uses the chronological design to arrange the main points of her speech and the categorical design to order the subpoints under them. This combination of patterns, which works perfectly well in Marie's speech, is evident in her preview:

> **In this speech I'm going to take you through the development of friendship, beginning in childhood, and going up through adolescence all the way to young adulthood (*chronological*). I'm going to talk about how we define our friends, the roles that friends play in our lives, and the effect conflicts have on friendship during each stage (*categorical*).**

Comparative Design

You may find a **comparative design** useful when your topic is unfamiliar, abstract, technical, or difficult to understand. This design can also help you describe dramatic changes in a subject. A comparative design should relate your topic to something the audience knows and understands. It can be especially useful in speeches of explanation and briefings. Three basic variations of the comparative design are literal analogy, figurative analogy, and comparison and contrast.

In a **literal analogy,** the subjects compared are drawn from the same field of experience. One student compared the game of rugger as played in his native Sri Lanka to the American game of football. Since both rugger and football are contact sports, the comparison between them was literal.

In a **figurative analogy**, the subjects are drawn from different fields of experience. Paul Ashdown, a professor of journalism at the University of Tennessee, used an extended figurative analogy comparing the World Wide Web to America's "Wild West."[10] Another example of a figurative analogy could relate the body's struggle against infection to a military campaign. In such a design, the speaker might identify the nature of the armies, the ways they fight, and the consequences of defeat and victory. Both literal and figurative analogy designs can be insightful and imaginative, helping listeners see subjects in surprising, revealing ways. But if the comparison seems strained or far-fetched, the speech will collapse and the speaker's ethos will be damaged.

A **comparison and contrast** design points out the similarities and/or differences between subjects or ideas. In this design, each similarity or difference becomes a main point. In the interest of simplicity, you should limit yourself to five or fewer points of similarity and difference in a short presentation. In the following example Don Carson emphasized contrast as he organized the body of his speech:

> *Preview:* Over the past forty years, the women seen in American advertising changed with respect to the products they pitched, their roles and ages, and the implicit atititudes expressed towards them.
>
> I. The products they advertised changed.
>   A. In the 1960s, most women were pitching products in the kitchen or bathroom.
>   B. By the year 2000, more women were selling high-ticket items.
>
> II. Women began to appear in different roles.
>   A. In the 1960s, most women were shown in domestic (wife/mother) roles.
>   B. By the year 2000, more women were shown in professional roles.
>
> III. The apparent ages of women changed.
>   A. In the 1960s, most women in ads appeared to be under thirty.
>   B. By the year 2000, older women were well represented in ads.
>
> IV. Attitudes toward women expressed in the ads also changed.
>   A. In the 1960s, most women were portrayed as dumb and dependent.
>   B. By the year 2000, more women were portrayed as intelligent and independent.

By now, we are not surprised to discover that Don's design actually blends chronology with contrast to produce still another example of combination design.

Causation Design

A **causation design**, often used in speeches of explanation, interprets a subject either as an effect of certain causes or as the cause of certain effects. The speaker usually begins by describing the subject and its importance, and then either asks how it came about or what its consequences may be. The major causes or consequences become main points in the body of the speech.

Speeches that use the causation design are subject to one serious drawback—the tendency to oversimplify. Any complex situation will generally have many underlying causes, and any given set of conditions may lead to many different future effects. Be wary of overly simple explanations and overly confident predictions. Such explanations and predictions are one form of faulty reasoning (fallacy), discussed further in Chapter 16.

Patsy Lenzini announced at the outset of her informative speech that research had revealed the existence of a new wonder drug—aspirin! In her classroom speech based on causation design, Patsy discussed aspirin therapy as the cause of many possible consequences. An abbreviated form of her outline follows:

> *Preview:* The humble aspirin can benefit your heart, prevent cancer, and help your brain avoid Alzheimer's, but it still has some serious possible drawbacks.

I. Daily small doses can benefit your heart.
   A. Reduce risk of first heart attack by 44%.
   B. Lower chance of second heart attack by 30%.
   C. Reduce risk of death during heart attack by 23%.
II. Daily doses can also prevent certain cancers.
   A. Lower risk of colon cancer by 40/50%.
   B. Reduce risk of esophageal cancer by 80/90%.
   C. Lower ovarian cancer risks by 25%.
III. Daily doses offer other great possible benefits.
   A. Reduce risk of stroke by 25%.
   B. Help counter dementia and Alzheimer's by increasing blood flow in the brain.
IV. Daily doses may also have some drawbacks.
   A. Can cause gastrointestinal bleeding.
   B. Delay blood clotting to stop bleeding.
   C. Could encourage another kind of stroke.
   D. May be of less benefit to women.

Any of the six design options we have discussed—either alone or in combination—can help you present information in ways that expand the knowledge and competency of your listeners, and that earn you their gratitude.

Rising to the Challenge of the Informative Speech

One dirty little secret we have learned in a lifetime of teaching public speaking is that informative speaking can pose a special challenge for speakers. Self-introductory speaking can offer revealing, fascinating glimpses into the minds and personalities of speakers. Persuasive speeches offer the drama of controversy and the excitement of watching speakers take public stands on issues. Ceremonial speeches can entertain and inspire us. In contrast, informative speeches can sometimes seem rather dull, even—in worst-case scenarios—downright boring.

On the other hand, many of the informative speeches we have heard in class, including those cited here, have managed to be very interesting. What can we learn from these successful speakers to help us avoid the information doldrums?

First, these speakers selected good topics, topics that offered information that was inherently interesting to listeners, fascinating to the speakers themselves, and important to the lives of listeners.

Second, these speakers planned their time well, finding topics well in advance of their speaking assignments and leaving plenty of time to research their topics and to reflect on what they learned.

Third, these speakers devised artful designs for their speeches, introducing topics in ways that grabbed and held attention, establishing a clear understanding of their purposes, developing ideas so that they satisfied the expectations of listeners, and finding a conclusion that would make it hard for audiences to forget their most important themes.

Fourth, these speakers filled these designs with colorful and striking content: facts and figures that confronted listeners with a reality they had not expected, examples and stories that awakened feeling and stirred the imagination. They used language in ways that made their ideas stick in the memory.

Fifth, they put a lot of energy into their presentations. They set a varied and lively pace, using pauses for emphasis. Their voices came alive with the importance of their messages, and their gestures emphasized what they were saying.

To avoid boring your audience, focus on

- finding a good topic.
- leaving yourself plenty of time for research and preparation.
- developing an artful overall structure for your speech.
- filling that structure with lively, striking content.
- making an energetic presentation of your speech.

If you follow these guidelines, chances are that at the end of your speech you won't be singing the information blues.

VideoLab

Review the "Do's" and "Don'ts" of informative speaking in **VideoLab Lesson 8's Coach: Tips to Remember.**

In Summary

Sharing knowledge is the essence of informative speaking. It helps us to live better and work smarter. In short, information is power.

Functions of Informative Speaking. Informative speaking serves four basic functions. First, informative speaking empowers listeners by sharing information and ideas. The *informative value* of a speech is measured by how much new and important information or understanding it provides the audience. Second, informative speaking can shape listener perceptions, preparing them for later persuasive speeches. Third, informative speaking serves an *agenda-setting function* by suggesting what we should be thinking about. Finally, informative speaking clarifies options for action. The ethical speaker will cover all the available options and present the most important information listeners will need to make responsible choices.

Types of Informative Speeches. Informative speeches include speeches of description, demonstration, and explanation. *Speeches of description* create word-pictures that help the audience visualize a subject. *Speeches of demonstration* show the audience how to do something. They may give listeners an understanding of a process or teach them how to perform it. Both speeches of description and speeches of demonstration are often more effective when presentation aids are used. *Speeches of explanation* inform the audience about abstract and complex subjects, such as concepts or programs. Such speeches normally present a more difficult challenge, especially when they contradict common knowledge or threaten cherished beliefs. *Briefings,* presented in organizational settings, are often informational. Briefings are usually status reports or updates on projects for which you have responsibility.

Helping Listeners Learn. You make it easier for listeners to learn by motivating them, showing how your subject fits their basic needs. To gain and maintain their attention, apply principles of intensity, repetition, novelty, activity, contrast, and relevance. The *intensity* of information measures the impact it makes upon listeners. Speakers use *repetition* to emphasize points, to help listeners follow the flow of ideas, and to embed their messages in audience memory. The *novelty* of information fascinates listeners, draws their attention, and raises their curiosity. *Activity* adds the sense of liveliness and often invites listeners to participate vicariously in the experience depicted. *Contrast* follows the principle that opposites attract attention. *Relevance* ties the subject to specific needs, interests, or concerns of the audience. Increase audience *retention* of what you say by organizing your message clearly and providing previews and summaries.

Speech Designs. The patterns that most frequently arrange the material in informative speeches are spatial, sequential, chronological, categorical, comparative, and causation designs. A *spatial design* orders the main points according to the arrangement of a subject within a physical setting. Spatial designs are especially appropriate for describing objects or places. Most speeches of demonstration use a *sequential design,* which follows a time pattern to present steps in a process. A *chronological design* follows the sequence of important events in the history of a subject. *Categorical designs* represent natural divisions of a subject or traditional ways of thinking about it. *Comparative designs* are especially effective when your topic is new to the audience, when it has undergone dramatic changes, or when you wish to establish right and wrong procedures. These designs are often based on *literal* or *figurative analogies,* depending on whether the compared subjects are drawn from the same or from different fields of experience. A *causation design* explains how one condition generates or is generated by others. Sometimes you may decide to combine several designs within the same speech.

Rising to the Challenge of the Informative Speech. Informative speakers must work hard to create and maintain attention and interest. Finding the right topic, taking the time to prepare, designing speeches artfully, developing striking and colorful content, and making an energetic presentation can ensure success.

Terms to Know

informative value
prepersuasive function
agenda-setting function
speech of description
speech of demonstration
speech of explanation
briefing
intensity
repetition
novelty
activity
contrast
relevance
retention
spatial design
sequential design
chronological design
categorical design
comparative design
literal analogy
figurative analogy
comparison and contrast
causation design

Discussion

1. The status of "information" concerning the presence of WMDs (weapons of mass destruction) in Iraq, a major rationale for our 2003 preemptive war on that country, was subject to a great deal of debate. A number of positions were argued:

   A. The information was faulty. Blame it on the CIA.

   B. The information was faulty, but the president was responsible for verifying it, especially when he used it to justify war. Blame it on him.

   C. The information was accurate, but it was used selectively to justify an *a priori* decision to invade Iraq. The "prepersuasive" function of information was manipulated to influence public opinion.

   D. Whether the information was or was not accurate is irrelevant. Either way, we made the right choice: to take Saddam out. The ends justified the means.

   Research this situation, and decide which of these or other possible arguments you favor. Be prepared to defend your position in classroom discussion. What does this situation teach you about the ethics of using information in speeches?

2. The power and importance of information are supported by the efforts governments make to hide it. How much secrecy of government information can we tolerate in a society that depends on fully informed citizens as the ultimate repositories of political power? Does this situation pose a dilemma for democratic governments? How can we ensure maximum access to information without compromising vital public interests? Research these questions, and bring your thoughts and findings to class to exchange in discussion.

3. You can probably recall one or several outstanding teachers who have helped you learn. How did they encourage learning? What can you learn about communicating information, using them as models of excellence?

Application

1. As you submit the outline for your informative speech, include a "strategy plan" as well. In your strategy plan, identify the following:

   A. The type and function of the informative speech you will present

   B. How you will apply principles of motivation, attention, and retention to help your listeners learn

   C. How specifically you will use attention factors (intensity, repetition, novelty, activity, contrast, relevance) to make your speech more effective

   D. Why you chose a specific design option to structure your speech

   E. How you will meet the challenge of presenting an interesting informative speech by applying the advice offered in the final section of this chapter

2. Study the headlines in two prominent daily newspapers over the period of a month.

   A. Do the headlines duplicate, or do they vary in content or emphasis? How do you explain this variation?

   B. To what extent might the headlines serve an agenda-setting function, as well as simply reflect what is actually happening in the world? What is the possible significance of this function?

   C. Might your analysis apply to the agenda-setting function of informative speeches as well?

3. Informative speeches presented within a context of controversy are often distorted and misunderstood by the fears, suspicions, and prejudices that abound in many audiences. As we write, for example, a controversy rages in many quarters concerning the legality and morality of gay marriage. If you wished to present an informative speech discussing the legal principles that might apply to this subject, what strategies might you employ to counter such negative feelings and receive a fair hearing before most audiences?

Notes

1. D. L. Shaw and M. E. McCombs, *The Emergence of American Political Issues: The Agenda-Setting Function of the Press* (St. Paul, Minn.: West, 1977).

2. Katherine E. Rowan, "Goals, Obstacles, and Strategies in Risk Communication: A Problem-Solving Approach to Improving Communication About Risks," *Journal of Applied Communication Research* 19 (1991): 314.

3. Ibid.

4. Paul R. Gamble and Clare E. Kelliher, "Imparting Information and Influencing Behavior: An Examination of Staff Briefing Sessions," *Journal of Business Communication* (July 1999): 261.

5. Ancil B. Sparks and Dennis D. Staszak, "Fine Tuning Your News Briefing: Law Enforcement Agency Media Relations," *FBI Law Enforcement Bulletin* (December 2000): 22.

6. See, for example, Joan Detz, *Can You Say a Few Words? How to Prepare and Deliver* (New York: St. Martin's Press, 1991); Dorothy Leeds, *PowerSpeak* (New York: Berkeley Books, 1991); Laurie Schloff and Marcia Yudkin, *Smart Speaking: Sixty-Second Strategies* (New York: Holt, 1991); and Lilly Walters, *Secrets of Successful Speakers: How You Can Motivate, Captivate and Persuade* (New York: McGraw-Hill, 1993).

7. J. E. Hollingsworth, "Oral Briefings," *Management Review* (August 1968): 2–10.

8. Institute for Learning Styles Research, "Seven Perceptual Styles," n.d. http://www.learningstyles.org (24 July 2001).

9. Adapted from material supplied by Randy Scott, Department of Communication, Weber State University, Ogden, Utah.

10. Paul Ashdown, "From Wild West to Wild Web," *Vital Speeches of the Day*, 1 Sept. 2000, pp. 699–701.

What Friends Are All About

Marie D'Aniello

It's nine o'clock at night. I'm curled up in the back seat of a new truck and my friends, Cammy and Joe, are in the front singing along with the radio. As I listen to them sing, and I'm lying there, I start to think about my life and all the changes that have occurred in the past year. A year ago I didn't even know who Cammy and Joe were. And now they're two of my dearest friends. It makes me wonder about friendship and its meaning.

■ Marie opens her speech of explanation with a narrative that gains attention by arousing curiosity: What happened in the truck? Why were Cammy and Joe singing? Quickly she shifts that attention to the focus of her speech.

According to Webster's dictionary, to be a friend means that you're someone who someone else feels comfortable with and is fond of. But friendship is so much more than that. According to Plato, true friendship rises out of basic human needs and desires, such as striving for goodness, reaching out to others, and seeking self-understanding. And loving and being loved. Friendship should benefit all who are involved in it and should occur between people who value each other's good qualities. As human beings we need friends in order to survive and grow.

Through our friends we learn who we are, and what we like and don't like. We learn about strengths we never knew we had, weaknesses that maybe we can overcome. Think about your friendships. I'll bet you've learned a great deal and grown a great deal because of them.

■ Throughout her opening, Marie leaves listeners waiting for a direct statement of her purpose. It soon becomes clear that she wants to share ideas and deepen audience understanding. She encourages attention by her interactive orientation: note the frequent use of "we" and how she invites listeners to "think about" their own friendships. She also sold this speech by her warm, vital manner of presentation. She stood in front of the lectern near listeners to encourage identification.

If you're like me you probably have one or two really close friends and a lot of great acquaintances. But that's what you need. According to Dr. John Litwac of the University of Massachusetts medical center, people in modern society require a variety of friends to meet their needs. And the variety of friends we need varies over time. In his book *Adult Friendship,* Dr. Litwac says that the friendships we enjoy when we are young differ from those we experience as we grow older. As we develop, so does the complexity and intimacy of our relationships.

In this speech I'm going to take you through the development of friendship, beginning in childhood, and going up through adolescence all the way to young adulthood. I'm going to talk about how we define our friends, the roles that friends play in our lives, and the effect conflicts have on friendship during each stage.

■ In her preview, Marie promises to follow a chronological design that will trace "the saga of friendship" to the point of young adulthood. Since this was where her listeners found themselves, the plan offered a then-to-now time pattern. At the subpoint level of her speech, Marie follows a categorical pattern, discussing the definitions, roles, and conflict resolution during each phase of development. She has researched her speech diligently, but she needs to establish the credentials of her experts and to document her evidence more carefully.

The saga of friendship begins when we are quite young. And the concepts we have of friendship change dramatically over the first decade of life. Psychologists classify childhood as the stage occurring between the ages of 4 and 10. During childhood our friends are those whom we have the most contact with, the children we play with. In childhood that's what friendship is all about. According to Dr. William Rawlings, friendships exist while children are playing together. For example, when I was in kindergarten, I was friends with Michelle when we were playing tag. But the next day I would go and play with others and make friends with them. The friendship vanished until the next time we played together. It had little to do with who Michelle really was. She was simply there and I could play with her.

But when we play as children, we're not only having fun, we're also learning how to assimilate into society and how to develop more lasting friendships. We learn to inhibit our actions, to deal with other people's emotions, and to follow rules. Because we're just starting out and just trying to figure out how everything works, we may run into a lot of conflicts with our friendships during childhood. We may get into silly fights about whose toy is this and whose toy is that, but the fights don't usually last very long and can be resolved fairly easily. Behavior is based on the moment, and the moment turns on what things appear to be.

During childhood friendship often depends on looks. Maybe that's why some children are so popular and others are ignored. In fact, a study conducted by Dr. William Lipit concluded that children between the ages of 4 to 9 base their descriptions of their friends completely on their looks. That may be sad, but it's just the way it is. Think of this as a phase in the process of growing up.

■ ***Marie relies especially on examples for her supporting material. In her first main point, she draws on personal experience. In the second main point, she invites listeners to supply examples from their own experience. She uses rhetorical questions to highlight the points and stimulate reflection. She also uses the contrast between play and talk to underscore the difference between the childhood and adolescent phases of friendship.***

At the end of childhood, friends become more than just playmates. They're people who share our interests—they're the ones we share our feelings with. Play becomes less, talk becomes more important. Friendship evolves steadily to a new level, called adolescence.

I'm sure you remember adolescence. It usually occurs between the ages of 11 and 17. As we live through it, friendship involves revealing and discussing one's personal thoughts and feelings. Just talking can be more important than anything, especially for girls. Boys, male friendships, still involve a good deal of activity, as in organized sports, but even here there is more verbal communication than before. The critical task of adolescence is to develop one's identity, and friends are crucial in that respect. Dr. Graham Allen observes in the book *Friendship* that people in adolescence, more than at any other time in their lives, need to share strong, often confusing emotions. Did you have a best friend in junior high school? A very special friend you would sit and talk with on the phone for hours on end? Well if you did, that's good, that's normal. According to Dr. Allen, that's what you needed.

Think back. Think back to friendship pins, and side ponytails and matching outfits, and sleep-over parties. Think of your first best friend. That person probably knew more about you than anyone in the whole world. She or he was probably your age, in your class, lived near you, and shared your social status. In adolescence we seek out those who are like us because they make us feel more normal. Because the level of intimacy is so much greater in adolescence, the potential for conflict and jealousy also increases. There's so much emotion at stake that an argument in adolescence can easily ruin a friendship. The way we learn to deal with such problems in adolescence prepares us for young adulthood.

■ ***In her final main point, Marie continues to engage listeners directly by asking rhetorical questions and by inviting them to consider their own friendships. She also continues to rely heavily on expert testimony, which reflects favorably on her ethos and builds the credibility of her speech. The listener gains the impression that this speech builds on a foundation of responsible knowledge.***

Now young adulthood is classified as the stage between 18 and 24, the stage we're all in now. Here at Vanderbilt and I suppose elsewhere, a "friend" can mean many things. Friends can be playmates, confidants, lovers, listeners. Rosemary Adams, writing in the book *Adult Friendship,* tells us that during the college years friends can provide crucial input regarding self-conceptions, career options, and recreational activities. Patterns of friendship vary a lot, and we have many different types of friends. We have party friends. We have classroom friends. And then we have our good, good friends. But you need all of those kinds of friends as you grow older because you are becoming a more complex individual.

Why do you like your good friends? Do you like them because of what they can do for you? Or do you like them because you can relate to them and share a bond with them? Our friends prevent us from being lonely. In fact 40 percent of college freshmen who reported they felt homesick also reported not having made new friends in college.

Why do some people make friends easily while others struggle to? Researchers speculate that how open and honest you are with others and how much you are willing to give of yourself can affect your forming friendships. Talking and sharing is important because it creates a sense of intimacy. Friendship also depends a great deal on attraction. Whatever attracts you to people is why you like them. Maybe you like people who smile a lot, or maybe you like those who are serious. Maybe you like people who are the complete opposite of you and who possess qualities you wish you had. Or maybe you like people who are just like you, who you feel you know inside and out.

When we're younger, friendships are based on what people appear to be. As we grow older, friendships are based more on what people really are. If you got in a fight with your best friend, would you tell him to hit the road? Chances are you'd probably try to work it out. As we get older, it's easier for us to accept differences in others. Serious betrayals could end friendships. But the researchers I read concluded that the older you get and the older the friendship is, the harder you will work to preserve it because it is all the more precious to you.

Friendship is hard to define and I think that's probably because it involves your heart and your soul. But out of all the research I've done and all the people I've talked to, no one said that they thought friendship was a bad thing. Of course there are downsides like peer pressure and conflict and sometimes stress, but 91 percent of the college freshmen studied by Dr. Adams felt that the benefits of friendship far outweigh the disadvantages. All I know is that from the day we're born until the day we die, other people affect the way we live. If we're lucky, maybe we'll come to know some of them as friends.

At this point, Marie reflects on the general meaning of her subject, signaling that she is moving into her conclusion. By citing Plato at the beginning of her speech and concluding with a quotation from Yeats, she dignifies her subject and emphasizes its importance in listeners' lives.

The dynamics of friendship change rapidly throughout our lives. During childhood friendship is based on play, while in adolescence it turns more on emotion. In young adulthood I think friendship is based on a combination of acceptance, respect, and trust. I remember the words of William Butler Yeats, who said, "Think where man's glory most begins and ends. And say my glory was to have such friends."

WORKS CONSULTED

Blieszner, Rosemary, and Rebecca G. Adams. *Adult Friendship.* Newbury Park: Sage Publications, 1992.

Brenton, Myron. *Friendship.* New York: Stein and Day, 1974.

Cates, Diana Fritz. *Choosing to Feel: Virtue, Friendship and Compassion for Friends.* Notre Dame: University of Notre Dame Press, 1997.

Gilligan, Carol, Nona P. Lyons, and Trudy J. Hammer. *Making Connections: The Relational Worlds of Adolescent Girls at the Emma Willard School.* Cambridge: Harvard University Press, 1990.

Gottman, John M., and Jeffrey G. Parker. *Conversation of Friends: Speculations and Affective Development.* Cambridge: Cambridge University Press, 1986.

Griffiths, Vivienne. *Adolescent Girls and Their Friends.* Aldershot: Avebury, 1995.

Meyer, Luanna H., et al. *Making Friends.* Baltimore: Paul H. Brookes Publishing Co., 1998.

Rawlins, William K. *Friendship Matters.* New York: Aldine de Gruyter, 1992.

Web Sources:

The Friendship Page. http://www.geocities.com/Athens/Acropolis/9761/quofrend.html.

http://www.ozemail.com.

Persuasive Speaking

15

OUTLINE

This chapter will help you

- realize how persuasive speaking differs from informative speaking
- appreciate the work persuasive speaking performs
- understand the process of persuasion
- adapt persuasive messages to different audiences
- confront the ethical challenges of persuasion

> ***Because there has been implanted in us the power to persuade each other . . . , not only have we escaped the life of the wild beasts but we have come together and founded cities and made laws and invented arts.***
>
> ISOCRATES

George Lazarus had a pretty negative reaction to his persuasive speaking assignment. "I'm just not a persuader," he told his roommate. "I make up my own mind on things, and I don't like others telling me what to do. As for what others do, that's their business. Live and let live, I say. I can live without persuasion."

"Not very persuasive," replied his roommate.

As a matter of fact, George had awakened that morning into a world of persuasion. As he rubbed the sleep out of his eyes, a DJ on the clock radio pushed tickets to a rock concert. As he brushed his teeth, his roommate tried to convince him that a trip to Florida would be both fun and affordable. As he walked to class, someone handed him a pamphlet protesting the lack of adequate medical care on campus. And so his day had gone.

For his part, George convinced himself that the concert would be fun, but that Florida was out of the question. On the way back from class, he stopped to argue with the person handing out brochures about the politics of medical care. Then he returned to his room to put on his best outfit preparing for a job interview on campus. Deep in his heart he knew that if he got this job, he would constantly have to sell himself and his ideas to others.

Clearly, George needed to rethink the importance of his persuasive speaking assignment. In our imperfect world of competing interests, values, and agendas—our world of problems and opportunities—persuasion thrives. It is unavoidable. The world of persuasion is one that we constantly shape and reshape with our words, either for better or for worse.

Persuasion works through other people, who are capable of advancing or impeding our interests and objectives. When we speak, we try to influence how others see things, how they feel, how they believe, and how they act in response to what they learn. We may not always succeed, nor *should* we always succeed: other views may be more persuasive, depending on the listener, the situation, and the merits of the case. But at least we can give our ideas an opportunity to be heard.

Persuasion, *therefore, is the art of gaining fair and favorable consideration for our points of view.* Persuasion can be ethical or unethical, selfless or selfish, inspiring or degrading. Persuaders may enlighten our minds or prey on our vulnerability. Ethical persuasion, however, is grounded in sound reasoning and is sensitive to the feelings and needs of listeners. Such persuasion gives us the chance to make the world better.

Beyond its personal importance to us, persuasion is essential to society. The right to persuade and be persuaded is the bedrock of the American political system, guaranteed by the First Amendment to the Constitution. According to the late Supreme Court justice Louis D. Brandeis, "Those who won our independence believed that the final end of the State was to make [citizens] free to develop their faculties; and that in its government the deliberative forces should prevail over the arbitrary."[1] Persuasion in the competing marketplace of ideas, before what one writer has called "the Court of Reason,"[2] is required for these "deliberative forces" to operate.

Deliberation involves the consideration of all sides of an issue before a decision is made. During the debate in the House of Representatives over the impeachment of President Clinton, Rep. Richard Gephardt was asked in a television interview whether the many speeches delivered on the floor of the House had any real purpose. Gephardt responded that persuasion is society's alternative to violence. We strongly agree. Our political system is based on the premise that persuasion is more ethical and more practical than force. We should make commitments because we are persuaded, not because we are coerced.

Although you may find the expression of some views to be objectionable, if not downright obnoxious, the freedom to voice unpopular opinions is the very soul of liberty. The English philosopher John Stuart Mill put the matter eloquently:

> **If all mankind, minus one, were of the one opinion, and only one person were of the contrary opinion, mankind would be no more justified in silencing that one person, than he, if he had the power, would be justified in silencing mankind.**
>
> **. . . We can never be sure that the opinion we are endeavoring to stifle is a false opinion; and if we were sure, stifling it would be an evil still.**[3]

There are also practical reasons for tolerating opposing opinions. Exposure to different perspectives can produce better decisions.[4] For example, even though Hailey may never agree with Nick's view that we should register guns, his arguments may prompt her to reexamine her thoughts, to understand her convictions better, or perhaps even to modify her position.

Although speaking out on public issues is important, many people ask: "What difference can one person make? My words don't carry much weight." Perhaps not, but words make ripples, and ripples can come together to make waves. Such was the case with Anna Aley, a student at Kansas State University who gave a persuasive speech on substandard student housing. Her classroom speech was later presented in a public forum on campus. The text of her speech, which appears in Appendix B, was reprinted in the local newspaper, which followed it up with investigative reports and a supportive editorial. Brought to the attention of the mayor and city commission, Anna's speech helped promote reforms in the city's rental housing policies. Her words are still reverberating in Manhattan, Kansas.

Perhaps your classroom speech will not have that kind of impact, but you never know who or what may be changed by it. In this chapter, we will examine the nature of persuasive speaking and help prepare you to meet the challenges of such speaking. In the next chapter, we will focus on building powerful arguments, which is the substance of ethical and enduring persuasion, and help you design your persuasive speech.

The Nature of Persuasive Speaking

We may best understand persuasive speaking if we contrast it with informative speaking, consider the major work that it does, and explore the process by which it works.

Seven Characteristics of Persuasive Speaking

Persuasive speaking differs from informative speaking in seven basic ways:

First, informative speeches reveal options: persuasive speeches urge a choice from among them. Informative speakers expand our awareness. For example, an informative speaker might say: "There are three different ways we can deal with the budget deficit. Let me explain these." In contrast, a persuasive speaker would weigh these options and urge support for one of them: "Of the three different ways to deal with the budget deficit, we should choose the following course of action."

Second, informative speakers function as teachers: persuaders work as advocates. The difference is often one of passion and engagement. Persuasive speakers are more vitally committed to a cause. This does not necessarily mean that persuaders are loud; the most passionate and intense moments of a speech can be very quiet.

Third, informative speeches offer supporting material to illustrate points: persuasive speeches transform such material into evidence that justifies advice. The ethical persuader interweaves facts and statistics, testimony, examples, and narratives into a compelling case that is based on responsible knowledge and sensitivity to the best interests of listeners.

Fourth, persuasive speeches ask for more audience commitment than do informative speeches. Although there is some risk in being exposed to new ideas, more is at stake when listening to a persuasive message. What if a persuasive speaker is mistaken or even dishonest? What if her proposed plan of action is defective? Doing always involves a greater risk than knowing. Your commitment could cost you dearly.

Fifth, leadership is even more important in persuasive than in informative speeches. Because persuasive speeches involve risk, listeners will weigh the character and competence of speakers more closely. Do they really know what they are talking about? Do they have their listeners' interests at heart? As a persuasive speaker, your ethos will be on public display and will be scrutinized carefully.

Sixth, appeals to feelings are more appropriate in persuasive than in informative speeches. Because of the risk involved, listeners may balk at accepting recommendations, even when they are supported by good reasons. To overcome such inertia, persuaders must often appeal to feelings.[5] This is why persuasive speakers often use emotional appeals to

The right to express controversial opinions is the mortar that holds democracy together.

open their speeches. For example, the informative statement "A 10 percent rise in tuition will reduce the student population by about 5 percent next term" might be transformed in the context of a persuasive speech in the following way:

Persuasive speeches can help raise support for worthy causes. Here actor Danny Glover speaks out in behalf of the National Kidney Foundation.

> **The people who are pushing for the tuition increase don't think a few hundred dollars more each semester will have that much effect. They think we can handle it.**
>
> **Well, let me tell you about my friend Tricia. She's on the Dean's List in chemistry, the pride and hope of her family. Tricia will get a great job when she graduates—if she graduates! But if this increase goes through, Tricia won't be back next term. Her dreams of success will be at least delayed, perhaps even denied! Do the legislators care about that? Do they care about Tricia's dreams?**
>
> **Perhaps you're in the same boat as Tricia—paddling like mad against the current. But even if you're not, she is one of us, and she needs our help now.**

Emotional and graphic language, often developed through examples, can help people see the human dimension of problems and move them to the right action.

Seventh, the ethical obligation for persuasive speeches is even greater than that for informative speeches. As Isocrates indicated in this chapter's opening quotation, persuasion can be a great blessing to humankind. At their best, persuasive speakers make us confront our obligation to believe and act in socially and morally responsible ways. By describing how they themselves became persuaded, they model how we should deliberate in difficult choice situations. By making intelligence and morality effective in public affairs, they can help the world evolve in more enlightened ways.

For all these reasons, you should take your assignment as persuasive speaker very seriously. The major differences between informative and persuasive speaking are summarized in Figure 15.1.

VideoLab

Watch the two persuasive speeches in **VideoLab Drill 9.1: Identifying Components of Persuasive Speeches** and think about the differences between informative and persuasive speeches.

Figure 15.1

Informative Versus Persuasive Speaking

Informative Speaking	Persuasive Speaking
1. Reveals options.	*1.* Urges a choice among options.
2. Speaker acts as teacher.	*2.* Speaker acts as advocate.
3. Uses supporting material to enlighten listeners.	*3.* Uses supporting material to justify advice.
4. Asks for little audience commitment.	*4.* Asks for strong audience commitment.
5. Speaker's credibilty is important.	*5.* Speaker's credibilty more important.
6. Fewer appeals to feelings.	*6.* More appeals to feelings.
7. High ethical obligation.	*7.* Higher ethical obligation.

The Work of Persuasion

Persuasion helps us resolve the uncertainties that constantly abound in our lives. Three basic questions reflect the nature of these uncertainties:

- What is the true state of affairs?
- How should I feel about a situation?
- What should I do about it?

These questions in turn prompt three fundamental types of persuasive speaking: *speeches that focus on facts; speeches that address attitudes, beliefs, and values; and speeches that advocate action and policy.*

Speeches That Focus on Facts.

People argue constantly over what the true state of affairs is, which becomes the central defining issue for **speeches that focus on facts**. Uncertainty can surround questions of past, present, and future facts.

Past Facts. Did something actually occur? Did the celebrity commit murder? Did the CEO defraud the company and her stockholders? Was the political candidate once actually convicted of marijuana possession? Persuaders argue questions of past facts before juries in courtrooms and newspaper editorial pages as well as on the public platform. Speeches concerning past facts try to shape the perceptions and control the memories of people and events. They will be successful if they do the following:

- Present facts that confirm what they claim. In the text of the speech reprinted at the end of this chapter, note how Joshua Logan uses charts and statistics to confirm the growth of greenhouse gases over the past thousand years.
- Call on supporting testimony from expert and widely respected sources. To support his factual claims about global warming, Joshua cites the "United Nations Intergovernmental Panel on Climate Change, reporting during the early part of this year." He describes this study as an "authoritative, thousand-page report, which correlates and tests the work of hundreds of environmental scientists from countries all around the globe."

  Note the subtle implications as Joshua establishes the authority of his source: the UNIPCC is *international*, not biased by national interests. Its work is *recent*, having reported "during the early part of this year." The work is *massive and exhaustive* ("thousand-page report"), and it escapes any possible *error or bias* that might result if it relied too heavily on any single scientist or program of research. Instead, it synthesizes "the work of hundreds of

Speeches that focus on fact may need visual supporting materials to function as evidence for their claims.

environmental scientists around the globe." Follow Joshua's example as you introduce supporting sources into your persuasive speeches.

- Re-create a dramatic and credible narrative of how events in a dispute actually happened. The renowned Roman orator Cicero, who was also one of the greatest courtroom lawyers who ever lived, was superb in creating narratives of past events that made his position seem not only credible but also inescapable. For an especially spicy example, which reflects the moral depravity of many people in the Rome of several thousand years ago, see his forensic speech, *Pro Caelius*.[6]

Successful speeches concerning past facts develop a compelling case that establishes that their versions of events are correct and reliable.

Present Facts. What is actually going on? Is the new medicine a boon or a threat to humankind? Is global warming actually happening? Is a certain rogue nation developing weapons of mass destruction? Questions involving present facts are of incredible importance to the fate of nations and individuals. Depending on our perceptions of present facts, we develop value judgments and plans of action. Policymakers in the Bush administration decided that Iraq was vitally engaged in efforts to develop weapons of mass destruction. That determination of present facts confirmed their value judgment that Saddam Hussein was an intolerable threat to the security of the United States. That conclusion in turn led to their policy decision to invade Iraq and to remove Hussein from power. Clearly, persuasive speeches on present facts can start a chain reaction of significant behaviors.

At times, questions of past and present facts will turn not on whether something happened or is happening, but on the *definition* of events. Yes, sexual activity occurred in the encounter between the sports star and the woman, but the sex was "consensual, not rape." A person has died, but the death resulted from "self-defense, not murder." Yes, Nation X possesses the alleged weapons, but they exist "for mass protection not for mass destruction. They don't portend war; they guarantee peace." To control the definitions of events is to control the perspectives and interpretations that people form about their meaning. This is why the definition of events is often the primary issue as persuaders compete to influence our thinking.

Future Facts. What will the future be like? And how should we plan to deal with it? Persuasive speeches regarding future facts are **predictions**, based on readings of the past and present. Therefore, they often depend on prior persuasion about past and present facts. Should we invest in stock in a certain company? That depends on predictions of the company's future earning potential. One persuader argues that the past record of earnings justifies a strong vote of confidence in the future. Another persuader answers that much of this past success occurred under a different leadership team and that present management has yet to prove itself. The first offers an enthusiastic "buy" recommendation: the second advises delay and caution. As a potential investor, you will have to consider these contending persuasions very carefully, weighing the evidence and testing the soundness of the reasoning.

Present and future facts were a central issue for Joshua Logan's speech reprinted at the end of this chapter. Joshua *says* that the question of whether global warming actually exists is no longer an issue, but he spends much of his time magnifying the meaning of the problem for his listeners. Joshua's persuasive strategy suggests that his listeners remain either uninformed, unconvinced, or in denial about the consequences of global warming. Therefore, his challenge must be to create in their minds a vivid sense of this present fact. Based on this heightened appreciation of danger, he offers a grim prediction of the future, unless these trends are altered by significant changes in the policies of nations and the practices of individuals. The companion speech, reprinted at the end of Chapter 16, offers his recommendations for these changes.

Speeches That Address Attitudes, Beliefs, and Values. The world of uncertainty in which we live often prompts **speeches that address attitudes, beliefs, and values**. As we noted in Chapter 5, at the heart of our *attitudes* are feelings we have developed toward specific kinds of subjects. For example, Cherie's intense dislike for those who practice "ethnic cleansing"—the removal and persecution of entire populations on the basis of religious faith or ethnic affiliation—illustrates her attitude toward them. *Beliefs* are conclusions we have formed about these subjects that may explain our attitudes about them. For example, Cherie's conviction that ethnic cleansing is an especially cruel and aggressive form of intolerance is her belief about that practice. *Values* are underlying general principles of behavior that justify our beliefs. Cherie's attitude and beliefs both rise out of her deep value commitment to a world of tolerance in which people tolerate, respect, and appreciate one another's differences.

Ideally, our attitudes, beliefs, and values should be in harmony, creating a coherent spiritual world within us. However, these elements are sometimes undeveloped, disconnected, or even opposed to one another, making that inner world narrow or confused. When this is the case, persuasive speakers have the opportunity to create or restore consistency and harmony to listeners. Thus persuasion can perform an important therapeutic and ethical role. For example, if Cherie suspects that her listeners are indifferent to ethnic cleansing, even though they strongly value tolerance, she has the opportunity to arouse and implant an appropriate attitude and belief about that practice through an effective persuasive speech. By providing her audience with vital information, examples, and stories and by appealing to their value of tolerance, she can expand their moral universe.[7]

In a similar instance, Sam sensed a disconnection—even a contradiction—among the attitudes, beliefs, and values of many classmates toward capital punishment. He sensed that many of them had an intense hatred for those accused of violent crimes. On the basis of that attitude, they had formed a belief that strongly favored capital punishment. Sam felt that these attitudes and beliefs were inconsistent with the religious values many of them held and with their other values of fairness and respect for life. In the persuasive speech he developed, Sam appealed to these values in an effort to change the attitudes and beliefs of his listeners.

Ethical persuasive speeches often focus on giving listeners good reasons to change or intensify their beliefs. In effect, such persuasion argues that beliefs should express our deeper values and should govern the attitudes we form. Such persuasion helps listeners form strong convictions. Beliefs that rest on our attitudes rather than on our values are often more shallow.

Because values are an integral part of our personality, deep changes in them can have a real impact on how we live. Therefore, we don't change values as readily as we change attitudes and beliefs, and speeches that attempt to change them may be perceived as radical and extreme. For this reason, such speeches are rare, usually occurring only in desperate times and situations. During the Great Depression of the 1930s, the civil rights struggle of the 1960s, and the Vietnam War of the 1960s and 1970s, one often heard on college campuses persuasive speeches that were critical of American values.

Speeches That Advocate Action and Policy. **Speeches that advocate action and policy** often build on earlier persuasive speeches that address facts and values. Such speeches encourage listeners to act as individuals or as members of a group to respond to the reality of a situation and to put into effect the values they profess. Therefore, in addition to promoting harmony in our inner spiritual world of attitudes, beliefs, and values, persuasive speeches can also establish a link among our perceptions, values, and actions. Clearly, a major goal of ethical persuasion is to create harmony and coherence in the lives of listeners.

Such was the goal of Amanda Miller, who presented a powerful indictment of the Western Hemisphere Institute for Security Cooperation, better known as the "School of the Americas." Amanda argued that this institute, conducted for many years at Fort Benning, Georgia, under U.S. sponsorship, had been "implicated in gross human rights violations in Latin America." The school, she said, trained its students in "techniques for torture, false imprisonment, extortion, and intimidation" and had been "responsible for the deaths of many thousands of people and countless acts of terrorism." Amanda painted a vivid picture of the gulf here between American values and American actions, and she urged her listeners to "support the cause" of shutting down the institute. In the process, they would be restoring coherence to the world of morality and action.

Speeches that advocate action encourage listeners to respond to a situation and put into effect the values that they profess.

The actions proposed by such speeches can be simple and direct, or they can involve complex policy plans, depending on the problem one is addressing. To meet the complex challenge of global warming, Joshua Logan developed an elaborate solution that called for listeners' direct personal action as well as their political support for changes in governmental policy. On a less complex issue, Bonnie Marshall asked her listeners to act individually to ensure their right to die with dignity. She urged them to draw up a living will, to assign durable power of attorney to a trusted friend or family member, and to let their personal physicians know their wishes.

When a speech advocates group action, the audience must see itself as having a common identity and purpose. As we noted in Chapter 12, the speaker can reinforce group identity by using inclusive pronouns (*we, our, us*); by telling stories that emphasize group achievements; and by referring to common heroes, opponents, or martyrs. Anna Aley used an effective appeal to group identity as she proposed specific actions:

> **What can one student do to change the practices of numerous Manhattan landlords? Nothing, if that student is alone. But just think of what we could accomplish if we got all 13,600 off-campus students involved in this issue! Think what we could accomplish if we got even a fraction of those students involved!**

By identifying and uniting them as victims of unscrupulous landlords, Anna encouraged her student listeners to act as members of a group.

Speeches advocating action usually involve risk. Therefore, you must present good reasons to overcome your audience's natural caution. The consequences of acting and not acting must be clearly spelled out. Your plan must be practical and reasonable, and your listeners should be able to see themselves enacting it successfully.

The world of uncertainty in which we live can quickly become a world of controversy. People often do see the world differently, develop different value priorities, and therefore respond to different proposals for action. It is not unusual to hear several competing points of view on the same subject.

Persuasive speeches often must arouse strong feelings to move people to action.

As you persuade, you may well have to justify your ideas and explain why you find other views less persuasive. This clash of ideas can be instructive, providing listeners with a richer sense of their alternatives. It can help reveal weak spots in the opposing positions. This verbal "trial by fire" occurs as **debate** when opponents confront each other directly. As listeners witness and evaluate the clash of ideas, they may come closer to the truth of a situation. We shall talk more about debate strategies when we discuss the refutative design of persuasion in the next chapter.

The Process of Persuasion

To function effectively as speakers and listeners, we must understand how persuasion works. William J. McGuire, professor of psychology at Yale University, suggests that successful persuasion is a complicated process involving up to twelve phases.[8] For our purposes, these phases may be grouped into five stages: awareness, understanding, agreement, enactment, and integration (see Figure 15.3). Familiarity with these stages helps us see that persuasion is not an all-or-nothing proposition. A persuasive message may be successful if it moves people through the process toward a goal.

Figure 15.2
The Work of Persuasive Speeches

Type	Function	Techniques
Speeches that Focus on Facts	Establish true state of affairs	Strengthen claims of past, present, and future fact by citing expert testimony and supporting factual and statistical evidence. Create lively pictures of the contested facts through narratives and images that lend them the aura of reality.
Speeches that address attitudes, beliefs, and values	Harmonize attitudes with beliefs, and beliefs with values	Reawaken appreciation for values through stories, examples, and vivid words. Inform listeners about situations that invite the application of these values, encouraging audience to form attitudes and beliefs that will make the values operational.
Speeches that advocate action and policy	Propose programs to remedy problems and put values into action	Show that the program of action will solve the problem by mentioning previous successes in similar situations. Prove that the plan is practical and workable. Picture audience enacting the plan of action. Show the consequences of acting and not acting. Visualize success.

Awareness

The first stage in the persuasive process is **awareness**. Awareness includes knowing about a problem, paying attention to it, and understanding how it affects our lives. This phase is sometimes called *consciousness raising*. As we noted in Chapter 14, informative speaking can build such awareness and help prepare us for persuasion.[9] In her persuasive speech indicting the School of the Americas, Amanda Miller shocked her audience into awareness with her introduction :

> **"If any government sponsors the outlaws and killer of innocents, they have become outlaws and murderers themselves, and they will take that lonely path at their own peril." President Bush spoke these words to the world, shortly after the attacks on the World Trade Towers, as he began the fight against terrorism.**
>
> **But we Americans have been training terrorists ourselves for many years right here in our own country, at a place known until just recently as the School of the Americas.**

Creating awareness is especially important when people do not believe that there actually is a problem. For example, before advocates could change the way females were depicted in children's books, they had to make listeners understand that always showing boys in active roles and girls in passive roles was a serious problem. They had to demonstrate that this could thwart the development of self-esteem or ambition in young girls.[10]

Beyond acquainting listeners with a problem, persuasive messages aimed at building awareness must demonstrate that the problem is important and show listeners how it affects them directly. Joshua Logan's speech "Global Burning," reprinted at the end of this chapter, had the task of raising awareness of the environmental threat posed by global warming. Persuasive speakers must raise such awareness before moving on to the next stage in the process.

Understanding

The second phase of the persuasive process is **understanding**. Listeners must grasp what you are telling them. They must be moved by your ideas and know how to carry out your proposals.

Amanda Miller developed her listeners' understanding of the School of the Americas by citing a number of examples:

> **In El Salvador, the United Nations Truth Commission found that of twelve officers responsible for the massacre of nine hundred villagers at El Mozote, ten of them were graduates of the School of the Americas.**
>
> **I wish this were a solitary case. According to an Inter-American Commission on Human Rights, School of the Americas graduate Raphael Samundio Molina led a massacre at the Colombian Palace of Justice, and three years later was inducted into the School of the Americas hall of fame. In the same country, an International Human Rights Tribunal found that of two hundred and forty-six officers cited for various crimes, one hundred and five of them were School of the Americas graduates.**
>
> **Finally, the School has produced at least twelve Latin American dictators, in countries such as Peru, Bolivia, Argentina, and Ecuador. This is the distinguished record of the School of the Americas that we continue to fund with our taxpayer dollars.**

Figure 15.3

McGuire's Model of the Persuasive Process

To provide understanding for her persuasive speech, Anna Aley used an "inside-outside" approach. She took listeners inside the housing problem in Manhattan, Kansas, by vividly describing her basement apartment. Then she took listeners outside the problem by showing them the total picture of substandard student housing in the city: the number of students involved and the causes of the problem. Ethical persuasion expands our knowledge, demonstrates how some arguments are stronger than others, and provides evidence to support a position.[11]

Finally, the audience must understand how to put the speaker's proposals into effect. In her persuasive speech, reprinted in Appendix B, Bonnie Marshall clearly spelled out the steps she wanted her listeners to take, enumerating these as she presented them.

Agreement

The third stage in the persuasive process is **agreement**. As they listen to you, audience members should go through a *series of affirmations*, such as: "He's right, this is a serious problem. . . . That's striking evidence, I didn't know about that. . . . I see how this can affect my life. . . . I've got to do something about this. . . . This plan makes sense. I believe it will work." These affirmations should build on each other, developing a momentum toward agreement at the end of the speech. Any doubt, any hesitation over the validity of a claim or the soundness of evidence or the accuracy of reasoning, will weaken the process of agreement.

Speakers themselves become important models for agreement. When Amanda Miller stood to speak against the School of the Americas, audience members were surprised to see this previously mild-mannered person so powerfully committed to a position. "If Amanda is this passionate about it," some of them reasoned, "there must really be something wrong here." As she laid out her evidence, other listeners were impressed by her research: "Amanda really knows what she's talking about," they concluded. As she painted vivid word-pictures of the abuse of human rights, her listeners shared her indignation. Her decisive gestures, emphatic voice, and eye contact all engaged her audience and convinced them that Amanda's cause truly deserved their agreement. In these many ways, Amanda had provided them with a model for their own commitment to her cause. When you speak as a persuader, you too must become a model for what you are asking of listeners.

Agreement can range from small concessions to total acceptance. Lesser degrees of agreement could represent success, especially to the extent that listeners have to change their attitudes, beliefs, or values or risk a great deal by accepting your ideas. During the Vietnam War, we often heard classroom speeches attacking or defending our involvement in that conflict. Feelings about the war ran so high that just to have a speech listened to without interruption could be an accomplishment. If a reluctant listener were to nod agreement or concede, "I guess you have a point," then one could truly claim victory.

Enactment

The fourth stage in the persuasive process is **enactment**. It is one thing to get listeners to accept what you say. It is quite another to get them to act on it. If you invite listeners to sign a petition, raise their hands, or voice agreement, you give them a way to enact agreement. By enacting their agreement, listeners make a commitment. The student speaker who mobilized his audience against a proposed tuition increase

- brought a petition to be signed.
- distributed the addresses of local legislators to contact.
- urged listeners to write letters to campus and local newspapers.

He channeled their agreement into constructive action.

Changing agreement to action may require the further use of emotional appeals. Stirring stories and examples, vivid images, and colorful language can arouse sympathy. As she told the story of Harry Smith, who died an agonizing death because he had not signed a living will, Bonnie Marshall moved her listeners to act on behalf of themselves and their loved ones. Anna Aley's concluding story of her neighbor's accident helped motivate her audience to take action against substandard student housing. In an especially interesting use of narrative technique, Elizabeth Tidmore asked her listeners to imagine themselves helping as volunteers for a Special Olympics weekend. As she told them the heartwarming story of what they would experience, she in effect invited them to transform this imaginative adventure into reality.

Integration

The final stage in the persuasive process is the **integration** of new attitudes and commitments with the listeners' previous beliefs and values. For a persuasive speech to have lasting effect, listeners must see the connection between the attitudes and actions you propose and their important values. Your ideas must fit comfortably within their belief system. As she presented her case for living wills, Bonnie Marshall anchored her appeals in the right to control one's own destiny. Anna Aley tied her attack on housing conditions to the values of fair treatment and safe living conditions. In the second of his two related persuasive speeches, "Cooling the World's Fever," reprinted at the end of Chapter 16, Joshua Logan urged listeners not just to accept his recommendations but to *become* the solution he advocated. He asked for total integration of attitudes, beliefs, values, and actions.

All of us seek consistency between our values and behaviors. For example, it would be inconsistent for us to march against substandard housing on Monday and contribute to a landlord's defense fund on Tuesday. This is why people sometimes seem to agree with a persuasive message, and then change their minds. It dawns on them later that this new commitment means that they must rearrange other cherished beliefs and attitudes.

To avoid such a delayed counterreaction, inoculate listeners by anticipating such problems and answering

InterConnections.LearnMore 15.1

Persuasion

Influence at Work
http://www.workingpsychology.com/intro.html.
Provides an in-depth but readable introduction to social influence, persuasion, and propaganda; an outstanding web site developed by Kelton Rhoades, Ph.D., consultant and lecturer at the University of Southern California and the Annenberg School for Communication.

Links to Social Psychology Topics
http://www.socialpsychology.org/social.htm
Comprehensive directory that links the study of social psychology to persuasive communication in a number of specific applications. See especially the section on "social influence."

Propaganda Analysis
http://www.propagandacritic.com/
A discussion of propaganda techniques, with examples from World War II as well as more contemporary applications; prepared by Aaron Delwiche, assistant professor in the Department of Communication, Trinity University.

Speaker's Notes 15.1

Applying McGuire's Model to Persuasive Speeches

1. Arouse attention with your introduction.
2. Relate your message to your listeners' interests and needs.
3. Define complex terms, use concrete examples, and organize your material clearly.
4. Emphasize facts, statistics, and expert testimony to gain acceptance of your point of view.
5. Include a clear plan of action.
6. Use vivid language to make your message memorable.
7. Ask listeners to make a public commitment.
8. Relate your proposal to your audience's values.

VideoLab

To test your skills and expand your understanding of the persuasive process, go to **VideoLab Lesson 9: Persuasive Speaking** and go through the videos, exercises, and tips provided.

them in the speech. Don't attempt too much persuasion in a single message. Remember that dramatic change may require a campaign of persuasion in which any single speech plays a small but vital role. Be content if you can move listeners just a small distance in a desirable direction.

To conclude, persuasion can be a complicated process. Any persuasive message must focus on the stage where it can make its most effective contribution: raising awareness, building understanding, seeking agreement, encouraging action, or promoting the integration of beliefs, attitudes, and values. Speaker's Notes 15.1 outlines several ways to apply McGuire's model to persuasive speeches. To determine where to focus your persuasive efforts, you must consider the challenges of the specific situation.

The Challenges of Persuasion

The challenges that persuaders face range from confronting a reluctant audience to framing messages that meet the most demanding ethical tests. As you plan a persuasive speech, you need to consider the audience's position on the topic, how listeners might react to you as an advocate, and the situation in which the speech will be presented. At this point, the information and techniques concerning audience analysis that we introduced in Chapter 5 become crucial to success.

Begin preparing your speech by determining where your listeners stand on the issue. Do they hold differing attitudes about the topic, or are they united? If listeners are divided, you might hope to unify them around your position. If listeners are already united—but in opposition—you might try to divide them and attract some toward your position. Also consider how your listeners might regard you as a speaker on the subject. If you do not have their respect, trust, and goodwill, use supporting testimony from sources they do trust to enhance your ethos and improve your chances for success.

Evaluating the relationships among the audience, the topic, and you as speaker will suggest further strategies for effective persuasion.

Enticing a Reluctant Audience to Listen

If you face an audience that opposes your position, success may be represented by small achievements, such as simply getting thoughtful attention. One way to handle a reluctant audience is to adopt a **co-active approach**, which seeks to bridge the differences between you and your listeners.[12] The major steps in this approach are as follows:

1. *Establish identification and goodwill early in the speech.* Emphasize experiences, background, beliefs, and values that you share with listeners.
2. *Start with areas of agreement before you tackle areas of disagreement.* Otherwise, listeners may simply "turn off and tune out" before you have a chance to state your position.
3. *Emphasize explanation over argument.* By explaining your position more than refuting theirs, you avoid provoking defensive behavior and invite listeners to consider the merits of your case.
4. *Cite authorities that the audience will respect and accept.* If you can find statements by such authorities that are favorable, you can gain "borrowed ethos" for your case. When he spoke before the Harvard Law School Forum, Charlton Heston, president of the National Rifle Association, attempted to disarm a chilly audience by citing his high regard for Dr. Martin Luther King Jr. and mentioning his attendance at King's "I Have a Dream" speech.[13]
5. *Set modest goals for change.* Don't try to push your audience too far, too fast. If reluctant listeners have listened to you—if you have raised their awareness and built a basis for understanding—you have accomplished a good deal.
6. *Make a multisided presentation that compares your position with others in a favorable way.* Show respect for opposing positions and understanding for why others might have supported them. Then reveal how these positions may not merit such support. Your attitude should be not to challenge listeners, but to help them see the situation in a new light.

Let's consider how you might apply these steps in a speech against capital punishment before an audience of largely reluctant listeners. You could build identification by pointing out the values you share with the audience, such as, "We all respect human life. We all believe in fairness." It might also help to take an indirect approach in which you sketch your reasoning before you announce your purpose.

What if I were to tell you that we are condoning unfairness, that we are condemning people to death simply because they are poor and cannot afford a good lawyer? What if I were to show you that we are sanctioning a model of violent behavior in our society that encourages more violence and more victims in return?

As you present evidence, cite authorities that your audience will respect and accept. "FBI statistics tell us that if you are poor and black, you are three times more likely to be executed for the crime of murder."

Persuasive speakers must often entice a reluctant audience to action, remove barriers to commitment, and move listeners to participate.

Keep your goals modest. Ask only for a fair hearing. Be aware that reluctant listeners may often struggle *not* to give you a fair hearing. Such listeners may distort your message so that it seems to fit what they already believe. Or they may simply deny or dismiss it, saying that it doesn't apply to them. Or they may discredit a source you cite in your speech, believing that any message that relies on *that* source cannot be taken seriously. Remember also that if you propose too much change, you may create a **boomerang effect**, in which the audience reacts by opposing your position even more strongly.[14]

For all these reasons, to hope for a major change on the basis of any single persuasive effort is what McGuire calls the **great expectation fallacy**.[15] Be patient with reluctant listeners. Try to move them a step at a time in the direction you would like them to go. Give them information that may eventually change their minds:

> **I know that many of you may not like to hear what I'm saying, but think about it. If capital punishment does not deter violent crime, if indeed it may encourage more violent crime, isn't it time we put capital punishment itself on trial?**

Finally, make a **multisided presentation**. Acknowledge the arguments in favor of capital punishment, showing that you respect and understand that position, even though you do not accept it.

> **I know that the desire for revenge can be strong. If someone I love had been murdered, I would want the killer's life in return. I wouldn't care if capital punishment wasn't fair. I wouldn't care that it condones brutality. I would just want an eye for an eye. But that doesn't mean you should give it to me. It doesn't mean that society should base its policy on my anger and hatred.**

A multisided approach helps make those you do persuade resistant to later counterattacks, because you show them how to answer such arguments. This is often called the **inoculation effect**, because you "inject" your listeners with a milder form of the arguments they may hear later in more vehement forms.[16]

When you acknowledge and then refute arguments, you also help your credibility in two ways. First, you enhance your trustworthiness by showing respect for your opposition. You suggest that their position deserves consideration, even though you have a better option. Second, you enhance your competence by showing your knowledge of the opposing position—both of the reasons why people may find it attractive and the reasons why it is defective.

After your speech, you should continue to show respect for the audience. Even if some listeners want to argue or heckle, keep your composure. Others may be impressed by your self-control and may be encouraged to rethink their position in light of your example.

There may be times when you and your audience are so far apart that you decide simply to acknowledge your disagreement. You might say that although you do not agree with listeners, you respect their right to their position and hope that they will respect yours. Such openness may help establish the beginnings of trust. Even if audience members do not see you as an ally, they may at least start to see you as an honest, committed opponent and give you a hearing. If you emphasize that you will not be asking them to change their minds, but simply to hear you out and to listen to the reasons why you believe as you do, you may have your day in court. And you may slightly erode the rock of their disagreement!

We once heard a student speak against abortion to a class that was sharply divided on that issue. She began with a personal narrative, the story of how her mother had been given a drug that was later found to induce birth defects. Her mother was then faced with a decision on terminating the pregnancy. The student concluded by saying that if her mother had chosen the abortion option, she would not be there speaking to them that day. She paused, smiled, and said, "Although I know some of

Figure 15.4

Audience Considerations for Persuasive Speeches

Audience Type	Strategies
Reluctant to listen, possibly hostile	Seek common ground and establish good will. Quote sources they respect. Explain more than you argue. Limit your goals: try for a fair hearing, and ask little from listeners. Try to weaken their resistance. Acknowledge opposing arguments, but show tactfully why you have a differentL commitment.
Uncommitted, even uninterested	Provide information needed to arouse their interest and encourage their commitment. Connect their values with your position. Become a model of commitment for them to follow.
Friendly, but not yet committed	Remind them of what is at stake. Show them why action is necessary now. Give them clear instructions and help them take the first step. Picture them undertaking this action successfully.

you may disagree with my views, I must say I am glad that you are here to listen and that I am here to speak. Think about it." If your reasons are compelling and your evidence is strong, you may soften the opposition and move waverers toward your position.

Do not worry if the change you want does not show up immediately. There often is a delayed reaction to persuasion, a **sleeper effect**, in which change shows up only after listeners have had time to integrate the message into their belief systems.[17] Even if no change is apparent, your message may sensitize your listeners to the issue and make them more receptive to future persuasion.[18]

Facing a reluctant audience is never easy. But you can't predict what new thoughts your speech might stimulate among listeners or what delayed positive reactions to it there might be.

Removing Barriers to Commitment

Undecided listeners may hesitate because they need more information, because they do not see a connection between their values and interests and the issue at hand, and because they may not feel certain that they can trust your judgment. To deal with these challenges, you should provide needed information, show listeners how your proposal relates to their values or interests, and strengthen your credibility.

Provide Needed Information. Often a missing fact or unanswered question stands in the way of commitment. "I know that many of you agree with me but are asking, 'How much will this cost?'" Anticipating reservations and supplying the necessary information can help move listeners toward your position.

Affirm and Apply Values. Persuasive speeches that threaten audience values are not likely to be effective. You must show listeners that your proposal agrees with their principles. For example, if your listeners resist an educational program for the financially disadvantaged because they think that people ought to take care of themselves, you may have to show them that your program represents "a hand up, not a handout." Show them that your proposal will lead to other favorable outcomes, such as reductions in crime or unemployment.

As we noted earlier, values are resistant to change. If you can reason from the perspective of your listeners' values, using them as the basis for your arguments, you will create identification and remove a barrier to commitment.

With sympathetic audiences, speakers may need to revitalize shared beliefs and demonstrate a need for involvement.

Strengthen Your Credibility. When audiences hesitate because they question your credibility, you can "borrow ethos" by citing expert testimony. Call on sources that your listeners trust and respect. Uncommitted audiences will scrutinize both you and your arguments carefully. Reason with such listeners, leading them gradually and carefully to the conclusion you would like them to reach and providing supporting material each step of the way. Adopt a multisided approach, in which you consider all options fairly, to confirm your ethos as a trustworthy and competent speaker.

When addressing uncommitted listeners, don't overstate your case. Let your personal commitment be evident through your sincerity and conviction, but be careful about using overly strong appeals to guilt or fear. These might cause cautious listeners to resist, resent, and reject both you and your message.[19] It is also important not to push uncommitted listeners too hard. Help them move in the desired direction, but let them take the final step themselves. Speaker's Notes 15.2 lists these ideas.

Moving from Attitude to Action

Just as opponents may be reluctant to listen, sympathetic audiences may be reluctant to act. It is one thing to agree with a speaker and quite another to accept the inconvenience and risk that action may require. Listeners may believe that the problem does not affect them personally. They may not know what they should do or how they should do it. Or, they may feel that the situation is hopeless.[20] To move people to action, you must give them reasons to act. You may have to arouse their enthusiasm, remind them of their beliefs, demonstrate the need for involvement, present a clear plan of action, and make it easy for them to comply.

Arouse Their Enthusiasm. Keep in mind that it may take strong feelings to move people to action. Declare your own commitment, and ask listeners to join you.

Speaker's Notes 15.2

Encouraging Uncommitted Listeners

1. Provide missing information that will help them decide in your favor.
2. Show how your proposal meets their needs and strengthens their values.
3. Borrow ethos by citing authorities they respect.
4. Do not overstate your case or rely too heavily on emotional appeals.

Once people have voiced their commitment, they are more likely to follow through on it.[21] Beth Tidmore, in her speech inviting listeners to become Special Olympics volunteers, followed such advice. Beth anticipated that her listeners already agreed with her—*in principle*. But she had not yet won their hearts. Beth decided that the best way to arouse enthusiasm would be to help listeners imagine themselves enacting her proposal. Here is the way she approached this challenge:

> **I've had so many great experiences, but these are hard to describe without overworking words like "fulfilling" and "rewarding." So I'm going to let you experience it for yourself. I want everybody to pack your bags—we're going to the Special Olympics summer games in Georgia! . . .**
>
> **Some of the athletes will be a little bit scared—it will be their first time away from home. All you've got to do is smile and reassure them that they'll have a great time—and you know they will. . . .**
>
> **Now we'll go to opening ceremonies. You walk onto a big field, and there's a huge tent, and they're playing loud music. All of the kids start dancing—they've never had such a moment! After that, each county marches by with a banner, and when your county comes by, you'd better be up and cheering.**
>
> **And then you hear something in the distance: a siren. Police cars and fire engines . . . and it's getting louder and louder. As it gets louder, it comes into the courtyard, and you catch your first glimpse of the Olympic torch runner. And as the runner gets closer and closer, the Special Olympics theme blares louder on the speakers, and the sirens are just absolutely piercing. They make a final hand-off, and one chosen athlete will light the cauldron. And the flame goes up in this huge whoosh. It's just incredible. All of the athletes cheer, and they're so proud to be part of this moment. . . . Then the athletes get very serious, because they know it's time to take that Special Olympics oath. . . .**
>
> **After the games are over, you get to see them all on the podium, because everyone gets a medal or a ribbon, everyone places. And it's great, because they're smiling and they're so proud, and there are flashbulbs going off, and the anthem is playing. And they turn and they congratulate their fellow competitors. . . .**
>
> **Sunday is a sad time, because you have to send them back home to their parents. But when they run off the buses to show their parents their medals, and their parents walk up to you, their simplest "thank you" is a great reward. And in the end your vocal chords are shot, you have a second degree sunburn on most of your body. Your feet hurt, your back aches, and you feel like you could sleep for a week. But you just can't stop smiling, because you know that you've just taken part in something magical.**

At the end of this speech, when Beth distributed commitment cards to her listeners, it was clear that she had moved her listeners to action.

Revitalize Shared Beliefs and Values. When speakers and audiences celebrate shared beliefs and values, the result is often a renewed sense of commitment. Such occasions may involve telling stories that resurrect heroes and heroines, giving shared beliefs new meaning.[22] At political conventions, Jefferson, Lincoln, Roosevelt, Kennedy, and Reagan are often invoked in speeches. These symbolic heroes can help bridge audience diversity by bringing different factions together.

In her speech, Beth Tidmore relied upon and revitalized the values of benevolence, generosity, and magnanimity—those large-hearted virtues that come into play when we reach out to those who do not share all of our blessings. Beth's narrative did not appeal directly and explicitly to such values—she simply assumed that they already existed in those who would respond to her story.

Demonstrate the Need for Involvement. Show your listeners how the quality of their lives depends on action, and demonstrate that the results will be satisfying. It often helps if you can associate the change with a vision of the future. In his final speech, Martin Luther King Jr. said, "I may not get there with you, but I can see the Promised Land." King's vision of the Promised Land helped justify the sacrifice called for in his plan of action.

Beth Tidmore's speech implied the need for listener involvement. If listeners did not show up to fill the roles she had described for them, the promise of the story would remain unfulfilled.

Present a Clear Plan of Action. Listeners may exaggerate the difficulty of enacting a proposal or insist that it is impossible. To overcome such resistance, tell them how others have been successful using the same approach. Develop examples or narratives that show them completing the project successfully. Stress that "we can do it, and this is how we can do it." A speaker urging classmates to work to defeat a proposed tuition raise said:

> **How many of you are ready to help defeat this plan to raise tuition? Good! I see your heads nodding. Now, if you're willing to sign this petition, hold up your hands. Good again! Now, I'm going to pass around this petition, and I want each of you to sign it. If we act together, we can make a difference.**

Be Specific in Your Instructions and Make it Easy to Comply. Your plan must show listeners what to do and how to do it. Instead of simply urging listeners to write their congressional representatives, provide them with addresses and telephone numbers, a petition to sign, or preprinted addressed postcards to complete and return. Beth Tidmore passed out information and cards at the end of her speech to help listeners confirm their commitment. Speaker's Notes 15.3 lists ways to move people to action.

The Challenge of Ethical Persuasion

Ours is a skeptical and cynical age, made more so by large-scale abuses of communication ethics. Ads assure us that their products will make us sexier or richer, often with no foundation in fact. Persuasive messages disguised as information appear in "infomercials" seen on television. They try to slip into our minds under the radar of critical listening. Public officials may present suspicious statistics, make dubious denials, or dance around questions they don't want to answer directly. Talk-show hosts may play fast and loose with facts and use inflammatory language. Little wonder that many people have lost trust in society's major sources of communication.

As a consumer of persuasive messages, you can at least partially protect yourself by applying the thinking skills we discussed in Chapter 4. As a producer of persua-

Speaker's Notes 15.3

Moving People to Action

1. Remind listeners of what is at stake.
2. Provide a clear plan of action.
3. Use examples and stories as models for action.
4. Visualize the consequences of acting and not acting.
5. Demonstrate that you practice what you preach.
6. Ask for public commitments.
7. Make it easy for listeners to take the first step.

Guidelines for Ethical Persuasion — Ethics Alert! 15.1

1. Avoid name calling: attack problems, proposals, and ideas—not people.
2. Be open about your personal interest.
3. Don't adapt to the point of compromising your convictions.
4. Argue from responsible knowledge.
5. Don't try to pass off opinions as facts.
6. Don't use inflammatory language to hide a lack of evidence.
7. Be sure your proposal is in the best interest of your audience.
8. Remember, words can hurt.

sive messages, you can help counter this trend toward unethical communication. Keep three simple questions in mind as you prepare your persuasive speech:[23]

- What is my ethical responsibility to my audience?
- Could I publicly defend the ethics of my message?
- What does this message say about my character?

These questions should light your way through the complexities of ethical persuasion.

As we noted in Chapter 1, an ethical speech is based fundamentally on respect for the audience, responsible knowledge of the topic, and concern for the consequences of your words. The guidelines in Ethics Alert! 15.1 should help you apply these precepts to persuasive messages.

VideoLab

Go to the **Lesson 7's VideoLab Coach: Tips to Remember** for a review of the "Do's" and "Don'ts" of persuasive speaking.

In Summary

Persuasion is the art of getting others to consider our point of view fairly and favorably. Persuasion is vital to our political system, which is based on the principle of rule by *deliberation* and choice rather than by force. Groups that have been exposed to different positions usually make better decisions because they are stimulated to examine a situation and to think about their options.

Characteristics of Persuasive Speaking. In contrast with informative speaking, persuasive speaking urges a choice among options and asks for a commitment. Rather than speaking as a teacher, the speaker assumes the role of advocate. Ethical persuasive speaking centers on good reasons based on responsible knowledge. Persuasive speeches rely more on emotional involvement than do informative speeches, and they carry an even heavier ethical burden.

The Work of Persuasion. Persuasion functions to help listeners resolve uncertainties surrounding the true state of affairs, how they should feel about these things, and what they ought to do about them. In turn, the three basic forms of persuasive speaking are speeches that focus on facts, speeches that address attitudes, beliefs, and values, and speeches that advocate action and policy.

Speeches that focus on facts concern questions of past fact (whether something actually occurred), present fact (what is actually going on), and future fact (what is likely to occur). Persuasive speeches on future fact function as *predictions*. Questions of past and present fact often depend upon the definitions of events.

Speeches that address attitudes, beliefs, and values strive to help listeners find harmony among these elements. Concentrate on adjusting attitudes and beliefs in light of deeper values.

Speeches that advocate action and policy encourage listeners to act as individuals or as members of a group to respond to the reality of a situation and to put into effect the values they profess. *Debates* occur when competing proposals for action and policy clash directly.

The Process of Persuasion. When persuasion is successful, people listen, learn, agree, and change as a result of what they hear. These behaviors parallel McGuire's categories of *awareness, understanding, agreement, enactment,* and *integration* of persuasive material.

Awareness suggests that we know of a problem and that it commands our serious attention. Understanding implies that we can see the connection between the problem and our lives and that we know how to carry out the speaker's proposals. Agreement implies our acceptance of a speaker's interpretations and recommendations. Enactment suggests our commitment and readiness to carry out the speaker's proposals. Integration involves consolidating the new attitudes and commitments into our overall belief and value system.

The Challenges of Persuasion. Persuading others can pose many challenges. You may have to entice a reluctant audience to listen, remove barriers that block commitment, and move listeners from agreement to action. In any of these situations, you must be scrupulously ethical.

To encourage reluctant listeners, use a *co-active approach* that seeks to bridge differences and to build identification. Avoid the *great expectation fallacy,* which asks for more change than one could reasonably expect after a single speech. Make a *multisided presentation* in which you acknowledge opposing positions in order to refute them.

Remove barriers to commitment by providing vital information, pointing out the relevance to listeners' lives, and building credibility. To move partisan listeners from agreement to action, use vivid language and examples to bring abstract principles to life; revitalize shared beliefs and values, prove the need for their involvement; present a clear plan, declare your own commitment to encourage the commitment of others, and make it easy for listeners to take the first step into involvement.

To be an ethical persuader, be sure that your messages are based on respect for the audience, responsible knowledge of the topic, and concern for the consequences of your words. Be sure that you could defend the ethics of your message if challenged.

Terms to Know

persuasion
deliberation
speeches that focus on facts
predictions
speeches addressing attitudes, beliefs, and values
speeches that advocate action and policy
debate
awareness
understanding
agreement
enactment
integration
co-active approach
boomerang effect
great expectation fallacy
multisided presentation
inoculation effect
sleeper effect

Discussion

1. Examine magazine ads and newspaper articles to find "infomercials"—persuasive messages cloaked as information. What alerts you to the persuasive intent? In what respects does such communication possess the characteristics of persuasion and information discussed in this chapter?
2. The letters-to-the editor section of the Sunday newspaper is often a rich source for the study of persuasive material. Using a recent Sunday paper, analyze the persuasion attempted in these letters. Which do you think are most and least effective and why?
3. The speech on slum housing that appears in Appendix B was prepared for a student audience at Kansas State University. What, if any, changes might you suggest in this speech if it were to be presented to a luncheon meeting of realtors in Manhattan, Kansas? Why?
4. Are there ever times when a speaker should give up trying to persuade a hostile audience and simply confront listeners directly with the position they appear to oppose? Why would a speaker bother to do this? Might speaker and audience gain anything from such a confrontation? Look for an example of such a speech. Do you agree with the strategy used in it? Discuss in class.

Application

1. Keep a diary for the next three days in which you identify all the moments in which you encounter and practice persuasion. When were you most and least persuaded and most and least persuasive? Why? Did you encounter (or commit) any ethical abuses? Discuss your experiences in class.
2. Read one of the persuasive speeches in Appendix B and identify the following:
   a. The work performed by the speech: whether it contends over facts, engages values, or proposes policies.
   b. The challenge the speech apparently confronted in addressing its particular audience

   How well does the speech perform this work and meet this challenge? Might it have done better?
3. Select a controversial subject and summarize the approach you might make in adapting a speech on this topic to
   a. an uncommitted audience.
   b. an audience in agreement.
   c. a reluctant audience.

   Discuss and explain these differences in approaches.

Notes

1. *Whitney v. California,* 274 U.S. 357, 375 (1927).
2. Stephen Edleston Toulmin, *The Uses of Argument* (Cambridge: Cambridge University Press, 1958), p. 8.
3. John Stuart Mill, *On Liberty* (Chicago: Henry Regnery, 1955 [originally published 1859]), p. 24.
4. Charlan Jeanne Nemeth, "Differential Contributions of Majority and Minority Influence," *Psychological Review* 93 (1986): 23–32.
5. Mark A. Hamilton and John E. Hunter, "The Effect of Language Intensity on Receiver Attitudes Toward Message, Source, and Topic," in *Persuasion: Advances Through Meta-Analysis,* ed. M. Allen and R. W. Preiss (Beverly Hills, Calif.: Sage, 1998).
6. This speech is made available in English translation by the Perseus Digital Library, sponsored by Tufts University <http://www.perseus.tufts.edu/cgi-bin/ptext?doc=Perseus%3Atext%3A1999.02.0020%3Ahead%3D%2311>
7. For a different view, which depicts persuasion in terms of manipulation and domination, see Sonja K. Foss and Cindy L. Griffin, "Beyond Persuasion: A Proposal for an Invitational Rhetoric," *Communication Monographs* 62 (1995): 2–18.
8. William J. McGuire, "Attitudes and Attitude Change," in *The Handbook of Social Psychology,* ed. Gardner Lindzey and Elliot Aronson (New York: Random House, 1985), vol. 1, pp. 258–261.
9. Roger Brown, *Social Psychology* (New York: Free Press, 1965), pp. 709–763.
10. Gloria Steinem, *Revolution from Within: A Book of Self-Esteem* (New York: Little, Brown, 1992), p. 120.
11. John C. Reinard, "The Empirical Study of the Persuasive Effects of Evidence: The Status After Fifty Years of Research," *Human Communication Research* 15 (1988): 3–59.
12. Adapted from Herbert W. Simons, *Persuasion: Understanding, Practice, and Analysis,* 2nd ed. (New York: Random House, 1986), p. 138.
13. Charlton Heston, "Winning the Cultural War," *Vital Speeches of the Day,* 1 Apr. 1999, pp. 357–359.
14. N. H. Anderson, "Integration Theory and Attitude Change," *Psychological Review* 78 (1971): 171–206.
15. McGuire, p. 260.
16. Mike Allen, "Meta-Analysis Comparing the Persuasiveness of One-Sided and Two-Sided Messages," *Western Journal of Speech Communication* 55 (1991): 390–404; M. Allen et al., "Testing a Model of Message Sidedness: Three Replications," *Communication Monographs* 56 (1990): 275–291; Jerold L. Hale, Paul A. Mongeau, and Randi M. Thomas, "Cognitive Processing of One- and Two-Sided Persuasive Messages," *Western Journal of Speech Communication* 55 (1991): 380–389; Carl I. Hovland, Arthur A. Lumsdaine, and Fred D. Sheffield, "The Effects of Presenting 'One Side' Versus 'Both Sides' in Changing Opinions on a Controversial Subject," in *Experiments on Mass Communication* (Princeton, N.J.: Princeton University Press, 1949), pp. 201–227; and William J. McGuire, "Inducing Resistance to Persuasion," in *Advances in Experimental Social Psychology,* ed. L. Berkowitz (New York: Academic Press, 1964), pp. 191–229.

17. Mike Allen and James B. Stiff, "Testing Three Models for the Sleeper Effect," *Western Journal of Speech Communication* 53 (1989): 411–426; and T. D. Cook et al., "History of the Sleeper Effect: Some Logical Pitfalls in Accepting the Null Hypothesis," *Psychological Bulletin* 86 (1979): 662–679.

18. M. E. McCombs, "The Agenda-Setting Approach," in *Handbook of Political Communication,* ed. D. D. Nimmo and K. R. Sanders (Beverly Hills, Calif.: Sage, 1981), pp. 121–140.

19. Franklin J. Boster and Paul Mongeau, "Fear-Arousing Persuasive Messages," in *Communication Yearbook 8*, ed. R. Bostrom (Beverly Hills, Calif.: Sage, 1984), pp. 330–377; and Richard E. Petty and Duane T. Wegener, "Attitude Change: Multiple Roles for Persuasion Variables," in *The Handbook of Social Psychology,* ed. Daniel T. Gilbert, Susan T. Fiske, and Gardner Lindzey, 4th ed. (Boston: McGraw-Hill, 1998), pp. 353–354.

20. Katherine E. Rowan, "Goals, Obstacles, and Strategies in Risk Communication: A Problem-Solving Approach to Improving Communication About Risks," *Journal of Applied Communication Research* 19 (1991): 322.

21. Michael Osborn, "Rhetorical Depiction," in *Form, Genre, and the Study of Political Discourse,* ed. Herbert W. Simons and Aram A. Aghazarian (Columbia: University of South Carolina Press, 1986), pp. 79–107.

22. R. A. Wicklund and J. W. Brehm, *Perspectives on Cognitive Dissonance* (Hillsdale, N.J.: Erlbaum, 1976).

23. Adapted from Richard L. Johannensen, *Ethics in Communication,* 3rd ed. (Prospect Heights, Ill.: Waveland, 1990), pp. 17–20.

Global Burning

Joshua Logan

Ten years ago, five years ago, reasonable people could argue and even disagree over some tough environmental questions: Is there really such a thing as "global warming"? Is the world really getting hotter at a rapid pace? And is it being fanned by humans? Are we really responsible for environmental conditions?

■ Joshua Logan presented this first of two persuasive speeches in his class at the University of Memphis (the second appears at the end of Chapter 16). Here his major challenge was to magnify the reality of global warming and its meaning for listeners. The speech is characterized by passion and good evidence.

Now there's no more room for argument. Fini. Case closed. The answer to all these questions is YES. This definitive answer has been provided by the United Nations Intergovernmental Panel on Climate Change, reporting during the early part of this year. This authoritative, thousand-page report, which correlates and tests the work of hundreds of environmental scientists from countries all around the globe, concludes that the process of global warming is now in motion and is accelerating. And the fire is fed largely by humans. The United States especially, with about 4 percent of the world's population, accounts for 25 percent of all global warming. We are the ones with our foot on the accelerator.

Today I want to sketch the dimensions of this problem, and what it might mean for you, your children, and your grandchildren. I will first track the causes of global warming, then trace its recent path and project its future. Sounds like an informative speech, doesn't it? But the most recent Gallup polls—published in April 2001—tell us that the people of the United States are pretty much in denial about global warming: yes, they believe it exists and, yes, they are concerned, but they're not that much concerned. Global warming is something of an abstract, distant problem for them, and they can't see the future all that clearly. That's why this is a problem for persuasion, why this is a challenge for this speech. We must recognize global warming for what it is, the monster we are creating by all our action and inaction. We must become scared—really scared! We must be willing to think green and act green, from the personal everyday decisions we make on disposing trash to the big consumer decisions we make on which cars to buy to the political decisions we make on which candidates to support. We must understand that this hot world is really ready to catch fire—and we must be willing to pay the price to help put the flames out. We must be committed to the proposition that global warming must not become global burning.

■ Josh announces his purpose and previews his speech. He wants to bring to life the reality of global warming and to arouse strong feelings in preparation for his second speech. Thus he addresses the present fact of global warming, predicts its future unless this trajectory is changed, and addresses relevant attitudes, beliefs, and values. With respect to the persuasive process, the speech concentrates on arousing awareness, sharing understanding, and securing agreement. The second speech will focus on enactment and integration. The challenge for this speech is to remove barriers that stand in the way of audience commitment.

Global warming begins with greenhouse gases—the tons of carbon dioxide that belch out of our smokestacks and our automobile exhausts; the vast clouds of methane gas that rise from our farms and ranches and landfills; the nitrous oxide from fertilizers, cattle feed lots, and chemical products. The world's forests are supposed to absorb much of this industrial and agricultural output, but guess what? We've also been busy cutting the rainforests and clear-cutting our own forests. We're tying nature's hands behind her back at just the wrong moment. So all these deadly gases mix and accumulate in the atmosphere, where they magnify the heat of the sun.

Now let's gain some perspective on where we now stand, because the world has already started to melt. I want to show you a chart that traces the human influence on the atmosphere over the past thousand years of history. This chart summarizes the history of greenhouse gases, according to the IPCC's *Summary for Policymakers* (page 6). Notice that the bottom border divides the time frame into two-hundred-year periods. The side frame measures the amount of the gas pouring into the atmosphere. Notice that for about eight hundred of these years, this amount is stable

■ Josh intensifies audience awareness by the use of graphic, concrete words like "belch" and "vast clouds" and by the vivid image of "tying nature's hands behind her back."

■ *Josh uses a chart to help create perspective concerning the recency and enormity of the problem. His use of contrast is especially effective, and the direct quotation reinforces the authenticity of his evidence. His careful research reinforces his credibility as Josh prepares to present the doomsday scenario that will follow.*

■ *Josh translates a complex situation into a simple word-picture that listeners can grasp. He asks listeners to imagine summer days made ten degrees hotter by global warming. His allusions to the fate of coral reefs and tigers hints of the impact on nature and wildlife. He adds dark humor by advising listeners to sell their beach property, and he personalizes the picture by suggesting the fate of the barrier islands he loved as a child.*

■ *Josh reassures listeners that the picture he has painted is not inevitable. He also prepares the ground for his next speech, which will complete the problem-solution design of his persuasion.*

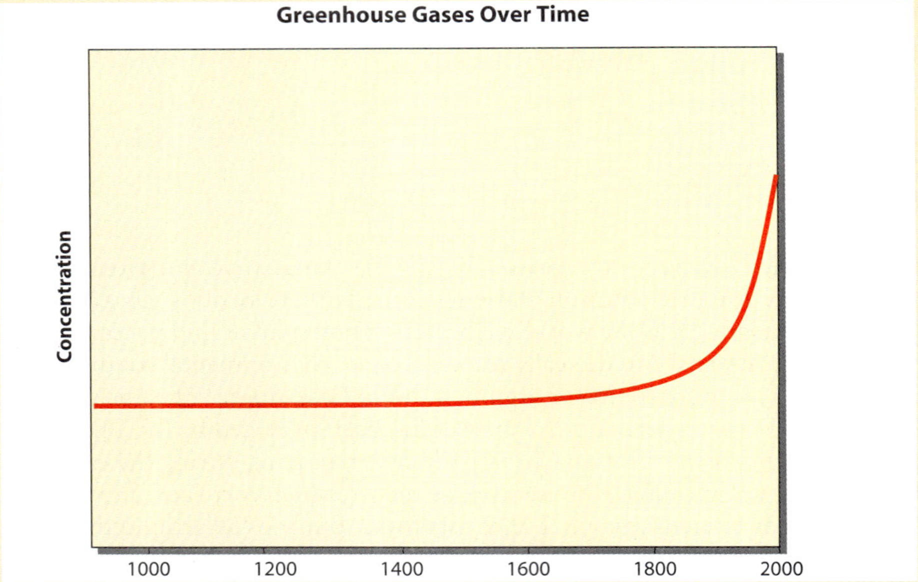

and even—almost a straight line. Then as the nineteenth century dawns on the Industrial Revolution, the lines begin to climb, at first gradually, then increasingly steeper until they almost reach the vertical during the past half-century. The dry technical language of the summary, speaking to carbon dioxide alone, carries the message of this chart with sharp clarity: "The atmospheric concentration of carbon dioxide (CO_2) has increased by 31 percent since 1750. The present CO_2 concentration has not been exceeded during the past 420,000 years and likely not during the past 20 million years. The current rate of increase is unprecedented during at least the past 20,000 years."

Another of the gases, nitrous oxide, is up 17 percent since 1750, more than in the past thousand years. Finally, methane gas has increased 151 percent–151 percent!—since 1750. The message is the same. We have a problem.

Now what does all this mean in human terms, especially if these lines continue to climb on the charts of the future? For one thing, it's hot, very hot. The decade of the 1990s was the hottest on record, probably reaching back for at least a thousand years. But it won't hold that record for long. The UN congregation of the world's scientists predicts that the earth's surface temperature could rise by as much as ten degrees over the next hundred years. Can you imagine what it will be like to add ten degrees to the average summer day in Memphis? But beyond that, the world's agriculture will be profoundly changed. Fertile lands will become deserts, and vast populations will be forced to relocate.

Moreover, it will soon get more lonely here on planet earth. The latest word is that more than one-third—that's one-third—of all species in several parts of the world could be destroyed over the next fifty years. Chris Leeds, conservation biologist of the University of Leeds, says: "Our analyses suggest that well over a million species could be threatened with extinction as a result of climate change." That's over a million species.

The story becomes more tragic when we contemplate the fate of the oceans. Some scientists had previously discounted global warming because some of the most dire predictions about rising temperatures had not come true. What they forgot was the capacity of the oceans to absorb heat and smother some of the immediate impact of global warming. But a recent issue of *Science* magazine has published reports that—as they put it—"link a warming trend in the upper 3,000 meters of the world's oceans to global warming caused by human activities." These reports are truly ominous for all living creatures. In particular, they confirm the IPCC predictions that most coral reefs will disappear within thirty to fifty years. And as the oceans continue to warm and melt the great ice shelves in the polar regions, the rise in sea level—perhaps as much as three feet over the next century—will wipe out vast lowland areas such as the Sundarbans in India and Bangladesh, the last, best habitat for the Bengal tiger. Large parts of Florida and Louisiana will surrender to the sea—sell your beach property soon! The barrier islands off Mobile Bay, where my parents took me camping as a boy and where I hope to take my own children, will recede into memory. These are just fragments, mere glimpses, of the future global warming has in store for us, our children, and grandchildren.

Well, I hope I have your attention. I hope you're willing to grant that we have a problem, a problem that threatens the quality of life here on earth. Can we do anything about it? I would like to give you a happy, simple answer to this question, but it is a complex one. It's not like we can just take our foot off the greenhouse accelerator, and bring the bus to a halt. Once it is heated, the ocean does not cool quickly. Once they have accumulated, greenhouse gases can linger for generations. But we can do something to change this picture for the better. The future is not an either-or proposition, and we can mitigate some of the worst possibilities. We can cool the fires under global warming to prevent it from becoming global burning. In my next speech I hope to show you how.

WORKS CONSULTED

"Americans Consider Global Warming Real, But Not Alarming." Gallup News Service. 9 Apr. 2001. 17 Apr. 2001<http://www.gallup.com/poll/Releases/PrO10409.asp>.

Davis, Robert. "Cost of Global Warming: 1 Million Species." *USA Today*. 7 Jan. 2004. 8 Jan. 2004 <http://www.usatoday.com/news/science/2004-01-07-global-warming_x.htm>.

"Feeling the Heat." *Time* 9 Apr. 2001: 22–39.

"Governments Agree: Global Warming Impact Serious." Environment News Service. 19 Feb. 2001. 17 Apr. 2001 <http://ens.lycos.com/ens/feb2001/20011-02-19-01.html>.

"Grim Future Forecast for World's Coastal Areas." Environment News Service. 17 Apr. 2001. 18 Apr. 2001 <http://ens-news.com/ens/apr2001/2001L-04-17-06.html>.

Lazaroff, Cat. "Warming Oceans Attributed to Greenhouse Gases." Environment News Service. 16 Apr. 2001. 17 Apr. 200l <http://ens.lycos.com/ens/apr2001/20011-04-16-06.html>.

Petit, Charles W. "Polar Meltdown." *U.S. News & World Report* 28 Feb. 2000: 65–74.

Shute, Nancy. "The Weather Turns Wild." *U.S. News & World Report* 5 Feb. 2001: 44–52.

Summary for Policymakers: A Report of Working Group I of the [United Nations] Intergovernmental Panel on Climate Change. January 2001. 17 Apr. 2001 <http://www.usgcrp.gov/ipcc/wg1spm.pdf>.

Building Powerful Arguments

16

OUTLINE

This chapter will help you

- support and prove your points
- develop effective patterns of reasoning
- select appropriate designs for your persuasive arguments
- avoid defects of evidence, proof, and reasoning

Speech is power: Speech is to persuade.

RALPH WALDO EMERSON

As he completed his speech, "Cooling the World's Fever," Joshua Logan knew that his persuasive effort had been effective. Listeners seemed concerned and attentive as he presented his *evidence*. They nodded in agreement as he developed compelling *proofs* to support his points. At the end of the speech, many of them seemed ready to accept his *argument* that global warming would require far-reaching changes both at the level of government and in the ways people lived (see his entire speech at the end of this chapter).

There is a kind of persuasion—**manipulative persuasion**—that has become part and parcel of life in media America. Such persuasion works by suggestion, colorful images, appealing music, and attractive spokespersons. It reveals itself in thirty-second television commercials that sell us everything from deodorant to political candidates. Such persuasion is not *always* unethical, because it often supports good and useful causes. But it is not inherently ethical, because it circumvents or ignores decisions that are based on a careful consideration of supporting evidence and arguments. It avoids the *ethical burden of justification.*

There is another kind of persuasion that is more a part of the Western tradition reaching back over several thousand years to the speeches of Pericles and Demosthenes in ancient Greece. This kind of persuasion—which we call **argumentative persuasion**—works by building arguments out of evidence and reasoning. It displays patterns of reasoning for critical inspection, and asks for audience agreement and action. It is not *always* ethical, because evil speakers can sometimes twist evidence and disguise bad reasoning, deceiving even careful listeners. But it is inherently ethical, because it takes up the burden of justification, addresses itself to our judgment rather than to our impulses, and honors the intellectual behaviors that make us human.

Argumentative persuasion is the business of this chapter. In this chapter we consider ways *to build powerful arguments that deserve respectful attention from thoughtful listeners.* We will cover how to develop evidence and proofs, build patterns of reasoning, find the right design for persuasive speeches, and avoid defective evidence, proofs, and reasoning.

Developing Evidence and Proofs

In Chapter 8 we explored the use of supporting materials. In persuasive speaking, these materials function as **evidence**, the foundation on which ethical argument builds.

Supporting Materials as Evidence

To test your skills and expand your understanding of the persuasive process, go to **Lesson 9: Persuasive Speaking** and go through the videos, exercises, and tips provided.

VideoLab

In their role as evidence in persuasive speaking, supporting materials do some special work. *Facts and figures, for example, are often the ultimate justification for asking us to believe or act in different ways.*[1] They can be especially important during the awareness phase of the persuasive process, when they expose a reality that calls for action.

In persuasive speaking, *examples can awaken feelings that make listeners want to act*. In her speech opposing discrimination against women in news organizations, LaDell Patterson wanted to arouse indignation over unfair treatment. She decided to offer the example of Laura Stepp, a reporter for the *Washington Post:*

> **Ms. Stepp recalled that while a *Washington Post* lawyer was reading one of her stories, she commented that she hoped it would land on the front page because of its importance. His reply to her was, "All you have to do is shake your little fanny and they'll put it on the front page." When she objected, he said he had no idea that the remark was offensive.**

This example, one of many in LaDell's speech, helped prepare her listeners emotionally for the reforms she would offer.

In persuasive speeches, *narratives can carry listeners to the scene of a problem and make them witnesses to a living drama*. Student speaker Kirsten Lientz illustrated this function when she opened a speech with the following narrative:

> **It's a cold, icy December afternoon. You hear a distant crash, then screams, and finally the unending moan of a car horn fills the silence. You rush the short distance to the scene of the crash, where you find an SUV overturned with a young woman and two small boys inside. The woman and one of the boys climb from the wreckage unhurt; the other boy, however, is pinned between the dashboard and the roof of the car, unconscious and not breathing.**
>
> **Would you know what to do? Or would you stand there wishing you did? These events are real. Bob Flath saved this child with the skills he acquired at his company's first aid workshop.**

After this dramatic narrative introduction, Kirsten's listeners were prepared to listen to her speech urging them to take the first aid course offered at her university.

When you use testimony in a persuasive speech, you call on experts as witnesses to support your position. Expert testimony is most effective when

- the audience knows little about the issue because it is new or complicated;
- listeners don't feel that the issue affects them directly; and/or
- listeners lack the ability or motivation to analyze the situation independently.[2]

Introduce your witnesses carefully, pointing out their credentials. To support her call for air safety improvements, one of our students, Juli Pardell, cited eight authoritative sources of information. In his plea for organ donors, Paul Fowler, another student, cited four reputable books. It was not just Juli or Paul speaking—it was *all* these sources of testimony together, supporting the speaker's voice.

Personal experience with a situation can qualify a speaker's testimony as was the case when former New York City Mayor Rudy Giuliani testified before the 9/11 commission.

Witnesses who testify *against* their apparent self-interest are called **reluctant witnesses**. They provide some of the most powerful evidence available in persuasion. For example, Joshua Logan's criticism of President Bush's environmental decisions in the speech reprinted at the end of this chapter was more effective because he spoke as a Republican who had voted for the president.

In ethical persuasive speaking, you should rely mainly on expert testimony. Use prestige or lay testimony as secondary sources of evidence. You can use prestige testimony to stress values you want listeners to embrace. You can use lay testimony to relate an issue to the lives of listeners. Keep in mind that when you quote others, you are associating yourself with them. Be careful with whom you associate!

As you search for evidence, keep an open mind. Consider different points of view, so that you don't simply present one perspective without being aware of others. Gather more evidence than you think you will need so that you have a wide range from which to choose. Be sure you have facts, figures, or expert testimony for each of the major points you want to make. Use multiple sources and types of evidence to strengthen your case.

Developing Proofs

VideoLab

After viewing the video clips in **VideoLab Drill 9.4: Aristotle's Persuasive Proofs**, complete the quiz to test your understanding of how persuasive speakers use different kinds of proof.

In building strong arguments, persuaders must develop powerful proofs. **Proofs** may be based on evidence, may tap into our emotional reactions, may be based on our social heritage, or may call on the personal leadership qualities of speakers in an effort to influence us.

The nature of proof has been studied since the Golden Age of Greece. In his *Rhetoric* Aristotle identified three forms of proof. The first, **logos**, recognizes that we respond to reason. *At least we like to think that we are reasonable creatures.* When speeches make good sense to us, when they are grounded in strong evidence and move logically to the conclusions they want us to accept, we find them hard to resist.

Ethics Alert! 16.1

Guidelines for the Ethical Use of Evidence

1. Provide evidence from credible sources.
2. Identify your sources of evidence.
3. Use evidence that can be verified by other experts.
4. Acknowledge disagreements among experts.
5. Do not withhold any important evidence.
6. Use expert testimony to establish facts, prestige testimony to enhance credibility, and lay testimony to create identification.
7. Quote or paraphrase testimony accurately.

The second, **pathos**, affirms that we can be touched by appeals to personal feelings such as fear, pity, and anger. Examples and narratives often provide the evidence this kind of proof emphasizes, just as Ladell Patterson aroused indignation with her story of Laura Stepp's humiliating experience as a woman journalist.

The third form, **ethos**, recognizes that we respond to the personal qualities of speakers, to our perceptions of their competence, character, good will, and dynamism. When we find these qualities attractive, we *want* to agree with speakers. When these qualities are negative or lacking, speakers will have a hard time winning us over. We are also affected by the credibility of the evidence cited in a speech. If we respect the people you quote in your speech, we will listen respectfully to their testimony. If we are not impressed by them, you have created an additional problem for yourself.

In our time, the work of many scholars has confirmed the presence of a fourth type of proof, **mythos**, which suggests that we respond to appeals to the traditions and values of our culture and to the legends and folktales that embody them.[3] We are social creatures who build much of our individual identity on our membership in groups, ranging from churches and universities to cities, states, and nations. If you can make a connection between your proposal and this social and cultural identity, listeners will give your ideas a careful hearing.

A persuasive speech rarely relies on a single kind of proof. Each type of proof brings its own coloration and strength to the fabric of persuasion. For this reason, perhaps, the traditional forms of proof are often discussed as though they were of equal importance to persuasion. But in manipulative persuasion, ethos, pathos, and mythos may be used more frequently than logos. Soft drink and automobile commercials rarely treat us as reasoning creatures.

On the other hand, the kind of ethical persuasion we stress in this chapter, argumentative persuasion, centers on logos and assigns supporting roles to ethos, mythos, and pathos. Even if these latter forms of proof are vital in adding life, color, and human interest to persuasion, they still serve to augment the central driving force of ethical persuasion, which is its appeal to our rational nature. These priorities among the forms of proof are shown in Figure 16.1.

In the section that follows, we discuss ethos, pathos, and mythos as we build up to the central importance of logos. We shall concentrate on the strengths and qualities of these proofs so that you may weave them effectively into your own persuasive speech.

Proof by Ethos. When you speak, listeners must sense that you are a person of strong conviction and that you know what you are talking about. Your sincerity and personal commitment must be beyond question. Listeners must feel that they can trust you—that you will not distort the truth for personal advantage. Ideally, they will also conclude that you are a likeable person who in turn likes them—that you are a person of goodwill.[4]

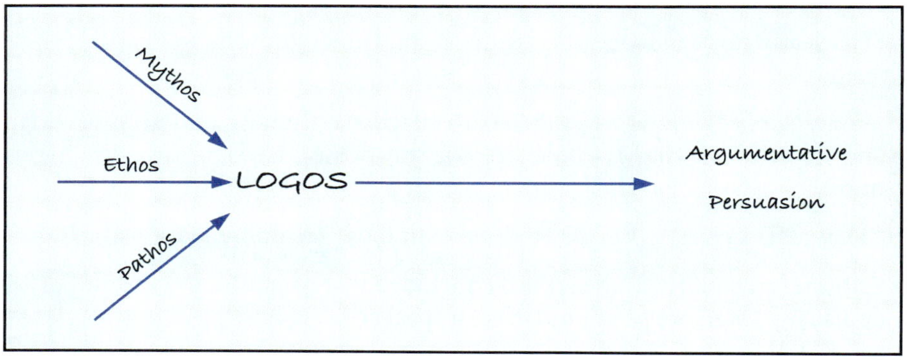

Figure 16.1
Proof Priorities in Argumentative Persuasion

Trustworthiness is an important dimension of proof by ethos. Former President Carter instills confidence when he speaks on humanitarian issues.

Clearly, listeners are influenced (both pro and con) by the credibility of speakers. Social scientists have discovered that credibility is a dynamic, not a stable quality: it changes constantly during a speech, according to the reactions of listeners.[5] Credibility cannot be separated clearly from anything you do or say. As you stand to speak, listeners may have already formed some impressions of your character, ability, good will, and confidence. This is your **initial credibility**. When you sit down after your speech, listeners will have definitely formed impressions of you, which is your **terminal credibility**. Even terminal credibility is dynamic, subject to revision as listeners discuss a speech in the moments and days after it is presented. Of course, the two moments of initial and terminal credibility may differ substantially, depending on how you impress listeners during your speech. Your terminal credibility when one speech concludes becomes your initial credibility when you present another.

What happens while you are actually speaking is what is known as your **emerging credibility**. These changes can be very complex, and sometimes quite dramatic. We recall a student who, as a result of some very unpleasant speaking experiences before taking our class, suffered from acute communication apprehension. His nervousness caused him to read his first two speeches, speaking in a monotone and avoiding eye contact. It was hard to tell whether his speeches had good content because they were presented so poorly. Outside class we had worked with him repeatedly, trying to build his confidence, exploring the basis of his fear, offering tips and encouragement. Finally, on one particular day, he broke through the wall he had built between himself and listeners. The process of his emerging credibility, as we experienced it that day, can be reconstructed in the following sequence of moments:

1. *Initial credibility* (as the moment of the speech approached): We are smiling encouragement, but thinking to ourselves, "This is going to be painful."
2. "Well, he does look more comfortable. He is actually making eye contact! He is even smiling, and what a nice smile! Lights up the room."
3. "He clearly cares a lot about arts education. Didn't know he was capable of such feeling."
4. "Wow, he really knows his stuff. That's effective testimony, and impressive facts and statistics. Moving example too. The way he just used language—first-class mind."
5. "That makes good sense. I'll go along with those recommendations."
6. *Terminal credibility* (as the speech concluded in a congratulatory round of applause): "Well, we've got ourselves a speaker!"

The interesting thing about this experience is that more than the audience changed their assessment of credibility that day. The speaker had risen in his own estimation, and he now believed in himself. The last time we heard from him, he had just finished law school and had accepted a position in San Francisco.

The sources of information you cite in your speech provide another form of proof by ethos. Listeners will also evaluate these sources in terms of their competence, character, goodwill, and power. If the evaluation of these sources is positive, audiences will be more inclined to accept your position. Let's look at how student speaker Heide Nord used the ethos of her sources to help persuade her listeners to change their attitudes about suntanning. To support the claim "We should avoid prolonged exposure to the sun," Heide emphasized expert testimony supplemented with lay testimony:

> **The most recent *Consumer Report* of the Food and Drug Administration tells us, "Prolonged exposure to sunlight without protection is responsible for about 90 percent of skin cancer." The article describes the case of Wendell Scarberry, a skin cancer patient who has had over a hundred surgeries. Wendell talks about the seriousness of the disease and urges us to be careful about sun exposure. "You can't cure skin cancer," he says, "by just having the doc whack it off." Finally, the American Cancer Society in its pamphlet *Fry Now Pay Later* says that skin cancer most often occurs among people who spend a lot of time in the sun, especially if they have been overexposed during their teens or twenties. Well, that's where most of us are right now. The FDA, the American Cancer Society, and Mr. Scarberry form a chorus of credibility, and we ought to listen to them.**

Heidi's obvious commitment, together with the combination of expert and lay testimony, made her speech highly credible.

Clearly, proof based on the testimony of reliable, competent, and trustworthy sources is extremely important in persuasive speaking. *Identify your sources and point out why they are qualified to speak on the subject.* It is also helpful if you can say that the testimony is recent. For maximum effect, quote experts directly rather than paraphrase them.

Proof by Pathos. People usually respond strongly when they feel angry, afraid, guilty, excited, or compassionate toward others. If used ethically, appeals to personal feelings can change bad attitudes or move people to act for good causes.[6]

When speakers tell personal stories, emotional appeals can be especially effective. Personal narratives blend the power of feeling with strong credibility. During a congressional debate on handgun control legislation, James Brady, the presidential press secretary who was shot during the assassination attempt on President Reagan, testified before the U.S. Senate Judiciary Subcommittee. Speaking from his wheelchair, he said:

> **There was a day when I walked the halls of this Senate and worked closely with many of you and your staffs. There was a wonderful day when I was fortunate enough to serve the President of the United States in a capacity I had dreamed of all my life. And for a time, I felt that people looked up to me. Today, I can tell you how hard it is to have people speaking down to me. But nothing has been harder than losing the independence and control we all so value in life. I need help getting out of bed, help taking a shower, and help getting dressed.**
>
> **There are some who oppose a simple seven-day waiting period for handgun purchases because it would inconvenience gun buyers. Well, I guess I am paying for their convenience. And I am one of the lucky ones. I survived being shot through the head. Other shooting victims are not as fortunate.[7]**

Motives	Personal Emotions	Possible Connection
Health/Safety	Fear/Security	Does my subject affect the personal well-being and safety of listeners?
Nurturance/ Altruism	Sympathy/Caring for others	Does my subject invite feelings of sympathy and benevolence for the fate of others?
Family/Significant Others	Love	Does my subject involve special feelings for loved ones?
Self-Actualization	Ambition	Does my subject envision success and promise self-satisfaction over some important achievement?
Fairness	Anger over injustice	Do my proposals promise to restore justice?

Figure 16.2

Connecting Pathos with Motives

Often, appeals to emotions are the only way to convince people of the human dimensions of a problem or the need for immediate action. So how can you use proof by pathos effectively? Consider again the section on motivation in Chapter 5. Motives, you may recall, drive our behavior. We tend to become emotional when our motives are either frustrated or satisfied. Therefore, effective appeals to pathos often connect the speaker's points in personal ways with this underlying bedrock of motives. Figure 16.2 illustrates how such connections might be made to relevant and productive motives.

As powerful as emotional proof may be, it should be used with caution. If an appeal to feeling is too obvious, audiences may suspect you are trying to manipulate them. Appeals to negative emotions such as fear or guilt are especially tricky because they can boomerang, causing listeners to discredit both you and your speech. When you use appeals to feeling, justify them with solid evidence. In your presentation, let your voice and body language understate rather than overstate the emotional appeal. Don't engage in theatrics.

Proof by Mythos. Appeals to the values, faith, and feelings that make up our social identity can be a powerful source of proof. Such appeals, often expressed in traditional stories, sayings, and symbols, assume that audiences value their membership in a culture and share its heritage. Communication scholar Martha Solomon Watson has noted, "Rhetoric which incorporates mythical elements taps into rich cultural reservoirs."[8]

Appeals to cultural identity often call on patriotism and remind us of our heroes or enemies. They may be based on political narratives, such as the story of George Washington's harsh winter at Valley Forge. They may reassure us that ours is "the land of opportunity."[9] Appeals to mythos also may be based on economic legends, such as American stories of success through hard work and thrift that celebrate the rise to power from humble beginnings. These stories justify economic power in our society while assuring the powerless that they too can make it, if only they have "the right stuff."

Appeals to cultural identity may also draw on religious narratives. Sacred documents such as the Bible provide a rich storehouse of parables, used not only for proof purposes in sermons but in political speeches as well.[10] Note how President Bush appealed to religious mythos in his 2003 State of the Union address to justify his faith-based initiative proposal: "There is power—wonder-working power—in the goodness and idealism and faith of the American people."[11] His "wonder-working power" allusion was to an old hymn well known to many of his audience, especially to his target audience of religious conservatives.

To create the sense of mythos, stories clearly need not be retold in their entirety each time they are invoked. Because they are so familiar, allusions to them may be sufficient. The culturetypes discussed in Chapter 12 are often called into service, because they compress myths into a few provocative words. Words like *progress, science,* and *education* have positive mythic overtones, and words like *terrorist, pollution,* and *weapons of mass destruction* are negatively charged with mythic meaning. In his speech accepting the Democratic presidential nomination in 1960, John F. Kennedy called on the myth of the American frontier to move Americans to action:

> **The New Frontier of which I speak is not a set of promises—it is a set of challenges. It sums up not what I intend to offer the American people, but what I intend to ask of them.[12]**

The Western frontier is a major source of mythos in American speeches. *American Progress,* a painting by American artist John Gast, portrays many icons and ideographs. Which ones can you identify?

This appeal to cultural identity emerged as a central theme of Kennedy's presidency. He didn't need to refer directly to the legends of Daniel Boone and Davy Crockett, or to the tales of wagons pushing west to meet the challenges that lay ahead—he was able to conjure up those thoughts in listeners with the phrase "the New Frontier." Such brief allusions can also be used to refute exploitative uses of the myth. For example, an antismoking billboard we saw in Montana shows two "Marlboro-type" cowboys with the caption, "Bob, I've got emphysema!"

How can you use proof by mythos in a classroom speech? Once again we return to the earlier discussion of motivation in Chapter 5. The social motives discussed there, which tend to engage group emotions, may also suggest guides to the development of proof by mythos. Figure 16.3 shows how connections might be made between mythos and motives.

Let's see how Robert Owens used such appeals to urge stronger action against drug traffic in urban slums. Robert wanted to establish that "we must win the battle against drugs on the streets of America." He supported this statement by creating a sense of outrage in listeners over the betrayal of the American dream in urban America:

> **Read the latest issue of *Time* magazine, and you'll meet an America you never sang about in the songs you learned in school. It's an America in which hope, faith, and dreams are nothing but a bitter memory.**

Figure 16.3

Connecting Mythos with Motives

Motives	Group Emotion	Possible Connection
Maintain Control/ Stability	Respect for/love of tradition	Does my proposal reaffirm traditions that my listeners want to protect?
Honor affiliations	Feelings of group pride/patriotism	Does my subject connect with audience feelings of loyalty to a group and pride in membership?
Preserve group identity	Respect for heroes/ great deeds	Does my speech connect with models of heroism and memories of great events? Does my speech call upon values that are vital to group identity?

> **They call America a land of hope, but it's hard to hope when your mother is a cocaine addict on Susquehanna Avenue in North Philadelphia.**
>
> **They call America a land of faith, but what faith can you cling to when even God seems to have abandoned the street corners to the junkies and the dealers!**
>
> **They call America a land of dreams, but what kind of dreams can you have when all you hear at night as you lie in bed are the curses and screams of buyers and dealers.**
>
> **We might be able to redeem the hope, the faith, and the dreams Americans like to talk about. But we have to do more than just declare war on drugs. We've got to *go* to war, and we've got to win! If we don't, the crack in the Liberty Bell may only symbolize a deadly drug that is destroying the American spirit all over this land.**

These appeals to a betrayed mythos justified Robert's concluding plea for a broad-based, aggressive campaign to rid America of its drug culture. *The unique function of appeals to cultural identity is to help listeners understand how the speaker's recommendations fit into the total belief and value patterns of their group.* This gives such proof a special role in the persuasive process we discussed in the last chapter. It can help integrate new attitudes and action into the group's culture.

Like appeals to personal feeling, appeals to cultural identity can be a great good or a considerable evil. At their best, such appeals heighten our appreciation of who we are *as a people* and promote consistency between cultural values and public policy. However, when misused, these appeals can make it seem that there is only *one legitimate culture.* Appeals to cultural identity can abuse those who choose not to conform to the dominant values. Such appeals can tear apart the social fabric of our society, and even of our world.

Speaker's Notes 16.1 summarizes the four forms of appeal.

Patterns of Reasoning

A persuasive speech that is both ethical and effective will contain a sufficient array of evidence and proofs based on ethos, pathos, and mythos. Yet these proofs are all secondary to the central focus of ethical persuasion: proof by logos. Thoughtful listeners must be convinced by the patterns of reasoning you develop in your speech to accept your conclusions and recommendations. Such listeners will intuitively apply the following critical tests:

- Have central issues and terms been clearly and fairly defined?
- Does the speech reason from acceptable principles of value and conduct?

Speaker's Notes 16.1

When and How to Use Proof

1. To increase awareness and understanding, use rational appeals based on facts, statistics, and expert testimony *(logos)*
2. To communicate the human dimensions of a problem, stir listeners with moving examples and stories *(pathos)*
3. To reassure listeners that you are a credible speaker, convince them that you know what you are talking about, that you are fair and honest in depicting a problem, and that you have their interests at heart *(ethos)*
4. To connect a problem with the general welfare, show how it relates to traditions, cultural values, and symbols of group identity. *(mythos)*

- Is the speech anchored firmly in reality?
- Does the speech reason acceptably from similar or parallel cases?
- Does the speech follow a clear persuasive design?
- Does the speech avoid classic flaws of reasoning?

In the sections that follow, we shall consider each of these tests, explain its meaning, and indicate how you might pass it successfully.

Definitions of Central Concepts

The Greek philosopher Socrates was one of the first to insist that all ethical persuasion must begin with clear agreement on the meanings of the important terms in dispute. In Plato's dialogue, the *Phaedrus*, Socrates criticizes Lysias, a popular rhetorician of the day, for not defining terms at the beginning of his speech.

Have you ever had a heated discussion with someone, only to discover later that the two of you were not even talking about the same things? If speakers and listeners don't share such understanding from the outset, it is difficult to communicate. When the speaker and audience come from different backgrounds, careful definitions are even more important. Opening his speech on "gender bending," Brandon Rader was careful to offer the following definition: "If you are a gender bender, you dress or act or think or talk like people in your community assume someone of the opposite sex would do or act or talk or dress." Having shared this understanding, Brandon went on to argue that most assumptions about gender benders are quite wrong. Definitions like Brandon's take a term that may be unfamiliar to many audience members and translate it into simpler, more familiar language.

Not all definitions involve translating technical language into familiar terms. Some of the most interesting definitions offered by speakers are efforts to change listeners' perspectives so that they will be more sympathetic to the arguments that will follow. Should alcohol be defined as a drug? Should a fetus be defined as a human being? Definitions that affirm or deny such questions can prepare the way for elaborate arguments advocating different kinds of public policy.

In the 1968 Memphis sanitation strike that led to the assassination of Dr. Martin Luther King Jr., the workers marched carrying signs that read, "I Am a Man." This simple definitional statement was actually the tip of a complex underlying moral argument. The strikers were claiming they were *not* treated like men in social and economic terms.

An especially interesting effort to redefine perspectives occurred in a speech by Richard Corlin, president of the American Medical Association, at the 2001 AMA annual meeting (see his speech

Definitions are an important component of arguments as demonstrated by sanitation workers marching following the assassination of Dr. Martin Luther King Jr. in Memphis.

in Appendix B). Alarmed over the rise in gun-related fatalities, Dr. Corlin wanted to redefine gun violence in America as a "public health crisis." Here is the section near the beginning of his speech in which he introduces this attempted change of perspectives:

> **With the preponderance of weapons these days, it comes as no surprise that gun violence—both self-inflicted and against others—is now a serious public health crisis. No one can avoid its brutal and ugly presence. No one. Not physicians. Not the public. And most certainly—not the politicians—no matter how much they might want to.**
>
> **Let me tell you about part of the problem. In the 1990s, the CDC [Centers for Disease Control] had a system in place for collecting data about the results of gun violence. But Congress took away its funding, thanks to heavy lobbying by the anti-gun control groups. You see, the gun lobby doesn't want gun violence addressed as a public health issue. Because that data would define the very public health crisis that these powerful interests don't want acknowledged. And they fear that such evidence-based data could be used to gain support to stop the violence. Which, of course, means talking about guns and the deaths and injuries associated with them.[13]**

Having introduced a perspective that was no doubt novel for many members of his audience, Dr. Corlin went on build his extensive arguments to support it. By the end of his speech, the "public health crisis" he had identified near the opening of his speech had evolved into a "uniquely American epidemic."As these examples make clear, definitions can be *the fundamental issues at the heart of controversies.* If you attempt to redefine your audience's perspective on a subject, you may have to defend your effort with all the evidence, proof, and sincerity you can muster.

Reasoning from Principle

As we absorb the folkways of our culture, we acquire principles that guide the way we think and live. Such guides often become part of our formal faith. For example "freedom of speech" is written into the Constitution of the United States as a principle of government.

When we **reason from principle**, we use such principles to justify our value judgments and our calls to action. Such reasoning is sometimes called **deductive**, because it deduces from some general principle a conclusion about a particular relevant case. Consider a hypothetical example. A speaker begins by reminding listeners of a principle she believes they all accept (or at least give lip service to): "We all believe in freedom of speech." In terms of formal logic, such a principle is known as the **major premise**. Next, the speaker relates a specific issue to that principle, creating what is called the **minor premise**: "Melvin would like to speak." Finally, the speaker reaches her **conclusion**: "We should let Melvin speak." Because of their respect for the principle expressed in the major premise, many listeners would nod assent, even though they might not particularly like Melvin.

This underlying pattern of major premise/minor premise/conclusion is known in formal logic as a "syllogism." When it occurs in persuasion about public issues, Aristotle called it an **enthymeme**. The difference is that public speakers must deal with matters that are uncertain and surrounded by contingencies, or "what ifs." The conclusions that they draw are probable, not the mathematical certainties of formal logic. Enthymemes are vital in public persuasion: Aristotle described them as the most important rhetorical resource. In his 2003 State of the Union address, President Bush announced a major premise that allowed him to justify conclusions ranging from a massive program to relieve AIDS in Africa to a threat to invade Iraq. Here is what he said:

> **The American flag stands for more than our power and our interests. Our founders dedicated this country to the cause of human dignity, the rights of every person and the possibilities of every life. This conviction leads us into the world to help the afflicted, and defend the peace, and confound the designs of evil men.[14]**

The wording of this principle reveals its dependence on mythos as a supporting form of proof. Because it begins by reminding listeners of shared values, reasoning from principle is useful for establishing common ground with reluctant audiences. Such reasoning can also point out inconsistencies between beliefs and behaviors—the gap between what we practice and what we preach. For example, if you can show that the censorship of song lyrics is inconsistent with freedom of speech, then you will have presented a good reason for people to condemn such censorship. *We are more likely to change a practice that is inconsistent with cherished principles or values than we are to change the principles or values.* Because people like to be consistent and maintain the integrity of their values, reasoning from principle becomes a powerful way to achieve harmony among attitudes, beliefs, and values.

Occasionally, the pattern of reasoning in an enthymeme will not be entirely visible in a speech. For example, the major premise may not be stated: speakers may simply assume that the principle it expresses is already accepted by listeners. When offered appropriate cues, listeners will think of these principles and complete the speaker's line of thought on their own. As she spoke of the problems of Native Americans, Ashley Roberson spent much of her time proving the reality of "social injustice on reservations," which functioned as the minor premise in her enthymeme. She did not think it necessary to state the implied major premise, "Social injustice in the United States should not be tolerated." Instead, she felt justified in concluding, "We must eradicate social injustice on reservations." As she indicted the School of the Americas, Amanda Miller concentrated on demonstrating that the school had been training terrorists. She did not think it necessary to state the major premise, "The United States should try to end terrorism, not perpetuate it." Instead, she felt justified in drawing her conclusion, "We ought to close the School of the Americas now."

We should realize, however, that not all members of the audience might accept principles that seem to us beyond question. For example, some researchers have discovered that if you read the Bill of Rights to people without telling them it is part of the United States Constitution, an alarming percentage will describe it as "radical" or "communistic." Therefore, you should not take such principles for granted. You may have to explain and defend them to reinforce your listeners' belief in them. You may need to reawaken faith in the principles by telling stories or offering examples that demonstrate their value.

Another point critical to such reasoning comes when a speaker tries to show that a condition or situation—the minor premise—actually exists. People may not argue passionately about the *principle* of environmental protection, but assertions about a specific case of pollution may be subject to dispute. Your persuasive efforts may have to focus on that issue, emphasizing the kind of reasoning we discuss in the next section.

As you develop a principled pattern of reasoning for your speech, keep these cautions in mind:

1. *Be certain your audience will accept the major premises on which your arguments are based.* Remind listeners why they believe as they do. Cite prestige sources who testify to the importance of such faith. Use appeals to feeling and to cultural identity to reinforce the principles. Use rational appeals to show their practical importance.

Speaker's Notes 16.2

Reasoning from Principle

1. If there is any doubt, remind listeners of why they honor the principles from which you reason.
2. Demonstrate that the conditions relevant to the principle you invoke actually exist.
3. Show how these conditions and principles are related and why that relationship requires action.
4. Check for flaws in your reasoning.
5. Make it easy for listeners to enact the conclusion you advance.

2. *Demonstrate the existence of relevant conditions.* This, as we shall see in the next section, is where empirical reasoning joins with principled reasoning to build convincing arguments.

3. *Explain the relationship between principles and conditions (the major and minor premises).* Don't expect your audience to get the point automatically. Listeners may not see the connection between their responsibility to maintain the natural beauty of their country and specific environmental conditions that need reform. Help them by drawing the point explicitly.

4. *Be certain your reasoning is free from flaws and fallacies.* We discuss such problems of argument in the final section of this chapter.

5. *Be sure your conclusion offers a clear direction for listeners.* Don't leave them foundering without a clear idea as to what you want them to do.

Speaker's Notes 16.2 reminds you of these points.

Dr. Richard Corlin, former president of the American Medical Association, used many types of evidence in his speech on gun control. His use of analogy was especially striking.

Reasoning from Reality

Thoughtful listeners must have no doubt that persuasive speakers have a true understanding of the situation they would like to change. **Reasoning from reality** depends either on the speaker's personal experience or on the observations of others. These latter observations appear in the facts, statistics, or expert testimony used in the speech. Reasoning from reality is sometimes called **inductive**, in that it draws general conclusions from a consideration of particular instances. Inductive reasoning is the classic method of scientific investigation, and "science" for many Americans remains a god term. If you can show that "science supports my argument," you will have strengthened your case.

Dr. Richard Corlin, in his presidential address before the American Medical Association on gun violence, was uniquely positioned to speak both from direct personal experience and as a careful observer of the work of other experts. In the section that follows, we can see how he reasons from reality, citing statistic after statistic, example after example, and uses contrast to highlight the importance of his evidence. Note also how he speaks *as a scientist addressing other scientists:*

> **In 1993 and 1994, we resolved that the AMA would, among other actions, "support scientific**

research and objective discussion aimed at identifying causes of and solutions to the crime and violence problem." Scientific research and objective discussion because we as physicians are—first and foremost—scientists. We need to look at the science of the subject, the data, and—if you will—the micro-data, before we make a diagnosis. Not until then can we agree upon the prognosis or decide upon a course of treatment.

First, let's go straight to the science that we do know. How does this disease present itself? Since 1962, more than a million Americans have died in firearm suicides, homicides, and unintentional injuries. In 1998 alone, 30,708 Americans died by gunfire:

- **17,424 in firearm suicides**
- **12,102 in firearm homicides**
- **866 in unintentional shootings**

Also in 1998, more than 64,000 people were treated in emergency rooms for non-fatal firearm injuries.

This is a uniquely American epidemic. In the same year that more than 30,000 people were killed by guns in America, the number in Germany was 1,164, in Canada, it was 1,034, in Australia 391, in England and Wales 211, and in Japan, the number for the entire year was 83.[15]

Although reasoning from principle and reasoning from reality may seem quite different, they actually work together. Reasoning from reality can reinforce principles so that they don't appear to be simply items of blind faith. For example, if we can demonstrate empirically that "free and open discussion actually results in better public decisions," then we bring both morality and practicality to the support of freedom of speech.

Even more to the point, reasoning from reality is critical for demonstrating the truth of the minor premise in an enthymeme. Is the censorship of song lyrics an actual threat, or is it merely some bogeyman in the minds of liberals? Again, testimony from those who wish to censor and who have the power to censor would authenticate the threat. Similarly, Ashley Roberson had to prove with facts, statistics, and examples that the problems existing on Native American reservations were of such magnitude that they constituted "social injustice." Clearly, reasoning from reality empowers reasoning from principle in persuasive speeches, and the two forms are often found woven together.

Reasoning from reality also implies an understanding of cause-effect relationships. In his speech on gun violence, Dr. Corlin, once he had described the magnitude of the actual problem, went on to explore its causes. One such cause identified the culture of violence accessible to young children through video games. As he put it:

The spread of gun-related injuries and death is especially tragic when it involves our children. Like young lungs and tar and nicotine—young minds are especially responsive to the deadliness of gun violence.

Lieutenant Colonel Dave Grossman, a West Point professor of psychology and military science, has documented how video games act as killing simulators, teaching our children not just to shoot—but to kill. Grossman, who calls himself an expert in "killology," cites as evidence the marksmanship of the two children, aged 11 and 13, in the Jonesboro, Arkansas shootings in 1998. Both shooters were avid video game players. And just like in a video game—they fired off 27 shots—and hit 15 people. Killing four of their fellow students—and a teacher. Such deadly accuracy is rare and hard to achieve—even by well-trained police and military marksmen.[16]

Speaker's Notes 16.3

Reasoning from Reality

1. Are your observations objective?
2. Have you observed enough?
3. Are your observations recent?
4. Are your observations representative of the situation?
5. Do your observations adequately justify your conclusion?
6. Have you read widely enough to see if experts agree?
7. If experts disagree, will you acknowledge this and explain your preference?
8. Have you verified your experts' credentials so you can present them in your speech?

As you incorporate reasoning from reality into your arguments, keep in mind these basic requirements (given as questions in Speaker's Notes 16.3):

- You must be objective enough to see the situation clearly. Be on guard not to let your biases warp your perceptions. Remind yourself that it is important to look at an issue from as many perspectives as possible.
- You must observe a sufficient number of instances. One or two isolated incidents cannot justify reality claims.
- Since situations surrounding relevant issues are constantly changing, you must be sure your observations are recent.
- Your observations must be truly representative of the situation. The exception does not prove the rule.
- Your observations must actually justify your conclusion. They must be relevant to the claim you wish to demonstrate.
- If your inductive exposure comes from library or Internet research, don't just accept the testimony of the first expert you encounter. Read more widely to see whether experts agree with each other, and if they disagree, decide which of them are most credible. Be prepared to justify and defend your decision in your speech.
- As you present facts, statistics, and expert testimony, be sure to introduce the experts who are the sources of the evidence. Establish their credentials to reassure thoughtful listeners. Beginning speakers often neglect this important requirement of successful persuasion.

InterConnections.LearnMore 16.1

Reasoning

Mission: Critical
http://www.sjsu.edu/depts/itl/
An interactive site containing explanations and exercises about the basic concepts of critical thinking; developed by Professor David Mesher for the Institute for Teaching and Learning at San Jose State University.

Inductive Reasoning
http://webpages.shepherd.edu/maustin/rhetoric/inductiv.htm
A website on inductive reasoning with good explanations, examples, and exercises; developed by Professor Michael Austin of Shepherd College.

Annual Review of Psychology (1999): Deductive Reasoning
http://www.findarticles.com/cf_0/m0961/1999_Annual/54442295/p1/article.jhtml
A scholarly review of theory and research on how people use deductive reasoning to reach decisions; authored by P. N. Johnson-Laird.

Argumentation and Critical Thinking Tutorial
http://sorrel.humboldt.edu/~act/
An interactive tutorial, with tests developed by Jay VerLinden, professor of communication at Humboldt State University.

Reasoning from Parallel Cases

Reasoning from parallel cases suggests that we can learn how to deal with a problem by considering a similar situation. This related situation becomes a model from which we can draw lessons.

Sometimes identified as **analogy**, such reasoning can be useful in helping us frame an unfamiliar, abstract, or difficult problem in terms of something that is more familiar, more concrete, or more easily understood. It also can be used to dramatize the speaker's claim: "If we don't deal with global warming, we might well find ourselves on the endangered species list—and not so far into the future! Just like the tiger and the elephant, our habitat is in crisis."

Dr. Corlin used a vivid analogy to underscore the importance of video games in acclimating susceptible young people into America's climate of gun violence. Here is how reasoning from parallel cases helped him both magnify the problem and bring it into the understanding of listeners:

> **I want you to imagine with me a computer game called "Puppy Shoot." In this game puppies run across the screen. Using a joystick, the game player aims a gun that shoots the puppies. The player is awarded one point for a flesh wound, three points for a body shot, and ten points for a head shot. Blood spurts out each time a puppy is hit—and brain tissue splatters all over whenever there's a head shot. The dead puppies pile up at the bottom of the screen. When the shooter gets to 1000 points, he gets to exchange his pistol for an Uzi, and the point values go up.**
>
> **If a game as disgusting as that were to be developed, every animal rights group in the country, along with a lot of other organizations, would protest, and there would be all sorts of attempts made to get the game taken off the market. Yet, if you just change puppies to people in the game I described, there are dozens of them already on the market—sold under such names as "Blood Bath," "Psycho Toxic," "Redneck Rampage," and "Soldier of Fortune."[17]**

As useful as analogical reasoning can be in dramatizing arguments, it can be even more useful in persuading listeners to accept solutions. For example, in the continuing debate over our nation's drug policy, those who favor legalizing "recreational" drugs frequently base their arguments on an analogy to Prohibition.[18] They claim that the Prohibition amendment caused more problems than it solved because it made drinking an adventure and led to the rise of a criminal empire. They then claim that our efforts to outlaw recreational drugs have had the same result. The reason, they say, is that it is impossible to ban a human desire—that to try to do so simply encourages contempt for the law. Moreover, they assert that legalizing drugs would help put the international drug dealers out of business, just as the repeal of Prohibition helped bring about the downfall of the gangsters of the 1930s. Finally, they argue, if drug sales were legal, it would be easier to control the quality of drugs, thus reducing the danger to users (parallel to the health problems associated with bootleg whiskey during Prohibition).

As this example shows, analogical reasoning emphasizes strategic points of comparison between similar situations. People on both sides of an issue will focus on these points, using evidence and proofs to defend or attack them. Opponents to legalizing drugs claim that there are many important differences between drugs and alcohol.[19] They say that alcohol is not as addictive for casual users as heroin or cocaine. They contend that legalization would multiply the drug problem, not reduce it, because it would make drugs more accessible and make them seem acceptable. They further suggest that since many drug abusers are prone to violence, the cost to society would be increased. Thus, the public debate rages on over these crucial points of comparison.

What makes analogical reasoning work? It is similar to the empirical reasoning from reality in that it seeks insight through careful observation. Analogy, however, concentrates *on one similar situation* rather than ranging across many. This means that although analogical reasoning may seem more concrete and interesting than some forms of inductive reasoning (such as that based often on statistical evidence), it can also be less reliable. Before you decide to develop an analogy as part of your

Speaker's Notes 16.4

Developing Powerful Arguments

1. Provide clear definitions of basic terms.
2. Justify arguments by reasoning from accepted principles.
3. Remind listeners of why they honor these principles.
4. Convince listeners that your arguments are based in reality.
5. Create a vivid sense of problem conditions.
6. In analogical reasoning, use a similar situation as a model from which to draw comparisons and conclusions that favor your position.
7. Build arguments to answer questions reasonable listeners might ask.

argument, be sure that the important similarities outweigh the dissimilarities. If you must strain to make an analogy fit, rely on other forms of reasoning.

Speaker's Notes 16.4 summarizes the essentials of powerful arguments.

The Interplay of Reasoning. Just as forms of proof must often be combined to establish the legitimacy and power of a speaker's proposal, so also do patterns of reasoning often interact in persuasive speeches. One model that displays this interaction clearly, and makes its components more visible, was developed by Stephen Toulmin, a British logician.[20] Toulmin's model of argument, shown in Figure 16.4, includes six primary elements: data, claim, warrant, backing, reservations, and qualifier.

Data. Data represent "hard" evidence in the form of facts, statistics, and expert testimony. The data confirm the existence of a given reality. Joshua Logan's speech, "Global Burning," reprinted at the end of the previous chapter, summarizes a considerable array of evidence to demonstrate the reality of global warming.

Claim. The claim is the conclusion the speaker draws from the data. The move from data to claim, because it involves drawing a general conclusion from particulars, is primarily inductive. Joshua wishes us to accept his claim that global warming is a threat to life on a global scale and that controlling it should be a personal, national, and international imperative.

Warrant. The warrant supplies the principle that justifies the movement from data to claim. It functions very much like a major premise, and it provides the deductive element of the model. When it authorizes us to draw conclusions from a similar case and the set of similarities is compelling and no significant dissimilarities exist, the warrant can also justify analogical reasoning. In Joshua's speech, the warrant is unspoken, but the sense of its power can be felt in the speech. We might reconstruct it as follows: "Whenever hundreds of scientists, working independently of each other in countries around the globe, come to the same or similar conclusions, we can place considerable faith in the results."

Figure 16.4

Toulmin's Model of Argument

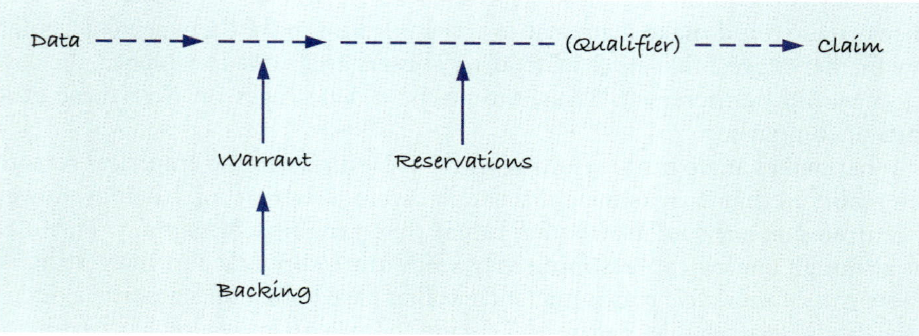

Ethics Alert! 16.2

Building Ethical Arguments

1. Emphasize logical reasoning built on the "hard" evidence of facts, statistics, and expert testimony.
2. Never compromise your integrity in a persuasive speech.
3. Always justify proof by pathos with hard evidence.
4. Never allow proof by mythos to become a mask for intolerance or an excuse to attack the rights of individuals who resist group values and culture.
5. Test the ethics of any persuasive proof or strategy by considering how it will be judged by a thoughtful listener.
6. Strive to achieve harmony among attitudes, beliefs, values, and actions.
7. As you research a problem, keep an open mind so that you can understand the various sides in a dispute.

Backing. In some arguments, the warrant may be contested, or several conflicting warrants may clash. To help resolve such disputes, backing in the form of additional justification may be introduced to strengthen the warrant. Had anyone questioned the principle implied in Joshua's warrant, he could have replied by pointing to past international research efforts on dread diseases or technological problems, such as the harnessing of atomic energy, to back his principle that when scientists agree on a global scale, you can rely on their conclusions.

Reservations. Reservations acknowledge conditions under which the claim may not follow. Ethical persuaders have an obligation to acknowledge such conditions when they are significant, and thoughtful listeners will expect them to. Not acknowledging such reservations risks real damage to one's ethos, should a critical listener point them out. Reservations are signaled by the word *unless*. Joshua might have introduced a reservation had he added, "Unless anyone can show that all these scientists were somehow mistaken, or in cahoots with each other to advance some political agenda, we must accept the ominous reality of global warming."

Qualifiers. Qualifiers are terms that express the force of the claim, taking into account possible reservations. Qualifiers often appear in such terms as *probably, almost certainly,* and *in all likelihood.* Joshua was especially confident of the power of his data and the certainty of his claim concerning global warming, so he did not find it necessary to introduce qualifiers.

You can use Toulmin's model of argument either as a critical template to help you become a more thoughtful listener, or to gain an overview of your own reasoning processes in a speech you are designing. In the latter case, you may be able to identify any weak points during preparation and correct them before you make your presentation.

Designs for Persuasive Speaking

Evidence, proof, and patterns of reasoning are not effective until they are framed into persuasive designs for your speech. Many of the designs used for informative speeches are also appropriate for persuasive speeches. Figure 16.5 provides guidelines on when to use them. The categorical design can be used to structure a

Figure 16.5

Selecting Persuasive Speech Designs

Design	Use When
Categorical	• Your topic invites thinking in familiar patterns, such as proving a plan will be safe, inexpensive, and effective. • Can be used to change attitudes or to urge action.
Comparison/ Contrast	• You want to demonstrate why your proposal is superior to another. Especially good for speeches in which you contend with opposing views.
Sequential	• Your speech contains a plan of action that must be carried out in specific order.
Problem-Solution	• Your topic presents a problem that needs to be solved and a solution that will solve it. Good for speeches involving attitudes and urging action.
Motivated-Sequence	• Your topic calls for action as the final phase of a five-step process that also involves, in order, arousing attention, demonstrating need, satisfying need, picturing the results, and calling for action.
Refutative	• You must answer strong opposition on a topic before you can establish your position. The opposing claims become main points for development. Attack weakest points first and avoid personal attacks.

persuasive argument, just as Joshua Logan develops three categories of technological improvement in the solution he offers to global warming (see his speech at the end of this chapter). The sequential design can outline the steps in a plan of action to make it seem practical. The comparative design works well for speeches that concentrate on developing proposals for action. Following this pattern, you might compare the superior features of your proposal with less adequate features of competing proposals.

Three designs are especially suited to persuasive speeches: the problem-solution design, the motivated sequence design, and the refutative design.

Problem-Solution Design

If you have chosen a speech topic that would work well with the Problem-Solution design, fill out the worksheet and double-check your work using the **Problem-Solution Design Outline Worksheet** and **Checklist** under **Selecting a Speech Design**.

Go to http://college.hmco.com/eduspace/

The **problem-solution design** first convinces listeners that there is a problem and then shows them how to deal with it. The solution can involve changing attitudes and beliefs or taking action. It is sometimes hard to convince listeners that a problem exists or that it is serious. People have an unfortunate tendency to ignore problems until they reach a critical stage. You can counteract this tendency by vividly depicting the crisis that will surely occur unless your audience makes a change.

As you focus on the problem, use substantive evidence and combinations of proof to demonstrate that a serious problem exists. Reason from the reality of the situation by using presentation aids, dramatic examples, and colorful imagery to make the problem loom large in the minds of listeners. Reasoning from principle can help justify a solution ("Because better education means a better future for our children, we must pass this tax increase to upgrade the school system"). Analogical reasoning can help convince listeners that a proposed solution will work ("Here's how New Yorkers solved this problem. . .").

A problem-solution speech opposing a tuition increase at your university might build on the following general design:

Thesis statement: We must defeat the tuition increase.

I. Problem: The proposal to raise tuition is a disaster!
  A. The increase will create hardships for many students.
    1. Many current students will have to drop out.
    2. New students will be discouraged from enrolling.
  B. The increase will create additional problems for the university and the community.
    1. Decreased attendance means decreased revenue.
    2. Decreased revenue will reduce the university's community services.
    3. Reduced service will mean reduced support from contributors.
    4. The ironic result will be: another tuition increase!

II. Solution: Defeat the proposal to raise tuition.
  A. Sign our petition against the tuition increase.
  B. Write letters to your state legislators.
  C. Write a letter to your local newspaper.
  D. Attend our campus rally next Wednesday.

When the problem can be identified clearly and the solution is concrete and simple, the problem-solution design works well in persuasive speeches.

As you are planning a problem-solution speech, make use of **stock issues,** those generic questions that a thoughtful person will ask before agreeing to a change in policies or procedures.[21] Be sure that your speech can answer these questions to the satisfaction of such listeners:

I. Is there a significant problem?
  A. How did the problem originate?
  B. What caused the problem?
  C. How widespread is the problem?
  D. How long has the problem persisted?
  E. What harms are associated with the problem?
  F. Will these harms continue and grow unless there is change?

II. What is the solution to this problem?
  A. Will the solution actually solve the problem?
  B. Is the solution practical?
  C. Would the cost of the solution be reasonable?
  D. Might there be other consequences to the solution?

III. Who will put the solution into effect?
  A. Are these people responsible and competent?
  B. What role might listeners play?[22]

Motivated Sequence Design

The **motivated sequence design**, first introduced by Professor Alan Monroe in 1935, offers a practical, step-by-step approach when speakers wish to move from the

Go to **VideoLab Lesson 9's Next Step: Using Monroe's Motivated Sequence** and take the quiz to better understand the speaker's use of this design.

VideoLab

awareness through the enactment phases of the persuasive process in a single speech.[23] The design offers five steps to persuasive success:

1. *Arouse attention.* As in any speech, you begin by stimulating interest in your subject. Vivid stories or examples, surprising claims, striking facts and statistics, eloquent statements from admired speakers—all can arouse the interest of your listeners.

2. *Demonstrate a need.* Show your listeners that the situation you want to change is urgent. Strong evidence arranged so that it builds in intensity and taps into audience motivations can help listeners see what they have to win and lose with regard to your proposal. By the end of this demonstration, listeners should be eager to hear your ideas for change.

3. *Satisfy the need.* Present a way to satisfy the need you have demonstrated. Set out a clear plan of action and explain how it will work. Show how this plan agrees with audience principles and values. Offer examples that show how your plan has already worked successfully in parallel cases.

4. *Visualize the results.* Paint verbal pictures that illustrate the positive results listeners can expect. Show them how their lives will be better when they have enacted your plan. A dramatic picture of the future can help overcome resistance to action. You could also paint a picture of what life will be like if listeners don't enact your suggestions. Place these positive and negative verbal pictures side by side to strengthen their impact through contrast.

5. *Call for action.* Your call for action may be a challenge, an appeal, or a statement of personal commitment. The call for action should be short and to the point. Give your listeners something specific that they can do right away. If you can get them to take the first step, the next will come more easily.

In the following, summarized version of a persuasive speech, we can see how the motivated sequence design works:

1. *Arouse attention*	Have you ever dreamed about being a hero or a heroine? Have you ever wished you could do something that would really make a difference in our world? Well, I'm here to show you how you can if you invest only three hours a week.
2. *Demonstrate a need*	Our community needs volunteers to help children who are lonely and neglected. Big Sisters and Big Brothers of Omaha have a program for these children, but it takes people to make the program work. Last year they had forty-eight student volunteers. This year only thirty have signed up to help. They need at least thirty more. They need you.
3. *Satisfy the need*	Volunteering to be a big brother or a big sister will help keep this vital program going. It will also make you a hero or heroine in the eyes of a child.
4. *Visualize the results*	Last year I worked with ten-year-old Kevin two afternoons a week. He needed help with his homework because his grades were just barely passing. But more than school help, he needed someone who cared about him. The first six weeks, his grades went from D's to C's, and I took him to a basketball game. The next six weeks, his grades went up to C's and C+'s, and I took him to a movie. This year Kevin is doing well in

school. He's making B's and above in all his courses, but we still meet and work together because I couldn't bear not to see him. I guess this is a small contribution to humankind, but not to Kevin. When I look in his eyes, I see a glorified reflection of myself. Put yourself in my place. There is a Kevin waiting for you.

5. *Call for action* — Won't you make the commitment to become one of the heroines or heroes of our community? Just one or two afternoons a week can make a difference in the life of a child and in our own future. The pay is not good—nothing!—but the rewards are enormous. I've got the applications with me. Let me sign you up now!

If you plan to develop your persuasive speech by using the motivated sequence, go to the **Outline Worksheet** and **Checklist for the Motivated Sequence Pattern** under **Selecting a Speech Design.**
Go to http://college.hmco.com/eduspace/

The motivated sequence design has helped many generations of persuasive speakers achieve success. If you use it, first determine where your listeners stand on the issue you wish to address; then concentrate on the steps that will carry persuasion forward. For example, if you are speaking to an audience that is already convinced of the need for a change but lacks a plan to make it work, you should spend more time on step 3, "Satisfy the need." However, if you are facing an audience that questions the need, your emphasis should be on step 2, "Demonstrate a need."

Refutative Design

The **refutative design** is appropriate when you need to counter opposing views. In this design, the speaker raises doubt about a competing position by revealing its inconsistencies and weaknesses. It is often wise to take on your opponent's weakest point first. Your refutation then raises doubt about other opposing arguments. The point of attack may be illogical reasoning, flimsy evidence, or self-interest and hidden agendas. However, avoid personal attacks unless credibility issues are central and inescapable. Above all, be fair.

Inductive reasoning from reality can be especially useful in refutative speeches. Such speeches often criticize specific weaknesses in evidence or proof, arguing that opponents have presented a distorted, flawed, or incomplete picture of reality.

There are five steps in developing an effective refutation. These five steps should be followed in sequence for each point you plan to refute.

1. State the point you are going to refute and explain why it is important.
2. Tell the audience how you are going to refute this point.
3. Present your evidence, using facts and figures, examples, and testimony. Cite sources and authorities that the audience will accept as competent and credible.
4. Spell out the conclusion for the audience. Do not assume that listeners will figure out what the evidence means. Tell them directly.
5. Explain the significance of your refutation—show how it discredits or damages the opposing position.

If you plan to develop your persuasive speech by using the refutative design, organize and double-check your speech under **Selecting a Speech Design**.
Go to http://college.hmco.com/eduspace/

See if you can follow each step in this pattern in the following refutation of an argument opposing sex education in public high schools:

Our well-intentioned friends would have you believe, and this is their biggest concern, that birth-control information increases teenage sexual activity. I want to share with you some statistical evidence that contradicts this contention—a contention that is simply not supported by the facts.

The latest study on this issue by the Department of Health, Education, and Welfare compared sexual activity rates in sixty high schools across the United States—thirty with sex education programs and thirty without. Their findings show that there are no significant differences in sexual activity rates between these two groups of schools.

Therefore, the argument that access to birth-control information through sex education programs increases sexual activity simply does not hold water. That's typical of the attack on sex education in the schools—to borrow a line from Shakespeare, it's a lot of "sound and fury, signifying nothing."

You can strengthen this design if you follow your refutation by proving a similar point of your own, thus balancing the negative refutation with a positive demonstration. The result gives the audience an alternative belief to substitute for the one you have refuted. Use the same five-step sequence to support your position. For example, you might follow the preceding refutation with the following demonstration:

I'm not going to try to tell you that birth-control information reduces sexual activity. But I want to tell you what it does reduce. It reduces teenage pregnancy. There is reliable evidence that fewer girls become pregnant in high schools with sex education programs. The same study conducted by Health, Education, and Welfare demonstrated that in high schools with sex education programs, the pregnancy rate dropped from one out of every sixty female students to one out of ninety within two years of the program's going into effect.

Therefore, sex education is a good program. It attacks a devastating social problem—the epidemic of children having children.

Any program that reduces unwanted teenage pregnancy is valuable—valuable to the young women involved, valuable to society. We all pay in so many ways for this personal and social tragedy—we should all support a program that works to reduce it. And we should reject the irrational voices that reject the program.

Combinations of these designs often work well in persuasive speeches. Amanda Miller's speech urging the close of the School of the Americas developed primarily in a problem-solution pattern, with the school itself constituting the problem and legislative proposals to close it providing the solution. But as she depicted what a serious problem the school had become, Amanda found it necessary to answer those who continued to defend it. In this section of her speech she followed a refutative pattern within the larger problem-solution design:

Those who argue in favor of the School claim that for many it is their only source of military education. But what kind of education are we providing?

I've already shown you what the textbooks teach—and that does not fit my idea of education. The School began as a line of defense against the U.S.S.R. in the Cold War. And with the Cold War long since completed, I can see little reason to continue spending millions of dollars each year funding a school that produces such negative results. That money might better be spent on education, or health care, or the environment.

A second argument in favor of the School is that the techniques taught are necessary for "self-defense" against civil wars. But what kinds of selves are these people defending? Are they themselves civil? In 1993, an International Human Rights Tribunal revealed that over one hundred School of the Americas graduates had committed war crimes. Among these crimes were

heading the concentration camps in Villa Grimaldi in Chile, organizing the Ocosingo Massacre in Mexico, and participating in drug trafficking and assassinations. How exactly do these activities qualify as "self defense," in any legitimate sense of the word?

Having completed the refutative part of her speech, Amanda was ready to move on to her solution.

Avoiding Defective Persuasion

It takes a lot of work to prepare a persuasive speech—analyzing your audience, researching your topic, planning your strategy, and developing arguments. Do not ruin all your hard work by committing **fallacies**, or errors of reasoning. Fallacies may crop up in the evidence you use, the proofs you develop, or the reasoning in your arguments. There are also fallacies particular to some speech designs. In this section we identify some of these major errors so that you can guard against them, both as speaker and as listener.

VideoLab

To assess your ability to detect and analyze fallacies in reasoning, go to **VideoLab Drill 9.3: Find the Fallacies** and complete the exercise.

Defective Evidence

Evidence is defective if the speaker misuses facts, statistics, or testimony, or uses evidence inappropriately.

Misuse of Facts. The **slippery slope fallacy** assumes that once something happens, it will establish an irreversible trend leading to disaster. The slippery slope fallacy often involves oversimplification and outlandish hyperbole. For example, a prominent religious leader once suggested that feminism was "a socialist, anti-family political movement that encourages women to leave their husbands, kill their children, practice witchcraft, destroy capitalism, and become lesbians."[24]

In an advertisement, the R. J. Reynolds Tobacco Company presented lay testimony by a Florida state employee:

> **The Government is considering a substantial increase in excise taxes as a deterrent to smoking. . . . And restricting smoking in your own home is also under review. . . . I don't think they'll be content with regulating tobacco. There isn't any reason they can't use a similar argument about other products such as meat, cheese, or anything they say we shouldn't consume. When they start regulating they rarely know when to stop.**

In the slippery slope fallacy, it is not logic but rather our darkest fears that drive the prediction of events.

A second misuse of evidence involves the **confusion of fact and opinion**. A factual statement is objective and verifiable, such as, "Most Republican

InterConnections.LearnMore 16.2

Fallacies

The Fallacy Files
http://gncurtis.home.texas.net/
An interactive site containing an extensive collection of fallacies and bad argument, with definitions and examples; well organized and entertaining as well as educational (see especially "Stalking the Wild Fallacy"); developed by Gary N. Curtis, Ph.D., an ontologist with an artificial intelligence company.

Stephen's Guide to the Logical Fallacies
http://datanation.com/fallacies/
The original "fallacies online" web site, with extensive information on critical thinking, logic, and fallacies; developed by Professor Steven Downes for the Institute of Professional Development, University of Alberta.

Fallacies Leading to Assumptions of Common Sense
http://www.kcmetro.cc.mo.us/longview/ctac/psychology/commonsense4.htm
A look at fallacious assumptions that may underlie arguments based on "common sense"; developed by Professor Matthew Westra, Longview Community College.

governors support the lowering of taxes." An opinion is a personal interpretation of information: a statement of belief, feeling, attitude, or value. Normally, factual and opinion statements stay in their proper places. The problem comes when speakers make impassioned claims based on opinions, such as: "The Republicans have done it now! They're violating our Constitution. They're tossing children out into the cold. They're depriving retired people of their right to a secure old age. These are the *facts* of what they're doing." Opinions can be useful in persuasive speeches when they represent careful interpretations that are supported by evidence. However, treating an opinion as a fact, or a fact as an opinion, is the source of many problems. It can make you seem to claim too much or too little and can raise questions about your competence and ethics.

At one time hunters used to distract their dogs from a trail by dragging a smoked herring across it. In our time, the **red herring fallacy** occurs when persuaders try to draw attention away from the real issues in a dispute, perhaps because they feel vulnerable on those issues or because they see a chance to vilify the opposition. Often the "red herring" they use is some sensational allegation. In the ongoing abortion controversy, some "pro-choice" advocates have discredited their opponents by associating them with terrorists, assassins, and bombers. In return, some "pro-life" advocates have smeared their opposition by suggesting that abortion clinics may be underwritten by "mafia money." Such charges from both sides divert attention from the central issues of the controversy.

Statistical Fallacies. Audiences are often intimidated by numbers. We've all been taught that "figures don't lie" without being reminded that "liars figure." Speakers can exploit this tendency by creating statistical deceptions. For example, consider the **myth of the mean**, the illusion of the average. If you've ever vacationed in the mountains, you know that a stream may have an "average depth" of six inches, yet a person could drown in one of its deep pools. A speaker could tell you not to worry about poverty in Plattsville because the average income is well above the poverty level. Yet this average could be skewed by the fact that a few families are very wealthy, creating an illusion of well-being that is not true for most people. Averages are useful to summarize statistical information, but be sure they do not hide the reality of a situation.

Another statistical fallacy occurs when we offer **flawed statistical comparisons** that start from unequal bases. Suppose you have two salespersons, George and John, working for you. George has just opened a new account, giving him a total of two. John has opened three new accounts for a total of thirteen. George comes to you and asks for a promotion, arguing, "My success rate this year rose by 100 percent, while John's rose only 30 percent." George would be guilty of fallacious reasoning, if not bad salesmanship.

Defective Testimony. Testimony can be misused in many different ways. Speakers may omit *when* a statement was made to hide the fact that the testimony is dated. They may leave out important facts about their experts, intimidating us with titles such as "*Dr.* Michael Jones reported that smoking does not harm health." What the speaker *didn't* reveal was that Dr. Jones was a marketing professor who was writing public relations material for the Tobacco Growers Association. Speakers also abuse testimony when they cite words out of context that are not representative of a person's actual position. This can happen when a qualifier is presented as though it represented a concession, misquoting a statement such as "unless the growers are no longer using poisons" as "Ah, hah! He admits—and I quote him—'growers are no longer using poisons.'" As we noted in Chapter 8, prestige and lay testimony can be misused if they replace expert opinion when facts must be established. Finally, the "voice of the people" can be easily misrepresented, depending on *which* people you choose to quote.

Inappropriate Evidence. Other abuses occur when speakers deliberately use one form of evidence when they should be using another. For example, you might use facts and figures when examples would bring us closer to the human truth of a situation. Welfare statistics are sometimes misused in this way. When a speaker talks about poverty in the abstract, it distances listeners from its human reality. George Orwell once complained that such language "falls upon the [truth] like soft snow, blurring the outlines and covering up all the details."[25] On the other hand, speakers may use examples to arouse emotions when what is needed is the dispassionate picture provided by facts and figures. Testimony is abused when it is used to compensate for inadequate facts. Narratives that create mythos may also be used inappropriately. Calling someone a "Robin Hood who steals from the rich to give to the poor" has been used to justify more than one crime.

Defective Proof

Any element of proof can be defective. We have already pointed out the danger when appeals to feelings overwhelm judgment and cloud the issue. Speakers might also misuse appeals to cultural identity to promote intolerance, such as, "When are Native Americans going to start being *good* Americans?"

Similarly, speakers may abuse appeals to credibility by attacking the person instead of the problem. This is called an **ad hominem fallacy**. Such persuaders try to avoid issues by calling the opposition derogatory names. For example, during a recent environmental dispute, one side charged that its opponents were "little old ladies in tennis shoes" and "outside agitators." Not to be outdone, the other side labeled their antagonists as "rapists of public parkland."[26] Senator Jennings Randolph, speaking before the U.S. Senate in the not-so-distant past, dismissed arguments in favor of the Equal Rights Amendment for women on grounds they were offered by a "small band of bra-less bubbleheads."[27] Proof by ethos also can be abused when speakers overuse it—when they try to intimidate listeners by citing an overwhelming list of authorities while neglecting to present information or good reasons for accepting their claims.

Finally, speakers neglect their responsibility to prove their points when they merely assert what they have not proved, thereby **begging the question**. Those who "beg the question" usually rely on colorful language to disguise the inadequacy of their proofs, so that the words themselves *seem* to establish the conclusion. Some antiabortion advocates may be guilty of this practice when they refer to the fetus as the "unborn *child*" without bothering to address the difficult moral question of when human life actually begins. A similar abuse may occur when the speaker taps into the mythos of the audience without adequate justification or preparation. A conclusion such as "Be *patriotic!* Support the *American way of life!* Speak out against gun control!"—tacked onto a speech without further explanation—begs the question, because the speaker has not proved that being against gun control is a form of patriotism.

Defective Patterns of Reasoning

Major fallacies may infest the basic patterns of reasoning in persuasion. It is unethical to commit them purposely, irresponsible to commit them accidentally. In your role as critical listener, be on guard against them at all times.

Errors of Reasoning from Principle. Reasoning from principle can only be as good as the underlying premise on which it is built. In the **shaky principle fallacy** the premise is not sound. *If the principle is faulty, the entire argument may crumble.*

We once heard a student begin a line of argument with the following statement of principle: "College athletes are not really here to learn." She was instantly in trouble. When her speech was over, the class assailed her with questions: How did she define *athletes?* Was she talking about intercollegiate or intramural athletes? How about the tennis team? How did she define learning? Was she aware of the negative stereotype at the center of her premise? Wasn't she being unfair, not to mention arrogant? It's safe to say that the speaker did not persuade many people that day. To avoid such a fiasco, be sure that you can defend each word in the principle that underlies your reasoning.

Omitted qualifiers, another fallacy common to reasoning from principle, occurs when a persuader claims too much, in effect confusing probability with certainty. The logic of everyday life is rarely certain. Suppose a friend from the Tau Beta fraternity calls you to set up a blind date. If the principle "Tau Betas are handsome" holds about 90 percent of the time in your experience, and if you are about 90 percent certain that your blind date is a Tau Beta, then your conclusion that your date will be attractive is an assumption qualified by at least two factors of uncertainty. It is better to say: "There is a *good chance* that my date will be handsome." If you point out the uncertainty factor in advance through proper qualification, you may not lose the audience's trust if a prediction does not come true.

Another error common in reasoning from principle is *assuming that if something happens after an event, it was caused by the event.* This **post hoc fallacy** confuses association with causation. It is the basis of many superstitious beliefs. The same people who wear their lucky boots and shirts to ball games may also argue that we should have a tax cut because the last time we had one we avoided war, increased employment, or reduced crime. One of our students fell into the post hoc trap when she argued that low readership of certain books in areas where the books are banned in public schools proves that the bans are effective. There may be many reasons why people don't read books—banning them in school libraries may or may not be among those reasons. It is just as likely that the book bans themselves are simply symptoms of deeper cultural conditions, and that the bans might actually create curiosity about their objects of scorn, resulting in more readership than might otherwise have happened. A speaker must demonstrate that events are causally connected, not just make the assumption based on association.

Finally, a **non sequitur fallacy** occurs when the principle and the observation discussed don't really relate to each other, when the conclusion does not necessarily follow from the relationship between them, or when the evidence presented is irrelevant. Former Speaker of the House Newt Gingrich, lecturing on why men are more suited than women to traditional military combat roles, provided a remarkable example that appears to fit all the conditions of non sequitur reasoning:

> **If combat means living in a ditch, females have biological problems staying in a ditch for 30 days because they get infections. . . . [Moreover,] males are biologically driven to go out and hunt for giraffes.**

Former Rep. Pat Schroeder responded to this wisdom as follows: "I have been working in a male culture for a very long time, and I haven't met the first one who wants to go out and hunt a giraffe."[28] And then there is the cockeyed non sequitur logic of the late Marge Schott, an owner of the Cincinnati Reds baseball team. Schott told a Denver radio audience that she would rather see children smoke than take drugs. Her reason? "We smoked a peace pipe with the Indians, right?"[29]

Errors of Reasoning from Observation. A common error in such reasoning is a **hasty generalization** that is based on insufficient or nonrepresentative observations. Suppose a student reasoned: "My big sister in Alpha Chi got a D from Professor Osborn. The guy who sits next to me in history got an F from her. I'm struggling to make a C in her class. Therefore, Professor Osborn is a tough grader." To avoid hasty generalization you would need to know what Professor Osborn's grade distribution looks like over an extended period of time and across courses, plus how her grades compare with other professors teaching the same courses.

Defective Analogy. A **faulty analogy** occurs when the things compared are dissimilar in some important way. For example, assume that you have transferred from a college with 1,500 students to a university with 15,000 students. You present a speech proposing new campus security measures, arguing that because they worked well at the college, they should also work well at the university. Would such analogical reasoning be valid? That would depend on similarities and dissimilarities between the two schools. Is the size difference important? Are the crime problems similar? Are the schools located in similar settings? Are the students from roughly the same social and economic backgrounds? Dissimilarity on any of these points could raise doubts about the analogy and make your persuasion less convincing.

Fallacies Related to Particular Designs

In addition to fallacies of evidence, proof, and argument, there are at least two major fallacies related to particular persuasive designs. **Either-or thinking**, sometimes called a *false dilemma,* makes listeners think that they have only two mutually exclusive choices. This fallacy is attractive because it is dramatic: it satisfies our need for conflict and simplicity. It occurs in policy issues when one hears statements such as, "It's either jobs or the environment" or, "If we pay down the debt, we sacrifice social security." Either-or thinking blinds listeners to other options, such as compromise or creative alternatives not yet considered. Such thinking often infests problem-solution speeches when speakers oversimplify the choices.

People with gardens sometimes make a "straw man" to scare off crows. As the name suggests, the straw is formed into the likeness of a man (presumably, a "straw woman" would work as well, as far as the crows are concerned). From this practice comes the **straw man fallacy**, creating a "likeness" of an opponent's view that makes it seem trivial, ridiculous, and easy to refute. As you might suspect, the straw man fallacy appears most often in speeches that contend with opposition. It understates and distorts the position of opponents and is unethical. Reducing the movement in favor of the Equal Rights Amendment for women to "an effort to abolish separate restrooms for men and women" or dismissing affirmative action as "a policy designed to give unfair advantage to minorities" are classic cases. As an ethical persuasive speaker, you have an obligation to represent an opposing position fairly and fully, even as you refute it. Only then will thoughtful listeners respect you and your arguments. The straw man fallacy is an implicit admission of weakness or desperation and can damage what may well be a legitimate case.

Persuasion is constantly threatened by flaws and deception. In a world of competing views, we often see human nature revealed in its petty as well as its finer moments. As you plan and present your arguments or listen to the arguments of others, be on guard against fallacies. Figure 16.6 lists and defines the fallacies we have been discussing.

For a final opportunity to test your knowledge of fallacies, go to **Find the Fallacy I and II** under **Selecting a Speech Design.**
Go to http://college.hmco.com/eduspace/

Figure 16.6

Gallery of Fallacies

Kind	Nature of the Problem
1. Evidential fallacies	
A. Slippery slope	• Arguing that one bad thing will result in many others
B. Confusing fact with opinion	• Asserting opinions as though they were facts, or discrediting facts as opinions
C. Red herring	• Distracting listeners with sensational, irrelevant material
D. Myth of the mean	• Using an average to hide a problem
E. Flawed statistical comparisons	• Using percentage increases or decreases to distort reality
F. Defective testimony	• Omitting when a statement was made or a speaker's credentials; quoting out of context
G. Inappropriate evidence	• Using facts when examples are needed, or examples when facts are needed, or an intimidating list of authorities as a substitute for information
2. Flawed proofs	
A. Ad hominem	• Attacking the person rather than the point
B. Begging the question	• Assuming as decided what has actually not been proved
3. Defective arguments	
A. Shaky principle	• Basing an argument on an unsound assumption
B. Omitted qualifiers	• Confusing probability with certainty by asserting a conclusion without qualification
C. Post hoc	• Assuming because one event follows another, it was caused by it
D. Non sequitur	• Reasoning in which principles and observations are unrelated to each other or to the conclusion drawn
E. Hasty generalization	• Drawing conclusions based on insufficient or nonrepresentative observations
F. Faulty analogy	• Comparing things that are dissimilar in some important way
4. Persuasive design fallacies	
A. Either-or thinking	• Framing choices so that listeners think they have only two options
B. Straw man	• Belittling or trivializing arguments to refute them easily

In Summary

Manipulative persuasion aims to influence our reflexive behavior; it evades judgment and reflection by thoughtful listeners, and it avoids bearing the ethical burden of justification. *Argumentative persuasion*, on the other hand, displays the grounds of its justification in the form of evidence, proofs, and patterns of reasoning.

Developing Evidence and Proofs. When used in persuasion, supporting materials become *evidence.* Facts and statistics alert us to a situation we must change. Examples move listeners, creating a favorable emotional climate for the speaker's recommendations. Narratives bring a sense of reality and help listeners identify with the issue. Testimony calls on witnesses to support a position. When you use evidence, strive for recent facts and figures, emphasize factual examples, engage listeners through stories that make your point, and rely primarily on expert testimony.

Proofs constitute appeals to our rational nature *(logos),* appeals to feeling *(pathos),* appeals to the credibility of speaker and sources cited within the speech *(ethos),* and appeals to cultural identity *(mythos).* Appeals to rationality assume that we are thinking creatures who respond to well-reasoned demonstrations. Appeals to feeling affirm that we are creatures of emotion as well. Appeals to credibility recognize that we respond to leadership qualities in speakers and to the authority of their sources of evidence. Appeals to cultural identity relate to our nature as social beings who respond to group traditions and values. Argumentative persuasion centers on the logos, but effective persuaders must be able to combine the strengths of these various forms.

Ethos may be discussed in terms of *initial credibility*, *emerging credibility*, and *terminal credibility*, depending on what happens during a given speech. Pathos appeals can add ingredients of humanity to the discussion, but they must avoid any impression of manipulation. Mythos appeals draw on powerful social motives to integrate proposed actions into the culture of accepted values and beliefs. At the same time, speakers must be careful to respect the individuality of listeners.

Patterns of Reasoning. Persuaders must define the meanings of key terms and concepts early in their speeches. Definitions can also attempt to change perspectives on subjects to make listeners more sympathetic to the arguments that will follow.

In *deductive reasoning*, speakers argue from accepted principles and values in order to justify their conclusions. Such reasoning originates in a principle *(major premise),* identifies some condition or situation relevant to the principle *(minor premise),* and makes some claim about the condition or situation that seems warranted by the principle *(conclusion).* Aristotle identified this pattern as the rhetorical syllogism, to which he gave the special name of *enthymeme.*

In *inductive reasoning*, speakers establish that their arguments are grounded in reality. Such *reasoning from reality* draws general conclusions from an inspection of particular related instances. It emphasizes evidence provided by facts, statistics, and expert testimony. Reasoning from reality can strengthen and authenticate reasoning from principle. Such reasoning must also demonstrate a clear grasp of cause-effect relationships.

In *analogical reasoning*, persuaders show how we can deal with a problem by considering a similar situation. Such *reasoning from parallel cases* can help clarify an abstract problem by relating it to a more concrete model. It can also add color and interest by relating a condition to a more dramatic parallel case. The legitimacy of such reasoning depends upon specific points of comparison.

Toulmin's model of argument provides an overview that displays the interaction of these patterns of reasoning. The model includes the following major components: *data, claim, warrant, backing, reservations,* and *qualifier.*

Designs for Persuasive Speaking. Evidence, proof, and patterns of reasoning are not effective until they are framed within persuasive designs that serve the purpose of your speech. Three designs in particular serve the needs of persuasive speaking. In a *problem-solution design,* you must first convince the audience that a problem exists and then advance a solution that corrects it. The *motivated sequence design* moves from the awareness through the enactment phases of the persuasive process in a single speech. The design has five steps: arousing attention, demonstrating a need, satisfying the need, visualizing results, and calling for action. The *refutative design* answers opposing views. Using this design, you state the point you intend to refute, tell how you will refute it, present your evidence, draw a conclusion, and explain the significance of the refutation.

Avoiding Defective Persuasion. Fallacies are errors in reasoning that can damage a persuasive speech. Evidence can be defective when the speaker misuses facts, statistics, and testimony. Common errors include the *slippery slope fallacy,* which assumes that a single instance will establish a trend; the confusion of fact with opinion; and the *red herring,* using irrelevant material to divert attention from the issue. Statistical fallacies include the *myth of the mean,* in which averages create illusions that hide reality, and faulty conclusions based on *flawed statistical comparisons*. Evidence can also be used inappropriately, featuring facts and figures when the situation calls for examples, examples when the audience needs facts and figures, testimony to hide the weakness of information, or narratives to justify unethical behavior.

Various defects can reduce the value of proof. Speakers misuse proof by credibility when they commit an *ad hominem fallacy*, attacking the person rather than the argument. When speakers merely assert and assume in their conclusion what they have not proved, they commit the fallacy of *begging the question.*

Fallacies are also common in the patterns of reasoning. If the principle you use as the base of your reasoning is faulty, your entire argument will crumble. Other frequent errors occur when probability is passed off as certainty and when the speaker confuses association with causation, reasoning that if something happened after an event, it therefore was caused by the event. The latter is called the *post hoc fallacy*. A *non sequitur fallacy* occurs when irrelevant conclusions or evidence are introduced into argument. Inductive reasoning can suffer from a *hasty generalization* drawn from insufficient or nonrepresentative observations. Analogical reasoning is defective when important dissimilarities outweigh similarities.

Either-or thinking can be a special problem in speeches calling for action. This fallacy reduces audience options to only two, one advocated by the speaker, the other undesirable. When speeches that contend with opposition understate, distort, or misrepresent an opposing position for the sake of easy refutation, they commit the *straw man fallacy.*

Terms to Know

manipulative persuasion
argumentative persuasion
evidence
reluctant witnesses
proofs
logos
pathos
ethos
mythos
initial credibility
terminal credibility
emerging credibility
reasoning from principle
deductive reasoning
major premise
minor premise
conclusion
enthymeme
reasoning from reality
inductive reasoning
reasoning from parallel cases
analogy
data
claim
warrant
backing
reservations
qualifiers
problem-solution design
stock issues
motivated sequence design
refutative design
fallacies
slippery slope fallacy
confusion of fact and opinion
red herring fallacy
myth of the mean
flawed statistical comparisons
ad hominem fallacy
begging the question
shaky principle fallacy
omitted qualifiers
post hoc fallacy
non sequitur fallacy
hasty generalization
faulty analogy
either-or thinking
straw man fallacy

Discussion

1. Bring to class examples of advertisements that emphasize each of the four forms of persuasive proof: logos, pathos, ethos, and mythos. What factors in the product, medium of advertising, or intended audience might explain this emphasis in each example? Do the ads combine other forms of proof as well? How effective is each ad?
2. Analyze the evidence, proofs, and patterns of reasoning that develop in the speech by Bonnie Marshall, reprinted in Appendix B. How powerful is this overall design of persuasive materials? Might it have been even stronger? How?
3. Look for examples of fallacies in the letters-to-the-editor section of your local newspaper over a week's period of time. Bring these specimens to class for discussion and analysis.
4. Apply the stock issues questions to Anna Aley's persuasive speech reprinted in Appendix B. Does Anna's speech stand up to the challenge of such questions? Does she answer them satisfactorily?

Application

1. Find a news story that interests you. Using the information in the story, (1) show how you might use this material as evidence in a persuasive speech, (2) indicate how this evidence might be used to develop a proof, and (3) explain how this proof might function as part of a pattern of reasoning.
2. About fifty years ago In *The Ethics of Rhetoric,* Richard Weaver observed that frequent controversy over the definitions of basic terms in public discourse are a sign of social and cultural division. Look and listen for examples of lively disagreement over the definitions of the following terms in contemporary argument:

   A. preemptive war

   B. faith-based initiatives

   C. gun control

   D. same-sex marriage

   E. abortion

   Do these disagreements reflect the kind of social division Weaver suggested?
3. Which patterns of reasoning do you plan to emphasize in your next persuasive speech? Why?
4. Attend a speech event on campus or observe a speech on television. Consider the speaker's ethos in terms of initial, emerging, and terminal credibility. What kinds of expectations of the speaker did you bring to the speech? What did he or she do during the speech to disappoint, satisfy, or surpass these expectations? How would you assess the speaker's ethos at the end of the speech? Submit a report of your observations to your instructor.
5. Evaluate a persuasive speech from Appendix B, using Toulmin's model of argument. Judge the adequacy of data, the acceptability of warrants, and the reasonableness of claims. Has the speaker provided sufficient backing for warrants? Does the speaker acknowledge any reservations, and qualify the claims accordingly?

Notes

1. Franklin J. Boster et al., "The Persuasive Effects of Statistical Evidence in the Presence of Exemplars," *Communication Studies* 51 (2000): 296–306.
2. Shelly Chaiken, Wendy Wood, and Alice H. Eagly, "Principles of Persuasion," in *Social Psychology: Handbook of Basic Principles,* ed. E. Tory Higgins and Arie W. Kruglanki (New York: Guilford, 1996), pp. 702–742.
3. Representative of this scholarship is Ernest G. Bormann, "Fantasy and Rhetorical Vision: The Rhetorical Criticism of Social Reality," *Quarterly Journal of Speech* 58 (1972): 396–407; Walter F. Fisher, "Narration as a Human Communication Paradigm: The Case of Public Moral Argument," *Communication Monographs* 51 (1984); 1–22; Michael C. McGee, "In Search of 'The People': A Rhetorical Alternative," *Quarterly Journal of Speech* 61 (1975): 235–249; Michael Osborn, "Rhetorical Depiction," in *Form, Genre and the Study of Political Discourse*, ed. Herbert W. Simons and Aram A. Aghazarian (Columbia: University of South Carolina Press, 1986), pp. 79–107; and Janice Hocker Rushing, "The Rhetoric of the American Western Myth," *Communication Monographs* 50 (1983): 14–32.
4. In recent times the importance of "goodwill" to impressions of ethos has been discounted by many social scientists. An experimental study that restores the importance of the "goodwill" factor is offered by James C. McCroskey and Mason J. Teven, "Goodwill: A Reexamination of the Construct and Its Measurement," *Communication Monographs* 66 (1999): 90–103.
5. The discussion that follows is based on James C. McCroskey, *An Introduction to Rhetorical Communication*, 8th ed. (Boston: Allyn and Bacon, 2000), pp. 93–103. We use the term *emerging credibility* in the place of McCroskey's *derived credibility* to emphasize the dynamic, interactive nature of the process.
6. Antonio R. Damasio, *Descartes' Error: Emotion, Reason, and the Human Brain* (New York: Putnam, 1994).
7. From a brochure distributed by Handgun Control, Inc., 1225 Eye Street NW, Washington, DC 20005 (1990).
8. Martha Solomon, "The 'Positive Woman's' Journey: A Mythic Analysis of the Rhetoric of STOP ERA," *Quarterly Journal of Speech* 65 (1979): 262–274.
9. Rushing, pp. 14–32.
10. Roderick P. Hart, *The Political Pulpit* (West Lafayette, Ind.: Purdue University Press, 1977).
11. George W. Bush, "State of the Union," *Washington Post*, 29 Jan. 2003, p. A10.

12. John Fitzgerald Kennedy, "Acceptance Address, 1960," in *The Great Society: A Sourcebook of Speeches,* ed. Glenn R. Capp (Belmont, Calif.: Dickenson 1969), p. 14.

13. Richard F. Corlin, "The Secrets of Gun Violence in America," *Vital Speeches of the Day,* 1 Aug. 2001, p. 611.

14. Bush, p. A10.

15. Corlin, p. 611.

16. Ibid., p. 612.

17. Ibid.

18. Lisa M. Ross, "Buckley Says Drug Attack Won't Work," Commercial Appeal *(Memphis),* 14 Sept. 1989, p. B2.

19. Mortimer B. Zuckerman, "The Enemy Within," *U.S. News & World Report,* 11 Sept. 1989, p. 91.

20. See Toulmin's discussion in *The Uses of Argument* (London: Cambridge University Press, 1958) and in Stephen Toulmin, Richard Rieke, and Allan Janik, *An Introduction to Reasoning,* 2nd ed. (New York: Macmillan, 1984).

21. J. W. Patterson and David Zarefsky, *Contemporary Debate* (Boston: Houghton Mifflin, 1983).

22. The structure of the stock issues design has been adapted from Charles U. Larson, *Persuasion: Reception and Responsibility,* 8th ed. (Belmont, Calif.: Wadsworth, 1998), pp. 293–295; and Charles S. Mudd and Malcolm O. Sillars, *Public Speaking: Content and Communication* (Prospect Heights, Ill.: Waveland, 1991), pp. 100–102.

23. The motivated sequence design was introduced in Alan Monroe's *Principles and Types of Speech* (New York: Scott, Foresman, 1935) and has been refined in later editions.

24. Gilbert Cranberg, "Even Sensible Iowa Bows to the Religious Right," *Los Angeles Times,* 17 Aug. 1992, p. B5.

25. George Orwell, *Shooting an Elephant and Other Essays* (London: Secker and Warburg, 1950), p. 97.

26. Michael M. Osborn, "The Abuses of Argument," *Southern Speech Communication Journal* 49 (1983): 1–11.

27. Howard Kahane, *Logic and Contemporary Rhetoric: The Use of Reason in Everyday Life*, 5th ed. (Belmont, Calif.: Wadsworth, 1988), p. 38.

28. *Newsweek,* 30 Jan. 1995, p. 17.

29. *Commercial Appeal (Memphis),* 6 Sept. 1996, p. C1.

Cooling the World's Fever

Joshua Logan

Our world has a fever. And after my last speech, we know the cause of it. Global warming, that threatens to become "global burning." Global burning, that could raise global temperatures by as much as ten degrees by the end of this century. Global burning, that could raise ocean levels by three feet all around the globe. Global burning, that could submerge coastal cities, turn fertile lands into deserts, and destroy vast populations of wildlife. Global burning, that threatens many people, especially those in poor areas of the world, with epidemics of disease and hunger and dislocation. In short, global burning that could disrupt civilization and all life on this planet.

■ *Josh summarizes the argument he developed in his speech at the end of Chapter 15. The argument depends on the convergence of inductive and deductive patterns of reasoning. His reasoning from reality draws from a broad range of factual and statistical evidence. His reasoning from principle rests on an implied warrant, that problems created by people can also be solved by them. Linked to this is the principle that listeners have a responsibility to future generations not to endanger the planet.*

We don't have time to argue anymore over whether global warming or global burning—call it what you will—is a serious problem. We know that it is, thanks to hundreds of scientists around the world whose work has been collected, tested, and reported by the United Nations Intergovernmental Panel on Climate Change. *Time* magazine has summarized the gravity of the problem in light of the IPCC report: "Except for nuclear war or a collision with an asteroid, no force has more potential to damage our planet's web of life than global warming."

Now you expect me to present you with an answer to this problem. But I ask a lot more from you than simply *accepting* a solution: I ask that you *become* the solution. I ask for deep changes in attitude and behavior, for your conversion to a new way of environmental living. I know that I ask for a lot, but frankly, there's no other way out of this mess we've made. Whether we are liberal or conservative, Republican or Democrat, Baptist or Episcopalian—global warming confronts us all.

■ *Josh announces the kind of persuasion he is seeking. His speech asks for persuasion in depth, close to religious conversion. It is not enough that listeners should enact his recommendations or integrate them into their value systems; they must also absorb them into their lifestyles.*

As I said last time, there's no easy or instant way out. It may take a hundred years before the earth benefits from some of the programs we put into place now. But we must begin. So what do you do when you've got a wild fire raging that you want to put out? You take away its fuel supply. What fuels global warming are the greenhouse gases, especially carbon dioxide, methane, and nitrous oxide.

The good news is, there is an emerging technology that could help us rearrange the bleak future I have painted. First, there are promising forms of energy that don't burn fossil fuels. Around the world, wind power is growing at 30 percent a year, with Europe leading the way. Already, this source of energy replaces the work of fifteen coal-fired power plants that would otherwise be belching tons of greenhouse gases into the atmosphere. Sound impractical for us? Just envision a new form of agriculture, wind farms. Already in North Dakota, farmers who have been earning $50 an acre from wheat are the new pioneers of power. Their wind farms will soon earn up to $2,000 an acre selling wind-generated power. Then of course there's solar power. Last year I enjoyed four days at an eco-resort in Mexico where there was no traditional electrical power. Each afternoon we took showers using hot water that had been warmed by solar power. The same source lighted the large dining room and powered its appliances. No harmful emissions there. Speaking of Mexico, that country is taking the lead in developing geothermal power—energy generated by natural underground heating, and is opening its national power grid to a range of alternative sources for electrical power. I don't even have time to talk about the promising technology of fuel cells that can power buildings and electric cars, or more efficient ways to use traditional forms of energy.

■ *Josh's argument for his solution relies on an additional set of warrants: that a program must be practical and affordable, that listeners must be able to enact its provisions, and that the graver the threat, the more effort and risk listeners should be willing to assume.*

■ *Josh relies heavily on inductive reasoning from facts and statistics. He uses personal experience to add authenticity and the power of his own ethos to the argument. He might have cited the sources of his information more frequently to reinforce credibility. He strengthens the design of his problem-solution speech by dividing the discussion of new technology into three categories.*

■ *Joshua asks listeners to combat global warming as citizens and energy consumers. He might have drawn this distinction more clearly. His criticism of President Bush is more effective because he is a Republican who speaks as a "reluctant witness." By contrasting the words of the president with the actions of China, he appeals to an implied principle of mythos: that Americans ought to lead, not reluctantly follow, competitor nations like China.*

Second, beyond these new forms of energy are also promising new products. Let me introduce you to the Toyota Prius and to the Honda Insight. These are hybrid gas-electric cars that run half the time on a traditional internal combustion engine and the rest of the time on batteries. As *Consumer Reports* describes the Prius, "Power comes from a 1.5 liter gasoline engine and a small electric motor. The Prius can automatically switch between one and the other, or run on both, based on conditions. Fuel economy came to 41 mpg in mixed driving. The Prius can seat 5 people comfortably, and is classified as a 'Super Ultra Low Emission Vehicle.'" The Honda did even better: 51 mpg in mixed driving. In fact, these new cars—now priced on the market under $20,000—reduce harmful emissions by 40 percent. Look for even better cars late in this decade: Ford, Chrysler, and Volkswagen have developed prototypes of cars that run very nicely on hydrogen fuel cells—no greenhouse gases!

Third, there are promising new ways to clean up fossil fuel power. British Petroleum has taken the lead in reducing greenhouse emissions from its oil fields and refineries. It and the Ford Motor Company are sponsoring research into what they call "sequestering," stripping harmful residues from greenhouse gases so that they can be stored in abandoned oil and gas wells. Other research programs are exploring how to convert harmful CO_2 gases into minerals to keep them out of the atmosphere.

So there's a great deal of hope out there. What is required is the political will to encourage these new initiatives on a large scale, the same way that the federal government once breathed life and hope into the fledgling airline industry. Here's where you come into the picture. By your votes and your letters, your contributions and your hard work, you can encourage politicians who make global burning a top priority. And once they are elected, we've got to hold their feet to the fire. Let me give just one example. I'm proud to be a Republican—most of the time! I voted for George W. Bush for president, encouraged by his promise to establish mandatory caps on power plant emissions. But once he was elected, President Bush announced there would be no such caps, and he has been dragging his feet over environment issues ever since. He also declared his opposition to the so-called Kyoto Protocol, a worldwide agreement to reduce greenhouse gas emissions. He said, "We will work together, but it's going to be what's in the interest of our country, first and foremost." What's in the interest of our country, first and foremost, is the health and well-being of this and future generations of Americans. Contrast the president's words with the actions of China, which reduced its greenhouse output 17 percent between 1997 and 1999, eliminating more than the entire CO_2 production of Southeast Asia. Surely, if China can do it, so can we.

What we need is a new, green way of thinking and acting. Through our letters to the president, and to our congressmen and senators as well, we've got to help him change his mind and get right on the environment. I urge you to write those letters.

The second thing I would like you to do is to make a personal commitment to change your behaviors. Keep an open mind to the new technologies and the new products like hybrid cars. Factor them into your energy and transportation decisions. Instead of always driving your car, walk or ride a bike. You will discover an added benefit: greater health! Instead of driving alone to work, learn to carpool. You may also make some new friends or deepen old friendships. Let me remind you of another old friend, trees. Trees cleanse the air of CO_2, and they shade our homes, reducing the need for air conditioning in the summer, but letting the sun through in the winter. So plant them, and join other green people who are working to encourage the wise management of forests. SOCM—"Save Our Cumberland Mountains"—is such a local group. These dedicated folks helped save Fall Creek Falls from strip mining, and they are working now to discourage the practice of clear-cutting, the large-scale destruction of forests in West Tennessee. I'm proud to belong to SOCM, and I invite you to join us at our next meeting this Thursday, where we are going to plan some serious environmental action.

You can make a difference, even in the small everyday choices you make. At the end of my speech I'm going to give you a list of other green things you can do to help take the red out of global warming. Planting a tree may not sound like much, but magnify every little act by a thousand, and then by a million, and then by a thousand million, as in China. We can make a difference—we must make a difference!

Someday, I hope to take my children, and my grandchildren, to Dauphin Island, Alabama, where they can walk on the sand and swim in the sea and enjoy the wildlife in the Audubon Bird Sanctuary. As I was preparing this speech, I developed an email conversation with Dr. George F. Crozier, executive director of the Sea Lab at Dauphin Island. From that fragile barrier island Dr. Crozier wrote me: "We are incorporating the message of global warming into our educational/outreach efforts in hopes that we can get the public's attention before it is too late." I don't think it's too late. And I hope what I've said in the last two speeches has gained your attention. Together we can cool the fever, and turn down the heat under our planet.

■ ***Joshua concludes with a personal vision. His reference to email correspondence with the executive director of the Dauphin Island Sea Lab again underscores his commitment.***

How You Can Cool Global Warming

1. Run your dishwasher only when full and use the speed-dry option.
2. Clean or replace air conditioner filters regularly.
3. Set your thermostat lower in winter and higher in summer.
4. Walk, bike, carpool, or use mass transit.
5. Insulate your water heater.
6. Set water heater thermostat below 120°.
7. Install low-flow showerheads.
8. Ask your utility company to conduct a free energy audit of your home.
9. Encourage recycling at school or work.
10. Plant trees next to your home.
11. Wash laundry in cold water.
12. Replace old refrigerators with more energy-efficient models.
13. Reduce garbage by buying reusable products and recycling.
14. Replace standard light bulbs with fluorescent bulbs.
15. When you buy a car, make fuel efficiency a major consideration.
16. When you have your car air conditioner serviced, make sure the coolant is recycled.
17. Install energy-saving windows in your home.
18. Caulk around doors and windows in your home.
19. Insulate all walls and ceilings.
20. If possible, select a utility company that does not produce electricity from fossil fuel sources.

Adapted from *Time*, 9 Apr. 2001, p. 39.

WORKS CONSULTED

■ ***Joshua's list of "Works Consulted" increased considerably over his first speech, reprinted at the end of Chapter 15. You should expand your research accordingly when you develop a topic over several speeches.***

"Americans Consider Global Warming Real, But Not Alarming." Gallup News Service. 9 Apr. 2001. 17 Apr. 2001 <http://www.gallup.com/poll/Releases/PrO10409.asp>.

Crozier, George. "Research on Global Warming and Dauphin Island." Email to Joshua Logan. 17 Apr. 2001.

"Feeling the Heat." *Time* 9 Apr. 2001: 22–39.

Fletcher, Susan R. "Global Climate Change Treaty: The Kyoto Protocol." National Council for Science and the Environment. 6 Mar. 2000. 19 Apr. 2001 <http://www.cnie.org/nle/clim-25.html>.

"Governments Agree: Global Warming Impact Serious." Environment News Service. 19 Feb. 2001. 17 Apr. 2001 <http://ens.lycos.com/ens/feb2001/20011-02-19-01.html>.

"Grim Future Forecast for World's Coastal Areas." Environment News Service. 17 Apr. 2001. 18 Apr. 2001 <http://ens-news.com/ens/apr2001/2001L-04-17-06.html>.

Lazaroff, Catherine. "New Method Could Reduce Carbon Dioxide Levels Safely." Environment News Service. 31 Aug. 1999. 17 Apr. 2001 <http://ens.lycos.com/ens/aug99/19991-08-31-07.html>.

Lazaroff, Cat. "Warming Oceans Attributed to Greenhouse Gases." Environment News Service. 16 Apr. 2001. 17 Apr. 2001 <http://ens.lycos.com/ens/apr2001/20011-04-16-06.html>.

Petit, Charles W. "Polar Meltdown." *U.S. News & World Report* 28 Feb. 2000: 65–74.

Shute, Nancy. "The Weather Turns Wild." *U.S. News & World Report* 5 Feb. 2001: 44–52.

"Snapshots of the 2001 Cars." *Consumer Reports* (April 2001): 44, 59.

Summary for Policymakers: A Report of Working Group I of the [United Nations] Intergovernmental Panel on Climate Change. January 2001. 17 Apr. 2001 <http://www.usgcrp.gov/ipcc/wg1spm.pdf >.

Summary for Policymakers: Climate Change 2001: Impacts, Adaptation, and Vulnerability. A Report of Working Group II of the [United Nations] Intergovernmental Panel on Climate Change. 13–16 Feb. 2001. 17 Apr. 2001 <http://usgcrp.gov/ipcc/wg2spm.pdf>.

Summary for Policy Makers of the IPCC WG III Third Assessment Report. 28 Feb.–3 Mar.2001. 4 Apr. 2001 <http://www.usgcrp.gov/ipcc/wg3spm.pdf>.

Ceremonial Speaking

17

OUTLINE

This chapter will help you

- understand the importance of ceremonial speaking
- present speeches of tribute and inspiration
- develop speeches introducing speakers and accepting awards
- prepare a toast or an after-dinner speech
- act as a master of ceremonies
- develop a speech using narrative design

[People] who celebrate . . . are fused with each other and fused with all things in nature.

ERNST CASSIRER

Your college has just concluded an ambitious fundraising campaign to create scholarships and attract outstanding teachers, artists, and scholars. As the leader of student volunteers who spent many hours soliciting contributions, you have been invited to be master of ceremonies at a banquet celebrating the campaign. At the banquet, you may both present and listen to many kinds of speeches: speeches offering tribute, speeches conferring and accepting awards, speeches introducing other speakers, speeches evoking laughter, and speeches inspiring listeners. They are all part of what we call ceremonial speaking.

There are other occasions when you may be called on to make a ceremonial speech. You may be asked to "say a few words" about a coworker or former teacher who is retiring, to toast a friend's wedding or anniversary, to welcome newcomers to an organization or community, or to present a eulogy at the memorial services for a dear friend or family member.

It is easy to underestimate the importance of ceremonial speaking. Informative speaking shares knowledge, and persuasive speaking influences attitudes and actions. In comparison, ceremonial speaking, with its occasional moments of humor or inspiration, may not seem that significant. But it can serve a very important purpose. **Ceremonial speaking** stresses the sharing of identities and values that unites people into communities.[1] The philosopher John Dewey observed that people "live in a community in virtue of the things which they have in common; and communication is the way in which they come to possess things in common. What they must have in common . . . are aims, beliefs, aspirations, knowledge—a common understanding."[2] It is ceremonial speaking that celebrates and reinforces our common aims, beliefs, and aspirations.

Rituals and ceremonies are important to all groups because they draw people together.[3] They provide larger-than-life pictures of our identities and ideals.[4] Ceremonial speaking addresses four basic questions: *Who are we? Why are we? What have we accomplished? and What can we become together?* As it answers these questions, ceremonial speaking provides people with a sense of purpose and helps create an "ordered, meaningful cultural world."[5]

Ceremonial speaking also serves a very practical purpose. As our opening example indicates, ceremonies put the spotlight on the speaker. As you conduct the college's celebration of its fundraising campaign as master of ceremonies, others will be looking at you and thinking, "Wouldn't she (or he) make a good student body president?" From the time of Aristotle, scholars have recognized that ceremonial speaking puts leadership on display.[6]

Ceremonial speeches also establish practical standards for action, advancing the principles that justify arguments and influence behavior.[7] The two student speeches at the end of this chapter illustrate this function. As Leslie Eason paid tribute to Tiger Woods for refusing to accept an identity based on race, she was, in effect, saying that we should not base our perceptions of ourselves or others on racial criteria. As Ashlie McMillan told the inspiring story of her cousin who is a dwarf, she was also urging her listeners not to let limitations block their own accomplishments. Both underlying messages could serve as principles justifying arguments and influencing behavior.

In this chapter we discuss the techniques and major forms of ceremonial speaking.

Techniques of Ceremonial Speaking

View the student speech in the **VideoLab Lesson 10 Screening Room** for an example of a ceremonial speech.

Two techniques, identification and magnification, are vital to the effectiveness of ceremonial speaking.

Identification

Identification occurs when a speech creates the feeling that speaker and listeners share goals, values, emotions, memories, motives, and cultural background. Kenneth Burke, perhaps the most important communication theorist of our time, suggested that *identification* was the key term of persuasive speaking.[8] People who *feel* together on issues will also reason and act together. Because ritual and ceremony draw people together, identification is also the heart of ceremonial speaking. Speakers promote identification through the use of narrative, the recognition of heroes and heroines, and the renewal of group commitment.

Complete the exercise in **VideoLab Drill 10.1: Identifying Effective and Ineffective Speaking Strategies** to learn more about the techniques of ceremonial speaking.

The Use of Narrative. Ceremonial speaking is the time for reliving shared golden moments. For example, if you were preparing a speech for the fundraising celebration mentioned at the beginning of this chapter, you could recall things that happened during those long evenings when student volunteers were making calls. You might remember moments of discouragement, followed by other moments of triumph when the contributions were especially large or meaningful. Your story would draw listeners closer together, as they remembered emotions they had shared. Stories that evoke humor are especially effective identifiers, because laughter itself is a shared group experience:

> **I don't think that any of us will forget the night that John tripped over a phone cord carrying a tray full of coffee and shorted out the computer network for the phone bank. Although many contributors got "cut off" by the accident, the returned calls netted the highest contributions of any night of the campaign.**

Just be certain your humorous stories don't belittle the people involved.

Ashlie McMillan showed how narrative can advance identification in her tribute to her cousin. In her introduction, she asked listeners to close their eyes and imagine themselves shrinking. As they imagined miniature versions of themselves, prompted by her skillful use of language, listeners could identify more closely with Tina and the enormous problems she had to confront as a dwarf.

We will say more about how to design effective narratives in the final section of this chapter.

Ritual and ceremony can reinforce feelings of identification between speakers and listeners.

The Recognition of Heroes and Heroines. As you speak of the trials and triumphs of fundraising, you may want to recognize people who made singular contributions. These heroes and heroines can function as role models to inspire future action. Because we try to be like them and act like them, the effect again is to draw people together around shared images of ideal conduct. You must be careful, however, in using this technique. You may leave out someone who deserves recognition and create division rather than identification. Therefore, recognize specific individuals only when they have made truly unusual contributions or when they are representative. You might say, for instance:

> **Let me tell you about Mary Tyrer. She is just one of the many who for the last two months have spent night after night on these phones—talking, coaxing, winning friends for our school, and raising thousands of dollars in contributions. Mary, and all the others like you, we salute you, and promise that we will follow your example in the years to come!**

Renewal of Group Commitment. Ceremonial speaking is a time both for celebrating what has been accomplished and for renewing commitments. Share with your listeners a vision of what the future can be like if their commitment continues. Plead with them not to be satisfied with present accomplishments. Renew their identity as a group moving toward even greater goals.

In his first inaugural address, delivered on the eve of the Civil War, Abraham Lincoln used the technique of identification in an effort to reunite the nation:

> **We are not enemies, but friends. We must not be enemies. Though passion may have strained, it must not break our bonds of affection. The mystic chords of memory, stretching from every battle-field, and patriot grave, to every living heart and hearthstone, all over this broad land, will yet swell the chorus of the Union, when again touched, as surely they will be, by the better angels of our nature.**[9]

Speaker's Notes 17.1

Promoting Identification

1. Tell stories that remind listeners of shared experiences.
2. Remember, listeners who laugh together are identifying with one another.
3. Create portraits of heroes and heroines as role models to draw listeners together.
4. Revive legends and traditions that remind listeners of their shared heritage and values.
5. Offer goals and visions to inspire listeners to work together.

Magnification

In his *Rhetoric*, Aristotle noted that when you select certain features of a person or event and then dwell on those qualities in your speech of tribute, the effect is to magnify those features until they fill the minds of listeners.[10] These magnified features then characterize the subject in terms of the values they represent. They focus listener attention on what is relevant, honorable, and praiseworthy. This vital inspirational technique is what we call **magnification**. For example, imagine that you are preparing a speech honoring Jesse Owens's incredible track and field accomplishments in the 1936 Olympic Games. In your research, you come up with a variety of facts:

- He had a headache the day he won the medal in the long jump.
- He had suffered from racism in America.
- He did not like the food served at the Olympic training camp.
- He won his four gold medals in front of Adolf Hitler, who was preaching the racial superiority of Germans.
- Some of his friends did not want him to run for the United States.
- After his victories, he returned to further discrimination in America.

If you used all this information, your speech might seem rather rambling and aimless. Which of these items should you emphasize, and how should you proceed? To make your selection, you need to know what themes are best to develop when you are magnifying the actions of a person. These themes include the following:

- Triumph over obstacles
- Unusual accomplishment
- Superior performance
- Unselfish motives
- Benefit to society

As you consider these themes, it becomes clear which items about Jesse Owens you should magnify, and how you should go about it. To begin, you would stress that Owens had to overcome obstacles such as racism in America to make the Olympic team. Then you would point out that his accomplishment was unusual, that no one else had ever won four gold medals in Olympic track and field competition. Moreover, the performance was superior, resulting in world records that lasted many years. Because Owens received no material gain from his victories, his motives were unselfish; his performance was driven solely by personal qualities such as courage and determination. Finally, you would demonstrate that because his victories repudiated Hitler's racist ideology, causing the Nazi leader public humiliation, Owens's accomplishments benefited our society. The overall effect would be to magnify the meaning of Jesse Owens's great performances, both for himself and for his nation.

In addition to focusing on these basic themes, magnification relies on effective uses of language to create dramatic word-pictures. Metaphor and simile can magnify a subject through creative associations, such as "He

InterConnections.LearnMore 17.1

Identification

The Kenneth Burke Society
http://www-home.cc.duq.edu/~thames/kennethburke/Default.htm
Gateway to greater understanding of the life and work of communication theorist Kenneth Burke; contains a discussion section and material on conferences on Burke's work; maintained by Professor Richard Thames, Department of English, Duquesne University.

On Kenneth Burke's Concept of Rhetorical Identification
http://www.libarts.ucok.edu/english/faculty/stein/rhetoric/report/Kenneth_Burke.htm
A brief, interesting explanation of Burke's treatment of identification; authored by Ricki Higdon.

Kenneth Burke and Identification
http://www.sla.purdue.edu/people/engl/dblakesley/burke/clark.html
Full text of a paper, "Kenneth Burke, Identification, and Rhetorical Criticism," by Professor Gregory Clark of Brigham Young University; presented at the Conference on College Compositition and Communication, March 1997; adapts the concept of identification to the teaching of writing.

Jesse Owens was both a great Olympic hero and a great inspirational speaker.

struck like a lightning bolt that day." Parallel structure, the repetition of key words and phrases, can also help magnify a subject and embed it in our minds. For example, if you were to say of Mother Teresa, "Whenever there was hurt, she was there. Whenever there was hunger, she was there. Whenever there was desperation, she was there," you would be magnifying her dedication and selflessness.

Magnification also favors certain speech designs over others. Comparison and contrast designs promote magnification by making selected features stand out. For example, you might contrast the purity of Owens's motives with the crassness of those of today's well-paid athletes. Chronological designs used to relate the history of a situation enhance magnification by dramatizing certain events as stories unfold over time. As Ashlie McMillan sketched incidents in the childhood and adulthood of her cousin, she magnified Tina's developing character. The causation design serves magnification when a person's accomplishments are emphasized as the causes of important effects: Jesse Owens's victories, a speaker might say, refuted Nazi propaganda for many people. The narrative design, which can highlight features of accomplishments, is a natural for ceremonial speaking. We will cover it more closely in the final section of this chapter.

Whatever designs ceremonial speeches use, it is important that they build to a conclusion. Speakers should save their best stories and their most dramatic points until the end of the speech. Ceremonial speeches should never dwindle to a conclusion.

Types of Ceremonial Speeches

Go to the **VideoLab Next Step: Types and Techniques of Ceremonial Speaking** to further your understanding of the types of ceremonial speaking. VideoLab

Ceremonial speeches include the speech of tribute (award presentations, eulogies, and toasts), the acceptance speech, the speech of introduction, the speech of inspiration, and the after-dinner speech (see Figure 17.1). A ceremonial speaker may also serve as a master of ceremonies.

Speaker's Notes 17.2

Magnification

1. Show how people have overcome obstacles to success.
2. Point out how unusual the accomplishments are.
3. Underscore superior features of the performance.
4. Emphasize unselfish motives behind the achievement.
5. Show how listeners and society as a whole have benefited.
6. Use the techniques of magnifying language power that are discussed in Chapter 12.
7. Use speech designs—comparison, chronological, causation, and narrative—that highlight magnification.

The Speech of Tribute

In magnifying the importance of accomplishments, the **speech of tribute** endorses the values of individual responsibility, striving, and achievement. For example, you might be called on to honor a former teacher at a retirement ceremony, present an award to someone for an outstanding accomplishment, eulogize a person who has died, or propose a toast to a friend who is getting married.

Speeches of tribute can serve several important purposes. If you have presented a series of speeches on related topics in your class, the speech of tribute gives you a chance to extend your efforts at informing and persuading listeners. For example, Holly Carlson chose the banning of books in public schools as the topic area for all her speeches. In her informative speech, she demonstrated how books are banned in schools all over the country, and she listed the books and authors most often targeted. In her persuasive speech she offered a stirring plea for intellectual freedom, urging her listeners to support the right to read and think for themselves. Then, for her ceremonial speech, she offered a tribute to one of the most victimized authors, J. D. Salinger. Her tribute to Salinger made her listeners want to read his works themselves. It also dramatized how hurtful censorship could be. Thus, all of Holly's speeches were woven into one fabric, which gave focus and cohesion to her semester's work.

Speeches of tribute blend easily with inspirational speeches. As Leslie Eason praised Tiger Woods, she also inspired listeners to apply his example of integrity to their own lives. Ashlie McMillan's tribute to her cousin offered listeners an inspiring model of determination to overcome obstacles to their own achievements.

Praiseworthy accomplishments are usually celebrated for two reasons. First, *they are important in themselves:* the influence of a teacher may have contributed to the success of many of her former students. Second, *they are important as symbols.* The planting of the American flag at Iwo Jima during some of the most intense fighting of World War II came to symbolize the fortitude of the entire American war effort; it represented commitment, and it was more important as a symbol than as an actual event. Sometimes the same event may be celebrated for both actual and symbolic reasons. A student speech honoring the raising of $60 million for famine relief celebrated this achievement both as a symbol of global generosity and for the actual help it brought to many starving people. When you plan a speech of tribute, you should consider both the actual and the symbolic values that are represented.

Figure 17.1

Types of Commercial Speeches

Type	Use When
Tributes	You wish to honor a person, group, occasion, or event. Subtypes include award presentations, eulogies, and toasts.
Acceptance	You need to acknowledge an award or honor.
Introductions	You must introduce a featured speaker in a program.
Inspiration	You want to motivate listeners to appreciate and commit to a goal, purpose, or set of values; this may be religious, commercial, political, or social in nature.
After-Dinner	You want to entertain the audience while leaving a message that can guide future behavior. Here, as elsewhere, brevity is golden.
Master of Ceremonies	You must coordinate a program and see that everything runs smoothly. The master of ceremonies sets the mood for the occasion.

The raising of the American flag at Iwo Jima during World War II became an important cultural symbol for courage and fortitude, themes echoed in the similar photograph of the raising of the flag by firefighters over the wreckage of the World Trade Center.

Developing Speeches of Tribute. As you prepare a speech of tribute, keep the following guidelines in mind:

- *Do not exaggerate the tribute.* If you are too lavish with your praise or use too many superlatives, you may embarrass the recipient and make the praise unbelievable.
- *Focus on the person being honored, not on yourself.* Even if you know what effort the accomplishment required because you have done something similar, don't mention that at this time. It will just seem as though you are tooting your own horn when the focus should be on the honoree.
- *Create vivid images of accomplishment.* Speeches of tribute are occasions for illustrating what someone has achieved, the values underlying those achievements, and their consequences. Tell stories that make those accomplishments come to life.
- *Be sincere.* Speeches of tribute are a time for warmth, pride, and appreciation. Your manner should reflect these qualities as you present the tribute.

When you honor a historical figure, your purpose will usually be to frame present goals in terms of the example you provide. This was the intention of Tommie Albright, Miss Florida Teen 2000 and a student at Daytona Beach Community College, as she spoke at the college's Martin Luther King Jr. Memorial Evening. Notice especially her use of contrast and parallel structure in the following section of her speech (reprinted in full in Appendix B):

> Martin Luther King had many dreams for us, each with its own challenge to us.
> Where he dreamed of peace, we must be peaceful and seek peace.
> Where he saw hope, we must provide fulfillment.
> Where he dreamed of equality, we must treat each other as equals.
> Where he dreamed of brotherhood, we must act as brothers and sisters.
> And where he dreamed of justice, we must provide a just society.[11]

Award Presentations. When you present an award, you often accompany it with a speech of tribute. An **award presentation** recognizes the achievements or contributions of those on whom the award is bestowed. Most award presentations have two main points: they explain the nature of the award, and they applaud what the recipient did to qualify for it.

Unless the award is quite well known, such as an Oscar or Nobel Prize, you should always begin an award presentation by explaining the award:

> Mary Beth Peterson was a graduate assistant in this department who exemplified the best qualities of a teacher: enthusiasm for her subject, the ability to impart it to others, and a real sense of caring for those whom she taught. After her untimely death, her parents and friends endowed the Mary Beth Peterson award, offered each year to the graduate assistant in our department

who best exemplifies the qualities Mary Beth brought so generously to the classroom.

The elegant use of language is important in ceremonial speaking. Here Toni Morrison accepts the Nobel Prize for Literature.

The second and most important part of an award presentation involves explaining why the honoree was chosen to receive the award. In talking about the recipient, you should emphasize the uniqueness, superiority, and benefits of his or her achievements. Provide specific examples that illustrate these accomplishments. Finally, you should name the recipient of the award and offer your congratulations and wishes for continued success. The complete text of an award presentation to Olympic track gold medalist Wilma Rudolph may be found in Appendix B.

Eulogies. Earlier we asked you to imagine yourself preparing a speech to honor Jesse Owens. Following his death in 1980, many such speeches were actually presented. A speech of tribute presented on the death of a person is called a **eulogy**. The following comments by Congressman Thomas P. O'Neill Jr., then Speaker of the House, illustrate how some of the major techniques we have discussed can work in a eulogy:

I rise on the occasion of his passing to join my colleagues in tribute to the greatest American sports hero of this century, Jesse Owens. . . . His performances at the Berlin Olympics earned Jesse Owens the title of America's first superstar. . . .

No other athlete symbolized the spirit and motto of the Olympics better than Jesse Owens. "Swifter, higher, stronger" was the credo by which Jesse Owens performed as an athlete and lived as an American. Of his performances in Hitler's Berlin in 1936, Jesse said: "I wasn't running against Hitler, I was running against the world." Owens's view of the Olympics was just that: he was competing against the best athletes in the world without regard to nationality, race, or political view. . . .

O'Neill's opening highlights the themes of unusual and superior accomplishment. He begins with the actual value of Owens's victories, and then he describes their symbolic value.

Jesse Owens proved by his performances that he was the best among the finest the world had to offer, and in setting the world record in the 100-yard dash, he became the "fastest human" even before that epithet was fashionable. . . .

In life as well as on the athletic field Jesse Owens was first an American, and second, an internationalist. He loved his country; he loved the opportunity his country gave him to reach the pinnacle of athletic prowess. In his own quiet, unassuming, and modest way—by example, by inspiration, and by performance—he helped other young people to aim for the stars, to develop their God-given potential. . . .

These comments magnify the values represented by Owens's life and develop the theme of benefit to the community.

As the world's first superstar Jesse Owens was not initially overwhelmed by commercial interests and offered the opportunity to become a millionaire overnight. There was no White House reception waiting for him on his return from Berlin, and as Jesse Owens once observed: "I still had to ride in the back of the bus in my hometown in Alabama."

That Owens remained a patriotic American in the face of racism and indifference magnifies his character.

Can one individual make a difference? Clearly in the case of Jesse Owens the answer is a resounding affirmative, for his whole life was dedicated to the elimination of poverty, totalitarianism, and racial bigotry; and he did it in his own special and modest way, a spokesman for freedom, an American ambas-

O'Neill's conclusion emphasizes the symbolic, spiritual values of Owens's life.

> **sador of good will to the athletes of the world, and an inspiration to young Americans. . . . Jesse Owens was a champion all the way in a life of dedication to the principles of the American and Olympic spirit.[12]**

When presented at memorial services, eulogies should also express the pain of loss and offer comfort.[13] Such eulogies are—indeed, must be—highly personal. One person responding to a special newspaper feature on eulogies commented:

> **There is nothing more depressing than a "generic" eulogy delivered by a celebrant that obviously did not know the deceased. The best eulogies are those that are very personal and celebrate the life of the deceased.[14]**

When you are asked to present a eulogy at a funeral or memorial service, you confront a special challenge. In addition to dealing with natural anxiety about speaking, you must also control your own feelings of grief. Plan your eulogy with these thoughts in mind:

- Remember that your primary purpose is to offer comfort to the living. Remind them of how much they meant to the deceased. Try to provide words that will continue to console them in the days, months, and years later.
- Share stories that highlight the humanity of the person. Use gentle humor to recall his or her endearing qualities.
- Focus on how wonderful it was to have shared the life of the person more than on the pain of the loss. Make the eulogy a celebration of life.
- Focus on the meaning of the person's life for those who live on.

Another respondent to the special issue on eulogies recalled fondly the eulogy delivered by her brother at the funeral of another brother.

> **At the end of his eulogy, Mike described some life lessons Kevin taught him . . . . He told about how Kevin would be happy just standing outside and gazing up at the stars at night or smelling the scent of honeysuckle on a cool spring evening. Mike talked about how Kevin had simple faith like a child. He would look at the stars in the sky or admire the beauty of the Ozark Mountains and know there was a Creator.[15]**

This speaker clearly was sensitive to the guidelines we have mentioned.

Noa Ben-Artzi eulogizes her grandfather Yitzhak Rabin, who was assassinated while serving as prime minister of Israel.

Toasts. A **toast** is a ceremonial speech in miniature, offered as a tribute to people and what they have done, as a blessing for their future, or simply as lighthearted enjoyment of the present moment. You might be asked to toast a coworker who has been promoted or a couple at a wedding reception, or simply to celebrate the beginning of a new year. The occasion may be formal or informal, but the message should always be eloquent. It simply won't do to mutter, "Here's to Tony, he's a great guy!" or "Cheers!" As one writer has said, such a feeble toast is "a gratuitous betrayal—of the occasion, its honoree, and the desire [of the audience] to clink glasses and murmur, 'Hear, hear' in appreciation of a compliment well fashioned."[16]

A toast, a ceremonial speech in miniature, is offered as a tribute to people, as a blessing for their future, or simply in light-hearted enjoyment of the moment.

Whenever you think you might be called on to offer a toast, plan your remarks in advance. Keep your toast brief, and build to a climax. You might toast the "coach of the year" in the following way:

> **I want to offer a toast to a woman who is being recognized tonight as "coach of the year." You talk to the young women in this community, and to many of their parents sitting in this hall, and they'll tell you we should be honoring her as "coach of the century." Friend, confidante, mentor, model, ambassador for the community, and, yes, coach of winning girls' basketball teams year after year, she means so much to so many of us. So here's to Nancy, who will always be our own "coach of the year!"**

Because a toast is a speech of celebration, you should refrain from making negative remarks.[17] For example, it would be inappropriate at a wedding reception to say, "Here's to John and Mary. I hope they don't end up in divorce court in a year the way I did!" Although most speeches are best presented extemporaneously, a toast should be memorized. Practice presenting your toast with glass in hand until it flows easily. If you have difficulty memorizing your toast, it is probably too long. Figure 17.2 presents samples of toasts for different occasions.

Acceptance Speeches

If you are receiving an award or honor, you may be expected to respond with a **speech of acceptance**. A speech of acceptance should express gratitude for the honor and acknowledge those who made the accomplishment possible. It should remain humble, should focus on the values the award represents, and should use language that matches the dignity of the occasion.

When Elie Wiesel was awarded the 1986 Nobel Peace Prize, he began his acceptance speech with these remarks: "It is with a profound sense of humility that I accept the honor you have chosen to bestow upon me."[18] (The complete text of Wiesel's acceptance speech may be found in Appendix B). Follow his lead and accept an award with grace and modesty.

In an acceptance speech, you should also give credit where credit is due. If your hometown historical society is awarding you a scholarship, it would be appropriate for you to mention some teachers who prepared you for this moment. You might say

Figure 17.2
Sample Toasts

- May you have warm words on a cold evening, a full moon on a dark night, and a road downhill all the way to your door. (Irish blessing)
- Here's looking at you, kid. (Humphrey Bogart toasting Ingrid Bergman in *Casablanca*)
- I drink to your charm, your beauty, and your brains—Which gives you a rough idea of how hard up I am for a drink. (Groucho Marx)
- To get the full value of joy, you must have someone to divide it with. (Mark Twain)
- May you have the hindsight to know where you've been, the foresight to know where you're going, and the insight to know when you're going too far.
- As you ramble through life, whatever be your goal, keep your eye upon the doughnut, and not upon the hole. (Offered by Sid Pettigrew)*
- May the road rise to meet you.
  May the wind be always at your back.
  May the sun shine warm upon your face.
  And rains fall soft upon your fields.
  And until we meet again,
  May God hold you in the hollow of His hand. (Irish blessing)

* From "Tom's Toasts: Irish Toasts and Blessings," March 1998. http://zinnia.umfacad.maine.edu/~donaghue/toasts01.html (16 Dec. 1998).

something like, "This award belongs as much to Mr. Del Rio as it does to me. He opened my eyes to the importance and relevance of history in our world." When Martin Luther King Jr. accepted his Nobel Peace Prize in 1964, he did so in these words:

> **I accept this prize on behalf of all men who love peace and brotherhood. . . . Most of these people will never make the headlines and their names will not appear in Who's Who. Yet when years have rolled past . . . men and women will know and children will be taught that we have a finer land, a better people, a more noble civilization—because these humble children of God were willing to suffer for righteousness' sake.[19]**

As you accept an award, express your awareness of its deeper meaning. In their acceptance speeches, both Mr. Wiesel and Dr. King stressed the value of freedom and the importance of involvement—of overcoming hatred with loving concern.

Finally, be sure the eloquence of your language fits the dignity of the situation. Dr. King relied heavily on an extended movement metaphor in his acceptance speech. He spoke of the "tortuous road" from Montgomery, Alabama, to Oslo, Norway, a road on which, in his words, "millions of Negroes are traveling to find a new sense of dignity." In a similar manner, Mr. Wiesel told the story of a "young Jewish boy discovering the kingdom of night" during the Holocaust. This personal, metaphorical narrative was introduced early in the speech and repeated in the conclusion when Mr. Wiesel remarked, "No one is as capable of gratitude as one who has emerged from the kingdom of night." Although you may not be as eloquent as these Nobel Prize winners, you should make a presentation that befits the dignity of the occasion.

If an award is presented as part of a ceremony involving presentations to more than one person, shorter acceptance speeches may be called for. Wilma Rudolph's brief words of acceptance on the National Sports Awards show were appropriate for that situation.

Speaker's Notes 17.3

Making an Acceptance Speech

1. Be modest.
2. Express your appreciation for the honor.
3. Acknowledge those who made your accomplishment possible.
4. Highlight the values that the award represents.
5. Be sure your language fits the formality of the occasion.

I'm excited. I'll get my breath. I receive this honor, and I dedicate it to the youth of America so they will know that their dreams too can come true. And also to my mother who is eighty-four years old, Blanche Rudolph. Thank you so much for this honor.

The Speech of Introduction

One of the more common types of ceremonial speeches is the **speech of introduction**, in which you introduce a featured speaker to the audience. The importance of this speech can vary, depending on how well the speaker is already known. At times a formal introduction may seem quite unnecessary. For example, when Madonna introduced Muhammad Ali at a gathering of New York sports personalities, she simply said:

We are alike in many ways. We have espoused unpopular causes, we are arrogant, we like to have our picture taken, and we are the greatest.[20]

A good speech of introduction will usually do three things: make the speaker feel welcome, establish or strengthen the ethos of the speaker, and prepare the audience for the speech that will follow. You make a speaker feel welcome both by what you say and how you say it. Deliver your words of welcome with warmth and sincerity.

As soon as you know you will be introducing someone, find out as much as you can about the person. You might ask the speaker what you might emphasize that would be most helpful to his or her speech. It may seem obvious, but be sure you know how to pronounce the speaker's name. One of our oldest friends is named Bakke, and there are various ways to mispronounce his name. We have heard him speak many times, and we have heard introducers butcher his name on more than one occasion.

The following guidelines will help you build ethos and lay the groundwork for speaker-audience identification:

- Create respect by magnifying the speaker's main accomplishments.
- Don't be too lavish with your praise. An overblown introduction can be embarrassing and distracting. One featured speaker was so overcome by an excessive introduction that he responded, "If you do not go to heaven for charity, you will certainly go somewhere else for exaggeration or downright prevarication."[21]
- Mention achievements that are relevant to the speaker's message, the occasion on which the speech is being presented, or the audience that has assembled.
- Be selective! If you try to present too many details and accomplishments, you may take up the speaker's time and make listeners weary. Introducers who drone on too long can create real problems for the speakers who follow.

Speaker's Notes 17.4

Introducing Featured Speakers

1. Be sure you know how to pronounce the speaker's name.
2. Find out what the speaker would like you to emphasize.
3. Focus on aspects of the speaker's background that are relevant to the topic, audience, and occasion.
4. Announce the title of the speech and tune the audience for it.
5. Make the speaker feel welcome. Be warm and gracious.
6. Be brief!

The final function of an effective introduction is to tune the audience. In Chapter 5 we discussed how preliminary tuning can establish a receptive mood. You tune the audience when you arouse anticipation for the message that will follow. However, this does not mean that you should attempt to preview the speech. Leave that job to the speaker!

The Speech of Inspiration

The **speech of inspiration** arouses an audience to appreciate, commit to, and pursue a goal, purpose, or set of values or beliefs. Speeches of inspiration help listeners see subjects in a new light. Inspirational speeches may be religious, commercial, political, or social. When a sales manager introduces a new product to marketing representatives, pointing up its competitive advantages and its glowing market potential, the speech is both inspirational and persuasive. The marketing reps should feel inspired to push that product with great zeal and enthusiasm. Speeches at political conventions that praise the principles of the party, such as keynote addresses, are inspirational in tone and intent. So also is that great American institution, the commencement address. As different as these speech occasions may seem, they have important points in common.

First, *speeches of inspiration are enthusiastic.* Inspirational speakers accomplish their goals through their personal commitment and energy. Both the speaker and the speech must be active and forceful. Speakers must set an example for their audiences through their behavior both on and off the speaking platform. They must practice what they preach. Their ethos must be consistent with their advice.

Second, *speeches of inspiration draw on past successes and frustrations to encourage future accomplishment.* At a Catalyst Awards Dinner, Sheila W. Welling, the organization president, evoked vivid memories of what the past was like for women as she urged continued progress toward equality in the workplace in the new millennium:

> **One hundred years ago, at the dawn of the last millennium, our bustled Victorian great-grandmothers could not run for a bus, let alone for Congress. If the race—as the Victorian poet claimed—went to the swift, women lost. Girdled, corseted, enveloped in yards of gingham and lace, women were balanced precariously on their pedestals.**
>
> **. . . Women couldn't vote when my mother was born. Every time I think about it, it startles me: even as Edith Wharton wrote her novels, as Helen Keller graduated from Radcliffe with honors, even as women manufactured the arms that led to victory in WWI and the nation's move to global primacy, women still could not vote.[22]**

Third, *speeches of inspiration revitalize our appreciation for values or beliefs.* Such speeches can strengthen our sense of mythos, the distinctive code of values underlying our society. In the later years of his life, when his athletic prowess had faded, Jesse Owens became known as a great inspirational speaker. According to his obituary in the *New York Times*, "The Jesse Owens best remembered by many Americans was a public speaker with the ringing, inspirational delivery of an evangelist. . . . [His speeches] praised the virtues of patriotism, clean living and fair play."[23] In the speech that follows below, Owens stresses the ideals of brotherhood and tolerance, as well as fair competition.

In his inspirational speeches to budding athletes, Jesse Owens frequently talked about his Olympic achievements. The following excerpts, taken from a statement protesting America's withdrawal from the 1980 Summer Olympic Games, illustrate his inspirational style. Jesse Owens was unable to deliver this message personally. He prepared it shortly before his death from cancer.

What the Berlin games proved . . . was that Hitler's "supermen" could be beaten. Ironically, it was one of his blond, blue-eyed, Aryan athletes who helped do the beating.

Owens's introduction suggests the larger meaning of his victories and sets the stage for identification.

I held the world record in the broad jump. Even more than the sprints, it was "my" event. Yet I was one jump from not even making the finals. I fouled on my first try, and playing it safe the second time, I had not jumped far enough.

The broad jump preliminaries came before the finals of my other three events and everything, it seemed then, depended on this jump. Fear swept over me and then panic. I walked off alone, trying to gather myself. I dropped to one knee, closed my eyes, and prayed. I felt a hand on my shoulder. I opened my eyes and there stood my arch enemy, Luz Long, the prize athlete Hitler had kept under wraps while he trained for one purpose only: to beat me. Long had broken the Olympic mark in his very first try in the preliminaries.

Note the use of graphic detail to recapture the immediacy of the moment.

"I know about you," he said. "You are like me. You must do it all the way, or you cannot do it. The same that has happened to you today happened to me last year in Cologne. I will tell you what I did then." Luz told me to measure my steps, place my towel 6 inches on back of the takeoff board and jump from there. That way I could give it all I had and be certain not to foul.

Owens's use of dialogue helps listeners feel they are sharing the experience.

As soon as I had qualified, Luz, smiling broadly, came to me and said, "Now we can make each other do our best in the finals."

And that's what we did in the finals. Luz jumped, and broke his Olympic record. Then I jumped just a bit further and broke Luz's new record. We each had three leaps in all. On his final jump, Luz went almost 26 feet, 5 inches, a mark that seemed impossible to beat. I went just a bit over that, and set an Olympic record that was to last for almost a quarter of a century.

I won that day, but I'm being straight when I say that even before I made that last jump, I knew I had won a victory of a far greater kind—over something inside myself, thanks to Luz.

This narrative leaves open the meaning of Owens's "inside" victory: perhaps it was over self-doubt or over his own stereotype of Germans. Perhaps it was over both.

The instant my record-breaking win was announced, Luz was there, throwing his arms around me and raising my arm to the sky. "Jazze Owenz!" he yelled as loud as he could. More than 100,000 Germans in the stadium joined in. "Jazze Owenz, Jazze Owenz, Jazze Owenz!"

This scene presents an inspirational model of international competition.

Hitler was there, too, but he was not chanting. He had lost that day. Luz Long was killed in World War II and, although I don't cry often, I wept when I received his last letter—I knew it was his last. In it he asked me to someday find his son, Karl, and to tell him "of how we fought well together, and of the good times, and that any two men can become brothers."

Owens shows how individuals can rise above ideologies, as Long's final message invites identification.

That is what the Olympics are all about. The road to the Olympics does not lead to Moscow. It leads to no city, no country. It goes far beyond Lake Placid or Moscow, Ancient Greece or Nazi Germany. The road to the Olympics leads, in the end, to the best within us.[24]

Owens ends with a metaphor of the "road to the Olympics."

Speaker's Notes 17.5

Presenting the Inspirational Speech

1. You must seem personally inspired by your own message.
2. Demonstrate sincerity and personal commitment in your presentation.
3. Set forth goals that will challenge listeners, but not discourage them.
4. Tell dramatic stories that catch listeners up in the inspiring action and revitalize their values.
5. Draw upon the past to portray an even better future that will reward audience commitment and effort.

The After-Dinner Speech

Occasions that celebrate special events or that mark the beginning or end of a course of action often call for special dinners and provide the setting for an **after-dinner speech.** Political rallies, award banquets, the kickoff for a fundraising campaign, or the end of the school year may constitute such occasions.

The after-dinner speech is one of the great rituals of American public speaking and public life. If you are the leader of the group holding the dinner, or have won some special recognition that makes people look up to you, or simply have the reputation for being an entertaining speaker, you may be invited to give such a speech. As these qualifications suggest, the purpose of such a speech may vary from celebrating group accomplishments and setting new goals to enjoying the company of the moment and the laughter that can enrich lives and bond groups more closely together.

Almost all after-dinner speeches, however, share certain features. In keeping with the nature of the occasion, they should not be too difficult to digest. Speakers making these presentations usually do not introduce radical ideas that require listeners to rethink their values or that ask for dramatic changes in belief or behavior. Nor are such occasions the time for anger or negativity. Rather, they are a time for people to savor who they are, what they have done, or what they wish to do. A good after-dinner speech typically leaves a message that can guide and inspire future efforts.

The Role of Humor. Humor is an essential ingredient in most after-dinner speeches. In the introduction, humor can place both the speaker and the audience at ease.[25] Enjoying lighter moments can remind us that there is a human element in all situations and that we should not take ourselves too seriously. At least one study has discovered that the use of humorous illustrations helps audiences remember the message of the speech.[26] In addition, humorous stories can create identification by building an "insider's" relationship between speaker and audience that draws them closer together. In sharing humor, the audience becomes a community of listeners.[27]

As we noted in Chapters 8 and 9, however, humor should not be forced on a speech. If you decide to begin with a joke simply because you think a speech should start that way, the humor may seem contrived and flat. Rather, humor must be functional, useful in making a point.

The humor in a speech is best developed out of the immediate situation. Dick Jackman, the director of corporate communications at Sun Company, opened an after-dinner speech at a National Football Foundation awards dinner by warning those in the expensive seats under the big chandelier that it "had been installed by the low bidder some time ago." In her keynote address at the Democratic National Convention in 1988, Texas state treasurer Ann Richards used pointed humor as she took her party to task for not involving women more frequently in major convention roles:

> **Twelve years ago Barbara Jordan, another Texas woman, . . . made the keynote address to the convention, and two women in 160 years is about par for the course.**
>
> **But if you give us a chance, we can perform. After all, Ginger Rogers did everything that Fred Astaire did. She just did it backwards and in high heels.[28]**

Humor requires thought, planning, and caution to be effective. If it is not handled well, it can be a disaster. For example, religious humor is usually dangerous, and racist or sexist humor is absolutely forbidden. The first runs the risk of offending some members of the audience and can make the speaker seem intolerant. The second reveals a devastating truth about the speaker's character, and it can create such negative reactions from the audience that the rest of the speech doesn't stand a chance. In general, avoid any anecdotes that are funny at the expense of others.

Often, the best kind of humor centers on speakers themselves. Speakers who tell amusing stories about themselves sometimes rise in the esteem of listeners.[29] When this technique is successful, the stories that seem to put speakers down are actually building them up. A rural politician once told the following story at a dinner on an urban college campus:

> **You know, I didn't have good schooling like all of you have. I had to educate myself for public office. Along the way I just tried not to embarrass myself like another fellow from around here once did. This man wanted to run for Congress. So he came up here to your college to present himself to all the students and faculty. He worked real hard on a speech to show them all that he was a man of vision and high intellect.**
>
> **As he came to the end of his speech, he intoned very solemnly, "If you elect me to the United States Congress, I'll be like that great American bird, the eagle. I'll soar high and see far! I won't be like that other bird that buries its head in the sand, the oyster!" There was a wonderful reaction from the audience to that. So he said it again—said he wasn't going to be no oyster.**
>
> **Well, I've tried hard not to be an oyster as I represent you, even though I know there's some folks who'd say, "Well, you sure ain't no eagle, either!"[30]**

This story, which led into a review of the politician's legislative efforts, was warmly appreciated both for its humor and its modesty. It suggests that humor takes time to develop and must be rich in graphic detail to set up its punch line. The story would not have been nearly as effective had the speaker begun with, "Did you hear the one about the politician who didn't know an ostrich from an oyster?"

Developing an After-Dinner Speech. After-dinner speeches are more difficult to develop than their lightness and short length might suggest. Like any other speech, they must be carefully planned and practiced. They must have an effective introduction that commands attention right away, especially since some audience members may be more interested in talking to table companions than in listening to the speaker. After-dinner speeches should be more than strings of anecdotes to amuse listeners. The stories told must establish a mood, convey a message, or carry a theme forward. Such speeches should build to a satisfying conclusion that conveys the essence of the message.

Above all, perhaps, after-dinner speeches should be mercifully brief. Long-winded after-dinner speakers can leave the audience fiddling with coffee cups and drawing pictures on napkins. After being subjected to such a speech, Albert Einstein once murmured: "I have just got a new theory of eternity."[31]

Master of Ceremonies

Quite often, ceremonial speeches are part of a program of events that must be coordinated with skill and grace if things are to run smoothly. Being the master of ceremonies is no easy task. A speaker who served in such a capacity for a community program once noted:

> **Being an MC was sort of like having to stand up and juggle a dozen oranges in front of an audience. I just kept standing there, fumbling everything and waiting for the whole thing to be over with.[32]**

It takes at least as much careful planning, preparation, and practice to function effectively as a master of ceremonies as it does to make a major presentation. As the **master of ceremonies**, you will be expected to keep the program moving along, introduce participants, and possibly present awards. You will also set the tone or mood for the program.

If at all possible, you should be involved in planning the program from the beginning. Then you will have a better grasp of what is expected of you, what events have been scheduled, what the timetable is, who the featured speakers are, and what special logistics (such as meal service) you might have to deal with. The following guidelines should help you function effectively as a master of ceremonies:[33]

- *Know what is expected of you.* Why were you chosen to emcee the program? Remember, as emcee, you are not the "star" of the program; rather, you are the one who brings it all together and makes it work.
- *Plan a good opener for the program.* Your opening remarks as an emcee are as important as the introduction to a major presentation. You should gain the attention of the audience and prepare them for the program. Be sure that the mood you set with your opener is consistent with the nature of the occasion.
- *Be prepared to introduce the participants.* Be sure you know who they are and can pronounce their names correctly. If you prepare the introductions for them, review the relevant material in this chapter. Find out all you can about them: check *Who's Who* and local newspaper clipping files, and, if possible, talk to them directly to see what they would like you to emphasize and to determine how you might tune the audience for their speeches.
- *Be sure you know the schedule and timetable so that you can keep the program on track.* Also, be sure that the participants get this information. They need to know how much time has been allotted for them to speak. Double-check this with them before the program and work out some way to cue them in case they should run overtime. If time restrictions are severe (as in a televised program), be ready to edit and adapt your own planned comments.
- *Make certain that any prizes or awards are kept near the podium.* You shouldn't be left fumbling around looking for a plaque or trophy at presentation time.
- *Plan your comments ahead of time.* Develop a key-word outline for each presentation on a running script of the program. Print the name of the person or award in large letters at the top of each outline so that you can keep your place in the program.
- *Practice your presentation.* Although you are not the featured speaker, your words are important (especially to the person whom you will introduce or who will receive the award you will present). Practice your comments the same way you would practice a speech.
- *Make advance arrangements for mealtime logistics.* Speak with the maitre d' be-

fore the program to be sure the waiters know the importance of "silent service." If you will be speaking while people are still eating, adapt your message to cope with this distraction by using the attention-gaining techniques discussed in Chapters 9 and 14.

- *Be ready for the inevitable glitches.* Despite your best efforts, Murphy's Law (If anything can go wrong, it will) will surely prevail. Be ready for problems like microphones that don't work or that squeal, trays of dishes being dropped, and people wandering in and out during the course of the program. As you respond to these events, keep your cool and good humor.
- *End the program strongly.* Just as a speech should not dwindle into nothingness, neither should a program. Review the suggestions for speech conclusions in Chapter 9. When ending your presentation, thank those who made the program possible, and then leave the audience with something to remember.

The tribute to Wilma Rudolph (the complete text appears in Appendix B) illustrates how one master of ceremonies, Tom Brokaw, performed that role.

Narrative Design

Throughout this book we have touched repeatedly on the importance of narrative. Narrative is an important form of supporting material when stories are embedded in speeches in order to illustrate points. In addition to these **embedded narratives**, there are two other types that need to be addressed, the master narrative and the vicarious experience narrative.

In the **master narrative**, the entire speech becomes a story that reveals some important truth. We saw a good example of this earlier in the chapter as Jesse Owens recounted his experience at the 1936 Olympic games. In the **vicarious experience narrative**, the speaker invites listeners to imagine themselves enacting the story that is the major business of the speech. Beth Tidmore's speech asking her listeners to imagine themselves as counselors at Special Olympics games, discussed in Chapter 15, exemplifies such a narrative.

In both of these latter forms, the story dominates and structures the entire speech. In short, the speech develops around a **narrative design**. Although speeches that follow narrative design can both inform and/or persuade listeners, the typical role for such speeches is ceremonial, as speakers tell stories that make social values come to life.

Narrative design is strikingly different from other forms we have discussed previously. Categorical, causation, and problem-solution designs—to mention just a few—are typical in that *they follow a linear, logical pattern of development*. Speeches that break out into categories divide the topic according to customary, rational patterns of discussion. Speeches that feature effects will also focus on causes, and discussions of problems will typically consider solutions. The outlines for such logically oriented speeches follow the patterns featured in Chapter 10: thesis statements and previews followed by main points, subpoints, sub-subpoints, and supporting materials, all tied together by transitions and followed by summaries and final reflections.

In contrast, *narrative design follows a dramatic pattern of development*. Speeches that build on narrative design don't make points as much as they describe selected scenes in a minidrama. Narrative design features three major components: prologue, plot, and epilogue.

InterConnections.LearnMore 17.2

More About Narrative Design

Narrative Design in Multimedia Presentations
http://www.multimediacreative.com.au/articles/narratives.htm
Explores the use of narrative in multimedia presentations; developed by Multimedia Creative, a design company based in Sydney, Australia.

Narrative Design in the Contemporary Sermon
http://www.preaching.org/Cahill.html
A paper, "Preaching by Design," prepared by Dennis M. Cahill; explores the role of narrative in developing new approaches to preaching.

Narrative Design on Websites
http://www.alistapart.com/articles/narrative/
Fascinating study of the role of narrative in designing web sites; in the process, it teaches us also about narrative; offered by Mark Bernstein, chief scientist at Eastgate Systems, in the April 20, 2001 issue of A List Apart, *an online magazine.*

Prologue

The **prologue** of narrative design sets the scene for what will follow. It orients listeners to the context of the action so that they can make sense of it. Very much like the preview of a logical design, it provides **foreshadowing**, hinting of the meaning of the story that will follow and suggesting its importance. It also introduces the important characters that will enact the story and whose ethos will develop as the story unfolds.

To see these elements in action, let's consider again the prologue to Jesse Owens's speech on the 1936 Olympics:

> **What the Berlin games proved . . . was that Hitler's "supermen" could be beaten. Ironically, it was one of his blond, blue-eyed, Aryan athletes who helped do the beating.**
>
> **I held the world record in the broad jump. Even more than the sprints, it was "my" event. Yet I was one jump from not even making the finals. I fouled on my first try, and playing it safe the second time, I had not jumped far enough.**

The first two sentences in this prologue *foreshadow* the meaning of the story. They help prepare listeners for the actions that will unfold within the plot. They also anticipate the major *character* who will develop within the speech, Luz Long. The final four sentences present the *context* and *setting* of the story, the fact that Owens held the world record and was favored, and the crisis he now had to confront.

Plot

The **plot** functions as the body of a speech organized by narrative design. Within the plot of a successful speech, two important things must happen. First, *the action of the story unfolds in a sequence of scenes designed to build suspense until there is a moment of climax.* Colorful detail, lively dialogue, and graphic imagery help this action come alive for listeners. Second, *the characters that are central to the story gain interesting complexity by the way they participate in the action.* They develop an ethos that often makes them idealized portraits that live on in our memories after the speech is over.

Consider again the Owens speech. The plot develops in a sequence of three closely connected scenes: (1) the moments before the actual competition, (2) a description of the competition, and (3) the aftermath of the competition.

In the first scene, we watch a crisis of self-doubt, as Owens kneels to pray. We are also introduced to the generous spirit of Luz Long, who appears on cue as though he were the answer to Owens's prayer, and who offers the advice Owens needs to qualify for his event. Owens recreates the immediacy of the moment by using actual dialogue as Long speaks.

The second scene, which describes the competition itself, is summarized rather quickly. It might have been quite colorful, had Owens wished to dwell upon it.

But he hurries on to the third scene, the aftermath, because the real business of this speech is to create the ethos of Luz Long as an Olympic ideal. The fact that Long is German, even that he represents a Nazi ideology, is relevant to this portrait only as irony. Owens's point is that good sportsmanship transcends both national origin and political affiliation and joins people as brothers and sisters. Thus we behold the extraordinary spectacle at the conclusion of the competition when Luz Long raises Owens's arms to the sky as he leads the throng of Germans in chanting "Jazze Owenz."

Epilogue

The **epilogue** of a story reflects upon the meaning of the action and offers final comments on the character of those who participated in it. Often, it draws lessons that listeners can apply in their own time and place. Thus, in the Owens example, we see the nobility of Luz Long reaffirmed in the final scene of the story:

> **Luz Long was killed in World War II and, although I don't cry often, I wept when I received his last letter—I knew it was his last. In it he asked me to someday find his son, Karl, and to tell him "of how we fought well together, and of the good times, and that any two men can become brothers."**

What Owens doesn't quite tell us, but we can infer it from what he says, is that Long and Owens had become good friends, that they corresponded often, and that Long knew that his end was near. These inferences only strengthen the underlying lesson for the audience Owens addressed in 1980:

> **That is what the Olympics are all about. The road to the Olympics does not lead to Moscow. It leads to no city, no country. It goes far beyond Lake Placid or Moscow, ancient Greece or Nazi Germany. The road to the Olympics leads, in the end, to the best within us.**

Just as the Olympic spirit could thrive in the bigoted atmosphere of Nazi Germany in 1936, so also could it blossom in the Cold War atmosphere of Moscow in 1980. Owens's speech, apparently commemorating a long past moment and honoring an obscure sports competitor, becomes finally an argument criticizing the action taken by the United States in boycotting the 1980 games.

From this discussion we can draw a number of guidelines to help you develop a speech using narrative design. Figure 17.3 summarizes these guidelines.

Develop the Prologue

- ☐ I have described the setting in which my story will play out.
- ☐ I have established the context in which my story occurs.
- ☐ I have aroused audience interest by foreshadowing the characters in my story.
- ☐ I have aroused curiosity by foreshadowing the meaning of my story.

Develop the Plot

- ☐ I have selected a scene (or scenes) in which the action of my story will unfold.
- ☐ I have used colorful detail, picturesque language, and lively dialogue to bring the action to life.
- ☐ I have developed characters who are interesting because of their roles in the action.
- ☐ I have built suspense to bring my story to a climax.

Develop the Epilogue

- ☐ I reflect on the meaning of my story so that listeners get the point.
- ☐ My story leaves listeners with the feeling that they have met an interesting character(s) they will want to remember.
- ☐ My story teaches an important lesson that listeners can apply.
- ☐ I have used language skills to help listeners remember the message.

Figure 17.3

Checklist for Developing a Narrative Design

Figure 17.4

Outline Format for Narrative Design

I. Prologue ______________________________
   A. Setting and context of story: ______________________________
   B. Foreshadowing characters: ______________________________
   C. Foreshadowing meaning: ______________________________

II. Plot ______________________________
   A. Scene 1: ______________________________
   B. Scene 2: ______________________________
   C. Scene 3: ______________________________

III. Epilogue ______________________________
   A. Final scene: ______________________________
   B. Lessons of the story: ______________________________

Works and People Consulted

We have also devised an outline format to help you plan the structure of a speech using narrative design. Figure 17.4 offers this format. Note that it asks you to list both the works and people consulted as you planned your speech.

And in Conclusion . . .

As you end this book, we offer our own speech of tribute: this one to you. Public speaking may not have been easy for you. But it is our hope that you have grown as a person as you have grown as a speaker. Our special wishes, expressed in terms of three underlying metaphors that provide the vision of this book, are that

- you have learned how to overcome the *barriers* that sometimes separate people and defeat communication.
- you have learned how to *build* speeches that are both powerful and ethical.
- you have learned how to *weave* words and evidence into eloquent thoughts and persuasive ideas.

We propose a toast: May you use your new speaking skills to improve the lives and lift the spirits of all who may listen to you.

VideoLab

Review the "Do's" and "Don'ts" of ceremonial speaking in **VideoLab Lesson 10's Coach: Tips to Remember**.

In Summary

Ceremonial speeches serve important social functions. They place the spotlight on leadership. They reinforce the values that hold people together in a community and give listeners a sense of order and purpose in their lives. They also establish principles that can be applied in later arguments.

Major Techniques of Ceremonial Speaking. Two major techniques of ceremonial speaking are *identification* and *magnification*. The first creates close feeling, and the second selects and emphasizes those features of a subject that will convey the speaker's message. Speakers build identification by using narratives that remind listeners of shared experiences. Recognizing heroes and heroines also provides ideal models of conduct to draw listeners and speakers closer together. Finally, appeals to group commitment can remind listeners of the values and goals they share. Themes worthy of magnification include overcoming obstacles, achieving unusual goals, performing in a superior manner, having unselfish motives, and benefiting the community. Eloquent uses of language can also magnify the subjects of ceremonial speeches.

Types of Ceremonial Speeches. *Speeches of tribute* recognize achievements or commemorate special events, helping listeners appreciate the values these represent. As they describe ideal models of conduct, speeches of tribute also perform an inspirational function. Achievements and events may be significant in themselves or in what they symbolize. *Award presentations* should explain the nature of the award and what the recipient has done to merit it. *Eulogies* are speeches of tribute presented on the death of a person or persons. *Toasts* are ceremonial speeches in miniature that pay tribute, offer blessings, or celebrate the moment.

Speeches of acceptance should begin with an expression of gratitude and an acknowledgment of others who deserve recognition. They should focus on the values that the honor represents. Acceptance speeches often call for more formal language than other speeches and for eloquence that suits the occasion.

Speeches of introduction should welcome the speaker, establish his or her ethos, and tune the audience for the message that will follow. Introductions should focus on information about the speaker that is relevant to the speech topic or the occasion or that has special meaning for the audience.

Speeches of inspiration help listeners appreciate values and make them want to pursue worthy goals. Such speeches often call on stories of past successes. After-dinner speeches should be lighthearted, serving up humor and insight at the same time. Humor should be functional in such speeches, illustrating a point or serving some larger purpose.

The *master of ceremonies* coordinates a program and sees that things run smoothly. He or she sets the mood of the program, introduces the participants, provides transitions, and sometimes presents awards.

Narrative Design. Speeches that center on a *master narrative* or that focus on engaging listeners in a *vicarious experience narrative* utilize *narrative design*. Such speeches follow a dramatic rather than a logical pattern of development. They feature a *prologue,* which sets the scene for what will follow by using *foreshadowing* techniques; a *plot,* which develops suspenseful action through a series of scenes and at the same time develops important characters; and an *epilogue,* which reflects upon the meaning of the story and draws out its lesson for listeners.

Terms to Know

ceremonial speaking
identification
magnification
speech of tribute
award presentation
eulogy
toast
speech of acceptance
speech of introduction
speech of inspiration
after-dinner speech
master of ceremonies
embedded narratives
master narrative
vicarious experience narrative
narrative design
prologue
foreshadowing
plot
epilogue

Discussion

1. Analyze Ashley Smith's "Three Photographs" (page 72) as a speech built on narrative design. Can you identify the prologue, plot, and epilogue and the major scenes of the speech? Who is the major character developed by the narrative? How might the narrative have been improved?
2. The speeches in Appendix B by Tommie Albright and Elie Wiesel are ceremonial addresses. How do they relate to the basic questions of "Who are we?" "Why are we?" "What have we accomplished?" and "What can we become together?" What values do they celebrate?
3. Is there a speech of inspiration you heard some time ago that you still remember? Why do you feel it made such an impression on you?
4. List five heroes or heroines who are often mentioned in ceremonial speeches. Why do speakers refer to them so frequently? What does this tell us about the nature of these admired persons, about the needs of contemporary audiences, and about the ceremonial speech situation? Be prepared to discuss these topics in class.

Application

1. Select a public figure that you admire and prepare a speech of tribute honoring that person. Which aspects of your subject's life did you choose to magnify and why?
2. Prepare a toast for a classmate who you feel either (a) has made the most progress as a speaker this term or (b) has given a speech you will likely long remember. Strive for brevity and eloquence in your toast. Be ready to present your toast in class.

Notes

1. Celeste Michelle Condit, "The Functions of Epideictic: The Boston Massacre Orations as Exemplar," *Communication Quarterly* 33 (1985): 284–299; Gray Matthews, "Epideictic Rhetoric and Baseball: Nurturing Community Through Controversy," *Southern Communication Journal* 60 (1995): 275–291; Randall Parrish Osborn, "Jimmy Carter's Rhetorical Campaign for the Presidency: An Epideictic of American Renewal," Southern States Communication Association Convention, Memphis, March 1996; Ch. Perelman and L. Olbrechts-Tyteca, *The New Rhetoric: A Treatise on Argumentation* (South Bend, Ind.: University of Notre Dame Press, 1971), pp. 47–54; and Richard M. Weaver, *The Ethics of Rhetoric* (Chicago: Henry Regnery, 1953), pp. 164–185.
2. John Dewey, *Democracy and Education* (New York: Macmillan, 1916), p. 4.
3. Bronislaw Malinowski, "The Problem of Meaning in Primitive Languages," in *The Meaning of Meaning: A Study of the Influence of Language upon Thought and of the Science of Symbolism*, ed. C. K. Ogden and I. A. Richards, 8th ed. (New York: Harcourt, Brace & World, 1946), p. 315.
4. Michael Osborn, *Orientations to Rhetorical Style* (Chicago: Science Research Associates, 1976), p. 32.
5. James W. Carey, "A Cultural Approach to Communication," *Communication* 2 (1975): 6.
6. Walter H. Beale, "Rhetorical Performance Discourse: A New Theory of Epideictic," *Philosophy and Rhetoric* 11 (1978): 221–246; and Bernard K. Duffy, "The Platonic Functions of Epideictic Rhetoric," *Philosophy and Rhetoric* 16 (1983): 79–93.
7. Christine Oravec, "Observation in Aristotle's Theory of Epideictic," *Philosophy and Rhetoric* 9 (1976): 162–174; and Perelman and Olbrechts-Tyteca.
8. See his discussion in "The Range of Rhetoric," in *A Rhetoric of Motives* (Berkeley and Los Angeles: University of California Press, 1969), pp. 3–43.
9. From *American Speeches*, ed. Wayland Maxfield Parrish and Marie Hochmuth (New York: Longmans, Green, 1954), p. 43.

10. See the discussion in *The Rhetoric of Aristotle*, trans. Lane Cooper (New York: Appleton-Century-Crofts, 1932), I.7, I.9, I.14 (pp. 34–44, 46–55, 78–79).

11. Tommie Albright, "Martin Luther King Jr.'s Legacy for Us," *Vital Speeches of the Day*, 1 Mar. 2000, p. 320.

12. *Congressional Record*, 1 Apr. 1980, pp. 7459–7460.

13. For a more detailed account of the functions of eulogies, see Karen A. Foss, "John Lennon and the Advisory Function of Eulogies," *Central States Speech Journal* 34 (1983): 187–194.

14. Carolyn Thomas, "Weeping Words for the People We've Loved & Lost," *(Memphis) Commercial Appeal*, 19 Oct. 2003, p. D6.

15. April Westmoreland, *(Memphis) Commercial Appeal* , 19 Oct. 2003, p. D6.

16. Owen Edwards, "What Every Man Should Know: How to Make a Toast," *Esquire*, January 1984, p. 37.

17. The advice that follows is adapted from Jacob M. Braude, *Complete Speaker's and Toastmaster's Library: Definitions and Toasts* (Englewood Cliffs, N.J.: Prentice Hall, 1965), pp. 88–123; and Wendy Lin, "Let's Lift a Glass, Say a Few Words, and Toast 1996," *(Memphis) Commercial Appeal*, 28 Dec. 1995, p. C3.

18. Elie Wiesel, "Nobel Peace Prize Acceptance Speech," *New York Times*, 11 Dec. 1986, p. A8.

19. Martin Luther King Jr., "Nobel Peace Prize Acceptance Statement," in *The Cry for Freedom: The Struggle for Equality in America*, ed. Frank W. Hale Jr. (New York: Barnes, 1969), pp. 374–377.

20. *(Memphis) Commercial Appeal*, 23 Oct. 1995, p. D2.

21. Cited in Morris K. Udall, *Too Funny to Be President* (New York: Holt, 1988), p. 156.

22. Sheila W. Welling, "Working Women: A Century of Change," *Vital Speeches of the Day*, 15 June 1995, pp. 516–517.

23. *Congressional Record*, 1 Apr. 1980, p. 7249.

24. *Congressional Record*, 1 Apr. 1980, p. 7248.

25. Roger Ailes, *You Are the Message* (New York: Doubleday, 1988), pp. 71–74.

26. Robert M. Kaplan and Gregory C. Pascoe, "Humorous Lectures and Humorous Examples: Some Effects upon Comprehension and Retention," *Journal of Educational Psychology* 69 (1977): 61–65.

27. For more on the social function of laughter, see Henri Bergson, *Laughter: An Essay on the Meaning of the Comic*, trans. Cloudsley Brereton and Fred Rothwell (London: Macmillan, 1911).

28. Ann Richards, "Keynote Address," delivered at the Democratic National Convention, Atlanta, Ga., 18 July 1988, *Vital Speeches of the Day*, 15 Aug. 1988, pp. 647–649.

29. Charles R. Gruner, "Advice to the Beginning Speaker on Using Humor—What the Research Tells Us," *Communication Education* 34 (1985): 142–147; and Christie McGuffee Smith and Larry Powell, "The Use of Disparaging Humor by Group Leaders," *Southern Speech Communication Journal* 53 (1988): 279–292.

30. Thanks for this story go to Professor Joseph Riggs, Slippery Rock University.

31. *Washington Post*, 12 Dec. 1978.

32. Cited in Joan Detz, *Can You Say a Few Words?* (New York: St. Martins, 1991), p. 77.

33. Adapted from Detz, pp. 77–78.

A Man for the New Age: Tribute to Tiger Woods

Leslie Eason

■ Leslie opens by taking her listeners on an imaginary trip to a golf tournament. Her skillful use of language, with its vigorous verbs and simple sentences arranged in parallel structure, fills her speech with color and action.

You're at the Western Open, where Tiger Woods could be Elvis reincarnated. People clap when he pulls out a club. They clap when he hits the ball. They clap no matter where that ball lands. They clap if he smiles. They clap because he is.

Not long ago, when not much else was going on and we were tired of O.J. and very much needed a hero, a young man in a red polo shirt materialized out of nowhere doing magical things with a stick in a sport we usually ignored. He was not just good or even outstanding. He was a miracle. His game all but laughed at records set by men twice his age. Nike threw forty million at him. Rolex threw fifty million at him. American Express lined up to give him millions more.

■ Leslie makes good use of the principles of tribute. Tiger Woods's sporting accomplishments are unique and exceptional. His attractiveness adds to his status as a hero. More important, his refusal to accept an identity based on race benefits society.

We started having to pay attention to things like the Masters, and Opens, and Invitationals, and other such things that applied to golf. Other people were playing, but he was all we could see, this young god in a red shirt. Suddenly we had to learn a new language—"fore," "eagle," "birdie," "par," and "bogie"—just to keep up with the latest news about him.

Some people watched him play, and bragged that black people could do just about anything. Then we heard that he was only one-fourth black, and that he did not describe himself as black. Now, in a society that honors the rule that one drop of blood is all it takes to be black, this didn't mean much. We ignored his Thai mother, disregarded the Native American and Chinese and Caucasian he said he had in him, and all we saw was his dark-skinned father, who was always there in the gallery cheering him on.

■ Leslie expresses her own attraction to Tiger through the way she describes him. She uses contrast, with the "gangsta" boys, and a striking summary description, "he's prep school and Pepsodent," to etch this description in the minds of listeners.

To us he continued to look a lot like other young black men we knew. Mothers with daughters of a certain age (including my own) said that they wished he was their son-in-law or future son-in-law. Six foot two, a hundred fifty-five pounds, smart—Stanford, remember—clean-cut in his creased khakis, curly hair, gorgeous teeth—gorgeous teeth. Skin the color of what they used to call "suntan" in the Crayola box. And rich—very, very rich.

He's the very opposite of the gangsta boys in the hood—boys who wear their pants hanging below their belt like some people in the penitentiary. Next to them he's prep school and Pepsodent. Some said he put a pretty face on blackness. Others said he couldn't possibly be black.

■ Leslie draws two important distinctions in this section. First, the world's way of assigning racial identity underscores what we are, not who we are. Second, Tiger's self-description as "Cablinasian" represents a revolt against the old "one drop is all it takes" rule. These distinctions allow her to conclude that Tiger has transcended the color barrier.

From the moment the world finally met him at the Nike press conference, people wondered *what,* not *who,* he was. He with the almond eyes, the great-colored skin, the photo-op smile. "What are you?" a reporter asked. He didn't seem quite ready for the question, suggesting he wasn't any one thing, but a lot of everything all rolled up into one. Started going into fractions—one-eighth of this, one-fifth of that, a fourth of something else. Told Oprah he didn't feel comfortable being called black. To describe his ethnicity, he came up with the name *Cablinasian,* combining his Caucasian, Black, Indian, and Asian ethnicities. It seemed both a naive plea for a color-blind, colorless America and a throwback to the quadroon days of old Louisiana when people measured their bloodlines by the teaspoon.

But in actuality, Tiger Woods was something the world needed very much. He transcended the color barrier. Not because he was the first black to do this or do that in golf, but because he refused to be defined by the color of his skin. In the midst of all his fame, fortune, contracts, money, and marriage offers, he had taken the step to destroy the old racist rule, *one drop is all it takes.* He offered instead a new principle: he was an equal representation of all he came from—Caucasian, Black, Indian, and Asian—but that was not *who* he was.

How does all this help Tiger? Well, to some he's considered the best golfer in the world. Not the best black player, but the best player, period. A perfect example of together and the same, instead of separate but equal. How does this help the rest of us? It shows us that race is just a small part of our identity. Our own personal racial equation does not determine who we are or where we're going. Or even what we can do.

You're back at the Western Open. The fan galleries finally look like America—Asian, white, black, Latino, fathers with sons, mothers pushing baby carriages, people who have been playing golf for years, people who didn't know what golf was before Tiger Woods and now want to try it. Everything revolves around Tiger. Even babies go silent when Tiger's about to swing. Once the ball is hit, people resume their conversation and stampede to the next hole to watch him, leaving the next player to struggle by himself.

So what are we to make of him? His father, Earl Woods, has said that his son would change the course of humanity. You can mark that up to a proud father's hyperbole, but perhaps Tiger has already pointed us in a new direction by his refusal to accept an identity imposed by racist custom. Hopefully one day we will see him as a young man who was simply ahead of his time, instead of viewing him as a naive child trying to escape his heritage.

■ ***In this section Leslie shifts the focus to Tiger's social significance. She dwells on the importance of creating our own identity rather than accepting a prearranged identity based on race. In the process she expands the idea of identity so that it applies more to traits of character and accomplishment.***

It's not clear yet who he is, but it's quite clear what he is not. His boundaries are not defined and confined by his complex racial background. Instead, he is what he told us, a complex mixture of heart, talent, dedication, attractiveness of person and personality, and grace under the pressure of constant media attention and tournament competition. The most important ingredient in that mixture is his stubborn refusal to accept the world's ways of limiting identity, and his polite insistence upon leaving himself open to change and growth. He did not inherit a prearranged identity imposed by race; rather, he is responsible for creating who he is and who he will become. Who he is will emerge over time, a product of his character and accomplishments.

As we watch him grow and become himself, we can only celebrate what he means for a nation and world that must become more comfortable with its incredible diversity of race and culture. Tiger Woods, you are a man for the New Age, and we salute you!

■ ***In her brief conclusion, Leslie sketches Tiger against the background of a New Age in which the world must come to accept and appreciate its cultural and racial diversity.***

WORKS CONSULTED

Garrity, John. "You the Kid." *Sports Illustrated* 9 March 1992. 12 Apr. 1998 <http://www.cnnsi.com/features/1996/sportsman/archive/920309.html>.

Lewis, Andrea. "A Public Course Win—Tiger's Victory Marks a New Stage in Cultural History." *JINN* 16 Apr. 1997. 11 Apr. 1998 <http://www.pacificnews.org/jinn/stories/3.08/970416-tiger.html>.

Montville, Leigh. "On the Job Training." *Sports Illustrated* 9 Sept. 1996. 12 Apr. 1998 <http://www.cnnsi.com/features/1996/sportsman/archive/960909.html>.

Reilly, Rick. "Goodness Gracious, He's a Great Ball of Fire." *Sports Illustrated* 27 Mar. 1995. 12 Apr. 1998 <http://www.cnnsi.com/features/1996/sportsman/archive/950327.html>.

Sirak, Ron. "Golf Owes Charlie Sifford a Great Deal." *GolfWeb Library* 24 Feb. 1998. 11 Apr. 1998 <http://services.golfweb.com/library/sirak/charlie980224.html>.

Van Sickle, Gary. "Jackpot!" *Sports Illustrated* 14 Oct. 1996. 10 Apr. 1998 <http://www.cnnsi.com/features/1996/sportman/archive/961014.html>.

Reach for the Stars!
Ashlie McMillan

In her speech of tribute to her cousin, Ashlie McMillan makes use of both identification and magnification, the major techniques of ceremonial speaking. Her opening asks listeners to imagine themselves as dwarfs. By picturing her cousin in simple, everyday situations, she invites identification with her.

Please close your eyes. Imagine now that you are shrinking. Can you feel your hands and feet getting smaller, your arms being pulled in closer to your shoulders? Can you picture your legs now dangling off the edge of your seat as your legs shrink up closer to your hips? Now you are only three feet tall. But don't open your eyes yet. This is your first day of being a diastrophic dwarf.

You wake up and get out of bed, which is quite a drop because the bed is almost as tall as you are. You go to the bathroom to wash your face and brush your teeth, but you must stand on a trash can because the faucet is out of your reach. Now you go back to your dorm room, and you're ready to put on your clothes. But again you can't reach the clothes hanging in your closet because you're too short. You have to struggle to get dressed.

Now you have errands that you must run. But how are you going to do them? If you walk, it will take you a long time because you must take many short steps. And you can't drive a car because you can't reach the pedals, much less see over the steering wheel. Finally you get to the bank. But it takes you about five minutes to get the teller's attention because she can't see you below the counter. Next you go to the grocery store. This takes forever because you can't push a cart. You're forced to use a carry basket and to find people who will reach high items for you. Frustrated yet? Okay, open your eyes.

In 1968 my cousin, Tina McMillan, was born. Today she's in her twenty-ninth year as a diastrophic dwarf. What does that mean? It means that she'll never be taller than three feet. It means that her hands will never be able to bend this way [gestures] because she will never have joints in her fingers or toes. She'll always have club feet, and she had to have a rod put in her spine because all diastrophic dwarfs are plagued with scoliosis.

After introducing her cousin and defining dwarfism, Ashlie begins magnification by selecting incidents that reveal Tina as a spirited, determined fighter who refuses to accept the role of a disabled person. Ashlie's entire speech is built on an inspiring irony: that someone so small in physique should be so large in spirit.

So what does her dwarfism mean to my cousin? Nothing. When you first meet Tina, you might be a little shocked at how tiny she is. But after a while you forget her physical size because her personality is so large and her spirit is so bright. Today I want to tell you the story of how this small person is reaching for the stars. Her life is a miracle that should teach us never to let obstacles stand in the way of our goals and dreams.

When my aunt and uncle were told that they were going to have a baby who was a diastrophic dwarf, they prepared themselves. They were ready to tell their child that she would never be able to have a Great Dane dog because it would be three times the size that she was. That she would never be able to ride a horse. That she would never be able to drive a car. And that she might not be able to attend college because the dormitories and other facilities were not built for people three feet tall.

What my aunt and uncle were *not* prepared for was a child with a physical disability who refused to see herself as disabled. I can tell you that growing up with Tina was quite an experience. She was always the ham of the cousins, always the center of attention. I remember going over to her house and playing with her *three* Great Dane dogs in the backyard. I remember every Sunday when my grandpa would take us out to the farm and we would fight over who got to ride the horses. And Tina would even fight my grandfather so she could get up on the horse all by herself. And I remember the day, some time after her sixteenth birthday, that she slid behind the wheel of a car. She had teamed up with some engineers down in Texas to have the pedals extended as well as hand gears made on the steering wheel so that she could drive herself. But perhaps my proudest and fondest memory was watching my cousin walk across the graduation stage at Texas Christian University in 1991. She not only got her degree in English, but she went on to get a master's degree in anthropology from TCU. After she graduated, the university invited her to come back to teach in the English Department. But by this time Tina had a new challenge: She declined the teaching job so that she could enter politics as campaign manager for the mayor of Dallas.

Tina has never stopped challenging the perception that she is disabled. Next April she will be marrying a person of normal stature, and once again she will defy society's assumption that something must be wrong about such a marriage. And then in the fall she plans on attending the University of Texas law school. Want to bet against her there?

Somehow, against the odds, my cousin has led a normal life. To many people, what she has accomplished might not seem that exceptional. To me, however, she is an inspiration. Whenever I think I've got problems that are too much for me, I think of her and of what she has done, this large and vital person stuffed into such a small body. I think of how she refuses to use her disability as a scapegoat or excuse. And I remember how she does not even consider quitting if something stands in her way. She simply views the obstacle, decides the best way to get around it, and moves on. And although she will lose the ability to walk, probably by the age of forty, I believe that she will still find the way to keep moving toward her goals.

■ As she nears the conclusion, Ashlie begins to draw lessons from her cousin's life to inspire listeners. The closing sentence suggests an analogy with a point made earlier in the speech: People must stand on dreams to reach distant goals.

The next time a large obstacle stands in your way, remember Tina, my small cousin who has achieved such noteworthy things. You too may seem too short to grasp your stars, but you never know how far you might reach if you stand upon a dream.

WORKS CONSULTED

Department of Orthopedics, Alfred I. Dupont Institute. Undated. 18 Apr. 1998 <http://gait.aidi.udel.edu.res695/homepage/pd_ortho/educat>.

Diastrophic Dwarfism. Undated. 18 Apr. 1998 <http://chorus.rad.mcw.edu/dpc/01027.html>.

Diastrophic Dysplasia. Undated. 18 Apr. 1998 <http://gasbone.herston.uq.edu.au/~ortho/regsum/genorth108>.

NORD Research Group. Undated. 18 Apr. 1998 <http://www.stepsn.com/nord/rdb_sum/482.htm>.

Texgene Genetics Network. "Methods of Inheritance." 4 Mar. 1998. 18 Apr. 1998 <http://www.tdh.texas.gov/texgene/inherit.htm>.

APPENDIX

A

Communicating in Small Groups

Many of the important communication interactions in your life happen in small groups. In school you may be assigned to a team working on a particular assignment. At work you may be appointed to a committee to plan a project for your department. In your community there may be problems that can only be solved by people working together. All of these interactions demand effective group communication skills. Moreover, members of groups must often make public presentations defending the recommendations produced by group deliberations.

To understand how groups communicate, we need to consider the nature of a group. Is any gathering of people a group? Not necessarily. For example, a gathering of people waiting for a bus would not be considered a group. *To be considered a **group**, a gathering of people must actively interact with one another over a period of time to reach a goal or goals.*

Let's suppose that the same people have been meeting at the bus stop every workday for several months. They may chat with one another while waiting for the bus, but this casual interaction is not enough to make them a group. Now, suppose that the Metropolitan Transit Organization (MTO) announces in the morning paper that it wants to raise fares from $2.00 to $3.00 each way for the trip downtown. That morning when the people get together, they begin to express their outrage about the problem that confronts them. One of them suggests that they gather at her apartment that evening to come up with a plan to persuade the MTO to reconsider its proposal. When these people get together that evening, they will be interacting as a group.

In this appendix we discuss how groups function and how good public communication skills can make you a better participant or leader in groups. We also consider the various types of group presentations that you may be called upon to make.

Advantages and Disadvantages of Group Problem Solving

When we listen to one speaker present information or make recommendations, we hear only a single version of a situation or problem. That version may be biased, based on self-interest, or simply wrong. When an issue or problem is important, we need to minimize the risk of such possibilities. One way to do this is to form a group to consider the situation and arrive at consensus recommendations about it.

Group problem solving has many advantages over individual efforts. When people share their various ways of seeing a problem, they create a richer picture of the situation. They begin to see the world as others see it. This sharing of perspectives has a self-correcting function. Misconceptions and bias may come to light as people share perceptions of problems. Listening to others' points of view also can stimulate creative thinking about solutions.

In well-managed problem-solving groups, people on all sides of an issue have a chance to discuss the similarities and differences of their perspectives. Through discussion, they may discover some areas of agreement that can help resolve differences. Additionally, small groups of people typically may be more willing to examine and confront their differences constructively, and they may feel more free to explore options for action. When these same people are on public display, communicating before larger audiences, they sometimes become inflexible. Because of these advantages, organizations often use small groups to work on important organizational problems. In fact, it is estimated that approximately 20 million meetings take place each day in the United States.[1]

Although working in groups has many advantages, some problems may arise that can reduce the effectiveness of group deliberations. **Cultural gridlock**, problems in communication that arise from profound cultural differences, can occur in groups whose participants come from different backgrounds. For example, people in marketing departments and the research and development scientists in an organization may bring different expectations to a meeting. Along with these differing professional expectations, participants from different social backgrounds may bring different perspectives, agendas, priorities, procedures, ways of communicating, and standards of protocol to meetings. These differences may sidetrack constructive discussions.

Dealing with cultural gridlock is never easy, but the following guidelines will help minimize its impact:

1. Allow time for people to get acquainted before starting to work.
2. Provide enough physical space so that people don't feel crowded.
3. Distribute an agenda in advance of the meeting so people know what to expect.
4. Summarize discussions as the meeting progresses. Post key points of agreement.
5. Avoid using jargon that some participants may not understand.
6. Be sensitive to cultural differences in protocol and nonverbal communication.[2]

Another problem groups may encounter is **groupthink**, the uncritical acceptance of a position.[3] Groupthink is most likely to occur when participants place a higher value on harmonious interpersonal interactions than on performing effectively. Other factors that contribute to groupthink include a leader's obvious preference for a certain position or the lack of a clear set of procedures for working through problems.

Groupthink can be dangerous because outsiders may assume that a group has deliberated carefully and responsibly when it has not. The problems in decision making that often accompany groupthink may include an inadequate exploration of the problem, slipshod information gathering and analysis, and an incomplete consideration of alternative solutions.

Dealing with groupthink is difficult, but there are some steps that can guard against it. First, groups need to be aware that groupthink can be a problem. The major symptoms of groupthink include pressuring dissidents within the group and censoring their ideas, defending and justifying opinions more than exploring alternate ways of thinking, and asserting the group's own moral righteousness and attacking the character of opposing groups.

Once a group is aware that groupthink is a problem, the leader can take action to minimize its effects. The leader should encourage the group to set standards for investigation and appraisal that discourage uncritical thinking and premature conclusions.[4] The following leadership behaviors can help reduce groupthink problems:

- Remind participants to critically evaluate all recommendations.
- Urge members to delay coming to conclusions until all have had a chance to express their views freely.
- Ask members to assume the role of devil's advocate and encourage critical questions.
- Bring in outsiders to talk about the issues under consideration.
- Encourage debate of all recommendations.

Group Problem-Solving Techniques

Group deliberations that are orderly, systematic, and thorough help people reach high-quality decisions. To function effectively, problem-solving groups can use a variety of methods.[5]

Reflective Thinking and Problem Solving

The approach recommended for most problem-solving groups is a modification of the reflective thinking technique first proposed by John Dewey in 1910. This systematic approach has five steps: (1) defining the problem, (2) generating potential solutions, (3) evaluating solution options, (4) developing a plan of action, and (5) evaluating the results.

Step 1: Defining the Problem. Sometimes what the group initially identifies as the problem is only a symptom of the actual problem. A group that begins with the problem of insufficient support for public education may discover that the actual problem is far more complicated, involving the lack of clearly articulated goals, poor communication with the public, and inadequate public participation. All problem-solving groups should take time to define the problem carefully before looking for solutions. The following guidelines can help define the problem:

1. Describe the problem as specifically as possible.
2. Gather enough information to understand the problem.
3. Explore the causes of the problem.
4. Investigate the history of the problem.
5. Determine who is affected by the problem.
6. Consider the consequences if the problem is solved or not solved.

Step 2: Generating Potential Solutions. Once the problem has been defined, the group can begin generating possible solutions. One useful technique at this stage is **brainstorming,** which encourages all group members to contribute to producing a large number of potential solutions.[6] Brainstorming works best when there are twelve or fewer members in the group.[7] During the brainstorming process, members should not attempt to evaluate the solutions or decide which option to follow.[8]

The following rules should govern brainstorming sessions:

- Contribute fully and enthusiastically.
- Present all your ideas, no matter how outrageous they may seem. Even outlandish ideas may develop into a workable solution. The more options the group generates, the better.
- During this step, don't pass judgment on your own or other people's ideas. Keeping the process of exploration free of criticism helps the group generate more and better eventual solutions.
- Don't be afraid to combine ideas to come up with additional options.
- Be sure that everyone contributes. Don't let the lack of organizational status or seniority stand in the way of a person's participating fully.

The process of brainstorming proceeds as follows:

1. The leader asks each member in turn to contribute a suggestion, one idea per person during each round of participation. If a member does not have an idea, he or she should pass. At this stage, emphasize full participation and the quantity of options over their quality.
2. A recorder writes down all ideas on a flip chart or marker board so everyone can see them.
3. Brainstorming continues through rounds of participation until the pool of possibilities is exhausted and all members have passed. *Do not try to streamline the process!*
4. The suggestions are reviewed for clarification, adding new options, or combining options.
5. The group identifies the most promising ideas.
6. The leader appoints members to research each idea and to bring additional information to a later evaluation meeting.
7. The process of gathering solution possibilities should remain open. Additional ideas may be considered during the next phase of the problem-solving process.

There are many creative variations of brainstorming. When time is short or when face-to-face participation may initially discourage the open exploration of ideas, one alternative may be **electronic brainstorming**, in which participants generate ideas in computer chat groups or by email before meeting face to face.[9] One advantage of these initial electronic explorations is that leaders can encourage participants to bring additional illustrative materials to the meetings in order to clarify options.[10]

Step 3: Evaluating Solution Options. As the meeting to generate options concludes, the group should schedule a later meeting to evaluate them. Between meetings, members can gather information on the feasibility of each option. When the group reconvenes, it should apply the following evaluation criteria:

- Costs of the option
- Probability of success
- Difficulty of enacting the option
- Time constraints

- Additional benefits to be expected
- Additional problems that might be encountered

Groups should summarize the evaluation of each option on a flip chart and then post the summaries so that members can refer to them as they compare options. As options are evaluated, some of them will seem weak and be dropped, and others may be strengthened and refined. The group also may combine options to generate new alternatives. For example, if the group is caught between option A, which promises improved efficiency, and option B, which promises lower cost, it may be possible to combine the best features of each into option C.

After each alternative has been considered, members should rank the solutions in terms of their acceptability. The option receiving the highest overall rank is the proposed solution.

It is not unusual for participants to become personally caught up with their own solutions. During evaluation, a leader must keep the group focused on ideas and not on participants. Accept differences of opinion and conflict as a natural and necessary part of problem solving. Discussing the strengths of an option before talking about its weaknesses can take some of the heat out of the process.

Step 4: Developing a Plan of Action. Once the group has selected a solution, it must determine how it can be implemented. For example, to improve company morale, a group might recommend a three-step plan: (1) better in-house training programs to increase opportunities for promotion, (2) a pay structure that rewards success in training programs, and (3) increased employee participation in decision making. As the group refines this plan, it should consider what might help or hinder it, the resources needed to enact it, and a timetable for completion.

If the group cannot develop a plan of action for the solution or if insurmountable obstacles appear, the group should return to step 3 and reconsider other options.

Step 5: Evaluating Results. Not only must a problem-solving group plan how to implement a solution, but it must also determine how to evaluate results once the plan is enacted. The group should establish evaluation criteria for what constitutes success, a timetable for when results can be expected, and contingency plans to use if the original plan doesn't work. To monitor the ongoing success of a solution, such as a three-part plan to improve morale, the group would have to determine reasonable expectations for each stage in the process. That way, the company could detect and correct problems as they occur, before they damage the plan as a whole. Having a scheduled sequence of expectations also provides a way to determine results while the plan is being enacted, rather than having to wait for the entire project to be completed.

Other Approaches to Group Problem Solving

Although the systematic process just described works well in many situations, there are times when a different approach may be needed. When a group consists of people from very diverse backgrounds, **collaborative problem solving** may work best.[11] For example, in many urban areas coalitions of business executives and educators have worked together on plans to train people for jobs in the community. In such situations, the problems are usually important and the resources are typically limited. Because there is no established authority structure and the factions may have different expectations or goals, these coalitions often have problems working together. To be effective, such groups need to spend considerable time defining the problem and exploring each other's perspectives. This should help them recognize their interdependence. In such groups, the participants must come to see themselves not as members of group A (the executives) or group B (the educators), but as members of group C (the coalition). Leadership can be especially difficult in such groups.

One useful approach in such situations is **dialogue groups**. According to William Isaacs, director of the Dialogue Project at the Massachusetts Institute of Technology Center for Organizational Learning, "Dialogue is a discipline of collective thinking and inquiry, a process for transforming the quality of conversation, and, in particular, the thinking that lies beneath it."[12] Such groups focus on understanding the different interpretations of the problem that participants bring to the interaction. Their purpose is to establish a dialogue from which common ground and mutual trust can emerge.

The role of the facilitator is critical in dialogue groups. According to Edgar Schein of the MIT Center, the facilitator must take the following steps:

1. Seat the group in a circle to create a sense of equality.
2. Introduce the problem.
3. Ask people to share an experience in which dialogue led to "good communication."
4. Ask members to consider what leads to good communication.
5. Ask participants to talk about their reactions.
6. Let the conversation flow naturally.
7. Intervene only to clarify problems of communication.
8. Conclude by asking all members to comment however they choose.[13]

The dialogue method is not a substitute for other problem-solving techniques, such as the reflective thinking process presented earlier. Instead, the dialogue method may be used as a precursor because deliberation usually works well only when members understand each other well enough to be "talking the same language."

When an organization wants to delve into the feelings or motivations of their customers or clients, they often put together a **focus group**.[14] Focus groups typically consist of six to ten members carefully selected to provide the type of information sought. In a focus group a trained moderator asks questions and encourages all of the participants to respond. Advertisements, brochures, other printed materials, or video clips may also be used to stimulate discussion. Interactions between members of the group often provide the most valuable information. The sessions are recorded on either audiotape or videotape for later analysis. Focus groups are typically face-to-face encounters, but they may also be conducted through telephone conference calls, in Internet chat rooms, or through videoconferencing.

Participating in Small Groups

To participate successfully in small groups, you must understand your responsibilities as a group member. You should also be prepared to assume leadership of the group.

Working as a Group Member

Becoming an effective group member means you must accept certain responsibilities:

- First, you should come to meetings prepared to contribute. You should have read background materials and completed any jobs assigned to you by the group leader.

- Second, you should be willing to learn from others. Try to contribute to the process rather than dominating the discussion. Don't be afraid to admit you are wrong, and don't become defensive when challenged. Willingness to change your views is not a sign of weakness, nor is obstinacy a strength.
- Third, listen constructively. Don't interrupt others. Object if you feel consensus is forming too quickly. You might save the meeting from groupthink.

Analyzing your group communication skills can help you become a more effective group communicator. Use the self-analysis form in Figure A.1 to steer yourself toward more constructive group communication behaviors.

Figure A.1

Group Communication Skills Self-Analysis Form

	Need to Do Less	Doing Fine	Need to Do More
1. I make my points concisely.	☐	☐	☐
2. I speak with confidence.	☐	☐	☐
3. I provide specific examples and details.	☐	☐	☐
4. I try to integrate ideas that are expressed.	☐	☐	☐
5. I let others know when I do not understand them.	☐	☐	☐
6. I let others know when I agree with them.	☐	☐	☐
7. I let others know tactfully when I disagree with them.	☐	☐	☐
8. I express my opinions.	☐	☐	☐
9. I suggest solutions to problems.	☐	☐	☐
10. I listen to understand.	☐	☐	☐
11. I try to understand before agreeing or disagreeing.	☐	☐	☐
12. I ask questions to get more information.	☐	☐	☐
13. I ask others for their opinions.	☐	☐	☐
14. I check for group agreement.	☐	☐	☐
15. I try to minimize tension.	☐	☐	☐
16. I accept help from others.	☐	☐	☐
17. I offer help to others.	☐	☐	☐
18. I let others have their say.	☐	☐	☐
19. I stand up for myself.	☐	☐	☐
20. I urge others to speak up.	☐	☐	☐

As you participate in groups, you should also keep in mind the following questions:

- What is happening now in the group?
- What should be happening in the group?
- What can I do to make this come about?

If you notice a difference between what the group is doing and what it should be doing to reach its goals, you have the opportunity to demonstrate leadership behavior.

Leading Small Groups

For over fifty years, social scientists have been studying leadership by analyzing group communication patterns. This research suggests that two basic types of leadership behaviors emerge in most groups. The first is **task leadership behavior**, which directs the activity of the group toward a specified goal. The second is **social leadership behavior**, which helps build and maintain positive relationships among group members.

Task leaders initiate goal-related communication, including both giving and seeking information, opinions, and suggestions. A task leader might say, "We need more information on just how widespread sexual harassment is on campus. Let me tell you what Dean Johnson told me last Friday." Or the task leader might ask, "Gwen, tell us what you found out from the Affirmative Action Office."

Social leaders express agreement, help the group release tension, and behave in a supportive manner. A social leader looks for chances to give compliments: "I think Gwen has made a very important point. You really helped us by finding that out." Sincere compliments help keep members from becoming defensive and help maintain a constructive communication atmosphere. In a healthy communication climate, the two kinds of leadership behavior support each other and keep the group moving toward its goal. When one person combines both styles of leadership, that person is likely to be highly effective.

Leadership has also been studied in terms of how the leader enacts the task and maintenance functions. An **autocratic leader** makes decisions without consultation, issues orders or gives direction, and controls the members of the group through the use of rewards or punishments. A **participative leader** seeks input from group members and gives them an active role in decision making. A **free-rein leader** lets members decide on their own what to do, how to do it, and when to do it. If you were working in an organization, you would probably say you "worked *for*" an autocratic leader, "worked *with*" a participative leader, and "worked *in spite of*" a free-rein leader.

Currently, work on leadership suggests that leadership styles are either transactional or transformational. **Transactional leadership** takes place in an environment based on power relationships and relies on reward and punishment to accomplish its ends. **Transformational leadership** appeals to "people's higher levels of motivation to contribute to a cause and add to the quality of life on the planet."[15] It carries overtones of stewardship instead of management. Transformational leaders have the following qualities:

- They have a vision of what needs to be done.
- They are empathetic.
- They are trusted.
- They give credit to others.
- They help others develop.

- They share power.
- They are willing to experiment and learn.

In short, transformational leaders lead with both their hearts and their heads. According to John Schuster, a management consultant who specializes in transformational leadership training, "The heart is more difficult to develop. It's easier to get smarter than to become more caring."[16] Recent research suggests that transformational leadership encourages communication from subordinates because they are less intimidated by their superiors and more willing to ask for advice or help.[17]

To understand leadership, you need to consider the major components of **ethos**: competence, integrity, goodwill, and dynamism. An effective leader is competent. This means the leader understands the problem and knows how to steer a group through the problem-solving process. An effective leader has integrity. This means the leader is honest and places group success above personal concerns. An effective leader is perceived as a person of goodwill, concerned less about the self and more about those whom the group serves. Finally, an effective leader is dynamic. Dynamism involves being enthusiastic, energetic, and decisive.

Don't be intimidated by this idealized portrait of a leader. Most of us have these qualities in varying degrees and can use them when the need for leadership arises. To be an effective leader, remember two simple goals: *Help others be effective* and *get the job done.* Cultivate an open leadership style that encourages all sides to air their views.

Planning for Meetings. In many situations, meetings seem to be time wasters. This may be because the people who conduct them do not know when to call meetings or how to run them.[18] Meetings should be called when members need to

- discuss the meaning of information face to face.
- decide on a common course of action.
- establish a plan of action.
- report on the progress of a plan, evaluate its effectiveness, and revise it if needed.

More than just knowing when to call meetings, you need to know how to plan them. The following guidelines should help you plan effective meetings:

- *Have a specific purpose for holding a meeting.* Unnecessary meetings waste time. If your goal is simply to increase interaction, plan a social event rather than a meeting.
- *Prepare an agenda and distribute it to participants before the meeting.* Having an agenda gives members time to prepare and assemble information they might need. Solicit agenda items from participants.
- *Keep meetings short.* After about an hour, groups get tired, and the law of diminishing returns sets in. Don't try to do too much in a single meeting.
- *Keep groups small.* You get more participation and interaction in small groups. In larger groups, people may be reluctant to ask questions or contribute ideas.
- *Select participants who will interact easily with each other.* In business settings, the presence of someone's supervisor may inhibit interaction. You will get better participation if group members come from the same or nearly the same working level in the organization.
- *Plan the site of the meeting.* Arrange for privacy and freedom from interruptions. A circular arrangement contributes to participation because there is no power position. A rectangular table or a lectern and classroom arrangement may inhibit interaction.

- *Prepare in advance.* Be certain that you have the necessary supplies, such as chalk, a flip chart, markers, note pads, and pencils. If you will use electronic equipment, check to be sure it is in working order.

Conducting an Effective Meeting. Group leaders have more responsibilities than other members. Leaders must encourage deliberations that proceed in good faith toward constructive ends. They should also be well informed on the issues so that they can answer questions and keep the group moving toward its objectives. The following checklist should be helpful in guiding your behavior as a group leader:

- Begin and end the meeting on time.
- Present background information concisely and objectively.
- Lead, don't run the meeting.
- Be enthusiastic.
- Get conflict out in the open so that it can be dealt with directly.
- Urge all members to participate.
- Keep discussion centered on the issue.
- At the close of a meeting, summarize what the group has accomplished.

As a group leader, you may need to present the group's recommendations to others. In this task, you function mainly as an informative speaker. You should present the recommendations offered by the group, along with the major reasons for making these recommendations. You should also mention reservations that may have surfaced during deliberations. Your job in making this report is not to advocate, but to educate. Later, you may join in any following discussion with persuasive remarks that express your personal convictions on the subject.

Communication Behavior and Group Effectiveness.

Certain communication and leadership behaviors may either encourage or thwart group effectiveness.[19] Better group decisions are made when all group members participate fully in the process; when members are respectful of each other and leaders are respectful of members; and when negative emotional behaviors are kept in check. More specific details of these findings are listed in Figure A.2.

Guidelines for Formal Meetings

The larger a group is, the more it needs a formal procedure to conduct meetings. Also, if a meeting involves a controversial subject, it is often wise to have a set of rules to follow. Having clear-cut guidelines helps keep meetings from becoming chaotic and helps ensure fair treatment for all participants. In such situations, many groups choose to operate by **parliamentary procedure**.

Parliamentary procedure establishes an order of business for a meeting and lays out the way the group initiates discussions and reaches decisions. Under parliamentary procedure, a formal meeting proceeds as follows:

1. The chair calls the meeting to order.
2. The secretary reads the minutes of the previous meeting, which are corrected, if necessary, and approved.

Figure A.2

Behaviors That Enhance or Impede Decision Making

Enhancing Behaviors	Impeding Behaviors
Opinions are sought out.	Members express dislike for others.
Creativity is encouraged.	Members personally attack others.
Participation is encouraged.	Members make sarcastic comments.
Opposing views are encouraged.	Leader sets criteria for solution.
Members provide information.	Leader makes the decision.
Group analyzes suggestions.	Leader intimidates members.
Members listen to one another.	Meeting becomes a gripe session.
Members respect others' ideas.	Disagreements are ignored, not aired.
Members support others' ideas.	Disagreement is discouraged.
Problem is thoroughly researched.	Members pursue personal goals.
Group sets criteria for solution.	
Members are knowledgeable on issue.	
Evidence for suggestions is presented.	
Group focuses on task.	

3. Reports from officers and committees are presented.
4. Unfinished business is considered.
5. New business is introduced.
6. Announcements are made.
7. The meeting is adjourned.

Business in formal meetings goes forward by **motions**, or proposals set before the group. Consider the following scenario. The chair asks: "Is there any new business?" A member responds: "I move that we allot $100 to build a Homecoming float." The member has offered a main motion, which proposes an action. Before the group can discuss the motion, it must be seconded. The purpose of a **second** is to ensure that more than one person wants to see the motion considered. If no one volunteers a second, the chair may ask, "Is there a second?" Typically, another member will respond, "I second the motion." Once a motion is made and seconded, it is open for discussion. It must be passed by majority vote, defeated, or otherwise resolved before the group can move on to other business. With the exception of a few technical motions (such as "I move we take a fifteen-minute recess" or "Point of personal privilege—can we do anything about the heat in this room?"), the main motion remains at the center of group attention until resolved.

Let us assume that, as the group discusses the main motion in our example, some members believe the amount of money proposed is insufficient. At this point, another member may say: "I move to amend the motion to provide $150 for the float." The **motion to amend** gives the group a chance to modify a main motion. It must be seconded and, after discussion, must be resolved by majority vote before discussion goes forward. If the motion to amend passes, then the amended main motion must be considered further.

How does a group make a decision on a motion? There usually is a time when discussion begins to lag. At this point the chair might say, "Do I hear a call for the question?" A motion to **call the question** ends discussion, and it requires a two-thirds vote for approval. Once the group votes to end discussion, it must then vote to accept or reject the motion. No further discussion can take place until the original or amended original motion is voted on.

Sometimes the discussion of a motion may reveal that the group is confused or sharply divided about an issue. At this point a member may move to **table the motion**. This is a way to dispose of a troublesome motion without further divisive or confused discussion. At other times, the discussion of a motion may reveal that the group lacks information to make an intelligent decision. At that point, we might hear from a member: "In light of the uncertainty over costs, I move we postpone further consideration until next week's meeting." The **motion to postpone consideration** gives the chair a chance to appoint a committee to gather the information needed. The move to adjourn ends the meeting.

These are just some of the important procedures that can help ensure that formal group communication remains fair and constructive (see Figure A.3). For more information on formal group communication procedures, consult the authoritative *Robert's Rules of Order.*

Making Group Presentations

After a group has completed its work, it may need to present its findings and recommendations to a larger audience of decision makers. To plan this presentation, the group leader may make assignments, deciding who can best present different areas of the report. The group should also develop an agenda for the presentation that indicates the order of topics to be covered and who will cover them. This planning should be done well in advance of the actual presentation so that participants have time to prepare.

Often the group's leader or designated spokesperson will simply offer an **oral report**. This report is an informative speech that generally follows a certain pattern. The introduction to the report should briefly review the problem the group has been assigned, introduce the members of the group (including their credentials) if they are not well known to the audience, and describe the process used by the group. The body of the report should cover the major findings or recommendations. The

Figure A.3

Guide to Parliamentary Procedure

Action	Requires Second	Can Be Debated	Can Be Amended	Vote Required	Function
Main Motion	Yes	Yes	Yes	Majority	Commits group to a specific action or position.
Second	No	No	No	None	Assures that more than one group member wishes to see idea considered.
Move to Amend	Yes	Yes	Yes	Majority	Allows group to modify and improve an existing motion.
Call the Question	Yes	No	No	Two-thirds	Brings discussion to an end and moves to a vote on the motion in question.
Move to Table the Motion	Yes	No	No	Majority	Stops immediate consideration of the motion until a later unspecified time.
Move to Postpone Consideration	Yes	Yes	Yes	Majority	Stops immediate discussion and allows time for the group to obtain more information on the problem.
Move to Adjourn	Yes	No	No	Majority	Formally ends meeting.

conclusion should summarize those findings and possibly make suggestions for further work. The report should be as succinct as possible and should allow for questions and answers following the formal presentation.

In addition to the oral report, group presentations may follow three other formats: a symposium, a panel discussion, or a forum.

A **symposium** features a moderator and certain members of the problem-solving group as presenters. This group should be selected on the basis of special competencies and communication skills. The primary role of the moderator is to introduce the topic and speakers at the beginning of the symposium and to summarize the findings as the presentation draws to a close. Each symposium speaker will typically cover one aspect of the topic, making a short (well-prepared and practiced) oral report on the group's findings or recommendations. The speaking in the symposium must be coordinated so that speakers are not simply repeating what earlier speakers have said. The moderator enforces time limits and keeps the presentations on track. The symposium is followed typically by a question-and-answer session.

A **panel discussion** is less formal than a symposium. It also has a moderator who introduces the topic and the participants, but it does not feature prepared speeches. Rather, it features a planned pattern of spontaneous conversational exchanges. Following the brief introductions the moderator asks questions of the group. Participants respond with brief impromptu answers. As we noted in Chapter 13, impromptu presentations should state a point, follow it up with a reason or example, and then restate or summarize what has been said. The moderator guides the discussion and keeps the group in focus. He or she should also see that no single participant dominates the discussion and that all panelists actually participate.

Although responses are impromptu, this does not mean that participants are in the dark about what will happen. Advance planning should indicate what questions will be asked so that panelists can prepare with these in mind. Panelists should review what went on in the group and organize their ideas before participating. The impromptu responses of panelists should be similar to the briefings covered in Chapter 14: that is, brief and to the point. Panelists should be prepared for tough follow-up questions either from the moderator or from the audience.

A **forum** presentation is much like a panel discussion except that the questions come from the audience rather than from the moderator. The basic job of the moderator of a forum is to keep the discussion on track. The moderator may introduce the topic and participants, and during the course of the forum he or she recognizes audience members who wish to ask questions. At times, the moderator may also have to "moderate"—act as a referee if questions or answers become heated on emotional topics. If the group anticipates controversy, it may wish to arrange for a parliamentarian to help keep the meeting constructive. Participants should follow the guidelines suggested for handling questions and answers in Chapter 13.

Notes

1. Scot Ober, *Contemporary Business Communication* (Boston: Houghton Mifflin, 1995), p. 498.
2. Adapted from Marc Hequet, "The Fine Art of Multicultural Meetings," *Training* (July 1993): 29–33.
3. Christopher P. Neck and Charles C. Manz, "From Groupthink to Teamthink: Toward the Creation of Constructive Thought Patterns in Self-Managed Work Teams," *Human Relations* (August 1994): 929–953.
4. I. L. Janis, *Groupthink: Psychological Studies of Policy Decisions and Fiascoes* (Boston: Houghton Mifflin, 1982), pp. 245–246.
5. For an overview of methods other than reflective thinking, see Patricia Hayes Andrews and Richard T. Herschel, *Organizational Communication: Empowerment in a Technological Society* (Boston: Houghton Mifflin, 1996), pp. 213–218.
6. Floyd Hurt, "Better Brainstorming," *Training and Development* (November 1994): 57–59.
7. Ron Zemke, "In Search of Good Ideas," *Training* (January 1993): 46–52.
8. "The Right Way to Brainstorm," *Inc.* (July 1999): 93.

9. Gail Kay, "Effective Meetings Through Electronic Brainstorming," *Management Quarterly* (Winter 1994): 15–26; Milam Aiken, Mahesh Vanjami, and James Krosp, "Group Decision Support Systems," *Review of Business* (Spring 1995): 38–42; and Michael C. Kettelhut, "How to Avoid Misusing Electronic Meeting Support," *Planning Review* (July–August 1994): 34–38.

10. Robyn D. Clarke, "For a Better Way to Brainstorm," *Black Enterprise* (January 2000): 114.

11. Jacqueline Hood, Jeanne M. Logsdon, and Judith Kenner Thompson, "Collaboration for Social Problem Solving: A Process Model," *Business and Society* (Spring 1993): 1–17.

12. William M. Isaacs, "Taking Flight: Dialogue, Collective Thinking, and Organizational Learning," *Organizational Dynamics* (Autumn 1993): 24–39.

13. Edgar H Schein, "On Dialogue, Culture, and Organizational Learning," *Organizational Dynamics* (Autumn 1993): 40–51.

14. The information on focus groups was synthesized from Carter McNamara, "Basics of Conducting Focus Groups" (undated posting), http://www.mapnp.org/library/ evaluatn/focusgrp.htm (downloaded 6 March 2004); George Silverman, "How to Get Beneath the Surface in Focus Groups" (undated posting), http://www.mnav.com/bensurf.htm (downloaded 6 March 2004); Townsend International, "How to Run a Focus Group" (undated posting), http://www.gdaymate.com/customer_service/focusgroup.html (downloaded 6 March 2004); and Thomas L. Greenbaum, "Ten Tips for Running Successful Focus Groups" (14 Sept. 1998), http://www.groupsplus.com/pages/mn091498.htm (downloaded 6 March 2004).

15. John P. Schuster, "Transforming Your Leadership Style," *Association Management* (January 1994): 39–43.

16. *Ibid.*

17. Svjetlana Madzar, "Subordinate's Information Inquiry: Exploring the Effect of Perceived Leadership Style and Individual Differences," *Journal of Occupational and Organizational Psychology* (June 2001): 221–232.

18. Much of the material in this section is adapted from Robert D. Ramsey, "Making Meetings Work for You," *Supervision* (February 1994): 14–16; and Becky Jones, Midge Wilker, and Judy Stoner, "A Meeting Primer," *Management Review* (January 1995): 30–32.

19. Michael E. Mayer, "Behaviors Leading to More Effective Decisions in Small Groups Embedded in Organizations," *Communication Reports* (Summer 1988): 123–132.

APPENDIX B

Speeches for Analysis

Self-Introductory

Sandra Baltz *My Three Cultures*
Rodney Nishikawa *Free at Last*
Elizabeth Tidmore *Lady with a Gun*

Informative

Marge Anderson *Looking Through Our Window: The Value of Indian Culture*
Stephen Huff *The New Madrid Earthquake Area*
Cecile Larson *The "Monument" at Wounded Knee*

Persuasive

Anna Aley *We Don't Have to Live in Slums*
Bonnie Marshall *Living Wills: Ensuring Your Right to Choose*
Richard F. Corlin *The Secrets of Gun Violence in America*

Ceremonial

Tommie Albright *Martin Luther King Jr.'s Legacy for Us*
A Tribute to Wilma Rudolph with presentations by Tom Brokaw, Bill Cosby, Gail Devers, Ed Temple, and Wilma Rudolph
Elie Wiesel *Nobel Peace Prize Acceptance Speech*

My Three Cultures

Sandra Baltz

Sandra Baltz first presented this self-introductory speech many years ago at the University of Memphis. She addressed the themes of cross-culturalism and family values long before these became fashionable. Sandra's deft use of comparison and contrast, and her example of foods illustrating how three cultures can combine harmoniously, are instructive. As her speech developed, she built her ethos as a competent, warm person, highly qualified to give later informative and persuasive speeches on issues involving medical care. Presented at a time when tensions in the Middle East were running high, Sandra's speech served as a gentle reminder that people of goodwill can always find ways to enjoy their differences, and to reaffirm their common membership in the human family.

Several years ago I read a newspaper article in the *Commercial Appeal* in which an American journalist described some of his experiences in the Middle East. He was there a couple of months and had been the guest of several different Arab families. He reported having been very well treated and very well received by everyone that he met there. But it was only later, when he returned home, that he became aware of the intense resentment his hosts held for Americans and our unwelcome involvement in their Middle Eastern affairs. The journalist wrote of feeling somewhat bewildered, if not deceived, by the large discrepancy between his treatment while in the Middle East and the hostile attitude that he learned about later. He labeled this behavior hypocritical. When I reached the end of the article, I was reminded of a phrase spoken often by my mother. "Sandra," she says to me, *"respeta tu casa y a todos los que entran en ella, trata a tus enemigos asi como a tus amigos."*

This is an Arabic proverb, spoken in Spanish, and roughly it translates into "Respect your home and all who enter it, treating even an enemy as a friend." This is a philosophy that I have heard often in my home. With this in mind, it seemed to me that the treatment the American journalist received while in the Middle East was not hypocritical behavior on the part of his hosts. Rather, it was an act of respect for their guest, for themselves, and for their home—indeed, a behavior very typical of the Arabic culture.

Since having read that article several years ago, I have become much more aware of how my life is different because of having a mother who is of Palestinian origin but was born and raised in the Central American country of El Salvador.

One of the most obvious differences is that I was raised bilingually—speaking both Spanish and English. In fact, my first words were in Spanish. Growing up speaking two languages has been both an advantage and a disadvantage for me. One clear advantage is that I received straight A's in my Spanish class at Immaculate Conception High School. Certainly, traveling has been made much easier. During visits to Spain, Mexico, and some of the Central American countries, it has been my experience that people are much more open and much more receptive if you can speak their language. In addition, the subtleties of a culture are easier to grasp and much easier to appreciate.

I hope that knowing a second language will continue to be an asset for me in the future. I am currently pursuing a career in medicine. Perhaps by knowing Spanish I can broaden the area in which I can work and increase the number of people that I might reach.

Now one of the disadvantages of growing up bilingually is that I picked up my mother's accent as well as her language. I must have been about four years old before I realized that our feathered friends in the trees are called "birds" not "beers" and that, in fact, we had a "birdbath" in our backyard, not a "beerbath."

Family reunions also tend to be confusing around my home. Most of my relatives speak either Spanish, English, or Arabic, but rarely any combination of the three. So, as a result, deep and involved conversations are almost impossible. But with a little nodding and smiling, I have found that there really is no language barrier among family and friends.

In all, I must say that being exposed to three very different cultures—Latin, Arabic, and American—has been rewarding for me and has made a difference even in the music I enjoy and the food I eat. It is not unusual in my house to sit down to a meal made up of stuffed grape leaves and refried beans and all topped off with apple pie for dessert.

I am fortunate in having had the opportunity to view more closely what makes Arabic and Latin cultures unique. By understanding and appreciating them I have been able to better understand and appreciate my own American culture. In closing, just let me add some words you often hear spoken in my home—*adios* and *allak konn ma'eck*—goodbye, and may God go with you.

Free at Last

Rodney Nishikawa

Rod Nishikawa presented this sensitive and moving self-introductory speech in his public speaking class at the University of California–Davis. Although most of his classmates were aware of prejudice, Rod's personal narrative—about his first encounter with prejudice as a child—introduced many of them to the Japanese American culture and helped them relate to the problem more closely. Rod's willingness to speak from the heart helped transform his class into a creative, caring community.

Three years ago I presented the valedictory speech at my high school graduation. As I concluded, I borrowed a line from Dr. Martin Luther King's "I Have a Dream" oration: "Free at last, free at last, thank God almighty we're free at last!" The words had only a joyful, humorous place in that speech, but for me personally they were a lie. I was not yet free, and would not be free until I had conquered an ancient enemy, both outside me and within me—that enemy was racial prejudice.

The event in my life that had the greatest effect on me happened over twelve years ago when I was eight years old. I was a shy, naive little boy. I knew I was Japanese, but I didn't consider myself different from my friends, nor did I realize anyone else noticed or even cared. But at least one person did. The "bully" in our class made it a point to remind me by calling me a "Jap." He told me I didn't belong in America, and that I should go back to Japan.

It was hard for me to understand what he meant, because like my parents I was born here in this country. This was my home. I didn't know what to do when I was taunted. All I can remember is going home after school and crying as though my heart were broken. I told my mom that I wished I wasn't Japanese, but that if I did have to be Japanese, why did I have to be born in this country?

Of course my mother knew exactly how I felt. She was about the age I was then when the Japanese attacked Pearl Harbor. She told me how she too had experienced prejudice at school, but that the prejudice she encountered was over a hundred times worse. When my father came home from work, my mom and I told him what had happened. Although my father was understanding, he said that I would never know the meaning of true prejudice because I did not grow up on the West Coast during World War II.

My encounter with the school bully was the beginning of my personal education about prejudice. What I have learned is that prejudice is not a disease that infects only the least educated among us. Rather, it is a bad part of human nature that lies buried deep within all of us. Some people, however, seem to enjoy their prejudice. These people like to feel good by putting others down. But I have also learned how to deal with such problems when they arise. It was the advice from my mother that helped me the most.

My mother explained to me the meaning of the Japanese word *gaman. Gaman* means to "bear within" or "bear the burden." It is similar to the American phrase "turn the other cheek," but it means more to "endure" than to "ignore." She told me that when I go back to school, I should practice *gaman*—that even if I am hurt, I should not react with anger or fear, that I should bear the burden within. She said that if I showed anger or fear it would only make things worse, but if I practiced *gaman* things would get better for me. She was right. When I went back to school, I remembered what she had said. I used *gaman.* I bore the burden within. It wasn't easy for an eight-year-old, but I did not show any anger. I did not show any fear to the bully, and eventually he stopped picking on me.

Prejudice has been a bitter teacher in my life, but *gaman* has been an even greater blessing. By learning how to practice it, I feel I have acquired a great deal of inner strength. Whereas Gary [another student in the class] said he is a "competitor," I believe I am a "survivor." I look around my environment, recognize my situation, and cope with it. Because *gaman* has been part of my daily life since I was eight years old, I rarely experience feelings of anger or fear—those negative emotions that can keep a person from really being "free."

Being freed from such negative feelings has also helped me to better understand and accept myself. When I first encountered prejudice, I was ashamed of who I was. I didn't like being different, being a Japanese American. But as I've grown to maturity, I have realized that I'm really proud to be Japanese American: Japanese by blood—with the rich culture and heritage of my ancestors behind me—and American by birth—which makes me equal to anyone in this room because we were all born in this country and we all share the same rights and obligations.

Practicing *gaman* has helped me conquer prejudice. Although my Japanese ancestors might not have spoken as boldly as I have today, I am basically an American, which makes me a little outspoken. Therefore, I can talk to you about racial prejudice and of what it has meant to my life. And because I can talk about it, and share it with you, I am finally, truly, "free at last."

Lady with a Gun

Elizabeth Tidmore

Beth Tidmore presented this self-introductory speech to her honors class in oral communication at the University of Memphis. The speech, offered as a tribute to her mother's faith in her, describes her dramatic development as a shooting champion. Beth's speech is noteworthy for its use of narrative design, especially dialogue. Her graphic descriptions, engaging her listeners' senses of sight, sound, touch, and smell, also helped her establish a vital, direct contact with her audience and transported them to the scenes she depicted. In addition, her colorful uses of voice and gesture helped achieve the ideal of integrated communication described in Chapter 13. By the end of the semester, Beth had won the National Junior Olympic Championship Women's Air Rifle competition at the Olympic Training Center in Colorado Springs. She was named to the All-America shooters team and was selected to the National team, where she will train for World Cup and Olympics competitions.

I'm sure everybody has had an April Fool's joke played on them. My father's favorite one was to wake me up on April first and tell me, "School's been cancelled for the day; you don't have to go," and then get all excited and say "April Fools!" I'd get up and take a shower . . .

Well, on April first 2000, my mother said three words that I was sure weren't an April Fools joke. She said, "We'll take it." The "it" she was referring to was a brand-new Anschutz 2002 Air Rifle. Now, this is $2,000 worth of equipment for a sport that I'd been in for maybe three months—not long. That was a big deal! It meant that I would be going from a junior-level to an Olympic-grade rifle.

Someone outside of the sport might think, "Eh, minor upgrade. A gun is a gun, right?" No. Imagine a fifteen-year-old who has been driving a used Toyota and who suddenly gets a new Mercedes for her sixteenth birthday. That's how I felt.

And as she was writing the check, I completely panicked. I thought, "What if I'm not good enough to justify this rifle? What if I decide to quit and we have to sell it, or we can't sell it? What if I let my parents down and I waste their money?" So later in the car I said, "Momma, what if I'm not good enough?" She said, "Don't worry about it—it's my money." Okay . . .

So my journey began. Most shooters start out when they're younger, and they move up through different rifles. Most of my peers had at least four years' experience on me. I had to jump right in and get a scholarship. And to get a scholarship I had to get noticed. And to get noticed I had to win, and to win, I had to shoot great scores immediately.

So my journey was filled with eight hours a day practice, five days a week. On weekends I shot matches and I traveled. I had to take my homework with me to complete it before I got back to school. I had to do physical training, I had dietary restrictions. When all my friends were out at parties and at Cancun for Spring Break, I was at the shooting range. My free time—if I had any—was spent lifting weights and running.

At times I really resented my friends, because I thought they must have all the fun. But you know what, it was worth it! My friends don't know what it's like to feel the cold, smooth wood of the cheekpiece against your face. And they don't know the rich smell of Hoppe's No. 9 [oil] when you're cleaning your rifle. And they've never been to the Olympic Training Center in Colorado and seen how they embroider the little Olympic logo on *everything* from the mattresses to the plates. And they don't know the thrill of shooting in a final and having everyone applaud when you shoot a ten or even a center ten, or standing on the podium and having them put a medal around your neck, and being proud to represent your school, your country. . . .

There's a bumper sticker that says, "A Lady with A Gun Has More Fun." After three years in this sport, I have had so much fun! I've been all over the U.S., I've been captain of a high school rifle team, I've been to matches everywhere, I've won medals, I've been to World Cups and met people from all over the world. And I've gotten to experience so many different people, places, and events through my participation in shooting sports.

So not long ago, I asked my mother, "Mom, how did you know?" She said, "Ah, I just knew." I said, "No, Mom—*really.* How did you know that you weren't going to waste your money?" She got very serious and she took me by the shoulders and she squared me up. She looked me right in the eye and she said, "When you picked up that gun, you just looked like you belonged together. I knew there was a sparkle in your eye, and I knew that you were meant to do great things with that rifle."

So, thanks, Mom.

Looking Through Our Window: The Value of Indian Culture

Marge Anderson

This presentation by Marge Anderson, chief executive of the Mille Lacs Band of the Ojibwe, shows that one speech can perform multiple general functions. Anderson both celebrates the values of her culture and persuades listeners to engage in a dialogue, which she defines, citing St. Thomas Aquinas, as "the struggle to learn from each other." The even more fundamental function of her speech is to inform *her mainstream Minnesota audience of how Native Americans view the world and their relationship to it. From the basis of that understanding, she explains specific accomplishments of her tribe and the rationale behind her people's business decisions. All of us are enriched, she argues, when we are able to look at the world through each other's windows. Therefore, she suggests, her listeners should honor and help preserve the authenticity of the Native American cultural perspective.*

Aaniin. Thank you for inviting me here today. When I was asked to speak to you, I was told you are interested in hearing about the improvements we are making on the Mille Lacs Reservation, and about our investment of casino dollars back into our community through schools, health care facilities, and other services. And I do want to talk to you about these things, because they are tremendously important, and I am very proud of them.

But before I do, I want to take a few minutes to talk to you about something else, something I'm not asked about very often. I want to talk to you about what it means to be Indian. About how my people experience the world. About the fundamental way in which our culture differs from yours. And about why you should care about all this.

The differences between Indians and non-Indians have created a lot of controversy lately. Casinos, treaty rights, tribal sovereignty—these issues have stirred such anger and bitterness.

I believe the accusations against us are made out of ignorance. The vast majority of non-Indians do not understand how my people view the world, what we value, what motivates us.

They do not know these things for one simple reason: they've never heard us talk about them. For many years, the only stories that non-Indians heard about my people came from other non-Indians. As a result, the picture you got of us was fanciful, or distorted, or so shadowy, it hardly existed at all.

It's time for Indian voices to tell Indian stories.

Now, I'm sure at least a few of you are wondering, "Why do I need to hear these stories? Why should I care about what Indian people think, and feel, and believe?"

I think the most eloquent answer I can give you comes from the namesake of this university, St. Thomas Aquinas. St. Thomas wrote that dialogue is the struggle to learn from each other. This struggle, he said, is like Jacob wrestling the angel—it leaves one wounded and blessed at the same time.

Indian people know this struggle very well. The wounds we've suffered in our dialogue with non-Indians are well documented; I don't need to give you a laundry list of complaints.

We also know some of the blessings of this struggle. As American Indians, we live in two worlds—ours, and yours. In the 500 years since you first came to our lands, we have struggled to learn how to take the best of what your culture has to offer in arts, science, technology and more, and then weave them into the fabric of our traditional ways.

But for non-Indians, the struggle is new. Now that our people have begun to achieve success, now that we are in business and in the headlines, you are starting to wrestle with understanding us.

Your wounds from this struggle are fresh, and the pain might make it hard for you to see beyond them. But if you try, you'll begin to see the blessings as well—the blessings of what a deepened knowledge of Indian culture can bring to you. I'd like to share a few of those blessings with you today.

Earlier I mentioned that there is a fundamental difference between the way Indians and non-Indians experience the world. This difference goes all the way back to the Bible, and Genesis.

In Genesis, the first book of the Old Testament, God creates man in his own image. Then God says, "be fruitful, multiply, fill the earth and conquer it. Be masters of the fish of the sea, the birds of the heaven, and all living animals on the earth."

Masters. Conquer. Nothing, nothing could be further from the way Indian people view the world and our place in it. Here are the words of the great nineteenth-century Chief Seattle:

"You are a part of the earth, and the earth is a part of you. You did not weave the web of life, you are merely a strand in it. Whatever you do to the web, you do to yourself."

In our tradition, there is no mastery. There is no conquering. Instead, there is kinship among all creation—humans, animals, birds, plants, even rocks. We are all part of the sacred hoop of the world, and we must all live in harmony with each other if that hoop is to remain unbroken.

When you begin to see the world this way—through Indian eyes—you will begin to understand our view of land and treaties very differently. You will begin to understand that when we speak of Father Sun and Mother Earth, these are not new-age catchwords—they are very real terms of respect for very real beings.

And when you understand this, then you will understand that our fight for treaty rights is not just about hunting deer or catching fish. It is about teaching our children to honor Mother Earth and Father Sun. It is about teaching them to respectfully receive the gifts these loving parents offer us in return for the care we give them. And it is about teaching this generation and the generations yet to come about their place in the web of life. Our culture and the fish, our values and the deer, the lessons we learn and the rice we harvest—everything is tied together. You can no more separate one from the other than you can divide a person's spirit from his body.

When you understand how we view the world and our place in it, it's easier to appreciate why our casinos are so important to us. The reason we defend our businesses so fiercely isn't because we want to have something that others don't. The reason is because these businesses allow us to give back to others—to our People, our communities, and the Creator.

I'd like to take a minute and mention just a few of the ways we've already given back:

We've opened new schools, new health care facilities, and new community centers where our children get a better education, where our elders get better medical care, and where our families can gather to socialize and keep our traditions alive.

We've built new ceremonial buildings, and new powwow and celebration grounds.

We've renovated an elderly center, and plan to build three culturally sensitive assisted living facilities for our elders.

We've created programs to teach and preserve our language and cultural traditions.

We've created a Small Business Development Program to help band members start their own businesses.

We've created more than twenty-eight hundred jobs for band members, people from other tribes, and non-Indians.

We've spurred the development of more than one thousand jobs in other local businesses.

We've generated more than fifty million dollars in federal taxes, and more than fifteen million dollars in state taxes through wages paid to employees.

And we've given back more than two million dollars in charitable donations.

The list goes on and on. But rather than flood you with more numbers, I'll tell you a story that sums up how my people view business through the lens of our traditional values.

Last year, the Woodlands National Bank, which is owned and operated by the Mille Lacs Band, was approached by the city of Onamia and asked to forgive a mortgage on a building in the downtown area. The building had been abandoned and was an eyesore on Main Street. The city planned to renovate and sell the building, and return it to the tax rolls.

Although the bank would lose money by forgiving the mortgage, our business leaders could see the wisdom in improving the community. The opportunity to help our neighbors was an opportunity to strengthen the web of life. So we forgave the mortgage.

Now, I know this is not a decision everyone would agree with. Some people feel that in business, you have to look out for number one. But my people feel that in business—and in life—you have to look out for every one.

And this, I believe, is one of the blessings that Indian culture has to offer you and other non-Indians. We have a different perspective on so many things, from caring for the environment, to healing the body, mind and soul.

But if our culture disappears, if the Indian ways are swallowed up by the dominant American culture, no one will be able to learn from them. Not Indian children. Not your children. No one. All that knowledge, all that wisdom, will be lost forever.

The struggle of dialogue will be over. Yes, there will be no more wounds. But there will also be no more blessings.

There is still so much we have to learn from each other, and we have already wasted so much time. Our world grows smaller every day. And every day, more of our unsettling, surprising, wonderful differences vanish. And when that happens, part of us vanishes, too.

I'd like to end with one of my favorite stories. It's a funny little story about Indians and non-Indians, but its message is serious: you can see something differently if you are willing to learn from those around you.

This is the story: Years ago, white settlers came to this area and built the first European-style homes. When Indian People walked by these homes and saw see-through things in the walls, they looked through them to see what the strangers inside were doing. The settlers were shocked, but it makes sense when you think about it: windows are made to be looked through from both sides.

Since then, my people have spent many years looking at the world through your window. I hope today I've given you a reason to look at it through ours.

Mii gwetch.

The New Madrid Earthquake Area

Stephen Huff

Stephen Huff's informative speech skillfully relates his subject to his immediate audience at the outset. He makes excellent use of comparison and contrast, of presentation aids, and of vivid description to make his subject come alive. After first establishing a basis of facts, he builds an imaginary disaster narrative to help his audience understand the magnitude of the problem being discussed. Thus he motivates listeners to take seriously his suggestions for earthquake preparation. A more adequate summary at the end of the speech might have made it even more effective.

How many of you can remember what you were doing around seven o'clock on the evening of October 17th? If you're a sports fan like me, you had probably set out the munchies, popped a cold one, and settled back to watch San Francisco and Oakland battle it out in the World Series. Since the show came on at seven o'clock here in Memphis for its pregame hype, you may not have been paying close attention to the TV—until—until—until both the sound and picture went out because of the Bay Area earthquake.

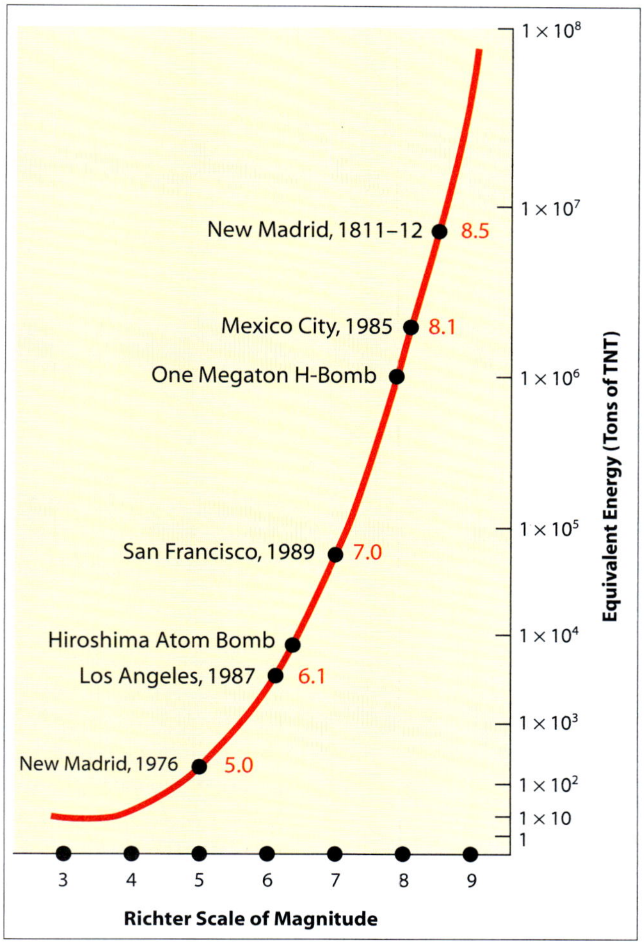

If you're like me, you probably sat glued to the TV set for the rest of the evening watching the live coverage of that catastrophe. If you're like me, you probably started thinking that Memphis, Tennessee, is in the middle of the New Madrid earthquake area and wondering how likely it would be for a large earthquake to hit here. And if you're like me, you probably asked yourself, "What would I do if a major earthquake hit Memphis?"

As I asked myself these questions, I was surprised to admit that I didn't know very much about the New Madrid earthquake area or the probability of a major quake in Memphis. And I was really upset to discover that I didn't have the foggiest idea of what to do if a quake did hit. So I visited the Center for Earthquake Research and Information here on campus; talked with Dr. Arch Johnston, the director; and read the materials he helped me find. Today, I'd like to share with you what I learned about the New Madrid earthquake area, how likely it is that Memphis may be hit by a major quake in the near future, what the effects of such a quake might be, and—most important—what you can do to be prepared.

Let's start with a little history about the New Madrid earthquake area. During the winter of 1811 to 1812, three of the largest earthquakes ever to hit the continental United States occurred in this area. Their estimated magnitudes were 8.6, 8.4, and 8.8 on the Richter scale. [He reveals magnitude chart.] I have drawn this chart to give you some idea of how much energy this involves. To simplify things, I have shown the New Madrid quakes as 8.5. Since a one-point increase in the Richter scale equals a thirtyfold increase in energy release, the energy level of these quakes was over nine hundred times more powerful than the Hiroshima atomic bomb and more than thirty times more powerful than the 7.0 quake that hit San Francisco last October. [He conceals magnitude chart.]

Most of the reports of these early earthquakes come from journals or Indian legends. The Indians tell of the night that lasted for a week and the way the "Father of Waters"—the Mississippi River—ran backwards. Waterfalls were formed on the river. Islands disappeared. Land that was once in Arkansas—on the west bank of the river—ended up in Tennessee—on the east bank of the river. Church bells chimed as far away as New Orleans and Boston. Cracks up to ten feet wide opened and closed in the earth. Geysers squirted sand fifteen feet into the air. Whole forests sank into the earth as the land turned to quicksand. Lakes disappeared and new lakes were formed. Reelfoot Lake—over ten miles long—was formed when the Mississippi River changed its course. No one is certain how many people died from the quakes because the area was sparsely settled with trappers and Indian villages. Memphis was just an outpost village with a few hundred settlers.

[He shows map of epicenters.] As you can see on this map, Memphis itself is not directly on the New Madrid Fault line. The fault extends from around Marked Tree, Arkansas, northeast to near Cairo, Illinois. This continues to be a volatile area of earthquake activity. According to Robert L. Ketter, director of the National Center for Earthquake Engineering Research, between 1974 and 1983 over two thousand quakes were recorded in the area. About 150 earthquakes per year occur in the area, but only about eight of them are large enough for people to notice. The others are picked up on the seismographs at tracking stations. The strongest quake in recent years occurred here in 1976. [He points to location on map.] This measured 5.0 on the Richter scale.

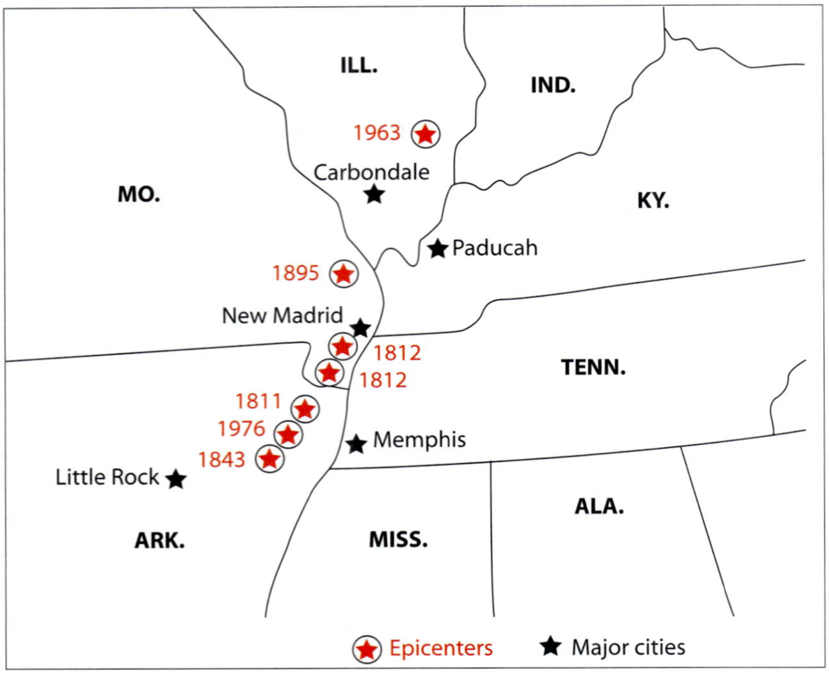

The New Madrid earthquake area is much different from the San Andreas Fault in California. Because of the way the land is formed, the alluvial soil transmits energy more efficiently here than in California. Although the quakes were about the same size, the New Madrid earthquakes affected an area fifteen times larger than the "great quake" that destroyed San Francisco in 1906.

Although scientists cannot predict exactly when another major quake may hit the area, they do know that the *repeat time* for a magnitude-6 New Madrid earthquake is seventy years, plus or minus fifteen years. The last earthquake of this size to hit the area occurred in 1895 north of New Madrid, Missouri. [He points to epicenter on map.] According to Johnston and Nava of the Memphis Earthquake Center, the probability that one with a magnitude of 6.3 will occur somewhere in the fault area by the year 2010 is 40 to 63 percent. By the year 2035 this probability increases to 86 to 97 percent. The probabilities for larger quakes are lower. They estimate the probability of a 7.6 quake within the next fifty years to be from 19 to 29 percent. [He conceals map of epicenters.]

What would happen if an earthquake of 7.6 hit Memphis? Allan and Hoshall, a prominent local engineering firm, prepared a study on this for the Federal Emergency Management Agency. The expected death toll would top 2,400. There would be at least 10,000 casualties. Two hundred thousand residents would be homeless. The city would be without electricity, gas, water, or sewer treatment facilities for weeks. Gas lines would rupture, and fires would sweep through the city. Transportation would be almost impossible, bridges and roads would be destroyed, and emergency supplies would have to be brought in by helicopter. The river bluff, midtown, and land along the Wolfe River would turn to quicksand because of liquification. Buildings there would sink like they did in the Marina area during the San Francisco quake. If the quake hit during daytime hours, at least 600 children would be killed and another 2,400 injured as schools collapsed on them. None of our schools have been built to seismic code specifications.

In fact, very few buildings in Memphis have been built to be earthquake resistant, so it would be difficult to find places to shelter and care for the homeless. The major exceptions are the new hospitals in the suburbs, the Omni Hotel east of the expressway, the Holiday Inn Convention Center, and two or three new office complexes. The only municipal structure built to code is the Criminal Justice Center. The Memphis Pyramid, built by the city and county, which seats over twenty thousand people for the University of Memphis basketball games, was not built to code. I'd hate to be in it if a major quake hit. The prospects are not pretty.

What can we do to prepare ourselves for this possible catastrophe? We can start out by learning what to do if a quake does hit. When I asked myself what I would do, my first reaction was to "get outside." I've since learned that this is not right. The "Earthquake Safety Checklist" published by the Federal Emergency Management Agency and the Red Cross makes a number of suggestions. I've written them out and will distribute them after my speech.

First, when an earthquake hits, if you are inside, stay there. Get in a safe spot: Stand in a doorway, stand next to an inside wall, or get under a large piece of furniture. Stay away from windows, hanging objects, fireplaces, and tall, unsecured furniture until the shaking stops. Do not try to use elevators. If you are outside, get away from buildings, trees, walls, or power lines. If you are in a car, stay in it; pull over and park. Stay away from overpasses and power lines. Do not drive over bridges or overpasses until they have been inspected. If you are in a crowded public place, do not rush for the exit. You may be crushed in the stampede of people.

When the shaking stops, check for gas, water, or electrical damage. Turn off the electricity, gas, and water to your home. Do not use electrical switches—unseen sparks could set off a gas fire. Do not use the telephone unless you must report a severe injury. Check to see that the sewer works before using the toilet. Plug drains to prevent a sewer backup.

There are also some things you can do in advance to be prepared. Accumulate emergency supplies: At home you should have a flashlight, a transistor radio with fresh batteries, a first-aid kit, fire extinguishers, and enough canned or dried food and beverages to last your family for 72 hours. Identify hazards and safe spots in your home—secure tall, heavy furniture; don't hang heavy pictures over your bed; keep flammable liquids in a garage or outside storage area—look around each room and plan where you would go if an earthquake hit. Conduct earthquake drills with your family.

There's one more suggestion that I would like to add. One that is specific to Memphis. Let our local officials know that you are concerned about the lack of preparedness. Urge them to support a building code—at least for public structures—that meets seismic resistance standards.

In preparing this speech, I learned a lot about the potential for earthquakes in Memphis. I hope you have learned something too. I now feel like I know what I should do if an earthquake hits. But I'm not really sure how I would react. Even the experts don't always react "appropriately." In 1971 an earthquake hit the Los Angeles area at about six o'clock in the morning. Charles Richter, the seismologist who developed the Richter scale to measure earthquakes, was in bed at the time. According to his wife, "He jumped up screaming and scared the cat."

Earthquake Preparedness Suggestions

1. If you are inside, stay there. Get in a safe spot: Stand in a doorway, stand next to an inside wall, or get under a large piece of furniture. Stay away from windows, hanging objects, fireplaces, and tall, unsecured furniture until the shaking stops. Do not try to use elevators.
2. If you are outside, get away from buildings, trees, walls, or power lines. If you are in a car, stay in it; pull over and park. Stay away from overpasses and power lines. Do not drive over bridges or overpasses until they have been inspected.
3. If you are in a crowded public place, do not rush for the exit. You may be crushed in the stampede of people.
4. When the shaking stops, check for gas, water, or electrical damage. Turn off the electricity, gas, and water to your home. Do not use electrical switches—unseen sparks could set off a gas fire. Do not use the telephone unless you must report a severe injury. Check to see that the sewer works before using the toilet. Plug drains to prevent sewer backup.

There are also some things you can do in advance to be prepared:

1. Accumulate emergency supplies: At home you should have a flashlight, a transistor radio with fresh batteries, a first-aid kit, fire extinguishers, and enough canned or dried food and beverages to last for 72 hours.
2. Identify hazards and safe spots in your home—secure tall, heavy furniture; don't hang heavy pictures over your bed; keep flammable liquids in a garage or outside storage area—look around each room and plan where you would go if an earthquake hit; conduct earthquake drills with your family.

The "Monument" at Wounded Knee

Cecile Larson

Cecile Larson's classroom speech serves two informative functions. First, it shapes the perceptions of the audience because of the way it describes the "monument" and the perspective it takes on the situation—most of her classmates had had little or no contact with Native Americans, and this might have been their first exposure to this type of information. Second, the speech serves the agenda-setting function in that it creates an awareness of a problem and the importance of that problem. The speech follows a spatial design. Cecile's vivid use of imagery and the skillful contrasts she draws between this "monument" and our "official" monuments create mental pictures that should stay with her listeners long after the words of her speech have been forgotten.

We Americans are big on monuments. We build monuments in memory of our heroes. Washington, Jefferson, and Lincoln live on in our nation's capital. We erect monuments to honor our martyrs. The Minuteman still stands guard at Concord. The flag is ever raised over Iwo Jima. Sometimes we even construct monuments to commemorate victims. In Ashburn Park downtown there is a monument to those who died in the yellow fever epidemics. However, there are some things in our history that we don't memorialize. Perhaps we would just as soon forget what happened. Last summer I visited such a place—the massacre site at Wounded Knee.

In case you have forgotten what happened at Wounded Knee, let me refresh your memory. On December 29, 1890, shortly after Sitting Bull had been murdered by the authorities, about 400 half-frozen, starving, and frightened Indians who had fled the nearby reservation were attacked by the Seventh Cavalry. When the fighting ended, between 200 and 300 Sioux had died—two-thirds of them women and children. Their remains are buried in a common grave at the site of the massacre.

Wounded Knee is located in the Pine Ridge Reservation in southwestern South Dakota—about a three-hour drive from where Presidents Washington, Jefferson, Theodore Roosevelt, and Lincoln are enshrined in the granite face of Mount Rushmore. The reservation is directly south of the Badlands National Park, a magnificently desolate area of wind-eroded buttes and multicolored spires.

We entered the reservation driving south from the Badlands Visitor's Center. The landscape of the Pine Ridge Reservation retains much of the desolation of the Badlands but lacks its magnificence. Flat, sun-baked fields and an occasional eroded gully stretch as far as the eye can see. There are no signs or highway markers to lead the curious tourist to Wounded Knee. Even the *Rand-McNally Atlas* doesn't help you find your way. We got lost three times and had to stop and ask directions.

When we finally arrived at Wounded Knee, there was no official historic marker to tell us what had happened there. Instead there was a large, handmade wooden sign—crudely lettered in white on black. The sign first directed our attention to our left—to the gully where the massacre took place. The mass grave site was to our right—across the road and up a small hill.

Two red-brick columns topped with a wrought-iron arch and a small metal cross form the entrance to the grave site. The column to the right is in bad shape: cinder blocks from the base are missing; the brickwork near the top has deteriorated and tumbled to the ground; graffiti on the columns proclaim an attitude we found repeatedly expressed about the Bureau of Indian Affairs—"The BIA sucks!"

Crumbling concrete steps lead you to the mass grave. The top of the grave is covered with gravel, punctuated by unruly patches of chickweed and crabgrass. These same weeds also grow along the base of the broken chainlink fence that surrounds the grave, the "monument," and a small cemetery.

The "monument" itself rests on a concrete slab to the right of the grave. It's a typical, large, old-fashioned granite cemetery marker, a pillar about six feet high topped with an urn—the kind of gravestone you might see in any cemetery with graves from the turn of the century. The inscription tells us that it was erected by the families of those who were killed at Wounded Knee. Weeds grow through the cracks in the concrete at its base.

There are no granite headstones in the adjacent cemetery, only simple white wooden crosses that tell a story of people who died young. There is no neatly manicured grass. There are no flowers. Only the unrelenting and unforgiving weeds.

Yes, Americans are big on monuments. We build them to memorialize our heroes, to honor our martyrs, and sometimes, even to commemorate victims. But only when it makes us feel good.

We Don't Have to Live in Slums

Anna Aley

Anna Aley was a student as Kansas State University when she presented the following persuasive speech to her public speaking class. Her classmates selected the speech for presentation at a campuswide forum. Anna's speech made such an impression there that the local newspaper printed the text of it and launched an investigation into the community problem Anna revealed. The speech, investigative news stories, and follow-up editorials all created a momentum for change. The mayor responded by establishing a rental inspection program in Manhattan, Kansas. The speech is noteworthy for its vivid language; its effective use of supporting materials, especially narrative; and the deft way in which it focuses listeners on a program of action.

Slumlords—you'd expect them in New York or Chicago, but in Manhattan, Kansas? You'd better believe there are slumlords in Manhattan, and they pose a direct threat to you if you ever plan to rent an off-campus apartment.

I know about slumlords, I rented a basement apartment from one last semester. I guess I first suspected something was wrong when I discovered dead roaches in the refrigerator. I definitely knew something was wrong when I discovered the leaks: the one in the bathroom that kept the bathroom carpet constantly soggy and molding and the one in the kitchen that allowed water from the upstairs neighbor's bathroom to seep into the kitchen cabinets and collect in my dishes.

Then there were the serious problems. The hot water heater and furnace were connected improperly and posed a fire hazard. They were situated next to the only exit. There was no smoke detector or fire extinguisher and no emergency way out—the windows were too small for escape. I was living in an accident waiting to happen—and paying for it.

The worst thing about my ordeal was that I was not an isolated instance; many Kansas State students are living in unsafe housing and paying for it, not only with their money, but their happiness, their grades, their health, and their safety.

We can't be sure how many students are living in substandard housing, housing that does not meet the code specifications required of rental property. We can be sure, however, that a large number of Kansas State students are at risk of being caught in the same situation I was. According to the registrar, approximately 17,800 students are attending Kansas State this semester. Housing claims that 4,200 live in the dorms. This means that approximately 13,600 students live off-campus. Some live in fraternities or sororities, some live at home, but most live in off-campus apartments, as I do.

Many of these 13,600 students share traits that make them likely to settle for substandard housing. For example, many students want to live close to campus. If you've ever driven through the surrounding neighborhoods, you know that much of the available housing is in older houses, houses that were never meant to be divided into separate rental units. Students are also often limited in the amount they can pay for rent; some landlords, such as mine, will use low rent as an excuse not to fix anything and to let the apartment deteriorate. Most importantly, many students are young and, consequently, naive when it comes to selecting an apartment. They don't know the housing codes; but even if they did, they don't know how to check to make sure the apartment is in compliance. Let's face it—how many of us know how to check a hot water heater to make sure it's connected properly?

Adding to the problem of the number of students willing to settle for substandard housing is the number of landlords willing to supply it. Currently, the Consumer Relations Board here at Kansas State has on file student complaints against approximately one hundred landlords. There are surely complaints against many more that have never been formally reported.

There are two main causes of the substandard student housing problem. The first—and most significant—is the simple fact that it is possible for a landlord to lease an apartment that does not meet housing code requirements. The Manhattan Housing Code Inspector will evaluate an apartment, but only after the tenant has given the landlord a written complaint and the landlord has had fourteen days to remedy the situation. In other words, the way things are now, the only way the Housing Code Inspector can evaluate an apartment to see if it's safe to be lived in is if someone has been living in it for at least two weeks!

A second cause of the problem is the fact that campus services designed to help students avoid substandard housing are not well known. The Consumer Relations Board here at Kansas State can help students inspect apartments for safety before they sign a lease, it can provide students with vital information on their rights as tenants, and it can mediate in landlord-tenant disputes. The problem is, many people don't know these services exist. The Consumer Relations Board is not listed in the university catalogue; it is not mentioned in any of the admissions literature. The only places it is mentioned are in alphabetically organized references such as the phone book, but you have to already know it exists to look it up! The Consumer Relations Board does receive money for advertising from the student senate, but it is only enough to run a little two-by-three-inch ad once every month. That is not large enough or frequent enough to be noticed by many who could use these services.

It's clear that we have a problem, but what may not seem so clear is what we can do about it. After all, what can one student do to change the practices of numerous Manhattan landlords? Nothing, if that student is alone. But just think of what we could accomplish if we got all 13,600 off-campus students involved in this issue! Think what we could accomplish if we got even a fraction of those students involved! This is what Wade Whitmer, director of the Consumer Relations Board, is attempting to do. He is reorganizing the Off-Campus Association in an effort to pass a city ordinance requiring landlords to have their apartments inspected for safety before those apartments can be rented out. The Manhattan code inspector has already tried to get just such an ordinance passed, but the only people who showed up at the public forums were known slumlords, who obviously weren't in favor of the proposed ordinance. No one showed up to argue in favor of the ordinance, so the city commissioners figured that no one wanted it and voted it down. If we can get the Off-Campus Association organized and involved, however, the commissioners will see that someone does want the ordinance, and they will be more likely to pass it the next time it is proposed. You can do a great service to your fellow students—and to yourself—by joining the Off-Campus Association.

A second thing you can do to help ensure that no more Kansas State students have to go through what I did is sign my petition asking the student senate to increase the Consumer Relations Board's advertising budget. Let's face it—a service cannot do anybody any good if no one knows about it. The Consumer Relations Board's services are simply too valuable to let go to waste.

An important thing to remember about substandard housing is that it is not only distasteful, it is dangerous. In the end, I was lucky. I got out of my apartment with little more than bad memories. My upstairs neighbor was not so lucky. The main problem with his apartment was that the electrical wiring was done improperly; there were too many outlets for too few circuits, so the fuses were always blowing. On day last November, Jack was at home when a fuse blew—as usual. And, as usual, he went to the fuse box to flip the switch back on. When he touched the switch, it delivered such a shock that it literally threw this guy the size of a football player backwards and down a flight of stairs. He lay there at the bottom, unable to move, for a full hour before his roommate came home and called an ambulance.

Jack was lucky, His back was not broken. But he did rip many of the muscles in his back. Now he has to go to physical therapy, and he is not expected to fully recover.

Kansas State students have been putting up with substandard living conditions for too long. It's time we finally got together to do something about this problem. Join the Off-Campus Association. Sign my petition. Let's send a message to these slumlords that we're not going to put up with this any more. We don't have to live in slums.

WORKS CONSULTED

Kansas State University. *K-State! Campus Living.*

Registrar's Office. Kansas State University. Personal interview. 10 Mar. 1989.

Residential Landlord and Tenant Act, State of Kansas, 1975.

Whitmer, Wade. Director, Consumer Relations Board. Personal interview. 10 Mar. 1989.

Living Wills: Ensuring Your Right to Choose

Bonnie Marshall

Bonnie Marshall was a student at Heidelberg College in Ohio when she made the following persuasive presentation. Her speech is noteworthy for its use of an opening narrative to heighten interest in the problem Bonnie was presenting. The speech is also strong in its use of personal and expert forms of testimony. Clearly, Bonnie had responsible knowledge of her subject. In her conclusion, she makes excellent use of repetition to underscore her message of personal responsibility. She presented the speech with great conviction, and its overall impact led to its selection as a finalist in the Midwest division of the 1991 Houghton Mifflin Public Speaking contest.

Harry Smith was a cranky, obstinate, old farmer. He loved bowling, Glenn Miller music, and Monday night football. He was also dying from cancer of the esophagus, which had metastasized to his lungs. He didn't like doctors, and he liked hospitals and modern medicine even less. Harry used to say that he remembered when three square meals, mom's mustard plaster, and an occasional house call from Doc Jones was all anyone ever needed to stay healthy. Harry didn't want to live in pain, and he hated being dependent on anyone else; yet like so many others, Harry never expressed his wishes to his family. When Harry's cancer became so debilitating that he could no longer speak for himself, his family stepped in to make decisions about his medical care. Since Harry never told them how he felt, his children, out of a sense of guilt over the things they had done and the love they hadn't expressed, refused to let Harry die. He was subjected to ventilators, artificial feedings, and all the wizardry that modern medicine can offer. Harry did die eventually, but only after months of agony with no hope of recovery.

Harry's doctor, my husband, agonized too, over the decisions regarding Harry's care. He knew that the children were acting out of grief and guilt, not for Harry's benefit. Yet because Harry had not documented his wishes, his doctor had no choice but to subject Harry to the senseless torture that he didn't want.

We all know of a similar case that gained national attention. On December 26, 1990, Nancy Cruzan died. The tragic young woman who became the focal point for the right-to-die movement was finally allowed to die after eight long years and a legal battle that reached the hallowed halls of the Supreme Court. Nancy's battle is now over, yet the issue has not been resolved and the need for action is more urgent than ever. Since the Supreme Court ruling on June 25, 1990, public interest in this issue has skyrocketed. From July 1990 to November 1990, the last month statistics were available, the Society for the Right To Die answered 908,000 requests for information. By comparison, in November of 1989, the first month that the Society kept monthly statistics, they answered only 21,000 requests.

Today I would like to explore this problem and propose some solutions that we all can implement.

The *Cruzan* v. *Missouri* decision was significant because it was the first time that the Supreme Court had rendered an opinion on the right-to-die issue. However, the message from the Court is anything but clear and complete. As Justice Sandra Day O'Connor wrote in her concurring opinion, "Today we decide only that one state's practice does not violate the Constitution. . . . The more challenging task of crafting appropriate procedures for safeguarding incompetents' liberty interests is entrusted to the 'laboratory' of the states." So while the Court has for the first time recognized a "constitutionally protected liberty interest in refusing unwanted medical treatment," it has also given the power over this issue back to the states. According to the July 9, 1990, issue of *U.S. News and World Report,* nine states, including Ohio, have no legislation recognizing the legality of living wills. Of the states that do have living will legislation, about one-half do not allow for the withdrawal of nutrition and hydration, even if the will says the patient does not want such treatment, according to Lisa Belken in the June 25th issue of the *New York Times.* Also according to the *Times,* only 33 states have health care proxy laws. Perhaps as a result of all this indecision and inconsistency, desperate patients with terminal illnesses will continue to seek out the "Dr. Deaths" of the medical community, those who, like Dr. Kevorkian of Michigan, are willing to surpass simply allowing the terminally ill to die, to actively bringing about death.

The right-to-die issue may seem far removed from you today, yet the American Medical Association estimates that 80 to 90% of us will die a "managed death." Even today, according to an editorial by Anthony Lewis in the June 29, 1990, *New York Times,* "The problem is far more acute and far-reaching than most of us realize. Almost two million people die in the United States every year, and more than half of those deaths occur when some life-sustaining treatment is ended." The decision to provide, refuse, or withdraw medical treatment should be made individually, personally, with the counsel of family, friends, doctors, and clergy, but certainly not by the state.

More and more, however, these personal decisions are being taken away from patients and their families and instead are being argued and decided in courts of law. Perhaps it began with Karen Ann Quinlan. It certainly continued with Nancy Cruzan, and these decisions could be taken away from you, if we do not act now to ensure that our right to refuse medical treatment is protected. And our right to refuse medical treatment includes the right to refuse artificial nutrition and hydration, just as it includes the right to refuse antibiotics, chemotherapy, surgery, or artificial respiration. According to John Collins Harvey, M.D., Ph.D from the Kennedy Institute of Ethics at Georgetown University, "The administration of food and fluid artificially is a medical technological treatment. . . . Utilizing such medical treatment requires the same kind of medical technological expertise of physicians, nurses, and dietitians as is required in utilizing a respirator for treatment of respiratory failure or employing a renal dialysis machine for the treatment of kidney failure. This medical treatment, however, is ineffective, for it cannot cause dead brain cells to regenerate; it will merely sustain biological life and prolong the patient's dying. Such treatment is considered by many physicians and medical ethicists to be extraordinary." Additionally, the Center for Health Care Ethics of St. Louis University, a Jesuit institution, prepared a brief for the Cruzan case which states that "within the Christian foundation, the withholding and withdrawing of medical treatment, including artificial nutrition and hydration, is acceptable."

So what can we do to protect ourselves and assure that our wishes are carried out? My plan is fourfold. First, we in Ohio must urge our legislators to pass living will legislation. Representative Marc Guthrie, from Newark, Ohio, has drafted a living will bill, House Bill 70. We must urge our legislators to pass this bill, since it is more comprehensive than the Senate version and will better protect our rights on this crucial issue.

Second, we must draw up our own living wills stating our philosophy on terminal care. I propose the use of the Medical Directive, a document created by Drs. Linda and Ezekiel Emanuel. This document details twelve specific treatments that could be offered. You can choose different treatment options based on four possible scenarios. You can indicate either that you desire the treatment, do not want it, are undecided, or want to try the treatment, but discontinue it if there is no improvement. This directive, which also includes space for a personal statement, eliminates much of the ambiguity of generic living wills and provides clearer guidelines to your physician and family.

Third, designate a person to make health care decisions for you should you become incompetent. This person should be familiar with your personal philosophy and feelings about terminal care and be likely to make the same decisions that you yourself would make. You should name this person in a Durable Power of Attorney for Health Care, a legal document that is now recognized in the State of Ohio.

Fourth, have a heart-to-heart talk with your doctor and be sure that he or she understands and supports your wishes on terminal care. Have a copy of your living will and Durable Power of Attorney for Health Care placed in your medical file. Finally, for more information on living wills, you can contact: The Society for the Right To Die, 250 West 57th St., New York, NY 10107, or send $1.00 to the Harvard Medical School Health Letter, 164 Longwood Ave., Fourth Floor, Boston, MA 02115 for a copy of the Emanuels' Medical Directive form.

I am interested in this issue because, through my husband, I have seen patients suffer the effects of not having an advance directive. You need to ask yourself how you feel about terminal care, but regardless of your personal response, we all must choose to protect our rights on this issue. WE must choose to pressure our legislators to adopt living will legislation. WE must choose to draw up our own living wills and health care proxies. And most importantly, WE must choose to discuss this most personal and sensitive issue with our families and loved ones, so that in the absence of a legal document, or even with one, they may confidently make the decisions concerning our life and death that we ourselves would make. Not all patients end up like Nancy Cruzan or Harry Smith. Many people are allowed to quietly slip away from the pain and suffering of life. But that can only happen after the careful, painful deliberation of a grieving family, who can at least take comfort in the fact that they are carrying out their loved one's wishes.

The Secrets of Gun Violence in America

Richard F. Corlin

Dr. Richard Corlin, president of the American Medical Association, presented this persuasive speech in 2001 at the AMA's annual meeting. The speech is noteworthy for its use of "all the available means of persuasion," as Aristotle once defined the function of rhetoric. Corlin uses a wide range of supporting materials—especially facts and statistics, examples, and expert testimony—to create a base of responsible knowledge for his claims. To activate the basic forms of proof—pathos, ethos, and mythos—he appeals to his listeners' feelings, to their respect for his position and experience, and to their faith in physicians and the institutional mission of the AMA. These forms feed into his central reliance on reasoning—the logos—as he builds his case. The speech illustrates how argumentative persuasion, while essentially rational and ethical, can also be quite passionate and committed. Note how Corlin makes repeated use of comparison and contrast to make his claims dramatic and vivid.

Thank you for joining me tonight. It's my great pleasure to introduce to you the friends, colleagues, and family members without whom, I would not have made it here tonight. And without whose presence, this wouldn't be a special evening for me.

I grew up in East Orange, New Jersey, in the 1940s and 1950s. My high school was a mosaic of racial and ethnic diversity—equal numbers of blacks and whites, some Puerto Ricans, and a few Asians. We'd fight among ourselves from time to time—sometimes between kids of the same race, sometimes equal opportunity battles between kids of different races and nationalities. Our fights were basically all the same: some yelling and shouting, then some shoving, a couple of punches, and then some amateur wrestling. They weren't gang fights—everyone but the two combatants just stood around and watched—until one of our teachers came over and broke it up.

My old high school reminds me a little of *West Side Story* only without the switchblades or a Leonard Bernstein score. And there were no Sharks or Jets. Remember, those were the days of James Dean and Elvis Presley. Nobody pulled out a gun—none of us had them and no one even thought of having one. The worst wound anyone had after one of those fights was a split lip or a black eye.

It was just like kids have always been—until today. Back then, no parents in that town of mostly lower-middle class blue collar workers had to worry that their children might get shot at school, in the park or on the front stoop at home. But then again, that was also a time when we thought of a Columbine as a desert flower, not a high school in Littleton, Colorado.

Even in my first encounter with medicine, when I was only fourteen years old and got a summer job at Presbyterian Hospital in Newark, New Jersey, there were no guns. I worked on what was called the utility team—moving patients back to their own rooms after surgery, starting IVs, taking EKGs, and passing N-G tubes. I told them I wanted to be a doctor and—unbelievably at the age of fourteen—they let me help the pathologist perform autopsies. I was so excited about helping with the autopsies that I used to repeat the details to my Mom and Dad over dinner. Before long, they made me eat by myself in the kitchen.

When I was old enough to get a driver's license, I got a job working as an emergency room aide and ambulance driver at Elizabeth General Hospital. In all that time, in five summers of working in two center city hospitals—in the recovery room, in the morgue, in the emergency room, and driving the ambulance—I never saw even one gunshot victim.

Today, it's very different. Guns are so available and violence so commonplace that some doctors now see gunshot wounds every week—if not every day. It's as if guns have replaced fists as the playground weapon of choice. The kids certainly think so. In a nationwide poll taken in March after two students were shot to death at Santana High School near San Diego, almost half of the 500 high school students surveyed said it wouldn't be difficult for them to get a gun. And one in five high school boys said they had carried a weapon to school in the last twelve months. One in five. Frightening, isn't it?

I began by telling you how I grew up in a world without guns. That has changed for me—as it has for so many Americans. Recently, the violence of guns touched me personally. Not long ago, Trish, one of our office staff members in my practice—a vibrant, hard-working young woman from Belize—was gunned down while leaving a holiday party at her aunt's home in Los Angeles.

Trish had done nothing wrong—some might say that she was in the wrong place at the wrong time—but I don't buy into that. Here was a woman who was where she should be—leaving a relative's home—when she was gunned down. Someone drove down the street randomly firing an assault weapon out the car window, and he put a bullet through her eye. Trish lingered in a coma for eight days—and then she died, an innocent victim of gun violence.

With the preponderance of weapons these days, it comes as no surprise that gun violence—both self-inflicted and against others—is now a serious public health crisis. No one can avoid its brutal and ugly presence. No one. Not physicians. Not the public. And most certainly—not the politicians—no matter how much they might want to.

Let me tell you about part of the problem. In the 1990s, the CDC had a system in place for collecting data about the results of gun violence. But Congress took away its funding, thanks to heavy lobbying by the anti-gun control groups. You see, the gun lobby doesn't want gun violence addressed as a public health issue. Because that data would define the very public health crisis that these powerful interests don't want acknowledged. And they fear that such evidence-based data could be used to gain support to stop the violence. Which, of course, means talking about guns and the deaths and injuries associated with them.

We all know that violence of every kind is a pervasive threat to our society. And the greatest risk factor associated with that violence—is access to firearms. Because—there's no doubt about it—guns make the violence more violent and deadlier.

Now my speech today is not a polemic. It is not an attack on the politics or the profits or the personalities associated with guns in our society. It isn't even about gun control. I want to talk to you about the public health crisis itself—and how we can work to address it, in the same way we have worked to address other public health crises such as polio, tobacco, and drunk driving.

At the AMA, we acknowledged the epidemic of gun violence when—in 1987—our House of Delegates first set policy on firearms. The House recognized the irrefutable truth that "uncontrolled ownership and use of fire-arms, especially handguns, is a serious threat to the public's health inasmuch as the weapons are one of the main causes of intentional and unintentional injuries and death." In 1993 and 1994, we resolved that the AMA would, among other actions, "support scientific research and objective discussion aimed at identifying causes of and solutions to the crime and violence problem."

Scientific research and objective discussion because we as physicians are—first and foremost—scientists. We need to look at the science of the subject, the data, and—if you will—the micro-data, before we make a diagnosis. Not until then can we agree upon the prognosis or decide upon a course of treatment.

First, let's go straight to the science that we do know. How does this disease present itself? Since 1962, more than a million Americans have died in firearm suicides, homicides, and unintentional injuries. In 1998 alone, 30,708 Americans died by gunfire:

- 17,424 in firearm suicides
- 12,102 in firearm homicides
- 866 in unintentional shootings

Also in 1998, more than 64,000 people were treated in emergency rooms for nonfatal firearm injuries.

This is a uniquely American epidemic. In the same year that more than 30,000 people were killed by guns in America, the number in Germany was 1,164, in Canada, it was 1,034, in Australia 391, in England and Wales 211, and in Japan, the number for the entire year was 83.

Next, let's look at how the disease spreads, what is its vector, or delivery system. To do that, we need to look at the gun market today. Where the hard, cold reality is—guns are more deadly than ever. Gun manufacturers—in the pursuit of technological innovation and profit—have steadily increased the lethality of firearms. The gun industry's need for new products and new models to stimulate markets that are already oversupplied with guns—has driven their push to innovate. Newer firearms mean more profits. With the American gun manufacturers producing more than 4.2 million new guns per year—and imports adding another 2.2 million annually—you'd think the market would be saturated.

But that's why they have to sell gun owners new guns for their collections—because guns rarely wear out. Hardly anyone here is driving their grandfather's 1952 Plymouth. But a lot of people probably have their grandfather's 1952 revolver. So gun manufacturers make guns that hold more rounds of ammunition, increase the power of that ammunition, and make guns smaller and easier to conceal.

These changes make guns better suited for crime, because they are easy to carry and more likely to kill or maim whether they are used intentionally or unintentionally. In fact, one of the most popular handgun types today is the so-called "pocket rocket:" a palm-sized gun that is easy to conceal, has a large capacity for ammunition and comes in a high caliber.

The *Chicago Tribune* reported that the number of pocket rockets found at crime scenes nationwide almost tripled from 1995 to 1997. It was a pocket rocket in the hands of a self-proclaimed white supremacist that shot five children at the North Valley Jewish Community Center and killed a Filipino-American postal worker outside of Los Angeles in August of 1999.

Now, we don't regulate guns in America. We do regulate other dangerous products like cars and prescription drugs and tobacco and alcohol—but not guns. Gun sales information is not public. Gun manufacturers are exempt by federal law from the standard health and safety regulations that are applied to all other consumer products manufactured and sold in the United States.

No federal agency is allowed to exercise oversight over the gun industry to ensure consumer safety. In fact, no other consumer industry in the United States—not even the tobacco industry—has been allowed to so totally evade accountability for the harm their products cause to human beings. Just the gun industry.

In a similar pattern to the marketing of tobacco—which kills its best customers in the United States at a rate of 430,000 per year—the spread of gun-related injuries and death is especially tragic when it involves our children. Like young lungs and tar and nicotine—young minds are especially responsive to the deadliness of gun violence.

Lieutenant Colonel Dave Grossman, a West Point professor of psychology and military science, has documented how video games act as killing simulators, teaching our children not just to shoot—but to kill. Grossman, who calls himself an expert in "killology," cites as evidence the marksmanship of the two children, aged 11 and 13, in the Jonesboro, Arkansas shootings in 1998. Both shooters were avid video game players. And just like in a video game—they fired off twenty-seven shots—and hit 15 people. Killing four of their fellow students—and a teacher. Such deadly accuracy is rare and hard to achieve—even by well-trained police and military marksmen.

I want you to imagine with me a computer game called "Puppy Shoot." In this game puppies run across the screen. Using a joystick, the game player aims a gun that shoots the puppies. The player is awarded one point for a flesh wound, three points for a body shot, and ten points for a head shot. Blood spurts out each time a puppy is hit—and brain tissue splatters all over whenever there's a head shot. The dead puppies pile up at the bottom of the screen. When the shooter gets to 1,000 points, he gets to exchange his pistol for an Uzi, and the point values go up.

If a game as disgusting as that were to be developed, every animal rights group in the country, along with a lot of other organizations, would protest, and there would be all sorts of attempts made to get the game taken off the market. Yet, if you just change puppies to people in the game I described, there are dozens of them already on the market—sold under such names as "Blood Bath," "Psycho Toxic," "Redneck Rampage," and "Soldier of Fortune." These games are not only doing a very good business—they are also supported by their own Web sites. Web sites that offer strategy tips, showing players how to get to hidden features, like unlimited ammunition, access more weapons, and something called "first shot kill," which enables you to kill your opponent with a single shot.

We do not let the children who play these games drive because they are too young. We do not let them drink because they are too young. We do not let them smoke because they are too young. But we do let them be trained to be shooters at an age when they have not yet developed their impulse control and have none of the maturity and discipline to safely use the weapons they are playing with. Perhaps worst of all, they do this in an environment in which violence has no consequences. These kids shoot people for an hour, turn off the computer—then go down for dinner and do their homework.

We need to teach our children from the beginning that violence does have consequences—serious consequences—all the time. Gunfire kills ten children a day in America. In fact, the United States leads the world in the rate at which its children die from firearms. The CDC recently analyzed firearm-related deaths in twenty-six countries for children under the age of fifteen—and found that 86 percent of all those deaths—occurred in the United States.

If this was a virus—or a defective car seat or an undercooked hamburger—killing our children, there would be a massive uproar within a week. Instead, our capacity to feel a sense of national shame has been diminished by the pervasiveness and numbing effect of all this violence.

We all are well aware of the extent of this threat to the nation's health. So why doesn't someone do something about it? Fortunately, people are. People we know, people we don't know, and people we have only heard about are working hard to abolish the menace of gun violence—of all forms of violence—from the American scene. Some of them are with us tonight.

One of them is Elizabeth Kagan, the newly inaugurated president of our AMA Alliance. Elizabeth will head the Alliance campaign for Safe Gun Storage.

Another is Dr. William Schwab, chief of trauma surgery at the University of Pennsylvania in Philadelphia. He is truly one of the heroes in this battle. His work has shown us just the kind of information we really need to reduce this violence. We are extremely pleased that he has agreed to be one of our ongoing advisors in this activity.

These are the people who stand and deliver when it comes to educating the nation about the threat of gun violence. Elizabeth and Bill, will you please stand? They certainly deserve a hand.

Elizabeth and Bill will be with us through the evening, and I urge as many of you as possible to spend a few minutes with them. They came here because they understand that gun violence in the United States is a problem that is bigger than every one of us. And the blood in America's streets—and classrooms—is a problem for all of us.

I was gratified when—earlier today—Terry Hillard, Superintendent of the Chicago Police Department, stopped by to join me in talking with reporters. We discussed the importance of data collection and how the physician community can work together with law enforcement to tackle this important issue of gun violence.

The question remains, what are we—the physician community—going to do about it? I can tell you first what we're not going to do. We're not going to advocate changing or abolishing the Second Amendment to the Constitution. We really don't have to, to make our point.

The gun lobby loves to use the Second Amendment as a smokescreen—to hide the reality of the damage that guns do—and to prevent our looking any deeper into the facts and statistics of that damage. We've all heard that tired old statement: Guns don't kill people—people kill people. But how does that explain these facts? A gun kept in the home for self-defense is twenty-two times more likely to be used to kill a family member or a friend than an intruder. The presence of a gun in the home triples the risk of homicide—and increases the risk of suicide fivefold.

And listen to this quote: "... the Second Amendment has been the subject of one of the greatest pieces of fraud, I repeat the word *fraud,* on the American people by special interest groups that I have ever seen in my lifetime. The very language of the Second Amendment refutes any argument that it was intended to guarantee every citizen an unfettered right to any kind of weapon. Surely the Second Amendment does not remotely guarantee every person the constitutional right to have a Saturday night special or a machine gun. There is no support in the Constitution for the argument that federal and state governments are powerless to regulate the purchase of such firearms."

These are the words of a respected conservative jurist, the late Chief Justice of the Supreme Court, Warren Burger.

As I said, our mission is not to abolish all guns from the hands of our fellow citizens. We're not advocating any limitations on hunting or the legitimate use of long guns, or for that matter, any other specific item of gun control. And we won't even be keeping a scorecard of legislative victories against guns in Congress and in the statehouses.

Why not? Because all these well-intentioned efforts have been tried by good people—and they have not met with success. Instead, they have been met with a well-organized, aggressive protest against their efforts by powerful lobbies in Washington and at the state and community levels. We—the American Medical Association—are going to take a different route—not just calls for advocacy—but for diplomacy and for statesmanship and for research as well. And make no mistake about this: We will not be co-opted by either the rhetoric or the agendas of the public policy "left" or "right" in this national debate about the safety and health of our citizens.

One of the ways we will do this is—to help assemble the data. Current, consistent, credible data are at the heart of epidemiology. What we don't know about violence—and guns—is literally killing us. And yet, very little is spent on researching gun-related injuries and deaths.

A recent study shows that for every year of life lost to heart disease, we spend $441 on research. For every year of life lost to cancer, we spend $794 on research. Yet for every year of life lost to gun violence, we spend only $31 on research—less than the cost of a taxi ride here from the airport.

That's bad public policy. It's bad fiscal policy. And it certainly is bad medical policy. If we are to fight this epidemic of violence, the Centers for Disease Control must have the budget and the authority to gather the data we need. As I mentioned earlier, the CDC's National Center for Injury Prevention and Control researched the causes and prevention of many kinds of injuries. But in the mid-90s the gun lobby targeted the NCIPC—and scored a bull's eye when Congress eliminated its funding. It wasn't a lot of money—just $2.6 million—budget dust to the federal government. But it meant the difference between existence and extinction for that project.

Just think—gun injuries cost our nation $2.3 billion dollars in medical costs each year—yet some people think $2.6 million dollars is too much to spend on tracking them. Every dollar spent on this research has the potential to reduce medical costs by $885.

The CDC is intent on doing its job and is now heading up the planning for a National Violent Death Reporting System—coordinated and funded at the federal level—and collecting data at the state level. Because knowing more about the who, what, when, where, why and how of violent homicides, suicides, and deaths—will help public health officials, law enforcement, and policy makers prevent unnecessary deaths.

We must further insist that such a system be expanded to cover data about nonfatal gunshot injuries so that we can prevent these as well. Such a system of data collection and analysis has already helped us address another national epidemic—motor vehicle fatalities. Prompting preventive measures like mandatory seat belt laws, air bags, improved highway signage, and better designed entry and exit ramps—not the confiscation of cars. The establishment of a National Violent Death and Injury Reporting System would help us establish similar preventive measures against violence. And help us fill in all the blanks about violent death and injury in America. Including such basics as:

- How do kids with guns get their weapons?
- Do trigger locks work?
- What can we do to reduce accidental, self-inflicted gun injuries?
- What are the warning signs of workplace or school shootings?
- During which hours of the week and in what specific parts of town (down to individual blocks—not just neighborhoods) do the shootings occur?
- Do we need to work with Police Departments to change patrolling patterns based on these data?
- And finally, the realization that the answers to these questions are apt to be different from one town to the next.

Today, we can't answer these questions—because we are not allowed to collect the data. Collecting and considering the facts isn't a matter of opinion or politics, it's essential. It's a matter of working with other committed leaders to get the job done.

The good news is that we have HELP—the Handgun Epidemic Lowering Plan—with membership of 130 organizations including the AMA, and, among others, the Rehabilitation Institute of Chicago, and the Minnesota Department of Health. We also have the Surgeon General's National Strategy for Suicide Prevention, released last month, which also supports the National Violent Death Reporting System.

We will not advocate any changes at all based on urban legend, anecdote or hunch. We will only base our conclusions on evidence-based data and facts. It's just good, common sense—the kind of solid epidemiology that has been brought to bear on other public health hazards—from Legionnaire's Disease to food-borne illnesses to exposure to dioxin or DDT. Trustworthy science that can help us prevent harm before it happens. For, as we physicians know, prevention is usually the best cure.

One of the giants of American medicine, Dr. William Osler, proposed using preventive medicine against serious public health threats like malaria and yellow fever. And the tools he advocated—education, organization and cooperation—sound like a pretty good definition of diplomacy to me. We will put these same tools to use in removing the threat of gun violence from our society.

As we have in the past, we have already sought the cooperation of the American Bar Association—and we are grateful that our invitation has been accepted. We will be working with the ABA on their Forum on Justice Improvements, taking place this October in Washington, D.C. The forum, set up by their Justice Initiatives Group, will focus on gun violence.

We are being advised by a panel of physicians and other experts, who have worked long and hard in tackling the many-headed monster of gun violence and its grisly outcomes. They have welcomed our involvement in this issue and look forward to a newly configured playing field with allies that command such clout as the ABA and the AMA.

People have told me that this is a dangerous path to follow. That I am crazy to do it. That I am putting our organization in jeopardy. They say we'll lose members. They say we'll be the target of smear campaigns. They say that the most extremist of the gun supporters will seek to destroy us. But I believe that this is a battle we cannot not take on.

While there are indeed risks—the far greater risk for the health of the public, for us in this room, and for the AMA, is to do nothing. We, as physicians, and as the American Medical Association, have an ethical and moral responsibility to do this—as our mission statement says—"to promote the science and art of medicine and the betterment of public health." If removing the scourge of gun violence isn't bettering the public health—what is?

As physicians, we are accustomed to doing what is right for our patients—and not worrying about our comfort, case or popularity. Our goal is to help cure an epidemic, not to win a victory over some real or imagined political enemy. Anyone who helps us in this fight is an ally—anyone.

We don't pretend to have all the answers. Nor do we expect the solution to be quick—and we certainly don't expect it to be easy. In fact, I am certain that we will not reach the solution during my term as your president. But, together as the American Medical Association—guided by our stated mission—we recognize our obligation to contribute our voice, our effort and our moral imperative to this battle. And we will.

Almost a century ago, in his book *Confessio Medici*, Stephen Paget, the British physician and author, referred to medicine as a divine vocation. This is part of what he said:

"Every year young people enter the medical profession . . . and they stick to it . . . not only from necessity, but from pride, honor, and conviction. And Heaven, sooner or later, lets them know what it thinks of them. This information comes quite as a surprise to them . . . that they were indeed called to be doctors . . . Surely a diploma . . . obtained by hard work . . . cannot be a summons from Heaven. But it may be. For, if a doctor's life may not be a divine vocation, then no life is a vocation, and nothing is divine."

We are here today as the guardians of that divine vocation and as such are dedicated to do what is right, whether or not it is comfortable, whether or not it is easy, and whether or not it is popular. Stephen Paget, you can rest well tonight. Your divine vocation is in good hands. We will guard it well. We will live up to our mission—we will do what is right.

Thank you.

From "The Secrets of Gun Violence in America" by Richard F. Corlin, *Vital Speeches of the Day*, 1 Aug. 2001, pp. 610–615.

Martin Luther King Jr.'s Legacy for Us

Tommie Albright

Tommie Albright, Miss Florida Teen 2000, presented this inspirational speech of tribute at a Dr. Martin Luther King Jr. Memorial Evening in Daytona Beach, Florida, on January 13, 2000. The evening was sponsored by Daytona Beach Community College, where Ms. Albright was a student. The speech is noteworthy for its eloquence, especially for the way it uses antithesis and parallel construction to achieve the dramatic effects of contrast and repetition. These stylistic techniques and effects are interwoven late in the speech as Albright interprets King's dreams in his own time as calls for action in ours. The speech also reveals an unusual ability to expand ideas to illuminate their larger significance for listeners. We see this trait as Albright develops the theme that "every generation stands on the shoulders of the generation that came before." To prepare her adult listeners for such lofty thoughts coming from such a young person, she acknowledges her youth and limitations at the beginning of the speech with disarming and becoming modesty.

Thank you, Professor Fuqua, for that very kind introduction. I hope you recognize that, as my English Professor and also as the one who invited me to speak here this evening, you must take at least partial responsibility for any faux pas I make.

In all seriousness, though, Professor Fuqua is one of those dream teachers, who inspires and nurtures as she teaches and instructs.

And—along with many other students—I have been really blessed by her brilliant intellect and warm and forgiving nature.

And, I hope she will forgive me for feeling a bit daunted, speaking at this memorable event tonight.

It's daunting because:

Not only am I a teenager speaking before a very intellectual and gifted audience of adults. . . .

But because my words will most likely appear somewhat mundane following those of a sophisticated English professor and coming before those of a practiced preacher.

I suppose I now feel a little like I might feel if our high school football coach came over to our cheerleading squad and sent me into the football game in the middle of all those 200 pound guys.

But, I will do my best.

I have been asked to speak to you this evening with a perspective on Dr. Martin Luther King Jr.'s life, focusing on the present.

And, in doing so, I feel quite fortunate, because I can build on the brilliant review shared with us by Doctor Offiah, who so richly described the work of Dr. King and the impact of the important events of his life on his times.

But, because I am neither a scholar nor a preacher, I can only share with you what I believe is Dr. Martin Luther King's influence on my life and on my times, neither of which are very long in the grand scheme of things.

So, once again, I hope you will bear with me.

Ladies and gentlemen, we young people growing up in America today often look to the celebrated acts and worthy thoughts of others around us upon which to form our own acts and our own thoughts.

Close at hand, I am fortunate to have the thoughts and guidance of a very loving and supportive mother and father and wonderful teachers and professors such as Professor Fuqua here at DBCC.

But when as a young teenager—looking for inspiration and example—beyond my family circle and my classrooms—the life of Martin Luther King Jr. came more naturally to mind than you might imagine.

Outwardly, there is nothing much that links my life directly to Dr. King.

He was a man; I am a woman.

He was black; I am white.

He was a man of the 50s and 60s, which was a generation of turbulent change, and I am a woman of a generation that is yet to be tested.

He was—and still is—one of the most important leaders of the past millennium and I am still a high school and college student, waiting to be tested by life.

But, the fact is that—through his inspired leadership and spellbinding language—Dr. King has become a symbol. . . .

A symbol of calming harmony in a world of angry conflict—for every generation.

A symbol of human understanding in a world of bigoted ignorance—for every generation.

A symbol of tolerance and unity in a world of parochial disharmony—for every generation.

And, therefore, in his teachings and through his leadership principles, Martin Luther King Jr. spoke:

Not just to African Americans, but to all Americans—and especially to me and those of my generation;

And—not just to Americans, but to Europeans, Asians, Africans and all the people of every race and nationality throughout the world.

And not only for harmony and justice in his time, but for harmony and justice in my time and in the time of my children yet to come.

Dr. King's lessons of justice, brotherhood and harmony should have no boundaries of race, nationality or time.

As a white woman in Florida, I am just as much the recipient of his legacy of racial harmony as a black man in Georgia.

Because of Dr. King's Dream, as a white girl attending both an integrated high school and an integrated college, I am blessed by the teaching of brilliant black teachers like Professor Fuqua.

Because of Dr. King's Dream, I now have the friendship of schoolmates I might never have met had it not been for him and the great movement he led for equality and integration.

Because of Dr. King's work, I live in a time of racial harmony, not racial conflict.

So when Dr. Martin Luther King dreamed of the day when "little black boys and black girls will be able to join hands with little white boys and white girls together as sisters and brothers," I believe I was one of the little white girls he dreamed about.

Now no one—least of all me—would say that the total fulfillment of Martin Luther King's Dream of a just society—devoid of bigotry and malice—was realized in his time. . . .

Nor was it realized in your time. . . .

Nor will it be realized in my time.

But, it is our challenge and our responsibility—in our time—to do our very best to follow his teachings and his principles, and to continue the great work he began. . . .

Not only through his nonviolent leadership in the counterculture of the 50s and 60s. . . .

But also through his teachings that every man and woman on this earth has value and deserves respect.

Clearly, Dr. King willed us a legacy to live by—a legacy that is just as vital in our new millennium as it was in his.

In his great ministry of love and brotherhood so brilliantly put forth in his "I Have a Dream" speech Dr. King spoke of his dream of what should be.

It is now the task and responsibility of your generation and my generation to take up his challenge to us of making what should be . . . what is . . . and what will be.

It is now our obligation to make sure that in everything we do, no man's right of life, liberty and the pursuit of happiness is impinged upon.

Dr. King spoke of 1963 as the dawn of the struggle for justice.

It is now our duty to ensure that . . . in our new millennium . . . we continue that struggle for full justice, for all races and nationalities.

Dr. King dreamed of a time when the full meaning of America's creed that all men are created equal would be realized.

It is now up to all of us to make sure that . . . in our time on this earth . . . all men are treated equally.

Dr. King dreamed that one day the sons of former slaves and the sons of former slave owners would be able to sit down at the table of brotherhood.

We have come a long way toward that dream and, today, many of us sit at that table of brotherhood of which Dr. King dreamed. But there are still far too many who do not have a seat at that table. And it is our task to make more room for those who do not yet have a place.

Now, in his ministry and in his famous speech before the Lincoln Memorial, Dr. King was most likely thinking of blacks having a place at the table with whites.

But—in that same spirit—both blacks and whites today must make room for yellows, reds and browns at the table as well.

And there will be many places needed at that table, because, within the next five years, Hispanics will become the largest minority in North America.

Dr. King dreamed of a time when his four little children would not be judged by the color of their skin, but by the content of their character.

So today, it is our obligation to be character conscious and color blind.

And it is just as important that whites and blacks do not judge others by the color of their skin, but by the content of their character as well.

We all should be judged by what we do rather than how we look or how we talk.

And, were he here, I would hope that—in his rich and powerful preacher's voice—Reverend King would say a resounding Amen to that.

Yes—ladies and gentlemen—Martin Luther King had many dreams for us, each with its own challenge to us.

Where he dreamed of peace, we must be peaceful and seek peace.

Where he saw hope, we must provide fulfillment. Where he dreamed of equality, we must treat each other as equals.

Where he dreamed of brotherhood, we must act as brothers and sisters.

And where he dreamed of justice, we must provide a just society.

Let me close my few thoughts with you this evening by saying that Martin Luther King Jr. became famous, not for providing solutions, but for providing challenges and by setting the example.

And, now, each of us must accept his challenge for greater understanding and follow his powerful example.

Each of us, in our time, must fight the good fight for justice and equality.

For it is true that every generation stands on the shoulders of the generation that came before.

Just as Martin Luther King stood on the shoulders of Mahatma Gandhi to see the promised land of brotherhood and non-violent protest. . . .

Your generation must stand on Martin Luther King's shoulders to fulfill the destiny of brotherhood, in your time.

And my generation must stand on your shoulders to fulfill the destiny of brotherhood in our time.

So the higher your generation lifts mine, the higher we can hold the next, and the better off each successive generation thereafter will be.

As a young woman who now walks in your footsteps, all I ask is that you show us the same path of brotherhood and set the same good example that Doctor Martin Luther King Jr. showed and set for you.

I know you have the courage and strength to do so.

And I hope my generation will as well.

Thank you for your time, and good night.

A Tribute to Wilma Rudolph

The following material was presented as part of the National Sports Awards program telecast on NBC, June 23, 1993. The script, transcribed from the telecast of the show and provided by NBC, includes the beginning of the program. Tom Brokaw, NBC Nightly News anchor, was the master of ceremonies. Speeches of tribute were presented by Bill Cosby, entertainer and former college track star; Gail Devers, 1992 Olympic Gold Medal winner in the 100-meter dash; and Ed Temple, Ms. Rudolph's mentor and track coach at Tennessee State University.

Tom Brokaw (Master of Ceremonies): Good evening and welcome. This is such a fitting national celebration because, after all, what would life be without the games that we play? The greatest athletes—the most memorable—are those who give us a sense of exhilaration off the field as well as on. Heywood Hale Broun once said, "Sports don't build character; they reveal it." What you'll share here tonight is the essence of character as revealed by the lives of these great athletes.

Sports are such an important part of our national culture, our language, our fantasies. Well, tonight the National Sports Awards honors those who played their games at the highest level—and lived their lives at the same heights. They lifted us all by their achievements and by their conduct. Four of them are here in Washington with us tonight; one of them, Ted Williams, has been asked by his doctor not to travel, so he's watching from his home. They were all nominated by a panel of leading sports journalists.

The first that we honor tonight is a woman. When she was born, one of twenty-two children in a Tennessee family, no one could have guessed at that time that her story would echo over the decades, or that it would make even a big impression on the 1962 Middle Atlantic Conference High Jump Champion.

Bill Cosby: She was five foot eleven, she was slender, and she had the manner of a duchess, and you know what they called her in Europe? La Gazelle—La Perle Noire—La Chattanooga Choo-Choo. Wouldn't it be nice to be called "La Chattanooga Choo-Choo?"

I had dreams of being a track star, so I have a particularly vivid memory of this woman who broke barriers, broke records, and brought glory to her country at the 1960 Rome Olympics. Very few Olympians have climbed a bigger mountain than the girl from Clarksville, Tennessee—and her story is one of the most powerful and poignant of the modern Olympics. Madame Choo-Choo, I join the nation in saluting you.

When she was four years old, she contracted polio. Watching other children at play was the cruelest hurt of all. She said, "Only my mother gave me the faith to believe I'd ever walk again." She was the twentieth of twenty-two children. The family scrimped to pay for her therapy at the clinic nearly 90 miles away. But in the end it was her own therapy that did it. She threw away the brace, gritted her teeth, and taught herself to walk . . . to run, to throw herself completely into the Burt High School basketball team. Then a visiting coach who saw her play suggested she try something else.

She was naturally blessed with burning speed—and the passion to push it. Long-legged—and glamorous, there had never been a woman runner who looked like *this* and ran like *that.*

The Tennessee Tigerbelles made their international debut at the '56 Olympics. She was sixteen and green, and while the team had won a bronze, she missed her golden moment in the 200. It would be four years before the next Olympics. The girls track team was at the bottom of the budget, so Coach Ed Temple picked up the tab. Going into the Rome Olympics she was among the world's fastest but she remembered her failure in '56 —the narrow margin between gold and bronze.

Coach Temple's home movies—occasionally in focus—show the athletes settling in. Here's Wilma, and her new hat . . . and her new friends. Then it got serious. "From the moment I walked into the stadium," she said, "I blocked out everything. Everything." Her first event was the 100 meters. Eleven seconds flat. She was the fastest woman in the world. Then came the 200—the excruciating demand of speed and stamina. She simply ran away from the rest of the world. Twenty-four flat. An Olympic record. She wasn't done yet. On the last day she ran the anchor leg of the 400-meter relay, and another record fell. It was her third Olympic gold. No American woman had done that in track before.

From out of these Olympic games, Wilma Rudolph entered the company of American heroines. She was honored at every turn. But the greatest reward was in the eyes of her parents. Her hometown set aside old differences. Everyone came out to greet her. That night, for the first time, black and white sat together at the same table. Thirty years ago she gave women a reason to run. She still encourages. She still inspires. It is the simplest, purest athletic endeavor—to run. And oh my—how Wilma could run.

Tom Brokaw: At last summer's Olympic games in Barcelona, we were reminded once again of the power of the human spirit by another American sprinter, gold medal winner Gail Devers.

Gail Devers: I was diagnosed with Graves Disease in 1990, and until I received the proper medication, I had come within two days of having my feet amputated. Long before any of this ever happened, I had heard of a woman named Wilma Rudolph. I read about her in books and I'd watched the Wilma Rudolph stories several times on television and just like Wilma, during my ordeal my first goal was just to walk again. And once I was back on the track running, I thought about her determination.

I knew that she had overcome a very serious illness and still went on to pursue her dream. I felt that if Wilma could do it, I could do it too. Her strong will and her never-give-up attitude had inspired so many of us to keep going despite any obstacles that we may be faced with. And I want to take this opportunity to tell you, Wilma, thank you from the very bottom of my heart. Not just for the example that you've given, not just to me, but to all women in track and field. We love you.

Tom Brokaw: And the man with the movie camera. He has come from Tennessee to present Wilma Rudolph with her award. Her coach and mentor, who retires this fall after forty-two years as coach of the Tennessee State Tigerbelles, Ed Temple, ladies and gentlemen.

Ed Temple: Wilma, you've worked long and hard to achieve these kinds of honors. I've always talked about the adversity that you've had. I tell people that you were able to meet it, to greet it, and defeat it. Wilma, you were an individual who opened up the doors for women's track and field in the United States, and that will always be your greatest legacy. It is an honor for me to be here tonight with you.

Tom Brokaw: And on this occasion the great ones do a great walk, so Wilma Rudolph, will you please come forward so that Gail Devers and Ed Temple can present you the first National Sports Award. Ladies and gentlemen, the object of our attention and affection, Wilma Rudolph.

Wilma Rudolph: I'm excited. I'll get my breath. I receive this honor, and I dedicate it to the youth of America so they will know that their dreams too can come true. And also to my mother who is eighty-four years old, Blanche Rudolph. Thank you so much for this honor.

On June 23, 1993, *The Great Ones: The National Sports Awards* was broadcast on NBC. The program was conceived and produced by George Stevens Jr., Don Mischer, and Michael Stevens, and written by George Stevens Jr. and Brian Brown.

Nobel Peace Prize Acceptance Speech

Elie Wiesel

Elie Wiesel delivered the following speech in Oslo, Norway, on December 10, 1986, as he accepted the Nobel Peace Prize. The award recognized his lifelong work for human rights, especially his role as "spiritual archivist of the Holocaust." Wiesel's poetic, intensely personal style as a writer carries over into this ceremonial speech of acceptance. He uses narrative very effectively as he flashes back to what he calls the "kingdom of night" and then flashes forward again into the present. The speech's purpose is to spell out and share the values and concerns of a life committed to the rights of oppressed peoples, in which, as he put it so memorably, "every moment is a moment of grace, every hour an offering."

It is with a profound sense of humility that I accept the honor you have chosen to bestow upon me. I know: your choice transcends me. This both frightens and pleases me.

It frightens me because I wonder: do I have the right to represent the multitudes who have perished? Do I have the right to accept this great honor on their behalf? I do not. That would be presumptuous. No one may speak for the dead, no one may interpret their mutilated dreams and visions.

It pleases me because I may say that this honor belongs to all the survivors and their children, and through us, to the Jewish people with whose destiny I have always been identified.

I remember: it happened yesterday or eternities ago. A young Jewish boy discovering the kingdom of night. I remember his bewilderment, I remember his anguish. It all happened so fast. The ghetto. The deportation. The sealed cattle car. The fiery altar upon which the history of our people and the future of mankind were meant to be sacrificed.

I remember: he asked his father: "Can this be true? This is the 20th century, not the Middle Ages. Who would allow such crimes to be committed? How could the world remain silent?"

And now the boy is turning to me: "Tell me," he asks. "What have you done with your life?"

And I tell him that I have tried. That I have tried to keep memory alive, that I have tried to fight those who would forget. Because if we forget, we are guilty, we are accomplices.

And then I explained to him how naive we were, that the world did know and remain silent. And that is why I swore never to be silent whenever and wherever human beings endure suffering and humiliation. We must always take sides. Neutrality helps the oppressor, never the victim. Silence encourages the tormentor, never the tormented.

Sometimes we must interfere. When human lives are endangered, when human dignity is in jeopardy, national borders and sensitivities become irrelevant. Wherever men or women are persecuted because of their race, religion or political views, that place must—at that moment—become the center of our universe.

Of course, since I am a Jew profoundly rooted in my people's memory and tradition, my first response is to Jewish fears, Jewish needs, Jewish crises. For I belong to a traumatized generation, one that experienced the abandonment and solitude of our people. It would be unnatural for me not to make Jewish priorities my own: Israel, Soviet Jewry, Jews in Arab lands.

But there are others as important to me. Apartheid is, in my view as abhorrent as anti-Semitism. To me, Andrei Sakharov's isolation is as much a disgrace as Iosif Begun's imprisonment. As is the denial of Solidarity and its leader Lech Walesa's right to dissent. And Nelson Mandela's interminable imprisonment.

There is so much injustice and suffering crying out for our attention: victims of hunger, or racism and political persecution, writers and poets, prisoners in so many lands governed by the left and by the right. Human rights are being violated on every continent. More people are oppressed than free.

And then, too, there are the Palestinians to whose plight I am sensitive but whose methods I deplore. Violence and terrorism are not the answer. Something must be done about their suffering, and soon. I trust Israel, for I have faith in the Jewish people. Let Israel be given a chance, let hatred and danger be removed from her horizons, and there will be peace in and around the Holy Land.

Yes, I have the faith. Faith in God and even in His creation. Without it no action would be possible. And action is the only remedy to indifference: the most insidious danger of all. Isn't this the meaning of Alfred Nobel's legacy? Wasn't his fear of war a shield against war?

There is much to be done, there is much that can be done. One person—a Raoul Wallenberg, an Albert Schweitzer, one person of integrity, can make a difference, a difference of life and death. As long as one dissident is in prison, our freedom will not be true. As long as one child is hungry, our lives will be filled with anguish and shame.

What all these victims need above all is to know that they are not alone: that we are not forgetting them, that when their voices are stifled we shall lend them ours, that while their freedom depends on ours, the quality of our freedom depends on theirs.

This is what I say to the young Jewish boy wondering what I have done with his years. It is in his name that I speak to you and that I express to you my deepest gratitude. No one is as capable of gratitude as one who has emerged from the kingdom of night.

We know that every moment is a moment of grace, every hour an offering; not to share them would mean to betray them. Our lives no longer belong to us alone; they belong to all those who need us desperately.

Thank you Chairman Aarvik. Thank you members of the Nobel Committee. Thank you people of Norway, for declaring on this singular occasion that our survival has meaning for mankind.

Glossary

accuracy Criterion for evaluating the correctness of information by checking it against other information.
acronym A word composed of the initial letters of a series of words.
activity Any movement that the speaker makes that attracts attention.
ad hominem fallacy An attempt to discredit a position by attacking the people who favor it.
advocacy website A website whose major purpose is to change attitudes or behaviors.
after-dinner speech A brief, often humorous, ceremonial speech, presented after a meal, that offers a message without asking for radical changes.
agenda-setting function The work of informative speeches in raising the importance of topics.
agreement The third stage in the persuasive process, which requires that listeners accept a speaker's recommendations and remember their reasons for doing so.
alliteration The repetition of initial consonant sounds in closely connected words.
amplification The art of developing ideas by finding ways to restate them in a speech.
analogical persuasion Creating a strategic perspective on a subject by relating it to something similar about which the audience has strong feelings.
analogous color scheme Colors adjacent on the color wheel; used in a presentation aid to suggest both differences and close relationships among the components.
analogy A connection established between two otherwise dissimilar ideas or things.
anticipatory anxiety The fear of public speaking that occurs before the actual presentation of a speech.
antithesis A language technique that combines opposing elements in the same sentence or adjoining sentences.
anxiety sensitivity The tendency to label weak symptoms of anxiety as fear and then to over-respond to them.
appreciative listening Phase of listening in which we enjoy the beauty of messages, responding to such factors as the simplicity, balance, and the eloquence of language.
argumentative persuasion Persuasion built on evidence and reasoning.
arrangement The placing of ideas in appropriate order.
articulation The manner in which individual speech sounds are produced.
assimilation The tendency of listeners to interpret the positions of a speaker with whom they agree as closer to their own views than they actually are.
attitude system The conglomerate of beliefs, attitudes, and values that affects how we conduct our lives.
attitudes Feelings we have developed toward specific kinds of subjects.
audience demographics Observable characteristics of listeners, including age, gender, educational level, group affiliations, and sociocultural backgrounds.
audience dynamics The motivations, attitudes, beliefs, and values that influence the behavior of listeners.
authority Criterion for evaluating the credentials of the author.
autocratic leader A leader who makes decisions without consultation, issues orders or gives direction, and controls the members of the group through the use of rewards or punishments.
award presentation A speech of tribute that recognizes achievements of the award recipient, explains the nature of the award, and describes why the recipient qualifies for the award.
awareness This first stage in the persuasive process includes knowing about a problem, paying attention to it, and understanding how it affects our lives.

backing Additional justification provided to strengthen the warrant in an argument.
balance Appropriate size allocation of the major parts of a presentation.
bar graph A graph that shows comparisons and contrasts between two or more items or groups.
begging the question Assuming that an argument has been proved without actually presenting the evidence.
beliefs Ideas about subjects that may explain our attitudes toward them.
belonging needs Our need to feel close to others.
body The part of a speech used to develop main ideas.
body language Communication achieved using facial expressions, eye contact, movements, and gestures.
boomerang effect A possible audience's reaction to a speech that advocates too much change.
brainstorming Technique that encourages the free play of the mind.
brief example A specific instance illustrating a general idea.
briefing A short informative presentation.
bulleted list A presentation aid that highlights ideas by presenting them as a list of brief statements.

call the question A motion that proposes to end discussion and bring a vote.
categorical design The use of natural or traditional divisions within a subject as a way of structuring an informative speech.
causation design A pattern for an informative speech that shows how one condition generates, or is generated by, another.

ceremonial speaking (ceremonial speech) Speaking that celebrates special occasions, such as speeches of tribute, inspiration, and introductions, eulogies, toasts, award presentations, acceptances, and after-dinner speeches. Their deeper function is to share identities and reinforce values that unite people into communities.

charisma Impact of speakers based on their perceived likeableness and forcefulness.

chronological design A pattern of speech organization that follows a sequence of important events in an historical pattern.

claim The conclusion the speaker draws based on the data in an argument. Also, conclusions that go beyond factual statements to make judgments about their subjects.

co-active approach A way of approaching reluctant audiences in which the speaker attempts to establish goodwill, emphasizes shared values, and sets modest goals for persuasion.

cognitive restructuring The process of replacing negative thoughts with positive, constructive ones.

collaborative problem solving In group communication, an approach that gathers participants from separate areas of the public or private sectors for their input on a problem.

communication anxiety The fear of public speaking, experienced by most novice speakers.

communication orientation Looking at public speaking as an interactive communication event rather than as a performance.

comparative design A pattern for an informative speech that relates an unfamiliar subject to something the audience already knows or understands.

comparison Using supporting material to point out the similarities of an unfamiliar or controversial issue to something the audience already knows or accepts.

comparison and contrast An informative speech design that points out similarities and differences between subjects or ideas.

competence The perception of a speaker as being informed, intelligent, and well prepared.

complementary color scheme Colors opposite one another on the color wheel; used in a presentation aid to suggest tension and opposition.

comprehensive listening Phase of listening in which we focus on, understand, and interpret spoken messages.

computer-assisted presentation The use of commercial presentation software to join audio, visual, textual, graphic, and animated components.

conclusion The ending of the speech, which summarizes the message and leaves listeners with something to remember. Also, the final statement of the relationship between the major and minor premises of an argument.

confusion of fact and opinion A misuse of evidence in which personal opinions are offered as though they were facts, or facts are dismissed as though they were opinion.

connotative meaning The emotional, subjective, personal meaning that certain words can evoke in listeners.

consequences The mental or behavioral impact of a speech after it has been presented.

constructive listening The involvement of the listener in the creation of meaning. Involves discovering the speaker's intention, tracing out the implications and consequences of the message, and applying the message to one's life.

contrast Using supporting materials to emphasize difference between two things.

contrast effect A tendency by listeners to distort the positions of a speaker with whom they disagree and to interpret those positions as even more distant from their own opinions than they actually are.

coordination The requirement that statements equal in importance be placed on the same level in an outline.

coverage Criterion for evaluating the breadth of information on a topic.

credibility Judgments of speakers based on their perceived competence and integrity.

critical listening Listening with careful analysis and evaluation of message content.

critique An evaluation of a speech.

cultural gridlock A problem that occurs when the cultural differences in a group are so profound that they create tensions that block constructive discussion.

cultural sensitivity The respectful appreciation of diversity within an audience.

culturetypes Terms that express the values and goals of a group's culture.

currency Criterion for evaluating whether or not the information on a website is up-to-date.

data The factual evidence in an argument.

debate The clash of opposing ideas, evaluations, and policy proposals on a subject of concern.

decoding The process by which the listener determines the meaning of the speaker's message.

deductive reasoning Arguing from a general principle to a specific case.

definition A translation of an unfamiliar word into understandable terms.

deliberation Considering the evidence, proofs and arguments before reaching a policy decision.

deliberative Speeches that debate issues of public policy.

delivery The presentation of ideas to an audience.

demagogues Political speakers who try to inflame feelings without regard to the accuracy or adequacy of their claims in order to promote their own agendas.

denotative meaning The dictionary definition or objective meaning of a word.

descriptions Word pictures that help listeners visualize information by evoking vivid, concrete images in their minds.

design The organizational pattern of a speech.

dialect A speech pattern associated with an area of the country or with a cultural or ethnic background.

dialogue Having the characters in a narrative speak for themselves, rather than paraphrasing what they say.

dialogue group A group assembled to explore the underlying assumptions of a problem but not necessarily to solve it.

direct quotation Repeating the exact words of another to support a point.

discovery phase Phase of the process of finding speech topics that identifies large topic areas.

discriminative listening Phase of listening in which we detect sounds of spoken communication.

disinformation Communication that offers what appears to be information, but that actually deceives listeners.

distance Principle of proxemics involving the control of the space.

dynamism The perception of a speaker as confident, decisive, and enthusiastic.

egocentrism Holding the view that one's own experiences and thoughts are the norm.

either-or thinking A fallacy that occurs when a speaker suggests that there are only two options, and only one is desirable.

electronic brainstorming A group technique in which participants generate ideas in computer chat groups or by email.

elevation Principle of proxemics dealing with power relationships implied when speakers stand above listeners.

embedded narrative Stories inserted within speeches that illustrate the speaker's points.

emerging credibility The changes in the audience's assessment of ethos that occur as you present your speech.

empathic listening Phase of listening in which we suspend judgment, allow speakers to be heard, and try to see things from their points of view.

empirical A form of thinking that emphasizes the close inspection of reality.

enactment The fourth stage of the persuasive process in which listeners take appropriate action as the result of agreement.

encoding The process by which the speaker combines words, tones, and gestures to convey thought and feelings to the audience.

enduring metaphors Metaphors of unusual power and popularity that are based on experience that lasts across time and that crosses many cultural boundaries.

enthymeme A syllogism based on uncertain principles or instances, in which the conclusions are probable rather than absolute.

enunciation The manner in which individual words are articulated and pronounced in context.

epideictic The classical term for ceremonial speaking.

epilogue The final part of a narrative that reflects upon its meaning.

esteem needs Our need for self-respect and respect from others.

ethics The moral dimension of human conduct, governing how we treat others.

ethnocentrism The tendency of any nation, race, religion, or group to believe that its way of looking at and doing things is right and that other perspectives have less value.

ethos Those characteristics that make a speaker appear honest, credible, and appealing; a kind of proof created by a speaker's own favorable impression and by association with credible testimony.

eulogy A speech of tribute presented upon a person's death.

evidence Supporting materials used in persuasive speeches, including facts and figures, examples, narratives, and testimony.

examples Verbal illustrations of the speaker's points.

expanded conversational style A presentational quality that, while more formal than everyday conversation, preserves its directness and spontaneity.

expert testimony Information derived from authorities within a field.

explanations A combination of information examples to clarify an idea.

exploration phase Phase of the process of finding speech topics that involves the close examination of large topic areas to identify more precise topics that might be developed.

extemporaneous presentation A form of presentation in which a speech, although carefully prepared and practiced, is not written out or memorized.

extended example A detailed illustration that allows a speaker to build impressions.

facts Information that can be verified by observation or expert testimony.

factual example An illustration based on something that actually happened or that really exists.

fallacies Errors in reasoning that make persuasion unreliable.

faulty analogy A comparison drawn between things that are dissimilar in some important way.

feedback The audience's immediate response to a speaker.

figurative analogy A comparison made between things that belong to different fields.

figurative language The use of words in certain surprising and unusual ways in order to magnify the power of their meaning.

filtering Listening to only part of a message, the part the listener wants to hear.

flawed statistical comparisons Statistical reasoning that offers fallacious conclusions by comparing unequal or unlike situations.

flow chart A visual method of representing power and responsibility relationships, or describing the steps in a process.

focus group A small group formed to reveal the feelings or motivations of customers or clients.

forensic Speeches that argue guilt and innocence in legal settings.

foreshadowing Hints to the meaning of the story that will follow.

formal outline The final outline in a process leading from the first rough ideas for a speech to the finished product.

forum Presentational format in which a group of specialists in different areas of a subject, respond to questions from an audience.

free-rein leader A leader who leaves members free to decide what, how, and when to act, offering no guidance.

gender stereotyping Generalizations based on oversimplified or outmoded assumptions about gender roles.

general purpose (general function) The speaker's overall intention to inform or persuade listeners, or to celebrate some person or occasion.

general search engine An Internet search engine that allows you to enter a keyword and find related websites.

global code of ethical conduct Values that are widely shared across many cultures.

good form A primary principle of structure, based on simplicity, symmetry, and orderliness.

goodwill The dimension of ethos by which listeners perceive a speaker as having their best interests at heart.

graphics Visual representations of information.

great expectation fallacy The mistaken idea that major change can be accomplished by a single persuasive effort.

group Gathering of people who interact with one another to reach goals.

groupthink Occurs when a single, uncritical frame of mind dominates group thinking and prevents the full, objective analysis of specific problems.

habitual pitch The level at which people speak most frequently.

hasty generalization An error of inductive reasoning in which a claim is made based on insufficient or nonrepresentative information.

hearing The physical reception of sounds.
hypothetical example A representation of reality, usually a synthesis of actual people, situations, or events.

identification The feeling of closeness between speakers and listeners that may overcome personal and cultural differences.
identification model The Burkean model of communication, which illustrates how the meaningful interaction between speaker and listeners leads to the development of common ground.
ideographs Words that convey in a compressed way a group's basic political faith.
immediacy A quality of successful communication achieved when the speaker and audience experience a sense of closeness.
imperialism An aggressive form of ethnocentrism that not only assumes the superiority of one's own way of life but also tries to impose it on others.
impromptu speaking A talk delivered with minimal or no preparation.
inductive reasoning Reasoning from specific cases to reach a general conclusion.
inferences Assumptions based on incomplete information.
information cards Research notes on facts and ideas obtained from an article or book.
information website A website designed to provide factual information on a subject.
informative speech Speech aimed at extending understanding.
informative value A measure of how much new and important information or understanding a speech conveys to an audience.
initial credibility The audience's assessment of your ethos before you begin your speech.
inoculation effect Preparing an audience for an opposing argument by answering it before listeners have been exposed to it.
integrated communication An ideal, harmonious convergence of voice, body language, and speech content to produce a self-reinforcing interplay of meanings.
integration Final stage of the persuasive process in which listeners connect new attitudes and commitments with previous beliefs and values to ensure lasting change.
integrity The quality of being ethical, honest, and dependable.
intensity Attention factor concerning how much an object contrasts with its background.
interference Physical noise or psychological distraction that impedes the hearing of a speech.
interest chart Visual display of a speaker's interests, as prompted by certain probe questions.
internal summary A transition that reminds listeners of major points already presented in a speech before proceeding to new ideas.
intertextual signifier Verbal and nonverbal references within a speech that connect with the meanings of previous speeches heard by a group.
introduction The first part of a speech, intended to gain the audience's attention and to prepare them for the rest of the presentation.
invention The discovery and selection of ideas, themes, and lines of argument for a speech.
inversion Changing the normal order of words to make statements memorable.
invisible web High-quality databases generally not included in the searches conducted by general or meta-search engines.

jargon Technical language related to a specific field that may be incomprehensible to a general audience.

key-word outline An abbreviated version of a formal outline that may be used in presenting a speech.

lay testimony Information derived from ordinary citizens.
line graph A visual representation of changes across time; especially useful for indicating trends of growth or decline.
listener A person who interprets the message offered by the speaker to construct its meaning.
literal analogy A comparison made between subjects within the same field.
logos A form of proof that makes rational appeals based on facts and figures and expert testimony.

magnification A speaker's selecting and emphasizing certain qualities of a subject to stress the values they represent.
main points The most prominent ideas of the speaker's message.
major premise The statement of a general principle on which an argument is based.
malapropisms Language errors that occur when a word is confused with another word that sounds like it.
manipulative persuasion Persuasion that works through suggestion, colorful images, music, and attractive spokespersons. It does not justify its conclusions by evidence and reasoning.
manuscript presentation A speech read from a manuscript.
marking Adding a gender, racial, or ethnic reference when none is needed—e.g., "a woman doctor."
master narrative Form of speaking in which the entire speech becomes a story that reveals some important truth.
master of ceremonies A person who coordinates an event or program, sets its mood, introduces, and, provides transitions.
maxims Brief and particularly apt sayings.
mechanical model The speaker, message, medium, interference, listener, feedback model of the communication process.
media prompts Sources such as newspapers, magazines, and the electronic media that can suggest ideas for speech topics.
medium Those elements conducting a message, such as the air, microphone, amplifiers, or electronic media.
memorized text presentations Speeches that are committed to memory and delivered word for word.
memory The storing of ideas in the mind for recall.
message The fabric of words, illustrations, voice, and body language that conveys the idea of the speech.
metaphor A figure of speech in which anticipated words are replaced by new, surprising language in order to create a new perspective.
meta-search engine A search engine that combines the results from several general search engines.
mind-mapping Changing certain basic habitual patterns of expression to free the mind for creative exploration of speech topics.
minor premise The statement of a specific instance that relates to the general principle on which an argument is based.
mirror questions Questions that repeat part of a previous response to encourage further discussion.
monochromatic color scheme Use of variations of a single color in a presentation aid to convey the idea of unity.

motion Formal proposal for group consideration.
motion to amend A parliamentary move that offers the opportunity to modify a motion presently under discussion.
motion to postpone consideration A motion that defers discussion until some specified time.
motivated sequence design A persuasive speech design that proceeds by arousing attention, demonstrating a need, satisfying the need, visualizing results, and calling for action.
motivation Internal forces that impel action and direct human behavior toward specific goals.
multisided presentation A speech in which the speaker's position is compared favorably to other positions.
myth of the mean The deceptive use of statistical averages in speeches.
mythos A form of proof that connects a subject to the culture and tradition of a group of narratives.

narrative A story used to illustrate some important truth.
narrative coherence Whether a narrative or story flows well and fits together smoothly.
narrative design Format in which the speech follows a dramatic rather than logical pattern of development.
narrative fidelity Whether a narrative seems true and makes sense.
non sequitur fallacy A deductive error occurring when conclusions do not follow from the premises that precede them.
novelty The quality of being new or unusual.

objectivity Criterion for evaluating whether or not a source is free from bias.
omitted qualifiers A reasoning error that occurs when a claim ignores conditions under which it might not hold.
onomatopoeia The use of words that sound like the subjects they signify.
opinions Expressions of personal attitude or belief offered without supporting material.
optimum pitch The level at which people can produce their strongest voice with minimal effort and that allows variation up and down the musical scale.
oral report Presentation that summarizes the deliberations of a small group to inform a larger audience of decision makers.
order A consistent pattern used to develop a speech.

panel discussion A group presentation that features an organized pattern of exchanges among speakers, directed and controlled by a moderator.
parallel construction Wording points in the same way to emphasize their importance and to help the audience remember them.
paraphrase Summarizing in your own words something said or written.
parliamentary procedure A set of formal rules that establishes an order of business for meetings and encourages the orderly, fair, and full consideration of proposals during group deliberation.
participative leader A leader who seeks input from group members and gives them an active role in decision making.
pathos Proof relying on appeals to emotions.
perfectionism Believing that you must be perfect to be effective.
personal website A website designed and maintained by an individual; contains whatever that person wishes to place on it.
personification A figure of speech in which nonhuman or abstract subjects are given human qualities.
persuasion The art of convincing others to give favorable attention to our point of view.
persuasive speech Speech intended to influence the attitudes or actions of listeners.
physiological needs Our survival need for food, air, and water, safety needs.
pictographs A visual image symbolizing information.
pie graph A circle graph that shows the size of a subject's parts in relation to each other and to the whole.
pitch The position of a human voice on the musical scale.
plagiarism Presenting the ideas and words of others without crediting them as sources.
plot The body of a speech that follows narrative design. Unfolds in sequence of scenes designed to build suspense.
post hoc fallacy A deductive error in which one event is assumed to be the cause of another simply because the first preceded the second.
predictions Forecasts of what we can expect in the future, often based on projections of trends from past occurrences.
preliminary tuning effect The effect of previous speeches or other situational factors in predisposing an audience to respond positively or negatively to a speech.
prepersuasive function The way in which informative speaking shapes listeners' perceptions, preparing them for later persuasive speeches on a topic.
PREP formula A technique for making an impromptu speech: state a point, give a reason or example, and restate the point.
presentation The act of offering a speech to an audience, integrating the skills of nonverbal communication with the speech content.
presentation aids Supplemental materials used to enhance the effectiveness and clarity of a presentation.
presentation anxiety The fear reactions that occur during the presentation of a speech.
prestige testimony Information coming from a person who is highly regarded, but not necessarily an expert on a topic.
preview The part of the introduction that identifies the main points to be developed in the body of the speech and presents an overview of the speech to follow.
principle of closure The need for a satisfactory end or conclusion to a speech.
principle of proximity The idea that things occurring together in time or space should be presented in the order in which they normally happen.
principle of similarity The principle that like things should be grouped together.
probes Questions that ask someone being interviewed to elaborate on a response.
problem-solution design A persuasive speech pattern in which listeners are first persuaded that they have a problem and then are shown how to solve it.
prologue An opening that establishes the context and setting of a narrative, foreshadows the meaning, and introduces major characters.
pronunciation The use of correct sounds and of proper stress on syllables when saying words.
proof An interpretation of evidence that provides a good reason for listeners to agree with the speaker.

proxemics The study of how human beings use space during communication.

public knowledge What a community decides is worth knowing.

qualifiers In an argument, expressions of the strength of a claim that take into account possible reservations.

quoting out of context An unethical use of a quotation that changes or distorts the original speaker's meaning or intent by not including parts of the quote.

rate The speed at which words are uttered.

reasoning from parallel cases Presenting a similar situation and how it was handled as the basis of an argument. Often called analogical reasoning.

reasoning from principle Argumentative reasoning that is based upon shared principles, values, and rules, sometimes called deductive reasoning.

reasoning from reality Presenting a number of cases from which you then derive a general principle in argumentation.

receiver apprehension Fear of misinterpreting, inadequately processing and/or not being able to adjust psychologically to messages sent by others.

recency Ensuring that the information in a speech is the latest that can be provided.

red herring fallacy The use of irrelevant material to divert attention.

refinement phase Identifying the general and specific purposes of a speech topic and framing its thesis statement.

refutative design A persuasive speech design in which the speaker tries to raise doubts about, damage, or destroy an opposing position.

reinforcer A comment or action that encourages further communication from someone being interviewed.

relevance A subject's importance or value to us. A criterion for evaluation that ensures that supporting material relates directly to the issue in question.

reliability The trustworthiness of information critical to the credibility of a speech.

reluctant testimony Highly credible form of supporting material in which sources speak against their apparent self-interest.

repetition Repeating sounds, words, or phrases to attract and hold attention.

representative A criterion for evaluation that ensures that supporting material is not an exception to the general situation.

research overview A listing of the main sources of information that could be used in a speech and of the major ideas from each source.

reservations Acknowledgment of conditions under which a claim may not be valid.

response What happens as the result of a speech.

responsible knowledge An understanding of the major features, issues, information, latest developments, and local applications relevant to a topic.

retention The extent to which listeners remember and use the speaker's message.

rhetoric Originally the study of public speaking, rhetoric now often includes the art of oral communication in general, the art of persuasion, and the study of communication as a social and political force.

rhetorical questions Questions that have a self-evident answer, or that provoke curiosity that the speech then proceeds to satisfy.

rhythm Rate patterns of vocal presentation within a speech.

Robert's Rules of Order The authoritative, traditional "bible" of parliamentary procedure.

second A motion must receive a "second" before group discussion can proceed; ensures that more than one member wishes to have the motion considered.

selective relaxation The technique of tightening and relaxing muscles on command, used to help reduce communication anxiety.

self-actualization need Our need to be the best we can by optimizing our potential.

self-awareness inventory A series of questions that a speaker can ask to develop an approach to a speech of introduction.

sequence chart Visual illustrations of the different stages of a process presented on separate charts.

sequential design A pattern for an informative speech that presents the steps involved in the process being demonstrated.

setting Physical and psychological context in which a speech is presented.

sexism Allowing gender stereotypes to control interactions with members of the opposite sex.

sexist language The use of masculine nouns and pronouns when the intended reference is to both sexes, or the use of derogatory, emotional, trigger words when referring to women.

shaky principle fallacy A reasoning error that occurs when an argument is based on a faulty premise.

simile A language tool that clarifies something abstract by comparing it with something concrete; usually introduced by "as" or "like."

simplicity A desirable quality of speech structure; suggests that a speech has a limited number of main points and that they be short and direct.

skills training Developing abilities and attitudes that help speakers control and transform communication apprehension into a positive factor.

slang The language of the street.

sleeper effect A delayed reaction to persuasion.

slippery slope fallacy The assumption that once something happens, an inevitable trend is established that will lead to disastrous results.

social leadership behavior Occurs when leaders focus upon building and maintaining positive, productive relationships among group members.

source cards Records kept of the author, title, place and date of publication, and page references for each research source.

source citation References in a speech to sources used.

spatial design A pattern for an informative speech that orders the main points as they occur in physical space.

speaker Person who initiates oral communication.

specific purpose The speaker's particular goal or the response that the speaker wishes to evoke.

speech of acceptance A ceremonial speech expressing gratitude for an honor and acknowledging those who made the accomplishment possible.

speech of demonstration An informative speech aimed at showing the audience how to do something or how something works.

speech of description An informative speech that creates word-pictures to help the audience understand a subject.
speech of explanation A speech that is intended to inform the audience about abstract and complex subjects.
speech of inspiration A ceremonial speech directed at awakening or reawakening an audience to a goal, purpose, or set of values.
speech of introduction A ceremonial speech in which a featured speaker is introduced to the audience.
speech of tribute A ceremonial speech that recognizes the achievements of individuals or groups or commemorates special events.
speeches that address attitudes, beliefs, and values Speeches designed to modify these elements and help listeners find harmony among them.
speeches that advocate action and policy Speeches that encourage listeners to change their behavior either as individuals or as members of a group.
speeches that focus on facts Speeches designed to establish the validity of past or present information or to make predictions about what is likely to occur in the future.
statistics Numerical Information.
stereotypes Generalized pictures of a race, gender, or group that supposedly represent its essential characteristics.
stock issues The major general questions a reasonable person would ask before agreeing to a change in policies or procedures.
straw man fallacy Understating, distorting, or otherwise misrepresenting the position of opponents for ease of refutation.
style The expression of ideas in effective language.
subject directory An organized list of links to websites on specific topics.
subordination The requirement that material in an outline descend in importance from main points to subpoints to sub-subpoints to sub-sub-subpoints.
subpoints The major divisions of a speech's main points.
sub-subpoints Divisions of subpoints within a speech.
summary statement The speaker's reinterpretation of the speech's main idea at the end of a presentation.
supporting materials The facts and figures, testimony, examples, and narratives that constitute the building blocks of successful speeches.
symbolic racism An indirect form of racism that employs code words and subtle, unspoken contrast to suggest that one race is superior to another.
symposium Group presentation in which speakers address different areas of an issue.

table the motion A parliamentary move to suspend indefinitely the discussion of a motion.
task leadership behavior A leadership emphasis that directs the attention and activity of a group toward a specified goal.
terminal credibility The audience's assessment of your ethos after you have made a presentation.
testimonial Lay testimony used to endorse a person, practice, or institution.
testimony Citing the opinions or conclusions of other people or institutions to clarify, support, and strengthen a point.
textual graphics Visual presentation using words.
thesis statement The speech's central idea.
thoroughness Providing complete and accurate information about a topic.
toast A short speech of tribute, usually offered at celebration dinners or meetings.
topoi of topic discovery Probe questions used to stimulate the mind during topic exploration, centering on places, people, activities, things, events, ideas, values, problems, and campus concerns.
topic analysis Using questions often employed by journalists to explore topic possibilities for speeches (who, what, why, when, where, and how).
topic area inventory chart A means of determining possible speech topics by listing topics you find interesting and subjects your audience finds interesting, and then matching them.
topic briefing Speech in which the speaker attempts to "sell" listeners on the importance of a topic proposed for a speech.
transactional communication The shaping and sharing of identities that can result from successful communication.
transactional leadership A leadership style based on power relationships that relies on reward and punishment to achieve its ends.
transformational communication The spiritual impact of ethical communication on the identity of participants.
transformational leadership A leadership style based on mutual respect and stewardship rather than on control.
transitions Connecting elements used in speeches.
trigger words Words that arouse such powerful feelings that they interfere with the ability to listen critically and constructively.

understanding This second phase in the persuasive process requires that listeners grasp the meaning of the speaker's message.
universal human values Values that transcend cultural differences such as love, truthfulness, fairness, freedom, unity, tolerance, responsibility, and respect for life.
universal listener Listening as though you represent all who might be affected by a message.

values Underlying principles or standards of desirable or ideal behavior that justify our beliefs and attitudes.
verifier A statement by an interviewer confirming the meaning of what has just been said by the person being interviewed.
vicarious experience narrative Speech strategy in which the speaker invites listeners to imagine themselves enacting a story.
visualization The process of systematically picturing oneself succeeding as a speaker and practicing a speech with that image in mind.
vocal distractions Filler words, such as "er," "um," and "you know," used in the place of a pause.

warrant The principle that justifies moving from data to claim in an argument.
working outline A tentative plan showing the pattern of a speech's major parts, their relative importance, and the way they fit together.
works cited A form of bibliography in an outline that lists those sources of supporting material actually used in the speech.
works consulted A form of bibliography that lists all sources of research considered in the preparation of the speech.

Photo Credits

Chapter 1: Page 1: Bob Daemmrich/Stock, Boston LLC; 5: © Bob Daemmrich/The Image Works; 6: © Bob Daemmrich/The Image Works; 8: Alinari Archives/Corbis; 13: © Dick Blume/The Image Works; 14: © R.W. Jones/Corbis.

Chapter 2: Page 30: © Chuck Savage/Corbis; 31: © Gary Newkirk/NewSport/Corbis; 33: Tony Freeman/PhotoEdit; 38: Bob Daemmrich; 44: © Chris Trotman/NewSport/Corbis.

Chapter 3: Page 50: Barbara Stitzer/PhotoEdit; 53: © David Pu'u/Corbis; 55: AP/Wide World Photos; 63: Bob Daemmrich/Stock, Boston LLC; 64: Terry Wild Studio.

Chapter 4: Page 76: Seth Resnick/Stock, Boston LLC; 78 (top): © Bob Daemmrich/The Image Works; 78 (bottom): Loren Santow; 79: © Lawrence Migdale/www,migdale.com; 81: Deborah Lerme Goodman; 85: Michael Newman/PhotoEdit; 91: © Erik Freeland/Corbis.

Chapter 5: Page 105: © Bob Daemmrich/The Image Works; 119: AP/Wide World Photos; 125: © Richard B. Levine; 128: Michael Newman/PhotoEdit.

Chapter 6: Page 142: © Warren Morgan/Corbis; 145: Chris Tagaki; 152: © Jeff Greenberg/The Image Works; 158: Photodisc/Getty Images.

Chapter 7: Page 166: Rob Crandall/Stock, Boston LLC; 168: Ghislain & Marie David de Lossy/Getty Images; 176: David Young-Wolff/PhotoEdit; 183: © James Marshall/The Image Works.

Chapter 8: Page 200: David Young-Wolff/PhotoEdit; 202: © Corbis; 203: Balfour Walker/Chris Mooney Photography; 206: Jean-Marc Giboux/Getty Images; 207: AP/Wide Wrold Photos; 208: © Martin Simon/Corbis.

Chapter 9: Page 230: Gary Conner/PhotoEdit; 232: Charles Gupton/Stock, Boston LLC; 243: Asahi Shimbun; 245: AP/Wide World Photos; 253: Ron Wurzer/Getty Images.

Chapter 10: Page 262: © Peter Beck/Corbis; 264: Stuart Dee/Getty Images; 270: Frank Clarkson/Getty Images; 276: David Young-Wolff/PhotoEdit.

Chapter 11: Page 289: © Kathy McLaughlin/The Image Works; 291: Patti McConville/Unicorn Stock Photos; 293: Michael Newman/PhotoEdit; 295: AP/Wide World Photos; 301 (top) Kiser/Glacier National Park Archives; 301 (bottom): Dan Fagre/U.S. Geological Survey; 301: Daniel Bosler/Getty Images.

Chapter 12: Page 324: © Chuck Savage/Corbis; 329: © Michael Newman/PhotoEdit; 330: © Lou Dematteis/The Image Works; 338: © Jacques Langevin/Corbis; 339: Jeff Greenberg/PhotoEdit; 340: © Flip Schulke/Corbis.

Chapter 13: Page 350: © Richard B. Levine; 351: © Joel Gordon 1993; 362: © Richard B. Levine; 363: AP/Wide World Photos; 364: AP/Wide World Photos; 370: Ghislain & Marie David de Lossy/Getty Images.

Chapter 14: Page 381: Bob Daemmrich/Stock, Boston LLC; 382: Michael Mewman/PhotoEdit; 386: © Bob Stern/The Image Works; 390: © Shmuel Taylor/Jeroboam; 391: © Steve Rubin/The Image Works; 392: © Al Campanie/Syracuse Newspapers/The Image Works; 396: AP/Wide World Photos.

Chapter 15: Page 410: © Bob Daemmrich/The Image Works; 412: Kevin Winter/Getty Images; 413: Frederick Brown/Getty Images; 414: © Charles Gupton/Corbis; 417: Barry Rosenthal/Getty Images; 418: © Peter Turnley/Corbis; 423: Jonathan Nourok/PhotoEdit; 426: Ryan McVay/Getty Images.

Chapter 16: Page 438: Photodisc/Getty Images; 440: AP/Wide World Photos; 442: © Rick Friedman/Corbis; 445: *American Progress*, John Gast, oil on canvas, 1987. Museum of the American West collection, Autry National Center; 447: © Bettmann/Corbis; 450: AP/Wide World Photos.

Chapter 17: Page 476: © Richard B. Levine; 478: Bruce Henderson/Stock, Boston LLC; 480 (left): James Burke/Getty Images; 480 (right): © Hulton-Deutsch Collection/Corbis; 482 (left): Alan Goldstein/Folio; 482 (right): © 2001 *The Record* (Bergen County, NJ); 483: AP/Wide World Photos; 484: AP/Wide World Photos; 485: Stewart Cohen/Getty Images.

Index